Popular Music Th

ROUTLEDGE MUSIC BIBLIOGRAPHIES

RECENT TITLES

COMPOSERS

Isaac Albéniz, 2nd Edition (2015)
Walter A. Clark

William Alwyn (2013)
John C. Dressler

Samuel Barber, 2nd Edition (2012)
Wayne C. Wentzel

Béla Bartók, 3rd Edition (2011)
Elliott Antokoletz and Paolo Susanni

Vincenzo Bellini, 2nd Edition (2009)
Stephen A. Willier

Alban Berg, 2nd Edition (2009)
Bryan R. Simms

Leonard Bernstein, 2nd Edition (2015)
Paul R. Laird and Hsun Lin

Johannes Brahms, 2nd Edition (2011)
Heather Platt

William Byrd, 3rd Edition (2012)
Richard Turbet

Frédéric Chopin, 2nd Edition (2015)
William Smialek and Maja Trochimczyk

Miles Davis (2017)
Clarence Henry

Frederick Delius, 2nd Edition (2009)
Mary Christison Huismann

Gaetano Donizetti, 2nd Edition (2009)
James P. Cassaro

Edward Elgar, 2nd Edition (2013)
Christopher Kent

Gabriel Fauré, 2nd Edition (2011)
Edward R. Phillips

Alberto Ginastera (2011)
Deborah Schwartz-Kates

Charles François Gounod (2009)
Timothy S. Flynn

Fanny Hensel (2018)
Laura K.T. Stokes

Paul Hindemith, 2nd Edition (2009)
Stephen Luttmann

Gustav Holst (2011)
Mary Christison Huismann

Charles Ives, 2nd Edition (2010)
Gayle Sherwood Magee

Quincy Jones (2014)
Clarence Bernard Henry

Franz Liszt, 3rd Edition (2009)
Michael Saffle

Alma Mahler and Her Contemporaries (2017)
Susan M. Filler

Bohuslav Martinů (2014)
Robert Simon

Felix Mendelssohn Bartholdy, 2nd Edition (2011)
John Michael Cooper with Angela R. Mace

Nikolay Andreevich Rimsky-Korsakov, 2nd Edition (2015)
Gerald R. Seaman

Gioachino Rossini, 2nd Edition (2010)
Denise P. Gallo

Ralph Vaughan Williams (2016)
Ryan Ross

Giuseppe Verdi, 2nd Edition (2012)
Gregory W. Harwood

Richard Wagner, 2nd Edition (2010)
Michael Saffle

Anton Webern (2017)
Darin Hoskisson

GENRES

Blues, Funk, R&B, Soul, Hip Hop, and Rap (2010)
Eddie S. Meadows

Chamber Music, 3rd Edition (2010)
John H. Baron

Choral Music, 2nd Edition (2011)
Avery T. Sharp and James Michael Floyd

Church and Worship Music in the United States, 2nd Edition (2017)
Avery T. Sharp and James Michael Floyd

Ethnomusicology, 2nd Edition (2013)
Jennifer C. Post

Free Jazz (2018)
Jeffrey Schwartz

The Madrigal (2012)
Susan Lewis Hammond

The Musical, 2nd Edition (2011)
William A. Everett

North American Fiddle Music (2011)
Drew Beisswenger

Piano Pedagogy (2009)
Gilles Comeau

Popular Music Theory and Analysis (2017)
Thomas Robinson

The Recorder, 3rd Edition (2012)
Richard Griscom and David Lasocki

String Quartets, 2nd Edition (2011)
Mara E. Parker

Women in Music, 2nd Edition (2011)
Karin Pendle and Melinda Boyd

POPULAR MUSIC THEORY AND ANALYSIS
A Research and Information Guide

Thomas Robinson

ROUTLEDGE MUSIC BIBLIOGRAPHIES

LONDON AND NEW YORK

First published 2017 by Routledge

2 Park Square, Milton Park, Abingdon, Oxfordshire OX14 4RN
52 Vanderbilt Avenue, New York, NY 10017

Routledge is an imprint of the Taylor & Francis Group, an informa business

First issued in paperback 2019

Copyright © 2017 Taylor & Francis

The right of Thomas Robinson to be identified as the author of this work has been asserted by him in accordance with sections 77 and 78 of the Copyright, Designs and Patents Act 1988.

All rights reserved. No part of this book may be reprinted or reproduced or utilised in any form or by any electronic, mechanical, or other means, now known or hereafter invented, including photocopying and recording, or in any information storage or retrieval system, without permission in writing from the publishers.

Notice:
Product or corporate names may be trademarks or registered trademarks, and are used only for identification and explanation without intent to infringe.

Library of Congress Cataloging-in-Publication Data
Names: Robinson, Thomas (Music bibliographer), author.
Title: Popular music theory and analysis : a research and information guide / Thomas Robinson.
Other titles: Routledge music bibliographies.
Description: New York ; London : Routledge, 2017. | Series: Routledge music bibliographies
Identifiers: LCCN 2016048698 (print) | LCCN 2016049693 (ebook) | ISBN 9781138206328 (hardback) | ISBN 9781315465289
Subjects: LCSH: Music theory—Bibliography.
Classification: LCC ML128.T5 R63 2017 (print) | LCC ML128.T5 (ebook) | DDC 016.78164/11—dc23
LC record available at https://lccn.loc.gov/2016048698

ISBN: 978-1-138-20632-8 (hbk)
ISBN: 978-0-367-87171-0 (pbk)

Typeset in Minion
by Apex CoVantage, LLC

Contents

Preface	*vii*
I. Articles	1
II. Books	83
III. Collections	95
IV. Dissertations	121
Song Index	125
Subject Index	271
Author/Editor Index	327
Year Index	335

Preface

For as long as popular music has been performed and recorded, writing about popular music has followed. From Theodor Adorno's "high" cultural critique of its standardized components to Charles K. Harris's "low" lessons from Tin Pan Alley in how to compose it oneself, popular music has inspired a wide variety of responses in the written word.[1]

By all accounts, however, the more scholarly examples were slow to give a detailed accounting of the musical materials. Peter Winkler recalls his experience as a music student in 1967: "Gradually I was able to build up a picture of the social, historical, and economic context in which this [popular] music existed. But rarely did the literature address the music *itself*. This, alas, is still largely true today [1997], even though the literature has multiplied enormously" (emphasis in original).[2] Just a few years after Winkler's early struggles, Wilfrid Mellers, one of the first musicologists to bring the weight of traditional music-theoretical apparatus to bear on popular music analysis, defended his methodology: "[T]here is no valid way of talking about the experiential 'effects' of music except by starting from an account of what actually happens in musical technique, the terminology for which has been evolved by professional musicians over some centuries."[3]

As the century drew to a close, international scholarly societies formed, journals proliferated, and the apparent gaps between music theory, social theory, and cultural theory seemed to close somewhat. Yet, as the new millennium approached, there lingered concern about the scarcity of work that dealt directly with the music, the sonic material, as opposed to its context. So pressing was this concern that an article of a structuralist bent customarily featured a preamble positioning the work as a step toward a solution to this problem. Even when musicologists and music theorists (when the distinction can be made) were inclined to tackle the "sounds themselves," they disagreed on the methodological specifics. Can Beethoven and the Beatles be analyzed with the same models? If so, to what extent? If the traditional attention to structure "usually take[s] us little further than triumphant revelations of banality," how does one proceed?[4] Even as the friction continued, and continues today to some degree, more scholarly writing on popular music theory and analysis continues to appear, bringing new possibilities to the table. Analyses of gesture, metaphor, narrative, gender, and intertextuality alternate with long-standing tonal theories of Heinrich Schenker, phrase rhythm, meter, and even pitch-class set theory. All are given serious and rigorous application.[5] In spite of the strife, or perhaps because of it, we sit today with an abundance of writing that, as a whole, both addresses the sounds we hear and connects those specific sounds to broader meaning.

This volume indexes representative writing published before 2015, yet it is not to be understood merely as a "greatest hits" package. Nor does it claim to be comprehensive or advocate one method of analysis over another. Rather, it includes all of the essential works in the field, while accurately reflecting the ever-expanding landscape. Writers are treating some genres and techniques, like hip-hop, mashups, sampling, music video, and record production, in innovative ways, and every effort was made to represent their work here. One may notice the attention given to pedagogical writings as well; however, textbooks or how-to manuals were avoided. Inclusion was limited to those articles, books, collections of essays, and dissertations that both engage popular songs directly, and are scholarly and analytical in intent. While newcomers to pop-music study will find the discipline's fundamental texts here, I hope that experienced scholars will find some surprises among the citations.

The music in question is limited mostly to North American and British pop-rock music of the 20th and 21st centuries, including but certainly not limited to Tin Pan Alley, the American Songbook, the blues, folk, R&B, country & western, soul, rock, funk, disco, pop, metal, hip-hop, rap, and the many variants (soft rock, death metal, etc.). Studies of music generally understood as art music were excluded. Jazz, film music, and video-game music are burgeoning sub-disciplines of their own and were generally excluded, unless the analytical focus was on a song's compositional structure. Of course, many of the popular songs found in the included works may turn up in movies or may become the basis for jazz performance, but the bottom-line criterion for inclusion in this volume is whether a particular work addresses the song itself. If nothing else, the book serves as the quickest and most direct means of finding published musical analyses of a given song.

Four indices assist the user in finding the most helpful entry. Because "the song's the thing" here, the Song Index is comprehensive. It lists every song mentioned in every cited article and book, except those songs appearing only in reference to other works also included in this volume. Scholars looking for more than a brief mention should take note of the boldface entry numbers, which indicate a song's non-trivial appearance in a stand-alone analytical example or figure. A simple transcription of the lyrics does not qualify; some aspect of the sonic content (whether harmonic progression or gestural pattern) must be addressed. Of course, many writers are adept at giving a thorough analysis exclusively in prose. Furthermore, some areas of investigation, such as timbre, currently lack a notational apparatus to support non-prose examples. Therefore, users are encouraged to investigate all corresponding entry numbers. The Subject Index is similarly rich. Here the user not only will find names of the musicians, groups, and scholars discussed in the sources, but also will locate musicological and music-theoretical topics and concepts. The Author/Editor Index provides quick reference to specific works, and the Year Index assists the user in finding coterminous works.

This volume was compiled and edited keeping in mind two hypothetical users and their particular needs. Consequently, the musicologist writing about, say, Led Zeppelin and looking for existing analyses of the band's music will appreciate the extensive Song Index. Likewise, the music theorist preparing a syllabus for a popular music class will make good use of the Subject Index. Each user ultimately will be led to annotated entries that give a sense of what methodologies are used (e.g. Schenkerian analysis, intertextual studies) and that indicate what types of examples and figures are included.

I would like to thank the staffs of the libraries at the University of Alabama and Bowdoin College for generous assistance, the anonymous reviewers for comments, and, of course, my family for endless patience. Finally, special appreciation is owed to my colleagues in the Society for Music Theory's Popular Music Interest Group for their collective efforts over the years to build and update our online bibliography. It was utterly

Preface

indispensable when I started this project; while its scope is broader than mine, it contains some hidden gems that I would not have discovered otherwise. I hope that this online resource will continue to thrive and be used in tandem with my printed contribution.

NOTES

1 Theodor Adorno, "On Popular Music," in Leo Lowenthal and Max Horkheimer, eds., *Studies in Philosophy and Social Science* 9: 17–48. New York: Institute of Social Research, 1941. Charles K. Harris. *How to Write a Song*. New York: Charles K. Harris, 1906.
2 Peter Winkler, "Writing Ghost Notes: The Poetics and Politics of Transcription," in David Schwarz, Anahid Kassabian, and Lawrence Siegel, eds., *Keeping Score: Music, Disciplinarity, Culture*: 169–203. Charlottesville and London: University Press of Virginia, 1997: 170.
3 Wilfrid Mellers, *Twilight of the Gods: The Beatles in Retrospect*. London: Faber and Faber, 1973: 15.
4 Richard Middleton, "Towards a Theory of Gesture in Popular Song Analysis," in Rossana Dalmonte and Mario Baroni, eds., *Secondo Convegno Europeo di Analisi Musicale*: 345–50. Trento: Università degli Studi di Trento, 1992: 345. Interesting exchanges can be found in Susan McClary and Robert Walser, "Start Making Sense! Musicology Wrestles with Rock," in Simon Frith and Andrew Goodwin, eds., *On Record*: 277–90. New York: Pantheon, 1990; Susan McClary, "Terminal Prestige: The Case of Avant-Garde Music Composition," in Schwarz, Kassabian, and Siegel, eds., Keeping Score: 54–74; Charlottesville and London: University Press of Virginia, 1997; John Covach, "We Won't Get Fooled Again," in Schwarz, Kassabian, and Siegel, eds., Keeping Score: 75–89; and John Covach, "Popular Music, Unpopular Musicology," in Nicholas Cook and Mark Everist, eds., *Rethinking Music*: 452–70. Oxford: Oxford University Press, 1997.
5 For an overview, see Jocelyn Neal, "Popular Music Analysis in American Music Theory," *Zeitschrift der Gesellschaft für Musiktheorie* 2, no. 2 (2005).

I
Articles

A1 **Adams, Kyle.** "Aspects of the Music/Text Relationship in Rap." *Music Theory Online* 14, no. 2 (2008).

A study of the interaction of music and text in rap. Adams, noting that the music in rap is customarily produced before the lyrics are composed, inverts the standard "text/music" relation to "music/text," arguing that rap lyrics often support the music, not the reverse. Using a table derived from Adam Krims's analytical method, Adams looks at the rhythmic placement of each word's syllables. The resulting rhythmic motives, syllable groupings, and patterns of rhymed syllables all are shown to incorporate drumbeats, pitch groupings, and motivic elements found in the music (the backing track). Includes transcriptions, musical figures, and lyrics from the music of OutKast, A Tribe Called Quest, and Big Boi.

A2 **Adams, Kyle.** "On the Metrical Techniques of Flow in Rap Music." *Music Theory Online* 15, no. 5 (2009).

An identification of specific metrical and articulative techniques in rap, enabling a more detailed analysis of "flow." Adams builds upon Adam Krims's definition and taxonomy, focusing primarily on three metrical techniques: the placement of accented syllables, the placement of rhymed syllables, and the correspondence of syntactical and metrical units. The various graphic musical examples show rhythmic patterns marking formal transition, complex enjambment, and rhythmic ambiguity matching that of the musical accompaniment, and changes in accentuation and syncopation mapping neatly onto similar changes in the lyrical narrative. Includes lyric charts, audio examples, and transcriptions from the music of Blackalicious, Madvillain, and N.W.A.

A3 **Amico, Stephen.** "Su Casa es Mi Casa: Latin House, Sexuality, Place." In Whiteley and Rycenga, eds., *Queering the Popular Pitch*. 2006: 131–51. See **C39**.

A study of Latin house music and gay Latino culture in New York City. Amico considers the "reverse diaspora," a migration of homosexuals to places more supportive of their identity, often urban centers. Through field study, he examines how people who make such a move frequently bring along elements of their former home. In this case, it is the carrying of a Latin musical influence into the house club scene in New York City. Amico studies the music (particularly with respect to clave and tresillo rhythms) as well as its reception in the clubs. Includes a couple of musical figures and a brief transcription.

A4 **Anderson, Roger L.** "Ian Anderson's Acoustic Guitar in the Early Recordings of Jethro Tull." *Journal of Popular Music Studies (Tracking: Popular Music Studies)* 1, no. 1 (1988): 23–9. [Reprinted in *Soundscapes* 3 (2000).]

An exploration of the increasingly prominent role of Ian Anderson's acoustic guitar technique in Jethro Tull's recorded output from *This Was* to *Aqualung*. Anderson, granting the flute its distinctive role in the music of Jethro Tull, attends to the dramatic formal and textural contrast provided by the instrument. Several musical examples, given in both tablature and traditional notation, show the idiosyncratic use of embellishments, open strings, and octaves. Includes several transcriptions.

A5 **Attas, Robin.** "Sarah Setting the Terms: Defining Phrase in Popular Music." *Music Theory Online* 17, no. 3 (2011).

An examination of phrase in popular music, using three songs by Sarah McLachlan as case studies. Attas defines phrase in popular music as a "musical unit with goal-directed motion towards a clear conclusion, created through the manipulation of text, harmony, rhythm, and melodic contour." The musical examples show how these musical domains shape phrases and phrase rhythm, even in the absence of a traditional marker such as a cadence. Includes several examples, which linearly display chords, lyrics, phrases, and hypermeter on pulse-lines.

A6 **Attinello, Paul.** "Closeness and Distance: Songs about AIDS." In Whiteley and Rycenga, eds., *Queering the Popular Pitch*. 2006: 221–31. See **C39**.

An analysis of two songs read as responses to AIDS, one by Tori Amos and one by James Taylor. Attinello surveys various musical responses to the AIDS crisis and notes both that they tend to be fewer in number than those from the other arts, and that they tend to be more reserved and less direct in their presentation of material deemed controversial to some. The two songs under analysis are unlike other popular responses to AIDS in that they are much more heavily coded. Attinello studies texture and metaphor in Amos's "Not the Red Baron" and reads the narrative and form in Taylor's "Never Die Young." Includes a formal diagram.

A7 **BaileyShea, Matthew L.** "From Me to You: Dynamic Discourse in Popular Music." *Music Theory Online* 20, no. 4 (2014).

A study of the effect on meaning in popular songs brought about by shifts in pronouns and in persona. BaileyShea focuses particularly on the motion from distant to intimate discourse. One example is the shift from first-person to second-person discourse. A distinction is made here between a switch in perspective ("substitution") and a perspective made clear through revealing more information ("clarification"). The shift can be made suddenly, gradually, or in a more complex or cyclic manner. BaileyShea also proposes a "double-address" through which a song can address its fictional characters as well as the real listening audience. Includes several diagrams of form and persona shift in music of Elvis Presley, The Beatles, U2, Patti Smith, and others.

A8 **Benadon, Fernando and Ted Gioia.** "How Hooker Found His Boogie: A Rhythmic Analysis of a Classic Groove." *Popular Music* 28, no. 1 (2009): 19–32.

A study that divides the 1948–51 output of John Lee Hooker into "blues" (60–110 beats per minute or bpm) and "boogie" (130–220 bpm) and draws upon the work of A.M. Cohen to identify examples of Hooker's characteristic guitar pattern ("isoriff") in various recordings. Benadon and Gioia, with attention to tempo, subdivision of the beat, and metric malleability, note cases where the upbeat is so heavily accented that there may be two parallel pulse streams. Additionally, they consider Hooker's playing to exhibit characteristics of both boogie-woogie piano and big-band swing. Includes musical figures and examples.

A9 **Bennighof, James.** "Fluidity in Paul Simon's 'Graceland': On Text and Music in a Popular Song." *College Music Symposium* 33/34 (1993/1994): 212–36.

An argument starting with the premise that aesthetic value in popular music cannot be found by examining the same musical relationships one would examine in art music. Bennighof concludes that text, instrumentation, and performer are far more relevant in value judgments of the former than of the latter, and he holds Paul Simon's song as an example. The blurred symmetry, the melodic variation in repeats, the loose background vocals, the vocal delivery, and even the avoidance of the leading tone all contribute to the characteristic "fluidity" of the song. Includes figures, transcriptions, and lyrics.

A10 **Berger, Harris M.** "Death Metal Tonality and the Act of Listening." *Popular Music* 18, no. 2 (1999): 161–78.

A call for more music analysts to consider perception, particularly that of music's practitioners, as meaning is so often dependent upon it. Berger, in reporting on his field work in an Ohio death-metal scene, gives an example that can be read in multiple ways. His straightforward analysis (with a particular tonal center and hierarchy) is directly contradicted by the composer/guitarist's perception of the structure. Traditional descriptions of tonality, he argues, fall short by treating it as an aspect of sound instead of something constituted in the listener's ear. Includes a few musical examples.

A11   **Bernard, Jonathan.** "Listening to Zappa." *Contemporary Music Review* 18, no. 4 (1999): 63–103.

An essay that proposes strategies for studying and listening to Frank Zappa's compositions for acoustic concert ensemble. Bernard argues that the music is better understood if one is aware of compositional and performance practices in Zappa's earlier jazz/rock style. He first discusses Zappa's early work in the Mothers of Invention, focusing on parody (of R&B) and quotation (of classical repertoire). He then discusses what he calls "retakes," different versions of earlier pieces for different ensembles, sometimes reworked into new pieces altogether. Six such pieces are explored in detail. Noting that it can be challenging to assess Zappa's purely orchestral compositional style, Bernard proposes two categories, forms dependent upon repetition (recurrent theme or ostinato) and episodic forms (narrative), and offers some examples of each. He closes with some thoughts of the most recent performances and recordings of Zappa's music by the Ensemble Modern. Includes several music examples, a table, and a detailed discography.

A12   **Bernard, Jonathan.** "The Musical World(s?) of Frank Zappa: Some Observations of His 'Crossover' Pieces." In Everett, ed., *Expression in Pop-Rock Music: Critical and Analytical Essays*, 2nd ed. 2008 [2000]: 1–44. See **C6**.

A survey of Frank Zappa's "crossover" pieces, those that were arranged and performed in both the popular and the art music idioms. Bernard, however, finds them to be more than mere "arrangements." He compares all multiple versions, whether studio or live recordings, and whether with Zappa's group The Mothers of Invention or orchestrated for large ensemble. "Dupree's Paradise" is shown to be similar in design to Stravinsky's "Agon." Bernard provides several transcribed excerpts as well as an appendix with discography and recording data.

A13   **Berry, David Carson.** "Dynamic Introductions: The Affective Role of Melodic Ascent and Other Linear Devices in Selected Song Verses of Irving Berlin." *Intégral* 13 (1999): 1–62.

An application of Schenkerian analytical techniques to some of the songs of Irving Berlin. Berry finds examples of strong coordination between melody and lyric. He discusses instances in which a verse's melody forms an initial ascent, leading to a *kopfton* appearing at the beginning of the refrain. This ascent is supported by the uncertainty, tension, anticipation, longing, and aching found in the lyrics. In this group of songs, he finds the ascending verse and the descending refrain to represent a kind of balance, which has ramifications in the large scale, as shown in numerous foreground and middleground graphs. Berry also comments on text painting, pentatonic elements, and performance implications.

Articles

A14 **Berry, David Carson.** "The Popular Songwriter as Composer: Mannerisms and Design in the Music of Jimmy Van Heusen." *Indiana Theory Review* 21 (2000): 1–51.

A study of the music of songwriter Jimmy Van Heusen. Berry's interest lies primarily in the music, so while he did not consider the lyrics in detail, he examined the original, published sheet music for 98 of Van Heusen's songs, and he details here their harmonic, linear, and formal characteristics. Features such as chromatic bass lines, linear intervallic patterns, flatted melody notes, motivic transformation, and contour all are discussed along with analysis from a Schenkerian perspective. Includes numerous musical examples, voice-leading graphs, and formal diagrams.

A15 **Biamonte, Nicole.** "Augmented-Sixth Chords vs. Tritone Substitutes." *Music Theory Online* 14, no. 2 (2008).

A study of the augmented-sixth chord and the tritone substitution. Biamonte points out that while the two chords are enharmonically equivalent, there are some fundamental differences. She surveys the literature on the topic, lays out a few basic examples, and discusses the commonalities: both chords are chromatic enhancements of diatonic chords, and both have non-essential fifths. Reference is made to jazz chord-scale theory and to Rameau and other music theorists. She ultimately focuses on the three key differences: harmonic function (dominant preparation versus substitute for the dominant itself), voice leading (contrary motion versus parallel), and possibilities for enharmonic reinterpretation. Includes numerous jazz and classical examples. Both chords, she notes, are found in both repertoires.

A16 **Biamonte, Nicole.** "Triadic Modal and Pentatonic Patterns in Rock Music." *Music Theory Spectrum* 32, no. 2 (2010): 95–110. [Reprinted in Spicer, ed., *Rock Music*. 2011: 227–42.] See **C35**.

A study of classic rock songs from the 1950s through the 1990s that examines harmonic function as well as pentatonic frameworks in rock music. Biamonte considers what chords may function as tonic, subdominant, and dominant in various modes, paying special attention to the double-plagal and Aeolian progressions. Noting the prevalence of major triads (or even power chords with no third) in rock, she points out that the roots of these chords often are arranged according to various modes of the pentatonic scale. Dozens of songs are cataloged accordingly, and the system is expanded to include hexatonic and heptatonic configurations. Includes several musical examples and song tables.

A17 **Biamonte, Nicole.** "Formal Functions of Metric Dissonance in Rock Music." *Music Theory Online* 20, no. 2 (2014).

Biamonte, following Kamisnky and Krebs, makes clear the distinction between displacement and grouping dissonance at the rhythmic, metric, and hypermetric levels, supplying musical examples of each. Considering where these tend to occur in the music, she proposes, after Caplin, three common types of small- and large-scale formal function: initiating, concluding, and transitional. Biamonte then examines seven rock corpuses (Beatles, Rolling Stones, and others), comparing the distinct treatments of metric dissonance and how they changed over time. Includes numerous musical examples and figures.

A18 **Bickford, Tyler.** "Music of Poetry and Poetry of Song: Expressivity and Grammar in Vocal Performance." *Ethnomusicology* 51, no. 3 (2007): 439–76.

A study of sound and gesture in singing. Bickford notes that as linguistic systems mediate the sensory and the semiotic, sung language mediates form and meaning. A single song, Bob Dylan's "Down the Highway," serves as a subject for investigation of rhythm and meter (particularly the placement of stress), enunciation (over-pronunciation as means of phrase distinction), and sonority (a parameter shown as a formal determinant when studied with rhyme). The form that emerges in the analysis would not have been discovered through traditional means. Includes rhythmic figures in grid notation, phonetic figures, and other formal diagrams.

A19 **Björnberg, Alf.** "On Aeolian Harmony in Contemporary Popular Music." Gothenburg: IASPM—Nordic Branch Working Papers, no. DK 1, 1989. [Appeared earlier as "There's Something Going On: om eolisk harmonik i rockmusik." In *Tvärspel: Trettioen artiklar om musik: Festskrift till Jan Ling*: 371–86. Gothenburg, Sweden: University of Gothenburg, 1984. Reprinted in Moore, ed., *Critical Essays in Popular Musicology*. 2007: 275–82.] See **C27**.

A look at a specific harmonic practice, which at the time of writing was becoming more prevalent: "Aeolian harmony." Björnberg defines this as the use of harmonic progressions coming exclusively from the Aeolian mode, such as i-♭VII-♭VI or i-iv-v. He traces potential connections to pentatonic origins and notes some consistent lyrical treatment of the progressions. Further, he suggests that Aeolian harmony, with its lack of goal-directed dominant or leading tone, is an alternative to conventional tonality, thus reflecting particular societal and ideological conflicts.

A20 **Björnberg, Alf.** "Sounding the Mainstream: An Analysis of the Songs Performed in the Swedish Eurovision Song Contest Semi-Finals 1959–1983." In Roe and Carlsson, eds., *Popular Music Research: An Anthology from NORDICOM Sweden*. 1990: 121–31. See **C32**.

An account of the changes in adult or mainstream popular music (as distinct from youth-oriented rock music) during the rock era. Björnberg uses, as a representative sample, the set of 201 songs entered in the Swedish semifinals of the Eurovision song contest from 1959 to 1983. A series of graphs plots over time the percentage of songs that feature certain musical elements. Björnberg includes form (AABA versus verse-chorus); symmetrical periodicity (deviation from even measure groupings); major versus minor; triplet subdivision of the beat; pitch range (for singers); chord progressions (II-V-I, Baroque, modal); and rhythmic density (measured against the beat). Further, he proposes considering some possible connections between these changes and those in society at large. Includes several graphs. Also see his dissertation, **D2**.

A21 **Björnberg, Alf.** "Structural Relationships of Music and Images in Music Video." *Popular Music* 13, no. 1 (1994): 51–74. [Reprinted in Middleton, ed., *Reading Pop: Approaches to Textual Analysis in Popular Music*. 2000: 347–78.] See **C23**.

A general application of "empirical semiotics." Björnberg explores the structural relationships of music and images in popular music video, focusing on syntax and, therefore, narrative. The quantifiable parameters in his analysis are discursive repetition (repetition of large units), demarcation (the number of musical dimensions that change from one section to the next), symmetry (and deviation from a formal norm), musematic repetition (repetition of smaller units), directionality (related to melodic activity and harmonic progression), motorial flow (regularity of rhythmic accompaniment), dynamics, sound processes (timbre and recording effects), and individual predominance factor or "IPF" (relation or proportion of individual (vocal) to background). Analyzing four music videos (by Bruce Springsteen, Bryan Adams, Michael Jackson, and Snap), he measures each of these musical elements over the course of each song. The visuals of each are then discussed in relation to the narrativity (or lack of it) in the music. Finally, he proposes that videos tend to fall into one of four categories, depending on whether the music and the visuals are either narrative or epic. Includes one table and an appendix with four complete analyses.

A22 **Blake, David K.** "Timbre as Differentiation in Indie Music." *Music Theory Online* 18, no. 2 (2012).

A defense of timbre, above all other parameters, as the primary marker of generic distinction, and an argument that an analysis with emphasis on timbre can connect music and social practices more easily than pitch- or harmony-based analyses can. Blake surveys the various methods of timbral analysis, acknowledging timbre's resistance to systemization. Relying on Maurice Merleau-Ponty (for his theory of motility, which connects timbre and identity) and Edward Casey (for his metaphors of place), Blake notes that timbre is subjectively experienced, thus emphasizing a subject's relationship with surroundings, and he employs four adjectives (full, distorted, digestible, and homogeneous) in three case studies: a song by My Bloody Valentine, another by Neutral Milk Hotel, and an album by the Shins. Includes numerous audio examples and a few figures.

A23 **Bolelli, Roberto.** "The Blue Chords in Rock Music: Some Possible Meanings." In Mario Baroni, Anna Rita Addessi, Roberto Caterina, and Marco Costa, eds., *Proceedings of the 9th International Conference on Music Perception and Cognition*: 1349–54. Bologna, Italy: Society for Music Perception & Cognition and European Society for the Cognitive Sciences of Music, 2006. ISBN 8873951554.

A look at "blue chords" in rock music, those chords built on the flatted third and flatted seventh scale degrees, and a study of their character as distinct from that of blue notes. Bolelli discusses the intersection of blues, modes, and tonality, but ultimately maps the horizontal and vertical dimensions in music onto the blue notes and blue chords, touching on some connections often not considered: playing by ear, bottleneck slide guitar, gesture, (electric guitar) timbre, emotion, and even music therapy. Includes no figures or examples.

A24 **Boone, Christine.** "Mashing: Toward a Typology of Recycled Music." *Music Theory Online* 19, no. 3 (2013).

A typology of mashups and a survey of various forms of "recycled" music. Boone identifies five principal aspects of mashups: they use pre-existing music, integrate songs vertically, use more than one song, use recognizable material (usually), and include at least one pop song (usually). She distinguishes mashups from other songs similarly constructed, such as cover songs, songs with samples, remixes, medleys, and collages, noting that though mashups may be considered a form of collage, they differ in intent and reception. She goes on to identify four types of mashup: the basic mashup (a vertical combination of two or three well-known songs using no new material); the cover mashup (like a basic mashup but performed without use of the original recordings); after Lawrence Lessig, the paint palette mashup (an interaction of three or more songs but heavily edited, leaving many samples unrecognizable); and the megamix mashup (a mashup with many songs creating a guessing-game effect for the listener). Includes several musical examples and transcriptions.

A25 **Boone, Graeme M.** "Tonal and Expressive Ambiguity in 'Dark Star.'" In Covach and Boone, eds., *Understanding Rock: Essays in Musical Analysis*. 1997: 171–210. See **C4**.

An analysis of "one of the most highly regarded renderings of one of the [Grateful] Dead's best-loved songs." Boone moves systematically through the piece from one formal juncture to the next, highlighting instances of tonal ambiguity, text-music correspondences, and the relation of local events to large-scale ones. Includes transcriptions of various sections, a couple figures, a formal diagram, and an appendix with reactions of band members to the essay.

A26 **Boone, Graeme M.** "Twelve Key Recordings." In Moore, ed., *The Cambridge Companion to Blues and Gospel Music*. 2002: 61–88. See **C25**.

A discussion of 12 representative blues and gospel recordings, with a focus on form, style, genre, and historical period. Boone looks at blues recordings by Fred McDowell (particularly for lyrics and form); Robert Johnson (riffs, strumming, harmonic progression); Bessie Smith and Louis Armstrong (mix of blues and popular form); Jimmy Preston (metric accentuation); Muddy Waters (melodic contour and downbeat); and B.B. King (vocal quality, guitar solo, arrangement). He examines gospel recordings of Reed, Hall, and Allison (rhythm and verse-refrain structure); The Golden Gate Quartet (*a cappella* effects), and The Edwin Hawkins Singers (form and vamp). He also compares three recorded versions of

"Take My Hand, Precious Lord" (Five Soul Stirrers of Houston, Clara Ward, and Mahalia Jackson) with the published song itself. Includes formal diagrams for nearly all songs.

A27 **Borders, James.** "Frank Zappa's 'The Black Page': A Case of Musical 'Conceptual Continuity.'" In Everett, ed., *Expression in Pop-Rock Music: Critical and Analytical Essays*, 2nd ed. 2008 [2000]: 45–61. See **C6**.

A comparison of the published notated versions, the live performances, and the recordings of Frank Zappa's work "The Black Page." Borders traces the transformation of the piece over time, considering authorized recordings as well as bootlegs. Changes in rhythm, harmony, and form are discussed, whether composed, "intentional," changes, or the result of musicians' performance and improvisation. Musical examples and formal diagrams are included.

A28 **Bowman, Durrell S.** "'Let Them All Make Their Own Music': Individualism, Rush, and the Progressive/Hard Rock Alloy, 1976–77." In Holm-Hudson, ed., *Progressive Rock Reconsidered*. 2002: 183–218. See **C15**.

A set of three analyses of large-scale works by Rush. Bowman notes that, while others have argued that progressive rock is an extension of the counterculture's mysticism, the subculture surrounding the genre is actually skeptical of the 1960s revolution and also challenged the blues-based guitar technique dominant in 1960s rock, pulling influence from jazz and a variety of other genres. Bowman outlines the differences between hard rock, heavy metal, and progressive rock, ultimately positioning Rush as "progressive hard rock," particularly because of their shift from hard rock to more extended structures inspired by British progressive rock. He goes on to analyze three examples: "2112," "Xanadu," and "Cygnus X-1." Here, the harmonic narratives are connected to themes of Ayn Rand-inspired individualism. Includes several musical examples and a formal diagram.

A29 **Bowman, Rob.** "The Stax Sound: A Musicological Analysis." *Popular Music* 14, no. 3 (1995): 285–320. [Translated as "Il 'sound Stax': un'analisi musicologica." *Rivista di Analisi e Teoria Musicale* 8, no. 2 (2002): 3–44. Reprinted in Perchard, ed., *From Soul to Hip Hop*. 2011: 3–38.] See **C28**.

An investigation of nine elements of style that contribute to the trademark sound of Stax Records, using 95 single recordings issued by the label as a corpus for study. Bowman gives a thorough treatment of instrumentation (consistently sparse), repertoire (from in-house writers), structure (a handful of forms), keys (tied perhaps to guitar, horns, or individual singers), harmony (progressions and voicing), time (rhythm as well as subtleties in performance), melody (carefully considered with horns), ornamentation (in voice and guitar), and timbre (equipment of both performers and engineers). With rich statistical data and concise musical examples, Bowman argues that all aspects of the "Stax sound" contribute to a successful aesthetic of "less is more." Includes several musical examples.

A30 **Bowman, Rob.** "The Determining Role of Performance in the Articulation of Meaning: The Case of 'Try a Little Tenderness.'" In Moore, ed., *Analyzing Popular Music*. 2003: 103–30. See **C26**.

A close analysis of four recorded performances of "Try a Little Tenderness" (Bing Crosby, 1933; Aretha Franklin, 1964; Sam Cooke, 1964; Otis Redding, 1966), with respect to form, melodic embellishment, vocal timbre, and instrumentation. Bowman situates the performances on a continuum from Crosby's (tight, controlled, and of a Northern, middle-class aesthetic) to Redding's (overtly emotional and rooted in Southern, African American culture). He concludes that Redding's version so transforms the song that the performance bears meaning not inherent in the lyrics, melody, and chords alone. Current copyright law is therefore out-of-date. In so far as meaning is often carried by a song's performance, he argues that performers can significantly transform a song to the extent that they should be considered authors of the (new) composition. Includes several musical examples and a tempo map.

A31 **Brackett, David.** "James Brown's 'Superbad' and the Double-Voiced Utterance." *Popular Music* 11, no. 3 (1992): 309–24. [Reprinted in Middleton, ed., *Reading Pop: Approaches to Textual Analysis in Popular Music*. 2000: 122–40. See **C23**. Revised for *Interpreting Popular Music*. 2000 [1995]: 108–56.] See **B4**.

A musical and textual analysis of a song by James Brown. Brackett, after Gates and Bakhtin, reads the recording as a double-voiced utterance, in which "a word can partake simultaneously of both black and white discursive worlds." The lyrics, pointing up distinctions between Black English and Standard English, are an example not only of signification but also of intertextuality, in its creative reuse of stock phrases. The melodic elements ("cells"), such as "Yaay," "I got soul," and "I'm superbad," are uttered multiple times with slight variations. Harmony also is double-voiced; the roles of subdominant and dominant here may be read as a commentary on Euro-American music. Includes lyrics, several melodic transcriptions, and one figure.

A32 **Brackett, David.** "The Politics and Practice of 'Crossover' in American Popular Music, 1963 to 1965." *The Musical Quarterly* 78, no. 4 (1994): 774–97. [Expanded version of "The Politics and Musical Practice of 'Crossover.'" In Straw, Johnson, Sullivan, Friedlander, with Kennedy, eds., *Popular Music—Style and Identity: International Conference on Popular Music Studies*. 1993: 23–31.] See **C36**.

An investigation of the musical and social aspects of R&B/pop crossover success in the mid-1960s. Brackett first discusses the Billboard charts' authority and the term "crossover" itself, looking specifically at how "pop" was positioned as mainstream while "hillbilly" and "race" records were marginalized. He then focuses on the 14-month period between 1963 and 1965 when Billboard did not publish an R&B chart. This gap purportedly was due to the greater prevalence of R&B songs on the Hot 100, but Brackett calls this into question and suggests possible alternative reasons for the chart's disappearance and reinstatement. He then analyzes five songs from late 1965 to correlate aspects of their musical style to their crossover success on the R&B and pop charts. Musical elements considered include phrase structure, repetition, timbre, and instrumentation, and whether the song highlights arrangement and form ("I Can't Help Myself") or features variations in repetition ("Papa's Got a Brand New Bag"). Brackett concludes that crossover success was not dependent upon a song's conforming to pop norms. There often were other, more arbitrary, forces at work. He demonstrates this with a brief discussion of "This Diamond Ring" by Gary Lewis and the Playboys. Includes several melodic transcriptions and a table.

A33 **Brackett, David.** "Elvis Costello, the Empire of the E chord, and a Magic Moment or Two." *Popular Music* 24, no. 3 (2005): 357–67. [Reprinted as "Magic Moments, the Ghost of Folk-Rock, and the Ring of E-Major." In Eric Weisbard, ed., *Listen Again: A Momentary History of Pop Music*: 103–19. Durham, NC: Duke University Press, 2007. ISBN 9780822340225; ML3470.L59 2007.]

A look at the history and possible meanings of the open-voiced E chord on the electric guitar. Brackett notes that the chord brings a certain satisfaction to the performer, given the number of open strings, including the lowest available pitch, but he also argues that this "sonic emblem" has far-reaching references. He provides examples of this chord, including instances in which a song is transposed specifically in order to accommodate this voicing. Brackett also discusses the treatment of the chord's third and other embellishments. Includes several musical examples.

A34 **Brackett, David.** "Questions of Genre in Black Popular Music." *Black Music Research Journal* 25, nos. 1/2 (2005): 73–92. [Reprinted in Perchard, ed., *From Soul to Hip Hop.* 2011: 39–58.] See **C28**.

A response to Phillip Tagg's "Open Letter," published in *Popular Music* (1989), which problematizes racial categorization of popular music. Brackett sees an important link between social identity and music making. He acknowledges that genres are fluid, ever-changing, and often unstable, but argues that through genre, one might better understand music as it was produced at a given moment in time. As a case study, he analyzes two recordings of Jimmy Webb's "By the Time I Get to Phoenix," released only two years apart. The vocal treatments, the arrangements, and even the singers' own (racial) identities show Glen Campbell to be participating in the middle-of-the-road (MOR) pop genre (and tangentially country), and Isaac Hayes squarely in the emerging soul genre.

A35 **Brackett, David.** "Black or White? Michael Jackson and the Idea of Crossover." *Popular Music and Society* 35, no. 2 (2012): 169–85.

A look at textual and musical elements in three songs and videos by Michael Jackson and how they address commonly held associations of music and groups of people. Brackett argues that Jackson's crossover work demonstrates the constructed nature of racial categories. He analyzes the play of genre (heavy metal and funk) in "Beat It," the rock/funk hybridity and utopian racial harmony in

"Black or White," and the use of racial stereotypes in "Bad." Brackett closes with some commentary on how Jackson's notions of race intersect with the star's own life. Includes a few musical examples.

A36 **Brackett, John.** "'Hand in Glove' and the Development of The Smiths' Sound." *Dutch Journal of Music Theory* 18, no. 2 (2013): 69–87.

An analysis of the musical sound of The Smiths, focusing on their recording and mixing techniques. Brackett, after detailing the band's recording history leading up to their first album, surveys their numerous recordings of the song "Hand in Glove," as well as one sung by Sandie Shaw and produced by Smiths' guitarist Johnny Marr, in order to track the subtle changes in their mixing practices. Building upon the work of Albin Zak and Allan Moore, he discusses reverb, texture, timbre, and effects, but the main focus here is on the stereo mix and the placement of instruments in the "sound-box" (after Moore). Includes several figures featuring various mixes and a table outlining the band's studio sessions.

A37 **Bradby, Barbara and Brian Torode.** "Pity Peggy Sue." *Popular Music* 4 (1984): 183–205. [Reprinted in Middleton, ed., *Reading Pop: Approaches to Textual Analysis in Popular Music*. 2000: 203–27.] See **C23**.

An analysis of the lyrics and rhythms of "Peggy Sue." The authors respond to Dave Laing's claim that Buddy Holly's voice is an integral example of rock and roll's rejection of the ballad's adoring sentimentality. For Laing, the vocal techniques, particularly the hiccupping, foreground the rhythm and personal style over any meaning carried by the lyrics. For Bradby and Torode, meaning can be recovered here, as can the adoration of the love-object thought lost to the ballad. Analysis of the lyrics, and of rhythm in the multiple iterations of verses with particular attention to syncopation and repetition, leads to the conclusion that the mother/child metaphor (as in "rock your baby") can be understood also as a metaphor for the sexual relation between man and woman. Includes lyrics and numerous rhythmic figures.

A38 **Bradby, Barbara.** "Oh, Boy! (Oh, Boy!): Mutual Desirability and Musical Structure in the Buddy Group." *Popular Music* 21, no. 1 (2002): 63–91. [Reprinted in Moore, ed., *Critical Essays in Popular Musicology*. 2007: 567–95.] See **C27**.

An analysis of a Buddy Holly song, focusing on the way in which Holly's vocal delivery, as well as that of the band members, genders the performance. Bradby builds upon Constantin Brailoiu's work in cross-cultural childrens' rhythms and details the song's treatment of anticipation and syncopation (and its "ironing out"). Further, connections are drawn to the rhythms of Bo Diddley. Ultimately, the masculinization in the song is shown to sharply contrast both with other "boy-group" songs, such as the Five Satins' "In the Still of the Nite," and with most "girl-group" songs. Includes numerous figures engaging rhythm and lyrics.

Articles

A39   **Brøvig-Hanssen, Ragnhild and Paul Harkins.** "Contextual Incongruity and Musical Congruity: The Aesthetics and Humour of Mash-ups." *Popular Music* 31, no. 1 (2012): 87–104.

A survey of mashups with particular attention to the musical elements in The Evolution Control Committee's "Whipped Cream Mixes" and Danger Mouse's *The Grey Album*. The authors review the literature on mashups, offering examples and definitions, and ultimately value mashups for their contextual incongruity and resulting humor. After investigating what exactly creates, or in some cases fails to create, humor, they note that successful mashups feature both contextual incongruity and musical congruity. Includes a discography.

A40   **Brown, Matthew.** "'Little Wing': A Study in Musical Cognition." In Covach and Boone, eds., *Understanding Rock: Essays in Musical Analysis*. 1997: 155–70. See **C4**.

An application of information processing theory to the composition process in rock music, using a Jimi Hendrix song as a case study. Brown suggests that little is known about the compositional process despite the best efforts of music theorists and musicologists to study scores and sketches, and he proposes the information process model as a way forward. Additionally, he considers Schenkerian analysis, with its built-in background states, transformations, and levels, to be a promising framework in which the process can be borne out. In the case of "Little Wing," the "starting state" is the basic pentatonic (guitar-driven) material; the "problem space" is the set of all pieces that can be composed using tonal principles; the "search strategy" is the experimentation with blues and psychedelic idioms, manifest in the middleground levels; and the "goal state" is the final piece. For Brown, examining various verses, even various performances of the same songs, confirms the observations. Includes a four-level Schenkerian sketch.

A41   **Buchler, Michael.** "Modulation as a Dramatic Agent in Frank Loesser's Broadway Songs." *Music Theory Spectrum* 30, no. 1 (2008): 35–60.

A case for direct modulation as dramatic device, not as evidence of multiple tonal centers. Buchler proposes that many songs with stepwise direct modulations, particulary those of Loesser, which often have tightly integrated words and music, need not be read as instances of directed tonality. In fact, monotonal, even Schenkerian, readings are possible if one continues to track scale degree and harmonic function but notates them in the original key. This suggests that the song can close monotonally but that certain portions have been raised one or more steps for specific dramatic effect. In several detailed examples from Loesser's Guys and Dolls, Buchler incorporates novel notations in his voice-leading graphs where this technique appears. Includes lyrics, voice-leading sketches, and other musical examples.

A42   **Burnett, Michael.** "Using Pop With Middle-School Classes." In Vulliamy and Lee, eds., *Pop, Rock and Ethnic Music in School*. 1982: 24–39. See **C37**.

An example of how popular music might be used in the classroom. Burnett takes four pop songs of the time and evaluates them in terms of form, rhythm, harmonic progression, riffs, and melody. He includes suggestions for the presentation of each principal component and instructions for class performance. Finally, Burnett discusses possibilities for composition and improvisation. Although the material is designed for middle-school students, much of it may be adapted for college freshmen. Includes several musical figures and a "pop-song kit," a set of basic melodic, harmonic, formal, and rhythmic material for the assembly of a "pop song."

A43 **Burns, Gary.** "A Typology of 'Hooks' in Popular Records." *Popular Music* 6, no. 1 (1987): 1–20.

A taxonomy of musical elements accompanied by numerous examples of how songwriters, performers, and producers manipulate them through repetition and variation to create musical hooks. Burns makes a distinction between textual elements, which relate to the composition, and non-textual elements, which relate to its performance or recording. Rhythm hooks, melody hooks, harmony hooks, and lyric hooks all are considered textual. Non-textual elements that can be hooks include instrumentation, tempo, dynamics, improvisation and accident, sound effects, editing, mix, channel balance, and signal distortion. Includes many song titles as examples but gives only one notated musical example.

A44 **Burns, Joe.** "The Music Matters: An Analysis of Early Rock and Roll." *Soundscapes* 6 (2003).

An analysis of a 100-song sample of early (1955–1959) rock-and-roll records. Burns focuses on three components (melody, time signature, and chord progression) in order to discover the basic musical principles of the genre. Time signature, almost universally 4/4, receives little attention, but the other parameters are reviewed from various angles, such as "number of progressions," "number of chords in each progression," specific chord progressions, key, cadence, and range. Burns concludes with some thoughts about repetition and how a common framework in rock and roll can support great variation. Includes tables of data and an appendix with the main chord progression from each song.

A45 **Burns, Lori.** "'Joanie' Get Angry: k.d. lang's Feminist Revision." In Covach and Boone, eds., *Understanding Rock: Essays in Musical Analysis.* 1997: 93–112. See **C4**.

A look at k.d. lang's cover of "Johnny Get Angry." Burns argues that in the original text, the songwriters uphold stereotypical views of women's subordination to men, and that k.d. lang's version is a feminist reading carrying this notion to its logical conclusion: physical violence. The music video makes this reading clear, but there are aural clues in the recording as well, and Burns's analysis is a detailed mapping of lyrics and vocal performance onto harmonies in a Schenkerian framework, exploring metaphors of strength, weakness, hierarchy, and closure. Includes a transcription, side-by-side vocal analysis, lyrics, and a voice-leading sketch.

A46 **Burns, Lori.** "Analytic Methodologies for Rock Music: Harmonic and Voice-Leading Strategies in Tori Amos's Crucify." In Everett, ed., *Expression in Pop-Rock Music: Critical and Analytical Essays*, 2nd ed. 2008 [2000]: 63–92. See **C6**.

A thorough analysis of Tori Amos's "Crucify." With close attention to voice leading, Burns proposes a modified Schenkerian methodology that can accommodate modal progressions. Because the different sections of the song (verse, pre-chorus, chorus, and bridge) contain different harmonic idioms and have different modal centers, she analyzes them separately. First, a governing model is found, and then a voice-leading graph reflects counterpoint between bass and vocalist. Ultimately the reductions of each section combine into a single narrative.

A47 **Burns, Lori and Alyssa Woods.** "Authenticity, Appropriation, Signification: Tori Amos on Gender, Race, and Violence in Covers of Billie Holiday and Eminem." *Music Theory Online* 10, no. 2 (2004).

A study of cover song as signification. Burns and Woods focus on voice as signifier in four distinct ways: voice as subject in the lyrical narrative (singer may have different roles or positions in the song); voice as the vehicle of social communication (vocal effects affect meaning); voice as participant in the musical codes, conventions, and styles (voice may affect structural elements); and voice as member of the instrumental ensemble (voice may be in dialog with instruments). With these four facets of vocal performance in mind, Burns analyzes Holiday's and Amos's performances of "Strange Fruit," and Woods analyzes Eminem's and Amos's performances of "'97 Bonnie and Clyde." In each case, Amos is shown to signify upon the earlier performance (and upon the original song), adding her own perspective and meaning. Includes transcriptions of portions of "Strange Fruit" for comparison of three versions.

A48 **Burns, Lori.** "Feeling the Style: Vocal Gesture and Musical Expression in Billie Holiday, Bessie Smith, and Louis Armstrong." *Music Theory Online* 11, no. 3 (2005).

A study of Billie Holiday's vocal performance as reflecting the "style" of Louis Armstrong and "feeling" of Bessie Smith, as Holiday herself described it. Burns surveys several critical interpretations of Smith and Armstrong, including those of Samuel Floyd, Henry Louis Gates, and others. Borrowing from Floyd, she maps the "what" of performance onto "style" of a vocal performance and maps the "how" onto its "feeling." Burns analyzes two songs, recorded explicitly as tributes to Armstrong ("Tain't Nobody's Biz-ness If I Do") and Smith ("I Gotta Right to Sing the Blues"), focusing on three components: vocal quality (result of physical attributes), vocal space (range, but relative to physical limitations), and vocal articulation (enunciation within a rhythmic and metric structure). Armstrong and Smith are shown to be the influence in the way Holiday described. Includes analytical examples of all three singers' performances as well as the published sheet-music versions.

A49 **Burns, Lori.** "Meaning in a Popular Song: The Representation of Masochistic Desire in Sarah McLachlan's 'Ice.'" In Deborah Stein, ed., *Engaging Music: Essays in Musical Analysis*: 136–48, 303–6. Oxford: Oxford University Press, 2005; 346p. ISBN 0195170105; MT90.E64 2004.

A close reading of a single that addresses both its social message and its musical content. Burns's analysis of "Ice" is threefold. First, there is a discussion of the multivalent social message of sexual subordination and domination. Second, these themes are interpreted through the lyrics in the chorus and several verses. Third, the bulk of the chapter is an analysis of harmony and voice leading from a Schenkerian perspective (but without formal notation, as it is part of a collection of essays intended for undergraduates as an introduction to analytical essays). Throughout the analysis, the musical narrative is explicitly connected to the lyrical one. Includes several voice-leading graphs and, in the book's appendix, a sheet-music score.

A50 **Burns, Lori, Marc Lafrance, and Laura Hawley.** "Embodied Subjectivities in the Lyrical and Musical Expression of PJ Harvey and Björk." *Music Theory Online* 14, no. 2 (2008).

An investigation of the connections between "the lived body and musical practice," specifically embodied female subjectivities as they are constituted in the music and lyrics of PJ Harvey and Björk. The authors focus on the timbral and textural qualities, as well as melody, harmony, and rhythm, in their dynamic analyses of musical and social meaning. They systematically address analytic concepts (content, settings, and dynamic expression); lyrical materials and strategies (verbal content, lyrical settings, and dynamic lyrical expression); and musical materials and strategies (sonic content, musical settings, and dynamic musical expression) in PJ Harvey's "The Letter" and Tori Amos's "Cocoon." Includes numerous transcriptions and tables.

A51 **Burns, Lori.** "Vocal Authority and Listener Engagement: Musical and Narrative Expressive Strategies in the Songs of Female Pop-Rock Artists, 1993–95." In Spicer and Covach, eds., *Sounding Out Pop: Analytical Essays in Popular Music*. 2010: 154–92. See **C34**.

A set of four song analyses exploring female vocal authority in Tori Amos, PJ Harvey, Ani DiFranco, and Alanis Morissette. Burns argues that female pop-rock in the 1990s introduced a particular style of vocal expression, in which musical elements are closely integrated with the lyrics' narrative and social meanings. Each of her analyses reveals this through the same four-part analytical framework: narrative agency (distinguishing implied author and narrator); narrative voice (identifying status of the narrator and determining whether voice is authorial, personal, or communal); modes of contact (public or private address, direct or indirect communication, and sincere or oppositional expression); and listener engagement (marking proximity, sincerity, and temporality). Despite the similarities in vocal style, the four analyses reveal an array of narrative strategies.

Articles

A52 **Butler, Mark.** "Taking it Seriously: Intertextuality and Authenticity in Two Covers by the Pet Shop Boys." *Popular Music* 22, no. 1 (2003): 1–19.

A study of authenticity in two cover songs by the Pet Shop Boys. Butler traces the long-standing relationship between rock music and authenticity, finding the cover of U2's "Where the Streets Have No Name" to be a total transformation. The Pet Shop Boys upend U2's seriousness with deliberate artificiality. In "Go West," however, the Village People's original sense of community and liberation is amplified. Includes lyrics and various musical excerpts.

A53 **Byrnside, Ronald.** "The Formation of a Musical Style: Early Rock." In Hamm, Nettl, and Byrnside, eds., *Contemporary Music and Music Cultures*. 1975: 159–92. See **C7**. [Reprinted in Moore, ed., *Critical Essays in Popular Musicology*. 2007: 217–50.] See **C27**.

An essay outlining and defining a rock-and-roll style. Byrnside first looks at five factors in the formation of a new musical style, using a historical example for each: new musical-aesthetic needs (opera), expansion of an older style (Ars Nova), rejection of inherited style (early 20th-century music), economics (the piano), and technology (the reproduction as well as the content of popular music). All of these factors are brought to bear on the formation of rock and roll. Byrnside discusses some of the fundamentals of the style, including rhythm, meter, accent, the 12-bar blues, ostinato, lyrics, and vocal style, focusing on the influence of R&B, country music, and white ballads. Includes lyrics and several musical figures.

A54 **Capuzzo, Guy.** "Neo-Riemannian Theory and the Analysis of Pop-Rock Music." *Music Theory Spectrum* 26, no. 2 (2004): 177–99.

A demonstration of a Neo-Riemannian approach to pop-rock analysis. Capuzzo argues that such a transformational approach is often effective where traditional harmonic (Roman-numeral) analysis fails to capture the structural essence of a passage or section of music. After a primer on Neo-Riemannian theory, with a distinction made between pitch parsimony and pitch-class parsimony, come various musical examples of sequence (from Ozzy Osbourne and Frank Zappa), chromatic motion with $\hat{8}$ or $\hat{5}$ (from Radiohead and Beck), and, through cross-type transformations, the interaction of triad and seventh chord (from King Crimson). The article concludes with a deeper analysis of a single song by Soundgarden. Includes numerous musical examples and transformational diagrams.

A55 **Capuzzo, Guy.** "A Pedagogical Approach to Minor Pentatonic Riffs in Rock Music." *Journal of Music Theory Pedagogy* 23 (2009): 39–55.

A pedagogically oriented study of rock and funk riffs as segments of the pentatonic scale. Capuzzo defines a scale-degree pattern (SDP) as a segment of adjacent pitch classes in the pentatonic scale (e.g., $<\hat{1},\hat{3},\hat{4}>$ = <E, G, A> in E-minor pentatonic) and discusses some vocal warm-up exercises that may be used in the undergraduate classroom. Three- and four-note segments are treated systematically with respect to how they are commonly situated as scale degrees and neighbors in various songs. The complete pentatonic scale is considered, too, as are its interactions with the blues scale and the altered blues scale. Finally, the pentatonic riff is situated in Dorian, Phrygian, and Aeolian modes. Includes several musical examples.

A56   **Capuzzo, Guy.** "Sectional Tonality and Sectional Centricity in Rock Music." *Music Theory Spectrum* 31, no. 1 (2009): 157–74.

A proposal for new perspectives on popular songs with multiple tonal centers. Capuzzo recognizes that many songs are not governed by a single tonic. Nor do they display a directional tonality. Furthermore, their multiple tonalities (sometimes numbering three or more) should not render the songs non-tonal, for each section operates tonally with a single center. He suggests that such songs have "sectional tonality," a "patchwork" tonality in which no one key is privileged over another. Capuzzo also recognizes that some songs, while not exhibiting key centers, do show multiple centricities as a result of shifting pitch-class collections (often pentatonic). After Joseph Straus, he suggests that the center in each collection can be determined by assessing the salience of various pieces. He offers analyses of two songs exhibiting this "sectional centricity," focusing on instrumentation, timbre, lyric content, and tonal allusion. Includes several musical examples and figures.

A57   **Cateforis, Theo.** "How Alternative Turned Progressive: The Strange Case of Math Rock." In Holm-Hudson, ed., *Progressive Rock Reconsidered*. 2002: 243–60. See **C15**.

A discussion of math rock, its connections to other genres, and its metaphors and meanings. Cateforis investigates this subgenre of "alternative rock" that, unlike, say, Nirvana or Soundgarden, bears affinity to progressive rock. After a discussion of the genre's history and a description of its basic features (mixed meter, contrasting scalar and harmonic patterns, more metaphoric than narrative), there follows an analysis of a track by the group Don Caballero, taking into account the many meter shifts and key areas, looped riffs, and references to minimalism as well as heavy metal. Cateforis closes with some thoughts on the problem-solving nature of transcribing, or even listening to, the music. Includes several musical examples and a formal diagram.

A58   **Cherlin, Michael and Sumanth Gopinath.** "'Somewhere Down in the United States': The Art of Bob Dylan's Ventriloquism." In Colleen J. Sheehy and Thomas Swiss, eds., *Highway 61 Revisited: Bob Dylan's Road from Minnesota to the World*. Minneapolis: University of Minnesota Press, 2009: 225–36. ISBN 9780816660995; ML420.D98H54.

A look at the many voices of Bob Dylan. Cherlin and Gopinath note the changes in voice from era to era and from song to song, but they are most interested in the moment-to-moment changes in technique. They detail vocal techniques (e.g., yodeling, swooping, laughing); spoken and sung timbres (e.g., choked, breathy, sneering); and linguistic accents (e.g., southern), which combine to form Dylan's various personae (e.g., country bluesman, drunken fool). The coordination of these techniques with the lyrics is examined in several songs from The Freewheelin' Bob Dylan. "Honey, Just Allow Me One More Chance" alone exhibits three distinct voices. Includes several figures.

A59 **Clement, Brett.** "Modal Tonicization in Rock: The Special Case of the Lydian Scale." *Gamut* 6, no. 1 (2013): 95–142.

An argument that the Lydian mode, having long been avoided or explained in terms of other modes or tonalities, actually plays a much larger role in rock music than previously thought. Clement defines "Lydian tonality" (major tonic and major supertonic are mode-defining; dominant is demoted) and proposes a set of stability rules for inclusion (resolution of the supertonic; proper realization of the tritone). Some analytical case studies serve as examples and introduce "secondary tonicization," in which scale degrees can become tonicized local centers by applying not a new dominant but the mode-defining chord (e.g., A♭-B♭ (as I and II) can be a Lydian tonicization of VI in C minor). Includes numerous musical figures, transcriptions, and tables.

A60 **Clement, Brett.** "A New Lydian Theory for Frank Zappa's Modal Music." *Music Theory Spectrum* 36, no. 1 (2014): 146–66.

A proposal to adopt a Lydian diatonic system as an alternative to major/minor tonality in the analysis of Frank Zappa's modal music. Clement summarizes George Russell's Lydian Chromatic Concept, on much of which his system is based. The system includes leading tones, fifth projections, modes (and modal interaction), harmonic progression (usually oscillations), and other scales ("minor Lydian"). Clement also shows how this Lydian language turns up in the compositional practice of Steve Vai, a long-time Zappa colleague. Includes many musical examples, transcriptions, tables, and diagrams.

A61 **Clements, Carl.** "Musical Interchange Between Indian Music and Hip Hop." In Hisama and Rapport, eds., *Critical Minded: New Approaches to Hip Hop Studies*. 2005: 125–41. See **C14**.

A look at various intersections of Indian music and mainstream hip-hop. Clements first discusses some superficial musical treatments of Indian elements in U.S. mainstream hip-hop that insensitively reinforce negative stereotypes. Second, he investigates the "Asian Underground" in the U.K., whose importing of a wide array of Asian influences supports their struggle against racism. Third, he examines bhangra, an Indian dance genre that incorporates hip-hop, thus reversing the direction of importation. Finally, he assesses the mainstream success of Panjabi MC. Includes a few melodic-rhythmic examples.

A62 **Cohen, Andrew M.** "The Hands of Blues Guitarists." *American Music* 14, no. 4 (1996): 455–79. [Reprinted in David Evans, ed., *Ramblin' on My Mind: New*

Perspectives on the Blues: 152–78. Urbana, IL: University of Illinois Press, 2008; 430p. ISBN 9780252032035; ML3521.R29 2008.]

A proposition that the position of the picking hand in folk and blues music varied regionally in the early 20th century, thus affecting the musical patterns. Cohen studied a broad sample of 94 African American guitarists from three regions of the U.S. In the "Eastern" region, fingering is characterized by an extended thumb and alternating bass. In the "Delta" region, players tend to use the thumb only as needed. Players in the "Texas" region tend to play with a "dead thumb" on quarter notes. Cohen details the various patterns that result from each style and considers what musical components (e.g., melody, bass runs, counterpoint) are possible in each. Complete statistics are sorted and presented in various configurations.

A63 **Collaros, Pandel.** "The Music of the Beatles in Undergraduate Theory Instruction." *Indiana Theory Review* 21 (2000): 53–78. [Appeared earlier in Heinonen, Heuger, Whiteley, Nurmesjärvi, and Koskimäki, eds., *Beatlestudies 3: Proceedings of the Beatles 2000 Conference*. 2001: 139–57.] See **C12**.

A call for the use of Beatles songs in the music theory classroom. Collaros presents several basic examples (scale, key relationships, triads and inversions, extended chords, non-harmonic tones, pedal tones, and modulation); an extended analysis (mixture, prolongation, and secondary dominants in "Something"); a study of rhythm (mixed meter); and advanced undergraduate concepts (symmetrical structures, modes, and polychords). Includes numerous musical examples and figures.

A64 **Comer, John.** "How Can I Use the Top Ten?" In Vulliamy and Lee, eds., *Pop, Rock and Ethnic Music in School*. 1982: 7–23. See **C37**.

An example of how popular music might be used in the classroom. Comer gives suggestions for performing chord progressions in various rhythms and how they might be notated for class use. Boney M's "Brown Girl in the Ring" inspires ideas about teaching form and improvising by embellishing the basic melodic structure. Wings's "Mull of Kintyre" works the same way but also is an opportunity for discussion about instrumentation. The Boomtown Rats' "Rat Trap" can be studied for the meaning in its lyrics. The exercises are directed at 13- and 14-year-olds, but most are suitable or can be adapted for college freshmen. Includes several musical examples and an appendix of open tunings for guitar.

A65 **Comer, John.** "Rock and Blues Piano Accompaniments." In Vulliamy and Lee, eds., *Pop, Rock and Ethnic Music in School*. 1982: 72–90. See **C37**.

An approach to popular piano styles for classically trained students. Comer lists nine reasons classical pianists have "problems of transfer" when attempting to learn popular styles, including matters of reading the score versus playing by ear, unfamiliarity with harmonic and rhythmic practices, and improvisation. The chapter approaches these problems with some specific exercises. Basic forms are introduced via a combination of left-hand bass lines and right-hand chords.

The blues scale serves as the backdrop of idiomatic right-hand articulations. Comer gives basic exercises covering harmonic progression, rhythm, and improvisation. Notably, the closing discussion is about how to interpret sheet music in a flexible manner. As it tends to simplify so many elements of the music, particularly the rhythm, sheet music should be a framework for interpretation and recreation. Comer suggests some first steps for students. Includes several musical examples and figures.

A66 **Cook, Nicholas.** "Credit Where It's Due: Madonna's 'Material Girl.'" In *Analyzing Musical Multimedia*: 147–73. New York: Oxford University Press, 1998; 278p. ISBN0198165897; ML3849.C73 1998.

A thorough analysis of the music video for Madonna's "Material Girl" inspired by Andrew Goodwin's "musicology of the image." Cook analyzes the video as music, finding connections between the music, the words, and the images, and relates the "song hierarchy" to the "narrative hierarchy." An analysis of the motives, mode, harmony, and large-scale metrical structure shows music and lyrics to be tightly knit. The video, however, seems to be in conflict with that form. It contributes a secondary, contradictory meaning, a reading apparently overlooked by some cultural commentators.

A67 **Cotner, John S.** "Music Theory and Progressive Rock Style Analysis: On the Threshold of Art and Amplification." In James R. Heintze and Michael Saffle, eds., *Reflections on American Music*. CMS Monographs and Bibliographies in American Music No. 16: 88–106. Hillsdale, NY: Pendragon Press, 2000; 428p. ISBN 1576470709; ML200.5.R45 2000.

An argument that British and American progressive rock represented musically the tensions between mind and body. Cotner writes that the various styles in the genre can be expressed on several continuums: formalist/eclectic, intensional/extensional (after Andrew Cheston), and time (1963–1974). Three songs serve as case studies. Cotner looks at Frank Zappa's "Hungry Freaks, Daddy" (intensional form/extensional riff), The Velvet Underground's "Heroin" (intensional style), and Jimi Hendrix's "Voodoo Child (Slight Return)" (extensional development in guitar solo). Includes two figures.

A68 **Cotner, John S.** "Pink Floyd's 'Careful With That Axe, Eugene': Toward a Theory of Textual Rhythm in Early Progressive Rock." In Holm-Hudson, ed., *Progressive Rock Reconsidered*. 2002: 65–90. [Translated as "Il ritmo testuale in Careful With That Axe, Eugene." *Rivista di Analisi e Teoria Musicale* 8, no. 2 (2002): 133–55.] See **C15**.

An analysis of a single studio recording of "Careful With That Axe, Eugene." Cotner gives a full accounting of the instrumentation and texture in the Pink Floyd track. The textural density is quantified after Wallace Berry, and the tension between meter and phrase is analyzed after Eyton Agmon's method of plotting musical duration. The track and its "textural rhythm" are considered with respect to the term "progressive." Includes numerous musical figures.

A69 **Covach, John.** "The Rutles and the Use of Specific Models in Musical Satire." *Indiana Theory Review* 11 (1990): 119–44. [Reprinted in Moore, ed., *Critical Essays in Popular Musicology.* 2007: 417–42.] See **C27**.

A study of the humor in two songs by "The Rutles," a fictitious 1960s group parodying the Beatles. Covach, after Schopenhauer, notes that caricature works when it successfully combines congruity and incongruity. Therefore, a listener to the Rutles' music will understand its humor only if its congruities and incongruities with the music of the Beatles are correctly inferred. Covach explains the specific musical parodies in terms of harmony, melody, timbre, and even recording techniques. Intertextual references are made clear with the aid of Leonard Meyer's distinctions between dialect, idiom, and intraopus style. Includes several musical examples and figures.

A70 **Covach, John.** "Stylistic Competencies, Musical Satire, and 'This is Spinal Tap.'" In Marvin and Hermann, eds., *Concert Music, Rock, and Jazz Since 1945: Essays and Analytical Studies.* 1995: 399–421. See **C20**.

A study of humor produced solely by musical means. Covach analyzes three songs of the fictional rock group Spinal Tap, featured in the comedy "This Is Spinal Tap." Influenced by Kant and Schopenhauer, he suggests that humor may arise from incongruity, and in these songs a certain level of stylistic competency is necessary. A listener may need to be sufficiently familiar with a particular style to detect when the incongruity lies in the exaggeration of specific elements of a style, as in a caricature. The strongest humor seems to occur when there is the right blend of stylistic congruity and incongruity. Analyses and transcriptions are included as well as listings of specific musical references found in the songs. Includes several musical examples.

A71 **Covach, John.** "Progressive Rock, 'Close to the Edge,' and the Boundaries of Style." In Covach and Boone, eds., *Understanding Rock: Essays in Musical Analysis.* 1997: 3–32. See **C4**.

An analysis of the composition "Close to the Edge" by progressive rock group Yes. Covach, after giving a history of progressive rock from its emergence in the late 1960s to its resurgence in the 1990s, discusses form, mode, transformation of motivic material, and stylistic references to art music in Yes's album-side-length 1972 recording. He argues that the musical elements, as do the lyrics based on Herman Hesse's novel *Siddhartha*, capture certain aspects of timelessness. Includes numerous musical examples and a form diagram.

A72 **Covach, John.** "Echolyn and American Progressive Rock." *Contemporary Music Review* 18, no. 4 (1999): 13–61.

A study of progressive rock in the U.S., focusing on the 1990s group echolyn. Covach offers an overview of progressive rock, particularly the American strains of the 1970s and 1980s. Groups like Starcastle, Kansas, Happy the Man, However, and Cartoon are all included and given close analysis. The bulk of the analysis is devoted to echolyn, a band who marks a return to the British influence of the 1970s. Covach employs serial and set-theoretical techniques as well as modal and harmonic analysis. Includes numerous transcriptions and musical examples. Also includes detailed discographies with both major releases, and releases by regional groups available only on small labels or by mail order.

A73   **Covach, John.** "Jazz-Rock? Rock-Jazz? Stylistic Crossover in Late-1970s American Progressive Rock." In Everett, ed., *Expression in Pop-Rock Music: Critical and Analytical Essays*, 2nd ed. 2008 [2000]: 93–110. See **C6**.

A discussion of the blending of progressive rock (prog) and jazz-rock (fusion). Covach draws a distinction between "chart crossover" and "stylistic crossover," arguing that the groups Happy the Man and the Dixie Dregs are examples of the latter. This crossover is evidenced in their instrumentation, form, and rhythm, and in the role of improvisation in their music. Brief musical examples are adduced in order to demonstrate the musical influence of groups like Return to Forever, the Mahavishnu Orchestra, and Yes, all groups argued to be either prog or rock but not fully crossover. Covach also discusses the problems with the analysis of crossover styles and suggests the alternate possibility of "hybrid" styles. Includes a few musical examples and tables.

A74   **Covach, John.** "Pangs of History in Late 1970s New-Wave Rock." In Moore, ed., *Analyzing Popular Music*. 2003: 173–95. See **C26**.

An argument that post-punk and new-wave music invoked 1950s rock and roll not only in visual style but also in the music itself, if in complex ways. Covach positions the new-wave music of The Cars as a blend of pre-psychedelic rock and corporate rock, as exemplified by the more mainstream rock of Foreigner. He reprises here his notion of "musical worlding," in which music is understood (or not) in terms of its similarity (or dissimilarity) to other songs the listener has heard. With this in mind, Foreigner's music is the known model, against which the Cars' music is evaluated. Despite the Cars' many timbral references to 1950s rock, its form, harmonic structure, and phrase rhythm evoke the mainstream rock techniques of the day. Includes numerous harmonic reductions and formal diagrams.

A75   **Covach, John.** "Form in Rock Music: A Primer." In Deborah Stein, ed., *Engaging Music: Essays in Musical Analysis*: 65–76. Oxford: Oxford University Press, 2005; 346p. ISBN 0195170105; MT90.E64 2004.

An introduction to some basic forms in rock music. Covach discusses 12-bar blues (and its 8- and 12-bar variants); AABA (with some discussion of Tin Pan Alley's "sectional" verse and "sectional" refrain); verse-chorus (with the modifiers "simple" and "contrasting" indicating whether the harmonic pattern is the same or different in the two sections); simple verse (verses without a chorus); and compound forms (verse-chorus embedded in AABA and AABA embedded in ABA). The 12-bar blues is understood not as a formal type but as an "organizational pattern." Includes numerous formal diagrams and references to many examples of songs.

A76   **Covach, John.** "From 'Craft' to 'Art': Formal Structure in the Music of the Beatles." In Kenneth Womack and Todd F. Davis, eds., *Reading the Beatles: Cultural Studies, Literary Criticism, and the Fab Four*: 37–53. Albany, NY: State University of New York Press, 2006; 249p. ISBN 9780791467163; ML421.B4R43 2006.

A look at the changes in the songwriting technique of the Beatles. Covach writes that Lennon and McCartney held American songwriting practices, particularly those of the Brill Buidling writers, as models for their own writing until they found individual compositional voices of their own. This gradual change from "craftsperson" to "artist" took place from 1964 to 1967 and is detailed in the chapter through close readings of several songs. Innovation appears in their treatment of the AABA form as well as large-scale design. Includes several musical examples.

A77   **Covach, John.** "Leiber and Stoller, the Coasters, and the 'Dramatic AABA' Form." In Spicer and Covach, eds., *Sounding Out Pop: Analytical Essays in Popular Music*. 2010: 1–17. See **C34**.

An identification and description of a unique form, the dramatic AABA, shown to emerge in short, dramatic, and humorous Lieber and Stoller songs, referred to by the songwriters as "playlets." Covach describes some basic forms (simple verse, simple verse-chorus, contrasting verse-chorus, AABA, and compund AABA) and notes that the Coasters frequently feature strong refrains at the end of their A-sections. This development gives rise to the positioning of B-section as dramatic climax, in contrast to its being downplayed in traditional AABA forms. Various musical elements are shown to shape this form in "Down in Mexico," "Little Egypt," and "Leader of the Pack." Includes a few form diagrams and a list of Coasters songs that fall into the various form types.

A78   **Daley, Mike.** "Patti Smith's 'Gloria': Intertextual Play in a Rock Vocal Performance." *Popular Music* 16, no. 3 (1997): 235–53.

An analysis of Patti Smith's "Gloria," a reworking of Van Morrison's original as recorded by Them. Daley acknowledges several musical domains in which the versions differ but focuses on the timbre of Smith's voice. By altering the tempo and adding her own text, Smith parodies the original; and by co-opting and manipulating Morrison's text, she plays on its gender coding. Through the analysis of the vocal manipulation, her version can be heard as a critique of the male-coded rock in the original. Includes a complete melodic transcription of Smith's version with phonetic and timbral analysis (after Cogan and Ladefoged). Includes a transcribed excerpt of the Them version.

A79   **Danielsen, Anne.** "His Name Was Prince: A Study of *Diamonds and Pearls*." *Popular Music* 16, no. 3 (1997): 275–91.

An analysis of a single album. Danielsen, using the work of Fredric Jameson as a point of departure, studies Prince's *Diamonds and Pearls*, combining both an aesthetic approach with a social one. To that end, she contrasts her analysis with Stan Hawkins's study of the same album. Where Hawkins presents the "bare facts," she examines how the album's elements (voice, intertextuality, parody and humor, collage) form a larger whole.

A80   **de Clercq, Trevor and David Temperley.** "A Corpus Analysis of Rock Harmony." *Popular Music* 30, no. 1 (2011): 47–70.

A statistical analysis of harmony in a rock music corpus. The authors review the work of three scholars (Stephenson, Moore, and Everett) and conclude that all refer in some way to common-practice principles, even if rock harmony stands distinct from them. A data-driven approach was thought possibly to reveal principles yet to be observed. For their corpus, the authors selected the top 20 songs from each decade as reported in *Rolling Stone* magazine's "500 Greatest Songs of All Time." Each author analyzed all 100 songs to extract harmonic data. The article explains their encoding methodology, and the resulting data are displayed in various tables. Distribution of roots (I, IV, and V are most common, in that order), chord transitions, root motions, distribution by decade, and correlations between multiple chords are tabulated and discussed. Potential critiques are acknowledged as well. Includes several tables, examples of coding, and a complete song list.

A81   **Derfler, Brandon.** "U Totem's 'One Nail Draws Another' as Art Music." *Indiana Theory Review* 21 (2000): 79–101.

An argument that the music of James Grigsby, particularly "One Nail Draws Another" by his group U Totem, draws more from art music than from rock. Derfler compares the piece's serial sections to the 12-tone technique of Schoenberg and Webern, and he details the relationship to the diatonic sections. He identifies quotations of both Blondie and "L'homme armé" and examines the complex integration of sonata form and arch form. Finally, he considers rock's influences, which are limited to instrumentation, studio techniques, and marketing. Includes several musical examples, figures, a formal diagram, and an appendix with lyrics and translations.

A82   **Dibben, Nicola.** "Pulp, Pornography, and Spectatorship: Subject Matter and Subject Position in Pulp's *This is Hardcore*." *Journal of the Royal Music Association* 126 (2001): 83–106. [Reprinted in Moore, ed., *Critical Essays in Popular Musicology*. 2007: 501–24.] See **C27**.

A study of Pulp's album *This is Hardcore* as a critique of constructed fantasies of sexuality, glamor, and fame. Dibben locates this critique in the album's artwork and two of its tracks, "The Fear" and "Seductive Barry." The artwork, the music, and the lyrics are shown to undermine constructions of macho masculinity. Dibben also points out the album's ambivalence toward the listener's voyeuristic position. Includes a few musical examples.

A83 **Doll, Christopher.** "Transformation in Rock Harmony: An Explanatory Strategy." *Gamut* 2, no. 1 (2009): 1–44. [Reprinted in Spicer, ed., *Rock Music*. 2011: 243–274.] See **C35**.

A look at how, in rock music, one harmonic progression can be understood as a transformation of another. Doll categorizes the types of transformation according to the difference in the number of chords between the transformee and the transformed. In "substitution," there is no change in the number of harmonies. This includes "Roman numeric chord substitution" (e.g., III for I), "coloristic chord substitution" (e.g., i for I), "functional chord substitution" (e.g., dominant for subdominant), and "hierarchical chord substitution" (e.g., embellishing chord for structural dominant). In "addition" or "subtraction," chords are added or omitted. He also categorizes the types of harmonic structure being transformed: the "norm," such as the standard I-vi-IV-V progression; the "precedent," referring to a specific instance in a song; and "(in)complete," in which either the transformee or the transformed is complete and the other is not. Includes numerous musical examples.

A84 **Doll, Christopher.** "Rockin' Out: Expressive Modulation in Verse-Chorus Form." *Music Theory Online* 17, no. 3 (2011).

A study of the "breakout chorus," a chorus that contrasts sharply with the preceding verse in some manner, whether in terms of dynamics, pitch (melodic or harmonic), rhythm, or timbre. Doll focuses on breakout choruses that assert a new tonal center, which, in conjunction with lyrical meanings, can be considered "expressive modulations." Most such modulations involve a shift of three semitones (typically relative major/minor) or five semitones. Shifts of six, five, two, and even one are possible, too, and Doll provides examples of each. Further, he investigates cases that are ambiguous, in which it is not clear whether modulation or mere tonicization is taking place;, and some stylizations of the breakout chorus, in which the creators are aware of the archetype and are playing with listeners' expectations. Includes numerous examples of harmonic progressions with accompanying audio examples.

A85 **Doll, Christopher.** "A Tale of Two Louies: Interpreting an 'Archetypal American Music Icon.'" *Indiana Theory Review* 29, no. 2 (2011): 71–103.

An investigation of the history and influence of "Louie Louie," particularly its signature riff. Doll finds the genesis of the song in a combination of the chord progression (I-IV-V-IV) and rhythmic pattern in "El Loco Cha Cha" by René Touzet with an upper-voice line ($\hat{5}$-$\hat{6}$-$\flat\hat{7}$-$\hat{6}$-$\hat{5}$) common in many R&B songs, what he calls the "rogue riff." He goes on to suggest that the incorporation of the flat-$\hat{7}$ may have led to a change in the chord progression itself from I-IV-V to I-IV-VII, as the subtonic was adopted as a root. Finally, he discusses more recent appearances of the rogue riff (with or without the chord progression) and considers the attendant meanings and themes carried. Includes numerous musical examples and figures.

Articles

A86   **Doll, Christopher.** "Definitions of 'Chord' in the Teaching of Tonal Harmony." *Dutch Journal of Music Theory* 18, no. 2 (2013): 91–106.

A proposal for a comprehensive methodology of chord definition that is rich enough to enable chord identification in classical as well as popular repertoires. Doll recognizes that music theory pedagogues who include pop-rock examples may decide not only to discuss them exclusively on their own terms, but also to define those terms in the way pop-rock musicians would, not in the way classical musicians would. To accommodate this, he offers five categories of chord identification (five ways to distinguish between chords): temporal location, color (broadly including timbre, pc content, voicing, and inversion), roman numeral, function, and hierarchical position. Chords in a Schumann song are discussed with respect to these distinctions, as are six pop-rock songs. Another song serves as a 12-bar-blues model, while each of the others bears a chord that is distinguished from this model according to one of Doll's five categories. Includes several musical examples and tables.

A87   **Duchan, Joshua.** "'Hide and Seek': A Case of Collegiate *A Cappella* 'Microcovering.'" In Plasketes, ed., *Play it Again: Cover Songs in Popular Music*. 2010: 191–204. See **C29**.

A comparative analysis of three *a cappella* covers of a single song by Imogen Heap. Duchan notes that while emulation of instruments is standard practice for *a cappella* groups, in this case the original version is itself *a cappella*, albeit laden with digital effects. Duchan's analyses explore the subtle differences in the three arrangements, including treatment of pitch, doubling, phonetics, melisma, word painting, chord substitution, and phrase structure. His term "microcovering" refers to the attempt not just to cover a song, but to reproduce its every recorded nuance. Includes two transcriptions.

A88   **Echard, William.** "Gesture and Posture: One Useful Distinction in the Embodied Semiotic Analysis of Popular Music." *Indiana Theory Review* 21 (2000): 103–28.

A demonstration of the utility of the distinction between gesture and posture. Echard notes that the latter is a fixed energetic state, while the former has temporal dynamics. The posture can be understood as a frozen instant in a gesture; the gesture, a series of postures. Building upon the work of David Lidov, Robert Hatten, and Naomi Cumming, he discusses four potential analytical benefits: timbre (the electric/acoustic duality as a postural distinction), the ineffable (after Cumming, the unnameable), tonal and modal tendencies (mobile and static connotations in each), and harmony itself (motion versus color). Includes numerous examples of harmonic progressions.

A89   **Endrinal, Christopher.** "Burning Bridges: Defining the Interverse in the Music of U2." *Music Theory Online* 17, no. 3 (2011).

A study of form in the music of U2, focusing particularly on the section in popular songs traditionally called a "bridge." Endrinal points out that very few bridges actually exhibit transitional characteristics, and that some may even be harmonically closed and somewhat independent. He therefore proposes the term "interverse" ("inter-" because it falls between sections and "-verse" because it carries lyrics) and uses several U2 songs as case studies. The article also serves as a broader study of U2's music, as it examines introductions, verses, choruses, codas, and other sections in many songs. The main focus, though, is on the interverse (as distinct from interlude) and its four main types: independent continuous, independent sectional, dependent continuous, and dependent sectional. Includes several musical examples and a glossary.

A90 **Everett, Walter.** "Fantastic Remembrance in John Lennon's 'Strawberry Fields Forever' and 'Julia.'" *The Musical Quarterly* 72, no. 3 (1986): 360–85. [Reprinted in Moore, ed., *Critical Essays in Popular Musicology*. 2007: 391–416.] See **C27**.

An examination of fantasy and memory in two songs by the Beatles. Everett shows these themes to be present in the music as well as in the lyrics. He presents several song excerpts bearing these themes, in modal mixture and instrumentation, before digging more deeply into the two titular John Lennon compositions. In "Strawberry Fields Forever," the manipulation of tape (speed and direction) and the obscuring of the dominant by the voice leading reflect childhood memories. In "Julia," imagery of Yoko Ono and Lennon's mother are evoked, and treatment of motive is of primary analytical concern. Includes lyrics, musical examples, and Schenkerian voice-leading graphs.

A91 **Everett, Walter.** "Voice Leading and Harmony as Expressive Devices in the Early Music of the Beatles: 'She Loves You.'" *College Music Symposium* 32 (1992): 19–37.

A demonstration of musical analysis, specifically Schenkerian, as a means of addressing the expressive content of a popular song. Everett provides a complete voice-leading analysis (background, middleground, foreground) of "She Loves You," and in the prose connects structural elements (registral contrast, prolongation, altered scale degrees) to key expressive points in the text. Passages from additional songs are discussed in support of this analysis, with emphasis on the descending chromatic line and the added-sixth chord. Includes several musical examples and voice-leading graphs.

A92 **Everett, Walter.** "The Beatles as Composers: The Genesis of *Abbey Road*, Side Two." In Marvin and Hermann, eds., *Concert Music, Rock, and Jazz Since 1945: Essays and Analytical Studies*. 1995: 172–228. See **C20**.

An analysis of the entirety of side two of the Beatles' *Abbey Road* as a single work of art. Everett details aspects of its composition, arrangement, and production. The song-by-song investigation touches upon the multitracking process and other recording techniques. Notably, the analyses draw upon the techniques and relevant music-theoretical literature usually reserved for classical repertoire. Includes transcriptions, harmonic and voice-leading analyses, lyrics, and tracking diagrams.

Articles

A93   **Everett, Walter.** "Swallowed by a Song: Paul Simon's Crisis of Chromaticism." In Covach and Boone, eds., *Understanding Rock: Essays in Musical Analysis*. 1997: 113–54. See **C4**.

A close look at Paul Simon's output between 1975 and 1980, during which his songwriting technique produced structures that were most unusual for pop-rock music of the time. Everett, using Schenkerian analytical techniques and making consistent reference to Simon's own words about his compositional process, investigates progressive key centers, chromatic ambiguity, structural tritone relationships, timbre and its connection to the lyrics, and the jazz-like treatment of non-harmonic tones. Consideration is also given to the diatonic periods that precede and follow Simon's "chromatic crisis." Includes numerous transcriptions and voice-leading sketches.

A94   **Everett, Walter.** "'High Time' and Ambiguous Harmonic Function." In Weiner, ed., *Perspectives on the Grateful Dead: Critical Writings*. 1999: 119–25. See **C38**.

A look at tonal and harmonic ambiguity in a song by the Grateful Dead. Everett first offers a brief discussion of conventional harmonic progression, goal-directed motion, and the roles of the bass and the upper voice (melody). The Grateful Dead's frequent departure from these musical norms is then linked to their position in the counterculture. The song "High Time" serves here as a case study. While its chorus is somewhat conventional, its verse exhibits ambiguity on at least four levels. Its mode (major/minor/Mixolydian) is unclear; a surplus of major triads introduces chromatic tones; numerous second-inversion chords contribute instability; and most of the chords are functionally ambiguous, making multiple analyses possible. Includes a few musical examples.

A95   **Everett, Walter.** "Detroit and Memphis: The Soul of *Revolver*." In Reising, ed., *"Every Sound There Is": The Beatles' Revolver and the Transformation of Rock and Roll*. 2002: 25–57. See **C30**.

A study of the numerous wide-ranging musical influences of soul and R&B music (particularly that on the Stax, Motown, and Atlantic labels) upon the music of the Beatles in general and the *Revolver* album in particular. Everett identifies musical elements such as bass lines, rhythms, tempos, horn writing, guitar voicings, tonic pedals, metric changes, vamps, applied dominants, and behind-the-beat playing in the Beatles, and locates their likely inspirations in the American R&B repertoire. Includes several musical examples and an appendix that lists, by date of chart entry, all 353 singles studied for the analysis.

A96   **Everett, Walter.** "A Royal Scam: The Abstruse and Ironic Bop-Rock Harmony of Steely Dan." *Music Theory Spectrum* 26, no. 2 (2004): 201–35.

An examination of the harmonic and voice-leading practices of Steely Dan. Everett, after discussing the multi-layered meaning in the group's lyrics, focuses on extended and inflected chords (including stacked fourths, altered chords, and slash chords), jazz and rock chord substitutions (tritone sub and ♭VII sub), transient modulations, and chords as agents of voice leading (linear intervallic patterns). Throughout, connections are drawn from the music to the jazz of Lennie Tristano, Dizzy Gillespie, and Thelonius Monk. Similarly, the irony and abstruseness in the lyrics find their direct correlates in the music. Includes many examples, transcriptions, lyrics, and voice-leading sketches.

A97   **Everett, Walter.** "Making Sense of Rock's Tonal Systems." *Music Theory Online* 10, no. 4 (2004). [Reprinted in Moore, ed., *Critical Essays in Popular Musicology*. 2007: 301–35.] See **C27**.

An argument that numerous tonal systems are evident in rock music, and that this can be seen in the varied approaches to harmony and voice leading. Everett argues that the tonal practices and principles in 1950s pop were the same as those of the common-practice era, but that by the 1990s, there existed a multitude of offshoots or competing versions of tonality. First, he defines and classifies nine distinct tonal systems (in six categories), ranging from major/minor tonality to blues to chromaticism. Numerous analytical examples from each system are provided. Second, he scores two corpuses of songs, from the late 1950s and from the late 1990s (482 in total), according to their adherence to 12 tonal principles (six voice-leading and six harmonic). Results are reported and graphed, confirming Everett's hypothesis. Finally, a single song by Beck is briefly discussed as an example of idiosyncratic approaches to harmony and voice leading. Includes numerous examples and voice-leading graphs as well as a complete song list and accompanying data.

A98   **Everett, Walter.** "Painting Their Room in a Colorful Way: The Beatles' Exploration of Timbre." In Kenneth Womack and Todd F. Davis, eds., *Reading the Beatles: Cultural Studies, Literary Criticism, and the Fab Four*: 71–94. Albany, NY: State University of New York Press, 2006; 249p. ISBN 9780791467163; ML421. B4R43 2006.

A chronological walk through the timbral innovations of the Beatles. Everett traces timbre from the group's early years, in which timbre was a matter of instrumentation, to the later years, in which timbral choices become essential aspects of the composition. His discussion covers the use of piano, guitar types, vocal expression, celesta, electronic effects, tremolo, cello, tuning, distortion, harmonium, overdubbing, tape loops, Mellotron, organ, Fender Rhodes, and harpsichord. Throughout, Everett draws specific connections to the musical structure in individual songs. Includes no stand-alone examples; analysis is in prose.

A99   **Everett, Walter.** "Pitch Down the Middle." In Everett, ed., *Expression in Pop-Rock Music: Critical and Analytical Essays*, 2nd ed. 2008 [2000]: 111–74. See **C6**. [Revision of "Confessions from a Blueberry Hell, or Pitch Can Be a Sticky Substance." In *Expression in Pop-Rock Music: A Collection of Analytical and Critical Essays*, 1st ed.: 269–345. New York and London: Garland, 2000; 372p. ISBN0815331606; ML3434.E985 2000.]

An argument that pitch is of central importance in the analysis of popular music and that other elements, such as timbre, rhythm, and form, are often better understood if considered with respect to pitch. Everett first investigates some basic elements: form, timbre (vocal and instrumental), rhythm, and tempo, offering many examples along the way. He explains his particular position on the use of Schenkerian analysis in pop-rock music, and several voice-leading graphs follow, with attention to non-triadic tones and linear progressions. Modal mixture and power chords are then shown to be important elements of the popular music vocabulary. Everett closes with some thoughts about the role of pitch in hip-hop, a genre often understood to downplay pitch in favor or rhythm or timbre, and the possibility of atonal rock. In all, over 400 songs are mentioned or analyzed in the chapter.

A100 **Everett, Walter.** "Any Time at All: The Beatles' Free Phrase Rhythms." In Womack, ed., *The Cambridge Companion to the Beatles*. 2009: 183–99. See **C40**.

A study of the free treatment of hypermeter and phrase rhythm in songs of the Beatles. Everett engages theories of Edward Cone, William Rothstein, and others to analyze dozens of metrically and rhythmically complex passages. Some excerpts simply show an irregular grouping or division, such as eight bars grouped as 3+3+2. Most, however, involve the manipulation of a simple four-bar prototype, such as a bar or bars tacked onto the end of a hypermeasure, sometimes forcing retrospective reassessment of weak measure as strong. There are measured fermatas, phrase extensions and expansions, elisions, enjambments, and linkages. In some cases the phrase rhythm itself speeds up with the harmonic rhythm. There is metric modulation as well. Throughout, Everett takes care to draw connections between these rhythmic practices and the lyrics or instrumentation.

A101 **Everett, Walter.** "'If You're Gonna Have a Hit': Intratextual Mixes and Edits of Pop Recordings." *Popular Music* 29, no. 2 (2010): 229–50.

A study of an overlooked site of intertextuality: alternate mixes and edited versions of popular music recordings. Everett details ten types of intertextuality found among recordings of popular music, and focuses on two in particular. The first type, "differing mixes of the same edit," includes comparisons of mono versus stereo mixes as well as a discussion of muting and other remixing effects. The second, "differing edits of the same recording," covers edits made due to the physical capacity of the 45 RPM single or to the expectations (limitations) of radio airplay. These include "edits to the coda," "the crossfade," "cuts to the intro and interior passages," "excised instrumental passages," and "recordings featuring multiple edits." Everett discusses many examples of such edits and analyzes the musical result. Special attention is given to Jethro Tull's *A Passion Play*, Mike Oldfield's *Tubular Bells*, Meat Loaf's "Paradise By the Dashboard Light," and Sugarhill Gang's "Rapper's Delight," albums or longer songs heavily edited for release as singles. Includes several tables and images of various record labels.

A102 **Everett, Walter.** "The Representation of Meaning in Post-Millenial Rock." *Beiträge zur Popularmusikforschung* 38 (2012): 149–69. [Reprinted in Dietrich Helms and Thomas Phleps, eds., *Black Box Pop. Analysen populärer Musik*:

149–69. Bielefeld, Germany: Transcript Verlag, 2012; 282p. ISBN 9783837618785; MT146.B53 2012.]

An examination, through a philosophical lens, of early-2000s rock and the musical representation of its textual themes. Everett, after Arnheim, reads structural tension in a song by Missy Elliott; after Peirce, iconic, symbolic and indexical signs in Randy Newman; and, after Goodman, Kivy, and others, the dialog between text and music in Wilco. He notes songs seem to have "inexhaustible interpretability," and he negotiates alternative meanings in Amy Winehouse. Everett ultimately argues that interpretation may lie in a song's adherence (or non-adherence) to the principles in an underlying tonal system (e.g., treatment of non-chord tones). Includes several musical examples, figures, illustrations, and voice-leading graphs.

A103   **Fast, Susan.** "Music, Contexts, and Meaning in U2." In Everett, ed., *Expression in Pop-Rock Music: Critical and Analytical Essays*, 2nd ed. 2008 [2000]: 175–197. See **C6**.

A study of music as discourse, featuring two songs by U2, each quite different in meaning. The lyrics of "Sunday Bloody Sunday," as well as the imagery and strong posture of lead singer Bono, are linked to specific political events and messages. While musical elements seem at first to contradict this message, contrapuntal and harmonic elements reinforce it. "Zoo Station," especially as performed on the "Zoo TV" tour, carries a different signification. Representative of the band's later dramatic change of style, the music, the lyrics, as well as Bono's vocal style and weaker posture, all seem to signify a reaction to contemporary technology, entertainment, and culture. A new postscript is included in this, the second edition.

A104   **Fink, Robert.** "ORCH5, or, the Classical Ghost in the Hip-Hop Machine." *Popular Music* 24, no. 3 (2005): 339–56. [Reprinted as "ORCH5, or the Classical Ghost in the Hip-Hop Machine." In Eric Weisbard, ed., *Listen Again: A Momentary History of Pop Music*: 231–55. Durham, NC: Duke University Press, 2007; 323p. ISBN 9780822340225; ML3470.L59 2007.]

A story of a single, digital, orchestral sample, from its creation, to its numerous instances and treatments, and to its multivalent associations and meaning. Fink describes how the programmers of the Fairlight CMI sampled a single chord from a recording of Stravinsky's Firebird Suite and included it as a stock sample, "ORCH5." The Fairlight's prohibitive cost kept the sample hidden until Arthur Baker and Afrika Bambaataa highlighted it in "Planet Rock." It is not the only "classical" music in the song, however. Fink traces its melody to Kraftwerk and even to Schubert. The story continues toward more modern reuses and recreations of the sample. Includes several musical examples.

A105   **Fink, Robert.** "Goal-Directed Soul? Analyzing Rhythmic Teleology in African American Popular Music." *Journal of the American Musicological Society* 64, no. 1 (2011): 179–238.

A musical and sociological study of two songs by the Temptations, calling into question the notions that "popular" (African American) music is strictly cyclic

Articles

and groove-oriented, and that "classical" is teleological and goal-oriented. Fink traces this dichotomy to Leonard B. Meyer and Charles Keil, and discusses two recent studies in rhythm. Anne Danielsen's study is shown to reinforce the cyclic orientation of funk's groove, while Mark Butler's study reveals instances of goal-directed motion in electronic dance music. In analyzing Norman Whitfiled's productions "Cloud Nine" and "Runaway Child, Running Wild," Fink positions the four-on-the-four beat as a "rhythmic tonic" and describes how transformations of the rhythm create and release musical tension. So, while the harmony may be static, the rhythm is goal-oriented. He also draws a connection to the goal-oriented aspirations of the black middle-class, as modeled by Berry Gordy and other soul music entrepreneurs. Includes a few musical figures and formal diagrams.

A106 **Fitzgerald, Jon.** "Motown Crossover Hits 1963–1966 and the Creative Process." *Popular Music* 14, no. 1 (1995): 1–11. [Expanded version of "Black or White? Stylistic Analysis of Early Motown 'Crossover' Hits: 1963–1966." In Straw, Johnson, Sullivan, Friedlander, with Kennedy, eds., *Popular Music—Style and Identity: International Conference on Popular Music Studies*. 1993: 95–8.] See **C36**.

A response to the apparent lack of research on Motown songwriters (Holland-Dozier-Holland and William "Smokey" Robinson) compared to the amount of research on their contemporaries (Lennon-McCartney, Goffin-King, and others). Fitzgerald discusses the interactive creative process at Motown as well as the gospel traditions from which the record company's house musicians came. Further, he questions the perceived unity of the Motown sound by contrasting Smokey Robinson's hits with those of Holland-Dozier-Holland. The latter writers' work is shown, through a series of statistical tables covering form, rhythmic devices, and harmonic progressions, to have a distinct, crossover style. Includes several tables and song lists.

A107 **Fitzgerald, Jon.** "Lennon–McCartney and the Early British Invasion, 1964–6." In Inglis, ed., *The Beatles, Popular Music and Society*. 2000: 53–85. See **C18**.

A documentation of the musical features of the British Invasion. Fitzgerald compares the songwriting style of Lennon and McCartney (the Beatles) to those of Dave Clark (The Dave Clark Five), Jagger/Richards (the Rolling Stones), and Ray Davies (the Kinks). After a brief comparison of their chart successes, he analyzes and compiles statistical data on all of the songwriters' U.S. Top 40 hits, focusing on six musical domains: lyrics (themes about relationships, use of satire and metaphor); melody (scale, mode, and distinctive interval); rhythm (tempo, subdivision, and riffs); harmony (diatonicity, modal mixture, and specific harmonies); form (AABA, strophic, verse-chorus); and production (mix, instrumentation, and background vocals). From these analyses, he is able to distinguish two distinct phases of the British Invasion. In the first, the songwriters (primarily Lennon/McCartney and Clark) share many structural elements, many of which closely resemble American songwriters of the Brill Building and Motown. In the second, the songwriters develop distinct songwriting styles, influenced in part by producers George Martin (Beatles) and Andrew Oldham (Rolling Stones). Includes numerous tables and (melodic) musical examples.

A108 **Fitzgerald, Jon.** "Black Pop Songwriting 1963–1966: An Analysis of U.S. Top Forty Hits by Cooke, Mayfield, Stevenson, Robinson, and Holland-Dozier-Holland." *Black Music Research Journal* 27, no. 2 (2007): 97–140. [Reprinted in Hawkins, ed., *Pop Music and Easy Listening*. 2011: 381–424.] See **C9**.

An analysis of all of the U.S. Top 40 hits of songwriters Sam Cooke, Curtis Mayfield, Smokey Robinson, Hollland-Dozier-Holland, and William Stevenson. Fitzgerald analyzes the songs' content in six domains: lyrics (themes and poetic devices); melody (range, mode, intervals, contour, and riffs); rhythm (tempo, subdivision, riffs, and common patterns); harmony (diatonicity, specific progressions, chord colorations, and sequences); form (duration, form type, solo instrumentation); and production (instrumentation, backing vocals). His study suggests that these songwriters introduced many techniques from the gospel tradition into mainstream popular music, and that Sam Cooke was particularly instrumental in this development. Includes song lists and tables of tabulated data.

A109 **Fitzgerald, Jon.** "Creating Those Good Vibrations: An Analysis of Brian Wilson's US Top 40 Hits 1963–66." *Popular Music and Society* 32, no. 1 (2009): 3–24.

An analysis of a group of 24 songs written by Brian Wilson and performed by the Beach Boys, Jan and Dean, and the Hondells. Fitzgerald, working from transcriptions of the recordings, investigated six musical parameters: lyrics (themes of positive relationships and teen interests); melody (mostly with wide range and rising contour); rhythm (fast tempos generally, with a shift from straight subdivision to shuffle in the later years); harmony (largely diatonic, some chromaticism, modulation, and sequence); form (mostly verse-chorus, some AABA); and production (complex vocal arrangements, influence of Phil Spector and of drugs). Includes several musical examples as well as tables showing traits within each musical parameter.

A110 **Flory, Andrew.** "Marvin Gaye as Vocal Composer." In Spicer and Covach, eds., *Sounding Out Pop: Analytical Essays in Popular Music*. 2010: 63–98. See **C34**.

A study of Marvin Gaye's recorded work, revealing that the singer blurred the distinction between composing, performing, and recording by simultaneously doing all three in the studio, directly to tape. Flory analyzes extant instances of multiple takes, different songs created from the same backing track, songs with multi-layered voice tracks, multiple versions of a single song, and early demo recordings. Throughout, the focus is on the recorded vocal performace, which is at the core of the melodic and harmonic structure of the songs. Includes several transcriptions, appendices listing songs written by Marvin Gaye, and a discography.

Articles

A111 **Folse, Stuart.** "Popular Music as a Pedagogical Resource for Musicianship: Contextual Listening, Prolongations, Mediant Relationships, and Musical Form." *Journal of Music Theory Pedagogy* 18 (2004): 65–79.

A suggestion for the incorporation of popular music in the classroom. Folse writes that popular music is full of pedagogically relevant examples for music theory curricula, particularly to support hearing tonal prolongation in aural skills classes. After reviewing some of the difficulties found in teaching harmonic dictation, he demonstrates how Shania Twain's "You're Still the One" can serve as an example of subdominant and tonic prolongation, and how the Eagles' "New Kid in Town" features transient tonicizations and mediant relationships. Includes several musical examples and a formal diagram.

A112 **Ford, Charles.** "'Gently Tender': The Incredible String Band's Early Albums." *Popular Music* 14, no. 2 (1995): 175–183. [Reprinted in Moore, ed., *Critical Essays in Popular Musicology*. 2007: 477–85.] See **C27**.

A brief survey of the songs from The Incredible String Band's first four albums. Ford focuses primarily on the relationship between the text and meter, highlighting numerous irregularities and complexities. Indian, Celtic, and Christian influences all are manifest in the music as well. Includes some figures displaying text and meter.

A113 **Forte, Allen.** "Secrets of Melody: Line and Design in the Songs of Cole Porter." *The Musical Quarterly* 77, no. 4 (1993): 607–47.

A study of the structural, motivic, and harmonic aspects of Cole Porter's melodies. Forte first discusses small-scale, surface elements such as the primary melodic tone (one might think of a Schenkerian *kopfton* here), the highest and lowest tones and their coordination with the form, special notes (such as blue notes or even the special nature of scale degree 1), motivic development, special chords (nearly every song has one chord that has a significant connection with the melodic structure), harmonic progression, and form (particularly exceptions to the AABA). He then discusses long-range aspects of the melody and linear concerns over whole songs. Though Forte does not use Schenkerian terminology, these last two sections discuss the equivalents of linear progression and the fundamental line, respectively. Includes numerous small musical examples and several voice-leading graphs.

A114 **Forte, Allen.** "Harmonic Relations: American Popular Harmonies (1925–1950) and Their European Kin." *Contemporary Music Review* 19, no. 1 (2000): 5–36.

An investigation into the correlations between the European avant-garde music of 1900–25 and the American popular ballads of 1925–50. Forte finds that many sonorities, although they may be employed in the two repertoires in different ways, are held in common. Pitch-class collections from diatonic, pentatonic, whole-tone, and octatonic scales (as well as some "atonal" examples) are cataloged. Forte points out, in closing, some commonalities in the critical response to the introduction of such harmonies in both repertoires. Includes numerous musical figures and examples of harmonic correspondence.

A115 **Garcia, Luis-Manuel.** "On and On: Repetition as Process and Pleasure in Electronic Dance Music." *Music Theory Online* 11, no. 4 (2005).

A study of repetition in electronic dance music (EDM) and an attempt to rescue it from critical and analytical aspersion. Garcia first discusses the (mostly negative) reputation of repetition and theorizes (more positively) the pleasure in repetition, starting with Karl Bühler's critique of Freud. He then focuses on three EDM tracks, each analyzed from one of three perspectives: looping as process (Plastikman's "ethnik" [sic] using Mark Spicer's "accumulative form"); looping as prolongation of pleasure (Tony Rohr's "Baile Conmigo" with an expansion of Mark Butler's model of dissonant textural layers); and process as pleasure (Afuken's "Deck the House" as dizzying collage of microsamples building on the work of Karl Bühler). Includes one musical figure and a few audio examples.

A116 **Gauldin, Robert.** "Beethoven, Tristan, and the Beatles." *College Music Symposium* 30, no. 1 (1990): 142–52.

An analysis of the Beatles' music, serving to reinforce musical principles found in Beethoven and Wagner. Gauldin first likens the motivic parallelism in "Something" to that in a Beethoven sonata. He then provides a large-scale analysis of Wagner's Tristan prelude (after Robert Morgan and Robert Bailey) and finds that side two of the Beatles' *Abbey Road* exhibits a similar key scheme and arrangement around a double tonic. Includes musical examples and formal diagrams.

A117 **Gaunt, Kyra.** "The Veneration of James Brown and George Clinton in Hip-Hop Music: Is it Live? Or Is it Re-memory?" In Straw, Johnson, Sullivan, Friedlander, with Kennedy, eds., *Popular Music—Style and Identity: International Conference on Popular Music Studies.* 1993: 117–22. See **C36**.

An argument that sampling is not simply a postmodern technique but that it is a continuation of African American practices that trace back to slave culture. Gaunt discusses James Brown's capturing of a "live" sound in the studio, which ultimately struggled on pop radio but succeeded with R&B audiences. George Clinton is shown to have similar ideals and even shared many musicians with Brown. The two artists are venerated by later hip-hop artists like Public Enemy and producer Hank Shocklee, who constructed "Fight the Power" with samples in much the same way that Brown used instruments in a percussive collage. Includes two transcribed excerpts.

A118 **Gelbart, Matthew.** "A Cohesive Shambles: The Clash's 'London Calling' and the Normalization of Punk." *Music and Letters* 92, no. 2 (2011): 230–72.

A study of the divide between music history and cultural history, as perceived by musicians, critics, and historians. Gelbart specifically focuses on the Clash's landmark album and its role in "normalizing" punk. While one can trace a coherent narrative across the double album's four sides, one also can point to the ways in which this coherence is disrupted. The article surveys deeply the critical reception but also looks analytically at key relationships and their relationships to lyrics. Includes several lyrics and a table of keys with commentary.

A119   **Givan, Benjamin.** "Duets for One: Louis Armstrong's Vocal Recordings." *The Musical Quarterly* 87, no. 2 (2004): 188–218.

An essay detailing the overdubbing technique found in some of Louis Armstrong's later recordings that allowed him more flexibly to add blues-inflected improvisations to his vocal performances. Givan notes that Armstrong already had employed innovative interpolations in his recordings with others, but the overdubbing process allowed him to duet with himself. Givan traces Armstrong's playing and singing styles in the early years, particularly the changes in his speech-like treatment (and truncation) of the lyrics, and shows how technology made modification of the sung melody no longer necessary, thus enabling more complex interaction of melody and improvisation. Includes several transcriptions.

A120   **Graziano, John.** "Compositional Strategies in Popular Song Form of the Early Twentieth Century." *Gamut* 6, no. 2 (2013): 95–131.

A close look at new harmonic possibilities brought about by the emerging AABA form, as found in 25 songs from the 1910s and 1920s. Graziano points out that as the refrain in the simpler verse-chorus structure more frequently exhibited AABA structure, it was able to accommodate more harmonic complexity. Examples include the prolongation of the subdominant in the bridge, the treatment of the mediant, the tonicization of the submediant, and the employment of the circle of fifths. Harmonic syntax itself became more surprising and unusual. Graziano concludes that the AABA could support such innovations due to the harmonic stasis and tonic centricity of the A-sections. Includes 25 excerpts from sheet music with accompanying voice-leading reductions.

A121   **Grier, James.** "Ego and Alter Ego: Artistic Interaction Between Bob Dylan and Roger McGuinn." In Spicer and Covach, eds., *Sounding Out Pop: Analytical Essays in Popular Music*. 2010: 42–62. See **C34**.

A comparison of Roger McGuinn's recordings (with or without The Byrds) of Bob Dylan songs with Dylan's own recordings. Grier traces significant differences in timbre, chords, harmonic rhythm, and form, but his primary focus is meter. He shows Dylan and McGuinn to be in a kind of dialog with one another through their performances, which continued for decades. Includes examples of harmonic progressions, side-by-side vocal parts, drum patterns, and a complete list of Dylan songs recorded by McGuinn.

A122   **Griffiths, Dai.** "Three Tributaries of 'The River.'" *Popular Music* 7, no. 1 (1988): 27–34. [Reprinted in Middleton, ed., *Reading Pop: Approaches to Textual Analysis in Popular Music*. 2000: 192–202.] See **C23**.

An analysis of the connections between the lyrics and the music in a song by Bruce Springsteen. Griffiths closely examines the lyrics with respect to rhyme, duality, and their coordination with harmonic rhythm, and he shows how chord progressions project a narrative path. Looking for more ("beyond content, beyond form"), Griffiths reveals how the first verse (imprecise, mythical) and the second verse (precise, factual) lead to self-revelation in the third and fourth. Includes a few musical examples and lyrics.

A123 **Griffiths, Dai.** "Cover Versions and the Sound of Identity in Motion." In Hesmondhalgh and Negus, eds., *Popular Music Studies*. 2002: 51–64. See **C13**.

An investigation of cover songs, with the original and the cover together giving rise to the study of cultural identity and political power. Griffiths focuses on numerous covers in which there is a shift in gender (e.g., Roberta Flack covering Bob Dylan), sexuality (e.g., multiple readings of "It's My Party"), or race (e.g., white-covering-black, black-covering white). He also includes examples of shifts in class, nation, and language. Includes one table with formal details.

A124 **Griffiths, Dai.** "From Lyric to Anti-Lyric: Analyzing the Words in Pop Song." In Moore, ed., *Analyzing Popular Music*. 2003: 39–59. See **C26**.

A discussion of the difficulty in analyzing lyrics. Can their meaning be determined independent of the music? Griffiths acknowledges the blurred lines between lyrics and poetry but proposes a view of lyrics in which they are on a continuum, the poles of which are poetry and prose ("lyric" and "anti-lyric"). His "verbal space" is where the lyrical phrase works within musical constraints, a kind of timeline on which a lyric's properties may be analyzed. The density of words in this space (particularly when comparing multiple iterations of a verse), the shifting of elements forward and back, rhyme (full, near, and non-), alliteration, parts of speech, and the novelty of certain words all help to distinguish lyric from anti-lyric. Includes several tables and musical examples.

A125 **Harrison, Daniel.** "After Sundown: The Beach Boys' Experimental Music." In Covach and Boone, eds., *Understanding Rock: Essays in Musical Analysis*. 1997: 33–58. See **C4**.

An analytical survey of the Beach Boys' phase of adventurous composition, starting with some of their earlier ballads, working through "Good Vibrations," and culminating in the more experimental albums that followed. Harrison highlights structural complexity, particularly with respect to hypermeter, formal ambiguity, and unusual harmonic shifts that enable modulation to remote keys. Includes several analytical examples and formal diagrams.

A126 **Hawkins, Stan.** "Prince: Harmonic Analysis of 'Anna Stesia.'" *Popular Music* 11, no. 3 (1992): 325–35. [Reprinted in Middleton, ed., *Reading Pop: Approaches to Textual Analysis in Popular Music*. 2000: 58–70.] See **C23**.

An examination of harmony in a single song. Hawkins begins his analysis with a complete assessment of phrase structure, harmonic structure, and textural levels, all in eight-measure units. A close examination of its chords reveals that the song is in Aeolian mode, and excursions from tonic are interpreted as transformations of i–iv–i. The impact of studio techniques (i.e., equalization, pitch shifting, compression, and mixing) on the harmony is considered. Ultimately, the song's meaning is found in these musical elements and their connection to the lyrics. Includes several musical examples, figures, and tables.

A127   **Hawkins, Stan.** "New Perspectives in Musicology: Musical Structures, Codes and Meaning in 1990s Pop." In Straw, Johnson, Sullivan, Friedlander, with Kennedy, eds., *Popular Music—Style and Identity: International Conference on Popular Music Studies.* 1993: 131–36. See **C36**.

An example of how one might analyze both the structure of popular music and how its meaning might be coded. Hawkins offers two case studies: "Harmony, Structure, and Vocal Timbre in 'Money Can't Buy It'" and "Timbre, Samples, and a Bass Riff in 'Fishin' for Religion.'" The first song, by Annie Lennox, is characterized by modal ambiguity and a rich set of timbre changes in the voice. The second, by Arrested Development, displays a verse-chorus form as call-and-response and features a striking authentic cadence in a predominantly Aeolian landscape. Includes musical examples, tables, and lyrics.

A128   **Hawkins, Stan.** "The Pet Shop Boys: Musicology, Masculinity, and Banality." In Sheila Whiteley, ed., *Sexing the Groove: Popular Music and Gender*: 118–33. London and New York: Routledge, 1997; 353p. ISBN 0415146712; ML3470.S46 1997.

An analysis of the Pet Shop Boys' musical style. Hawkins first surveys the politics of gender surrounding the group's rise to fame in the 1980s. Due to their combining Hi-NRG disco with serious lyrical content, as evidenced in the music video for their song "Domino Dancing," multiple gender and sexual readings inevitably arise. As a result, the music is always open to interpretation. Their song "Yesterday, When I Was Mad" becomes the site for analysis of the band's lyrics of "gloom" being "cushioned by easy harmonic progressions." This banality should not be dismissed, however, for this is where Hawkins locates their style: detailed and intricate rhythm, an expressionless vocal style, and a deliberately synthetic production. Includes a few musical examples.

A129   **Hawkins, Stan.** "Feel the Beat Come Down: House Music as Rhetoric." In Moore, ed., *Analyzing Popular Music.* 2003: 80–102. See **C26**.

An evaluation of the erotic dance track "French Kiss" by Lil' Louis (and house music in general) that considers its musical elements to understand how the track (and the genre) works in its cultural context. Hawkins gives a brief history of house music, describes its technological elements while emphasizing improvisation, and focuses on the important role of repetition ("cellular groove patterns") in the compositional design. Hawkins also looks at the direct connections between the music production and the genre-specific activity on the dance floor. Includes a few visual analyses and a brief transcription.

A130 **Hawkins, Stan.** "'Chelsea Rogers' was a Model: Vocality in Prince of the Twenty-First Century." In Scott, ed., *The Ashgate Research Companion to Popular Musicology*. 2009: 335–48. See **C33**.

An analysis of vocal performance in a song by Prince. Hawkins gives a basic account of the track's groove, rooted in the bass and drums. The primary focus, however, is on the voice in its many articulations and on Prince's interactions with featured singer Shelby Johnson, whose presence highlights Prince's "construction of masculinity, sexuality, and race." He also discusses the arrangement and production details that sustain the listener for the duration of the track. Includes two musical examples and two tables.

A131 **Headlam, Dave.** "Does the Song Remain the Same? Questions of Authorship and Identification in the Music of Led Zeppelin." In Marvin and Hermann, eds., *Concert Music, Rock, and Jazz Since 1945: Essays and Analytical Studies*. 1995: 313–63. See **C20**.

A study of Led Zeppelin's authorial mark: its distinctive treatment of riffs, juxtaposed "formal blocks," vocal delivery, timbre, and rhythm. Headlam summarizes contemporary writing on music from both the socio-cultural and the music-structural camps. Drawing upon Foucault, he then focuses on the tricky matter of authorship. Three songs by Led Zeppelin, many of whose songs are not originally composed by the group but are based on pre-existing sources, serve as case studies in which true authorship can be found in the reworking of a pre-existing song. Includes extensive analyses and transcriptions of Led Zeppelin's versions and the originals.

A132 **Headlam, Dave.** "Blues Transformations in the Music of Cream." In Covach and Boone, eds., *Understanding Rock: Essays in Musical Analysis*. 1997: 59–92. See **C4**.

A study of the rock group Cream and their adaptations of blues songs. Headlam, after reviewing the relationship of Chicago blues and British blues, focuses on Cream's treatment of three songs: "Cross Road Blues" (riff is repeated and regularized), "Rollin' and Tumblin'" (syncopation of original is exaggerated and formal design is modified to accommodate improvisational elements), and "Sittin' on Top of the World" (tempo is slowed and harmonies are jazzed up). The essay ends with some proposals for future research, including questions of harmony versus scale, the study and cataloging of riffs, the matter of rhythm versus meter, and finally timbre, the sound itself. Includes several transcriptions and formal diagrams.

A133 **Heinonen, Yrjö.** "Michelle, Ma Belle: Songwriting as Coping with Inner Conflict." In Heinonen, Eerola, Koskimäki, Nurmesjärvi, and Richardson, eds., *Beatlestudies 1: Songwriting, Recording, and Style Change*. 1998: 147–59. See **C10**.

A demonstration that composition may have therapeutic ends as well as artistic ones. Heinonen, using Freud's theories on creativity and subsequent work by

Maynard Solomon and Endel Tulving, proposes that the creative process involves the mixing of some recent event with an event in the past (usually childhood). Measuring a harmonic and melodic analysis of Paul McCartney's "Michelle" against those of 2,500 popular songs from 1920 to 1965, Heinonen discovered nine songs that not only are similar to "Michelle" but also may be subconscious inspirations for the song due to their contemporaneity to the past event (death of McCartney's mother) and the recent (break with Jane Asher). A study of lyric themes is made in support of the thesis. Includes tables of harmonic analyses and lyric themes.

A134 **Heinonen, Yrjö.** "In Search of Lost Order: Archetypal Meanings in 'Lucy in the Sky with Diamonds.'" In Heinonen, Koskimäki, Niemi, and Nurmesjärvi, eds., *Beatlestudies 2: History, Identity, Autheticity*. 2000: 207–55. See **C11**.

A reading of the Beatles' song that draws upon the work of Carl Jung (ego and self) and Daniel Stern (the four senses of self) and interprets the archetypes found in the lyrics and music. Heinonen acknowledges its potential connection to LSD specifically, but he reads the song as a search for inner order and self-understanding. He leads the reader through the archetypes in the lyrics (diamond, mandala, mantra, anima, water, tree, flower) as well as those in the music, which is compared melodically to various church modes (Hypomixolydian, Dorian) and considered for the expressive character of individual keys (with reference to classical notions of musical affect). Includes several musical examples, figures, and tables.

A135 **Hesselink, Nathan D.** "Radiohead's 'Pyramid Song': Ambiguity, Rhythm, and Participation." *Music Theory Online* 19, no. 1 (2013).

An analytical look at the many ways in which fans and listeners perceive the ambiguous meter in a song by Radiohead. Hesselink situates "Pyramid Song" in the band's overall output and gives an overview of the song's metrical complexity. In online communities, the song has inspired a host of insightful, analytical responses from musicians and non-musicians alike. Hesselink collates many of them and organizes them according to the salient aspects of their interpretations: regular meter, no meter identified, non-isochronous meters, compound meters, 4/4 with swung eighth notes, four-bar cycle, two-bar cycle, and mixed meter. The diversity of responses and the broad array of disciplines that inform them hold this case study as an example of crowdsourcing or mass collaboration. Includes several musical figures and an appendix with a "listening challenge."

A136 **Hisama, Ellie M.** "Voice, Race, and Sexuality in the Music of Joan Armatrading." In Elaine Barkin and Lydia Hamessley, eds., *Audible Traces: Gender, Identity, and Music*: 115–31. Zürich and Los Angeles: Carciofoli Verlagshaus, 1999; 358p. ISBN 3905323001; ML82.A93 1999.

An exploration of gender, sexuality, and race in the music and identity of Joan Armatrading. Hisama argues that the singer-songwriter's unconventional, genre-crossing music can be heard as challenging traditional notions of what it means to be black, British, and female. Several songs are analyzed in order to address vocal register as the site of power or gender, ambiguity and multiple readings in the lyrics, and the mix of musical influences. Includes two musical examples and several lyrics.

A137 **Hisama, Ellie M.** "From L'Étranger to 'Killing and Arab': Representing the Other in a Cure Song." In Everett, ed., *Expression in Pop-Rock Music: Critical and Analytical Essays*, 2nd ed. 2008 [2000]: 199–213. See **C6**.

An analysis of "Killing an Arab" by The Cure. After its release in a greatest hits compilation, the song was widely criticized as anti-Arab, but the band claimed that it carried no such sentiment and that it was based on a scene in Albert Camus's novel *L'Etranger*. Hisama ultimately concludes, after a survey of the literature on *L'Etranger*, that the song can be read as an alignment with the victim of murder, not the narrator. Some musical elements adduced in support: signification of the Orient through ironically inauthentic scale degrees in vocal line, interaction of the instruments, and the relationship of music and lyrics.

A138 **Holm-Hudson, Kevin.** "The 'American Metaphysical Circus' of Joseph Byrd's United States of America." In Holm-Hudson, ed., *Progressive Rock Reconsidered*. 2002: 43–62. See **C15**.

A look at the music of The United States of America, a group far more avant-garde and "serious" than given credit for at the time. Holm-Hudson details the meeting of the band members, who had backgrounds in contemporary art music. The band's sole album, from 1968, which features synthesizers, Ivesian collage, 12-bar blues, and pop-culture parody, is shown to be a unique blend of highbrow and lowbrow culture. Includes one musical figure highlighting chromatic mediants.

A139 **Holm-Hudson, Kevin.** "A Promise Deferred: Multiply Directed Time and Thematic Transformation in Emerson Lake and Palmer's 'Trilogy.'" In Holm-Hudson, ed., *Progressive Rock Reconsidered*. 2002: 111–20. See **C15**.

A study of large-scale tensions in a progressive-rock work. Holm-Hudson first discusses the coordination of the tonal areas into a "macroprogression." He further notes that some sections are frustrated or interrupted by following ones, and their resolution or completion is delayed. He refers here to Jonathan Kramer's "multiply directed time." The second discussion is a charting of the thematic transformation over the entire work. Includes a few musical examples and a large formal diagram.

A140 **Holm-Hudson, Kevin J.** "Your Guitar, It Sounds So Sweet and Clear: Semiosis in Two Versions of 'Superstar.'" *Music Theory Online* 8, no. 4 (2002).

A semiotic comparison of two versions of the same song, showing the influence and effect of timbre and recording techniques. Holm-Hudson interprets the recording across three levels of analysis: the poietic (details of the creation of both the Carpenters' version and an earlier one by Bette Midler); the esthesic (the song's critical reception with attention to the vocal delivery); and the neutral (analysis of the two recordings themselves). At the neutral level, Holm-Hudson discovers numerous signs ("genre-synecdoches") from the pop and classical genres in the Carpenters' version, referring at times to the work of Deryck Cooke and of Eero Tarasti. The Sonic Youth version shows timbre to aid in a reading with a changed gender persona and a sense of ironic nostalgia. An informal survey of students hearing the song (just the introduction—no lyrics) seemed to support these observations. Includes musical transcriptions of song excerpts, several audio examples, and survey results.

A141 **Holm-Hudson, Kevin.** "'Come Sail Away' and the Commodification of 'Prog Lite.'" *American Music* 23, no. 3 (2005): 377–94.

An analysis of specific intertextual references and gendered coding in a song by Styx. Holm-Hudson traces both the emergence of "prog-lite," seen in some ways as an imitation of an imitation of classical music, and its relationship to album-oriented rock (AOR). Influenced by Robert Hatten, he highlights the song's reference to Mozart (in the piano figure), The Who (the rock guitar pattern), and Terry Riley (the synth interlude), but he also notes the ways in which the borrowings are modified or simplified. Influenced by Edward Macan, he points out gender codes in the timbre. Includes a few musical examples and transcriptions.

A142 **Holm-Hudson, Kevin.** "A Study of Maximally Smooth Voice Leading in the Mid-1970s Music of Genesis." In Spicer and Covach, eds., *Sounding Out Pop: Analytical Essays in Popular Music*. 2010: 99–123. See **C34**.

A presentation of the Neo-Riemannian voice-leading techniques in the music of Genesis in the 1970s. Holm-Hudson, after summarizing basic Neo-Riemannian transformations, uses the techniques of Cohn, Lewin, Roeder (voice-leading vector), and Capuzzo to trace pitch parsimony in the group's songs, particularly those composed by keyboardist Tony Banks. He notes that as the group shifted toward a more popular radio-friendly sound in the 1980s, the techniques became less prevalent but were still evident in some album tracks, unreleased music, and also in a Banks solo album. There also is a discussion of the band's frequent use of pedal point. Includes numerous musical examples and figures.

A143 **Hubbs, Nadine.** "The Imagination of Pop-Rock Criticism." In Everett, ed., *Expression in Pop-Rock Music: Critical and Analytical Essays*, 2nd ed. 2008 [2000]: 215–37. See **C6**.

An argument for a pop-rock criticism that directly engages the music itself. Seeking to bridge the gap between musical discourse and musical experience, Hubbs doesn't propose the abandoning of music-theoretical tools but cautions against their use at the expense of other experiential elements. In response to Edward Macan's critique of "analysis for its own sake," she sympathizes with Allan F. Moore, who advocates a broader approach. As an example of the type of analysis (criticism) she advocates, one that is more useful to a wider audience, Hubbs investigates Radiohead's "Exit Music (For a Film)."

A144 **Hughes, Tim.** "Trapped Within the Wheels: Flow and Repetition, Modernism and Tradition in Stevie Wonder's 'Living for the City.'" In Everett, ed., *Expression in Pop-Rock Music: Critical and Analytical Essays*, 2nd ed. 2008 [2000]: 239–65. See **C6**.

A thorough analysis of a single song, "Living for the City," one of many politically and socially conscious songs from the 1960s and 1970s. Hughes, examining chord, cadence, rhythm, meter, and rhyme, finds multiple cycles in the song, all occurring at different levels, creating a "compound flow." He starts with the basic vamp and leads to a dramatic shift brought about by a disorienting chorus, with its irregular metric pattern and bass motion. The subsequent vignette of a youth unjustly arrested, followed by unfulfilled expectations in harmony and meter, is linked to the African American experience in America. Multiple live performances of the song from different decades are compared and contrasted as well. The chapter includes several musical examples and diagrams of form, meter, and lyrics.

A145 **Huron, David and Ann Ommen.** "An Empirical Study of Syncopation in American Popular Music, 1890–1939." *Music Theory Spectrum* 28, no. 2 (2006): 211–31.

A focused study of the popular music of a particular time and place, testing for the prevalence of syncopation in the U.S. in the late 19th and early 20th centuries. The authors provide an operational, yet theoretically neutral, definition of the syncopation: the lacuna (strong metric position with no note onset), the pre-lacuna, and the post-lacuna. Their sample (1,131 recordings) and their methodology are detailed, and their hypotheses (density of syncopated moments increases in the early 20th century; variety of syncopation increases; syncopated patterns become more adventurous) are shown mostly to be correct. Generally, syncopation was shown to increase in quality, if not in quantity, in the time period considered. Includes several graphs, tables, and musical examples.

A146 **Jarman-Ivens, Freya.** "Queer(ing) Masculinities in Heterosexist Rap Music." In Whiteley and Rycenga, eds., *Queering the Popular Pitch*. 2006: 199–219. See **C39**.

An investigation of masculinity in rap music, particularly that of Eminem. Jarman-Ivens notes that although rap groups are often read as both hypermasculine and homophobic, some incongruities exist. She discusses paradoxes in gender and language, and considers language as patriarchal structure in a gendered reading of rhythmic displacement in voice and drum in an Eminem track. After Susan McClary, she finds in two other songs the persistence of the long-held associations of closure with the masculine and cyclic movement or repetition with the feminine. Ultimately she wonders whether the associations held above are problematically essentialist, and questions whether there is anything queer in rap at all. Includes one stand-alone figure and several rhythmic notations embedded in the prose.

A147   **Johns, Donald.** "Funnel Tonality in American Popular Music, ca. 1900–70." *American Music* 11, no. 4 (1993): 458–72.

A study of a particular syntactical practice in 20th-century songwriting. Johns notes that many songs, from Tin Pan Alley to the 1960s, do not begin with a statement of the tonic harmony. Often they will begin off-tonic, perhaps on a secondary dominant. What may follow is a dynamic process of reaching for the stable tonal state, through circles of fifths or chord substitutions. With the term "funnel tonality," Johns seeks to incorporate Schoenberg's "suspended" and "fluctuating" tonality into one metaphor. The "funnel" can be the length of a few chords or it can span an entire song form, as in Burt Bacharach's "What the World Needs Now," in which the tonic arrives in the coda. In ABAB' forms, the first funnel may last through the first AB, with a brief touchdown on tonic and with a second funnel reaching tonic at the end of the form. In AABA form, the B-section is frequently the site of this phenomenon. Johns concludes that tonic emphasis is not required for tonal coherence. Includes numerous musical examples and formal diagrams.

A148   **Johnson, Nicholas.** "Jack White and the Music of the Past, Present, and Future." *Rock Music Studies* 1, no. 2 (2014): 111–31.

An exploration of the influence of Jack White and his postmodern blues revival. Johnson argues that White's influence is the product of his approaches to past musical influences (Delta blues), to gaining attention (mythological persona and simplicity in imagery), and to profiting in the music business (promotion of the resurging vinyl LP through his label, Third Man Records). Johnson discusses several songs by White (and by his band, The White Stripes), comparing harmony, riffs, and form with recordings of Muddy Waters and Son House.

A149   **Josephson, Nors S.** "Bach Meets Liszt: Traditional Formal Structures and Performance Practices in Progressive Rock." *The Musical Quarterly* 76, no. 1 (1992): 67–92.

A study of the formal structures and performance practices in progressive rock. Josephson outlines various idioms according to the historical era from which the influence comes. Some examples from the Renaissance and the Baroque are covered (e.g., madrigal in Gentle Giant and chaconne in the Beatles and Klaatu), but variation structures from the Classical and Romantic eras receive the most attention (instrumental coloration, cantus-firmus variation, melodic variation, and even sonata form). He also considers 20th-century elements such as the synthesizer timbre, modes, non-diatonic scales, and quartal harmony. The article is notable for its inclusion of progressive rock from New Zealand, Greece, Venezuela, Spain, Germany, and Japan. Includes several musical examples and formal diagrams.

A150   **Kaminsky, Peter.** "The Popular Album as Song Cycle: Paul Simon's *Still Crazy after All These Years*." *College Music Symposium* 32 (1992): 38–54.

An analysis of long-range structure in an album by Paul Simon. Kaminsky correlates specific musical elements with themes in the lyrical narrative, revealing coherence and closure. Two governing principles throughout are pattern completion (syntactical), such as the sequence of keys on each side, and association (expressive), such as Simon's references to numerous genres and idioms. The article closes with some thoughts about similarities to some Romantic-era song cyles. Includes several voice-leading reductions, musical excerpts, and a large-scale formal diagram.

A151 **Kaminsky, Peter M.** "Revenge of the Boomers: Notes on the Analysis of Rock Music." *Music Theory Online* 6, no. 3 (2000).

A commentary on the state of popular music theory and an analysis of a song by Sting. Kaminsky surveys and contrasts recent work by Philip Tagg, Richard Middleton, and Walter Everett. He then offers an analysis of "Lithium Sunset," connecting structural elements (such as harmony and mode mixture) with metaphor in the lyrics, by way of the appropriation of elements of country music (such as the pedal-steel guitar and use of irony). Originally delivered in a plenary session at the 2000 meeting of the New England Conference of Music Theorists. Includes a few musical examples and figures.

A152 **Karl, Gregory.** "King Crimson's Larks' Tongues in Aspic: A Case of Convergent Evolution." In Holm-Hudson, ed., *Progressive Rock Reconsidered*. 2002: 121–42. See **C15**.

An argument that King Crimson's "Lark's Tongues in Aspic" (Parts One and Two) developed organically out of their compositional practices in prior works. Karl notes that while one cannot prove that compositional elements, whether superficial or structural, were not borrowed or learned from Western art music, there is enough musical evidence in the band's compositional record to suggest that it is a case of "convergent evolution," in which the band reached the same compositional ends but on a different evolutionary track: popular music. Form and narrative in the tracks are compared side-by-side with those in earlier ones, and a harmonic and motivic analysis is offered. Aspects of the sonata-form narrative are present, albeit in a popular-song form. Includes a formal diagram and small motivic examples.

A153 **Kerton, Sarah.** "Too Much, Tatu Young: Queering Politics in the World of Tatu." In Whiteley and Rycenga, eds., *Queering the Popular Pitch*. 2006: 155–67. See **C39**. [Reprinted in McQuinn, ed., *Popular Music and Multimedia*. 2011: 407–19.] See **C21**.

A reading of "All the Things She Said" by Russian pop duo t.A.T.u. Kerton identifies a number of juxtaposed musical elements (European pop, Russian folk, metal riffs) and defiant lyrical themes (independence and assertion of sexuality) in the music and the music video. Both are shown to challenge cultural and gender norms. However, multiple readings are possible, and Kerton explores the song's mixed reception history. Some see a challenge to restraints on female expression, while others may read it as appealing to normative male fantasies by staging their sexuality. Includes a musical figure; analysis is mostly prose.

A154 **Koozin, Timothy.** "Fumbling Towards Ecstasy: Voice Leading, Tonal Structure, and the Theme of Self-Realization in the Music of Sarah McLachlan." In Everett, ed., *Expression in Pop-Rock Music: Critical and Analytical Essays*, 2nd ed. 2008 [2000]: 267–84. See **C6**.

An analysis of four songs by Sarah McLachlan, in which voice leading is connected to the singer-songwriter's larger narratives of self-actualization. Modal inflections, chord extensions, and cyclic harmonic patterns all are shown to relate directly to the lyrics. Several voice-leading graphs are included.

A155 **Koozin, Timothy.** "Guitar Voicing in Pop-Rock Music: A Performance-Based Analytical Approach." *Music Theory Online* 17, no. 3 (2011).

An amalgamation of guitar fingering and transformational theory that shows patterns of guitar voicings to bear cultural meaning. Koozin tracks physical motion on the guitar fretboard, via tablature, and interprets the motions as expressive gestures that contribute to the small- and large-scale form. He introduces a "fret-interval" type for labeling barre-chord shapes, which forms the basis of his (Neo-Riemannian) transformational networks. He also investigates open-string chord voicings and the idiomatic treatment of dissonance. Includes numerous musical examples, tablature figures, audio and video examples, and transformational diagrams.

A156 **Koskimäki, Jouni and Yrjö Heinonen.** "Variation as the Key Principle of Arrangement in 'Cry Baby Cry.'" In Heinonen, Eerola, Koskimäki, Nurmesjärvi, and Richardson, eds., *Beatlestudies 1: Songwriting, Recording, and Style Change*. 1998: 119–45. See **C10**.

A study of variation in the practice of musical arrangement. Koskimäki and Heinonen lay out basic principles of variation (after Tyndall and Bent), discuss the distinction between transcription and arranging, and make note of George Martin's role as arranger in the recording process. They propose to study arrangement in popular music in the same way that one would study orchestration in classical music; one needs only to make an accurate transcription in lieu of a score. In their analysis of "Cry Baby Cry," the simple AAB form is repeated several times, but variation is nonetheless manifest in three ways: the internal variation in the A-sections themselves, the varying number of instruments throughout the scoring, and the panning of instruments in the stereo mix. Includes several tables and diagrams related to form, arrangement, and mix.

A157 **Koskimäki, Jouni.** "Happiness Is . . . A Good Transcription: Shortcomings in Sheet Music Publications of 'Happiness is a Warm Gun.'" In Heinonen, Koskimäki, Niemi, and Nurmesjärvi, eds., *Beatlestudies 2: History, Identity, Autheticity*. 2000: 169–205. See **C11**.

A discussion of the problems and pitfalls in transcribing rhythmically complex pop music for publication as sheet music. Koskimäki surveys the various formats of sheet music (vocal/piano, lead sheet, full score, partial transcription, and simplified) and discusses the numerous problems, particularly rhythmic, one encounters when transcribing. He then compiles ten published versions of a single Beatles song and compares them with his own, again primarily with respect to meter, pointing out the relative merits of each. Includes numerous transcriptions, musical examples, and tables.

A158 **Krims, Adam.** "Marxist Music Analysis Without Adorno: Popular Music and Urban Geography." In Moore, ed., *Analyzing Popular Music*. 2003: 131–57. See **C26**.

An example, as the title suggests, of Marxist analysis of popular analysis with the obstacle of Adorno. Krims notes in the first half of the article that analysis of popular music has not been able to avoid Adorno's two principal critiques of popular music: cultural imperialism and standardization of production. However, under Flexible Accumulation, or Post-Fordism, capitalism has shown Adorno's critique to be insufficient. In the second half, Krims proposes a non-Adornian Marxism, relating changes in urban geography to changes in rap music and contrasting reality rap with knowledge rap. Includes two musical excerpts.

A159 **Lacasse, Serge.** "Intertextuality and Hypertextuality in Recorded Popular Music." In Michael Talbot, ed., *The Musical Work: Reality or Invention?*: 35–58. Liverpool: Liverpool University Press, 2000; 260p. ISBN 0853238251; ML3800.L69 1998. [Reprinted in Moore, ed., *Critical Essays in Popular Musicology*. 2007: 147–70.] See **C27**.

Mapping Gerard Gennette's terminology onto popular music, Lacasse develops a taxonomy of intertextuality and hypertextuality. He adapts subcategories of the former (quotation, allusion) and of the latter (parody, travesty, pastiche), but he extends these concepts adding copy, cover, translation, and instrumental cover. Examples include the music of Puff Daddy, David Bowie, Oasis, Jimi Hendrix, and others. The chapter closes by arranging these categories ontologically, with style and content as paradigm and syntagm, respectively.

A160 **Lambert, Philip.** "Brian Wilson's *Pet Sounds*." *Twentieth-Century Music* 5, no. 1 (2008): 109–33.

A close analytical reading of the songs on a single, unified album. Lambert focuses on the musical interrelationships that lend coherence to the large-scale work. He discusses Brian Wilson's influences, like The Four Freshman and Phil Spector, gives details about the making of the album, and outlines a single, lyric-derived narrative. The chief analytical aim here, however, is to highlight key relations, motive (particularly arch shapes and stepwise bass descents), vocal layering, chromaticism in harmony and voice leading, and details in the arrangements. Includes numerous musical examples, voice-leading reductions, and tables.

A161 **Legg, Andrew.** "A Taxonomy of Musical Gesture in African American Gospel Music." *Popular Music* 29, no. 1 (2010): 103–29.

A taxonomy of gospel singing techniques and a system for their notation. Legg compiles the techniques outlined by Pearl Williams-Jones and Horace Clarence

Boyer, and discusses several musical examples for each. They fall into two broad categories: timbre (gravel and grunts; screams and shouts; song-speech and vibrato; timbre and register shifts) and pitch (slides, glides, wails and the hi-who; blues inflection; passing tones, bends, neighbor notes, and the gospel gruppetto). Includes numerous examples. Also includes, as an appendix, a complete taxonomy with concise descriptions of each element and explanation of the corresponding notations used throughout the article.

A162 **Letts, Marianne Tatom.** "'I'm Not Here, This Isn't Happening': The Vanishing Subject in Radiohead's *Kid A*." In Spicer and Covach, eds., *Sounding Out Pop: Analytical Essays in Popular Music*. 2010: 214–43. See **C34**.

An examination of the musical contributions to an album's cohesion. Letts notes that concept albums are usually understood to exhibit narrative, lyrically thematic, or musically thematic unity. She argues, however, that cohesion in Radiohead's *Kid A* is demonstrated by consistent resistance to such unity and as such is a "resistant" concept album. Through analysis of binary oppositions (sense/nonsense, music/noise) and investigating key schemes, instrumentation, harmonic progression and ambiguity, groove, and texture, Letts details the protagonist's appearance and ultimate dissolution. Includes several musical examples and tables.

A163 **Leydon, Rebecca.** "Recombinant Style Topics: The Past and Future of Sampling." In Spicer and Covach, eds., *Sounding Out Pop: Analytical Essays in Popular Music*. 2010: 193–213. See **C34**.

A study of topics, sampling, and authorship. Leydon, by adapting the topic theories of Leonard Ratner and others, finds "stylistic topoi" to be the means by which some contemporary musicians continue to participate in the culture of digital sampling while avoiding some of its biggest criticisms. Through stylistic allusions, as opposed to direct sampling, musicians can continue the eclectic and referential qualities of the music while also retaining instrumental prowess and authorship, two things precluded by traditional digital sampling. The musician Beck is shown to make this move from samples (in *Odelay*) to style topics (in *Midnite Vultures*) by pairing extreme or opposing styles in the latter album. A song by the group Mr. Bungle is examined in detail with respect to its style topics: antique mechanical/carnival music, retro-futurism, bubblegum, funk, and cool jazz. Includes musical examples and a formal diagram.

A164 **London, Justin.** "One Step Up: A Lesson from Pop Music." *Journal of Music Theory Pedagogy* 4, no. 1 (1990): 111–14.

A look at a Bruce Springsteen song and a discussion of how it may be used in the classroom. London points out that the ostinato in the bass and the harmonic progression reflect the text. Further, the strongly cadential bass motion $\hat{3}$ $\hat{4}$ $\hat{5}$ renders the following move to IV a true retrogression, again reflecting the text ("One step up and two steps back"). Class discussion can ensue about whether the IV–I^6 progression is better heard as I–V^6 and whether guitar fingering plays a role in the decision. Includes no musical figures; analysis is in the prose.

A165 **Losseff, Nicky.** "Cathy's Homecoming and the Other World: Kate Bush's 'Wuthering Heights.'" *Popular Music* 18, no. 2 (1999): 227–40. [Reprinted in Moore, ed., *Critical Essays in Popular Musicology*. 2007: 487–500.] See **C27**.

An analysis of the meaningful interaction of music and lyrics in a single song by Kate Bush. Losseff proposes that through key structure (two tonal centers) and vocal timbre (multiple registers), dualities in the music reflect those in the text. The song is an interpretation of the Brontë novel, and Losseff relates Bush's modulatory procedure, as well as her vocal technique, to the novel's specific themes and plot elements.

A166 **Lundberg, Mattias.** "'To Let it Be Without Pretense': Canon, Fugue, and Imitation in Progressive Rock 1968–1979." *Music Theory Online* 20, no. 3 (2014).

An examination of contrapuntal writing in progressive rock. Lundberg details the critical reception of progressive rock, which usually entails themes either of "pretension" (appropriation of classical music) or "contention" (critique of the cultural establishment). His essay discusses how the genre can be situated in the counterculture while adopting high-culture classical techniques in the surface of the music as well as in its structure. From a survey of thousands of progressive rock works dating from 1969–80, Lundberg finds and discusses 24 pieces that contain canon, quodlibet, fugato, or fugue, including music from Gentle Giant, Van der Graaf Generator, and others. Includes several musical examples, transcriptions, and audio examples.

A167 **MacLachlan, Heather.** "Teaching Traditional Music Theory with Popular Songs: Pitch Structures." In Biamonte, ed., *Pop-Culture Pedagogy in the Music Classroom: Teaching Tools from* American Idol *to YouTube*. 2011: 73–94. See **C2**.

A guideline for the incorporation of popular music in the music theory classroom. MacLachlan recounts experiences in which her students benefitted greatly from learning new concepts in the context of music they already knew, but she also addresses the inherent challenges in such an approach. She supplies specific examples of songs that suit numerous theoretical topics: the diatonic major scale; intervals; tonic, subdominant, and dominant chords; inverted chords; nonharmonic tones; seventh chords; secondary dominants; the circle of fifths; modal mixture; modulation; four-part homophony; motive; and sequence. Includes several musical examples and an appendix, compiled by Nicole Biamonte, of popular-music examples sorted by music-theoretical concept.

A168 **Magee, Jeffrey.** "Irving Berlin's 'Blue Skies': Ethnic Affiliations and Musical Transformations." *The Musical Quarterly* 84, no. 4 (2000): 537–80.

An exploration of a single song's compositional and performance history, tracking the changes in meaning over time. Magee coins the term "song profile" for such a study, and points out several forerunners in Amercian music scholarship. His profile of "Blue Skies" spans the 20th century, covering the song's common thread of assimilation: its signifiers of "Jewishness" often perceived in Tin Pan

Alley songs (minor mode with non-sad affect, lament-like bass); its last-minute interpolation in a Belle Baker show, with themes of assimilation and with a Jewish protagonist; its inclusion in the film *The Jazz Singer* when jazz was understood as a fusion of Jewish and African American music; its later arrangement by Fletcher Henderson (performed by Benny Goodman) and Mary Lou Williams (performed by Duke Ellington); its adoption as popular ballad (Bing Crosby in the film *Blue Skies*) and jazz standard (Thelonius Monk's contrafact "In Walked Bud"); its cover versions by Ella Fitzgerald and Willie Nelson; and finally its championing by Pete Seeger. Includes several music examples, a table, and complete sheet-music version of the song.

A169 **Malawey, Victoria.** "Ear Training With the Music of Radiohead." *Indiana Theory Review* 30, no. 2 (2012): 27–64.

A proposal for the integration of music by Radiohead into aural skills curricula. Malawey has suggestions for use in interval identification (ID) (specific examples for each of the diatonic intervals); scale-type ID (collections or fragments both ordered and unordered, including major, minor, modes, and octatonic); meter ID (including hypermeter and composite meter); chord ID (quality and function); melodic dictation (with some reference to lyrics and scale degree); and aural analysis (directed analyses on worksheets). She also provides suggestions for sequencing of topics and supplies for specific exercises, including sample worksheets. Throughout, she refers to appropriate ancillary readings for students who wish to dig deeper into the theoretical literature. Includes numerous examples, worksheets, and tables.

A170 **Malawey, Victoria.** "'Find Out What It Means to Me': Aretha Franklin's Gendered Re-Authoring of Otis Redding's 'Respect.'" *Popular Music* 33, no. 2 (2014): 185–207.

A comparison of two versions of "Respect," describing how the latter version, through various modifications of Otis Redding's original (use of blue notes, level of syncopation, phrasing, addition of new material), and through its adoption as anthem by multiple social movements, came to be the definitive version, transferring "ownership" of the song to its author, Aretha Franklin. The first half covers the musical analysis, while the second draws upon various scholars in a review of the song's critical reception and its relationship to feminism. Includes transcribed excerpts of the two versions, lyrics, and formal diagrams.

A171 **Malvinni, David.** "'Now is the Time Past Believing': Concealment, Ritual, and Death in the Grateful Dead's Approach to Improvisation." In Meriwether, ed., *All Graceful Instruments: The Contexts of the Grateful Dead Phenomenon*. 2007: 1–18. See **C22**.

An essay focused on what goes missing, denied, or concealed in performances by the Grateful Dead. Malvinni "elucidate[s] an aesthetic force around improvisation" and addresses the transformational nature of the music. Specifically, he discusses ambiguity in "Eleven" and ritual in "Dark Star." Includes a few transcribed excerpts from "Eleven."

A172 **Martin, Henry.** "Balancing Composition and Improvisation in James P. Johnson's 'Carolina Shout.'" *Journal of Music Theory* 49, no. 2 (2005): 277–99.

An argument that James P. Johnson, although considered a jazz musician, had an approach to performance that was more compositional than improvisational. Martin studies Johnson's composition "Carolina Shout" and details elements of his approach to stride piano, which is a unique blend of ragtime, the blues, and the ring shout. Martin discusses features such as "backbeating" (not related to the "backbeat" in later popular music); the groove (a small, repeated cell, closely related to later concepts of groove in popular music); and the "thematic block," which he proposes as its principal formal component. These blocks combine to comprise the various "strains," which are not intended for improvisation. Multiple recorded performances by Johnson reveal that he was faithful to the development of these thematic blocks and eschewed improvisation in these sections. Includes several musical examples and a reproduction of the published score.

A173 **Mather, Olivia Carter.** "Taking It Easy in the Sunbelt: The Eagles and Country Rock's Regionalism." *American Music* 31, no. 1 (2013): 26–49.

An analysis of the Eagles' country-rock sound. Mather describes how adopting the symbolism of the mythical West and of Native Americans allowed country rock to emerge as the counterculture's version of country and to participate in the broader culture of the "Sunbelt" without carrying negative connotations of the older "South." After first looking at some details of a song by Poco, a possible precursor, she investigates the Eagles' "Take it Easy" for its instrumentation (particularly the banjo but in just the right amount); vocals (influenced by bluegrass and Crosby, Stills, and Nash); lyrics (themes of female entrapment); harmony (plagal motion); and structure (non-tonic ending). Includes a couple of musical examples; most analysis is in the prose.

A174 **Maus, Fred E.** "Glamour and Evasion: The Fabulous Ambivalence of the Pet Shop Boys." *Popular Music* 20, no. 3 (2001): 379–93. [Reprinted in Moore, ed., *Critical Essays in Popular Musicology*. 2007: 525–39.] See **C27**.

A study of meaning in the music of the Pet Shop Boys. Maus notes that fans of the group disagree about whether their music has a "gay sensibility," but many do hear a "double-voicedness," in which situations and feelings lack sufficient specificity to be read as just gay or just straight. Maus details several other ambivalences in the group's work, including multiple interpretations of harmony and voice leading, the coupling of cover songs in live performance and on record, modal mixture, and placement of instruments in a stereo mix. Includes two musical figures; the analysis is primarily in prose.

A175 **McCandless, Gregory R.** "Metal as a Gradual Process: Additive Rhythmic Structures in the Music of Dream Theater." *Music Theory Online* 19, no. 2 (2013).

A study of rhythm in progressive metal band Dream Theater. McCandless focuses on a particular technique he calls the "ABAC Additive Metrical Process," in which, for example, a four-hypermeasure consists of a 3/4 bar (A), a 4/4 bar

(B), a 3/4 bar (A), and a 5/4 bar (C); C is necessarily larger than B, hence the additive process. McCandless finds this to be characteristic of the band's process in particular and of the genre's generally. He locates numerous examples, both in Dream Theater's songs, and traces the practice back to minimalist composers. Includes numerous musical examples and figures, as well as a "Catalog of Metrical Complexities in Dream Theater's Music" as an appendix.

A176 **McClary, Susan.** "Thinking Blues." In *Conventional Wisdom: The Content of Musical Form*: 32–62. Berkeley: University of California Press, 2000; 205p. ISBN 0520221060; ML3795.M35 2000.

An essay that recognizes both the conventions of the blues and the nuances of its many performed variations. McClary notes that the blues undergird a great deal of 20th-century music, in part due to artists' ability to balance strict convention with expressive creativity. After narrating the tension in a 12-bar blues form, she investigates three specific examples: a classic blues (Bessie Smith, "Thinking Blues"), a Delta blues (Robert Johnson, "Cross Road Blues"), and a British-rock blues (Cream, "Crossroads"). Vocal delivery is the focus of the first two, and Clapton's adaption of Johnson, the latter. Includes one figure.

A177 **McDonald, Chris.** "Exploring Modal Subversions in Alternative Music." *Popular Music* 19, no. 3 (2000): 355–63.

An examination of an emerging harmonic idiom in guitar-based alternative rock. McDonald demonstrates how third relations in certain progressions have a tendency to obscure the mode to varying degrees, from "simple" to "complex" to "extreme." Large-scale relations also are considered. The power chord is an important factor, as its omitted third (or sometimes its implied third) can contribute to modal ambiguity. Includes examples of modal subversion found in the songs of Nirvana, Mudhoney, Soundgarden, and others.

A178 **McLeod, Ken.** "Bohemian Rhapsodies: Operatic Influences on Rock Music." *Popular Music* 20, no. 2 (2001): 189–203.

A study of the use of operatic elements in rock music. McLeod notes that, despite commonalities between the genres, and despite various attempts at crossover in one direction or the other, there have been few examples of true integration of the styles. From the 1970s comes Queen's "Bohemian Rhapsody"; and from the post-punk scene of the 1980s come Nina Hagen's opera-pop-disco, Klaus Nomi's new-wave countertenor, and Malcolm McLaren's rock versions of arias. McLeod provides some analysis of all four and closes with commentary on gender and sexuality. Includes a few musical examples and transcribed excerpts.

A179 **McLeod, Ken.** "'A Fifth of Beethoven': Disco, Classical Music, and the Politics of Inclusion." *American Music* 24, no. 3 (2006): 347–63. [Reprinted in Hawkins, ed., *Pop Music and Easy Listening*. 2011: 425–41.] See **C9**.

An analysis of two disco tracks that incorporated specific classical works. McLeod writes that disco was far from monolithic. Its simple production techniques allowed for a wide range of stylistic influences as can be found in the motion picture *Saturday Night Fever*. The film's soundtrack includes two disco adaptions of classical works. Walter Murphy's "A Fifth of Beethoven" includes the "fate motive" of Beethoven's Symphony No. 5, preserving its ambiguity at first; but, as McLeod describes, the motive is incorporated into the "inclusive homogeneity" of the body of the track. David Shire's "Night of Disco Mountain" adapts Mussorgsky's "Night on Bald Mountain" but uses a wider array of timbres and adds layers of seemingly incongruous instruments. McLeod comments upon disco's history as well as the reception of (and meaning in) this appropriation. Includes a few musical examples (of "A Fifth").

A180 **Mellers, Wilfrid.** "God, Modality and Meaning in Some Recent Songs of Bob Dylan." *Popular Music* 1 (1981): 142–57.

An analytical critique of the songs on Bob Dylan's albums *Street Legal* (1978), *Slow Train Coming* (1979), and *Saved* (1980). Mellers addresses gradual sophistication of resources toward (communal) consciousness against a historical backdrop of "black melody" and "white harmony." The analyses are driven primarily by lyrics but consistently touch upon structural elements such as scale and mode (pentatonic, Aeolian, Mixolydian), harmonic progression, intervallic relationships, and blue notes. Includes no musical examples; musical analysis is in the prose.

A181 **Mercer-Taylor, Peter.** "Stupid, Stupid Signs: Incomprehensibility, Memory, and the Meaning (Maybe) of R.E.M.'s 'Sidewinder Sleeps Tonite.'" *The Musical Quarterly* 88, no. 3 (2005): 456–86.

An analysis of a song by rock band R.E.M., arguing that it marks a turning point for singer/lyricist Michael Stipe. Mercer-Taylor suggests that while fans found meaning in their previous inscrutable lyrics, Stipe remained indifferent to any specific meaning. "The Sidewinder Sleeps Tonite," however, signals Stipe's realization that their music may have a positive meaning for the current generation and that he has some responsibility to bear. The analysis rests on two main points. First, the lyrics of "The Sidewinder Sleeps Tonite" (and their melodic setting) make a distinct passage from incomprehensibility to comprehensibility. Second, the quotation from "The Lion Sleeps Tonight" evokes a recollection from childhood, and its "misremembered" melodic variation performs an important structural function. Includes complete lyrics and melodic transcription.

A182 **Mercer-Taylor, Peter.** "'The Calliope Crashed to the Ground': Linear and Cyclic Time in Manfred Mann's Earth Band's 'Blinded by the Light.'" *Music Theory Spectrum* 35, no. 2 (2013): 147–65.

An analysis of a single song, written by Bruce Springsteen and recorded by Manfred Mann's Earth band, in which its treatment of linear time (through traditional formal functions of verse, chorud, etc.) and cyclic time (through repetitive, patterned processes) is emblematic of the contemporary blending of repetitive music (disco, minimalism) and traditional popular forms. Mercer-Taylor, after considering the numerous intertextual references (to Mike Oldfield, to Bruce Springsteen, and even to other music by Manfred Mann), considers manipulation of time in three main formal sections: the verse/pre-chorus/chorus (cycles and closure), the guitar solo (disorientation and climax), and the closing ("Chopsticks" as de-mystification of repetitive music). Includes several musical examples.

A183 **Middleton, Richard.** "Popular Music Analysis and Musicology: Bridging the Gap." *Popular Music* 12, no. 2 (1993): 177–90. [Reprinted in Middleton, ed., *Reading Pop: Approaches to Textual Analysis in Popular Music.* 2000: 104–21. See **C23**. [An earler version appeared as "Towards a Theory of Gesture in Popular Song Analysis." In Rossana Dalmonte and Mario Baroni, eds., *Secondo Convegno Europeo di Analisi Musicale*: 345–50. Trento, Italy: Università degli Studi di Trento, 1992; 733p. ISBN8886135092; MT90.E87 1992.]

A theory of gesture that addresses both meaning and the "sounds themselves." Middleton recognizes a schism between music scholars of a formalist bent and those more interested in a search for meaning. To close that gap, he proposes a theory of gesture, in which gestures are shown to have deeper, more general, generating gestures. In a song by Madonna, the groove, chords, phrases, microgestures, and texture all are connected to specific bodily motions and are notated with graphic notation. Plagal motions in a song by Bryan Adams get similar treatment. Because structuralism has been called into question by some, Middleton suggests that the division between "popular" and "classical" music, usually bolstered by structuralists' claims, should likewise be questioned. His theory of gesture, then, should apply equally well to the classical repertoire. Includes two figures.

A184 **Middleton, Richard.** "Form." In Horner and Swiss, eds., *Key Terms in Popular Music and Culture.* 1999: 141–55. See **C17**.

An essay discussing form not according to the traditional dichotomy of form-and-content, but in terms of process. Middleton highlights two formal processes. One involves starting with small components and developing them into larger structures. The other starts with a framework, repeats it, and introduces variety by way of the details within. The latter process is what Euro-American popular music has moved toward historically, as a result of the African American influence. He further distinguishes between two types of repetition: musematic (repetition of a small figure to build the whole, such as a riff) and discursive (repetition of a section to contribute to the larger whole, such as a phrase). Examples from the popular and rock repertoires follow, displaying both types as well as their combination. He closes with some thoughts about how these forms are mediated by genre, style, and technology. Includes a few musical figures.

A185 **Moore, Allan.** "Patterns of Harmony." *Popular Music* 11, no. 1 (1992): 73–106.

A catalog of harmonic patterns found in hundreds of pop-rock songs. Moore, in an effort to determine empirically the differences between the harmonic practices of various styles of popular music, analyzes data he had collected originally for pedagogical purposes. He introduces a hierarchic alphabetical code in which the first letter represents a class of patterns (defined in most cases by the initial harmonic progression), and subsequent letters indicate the particular group within the class. The patterns themselves reflect a Roman numeral system based not on major/minor tonality but on modes. Moore discusses various difficulties such as determination of tonic and distinguishing appoggiaturas from chords. He comments on the prevalence and function of different patterns but also suggests that a generative theory of pop-rock grammar may arise from these data. Includes a few musical examples and a comprehensive appendix listing all songs and patterns in each class and group.

A186 **Moore, Allan.** "The So-Called 'Flattened Seventh' in Rock." *Popular Music* 14, no. 2 (1995): 185–201. [Reprinted in Moore, ed., *Critical Essays in Popular Musicology*. 2007: 283–99.] See **C27**.

A close look at the ways in which the flatted seventh is employed in rock, both melodically as a scale degree and harmonically as a ♭VII triad. Moore argues that rock's tonality is quite distinct from common-practice tonality, and the flatted seventh should not be read as a departure from a major-scale norm. He shows, through many excerpts, how in modal music (i.e., rock), cadence and modulation both can be effected without the use of a leading tone. Includes numerous musical examples

A187 **Moore, Allan F.** "In a Big Country: The Portrayal of Wide Open Spaces in the Music of Big Country." *Contemporary Music Review* 17, no. 3 (1998): 1–6.

An examination of a commonly asserted signification in the music of rock band Big Country. Moore quotes several journalistic accounts of the band's music as evoking "wide open spaces" and wonders whether listeners take the impression for granted without any musical support for the signification. He finds, however, that the distancing of instruments in the sound field, a preference for "harmonic fields" over discrete chords, and a guitar technique evoking the Scottish Highland all seem to support the prevailing view. Includes no examples or figures; analysis is in the prose.

A188 **Moore, Allan F.** "Jethro Tull and the Case for Modernism in Mass Culture." In Moore, ed., *Analyzing Popular Music*. 2003: 158–72. See **C26**.

A study of Jethro Tull's music as modernism. Moore argues that idiolect is not subordinate to style and that the changes in the band's style reveal a single, consistent musical idiolect: binary oppositions such as individual/society, rural/urban, and happiness/disillusionment. This idiolect manifests musically as rhythmic displacement, rhythmic complexity, acoustic/electic contrast, or breaks in surface continuity. The music, while popular, is decidedly modernist as it reworks the past in the present. Includes a few musical examples.

A189 **Neal, Jocelyn.** "The Metric Makings of a Country Hit." In Cecelia Tichi, ed., *Reading Country Music: Steel Guitars, Opry Stars, and Honky-Tonk Bars*: 322–37.

Durham, NC: Duke University Press, 1998; 408p. ISBN 0822321564; ML3524. R43 1998.

A study of country music's metric and rhythmic structures, country dancing, and their influence upon one another. Neal discusses the simple metric structure that undergirds country songs but also explores metric irregularities on the surface, such as phrase overlap, phrase extension, irregular groupings, and half-bar units. She then looks at the rhythmic expectations in a number of line dances and studies the interaction of the metric patterns and the dance patterns. Includes several musical examples, figures, and tables.

A190   **Neal, Jocelyn.** "Songwriter's Signature, Artist's Imprint: The Metric Structure of a Country Song." *Country Music Annual* (2000): 112–40.

An investigation of the relationship of a country song's metric structure with its recorded performance. Neal, for each of several examples, finds both the simpler, underlying metric structure (the "prototype") and the hypermetric manipulation in the performance. The latter is said to reflect the personal stamp of the performer. Written for a broader audience that is non-scholarly, yet musically literate and familiar with country music songwriting, the article discusses principles of hypermeter; gives examples of elision, phrase overlap, and phrase expansion; and considers strong and weak placement of cadences. In one case, two different recordings of the same song are considered. Includes numerous musical examples.

A191   **Neal, Jocelyn R.** "Narrative Paradigms, Musical Signifiers, and Form as Function in Country Music." *Music Theory Spectrum* 29, no. 1 (2007): 41–72.

A study of "narrative paradigms" in country music, specific formal designs working in conjunction with standard lyrical and melodic signifiers to transmit meaning. Neal shows how one paradigm in particular, the "time-shift narrative," integrates specific formal and harmonic strategies with a common lyrical theme: the life cycle from birth to death. She also discusses how, particularly in songwriter Darrell Scott's "Long Time Gone" (recorded by The Dixie Chicks) and "Title of the Song," the paradigm affords songwriters the opportunity to participate in the standard practices of country music as an insider, while also commenting upon them as an outsider. Includes several musical examples and formal diagrams. Also includes an appendix listing songs featuring the time-shift narrative.

A192   **Neal, Jocelyn R.** "When Recollection is All We've Got: Analytical Exploration of 'Catchy' Songs." *College Music Symposium* 47 (2007): 12–22.

A discussion of how amateur or impromptu performances can offer insight into what constitutes the most basic communicable elements of a song and even what makes a particular song catchy. Neal analyzes two instances. In one, the 4+3+4 metric grouping causes an alternation of off-beat and downbeat clapping in Burt Bacharach's "I Say a Little Prayer" as staged in an on-screen singalong. In another, the extended series of direct modulations up a major second in Shania Twain's "If You Wanna Touch Her, Ask" necessitate a memorable timbral switch in the pop-country star's voice, but wreaks havoc on unsuspecting karaoke participants. In each example, it is a non-professional performance that reveals certain aspects of the song's character.

A193 **Neal, Jocelyn R.** "Country-Pop Formulae and Craft: Shania Twain's Crossover Appeal." In Everett, ed., *Expression in Pop-Rock Music: Critical and Analytical Essays*, 2nd ed. 2008: 285–311. See **C6**.

An examination of the songs of singer Shania Twain and producer Robert John "Mutt" Lange. Primary focus is on *Up!*, an album sold as three CDs, each containing different versions (country-pop, pop-rock, and international) of the same 19 songs. Through different versions, one can identify salient markers of the songs: the hooks, the harmony, and distinctive metric devices. After setting the stage for Twain's arrival by briefly surveying the history of country/pop crossovers in the 1980s and 1990s, Neal details the unusual modulations, hypermetric quirks, and sonic disruptions unique to her songs. These Twain/Lange markers are shown to be evident in other artists produced by Lange, such as the Corrs. Includes musical excerpts, metric and formal diagrams, and waveform analyses.

A194 **Nobile, Drew F.** "Form and Voice Leading in Early Beatles Songs." *Music Theory Online* 17, no. 3 (2011).

A study of the integration of form and voice leading in ten early Beatles songs. Nobile, borrowing Everett's "statement-restatement-departure-conclusion" (SRDC), identifies a consistent "SRDC-B form" in this repertoire. This is an AABA form in which each A is composed of a complete SRDC and the B represents a bridge. He demonstrates, in Schenkerian voice-leading graphs, how this form and the voice leading in each case is mutually reinforcing. Generally, "S" and "R" prolong the tonic and the primary soprano tone; "D" begins on some predominant with an unstable tone in the top voice; "C" completes the cadential motion and the upper-voice motion (not necessarily a descent to $\hat{1}$); and finally, "B" starts off-tonic and ends with a dominant retransition, an interruption with $\hat{2}$ in upper voice. Additional attention is given to neighbor, back-relating, and cadential subdominants as well as off-tonic beginnings. Includes numerous musical examples and voice-leading graphs.

A195 **Nurmesjärvi, Terhi.** "The Concept of Form and its Change in the Singles of the Beatles." In Heinonen, Eerola, Koskimäki, Nurmesjärvi, and Richardson, eds., *Beatlestudies 1: Songwriting, Recording, and Style Change*. 1998: 61–88. See **C10**.

A statistical analysis of musical form in the 22 singles (44 songs) by the Beatles officially released in the U.K. Nurmesjärvi tests the hypothesis that the Beatles' use of standard song forms was more prevalent in their early material. The results show this to be true, but their use of standard forms did not decline until much later than expected. Additional aims of the study include finding the songs most prototypical of the whole sample, examining the way the basic forms were extended (through repetition and/or addition of other sections), and identifying differences between A- and B-sides. Includes numerous tables and graphs, as well as an appendix displaying prototypicality, form, and recording/mixing/release data.

A196 **Nurmesjärvi, Terhi.** "You Need Another Chorus: Problems With Formal Concepts in Popular Music." In Heinonen, Koskimäki, Niemi, andNurmesjärvi, eds., *Beatlestudies 2: History, Identity, Autheticity*. 2000: 147–68. See **C11**.

An essay specifically focused on one specific element of popular music: form. Nurmesjärvi recognizes a certain complacency in the musicology that regards form in popular music as simple or having a few standard types. Noting that things are a bit more complex than is usually acknowledged, he offers a historical survey, in which he finds the roots of the Tin Pan Alley verse in recitative, covers strophic and AABA forms, and explains the newer verse-chorus model (as distinct from earlier verse-refrain forms). An analysis of the Beatles' "I Saw Her Standing There" is compared side-by-side with two other published analyses of the same song in order to show how different interpretations (ABAB+C or AABA or verse-bridge) may arise. Includes one figure and one formal diagram.

A197 **O'Donnell, Shaugn.** "Space, Motion, and Other Musical Metaphors." In Weiner, ed., *Perspectives on the Grateful Dead: Critical Writings*. 1999: 127–35. See **C38**.

A look at basic metaphorical concepts as evidenced in the Grateful Dead's music and thought. O'Donnell, after Saslaw, Zbikowski, and others, discusses two schemata: the container and the source-path-goal. With reference to quotes from band members, he suggests the Dead often made use of such metaphors, imagining their songs as containers one can inhabit, for instance, or conversely imagining themselves the container, containing the song. Their music itself is shown to negotiate special metaphors, too, through its incorporation of "outside" elements and through adventurous performances that suggest motion from one container to another. Includes a few musical examples and figures.

A198 **O'Donnell, Shaugn.** "Sailing to the Sun: *Revolver*'s Influence on Pink Floyd." In Reising, ed., *"Every Sound There Is": The Beatles'* Revolver *and the Transformation of Rock and Roll*. 2002: 69–86. See **C30**.

A study of influence in late-1960s rock. O'Donnell recognizes the Beatles' *Revolver* as an influence upon Pink Floyd's early singles and albums, predating the oft-cited influence of *Sgt. Pepper*. After comparing the timelines of the groups (1966–67), he details specific instances of commonality in the groups' use of metric irregularity, ostinato, form, harmonic rhythm, instrumentation (strings, winds, and sound effects), and Eastern textual influence. This suggests a direct influence at a time when contemporary accounts positioned the two bands as opposites of sorts. Includes several musical examples and a timeline.

A199   O'Donnell, Shaugn. "'On the Path': Tracing Tonal Coherence in *The Dark Side of the Moon*." In Reising, ed., *"Speak to Me": The Legacy of Pink Floyd's* The Dark Side of the Moon. 2005: 87–103. See **C31**.

A study of large-scale tonal unity in Pink Floyd's classic album. O'Donnell argues that the songs work together as a cycle, not just because of coherence in their poetic themes or studio techniques, but also in their tonal and motivic unity. He works through each of the album's eight songs, consistently plotting its form and voice leading and outlining its harmonic and modal details. Between songs, too, he reveals harmonic and voice-leading connections, ultimately displaying the unified structure of the entire album in a single background graph, complete with interruption at the subtonic ("rock dominant"). Includes numerous musical examples and voice-leading graphs.

A200   O'Donnell, Shaugn. "Bobby, Béla, and Borrowing in 'Victim or the Crime.'" In Meriwether, ed., *All Graceful Instruments: The Contexts of the Grateful Dead Phenomenon*. 2007: 38–51. See **C22**.

A study of the connections between The Grateful Dead's "Victim or the Crime" (music written by Bob Weir) and Béla Bartók's "Music for Strings, Percussion, and Celesta," to which Weir alluded in an interview. O'Donnell follows this thread with a more thorough analysis. After introducing the form in Bartók's first movement, noting the symmetrical structure, he highlights some specific moments of Weir's paraphrasing of Bartók, which leads ultimately to some direct quotation and transposition of the movement's climactic material in the song's bridge. There is also a specific connection drawn between Bartók's celeste and Mickey Hart's percussive instrument, the "beam." Includes musical examples, figures, and formal diagrams for both the Bartók composition and the Weir song.

A201   Oliver, Paul. "Blues and the Binary Principle." In Horn and Tagg, eds., *Popular Music Perspectives: Papers from the First International Conference on Popular Music Research, Amsterdam, June 1981*. 1982: 163–73. See **C16**.

An application of binary analysis to early blues. Oliver argues that quality, tied to meaning, can be addressed through binary analysis, which attends to an artwork's dualistic properties. Using examples discussed in Titon's work (see **B26**), he discusses various binaries in the blues, such as textural shifts from vocal to instrumental, rising and falling contour, rhythm against melody, pitch variability in blue notes, and parallelism in the lyrics. Includes lyrics.

A202   Orosz, Jeremy W. "'Can't Touch Me': Television Cartoons and the Paraphrase of Popular Music." *Contemporary Music Review* 33, no. 2 (2014): 223–40.

A look at music composed to paraphrase other music as closely as possible without risking copyright infringement. Orosz calls this technique "copyphrase," and he analyzes its use in the animated sitcoms *The Simpsons* and *Family Guy*. He offers several examples from both series, showing original and copyphrase side-by-side to highlight the variation, often found in the contour or the intervallic content. Orosz details the effects of copyright lawsuits on the shows' music and discusses their current musical treatments. Includes several musical examples and transcriptions.

A203 **Osborn, Brad.** "Beats that Commute: Algebraic and Kinesthetic Models for Math-Rock Grooves." *Gamut* 3, no. 1 (2010): 43–67.

A two-part modeling of the characteristic rhythmic and metric structures of math rock. Osborn's algebraic formulation applies both to the metric structures and to the physical movements of performers and listeners. The discussion focuses on a "pivot pulse," a pulse stream common to both meters in a metric modulation inspired by the common left-foot practice of rock drummers, and applies the concept in three ways: pulses between non-isochronous tactuses, pulses between binary and compound meters, and the addition or subtraction of pulses. The essay concludes with an analysis of a single song by Dillinger Escape Plan. Includes numerous musical examples and transcriptions.

A204 **Osborn, Brad.** "Understanding Through-Composition in Post-Rock, Math-Metal, and Other Post-Millennial Rock Genres." *Music Theory Online* 17, no. 3 (2011).

A taxonomy of through-composed forms in contemporary experimental rock. Osborn suggests that rock bands outside the mainstream are not bound by commercial expectations and can therefore employ less conventional forms in their composition. He identifies, according to the number of sections and themes, four main types frequently used: one-part monothematic, multi-part monothematic, one-part polythematic, and multi-part polythematic. The study engages several musical domains (melody, motive, groove, and meter) to show how the bands sustain interest and provide closure. Includes numerous examples, figures, waveforms, audio examples, and excerpts from the author's interviews with band members.

A205 **Osborn, Brad.** "Subverting the Verse-Chorus Paradigm: Terminally Climactic Forms in Recent Rock Music." *Music Theory Spectrum* 35, no. 1 (2013): 23–47.

An observation of a compositional trend in post-millennial (post-1990s) rock songs: the "terminally climactic form" (TCF). Osborn notes that the TCF, distinct from verse/chorus forms, forms with codas, and cumulative forms, contains an autonomous and non-recapitulatory closing section, which, surpassing the chorus in intensity, serves as the climax of the song. Osborn first lays out his theory of sectional climax, then visits examples by Dashboard Confessional, Coheed and Cambria, and others, to demonstrate how sections in two-part, three-part, and (more cautiously) extended TCFs are delineated and how they create a trajectory toward the terminal climax. Includes figures, musical examples, formal diagrams, and waveform analyses.

A206 **Osborn, Brad.** "Kid Algebra: Radiohead's Euclidean and Maximally Even Rhythms." *Perspectives of New Music* 52, no. 1 (2014): 81–105.

An investigation of rhythm and meter in the music of Radiohead. Osborn proposes a "Euclidean rhythm" as one in which the number of beats in a rhythm cannot be divided by the number of onset points evenly but can be divided maximally evenly (e.g., 16 beats divided by 5 results in the grouping 4+3+3+3+3). Such rhythms are modeled as points on a circle and represented as ordered and unordered collections. Osborn provides several examples in Radiohead's repertoire and considers how these may connect to the lyrics and the instrumentation in meaningful ways. Knowing that humans are entrained to hear rhythms in groupings of four or three, he also gives a prescriptive model for hearing Euclidean rhythms. Includes several musical examples and figures.

A207 **Palmer, John R.** "Yes, 'Awaken', and the Progressive Rock Style." *Popular Music* 20, no. 2 (2001): 243–61.

An account of the elements of Yes's language in a single song, "Awaken," one of the band's more overlooked long-form compositions. Palmer reviews the environment from which the recording comes, a time of longer album tracks and studio experimentation, exemplified by groups like Soft Machine, Pink Floyd, and others. Palmer finds compositional unity, in spite of its length (15:34), in the consistent treatment (serial operations such as inversion, retrograde, etc.) of short motives in multiple instruments and in multiple sections, including in a seemingly improvisatory, yet carefully planned, middle section. A smooth modal transition and a passage with complex harmonic rhythm add variety to the tight-knit structure. Throughout, Palmer ties the compositional elements to the spiritual nature of lyrics. Includes musical examples, figures, and a formal diagram.

A208 **Pieslak, Jonathan.** "Re-casting Metal: Rhythm and Meter in the Music of Meshuggah." *Music Theory Spectrum* 29, no. 2 (2007): 219–45.

An investigation of the complex rhythmic and metric design in the music of the Swedish metal band Meshuggah. Pieslak discusses several examples of the band's general employment of mixed meter, metric dissonance, and polymeter, all of which are analyzed in conventional terms. The 21-minute composition "I," however, eschews surface-level meter altogether in favor of a multi-layered approach. Pieslak's analysis of the multiple layers, or strata, in the music bring to bear Lerdahl and Jackendoff's "grouping structure," Joel Lester's "textural accent," John Roeder's "pulse stream," and Maury Yeston's "attack-point interval" and "pattern recurrence." Includes numerous musical figures and analysis.

A209 **Prather, Ronald E.** "The Popular Songs of Alec Wilder." *The Musical Quarterly* 74, no. 4 (1990): 521–49.

A set of analyses of 22 songs by Alec Wilder. Prather notes that Wilder's book on popular music (see **B30**) contains no reference to his own songs, and he remedies this by giving Wilder's songs similar analytical treatment. Following Wilder's model, Prather focuses on form, harmony, and stylistic melodic features. He reveals forms such as AABA, ABAB, and ABAC, and unconventional harmonic progressions and the use of chromatic medants; and he gives attention both to scale-degree 6 and to the interval of a sixth generally. Includes numerous musical examples (sheet-music style) and melodic excerpts.

A210   **Rapport, Evan.** "Hearing Punk as Blues." *Popular Music* 33, no. 1 (2014): 39–67.

An analysis of the musical elements of punk. Rapport begins with the premise that punk, like all rock, is based on blues resources, notwithstanding punk's being read frequently as "white" and the deliberate rejection of tradition by many of its practitioners. He discusses the proto-punks' treatment of blues formal designs and harmonic progressions as well as their distinctive transformation of blues vocal performance style, both of which gave rise to the punk style. The melodic and harmonic innovations that followed are traced through the 1980s and beyond. Includes several musical examples and formal diagrams.

A211   **Reily, Suzel Ana.** "Tom Jobim and the Bossa Nova Era." *Popular Music* 15, no. 1 (1996): 1–16. [Reprinted in Langlois, ed., *Non-Western Popular Music*. 2011: 472–87.] See **C19**.

An analysis of the elements of the bossa nova style. Reily notes the origins of the term, points out early examples "Desafinado" and "Chega de Saudade," and discusses the style's popularity with middle-class youths of the late 1950s and early 1960s. However, most attention is given to the meeting of its three chief minds in Rio de Janeiro. Composer Antônio Carlos Jobim bore a strong jazz and classical influence, particularly from Debussy by way of Villa-Lobos. Lyricist Vinícius de Moraes worked from a rich literary background, using commonplace language as well as techniques of the concrete poets. Guitarist and singer João Gilberto created the genre's fundamental rhythm, which is analyzed here. In closing, Reily also considers bossa nova's influence on the quickly following Música Popular Brasileira (MPB) movement. Includes a few musical examples.

A212   **Renzo, Adrian.** "'Sounds Like an Official Mix': The Mainstream Aesthetics of Mash-Up Production." In Sarah Baker, Andy Bennett, and Jodie Taylor, eds., *Redefining Mainstream Popular Music*: 139–49. New York and London: Routledge, 2013; 222p. ISBN 9780415807821; ML3470.R425 2013.

An argument that, despite being outside the mainstream, mashup producers use the aesthetic criteria of mainstream Top 40 music when creating their work. Renzo writes that such producers necessarily are outside the mainstream, with unofficial status, primarily because of their unauthorized use of samples. Their work, however, aspires toward "official" status in two ways. First, in the absence of official gatekeepers such as record companies, the musicians police themselves and each other, often in online communities, holding up standards of popular songwriting conventions. Renzo quotes several people in these communities. Second, the producers tend to make every effort to "sound official." A producer himself, Renzo describes the many microedits that he makes when creating a mashup. Includes a couple of musical figures.

A213   **Reynolds, M. Fletcher.** "'Selle V. Gibb' and the Forensic Analysis of Plagiarism." *College Music Symposium* 32 (1992): 55–78.

An examination of the complications in a legal case, in which The Bee Gees were accused of plagiarism, and a proposal for how to avoid pitfalls in future cases.

Reynolds covers the basics of copyright infringement and reviews the testimony in this particular case. The two songs in question had numerous, though superficial, pitch and rhythmic similarities, as shown by the plaintiff's expert witness, who concluded that the songs are so similar, they could not have been composed independently. The plaintiff ultimately lost the case in part due to the expert's admission of unfamiliarity with popular music and his failure to apply the full depth and strength of music analysis. Reynolds also proposes a set of forensic guidelines, including a call for hierarchical analysis in such cases, to distinguish the superficial from the structural. Includes melodic transcriptions and analyses used in the case.

A214 **Ricci, Adam.** "A 'Hard Habit to Break': The Integration of Harmonic Cycles and Large-Scale Structure in Two Songs by Chicago." *Indiana Theory Review* 21 (2000): 129–46.

A look at the tonal ramifications of the "pump-up" modulation, particularly nontrivial cases, in which the modulation enables a harmonic cycle and is thus intergral to the structure. Ricci finds two such modulations in the music of Chicago: "Hard Habit to Break" (half step up) and "You're the Inspiration" (whole step up). In the former, the cyle is embedded in the harmonic progression; in the latter, the progression is embedded in the cyle. Includes several musical examples, formal diagrams, and voice-leading graphs.

A215 **Ricci, Adam.** "Non-Coinciding Sequences." *Music Theory Spectrum* 33, no. 2 (2011): 124–45.

An identification of a melodic sequence in which two melodic elements are transposed by different intervals; the two elements are typically soprano and bass voices. Ricci enumerates such sequences based on harmonic and melodic content and proposes a typology according to "configuration classes." The article's analytical core features four popular songs (by Nelly, Rick Astley, Billy Joel, and Gwen Stefani) and four examples from the classical repertoire. Ricci also shows the sequences to have compositional function, such as disorientation, disruption, modulation, or various rhetorical functions. Includes numerous musical examples and reductions. Also includes appendices with mathematical formalizations of the concepts within.

A216 **Rings, Steven.** "A Foreign Sound to Your Ear: Bob Dylan Performs 'It's Alright, Ma (I'm Only Bleeding),' 1964–2009." *Music Theory Online* 19, no. 4 (2013).

A study of a single song and its performances over 45 years. Rings investigates sonic details, intertextual references, and meanings in the song's many incarnations. The first half of the article is focused on the 1965 studio recording and includes analysis of meter in the text, stylistic associations, the many signifiers in the vamp, and meter, voice leading, and harmony in the verse and refrain. The second half compares various performances from 1964 to 2009. There is some statistical information and commentary on the number of performances as well as the keys in which the song was performed. Performances from several tours

Articles

are then analyzed with respect to vocal timbre, instrumentation, rhythm, and intertextual or historical meaning. Includes numerous musical examples, audio examples, transcriptions, and spectrograms.

A217 **Robinson, Thomas.** "The Singer and the Song: Core Components in Jimmy Webb's 'Didn't We.'" *Popular Music* 33, no. 2 (2014): 315–36.

An analytical essay that, starting from the idea that a song's core components lie at a level more abstract than even a lead sheet reveals, proposes a methodology for comparing various recordings of a single song to separate the elements attributed to the performances from those attributed to this core. Robinson, focusing only on melody, uses "Didn't We" as a case study and examines several versions of the song. Each melodic performance is graphed on simple pitch/time axes and all versions are compared. Each note event is then assigned a numerical value according to the number of performances that include that event. Events unique to one performance are assigned to the individual performers, and those included in most or all versions comprise the core melodic contour, a background of sorts. Includes several graphs, a table, and a musical example.

A218 **Robison, Brian.** "Somebody is Digging My Bones: King Crimson's 'Dinosaur' as (Post)Progressive Historiography." In Holm-Hudson, ed., *Progressive Rock Reconsidered*. 2002: 221–42. See **C15**.

A semiotic reading of the King Crimson track "Dinosaur" (1995). Robison writes that it contains non-intentional signs, which sometimes overpower the intentional ones. The lyrics, written by guitarist Adrian Belew, are about his own personal history but commonly are taken to be about that of King Crimson of progressive rock. This perceived meaning seems to be consistent across many different groups of fans, and for Robison it is the music that makes this so. He compares five performances, including live recordings and Belew's solo one, noting that the timbre (with references to the Mellotron), mixed meters, and even one paraphrase all connect to various points in the band's history. Includes diagrams of the form and of the band's history.

A219 **Robison, Brian.** "'A Prayer from Your Secret God': The 'Sensitive Female Chord Progression' as a Veiled Symbol of Religiosity." In Teresa Malecka and Małgorzata Pawłowska, eds., *Music: Function and Value: Proceedings of the 11th International Congress on Musical Signification*: 656–66. Krakow: Akademia Muzyczna w Krakowie, 2013; 825p. ISBN 9788362743186; ML3845.I68 2013.

A closer look at the sudden proliferation of a particular four-chord progression dubbed by journalist Marc Hirsh as the "Sensitive Female Chord Progression" for its apparently exclusive employment by female singers and/or songwriters bearing a certain sensitivity. (Robison prefers the affects "sincerity" or "gravitas.") Robison investigates the progression (vi-IV-I-V or its rotation I-V-vi-IV), noting that its late-20th-century use is only indirectly related to common-practice-era practices or blues-derived musics. A more direct connection is made to American Protestant hymnody by way of the uninflected vocal, lack of syncopation, diatonicity, and slow tempos. Additionally, many of the songs' lyrics carry religious or spiritual themes. Includes a musical example, a chart, and a table.

A220 **Rockwell, Joti.** "Banjo Transformations and Bluegrass Rhythm." *Journal of Music Theory* 53, no. 1 (2009): 137–62.

An application of transformational theory to the rhythm and hand patterns of bluegrass banjo playing. Rockwell, after Blacking, theorizes the music not as notes on a staff, but as physical motions on the instrument (though examples include standard notation as well as tablature). He proposes an ordered set whose elements are the finger, the fret, the string, and the time point assigned to each note. Standard picking patterns, then, are represented as Lewinian transformational networks of the set, more specifically of the permutations of picking-finger patterns. He also uses beat-class theory to approach a deeper structural background. All of this is brought to bear on analysis of music by Earl Scruggs, Alison Brown, and Béla Fleck. Includes several transcriptions and musical figures.

A221 **Rosenberg, Nancy.** "Popular Music in the College Music Theory Class: Rhythm and Meter." In Biamonte, ed., *Pop-Culture Pedagogy in the Music Classroom: Teaching Tools from* American Idol *to* YouTube. 2011: 47–71. See **C2**.

A group of suggestions for including popular music in the study of rhythm and meter. Rosenberg discusses some of the advantages of such an approach, emphasizing the benefits of using student-chosen examples. Her examples are focused on transcription of drum patterns, turntablism, tempo and beat matching, and complex metrical procedures. Includes a few musical examples and two appendices, containing a list of online and software resources, and a list of songs with simple and complex meters, all organized by specific meter.

A222 **Rosenberg, Nancy.** "Bach, Beck, and Björk Walk into a Bar: Reclassifying Harmonic Progressions to Accommodate Popular Music Repertoire in the Traditional Music Theory Class." *Journal of Music Theory Pedagogy* 28 (2014): 163–209.

A proposal for a music theory curriculum that teaches harmonic progressions in a single paradigm that can accommodate both popular and common-practice-era music. Rosenberg finds that traditional sequencing of material in theory textbooks does not suit popular music well and proposes a different framework with four main units. Including examples from both repertoires along with suggestions for their employment in class, the units are arranged as follows. Unit I: single-chord works, allowing for focus on such rudiments as rhythm and scales; Unit II: two- and three-chord progressions, allowing for study of classical music that doesn't adhere to standard common-practice syntax; Unit III: standard chord progressions of four or more chords, which can introduce students to chromaticism; and Unit IV: other progressions of four or more chords, which may include a variety of progressions, some less orthodox than others. Includes several musical examples, a formal diagram, and an appendix listing recommended songs for each of the four units.

A223 **Rycenga, Jennifer.** "Endless Caresses: Queer Exuberance in Large-Scale Form in Rock." In Whiteley and Rycenga, eds., *Queering the Popular Pitch*. 2006: 235–47. See **C39**.

A proposal, influenced by the work of philosopher Georges Bataille and biologist Bruce Bagemihl, for a non-normative notion of musical form, one that encourages sensuous engagement and immersion, but also thwarts, even rejects, form's rational clarity and reproductive value. Rycenga offers two examples of such "queering the form": "The Ancient," a track from Yes's *Tales of Topographic Oceans*, and the entirety of *Is This Desire?*, an album by PJ Harvey. Avoiding a rigid template, Yes's fluid composition lacks narrative cohesion and eschews an external, controlling form. PJ Harvey's songs, on the other hand, display traditional forms, but the inter-referential and fragmentary narratives of the vignettes inspire repeated listening of the physical as well as intellectual kind. Ultimately, Rycenga finds pleasure to be an intrinsically valuable function of musical form. Includes a formal diagram.

A224 **Salley, Keith.** "On the Integration of Aural Skills and Formal Analysis through Popular Music." In Biamonte, ed., *Pop-Culture Pedagogy in the Music Classroom: Teaching Tools from* American Idol *to* YouTube. 2011: 109–32. See **C2**.

An approach to the aural apprehension of formal function, hypermeter, and phrase rhythm using songs from the broad jazz and theater repertoires (which overlap in the American Songbook). Salley refers to theories of Caplin, Ratz, Rothstein, and others in discussions of function (through melody and harmony), of hypermeter (through expansion and contraction), and phrase structure (through hypermeter and phrase rhythm). He argues that while this repertoire may be somewhat removed from that bearing classical sonata form, the skills students learn when studying smaller forms can prepare them for studying larger ones. Furthermore, these songs more closely resemble common-practice-era music than much pop and rock, which tends to be modally based. Includes several musical examples and sample student assignments.

A225 **Salley, Keith.** "On the Interaction of Alliteration with Rhythm and Metre in Popular Music." *Popular Music* 30, no. 3 (2011): 409–32.

A study of how the interaction of accented alliterative patterns with rhythm and meter make certain pop melodies "roll off the tongue." Salley, concerned more with vowel sounds than with rhyme, is interested in how recorded vocal melodies in popular music of the 1960s, 1970s, and 1980s engage at the level of the phoneme. After a survey of literature on analysis of recorded voice and an introduction to phonetics and International Phonetic Alphabet (IPA) notation, some detailed phonetic and rhythmic analyses of songs by the Beatles, Bob Dylan, Elton John, and others follow. Different types of alliteration are featured, connecting with the musical structure in meaningful ways. Includes many musical examples and figures.

A226 **Schenkius, Patrick.** "Slash Chords: Triads with a 'Wrong' Bass Note?" *Dutch Journal of Music Theory* 16, no. 1 (2011): 47–52.

An examination of the slash chord, how its various versions can function in a tonal settings, and which notation is most appropriate. Schenkius organizes nearly all the slash chords into three categories: those that are simple inverted triads, those that can be understood as incomplete seventh chords, and those that can be interpreted in multiple ways. In the analysis of a Pat Metheny arrangement, he spells out the various ways in which one of the chords can be interpreted. Additional focus is placed on the "pop dominant" (IV/$\hat{5}$). Includes a few musical examples and figures.

A227 **Scott, Derek B.** "Incongruity and Predictability in British Dance Band Music of the 1920s and 1930s." *The Musical Quarterly* 78, no. 2 (1994): 290–315. [Reprinted in Moore, ed., *Critical Essays in Popular Musicology*. 2007: 337–62.] See **C27**.

An introduction to the aesthetics of British dance band music in the 1920s and 1930s. Scott advocates understanding the incongruity and predictability embedded in the style. Incongruity is manifest in the mixing of the classical and the popular, of the classically trained voice and the crooner with a microphone. Incongruity is also found between the music and the lyrics. Critics often attack this repertoire for its predictability, but this music, and jazz more generally, is to be understood for the (performed) variation on the predictable (written) harmonies and standard forms. A mixture of predictability and incongruity is possible, too, such as when an arrangement directly quotes classical repertoire, a second-order semiological system, in Barthes's terms. Includes a few musical examples.

A228 **Shaftel, Matthew.** "From Inspiration to Archive: Cole Porter's 'Night and Day.'" *Journal of Music Theory* 43, no. 2 (1999): 315–47.

An in-depth analysis of "Night and Day." Shaftel first establishes Porter's "complete authorship" of the song. Unlike many other popular songwriters of his day, Porter was a classically trained musician with a deep knowledge of the classical repertoire; he had a fair amount of control over who was to perform his music; he submitted to the publisher complete melodic and harmonic scores, as opposed to producing a harmonic sketch or just the melody and leaving the rest to copiers and arrangers; and he was heavily involved in the publication process, checking proofs. Second, Shaftel places the song in the contexts of its early performances, noting how Porter changed the song to suit the voice of Fred Astaire. Third, Shaftel comprehensively analyzes the authoritative sheet-music edition, even including elements in the four-bar piano introduction (often overlooked in this type of analysis), which foretell of structure in the song proper. Among the facets of analysis: motivic development of the chromatic trichord, harmonic oscillation, and the flat-mediant harmony. Includes musical examples, voice-leading graphs, and a complete piano/vocal score.

A229 **Sheinbaum, John J.** "Progressive Rock and the Inversion of Musical Values." In Holm-Hudson, ed., *Progressive Rock Reconsidered*. 2002: 21–42. See **C15**.

An example of how progressive rock can balance seemingly competing value systems. Sheinbaum notes that critics generally found progressive rock to be inauthentic or full of empty virtuosity. However, most of the very elements esteemed in Western music broadly are disdained by critics in a rock context. Sheinbaum lists many such elements arranged as dichotomies (e.g., complicated/simple, innovative/derivative). He argues, however, that progressive rock operates in the middle and negotiates both "high" and "low" elements. As a case study, Yes's "Roundabout" is analyzed as the site of tensions between "high" versus "low," fixity versus improvisation, and structural versus cultural understanding. Includes a few tables and transcribed excerpts.

A230 **Sheinbaum, John J.** "'Think About What You're Trying to Do to Me': Rock Historiography and the Construction of a Race-Based Dialectic." In Beebe, Fulbrook, and Saunders, eds., *Rock Over the Edge: Transformations in Popular Music Culture*. 2002: 110–32. See **C1**.

An examination of the assumptions behind the common historical treatments of "white" and "black" rock. Sheinbaum points out that white rock artists, such as Bob Dylan or the Beatles, are frequently positioned as artists, even composers, while black artists, such as many Motown performers, are portrayed as laboring under a commercial regime imposed from above. Discussions of soul music tend to focus on the improvisational or intuitive elements, rendering its performances beyond the reach of traditional structural analysis. Sheinbaum questions this race-based dichotomy with analyses of the Beatles' "Eleanor Rigby" and Aretha Franklin's "Think." The songs (in their harmonic rhythm, vocal delivery, instrumentation, and form) are racially coded, but they also challenge the structural conventions on which they are based. Includes a few musical examples and formal diagrams.

A231 **Spencer, Piers.** "Reggae." In Vulliamy and Lee, eds., *Pop, Rock and Ethnic Music in School*. 1982: 154–70. See **C37**.

A recommendation for how to incorporate reggae into a music curriculum. Spencer, after explaining the basic instrumental roles in a reggae texture, suggests several assignments for classroom use: graded rhythmic patterns, a complete arrangement of a reggae song, and ideas for improvising and composing in the style. Spencer explains the basics of the "dub" practice in which the B-side of a reggae single is more stripped down with no lead vocal and with heavy effects, like echo or delay. He recommends a few specific recorded examples and offers a few classroom exercises that make use of this "version" side. Finally, he discusses how student reggae bands might be organized and developed. Includes several musical examples and arrangements.

A232 **Spicer, Mark.** "Large-Scale Strategy and Compositional Design in the Early Music of Genesis." In Everett, ed., *Expression in Pop-Rock Music: Critical and Analytical Essays*, 2nd ed. 2008 [2000]: 313–44. See **C6**.

A combination of formalist and intertextual approaches in the analysis of a large-scale (23-minute) work of progressive rock, "Supper's Ready" by Genesis.

Discussing the meter, harmony, and texture in each of the piece's seven sections, Spicer finds connections and references to Schumann, Liszt, Debussy, Stravinsky, and 1960s rock. Then, after Edward Macan, he finds "systematic juxtapositions" of "electronic and acoustic" sections to be one evident large-scale strategy, but he also discusses the roles of harmonic elements and the overall key scheme. Includes lyrics with program notes from early live concerts, album chronology, excerpts, and transcriptions.

A233 **Spicer, Mark.** "(Ac)cumulative Form in Pop-Rock Music." *twentieth-century music* 1, no. 1 (2004): 29–64. [Reprinted in Spicer, ed., *Rock Music*. 2011: 295–330.] See **C35**.

An investigation of pop-rock songs whose formal structures do not conform to standard verse-chorus types but seem to build gradually, sometimes over extended spans of time, developing a complex texture. Spicer builds upon J. Peter Burkholder's notion of cumulative form (usually a whole piece in which an initial presentation of themes ultimately is followed by their amalgamation into a unified whole) and proposes an "accumulative" form (usually the beginning of a song that deliberately builds up a groove, one instrument at a time) as well, highlighting examples of each in detailed analyses of the music of Yes, New Order, The Police, and others. Includes numerous musical examples.

A234 **Spicer, Mark.** "Strategic Intertextuality in Three of John Lennon's Late Beatles Songs." *Gamut* 2, no. 1 (2009): 347–75.

An analysis of Lennon's intertextual references in three late Beatles' songs. Spicer notes Robert Hatten's distinction between stylistic and strategic intertextuality, and while he acknowledges the Beatles' use of the former (broad references to a particular musical style), he is more interested here in the latter (focused references to a particular musical work). "All You Need is Love" plainly features multinational quotes in its fadeout, contributing to its positive trans-cultural message. Less overt are the five references to other Beatles' songs in "Glass Onion," a deliberate effort to confuse journalists who tended to misinterpret Lennon's use of metaphor. These are embedded in the melody, harmony, timbre, and instrumentation. The harmonies in "Because" bear a well-known resemblance to those in Beethoven's "Moonlight" sonata. Spicer details the connection between the two, as well as the syntactical differences, particularly with respect to the Neapolitan and diminished-seventh chords. Includes several musical examples.

A235 **Spicer, Mark.** "'Regatta de Blanc': Analyzing Style in the Music of The Police." In Spicer and Covach, eds., *Sounding Out Pop: Analytical Essays in Popular Music*. 2010: 124–53. See **C34**.

An analysis of stylistic eclecticism in the music of The Police. Spicer notes that the band is tagged frequently with the label "white reggae," but he argues that there is much more to their style. After Kofi Agawu, he proposes a "universe of style" for the band, including punk, jazz, progressive rock, synth-pop, music hall, blues, Baroque lament, and even the composer Villa-Lobos. Reggae and punk are the largest "planets" in that "universe," given that the band's primary idiolect is a combination of reggae's displacement of the apparent downbeat and punk's forthright riffs, but the other styles are shown to play a role as well. Includes numerous musical examples and figures.

A236 **Spicer, Mark.** "(Per)Form in(g) Rock: A Response." *Music Theory Online* 17, no. 3 (2011).

A response to the seven articles compiled in a special issue of *Music Theory Online*, the first four of which were presented at a meeting of the Society for Music Theory. Spicer offers some analyses that were inspired by the articles in question. After Doll (see **A84**), he considers a modulation that employs Lewin's SLIDE transformation. After Koozin (see **A155**), he considers keyboard topography and the ramifications of white- and black-key riffs. After Osborn (see **A204**), he considers post-millenium synth-pop. After Summach and his study of the pre-chorus (see **A241**), he proposes a "post-chorus" evident in the 1970s and later. An animated formal analysis of Lady Gaga's "Bad Romance" follows, bringing many of these ideas to bear. Spicer closes with some comments and responses to Nobile, Attas, and Endrinal (see **A194**, **A5**, and **A89**, respectively). Includes musical examples, audio examples, and an animation.

A237 **Stephenson, Ken.** "A Hit by Varèse: Idiomatic Syntax in the PC Counterpoint of Three Songs by Chicago." *Theory and Practice* 29 (2004): 125–31.

Stephenson, after William Benjamin, considers voice leading of pitch classes (pcs) rather than pitches, finding many instances of a perfect fifth (interval-class 5 (ic5)) moving by semitone (in pc space). Three songs by Chicago feature this design in distinct ways. In "Goodbye," the chords are rich and full of ic5's, so chord successions often feature multiple stepwise ascents, contributing to a restless quality. In "Call on Me," rising fifths are balanced by descending ones in a manner akin (after Salzer) to Hindemith. In "Woman Don't Want to Love Me," a large-scale tritone connection conceals stepwise motion. Includes several musical examples.

A238 **Stewart, Alexander.** "'Funky Drummer': New Orleans, James Brown and the Rhythmic Transformation of American Popular Music." *Popular Music* 19, no. 3 (2000): 293–318. [Reprinted in DeWitt, ed., *Roots Music*. 2011: 251–76. See **C5**. Reprinted in Perchard, ed., *From Soul to Hip Hop*. 2011: 123–48.] See **C28**.

An investigation into the New Orleans roots of funk. Stewart identifies a mid-century shift in popular music's basic metric subdivision from swing eighth notes to straight, which opened the door for the 16th-note rhythms of R&B, rock and roll, and funk. He discusses three principal components of the shift: the mixture of straight and swing (e.g., Earl King's drums and Professor Longhair's piano), the feel of the New Orleans march in second-line patterns, and the Caribbean influence (mambo, clave, percussion instruments). The funk style of James Brown, whose career spans this shift, is given close analysis with special attention to the drum patterns. The article closes with a discussion of funk styles in the 1970s. Includes numerous transcriptions and rhythmic examples.

A239 **Stoia, Nicholas.** "Mode, Harmony, and Dissonance Treatment in American Folk and Popular Music, c. 1920–1945." *Music Theory Online* 16, no. 3 (2010).

A study of dissonance treatment that cannot be explained by conventional means. Stoia applies Peter van der Merwe's "hanging third" and "dropping third" to the major triad using examples of recorded popular music of the 1920s and 1930s. Given the stable tones $\hat{1}$ and $\hat{5}$, a dropping third may be, for example, the flatted $\hat{3}$ over a IV leaping to the consonant $\hat{1}$. An example of a hanging third might be the oscillation between $\hat{5}$ and $\hat{3}$ over a V chord. Stoia examines a dozen recordings and notes that in many cases the mode will change along with the harmony, thus stabilizing some scale degrees and destabilizing others. This shift in stability seems to reinforce or confirm some harmonic and cadential practices in the genre. Includes several musical examples and audio excerpts.

A240 **Stoia, Nicholas.** "The Common Stock of Schemes in Early Blues and Country Music." *Music Theory Spectrum* 35, no. 2 (2013): 194–234.

A comparative analysis of the schemes (foundational harmonic and melodic patterns) common to black and white musical traditions in the American South from the 1920s to the 1940s. Stoia expands Tony Russell's "common stock" of songs to include these underlying schemes, and, unlike scholars who focus only on length of scheme and harmonic progression, he considers the ways in which different musicians realize these schemes, especially with respect to rhythm and melody. From the hundreds of "race" and "hillbilly" records studied, he identifies 15 specific schemes; some are named for the song with which a scheme is commonly associated, and some already hold well-known titles (e.g., 12-bar blues). These schemes fall into five broad categories: progressions with a specific discant, progressions with some specific discants but that can support original ones, progressions with original discants, a melodic structure with a basic harmonic plan, and a melodic structure with no shared conception of harmonic pattern. After discussing analytical matters that arise in transcription (i.e., how to parse the text, how to handle accent, stress, and syncopation), the article examines songs from each category in depth, side-by-side and transposed to C. Includes numerous transcriptions, musical examples, and tables.

A241 **Summach, Jay.** "The Structure, Function, and Genesis of the Prechorus." *Music Theory Online* 17, no. 3 (2011).

A survey of the Billboard's annual top-20 songs from 1955 to 1989 (700 total) that tracks the development of the formal pre-chorus in pop/rock music. Summach first identifies three basic forms in popular music: strophic, AABA, and verse-chorus. He then locates a sentence structure found in many strophic (and AABA) forms and, after Everett, labels its components "statement," "restatement," "departure," and "conclusion." After the presence of the sentential pattern increases in the 1960s, the first two components develop into independent verses, the departure develops into an independent pre-chorus, and the conclusion develops into a chorus. Includes numerous musical examples, figures, formal diagrams, audio examples, and statistical data spanning decades.

A242 **Tagg, Philip.** "Analysing Popular Music: Theory, Method and Practice." *Popular Music* 2 (1982): 37–67. [Reprinted in Middleton, ed., *Reading Pop: Approaches to Textual Analysis in Popular Music*. 2000: 71–103.] See **C23**.

A model for the analysis of how and what popular music communicates. Tagg, after a defense of why the study of popular music must be taken seriously, discusses the problem of musical notation and the limits of existing analytical methods (hermeneutics, semiotics, intonation theory, and others). He then outlines steps of the analytical procedure: checking all musical parameters, identifying smallest musical unit, establishing figure/ground relationships, analyzing melodic transformation, finding congruence between musical and extramusical processes, and falsifying conclusions with hypothetical substitution. The process is demonstrated in analyses of the Kojak theme and ABBA's "Fernando." Includes several melodic analyses and large analytical figures.

A243 **Tatom, Marianne.** "Mining for 'Goldheart': A Sketch Study in Popular Music." *Indiana Theory Review* 21 (2000): 141–67.

An analysis of a single song by the group Guided by Voices and its incarnations from demos to studio recording to live performances. Tatom discusses the band's history, from the early low-fidelity recordings, which earned them a prized position in the "lo-fi" genre, to the later albums, which were more richly produced. Her analysis of "The Goldheart Mountaintop Queen Directory" includes comparison of melody and form among the versions as well as lyrics (rhyme, inter-version references, interaction of voices), instrumentation, texture, and modal ambiguity. Includes several musical examples and formal diagrams.

A244 **Taylor, Timothy D.** "His Name Was in Lights: Chuck Berry's 'Johnny B. Goode.'" *Popular Music* 11, no. 1 (1992): 27–40. [Reprinted in Middleton, ed., *Reading Pop: Approaches to Textual Analysis in Popular Music*. 2000: 165–82.] See **C23**.

A comparison of two versions of "Johnny B. Goode," both by Chuck Berry, recorded nine years apart. Taylor first discusses the song itself and its original recording. Its lyrics exemplify classic American myths with broad appeal, its form retains the African American 12-bar blues pattern but with minor modifications, and it features "inverse hemiola" in the guitar and a strong backbeat. He then considers the numerous differences in the second version. Where the first is positioned as intimate storytelling, the second is more sanitized, drenched in a distancing reverb. Taylor notes that this aestheticization, this interest in music as sound, is probably due to Berry's move to a bigger record label, but he also hypothesizes that it was also part of an attempt to reach a broader (whiter) audience. Includes lyrics and several melodic excerpts.

A245 **Temperley, David.** "Syncopation in Rock: A Perceptual Perspective." *Popular Music* 18, no. 1 (1999): 19–40.

An application of the concepts developed in cognitive music theory to some instances of syncopation in rock music. Temperley argues that in rock music, syncopation is not just the placement of accent on weak beats; it crucially involves displacement of events. He formalizes the displacement rule, using the metrical preference rules in Lerdahl and Jackendoff's Generative Theory of Tonal Music. He suggests that listeners infer the deep structure from the forward-shifted (syncopated) surface structure. Vocal as well as instrumental syncopation is analyzed in various exceprts, as are the implications on harmony and other types of music. Includes numerous examples and figures.

A246 **Temperley, David.** "The Melodic-Harmonic 'Divorce' in Rock." *Popular Music* 26, no. 3 (2007): 323–42. [Reprinted in Spicer, ed., *Rock Music*. 2011: 207–26.] See **C35**.

A close study of the structural independence of melody and harmony, commonplace in rock music. Temperley notes that, in common-practice music, non-harmonic tones are treated in specific and prescribed ways. This is shown not to be the case in many pop-rock examples. Temperley proposes a stratified arrangement, borrowing a tiered chromatic-diatonic-triadic framework from Fred Lerdahl for the harmonic structure and modifying it into a chromatic-pentatonic framework for the melodic structure. He goes on to demonstrate how, for many songs, this scheme is active in the verse, while the melody and harmony in the chorus are integrated. His examples show that this "loose-verse/tight-chorus model" is frequently bolstered by lyrics. Includes numerous musical examples and figures.

A247 **Temperley, David.** "The Cadential IV in Rock." *Music Theory Online* 17, no. 1 (2011).

A study of large-scale plagal cadences, ending an entire section (sectional cadences at the end of a verse-chorus unit (VCU)) or an entire song. Temperley, using data from a previous study, shows that while the dominant most commonly precedes the cadential tonic in a VCU, the subdominant is a close runner-up. Temperley investigates four common uses of the cadential subdominant. In a "plagal stop cadence," the subdominant arrives on a downbeat and is followed by (after a rest or break in the accompaniment) a tonic on a downbeat. The melody carries through the break and concludes on the tonic. A "grand plagal cadence" is an exaggerated plagal stop cadence that closes not a section but an entire song. A subdominant that arrives when an authentic-cadential tonic is expected is called a "deceptive IV." Finally, Temperly discusses instances in which such cadential subdominants are tonicized. Includes numerous musical examples and tables.

A248 **Temperley, David.** "Scalar Shift in Popular Music." *Music Theory Online* 17, no. 4 (2011).

An examination of pop-rock songs uncovering instances of scalar shift, a shift in the underlying scale of the song. Temperley is not satisfied with conventional tonal (major/minor) or modal explanations of such phenomena and proposes a model in which the circle of fifths is stretched into a line, and sections of a song occupy regions on this line. Shifting from region to region, then, gives the impression of scalar shift. After discussing his model with respect to modes and experimental data, he discusses small-scale shifts, large-scale shifts, and ambiguous cases. Includes numerous musical examples, audio examples, and diagrams.

A249 **Toft, Robert.** "Hits and Misses: Crafting a Pop Single for the Top-40 Market in the 1960s." *Popular Music* 29, no. 2 (2010): 267–81. [Reprinted in Hawkins, ed., *Pop Music and Easy Listening*. 2011: 141–55.] See **C9**.

An investigation into how a song's arrangement can determine its success or failure. Toft studies three different versions of Burt Bacharach's "(They Long to Be) Close to You." Richard Chamberlain sang the first, and Dionne Warwick the second. Both were arranged by Bacharach but were deemed failures, even by the composer himself. Richard Carpenter's arrangement for the Carpenters' recording, however, was an undeniable success. Toft details Bacharach's meticulousness in the recording studio and reports on his process of recording. Side-by-side comparisons of all three songs are made, including decisions about form, instrumentation, tempo, modulation, and groove. Includes melodic excerpts and formal diagrams.

A250 **Traut, Don.** "'Simply Irresistible': Recurring Accent Patterns as Hooks in Mainstream 1980s Music." *Popular Music* 24, no. 1 (2005): 57–77.

An examination of the structural properties of hooks in rock and pop of the 1980s. Traut acknowledges (after Gary Burns) that "rhythm hooks" depend on their standing out in their context, not on their repetition. However, he also notes (after Charles Keil) that some hooks have a "vital drive" in spite of (or because of) their repetition. The distinction between the two is not always clear. Traut represents basic hook rhythms in over 100 songs, using a notation in which ordered integers stand for note durations in eighth notes (e.g., <3,3,2> = two dotted eighth notes followed by a quarter; <3,3,3,3,2,2>, etc.). In this body of songs, he observes three principal kinds of rhythmic hook: those that set the title lyric (which usually are set apart, distinct from their surroundings, as in Burns); those that support some additional gesture, like a pre-chorus or a formal transition; and those that establish the main groove. Traut closes with some comments on hooks in earlier decades. Includes numerous musical examples, figures, and tables.

A251 **van der Merwe, Peter.** "The Italian Blue Third." In Hautamäki and Rautiainen, eds., *Popular Music Studies in Seven Acts: Conference Proceedings of the Fourth Annual Conference of the Finnish Society for Ethnomusicology*. 1995: 55–66. See **C8**.

A look at another likely source for the "blue third." van der Merwe acknowledges West African music and folk music of the British Isles as influences, but adds another. He identifies the "Italian blue third" as a lowered third scale degree (often in a diminished-seventh chord) preceding a natural ("major") third (as in a cadential 6/4), ultimately leading stepwise down to tonic. He also notes the tone's dual resolution up to $\hat{3}$ and down to $\hat{2}$. In later African American examples, however, the resolution to $\hat{2}$ may be elided and the "blue" third may resolve directly to tonic. van der Merwe additionally locates an early instance of the tone's incorporation into 12-bar blues form. Includes several musical examples and a transcript of the brief discussion that followed the conference paper.

A252 **Vernallis, Carol.** "The Aesthetics of Music Video: An Analysis of Madonna's 'Cherish.'" *Popular Music* 17, no. 2 (1998): 153-85. [Reprinted in Moore, ed., *Critical Essays in Popular Musicology*. 2007: 443-75.] See **C27**.

A close reading of a single music video, detailing musical and visual codes in time. Vernallis divides the article into three main segments: the individual components of analysis (flow, continuity, contour, form, basic shape, motive, phrase, timbre and texture, harmony, and rhythm); a chronological reading of the entire video using the analytical components; and a discussion of race, gender, and sexuality. Vernallis notes that the possible narratives proposed in the third segment are possible only after a thorough reading in the manner of the second.

A253 **Wagner, Naphtali.** "Tonal Oscillation in the Beatles' Songs." In Heinonen, Heuger, Whiteley, Nurmesjärvi, and Koskimäki, eds., *Beatlestudies 3: Proceedings of the Beatles 2000 Conference*. 2001: 87-96. See **C12**.

A look at the "bifocal tonality" in nine songs by the Beatles. Wagner, after Charles Rosen, suggests that the oscillation between tonal centers can stop time, and through Schenkerian readings he links this notion to the lyric content, to the songs' meanings, and to precedents in Schubert and Schumann. The oscillation is found between relative keys, parallel keys, various modes, pentatonic scales, blues elements, and even foreign keys. Includes several voice-leading graphs.

A254 **Wagner, Naphtali.** "'Domestication' of Blue Notes in the Beatles' Songs." *Music Theory Spectrum* 25, no. 2 (2003): 353-65.

A study of the "consonantization" of blue notes in the Beatles' repertoire. Wagner points out that blue notes, such as flat-$\hat{3}$ and flat-$\hat{7}$, not only may be incorporated directly into chords, such as "Primary Blues Chords" I♭7, IV♭7, and V7, but also may be given consonant support (may be "domesticated") by employing chords like ♭III or ♭VI. The blue notes, then, are no longer surface elements but are part of a deeper structure. Wagner also shows how the Beatles use the techniques to highlight formal contrast in their songs and how their modal songs interact with blue notes. Includes numerous voice-leading graphs.

A255 **Walser, Robert.** "Rhythm, Rhyme, and Rhetoric in the Music of Public Enemy." *Ethnomusicology* 39, no. 2 (1995): 193-217. [Reprinted in Moore, ed., *Critical Essays in Popular Musicology*. 2007: 363-87. See **C27**. Originally appeared as "Clamor and Community: Rhythm, Rhyme, and Rhetoric in the Music of Public Enemy." In Straw, Johnson, Sullivan, Friedlander, with Kennedy, eds., *Popular*

Music—Style and Identity: International Conference on Popular Music Studies. 1993: 291–307.] See **C36**.

A discussion of the musical details in Public Enemy's "Fight the Power" to reveal coherence and complexity. Walser writes that the lyrics and social context of rap are often discussed, but these should not be separated from the music. Therefore, after a look at the popular debate about whether rap is or isn't music (which tends to focus on its reuse of existing material, its lack of traditional melody (its "noisiness"), and the lack of traditional musical skills), he directs his attention to the specifics of the rhythm (the groove) and the rhetoric in the rapping. Polyrhythmic complexity is found, particularly in the interaction of the two. Walser closes with some thoughts on African and African American music. Includes several transcriptions.

A256 **Weisethaunet, Hans.** "Is There Such a Thing as the 'Blue Note'?" *Popular Music* 20, no. 1 (2001): 99–116.

A proposal for new conceptions of harmony and of consonance and dissonance in the blues. Weisethaunet argues that the concept of the blue note is often described as the addition of a "blue" element to a pre-existing major/minor tonality, whether at the third and seventh scale degrees (van der Merwe) or at any of them (Titon). The "blue harmony" proposed here, and its attendant consonance and dissonance, is based instead on the musical texture, which is linked to the specific performed roles of each instrumentalist. Given the difference between harmonic and melodic roles, for example, a major third in a major triad may be understood as more dissonant than the minor third on the same chord. Weisethaunet focuses principally on the guitar, including riffs of Stevie Ray Vaughan and others, and he includes excerpts from his interviews with guitarists Steve Cropper, John Scofield, and John McLaughlin. Includes a table, examples of riffs, and a few guitar transcriptions.

A257 **Whiteley, Sheila.** "Progressive Rock and Psychedelic Coding in the Work of Jimi Hendrix." *Popular Music* 9, no. 1 (1990): 37–60. [Reprinted in Middleton, ed., *Reading Pop: Approaches to Textual Analysis in Popular Music*. 2000: 235–61.] See **C23**.

An analysis of the musical elements of various Jimi Hendrix songs to determine what social and cultural meanings they carry, particularly with respect to the counterculture of the 1960s. Each song studied is reviewed for "progressive elements" as well as "psychedelic coding." The blues influence, the fuzz tone (and other effects), repetition, phrasing, and motivic patterning all contribute to meaning. Includes numerous transcriptions and a brief appendix on electric guitar distortion.

A258 **Whiteley, Sheila.** "Seduced By the Sign: An Analysis of the Textual Links Between Sound and Image in Pop Videos." In Sheila Whiteley, ed., *Sexing the Groove: Popular Music and Gender*: 259–76. London and New York: Routledge, 1997; 353p. ISBN 0415146712; ML3470.S46 1997.

A study of the links between visuals and music that establish meaning in Madonna's music video "Justify My Love." Whiteley first analyzes the song and then follows with a reading of the erotic music video. Her analyses draw upon two principal components. First there is an application of Barthes's narratological codes, both syntagmatic (proairetic, hermeneutic) and paradigmatic (semic, cultural, symbolic). Second, numerous responses from Whiteley's student questionnaire are incorporated. She asked participants who had heard the song before seeing the video whether the video confirmed their perception of the song. She also asked whether they thought the video engages male viewers, female viewers, or both. Whiteley's own reading highlights the positive as well as the problematic sexual signs. Includes a couple of musical examples. Also includes the questionnaire as an appendix.

A259 **Whiteley, Sheila.** "'Love, Love, Love': Representations of Gender and Sexuality in Selected Songs by the Beatles." In Kenneth Womack and Todd F. Davis, eds., *Reading the Beatles: Cultural Studies, Literary Criticism, and the Fab Four:* 55–69. Albany, NY: State University of New York Press, 2006; 249p. ISBN 9780791467163; ML421.B4R43 2006.

An essay that assesses whether the Beatles' framing of femininity was oppressive or evolutionary. Whiteley explores connections between musical, narrative, and lyrical meaning in the Beatles' songs from 1962 to 1969. She covers the elements in their early sound, particularly the vocal harmonies, that held such an appeal to teenaged girls. Later music introduces vulnerability and less self-assuredness. She also details the categories into which the women in their later songs fall. Ultimately she finds that the music conservatively positions women within the patriarchy, though the later songs introduce some cynicism and self-mockery. Includes a few musical examples.

A260 **Whitesell, Lloyd.** "Harmonic Palette in Early Joni Mitchell." *Popular Music* 21, no. 2 (2002): 173–94.

A survey of dozens of songs from Joni Mitchell's early career (1966–72). Whitesell analyzes the role of Mixolydian, Aeolian, and Lydian modes; the combination of modes; harmonic progression; the use of thirds in the equal division of the octave; the occasional polytonality, where a song exhibits two tonal centers; and the structural and dramatic roles of pedal point. In a brief postlude, he considers how these concepts are treated in later Mitchell works. Includes numerous musical examples, formal diagrams, and a comprehensive table summarizing modal features.

A261 **Williams, Justin A.** "Theoretical Approaches to Quotation in Hip-Hop Recordings." *Contemporary Music Review* 33, no. 2 (2014): 188–209.

A discussion and analysis of different kinds quotation in hip-hop. Williams acknowledges existing theories of Signifyin(g) and intertextuality, but focuses primarily on digitally sampled ("autosonic") versus borrowed ("allosonic"), in Serge Lacasse's terms. He also distinguishes (after Richard Dyer) between borrowings that are acknowledged as such by the text itself (i.e., "textually signalled") and those that are not. These notions are brought to bear on a detailed analysis of Xzibit's "Symphony in X Major," whose multi-layered quotations include Wendy Carlos's version of Bach's Brandenburg Concerto No. 3. Includes several examples and tables.

A262 **Wilson, Olly.** "The Significance of the Relationship Between Afro-American Music and West African Music." *The Black Perspective in Music* 2, no. 1 (1974): 3–22. [Reprinted in DeWitt, ed., *Roots Music*. 2011: 291–310.] See **C5**.

An argument that West African musical practices were retained and adapted by African Americans. Wilson, building on the work of Melville J. Herskovitz, applies Alan P. Merriam's proposed characteristics of sub-Saharan African music, but he expands the sphere of African and African-descendant peoples, including parts of South America and the Carribean. One of Merriam's characteristics is critiqued ("metronomic sense"), but another ("polymeter") forms the basis of a comparison of an Ewe social dance to James Brown's "Superbad," both given in transcription. Includes several music examples.

A263 **Winkler, Peter K.** "Toward a Theory of Popular Harmony." In *Theory Only* 4, no. 2 (1978): 3–26. [Reprinted in Moore, ed., *Critical Essays in Popular Musicology*. 2007: 251–74.] See **C27**.

A close inspection of a harmonic/voice-leading cliché in jazz and popular music. Winkler analyzes eight examples, all of which, from the perspective of harmony and voice leading, are different instances of the same paradigm, defined by parallel chromatic motion and root motion by the circle of fifths. Through more extended analyses, he shows the paradigm extended through repetition, prolonged, and employed at various levels from background to foreground. The treatment of this paradigm by jazz soloists (Basie, Young, Parker) is also considered. Although Winkler acknowledges that the use of this paradigm has become less common, he finds its influence in a song by Earth, Wind, and Fire. Includes numerous musical examples, transcriptions, and voice-leading graphs.

A264 **Winkler, Peter.** "Randy Newman's Americana." *Popular Music* 7, no. 1 (1988): 1–26. [Reprinted in Middleton, ed., *Reading Pop: Approaches to Textual Analysis in Popular Music*: 27–57.] See **C23**.

An analysis of a songwriter's style. Winkler directly compares Randy Newman's work to songs from various other sources and identifies four primary elements of the songwriter's style. A barbershop paradigm (often with unresolved suspensions), a gospel-blues connection (in melodic countour and bluesy inflections), a nineteenth-century parlor music sound (by pianistic traits), and a grand film-music quality (pandiatonicism) are detailed in musical transcription and reduction. Winkler takes care to connect these features to Newman's lyrical traits, particularly irony. Includes several musical examples, figures, and transcriptions.

A265 **Winkler, Peter.** "Writing Ghost Notes: The Poetics and Politics of Transcription." In David Schwarz, Anahid Kassabian, and Lawrence Siegel, eds., *Keeping*

Score: Music, Disciplinarity, Culture: 169–203. Charlottesville, VA: University Press of Virginia, 1997; 307p. ISBN 0813916992; MT1.K32 1997.

An investigation of transcription as a perceptual and cognitive act with Aretha Franklin's "I Never Loved a Man (The Way I Love You)" as a case study. Winkler, noting that because scholars tend not to discuss the "music itself," transcription is largely absent from popular music study, draws upon discussions in ethnomusicology and jazz, where transcription is essential. He was interested in questioning the act of transcription to determine its meaning, use, and value. Though aware of its potential dangers, Winkler ultimately argues for the importance of transcription. In his analysis of the Franklin recording, he recounts the difficulties faced, particularly with respect to pitch and rhythm in the voice. He turned to forms of automatic transcription—waveform analysis and samplers—but found them insufficient. He closes with five reasons scholars might choose to transcribe: to show what is in the recording, to support historical arguments, to establish legitimacy, to reproduce music live, and to appropriate for scholarship. Includes a lead sheet, transcriptions, and several musical figures.

A266 **Wise, Timothy.** "Jimmie Rodgers and the Semiosis of the Hillbilly Yodel." *The Musical Quarterly* 93, no. 1 (2010): 6–44.

A broad analysis of Jimmie Rodgers's yodeling, focusing on its key structural aspects and how they correspond to the lyrics or mood of the songs. Wise, after a brief survey of the existing literature, introduces a three-part typology of Rodgers's yodeling. The first species is wordless yodeling, the second is yodeling occurring while singing words, and the third is the yodeled grace note. He discusses where in a song's form each of these may be employed (the turnaround, the refrain, or the yodel break) as well as the numerous tropes employed, including nostalgia for home, the interval of a sixth, blues tropes as in the "Blue Yodel" songs, and hummed yodeling. Includes several musical examples and an appendix showing the yodel species type, location in the form, and the meter for 111 Jimmie Rodgers songs.

A267 **Yakô, Masato.** "Classification of Rhythm Patterns." In Mitsui, ed., *Popular Music: Intercultural Interpretations: International Association for the Study of Popular Music, Ninth International Conference on Popular Music.* 1998: 398–411. See **C24**.

A system for classifying pop-rock rhythm patterns by structure and shape. Yakô notes that the style-blending afforded by the digital technology has rendered obsolete analysis based on traditional styles or genres. The method here, after Mickey Earnshaw, involves the encoding of 1,500 textbook rhythm patterns for drumset, each drum or symbol being assigned a string of 0s and 1s. One analysis of the data plots the similarities between the rhythms and groups them into families. Another analysis takes into account accent or emphasis on particular instruments. Includes several charts, graphs, and figures.

A268 **Zak, Albin J., III.** "'Edition-ing' Rock." *American Music* 23, no. 1 (2005): 95–107.

An essay that considers how one might attempt a written "edition" of a work of rock music. Zak reconciles the written notation of a printed edition with the sonic imagery of a recording, and proposes three possible components of such an enterprise: transcription, historical essay, and analysis. He acknowledges that transcription will always be a reduction, as will any effort to isolate a single element that contributes to the overall sound of a record, but it will be useful if used judiciously and if combined with the appropriate analysis. The writing should complement the transcription, addressing things like timbre, production techniques, and mood. He provides some examples of what this might look like using songs by Elvis and by John Hiatt. Includes one musical example.

A269 **Zak, Albin.** "Rock and Roll Rhapsody: Pop Epics of the 1970s." In Everett, ed., *Expression in Pop-Rock Music: Critical and Analytical Essays*, 2nd ed. 2008: 345–60. See **C6**.

A look at the grandiose in 1970s rock. Extended musical forms did not belong only to progressive rock, but also to rock and pop more broadly. In this chapter, Zak is less concerned with length than with the unusual formal structures that can tend toward the epic. After discussing the influence of FM radio and of the long-playing album, he examines texture and lyrics in Led Zeppelin, the "stylistic sprawl" of Queen's "Bohemian Rhapsody," and the manipulation of form in the music of several other artists. He closes by touching upon 1980s rock and new wave. Includes a few musical examples.

A270 **Zak, Albin.** "'Only the Lonely': Roy Orbison's Sweet West Texas Style." In Spicer and Covach, eds., *Sounding Out Pop: Analytical Essays in Popular Music*. 2010: 18–41. See **C34**.

A look at Roy Orbison's stylistic development across several years, producers, and record labels. Zak identifies "Only the Lonely" as the apotheosis of Orbison's songwriting, arranging, performance style, and sonic representation. In this song, as well as "An Empty Cup," "In Dreams," and others, Zak finds irregular harmonic rhythm with unusual phrase lengths and metric shifts; strophic variation involving a dramatic, rising vocal tessitura, even falsetto; a lush instrumentation bordering on orchestral pop; and elements of background and vocal figuration as integral parts of the composition, not mere embellishment. Includes a few musical examples.

A271 **Zbikowski, Lawrence M.** "Modelling the Groove: Conceptual Structure and Popular Music." *Journal of the Royal Musical Association* 129, no. 2 (2004): 272–97. [Reprinted in Hawkins, ed., *Pop Music and Easy Listening*. 2011: 425–41.] See **C9**.

An answer to the question "what is it that musicians know when they know a good groove?" Zbikowski writes that musicians, when performing and improvising, use "knowledge structures," which are built up from more basic "conceptual models." His models for musical rhythm are based on the concepts of regularity, difference, and cyclicity, which are embodied by physical motions, real or imagined. He uses this model when discussing the grooves (as in multi-layered R&B or popular grooves, not as in the subtleties of jazz swing) of three contrasting recordings. Layers in Eric Clapton's "It All Depends," beat division in Miles Davis's "If I Were a Bell," and stability/instability in James Brown's "Doing It to Death" are modeled and discussed. Includes several musical examples and diagrams.

II
Books

B1 **Bennighof, James.** *The Words and Music of Paul Simon.* Westport, CT: Praeger, 2007; 205p. ISBN 0275991636; ML420.S563B46 2007.

A survey of the entire recorded output of Paul Simon, song by song. Bennighof focuses primarily on meter, form, and harmonic structure, examining the relationship of music and text. Working chronologically, he is able to track changes in Simon's style over time. In a concluding essay, Bennighof discusses the synthetic nature of Simon's songs. Often, before the words, chords, and melody are even composed, the song is conceived as a selection and assembly of disparate elements. The book's chapters are organized by album, and a complete discography is included. Not only is there an extensive musical glossary, but also there is, for the novice musician, a 14-page tutorial on tonality; keys and harmonic progression; modulation; chords; and diatonic, modal, and chromatic harmony. Every song is analyzed, but no notated musical analyses are present; all musical elements are detailed in prose.

B2 **Berger, Harris M.** *Metal, Rock, and Jazz: Perception and the Phenomenology of Musical Experience.* Hanover, NH: Wesleyan University Press, University Press of New England, 1999; 334p. ISBN 0819563714; ML3838.B439 1999.

An ethnography of three music scenes in northeastern Ohio. The first section examines the compositional and performance practice of two hard rock bands, Dia Pason and Max Panic; two heavy metal bands, Winter's Bane and Sin-Eater; and Whisler's Quartet, a jazz group. Performance space, social context, and crowd response are primary considerations in the rock and metal scenes, while the jazz scene receives additional attention to groove, arrangement, and soloing. The second section is a phenomenological examination of the relationship of the musical elements to the musicians' experience of the world, and it outlines distinct differences between the three scenes. Here there are complete transcriptions and in-depth analyses of two songs. The third section touches, through interviews, upon the musicians' perspectives on politics, economics, race, and class. A glossary of terms, defined from the Ohio musicians' perspective, is incuded.

B3 **Bobbitt, Richard.** *Harmonic Technique in the Rock Idiom: The Theory and Practive of Rock Harmony.* Belmont, CA: Wadsworth, 1976; 246p. ISBN 0534004741; MT50.B65 1976.

A study of harmonic practice in rock, using more than 200 songs from the 1960s, referred to as the "rock period." Bobbitt explores the main harmonic principles in the music and presents numerous voice-leading reductions and paraphrases playable at the piano. Each concept is accompanied by a list of songs for reference. Part One introduces the techniques in the abstract: building and labeling 3-, 4-, 5-, 6-, and 7-note chords from different scales and modes; diatonic, mixed-diatonic, chromatic, and symmetrical progressions; idiomatic use, focusing on chord degrees and common tones; chord substitution; modes; and the blues scale. Part Two is an application of the concepts to analysis, including minor dominant, prolongation, subdominant, substitution, chromaticism, secondary dominants, characteristic "sus4" and dom7#9 chords, and form. A large appendix provides historical perspective with classical examples from the Renaissance to the modern era. There also is an accompanying workbook for self-study. Includes copious musical examples and figures.

B4 **Brackett, David.** *Interpreting Popular Music.* Cambridge: Cambridge University Press, 1995; 260p. ISBN 9780520225411; ML3470.B73 1995. [Reprinted in 2000 with a new preface by the author.]

A work that bridges the gap between the sociological and musicological approaches to popular music. Brackett finds it important to study the musical sounds themselves, but also notes that meaning tends to be socially constructed. His primary analytical interests, then, are the contexts in which meanings are allowed to form. The introduction lays the groundwork (Middleton's codes and signification, Stefani's musical competence, the complexities of authorship, the use of metaphor, and the limits of transcription) for the analyses that follow. Each remaining chapter focuses on a single song and the questions of meaning that surround it. Bing Crosby's and Billie Holiday's versions of "I'll Be Seeing You" are compared side-by-side using traditional notation as well as spectral analysis; Hank Williams's "Hey Good Lookin'" engages metanarratives in country music; James Brown's "Superbad" exemplifies African American music as discourse; and Elvis Costello's "Pills and Soap" is discussed in terms of competing aesthetics of the 1960s and 1970s. Includes several musical examples, transcriptions, figures, spectrum photos, and tables. [Revision and expansion of author's dissertation.] See **D6**.

B5 **Butler, Mark J.** *Unlocking the Groove: Rhythm, Meter, and Musical Design in Electronic Dance Music.* Bloomington: Indiana University Press, 2006; 346p.

ISBN 0253346622. MT146.B88 2006. [Chapter 2 reprinted in Butler, ed., *Electronica, Dance, and Club Music*. 2012: 21–63.] See **C3**.

A close investigation of the beats and rhythms of electronic dance music (EDM). Butler studies the music's design from the small to the large scale. He notes that he focuses on the sound and that many scholars have neglected to do so with precision. There are detailed analyses of more than a dozen EDM tracks, and his commentary is supported by field research. The book outlines a history of EDM and of the technology used in its creation; builds upon theories of Krebs, Lerdahl and Jackendoff, Temperley, Hasty, and others to show how the genre's rhythm and meter may be conceived, and to reveal metric ambiguity and various kinds of metric dissonance; and discusses larger-scale issues of hypermeter, combination of tracks, and form. Ultimately the genre is shown to be a rich one, from its subdivisions of the beat, to the interaction of its layers, to its turning the beat around. Includes numerous musical examples, figures, and transcriptions. Also includes appendices covering issues related to transcription and field research and providing complete transcriptions, a glossary of terms, and a CD containing recordings of the musical examples.

B6 **Echard, William.** *Neil Young and the Poetics of Energy*. Bloomington, IN: Indiana University Press, 2005; 260p. ISBN 0253345812; ML420.Y75E34 2005.

A study of Neil Young and his music, making use of semiotics, metaphor, and energetics, with special focus on Young's changing persona. Echard, after an overview of Young's reception history, investigates style, genre, performance, and Young's improvisational style. A survey of the musical semiotics of David Lidov and others leads to musical analyses of various songs. Harmonic elements are discussed in the prose, but some melodic excerpts are included in examples. The book concludes with a thorough, chapter-length, energetic analysis of Young's "Will to Love."

B7 **Everett, Walter.** *The Beatles as Musicians:* Revolver *through the Anthology*. Oxford: Oxford University Press, 1999; 395p. ISBN 0195129415; MT146.E94 1999.

A chronologically arranged, song-by-song examination of the musical techniques employed by the Beatles as composers, performers, and recording artists during the second half of the group's career. (See also **B8**.) Everett analyzes every known recording, not just the canonical records, but the demos and unreleased recordings as well. He assesses harmony, melody, riffs, or voice leading, whatever the particular song warrants, but he also comments upon recording techniques, instrumentation, arrangement, and other details of production. In short, he is interested in what constitutes the sound of the Beatles. Includes copious musical examples, figures, and voice-leading graphs, lists, tables, a map, timelines, an appendix describing the musical instruments of the band's early period, an appendix covering musical friends of the Beatles, a table of chord functions, and a glossary of terms.

B8 **Everett, Walter.** *The Beatles as Musicians: The Quarry Men Through* Rubber Soul. Oxford: Oxford University Press, 2001; 452p. ISBN 0195141059; MT146.E95 2001.

A chronologically arranged, song-by-song examination of the musical techniques employed by the Beatles as composers, performers, and recording artists during the first half of the group's career. (See also **B7**.) Everett analyzes every known recording, not just the canonical records, but the demos and unreleased recordings as well. He assesses harmony, melody, riffs, or voice leading, whatever the particular song warrants, but he also comments upon recording techniques, instrumentation, arrangement, and other details of production. In short, he is interested in what constitutes the sound of the Beatles. Includes copious musical examples, figures, voice-leading graphs, lists, tables, maps, timelines, an appendix describing the musical instruments of the band's early period, a table of chord functions, and a glossary of terms.

B9 **Floyd, Samuel A., Jr.** *The Power of Black Music: Interpreting Its History from Africa to the United States.* New York: Oxford University Press, 1996; 316p. ISBN 0195082354; ML3556.F65 1995.

A study of the origin and development of African American music and musical culture. Floyd argues that African traits, practices, and musical tendencies not only retained but also continuously influence the development of African American Music. He first traces African music, the survival of its traditions, and its syncretization with European music. He then follows its development through African American modernism, the Negro Renaissance, concert-hall developments, political and sociological influence, and music as Signifyin(g). He concludes by discussing the philosophical ideas of Peter Kivy and others. Without concern for barriers between "high" and "low" music, which in fact inform one another, Floyd investigates the full breadth of the African influence.

B10 **Forte, Allen.** *The American Popular Ballad of the Golden Era: 1924–1950.* Princeton, NJ: Princeton University Press, 1995; 366p. ISBN 069104399; ML3477.F67 1995.

A collection of close analyses of ballads from the American Songbook, largely from a Schenkerian perspective. Forte begins with brief introductory chapters on harmony (nomenclature, blue notes, mode mixture, embellishing chords, and progression); rhythm and meter (idiomatic figures and motives); melody (head note, primary tone, highpoint, and lowpoint); the lyric (rhyme, alliteration, and versification); formal nomenclature (period, double period, verse, refrain, chorus, and bridge); and the large-scale view (introduction to Schenkerian notation). What follows are chapters on each of the "big six" songwriters of the era: Kern, Berlin, Porter, Gershwin, Rodgers, and Arlen. Six songs from each composer are treated with melodic, motivic, and harmonic analysis, all with an eye toward voice leading and how the musical structure coordinates with the lyrics. Additional chapters feature a song from each of seven more songwriters, with one chapter featuring a special focus on women composers. Each analysis includes numerous musical figures and voice-leading graphs.

B11 **Forte, Allen.** *Listening to Classic American Popular Songs.* New Haven, CT: Yale University Press, 2001. ISBN 0300083386; ML3477.F672 2001.

A set of 23 individual analyses of standards by Gershwin, Porter, Rogers, Berlin, and others. Forte makes observations about melody, harmony, form, lyrics, and rhythm. These five terms are defined in Chapter 1 for the novice, but the ability to read a lead sheet (melody and chord symbols) is assumed. While there is nothing overtly Schenkerian here, many analysts will appreciate the attention to large-scale connections. Throughout, Forte pays special attention to connections between lyrics and musical structure. There is a glossary of terms, a brief bibliography, and a general index. Includes a CD with recorded performances by Richard Lalli and Gary Chapman of all but one of the analyzed songs, some of which are arranged as medleys.

B12 **Gottlieb, Jack.** *Funny, It Doesn't Sound Jewish: How Yiddish Songs and Synagogue Melodies Influenced Tin Pan Alley, Broadway, and Hollywood.* Albany, NY: State University of New York in Association with Library of Congress, 2004; 306p. ISBN 0844411302; ML3776.G65 2004.

A study of the Jewish influence on American popular music. Gottlieb investigates the music of Tin Pan Alley and Broadway, and he details its many connections to Yiddish music and Synagogue melodies. Looking primarily at the melodies, modes, and motives, he outlines the clustering of the music material into groups of shared influence. Includes numerous melodic examples, both popular excerpts and source influences. Also includes a photo gallery of Yiddish songwriters and poets, appendices listing composers, authors, performers, "Yingish" song titles, musical example titles, and a CD with 50 recorded examples.

B13 **Hawkins, Stan.** *Settling the Pop Score: Pop Texts and Identity Politics.* Burlington, VT: Ashgate: 2002; 220p. ISBN 0754603520; ML3918.P67H39 2002.

A collection of five case studies examining identity politics through musical codes and signification in the music and visuals of five highly commercial artists. Hawkins analyzes the music of Madonna, Morrissey, Annie Lennox, the Pet Shop Boys, and Prince, detailing formal properties, harmonic idioms, recording and production techniques, and rhythmic syntax. Includes numerous musical examples, tables, and images.

B14 **Krims, Adam.** *Rap Music and the Poetics of Identity.* Cambridge: Cambridge University Press, 2000; 217p. ISBN 0521632684; ML3531.K75 2000.

A study of the musical components of rap and their essential role in the formation of ethnic and geographic identities. Krims discusses the role of music theory in the cultural studies of rap; studies rhythm, texture, timbre, and flow to develop a set of rap genres (party rap, mack rap, jazz rap, and reality rap); analyzes the close integration of text, music, and identity at the individual level in a song by

Ice Cube and at the geographic level in the music of the Goodie MoB; and ultimately examines rap poetics at the global level (including Dutch and Canadian rap), which in turn aids understanding of the local level.

B15 **Lambert, Philip.** *Inside the Music of Brian Wilson: The Songs, Sounds, and Influences of the Beach Boys' Founding Genius.* New York: Continuum, 2007; 404p. ISBN 9780826418777; ML420.W5525L36 2007.

A comprehensive study of the songs and productions of Brian Wilson. Lambert focuses expressly on the music. While making necessary biographical and historical references, he explores the evolution of Wilson's musical practice, trends that emerged along the way, and the connections that can be found both among his songs and between his songs and others'. Starting with Wilson's early musical influences, particularly that of the Four Freshmen, and leading through *Pet Sounds*, *Smile*, and on into the later solo projects, Lambert discusses structural elements (harmony and form) as well as surface details. All analysis is presented in prose, in formal diagrams, or in tables—there is no musical notation—but this does not preclude examination of key, melodic contour, interval, and other musical details. Includes numerous formal diagrams, a chronology of all of Wilson's work as writer, producer, and/or performer (with alphabetized song list as cross-reference), a list of relevant Four Freshmen albums with track listings, and an annotated list of Wilson's early favorite songs.

B16 **Lee, Edward.** *Music of the People: A Study of Popular Music in Great Britain.* London: Barrie and Jenkins, 1970; 274p. ISBN 9780214660672; ML3650.L33 1970.

A critical survey of popular music in England from the earliest British history to the present day, the second half of which ("Part Two: English Popular Music of the Twentieth Century") may be of most interest to popular music scholars. Lee traces the development of popular music, noting the influence of jazz and rock and roll. He also discusses specific problems that arise, particularly notational and rhythmic, when attempting to use common-practice analytical techniques. He further discusses the basics of instrumentation, vocal timbre, chord voicing, and harmonic language. There are chapters on the effects popular music had on classical composers (Stravinsky, Ravel, Copland) and on folk music (particularly in its meter and arrangements). There are chapters, too, on the attitudes of musicians and audience. A chapter on melody touches on form and chromatic harmony but focuses mostly on contour and dissonance treatment. A chapter on lyrics highlights rhythmic pitfalls of text setting; songs from the Beatles and others are taken to task. Includes numerous musical examples and lyrics.

B17 **Malvinni, David.** *Grateful Dead and the Art of Rock Improvisation.* Lanham, MD: Scarecrow Press, 2013; 296p. ISBN 0810882558; ML421.G72M25 2013.

A study of "deadness," an aesthetic category exemplified by the Grateful Dead's openness to change, transcendental outlook, collective improvisation, and risky performance. Malvinni, with a focus on improvisation over composition and on performance over songwriting, approaches "deadness" through analyses engaging the music-theoretical (harmony, mode, form) as well as the philosophical (Deleuze, Derrida, and Heidegger). Malvinni considers the band's improvisations in their entire repertoire, from early R&B- and folk-influenced material, in which improvisations may arise in extended, single-chord vamps; through the jazz-rock period, in which harmonic vocabulary is extended; and to the late period, usually thought of as less improvisatory. Throughout the book, emphasis is on the transformative quality of improvisation. Includes a few musical examples, but there is a fair amount of analysis with roman numerals built into the prose.

B18 **Mellers, Wilfrid.** *Twilight of the Gods: The Beatles in Retrospect*. London: Faber and Faber, 1973; 215p. ISBN 0571103413; ML421.B4M44. [Published in the U.S. as *Twilight of the Gods: The Music of The Beatles*. New York: The Viking Press, 1973; 215p. ISBN 0670735981. Includes a "Note to the American Reader," which explains crotchets, quavers, etc.]

A chronologically arranged, analytical walk through the Beatles' repertoire from the early recordings to the first solo albums. Mellers mostly identifies keys, chords, motives, instrumentation, and other surface elements, but they are connected throughout to themes in the lyrics and to musical influences. It is notable as an early contribution to the study of Beatles' music and especially for its inclusion of solo material. Includes piano/vocal excerpts for many of the songs discussed and a glossary of terms.

B19 **Middleton, Richard.** *Studying Popular Music*. Milton Keynes, UK: Open University Press, 1990; 328p. ISBN 033515275; ML3470.M5 1990.

A wide-ranging study that is both cultural and musical. Middleton considers the history, philosophy, and analysis of popular music, which at the time was "banished" by musicologists for its apparent low quality and "neglected" by cultural theorists for its alienating technicality. He first establishes a historical framework, answers fundamental questions about how popular music is distinct from art music, and responds to philosophers and cultural commentators, such as Adorno and McLuhan. He then reviews the early analytical approaches of Charles Hamm and Wilfred Mellers and goes on to propose several other avenues: ethnomusicology, paradigmatic analysis, Schenkerian analysis, and the theories of Eugene Narmour. He closes by considering ideology in popular music. Includes numerous musical examples, figures, and tables.

B20 **Moore, Allan** F. *Rock: The Primary Text: Developing a Musicology of Rock*, 2nd ed. Burlington, VT: Ashgate, 2001 [1993]; 253p. ISBN 9780754602996; ML3534. M66 1993.

A set of analytic criteria for rock music (generally British rock and particularly progressive rock) that acknowledges a diversity of styles but also recognizes consistency of basic materials. Moore discusses current musicology—"the pop-classical split"—and concludes that pop/rock requires a distinct musicology from that practiced in classical music. He then systematically proposes primary materials: rhythm, voice, melody, and (mode-based) harmony. These are brought to bear in a chapter explicating the diversity and consistency in progressive rock's language (with numerous analyses of the music of Led Zeppelin; Emerson, Lake, & Palmer; The Kinks; The Incredible String Band; Pink Floyd; and many others). Another chapter covers the "profusion of styles" following in the wake of progressive rock (including music of The Clash, Madness, The Jam, U2, Big Country, and others). While these two chapters deal with the primary text, the sounds of the music, the closing chapter is a search for meaning in the music. This project is in part to "demystify" the musicological meaning, but it does not preclude the sociological. Includes numerous musical figures and examples.

B21 **Moore, Allan F.** *Song Means: Analysing and Interpreting Recorded Popular Song.* Burlington, VT: Ashgate, 2012; 395p. ISBN 9781409428640; MT146.M66 2012.

A comprehensive study about *how* songs mean; it is about the means by which songs mean things, not about *what* they mean. It is a methodology of both analysis and interpretation concerned primarily with meanings derived from the sound rather than socio-cultural meanings. Moore devotes each half of the book to a different enterprise. Though the two are related, neither is sufficient alone. The first half covers what one would consider traditionally analytical matters: "shape" (layers, soundbox—the stereo imaging of instruments in the sound field, and timbre); "form" (meter, hypermeter, phrase, syncopation, modal theory, loops, periods); and "delivery" (melodic contour, period, voice, lyrics). The second half is more hermeneutic with four main components. "Friction" is the result when what was expected to happen does not. This chapter is concerned with a norm—what it is and how songs vary from it, whether texturally or formally. A "persona" is projected by the performer, and the listener interacts with or relates to this persona in specific ways. A song makes "reference" to itself or within itself, and music theory is helpful here, but it also refers outside itself, which is when semiotics comes into play. Finally, both intertextuality and authenticity contribute to a sense of "belonging." The two halves are connected by a chapter on the history of style, a chronological walk through the popular styles of the 20th century. The theoretical and the hermeneutical are synthesized in the penultimate chapter, and the book closes, since Moore's approach is chiefly interrogative, with a set of questions one might ask oneself of a song under study. Includes numerous musical examples, figures, and tables.

B22 **Schloss, Joseph.** *Making Beats: The Art of Sample-Based Hip Hop.* Middletown, CT: Wesleyan University Press, 2004; 225p. ISBN 0819566969; ML3531.S35 2004.

An ethnographic study of the process of making sample-based beats in hip-hop. Schloss eschews transcription in favor of the perspective of hip-hop's practitioners gleaned from numerous interviews. He doesn't find transcriptions to be incorrect, just inadequate. They may distort the sounds in question, miss important subtleties, or, most importantly, disguise the actual process of sample combination when "instruments" from a single sample are notated individually. The

Books 91

book covers the history of sampling, deejaying practices, the reasons for rejection of live, "crate digging" for record albums to sample, the ethics of sampling, and community influences. Of most interest to music theorists and musicologists, perhaps, is Chapter 6, "Elements of Style: Aesthetics of Hip-Hop Composition." Here Schloss discusses the choices producers make when making a beat. The structure of the beat, the internal characteristics of individual samples, the relationship between samples, and the interpretive context of the samples, all comprise the chapter. Includes no stand-alone figures; analysis is in the prose.

B23 **Schwarz, David.** *Listening Subjects: Music, Psychoanalysis, Culture.* Durham, NC: Duke University Press, 1997; 211p. ISBN 0822319292; ML3830.S28 1997.

A blending of psychoanalysis, music theory, musicology, and music history in order to understand what happens to listeners when listening to music. Schwarz, arguing that music theory and cultural studies are mutually reinforcing, notes that listening can be a "fantasy thing," involving structural elements (theory) and a "fantasy space," involving the personal (psychoanalysis, cultural). Considering the Beatles' "I Want You (She's So Heavy)," Schwarz couples a harmonic analysis with a discussion of Lennon's scatting to show representations of frustration and desire, with attention to the deliberately abrupt end of the song. Peter Gabriel's "Intruder," through its timbres, vocal delivery, and synthesizer riff, invites the male listener to relate to violent sexual fantasy. This recording is contrasted with Primus's version of the same song. Schwarz gives a brief history of Oi Musik and explains how properties of post-rock enable a connection between Oi's musical, textual, and ideological structure to right-wing "skinhead" culture. Other chapters discuss the music of Schubert and of 20th-century performance artist Diamanda Galas. Includes numerous musical examples.

B24 **Stephenson, Ken.** *What to Listen for in Rock: A Stylistic Analysis.* New Haven, CT: Yale University Press, 2002; 253p. ISBN 0300092393; MT146.S74 2002.

A comprehensive study of the musical techniques of rock music, broadly construed as popular music after 1954, written for the mid-level undergraduate. Stephenson responds to critics who argue that analysis of rock should be rooted in cultural and sociological analysis by investigating phrase rhythm (including extension and elision); key and mode (with a discussion of the distinction as well as the possibilities of multiple keys and modes); cadence (melodic and harmonic aspects); harmony (chord type and progression); and form (and its relationship to lyrics and harmony). Includes copious musical examples and formal diagrams. Also includes a set of exercises for each chapter.

B25 **Tagg, Philip.** *Fernando the Flute: Analysis of Musical Mea Hit,* 3rd ed. New York: Mass Media Music Scholars' P 140p. ISBN 0970168411; MT130.F37T23 2001.

A detailed semiotic reading of ABBA's "Fernando." abundant musical meanings as well as its historic structural elements come first: a look at the song of meaning. They include pitch and rhythmic figures marked "bolero," "legato sincerity," and even "Fernando museme" for the song's title motive. Tagg then shows how the musemes combine in the formal process. He also discusses connections between lyrics (including Swedish and Spanish versions) and the music. Finally, a discussion of context includes the history of Chile under Pinochet and the reception of the song in Sweden and elsewhere. Includes numerous musical examples, a complete transcription of the song, a table of the 11 musemes, and a table of the musematic occurences, a formal diagram of sorts.

B26 **Titon, Jeff Todd.** *Early Downhome Blues: A Musical and Cultural Analysis.* Urbana: University of Illinois Press, 1977; 297p. ISBN 0252001877; ML3561. B63T58 1977.

An in-depth study of downhome (or "country") blues of the 1920s. Titon, after distinguishing the primarily male downhome blues (with raspy timbres, guitar accompaniment, and intimate, informal folk delivery and transmission) from the mostly female vaudeville blues (with roots in Tin Pan Alley and an often comic delivery), considers its cultural context in the first half of the 20th century. He then provides detailed textual and musical analysis of a representative 48 tracks. Transcriptions are followed by a systematic analysis covering form, timbre, rhythm, pitch complexes, modes, and a typology of contour. Finally, he investigates the record industry's response, analyzing the marketing and advertising of race records. Includes numerous musical examples, figures, transcriptions, and illustrations.

B27 **van der Merwe, Peter.** *Origins of the Popular Style: The Antecedents of Twentieth-Century Popular Music.* Oxford: Oxford University Press, 1989; 352p. ISBN 019816053. ML3470.V36 1988.

An expansive project based on the premise that the principal features of popular music have been in existence long before the 20th century. van der Merwe surveys music from antiquity to 1900, finding early precedents for the numerous structural, tonal, melodic, and formal elements particular to popular music of the English-speaking world. The book is composed of four parts: a historical survey of Europe, Africa, and North America; a discussion of theoretical fundamentals; a study of the blues and its connections to African and British music, from blue notes to the 12-bar blues form; and a look at "parlour music," a term used here to refer generally to European popular music. Includes an abundance of musical examples and a glossary of terms.

B28 **Walser, Robert.** *Running with the Devil: Power, Gender, and Madness in Heavy Metal Music.* Middletown, CT: Wesleyan University Press, 2014 [1993]; 230p. ISBN 0819552526; ML3534.W29 2014. [Chapter 3 appeared previously as "Eruptions: Heavy Metal Appropriations of Classical Virtuosity." *Popular Music* 11, no. 3 (1992): 263–308.]

A study of the social practices and the processes of music making in heavy metal of the 1980s. Walser is interested in the activities that produce texts and therefore, more than other scholars of the genre, pays close attention to specific musical detail. Chapter 1 explores what defines the genre and what it means to musicians, fans, and scholars. Chapter 2 discusses heavy metal as a discourse, first by reviewing the theoretical and semiotic background, then by identifying key musical components (timbre, rhythm, melody, guitar solo), and finally by analyzing a single song (Van Halen's "Runnin' With the Devil"). Chapter 3 examines the intersection of heavy metal and classical music and studies the similarities in technique and virtuosity. Four metal guitarists and their music are specifically showcased here. Chapter 4 studies gender construction in the lyrics, music, and videos of this male-dominated genre and also considers the role of female metal musicians. Chapter 5 is concerned with violence, horror, mysticism, and the controversy and lawsuits that often surround the genre. Includes several transcriptions in Chapter 3 and some prose analysis in Chapter 2. Appendices include canonical lists and the survey referred to in Chapter 1. The 2014 edition contains a foreword by Harris Berger and a new afterword from Walser, which includes a discussion of drum fills.

B29 **Whiteley, Sheila.** *The Space Between the Notes: Rock and the Counter-Culture.* London and New York: Routledge, 1992; 139p. ISBN 0415068150; ML3534. W555 1992.

A contextual analysis of various examples of progressive rock, with a focus on the countercultural. Despite the great variety of music in the genre, different musicians and rock groups have a common code, a set of shared musical elements that carry specific meaning. This notion is borne out in the analyses of music by Cream, Jimi Hendrix, Pink Floyd, the Beatles, and the Rolling Stones, in which harmony, meter, melody, form, timbre, and style all are shown, in coordination with lyrical elements, to intersect with psychedelia, each in its own way.

B30 **Wilder, Alec.** *American Popular Song: The Great Innovators 1900–1950.* Oxford: Oxford University Press, 1990 [1972]; 536p. ISBN 9780195014457; ML3551. W54.

A survey of hundreds of songs from American songwriters of the early 20th century. Wilder studies the musical characteristics that distinguish American popular songs from their European predecessors. Using published sheet music as his primary text, he investigates the musical details of those composers he finds most innovative: Kern, Berlin, Gershwin, Rogers, Porter, Arlen, Youmans, Schwartz, Lane, Martin, and Duke. Their work originates primarily in the theater, while the pop songwriters, the "great craftsmen" such as Carmichael, Ellington, and others, receive treatment in a large additional chapter, as do various other individual songs from other writers. Throughout, Wilder does not offer analysis per se, structural or otherwise. Rather, he highlights the most distinctive features in each song, whether they are melodic devices, unusual intervals, or metric curiosities. His observations are enhanced by critical commentary based on his personal experience as a songwriter and composer. For instance, he will recollect performance practices that vary from the sheet music, or he will note how certain arrangements suit certain songs for specific reasons. Contains an introduction by the editor, James T. Maher, and the 1990 reprint edition also contains a foreword by Gene Lees. Includes numerous musical excerpts.

B31 **Williams, Justin A.** *Rhymin' and Stealin': Musical Borrowing in Hip-Hop.* Ann Arbor: University of Michigan Press, 2013; 256p. ISBN 9780472118922; ML3531.W55 2013.

A study of hip-hop concerned with its defining feature, the use of pre-existing material, which is traced back to the use of funk drum breaks (i.e., "breakbeats"). Williams presents five types of borrowing: intrageneric borrowing as authenticity (Mos Def's borrowing of "Planet Rock"); intergeneric borrowing, specifically from jazz (A Tribe Called Quest, Digable Planets); borrowing for specific places, in this case the automobile (Dr. Dre's "Jeep Beats"); post-mortal borrowing, or sampling the voice of a deceased artist (memorializing of Notorious B.I.G.); and contemporary borrowing to establish a lineage (Eminem's borrowing of 2Pac). The analyses connect text and context, featuring form, harmony, lyrics, and instrumentation. Includes numerous musical examples and transcriptions.

B32 **Zak, Albin.** *The Poetics of Rock: Cutting Tracks, Making Records.* Berkeley: University of California Press, 2001; 259p. ISBN 0520218094; ML3534.Z35 2001.

A study of the techniques and processes of "recordists," the arrangers, producers, engineers, and others who contribute artistic elements, beyond the composition itself, to the production of a rock record. Zak offers a historical overview of the recording process; distinguishes frequently conflated elements in a track (i.e., separates the song from the performance); proposes five principal categories of aural components in a record: performance, timbre, echo, ambience, and texture; investigates the aesthetic contributions of electronic equipment and physical spaces; surveys various recording strategies that recordists employ at various stages of the recording process; discusses the roles of producer and engineer; and closes with some comments on the language and rhetoric of record making. Includes a glossary, discography and a few notated musical figures.

III
Collections

C1   **Beebe, Roger, Denise Fulbrook, and Ben Saunders, eds.** *Rock Over the Edge: Transformations in Popular Music Culture.* Durham, NC: Duke University Press, 2002; 392p. ISBN 082232900; ML3534.R6336 2002.

Thirteen essays on assessing the status and definition of "rock" in contemporary culture, particularly in light of the deconstruction of the mythic opposition between authenticity and commercialism. *Contents*: Introduction/Roger Beebe, Denise Fulbrook, and Ben Saunders—*I. Discourses/Histories.* Reflections of a Disappointed Popular Music Scholar/Lawrence Grossberg—Elvis Everywhere: Musicology and Popular Music Studies at the Twilight of the Canon/Robert Fink—"Think About What You're Trying to Do to Me": Rock Historiography and the Construction of a Race-Based Dialectic/John J. Sheinbaum (**A230**)—Hijacked Hits and Antic Authenticity: Cover Songs, Race, and Postwar Marketing/Michael Coyle—*II. New Spaces / New Maps.* Why Isn't Country Music "Youth" Culture?/Trent Hill—Just a Girl? Rock Music, Feminism, and the Cultural Construction of Female Youth/Gayle Wald—Satellite Rhythms: Channel V, Asian Music Videos, and Transnational Gender/Lisa Parks—The "Feminization" of Rock/Tony Grajeda—Rock's *Reconquista*/Josh Kun—*III. Desires/Affects.* A Fan's Notes: Identification, Desire, and the Haunted Sound Barrier/R.J. Warren Zanes—Mourning Becomes . . . ? Kurt Cobain, Tupac Shakur, and the "Waning of Affect"/Roger Beebe—D.C. Punk and the Production of Authenticity/Jason Middleton—Queen Theory: Notes on the Pet Shop Boys/Ian Balfour.

C2   **Biamonte, Nicole, ed.** *Pop-Culture Pedagogy in the Music Classroom: Teaching Tools from American Idol to YouTube.* Lanham, MD: Scarecrow Press, 2011; 344p. ISBN 9780810877368; MT1.P638 2011.

Fifteen essays on the use of aspects of popular culture in the college and secondary-school music classroom. *Contents*: Introduction/Nicole Biamonte—*I. General Tools*. Appreciating the Mix: Teaching Music Listening Skills through Sound-Mixing Techniques/Benjamin Biermann—Pod-Logic: A Guide to Getting the Most out of Your iPod in the Music Classroom/Kathleen Kerstetter—Global Connections via YouTube: Internet Video as a Teaching and Learning Tool/Hope Munro Smith—*II. Teaching Musicianship and Music Theory*. Popular Music in the College Music Theory Class: Rhythm and Meter/Nancy Rosenberg (**A221**)—Teaching Traditional Music Theory with Popular Songs: Pitch Structures/Heather MacLachlan (**A167**)—Using Pop-Culture Tools to Reinforce Learning of Basic Music Theory as Transformations/James R. Hughes—On the Integration of Aural Skills and Formal Analysis through Popular Music/Keith Salley (**A224**)—Musical Representation in the Video Games Guitar Hero and Rock Band/Nicole Biamonte—DDR at the Crossroads: A Report on a Pilot Study to Integrate Music Video-Game Technology into the Aural-Skills Classroom/Brent Auerbach, Bret Aarden, and Mathonwy Bostock—Turntablism: A Vehicle for Connecting Community and School Music Making and Learning/Karen Snell—*III. Teaching Music Analysis and Criticism*. Using *American Idol* to Introduce Music Criticism/James A. Grymes—An Analytical Model for Examining Cover Songs and Their Sources/Victoria Malawey—Contextuality in Music Video: Covering and Sampling in the *Cover Art* Video of "Umbrella"/Lori Burns, Tamar Dubuc, and Marc Lafrance—Vocal Practices and Constructions of Identity in Rap: A Case Study of Young Jeezy's "Soul Survivor"/Alyssa Woods—Crunkology: Teaching the Southern Hip-Hop Aesthetic/Ali Colleen Neff—Mashup Poetics as Pedagogical Practice/Wayne Marshall.

C3 **Butler, Mark J., ed.** *Electronica, Dance, and Club Music*. Burlington, VT: Ashgate Publishing, 2011; 536p. ISBN 9780754629658; ML3540.5.E44 2011.

A volume in The Library of Essays on Popular Music (Allan Moore, series editor) containing 28 previously published essays. *Contents*: Introduction/Mark Butler—*I. Production, Performance, and Aesthetics*. When Sound Meets Movement: Performance in Electronic Dance Music/Pedro Peixoto Ferreira—From Refrain to Rave: The Decline of Figure and the Rise of Ground/Philip Tagg—Conceptualizing Rhythm and Meter in Electronic Dance Music/Mark Butler (from **B5**)—Producing Kwaito: *Nkosi Sikelel' iAfrika* after Apartheid/Gavin Steingo—The Disc Jockey as Composer, or How I Became a Composing DJ/Kai Fikentscher—On the Process and Aesthetics of Sampling in Electronic Music Production/Tara Rodgers—The Aesthetics of Failure: "Post-Digital" Tendencies in Contemporary Computer Music/Kim Cascone—"A Pixel is a Pixel. A Club is a Club": Toward a Hermeneutics of Berlin Style DJ & VJ Culture/Sebastian Klotz—*II. The Body, the Spirit, and (the Regulation of) Pleasure*. In Defence of Disco/Richard Dyer—In the Empire of the Beat: Discipline and Disco/Walter Hughes—"I Want to See All My Friends at Once": Arthur Russell and the Queering of Gay Disco/Tim Lawrence—I Feel Love: Disco and Its Discontents/Tavia Nyong'o—Sampling Sexuality: Gender, Technology, and the Body in Dance

Music/Barbara Bradby—Sampling (Hetero)sexuality: Diva-ness and Discipline in Electronic Dance Music/Susana Loza—Dancing With Desire: Cultural Embodiment in Tijuana's Nor-tec Music and Dance/Alejandro L. Madrid—The Spiritual Economy of Nightclubs and Raves: Osho Sannyasins as Party Promoters in Ibiza and Pune/Goa/Anthony D'Andrea—Electronic Dance Music Culture and Religion: An Overview/Graham St. John—Soundtrack to an Uncivil Society: Rave Culture, the Criminal Justice Act and the Politics of Modernity/Jeremy Gilbert—*III. Identities, Belongings, and Distinctions.* Genres, Subgenres, Sub-Subgenres and More: Musical and Social Differentiation Within Electronic/Dance Music Communities/Kembrew McLeod—Exploring the Meaning of the Mainstream (or Why Sharon and Tracy Dance around Their Handbags)/Sarah Thornton—Women and the Early British Rave Scene/Maria Pini—Roomful of Asha: Gendered Productions of Ethnicity in Britain's "Asian Underground"/Falu Bakrania—"I Want Muscles": House Music, Homosexuality, and Masculine Signification/Stephen Amico—Mr. Mesa's Ticket: Memory and Dance at the Body-Positive T-Dance/Fiona Buckland—The Death of the Dance Party/Kane Race—Post-Soul Futurama: African American Cultural Politics and Early Detroit Techno/Sean Albiez—Music Tourism and Factions of Bodies in Goa/Arun Saldanha—The Dancer from the Dance: The Musical and Dancing Crowds of Clubbing/Ben Malbon.

C4 **Covach, John and Graeme M. Boone, eds.** *Understanding Rock: Essays in Musical Analysis.* Oxford: Oxford University Press, 1997; 219p. ISBN 01951000042; ML3534.U53 1997.

Seven essays featuring close musical analysis of rock music. *Contents*: Preface/Graeme Boone and John Covach—Progressive Rock, "Close to the Edge," and the Boundaries of Style/John Covach (**A71**)—After Sundown: The Beach Boys' Experimental Music/Daniel Harrison (**A125**)—Blues Transformations in the Music of Cream/Dave Headlam (**A132**)—"Joanie" Get Angry: k.d. lang's Feminist Revision/Lori Burns (**A45**)—Swallowed by a Song: Paul Simon's Crisis of Chromaticism/Walter Everett (**A93**)—"Little Wing": A Study in Musical Cognition/Matthew Brown (**A40**)—Tonal and Expressive Ambiguity in Dark Star/Graeme Boone (**A25**).

C5 **DeWitt, Mark F., ed.** *Roots Music.* Burlington, VT: Ashgate Publishing, 2011; 502p. ISBN 9780754629627; ML3545.R66 2011.

A volume in The Library of Essays on Popular Music (Allan Moore, series editor) containing 21 previously published essays. *Contents*: Introduction/Mark DeWitt—*I. Roots, Deconstructed.* The Popular Marketing of "Old Ballads": The Ballad Revival and Eighteenth-Century Antiquarianism Reconsidered/Dianne Dugaw—Another History of Bluegrass: The Segregation of Popular Music in the United States, 1820–1900/Allen Farmelo—Analogies and Differences in African-American Musical Cultures across the Hemisphere: Interpretive Models and Research Strategies/Gerhard Kubik—Love and Theft: The Racial Unconscious of Blackface Minstrelsy/Eric Lott—"That Wild Mercury Sound": Bob Dylan and the Illusion of American Culture/Barry Shank—*II. Roots, Experienced.* Zydeco/Zarico: Beans, Blues, and Beyond/Barry Jean Ancelet—Sounding out the City: Music and the Sensuous Production of Place/Sara Cohen—Techniques of Blues Composition among Black Folksingers/David Evans—Changing Contexts for Traditional Dance Music in Ireland: The Rise of Group Performance Practice/Hazel Fairbairn—"A Special Kind of Courtesy": Action at a Bluegrass Festival Jam Session/Michelle Kisliuk—Composition, Authorship, and Ownership in Flamenco, Past and Present/Peter Manuel—"Funky Drummer": New Orleans, James Brown, and the Rhythmic Transformation of American Popular Music/Alex Stewart (**A238**)—Afro-American Gospel Music: A Crystallization of the Black Aesthetic/Pearl Williams-Jones—The Significance of the Relationship between Afro-American Music and West African Music/Olly Wilson (**A262**)—*III. Offshoots.* Metaphors of Power, Metaphors of Truth: The Politics of Music Professionalism in Bulgarian Folk Orchestras/Donna A. Buchanan—Native American Contemporary Music: The Women/Beverley Diamond—The Jukebox of History: Narratives of Loss and Desire in the Discourse of Country Music/Aaron A. Fox—Searching for Rockordion: The Changing Image of the Accordion in America/Marion S. Jacobson—From *Ranchero* to *Jaitōn*: Ethnicity and Class in Texas-Mexican Music (Two Styles in the Form of a Pair)/Manuel Peña—Encounter with "The Others from Within": The Case of Gypsy Musicians in Former Yugoslavia/Svanibor Pettan—The Whole and the Sum of the Parts, or, How Cookie and the Cupcakes Told the Story of Apache history in San Carlos/David Samuels.

C6   **Everett, Walter, ed.** *Expression in Pop-Rock Music: Critical and Analytical Essays*, 2nd ed. New York: Routledge, 2008 [2000]; 392p. ISBN 0415979580; ML3534. E985 2008.

Thirteen essays drawing from various theoretical and analytical methodologies, most focusing more on the musical material and less on its sociological or historical contexts. *Contents*: Preface/Walter Everett—The Musical World(s?) of Frank Zappa: Some Observations of His "Crossover" Pieces/Jonathan W. Bernard (**A12**)—Frank Zappa's "The Black Page": A Case of Musical "Conceptual Continuity"/James Borders (**A27**)—Analytic Methodologies for Rock Music: Harmonic and Voice-Leading Strategies in Tori Amos's "Crucify"/Lori Burns (**A46**)—Jazz-Rock? Rock-Jazz? Stylistic Crossover in Late-1970s American Progressive Rock/John Covach (**A73**)—Pitch Down the Middle/Walter Everett (**A99**)—Music, Contexts, and Meaning in U2/Susan Fast (**A103**)—From *L'Étranger* to "Killing an Arab": Representing the Other in a Cure Song/Ellie M. Hisama (**A137**)—The Imagination of Pop-Rock Criticism/Nadine Hubbs (**A143**)—Trapped Within the Wheels: Flow and Repetition, Modernism and Tradition in Stevie Wonder's "Living for the City"/Tim Hughes (**A144**)—Fumbling Towards Ecstasy: Voice Leading, Tonal Structure, and the Theme of Self-Realization in the Music of Sarah McLachlan/Timothy Koozin (**A154**)—Country-Pop Formulae and Craft : Shania Twain's Crossover Appeal/Jocelyn R. Neal (**A193**)—Large-Scale Strategy and Compositional Design in the Early Music of Genesis/Mark Spicer (**A232**)—Rock and Roll Rhapsody: Pop Epics of the 1970s/Albin Zak (**A269**).

Collections

C7 **Hamm, Charles, Bruno Nettl, and Ronald Byrnside, eds.** *Contemporary Music and Music Cultures.* Englewood Cliffs, NJ: Prentice-Hall, Inc., 1975; 270p. ISBN 0131701754; ML197.H245C6 1975.

Nine essays (three from each contributor) assembled as an introduction to music that considers the breadth of contemporary music and world cultures. *Contents*: Preface/Ronald Byrnside, Charles Hamm, and Bruno Nettl—Introduction: Concepts and Terminology/Ronald Byrnside—Changing Patterns in Society and Music: The U.S. Since World War II/Charles Hamm—The Role of Music in Culture: Iran, a Recently Developed Nation/Bruno Nettl—The Western Impact on World Music: Africa and the American Indians/Bruno Nettl—The Acculturation of Musical Styles: Popular Music, U.S.A./Charles Hamm—The Formation of a Musical Style: Early Rock/Ronald Byrnside (**A53**)—Words and Music: English Folksong in the United States/Bruno Nettl—The Performer as Creator: Jazz Improvisation/Ronald Byrnside—Technology and Music: The Effect of the Phonograph/Charles Hamm.

C8 **Hautamäki, Tarja and Tarja Rautiainen, eds.** *Popular Music Studies in Seven Acts: Conference Proceedings of the Fourth Annual Conference of the Finnish Society for Ethnomusicology.* Tampere, Finland: Tampere University, 1995; 118p. ISBN 9529719043; ML3470.S85 1995.

Seven papers on the conference theme: the study of the history of popular music. *Contents*: Prologue/Tarja Hautamäki and Tarja Rautiainen—Who May Speak? From a Politics of Popular Music to a Popular Politics of Music/Richard Middleton—The Sounds of Swedish Rock/Lars Lilliestam—The Italian Blue Third/Peter van der Merwe (**A251**)—Popular Musical Theatre as Auditory Mirror: Reflection of Time and Culture/Michael Eigtved—Defining Minority Identity in Music: A Study of Swedish-Finnish Popular Music in the Dancehalls of Gothenburg/Pekka Suutari—Some Aspects of Brigitte Bardot: A Comparative View/Vesa Kurkela and Risto Pekka Pennanen—Culture, Society, Tradition, and Identity: A System-Based View on the Concepts/Timo Leisiö.

C9 **Hawkins, Stan, ed.** *Pop Music and Easy Listening.* Burlington, VT: Ashgate Publishing, 2011; 523p. ISBN 9780754629528; ML3470.P6583 2011.

A volume in The Library of Essays on Popular Music (Allan Moore, series editor) containing 24 previously published essays. *Contents*: Introduction/Stan Hawkins—*I. Aesthetics and Authenticity.* "Sing it for Me": Posthuman Ventriloquism in Recent Popular Music/Joseph Auner—Art Versus Technology: The Strange Case of Popular Music/Simon Frith—Pearls and Swine: The Intellectuals and the Mass Media/Simon Frith and Jon Savage—Remodeling Britney Spears: Matters of Intoxication and Mediation/Stan Hawkins and John Richardson—The Production of Success: An Anti-Musicology of the Pop Song/Antoine Hennion—In Excess? Body Genres, "Bad" Music, and the Judgement of Audiences/Leslie M. Meier—Hits and Misses: Crafting a Pop Single for the Top-40 Market in the 1960s/Robert Toft (**A249**)—*II. Groove, Sampling and Production.* Frank Sinatra:

The Television Years: 1950–1960/Albert Auster—Mediating Music: Materiality and Silence in Madonna's "Don't Tell Me"/Anne Danielsen and Arnt Maasø—Sample and Hold: Pop Music in the Digital Age of Reproduction/Andrew Goodwin—"Caught in a Whirlpool of Aching Sound": The Production of Dance Music in Britain in the 1920s/Mark Hustwitt—Spice World: Constructing Femininity the Popular Way/Dafna Lemish—Modelling the Groove: Conceptual Structure and Popular Music/Lawrence M. Zbikowski (**A271**)—*III. Subjectivity, Ethnicity and Politics.* Like a Virgin-Mother? Materialism and Maternalism in the Songs of Madonna/Barbara Bradby—"That Ill, Tight Sound": Telepresence and Biopolitics in Post-Timbaland Rap Production/Dale Chapman—Sex, Pulp, and Critique/Eric F. Clarke and Nicola Dibben—Pop and the Nation-State: Towards a Theorisation/Martin Cloonan—"Believe"? Vocoders, Digitalised Female Identity and Camp/Kay Dickinson—Music and Canadian Nationhood Post 9/11: An Analysis of *Music Without Borders: Live*/Susan Fast and Karen Pegley—Black Pop Songwriting 1963–1966: An Analysis of U.S. Top Forty Hits by Cooke, Mayfield, Stevenson, Robinson, and Holland-Dozier-Holland/John Fitzgerald (**A108**)—"A Fifth of Beethoven": Disco, Classical Music, and the Politics of Inclusion/Ken McLeod (**A179**)—"The Digital Won't Let Me Go": Construction of the Virtual and the Real in Gorillaz' "Clint Eastwood"/John Richardson—Navigating the "Channel": Recent Scholarship on African-American Popular Music/David Sanjek—Prince as Queer Poststructuralist/Robert Walser.

C10 **Heinonen, Yrjö, Tuomas Eerola, Jouni Koskimäki, Terhi Nurmesjärvi, and John Richardson, eds.** *Beatlestudies 1: Songwriting, Recording, and Style Change.* Jyväskylä, Finland: University of Jyväskylä, Research Reports 19, 1998; 182p. ISBN 9513903761; ML421.B4B48v1.

Seven essays on the Beatles, dealing with issues of psychology, historiography, and music analysis. The second publication of the BEATLES 2000 project. *Contents*: Introduction: (Being a Short Diversion to) Current Perspectives in Beatles Research/Yrjö Heinonen, Tuomas Eerola, Jouni Koskimäki, and Terhi Nurmesjärvi—*I. Quantitative Style Analysis.* Songwriting, Recording, and Style Change: Problems in the Chronology and Periodization of the Musical Style of the Beatles/Yrjö Heinonen and Tuomas Eerola—The Rise and Fall of the Experimental Style of the Beatles/Tuomas Eerola—The Concept of Form and Its Change in the Singles of the Beatles/Terhi Nurmesjärvi (**A195**)—The Beatles as a Small Group: The Effect of Group Development on Group Performance/Yrjö Heinonen—*II. Qualitative Case Studies.* Variation as the Key Principle of Arrangement in "Cry Baby Cry"/Jouni Koskimäki and Yrjö Heinonen (**A156**)—Michelle, ma belle: Songwriting as Coping with Inner Conflicts/Yrjö Heinonen (**A133**)—"Black and White" Music: Dialog, Dysphoric Coding and Death Drive in the Music of Bernard Herrmann, the Beatles, Stevie Wonder, and Coolio/John Richardson.

C11 **Heinonen, Yrjö, Jouni Koskimäki, Seppo Niemi, and Terhi Nurmesjärvi, eds.** *Beatlestudies 2: History, Identity, Authenticity.* Jyväskylä, Finland: University of Jyväskylä, Research Reports 23, 2000; 255p. ISBN 9513907333; ML421.B4B48v2.

Seven essays on the Beatles, dealing "with questions of history, identity, or authenticity." The second publication of the BEATLES 2000 project. *Contents*: Preface/ Yrjö Heinonen, Jouni Koskimäki, Seppo Niemi, and Terhi Nurmesjärvi—The Beatles and Their Times: Thoughts on the "Relative Autonomy" of Style Change/ Yrjö Heinonen and Tuomas Eerola—Band on the Record: The Beatles' Recordings from the Historical and Technological Points of View/Seppo Niemi— Liverpudlian Identity of the Early Beatles (1957–62)/Terhi Nurmesjärvi—A Man on a Flaming Pie: The Dubious Origin of the Beatles Revisited/Yrjö Heinonen— You Need Another Chorus: Problems with Formal Concepts in Popular Music/ Terhi Nurmesjärvi (**A196**)—Happiness is . . . A Good Transcription: Shortcomings in the Sheet Music Publications of "Happiness is a Warm Gun"/Jouni Koskimäki (**A157**)—In Search of Lost Order: Archetypal Meanings in "Lucy in the Sky with Diamonds"/Yrjö Heinonen (**A134**).

C12 **Heinonen, Yrjö, Markus Heuger, Sheila Whiteley, Terhi Nurmesjärvi, and Jouni Koskimäki, eds.** *Beatlestudies 3: Proceedings of the Beatles 2000 Conference.* Jyväskylä, Finland: University of Jyväskylä, 2001; 312p. ISBN 9789513908096; ML421.B4B5 1998.

Twenty-five papers on the Beatles, delivered at the BEATLES 2000 conference. The third publication of the BEATLES 2000 project. *Contents*: Preface/ Yrjö Heinonen, Markus Heuger, Sheila Whiteley, Terhi Nurmesjärvi, and Jouni Koskimäki—*I. Keynote Addresses*. No Fixed Agenda: The Position of the Beatles Within Popular/Rock Music/Sheila Whiteley—Drive My Car: 60s Soulsters Embrace Lennon-McCartney/Tim Riley—The Future of Beatles Research/ Walter Everett—*II. Culture, History, Cultural History*. The Greatest Story of Pop Music? Challenges of Writing the Beatles History/Janne Mäkelä—The Beatles in the Internet: An Analysis of the Presentation of the Beatles in the World Wide Web/Einbrodt, Ulrich D.—The Beatles in Australia/Bruce Johnson—The Beatles: High Modernism and/or Postmodernism?/Kenneth Gloag—*III. Music Theory, Psychology, Education*. Tonal Oscillation in the Beatles' Songs/Naphtali Wagner (**A253**)—Words and Chords: The Semantic Shifts of the Beatles' Chords/ Ger Tillikens—Semantic Shifts in Beatles' Chord Progressions: On the Perception of Shifts in Song Contexts Induced by Chords/Juul Mulder—Dynamics of Polylinearity in Popular Music: Perception and Apperception of 64 Seconds of "Please Please Me"/Tomi Mäkelä—The Music of the Beatles in Undergraduate Music Theory Instruction/Pandel Collaros (**A63**)—*IV. Roots and Heritage*. You're Going to Lose That Girl: The Beatles and the Girl Groups/Jacqueline Warwick— Ladies and Gentlemen, The Beatelles! The Influence of Sixties Girl Groups on the Beatles/Matthew Bannister—American with Liverpudlian Accent: The First Two Beatles' EMI Singles/Charles Gower Price—"Do You Want to Know a Secret": The Music of the Beatles and the Finnish Cover Versions in the 1960s/Hannu Tolvanen—(What's the Copy?) The Beatles and Oasis/Derek Scott—*V. Musical Style and Its Change*. Slow Down! How the Beatles Changed the Rhythmic Paradigm of Pop & Rock/Len McCarthy—Melodicism in Paul McCartney's Bass Playing/Michael Hannan—Vocal Harmony as a Structural Device in the

Commerical Recordings of the Beatles 1962–70/Stephen Valdez—Variation as the Key Principle in the Vocal Parts of "Cry Cry Cry"/Jouni Koskimäki—*VI. Making Music.* Everything I Need to Know About Music I Learned from the Fifth Beatle: An Introspection into George Martin's Influence on the Beatles/Kari McDonald and Sarah Hudson-Kaufman—Let Me Take You Down—To the Subdominant: Tools of Establishment and Revealing the Establishment/Gordon Thompson—John Lennon's and Paul McCartney's Different Ways of Recording a Song in the Studio (exemplified by "Strawberry Fields Forever" and "Penny Lane")/Rolf Berger—The Mystery of Eleanor Rigby: Meditations on a Gravestone/Yrjö Heinonen.

C13 **Hesmondhalgh, David and Keith Negus, eds.** *Popular Music Studies.* London: Arnold, 2002; 272p. ISBN 0340762470; ML3470.P69 2002.

Sixteen interdisciplinary essays surveying popular music studies and examining developments post-1990. *Contents*: Introduction: Popular Music Studies: Meaning, Power and Value/David Hesmondhalgh and Keith Negus—*I. Musical Meaning and History.* Music, Masculinity, and Migrancy Under Early Apartheid: Gender and Popular Song in South Africa, c. 1948–1960/Christopher Ballantine—Analysing Popular Songs/Luiz Tatit (translated by Lorraine Leu)—Cover Versions and the Sound of Identity in Motion/Dai Griffiths (**A123**)—(In Search of) Musical Meaning: Genres, Categories, and Crossover/David Brackett—*II. Audiences, Consumption, and Everyday Life.* Raving, Not Drowning: Authenticity, Pleasure and Politics in the Electronic Dance Music Scene/Rupa Huq—The Curse of Fandom: Insiders, Outsiders and Ethnography/Ian Maxwell—Popular Music Audiences and Everyday Life/David Hesmondhalgh—Ubiquitous Listening/Anahid Kassabian—*III. Productions, Institutions, and Creativity.* Mainstreaming, from Hegemonic Centre to Global Networks/Jason Toynbee—Value and Velocity: The 12-Inch Single as Medium and Artifact/Will Straw—Creativity and Musical Experience/Keith Negus and Michael Pickering—The Politics of Calypso in a World of Music Industries/Jocelyne Guilbault—*IV. Place, Space, and Power.* Locating Salsa/Patria Román-Velázquez—Blacking Japanese: Experiencing Otherness from Afar/Shuhei Hosokawa—India Song: Popular Music Genres since Economic Liberalization/Nabeel Zuberi—The "Pop-Rockization" of Popular Music/Motti Regev.

C14 **Hisama, Ellie and Evan Rapport, eds.** *Critical Minded: New Approaches to Hip Hop Studies.* Brooklyn, NY: Institute for Studies in American Music, 2005; 144p. ISBN 9780914678373; ML3531.C75 2005.

Eight essays, written from a variety of disciplinary perspectives, whose origins lie in a 2004 doctoral seminar on hip-hop. *Contents*: Preface/Ellie Hisama—"We're All Asian Really": Hip Hop's Afro-Asian Crossings/Ellie Hisama—"You Ain't Heard Us 'Til You Seen Us Live": The Alter Egos' Live Alternative to Mass Market Hip Hop/David G. Pier—Uptown-Downtown: Hip Hop Music in Downtown Manhattan in the Early 1980s/Jonathan Toubin—Gender Dynamics in the Film *Anne B. Real*/Stephanie Jensen-Moulton—Listening to the Music of the Brooklyn-Based Rapper Sensational/Evan Rapport—Wallowing in Rupture: Cultural Hybridity, Alienation, and Andre Benjamin's "A Life in the Day of Benjamin André (Incomplete)"/Robert Wood—A Preliminary Step in Exploring *Reggaetón*/Ejima Baker—Musical Interchange between Indian Music and Hip Hop/Carl Clements (**A61**).

C15 **Holm-Hudson, Kevin, ed.** *Progressive Rock Reconsidered.* New York and London: Routledge, 2002; 280p. ISBN0815337140; ML3534.P76 2002.

Eleven essays on the music of Pink Floyd, King Crimson, Yes, and others, bringing a variety of disciplines to bear on musical analysis. *Contents*: Introduction/Kevin Holm-Hudson—*I. History and Context*. Progressive Rock and the Inversion of Musical Values/John J. Sheinbaum (**A229**)—The "American Metaphysical Circus" of Joseph Byrd's United States of America/Kevin Holm-Hudson (**A138**)—*II. Analytical Perspectives*. Pink Floyd's "Careful with that Axe, Eugene": Toward a Theory of Textural Rhythm in Early Progressive Rock/John S. Cotner (**A68**)—Progressive Rock as Text: The Lyrics of Roger Waters/Deena Weinstein—A Promise Deferred: Multiply Directed Time and Thematic Transformation in Emerson, Lake, and Palmer's "Trilogy"/Kevin Holm-Hudson (**A139**)—King Crimson's *Larks' Tongues in Aspic*: A Case of Convergent Evolution/Gregory Karl (**A152**)—Tales of Change Within the Sound: Form, Lyrics, and Philosophy in the Music of Yes/Jennifer Rycenga—Precarious Pleasures: Situating "Close to the Edge" in Conflicting Male Desires/Dirk von der Horst—"Let Them All Make Their Own Music": Individualism, Rush, and the Progressive/Hard Rock Alloy, 1976–77/Durrell S. Bowman (**A28**)—*III. "Don't Dare Call us 'Progressive'": "Post-Prog" and Other Legacies*. Somebody is Digging My Bones: King Crimson's "Dinosaur" as (Post)Progressive Historiography/Brian Robison (**A218**)—How Alternative Turned Progressive: The Strange Case of Math Rock/Theo Cateforis (**A57**).

C16 **Horn, David and Philip Tagg, ed.** *Popular Music Perspectives: Papers from the First International Conference on Popular Music Research, Amsterdam, June 1981.* Gothenburg and Exeter: International Association for the Study of Popular Music, 1982; 250p. ISBN917260610; ML36.I625 1982.

Thirteen conference papers comprising the first major publication of the International Association for the Study of Popular Music, intended to bring "coordination and cooperation" among the varied international and interdisciplinary approaches. *Contents*: Preface/Philip Tagg and David Horn—Speech of Welcome/Simon Vinkenoog—Some Thoughts on the Measurement of Popularity in Music/Charles Hamm—Problems of Method in the Historical Study of Popular Music/Vic Gammon—Popular Music as Social Production/Antoine Hennion—Music in Advertising/Helmut Rosing—A Theory of Musical Genres: Two Applications/Franco Fabbri—Et Si L'On Reparlait d'Adorno/Paul Beaud—The Interdependency of Broadcasting and the Phonogram Industry: A Case Study Covering Events in Kenya in March 1980/Roger Wallis and Krister Malm—Popular Music in West Africa: Suggestions for an Interpretive Framework/John

Collins and Paul Richards—The Sociology of Rock: Notes from Britain/Simon Frith—Popular Music in the USSR: Problems and Opinions/Israel Nestiev—Blues and the Binary Principle/Paul Oliver (**A201**)—Tradition and Acculturation as Polarities of Slovenian Popular Music/Alenka Barber-Kersovan—Salvaging a Treasure: Pop Songs in the New York Public Library/Richard Jackson.

C17 **Horner, Bruce and Thomas Swiss, eds.** *Key Terms in Popular Music and Culture.* Malden, MA: Blackwell, 1999; 260p. ISBN 0631212639; ML3470.K49 1999.

Eighteen essays exploring the relationships between popular music and the words that define, describe, and explain it. *Contents*: Putting It into Words: Key Terms for Studying Popular Music/Bruce Horner and Thomas Swiss—*I. Locating Popular Music Culture.* Ideology/Lucy Green—Discourse/Bruce Horner—Histories/Gilbert B. Rodman—Institutions/David Sanjek—Politics/Robin Balliger—Race/Russell A. Potter—Gender/Holly Kruse—Youth/Deena Weinstein—*II. Locating Culture in Popular Music.* Popular/Anahid Kassabian—Music/David Brackett—Form/Richard Middleton (**A184**)—Text/John Shepherd—Images/Cynthia Fuchs—Performance/David Shumway—Authorship/Will Straw—Technology/Paul Théberge—Business/Mark Fenster and Thomas Swiss—Scenes/Sara Cohen.

C18 **Inglis, Ian, ed.** *The Beatles, Popular Music and Society.* New York: St. Martin's Press, 2000; 211p. ISBN 0312222351; ML421.B4B436 2000.

Eleven essays on the Beatles and their music, primarily from culture-theoretical and sociological perspectives. *Contents*: Introduction: A Thousand Voices/Ian Inglis—Men of ideas? Popular Music, Anti-Intellectualism, and the Beatles/Ian Inglis—Coming Out of the Rhetoric of "Merseybeat": Conversations with Joe Flannery/Mike Brocken—The Beatles and the Spectacle of Youth/John Muncie—Lennon-McCartney and the Early British Invasion, 1964–66/Jon Fitzgerald (**A107**)—From Me to You: Austerity to Profligacy in the Language of the Beatles/Guy Cook and Neil Mercer—The Postmodern White Album/Ed Whitley—You Can't Do That: The Beatles, Artistic Freedom, and Censorship/Martin Cloonan—Tell Me What You See: The Influence and Impact of the Beatles' Movies/Bob Neaverson—The Celebrity Legacy of the Beatles/P. David Marshall—Refab Four: Beatles for Sale in the Age of Music Video/Gary Burns—"Sitting in an English Garden": Comparing Representations of Britishness in the Songs of the Beatles and 1990s Britpop Groups/Andy Bennett.

C19 **Langlois, Tony, ed.** *Non-Western Popular Music.* Burlington, VT: Ashgate Publishing, 2011; 600p. ISBN 97880754629849; ML3470.N66 2011.

A volume in The Library of Essays on Popular Music (Allan Moore, series editor) containing 25 previously published essays. *Contents*: Introduction/Tony Langlois—*I. Power, Pop, and Identity.* Islam, the Turkish State and Arabesk/Martin Stokes—Starting from Nowhere? Popular Music in Cambodia after the Khmer Rouge/Stephen Mamula—Soccer, Popular Music and National Consciousness in Post-State-Socialist Bulgaria, 1994–96/Donna A.

Buchanan—Music and Cultural Politics: Ideology and Resistance in Singapore/Lily Kong—"The Morning Freedom Rose Up": Kurdish Popular Song and the Exigencies of Cultural Survival/Stephen Blum and Amir Hassanpour—Saida Sultan/Danna International: Transgender Pop and the Polysemiotics of Sex, Nation and Ethnicity on the Israeli-Egyptian Border/Ted Swedenburg—Re-thinking "Whiteness"? Identity, Change and "White" Popular Music in Post-Apartheid South Africa/Christopher Ballantine—Borderland Pop: Arab Jewish Musicians and the Politics of Performance/Galit Saada-Orphir—*II. Global Perspectives*. Are We Global Yet? Globalist Discourse, Cultural Formations and the Study of Zimbabwean Popular Music/Thomas Turino—Interpreting World Music: A Challenge in Theory and Practice/Jocelyne Guilbault—Between Globalisation and Localisation: A Study of Hong Kong Popular Music/Wai-Chung Ho—Hip Hop Revolución! Nationalizing Rap in Cuba/Geoffrey Baker—Bandiri Music, Globalization, and Urban Experience in Nigeria/Brian Larkin—*III. Music Industries*. The Cassette Industry and Popular Music in North India/Peter Manuel—Recycling Indian Film-Songs: Popular Music as a Source of Melodies for North Indian Folk Musicians/Scott Marcus—Charisma's Realm: Fandom in Japan/Christine Yano—Cross-Cultural Perspectives in Popular Music: The Case of Afghanistan/John Baily—Trends and Taste in Japanese Popular Music: A Case Study of the 1982 Yamaha World Popular Music Festival/Judith Ann Herd—Popular Music in Indonesia Since 1998, in Particular, Fusion, Indie and Islamic Music on Video Compact Discs and the Internet/Bart Barendregt and Wim van Zantem—"The World is Made by Talk": Female Fans, Popular Music, and New Forms of Public Sociality in Urban Mali/Dorothea E. Schulz—*IV. Historical Approaches*. Tom Jobim and the Bossa Nova Era/Suzel Ana Reily (**A211**)—Haitian Dance Bands, 1915–1970: Class, Race, and Authenticity/Gage Averill—You Can't Rid a Song of its Words: Notes on the Hegemony of Lyrics in Russian Rock Songs/Yngvar B. Steinholt—The Rise and Generic Features of Shanghai Popular Songs in the 1930s and 1940s/Szu-Wei Chen—Commerce, Politics, and Musical Hybridity: Vocalizing Urban Black South African Identity during the 1950s/Lara Allen.

C20 **Marvin, Elizabeth West and Richard Hermann, eds.** *Concert Music, Rock, and Jazz Since 1945: Essays and Analytical Studies*. Rochester, NY: University of Rochester Press, 1995; 449p. ISBN 1580460968; ML160,C737 1995.

Fourteen essays reflecting the diverse repertoire of studied and varied methodologies in use in late 20th-century scholarship. Popular music is placed on equal footing with jazz and art music. *Contents*: Introduction/Elizabeth West Marvin and Richard Hermann—*I. Compositional Poietics*. Beyond Unity: Toward an Understanding of Musical Postmodernism/Jonathan D. Kramer—The Art-Science of Music after Two Millennia/Robert Cogan—Aspects of Confluence between Western Art Music and Ethnomusicology/Robert D. Morris—*II. Some Structuralist Approaches*. Twelve-Tone Composition and the Music of Elliott Carter/Andrew Mead—An Analysis of Polyrhythm in Selected Improvised Jazz Solos/Cynthia Folio—A Generalization of Contour Theory to Diverse Musical

Spaces: Analytical Applications to the Music of Dallapiccola and Stockhausen/ Elizabeth West Marvin—The Beatles as Composers: The Genesis of Abbey Road, Side Two/Walter Everett (**A92**)—Structural Factors in the Microcanonic Compositions of György Ligeti/Jane Piper Clendinning—*III. Insights from Other Disciplines.* Theory, Analysis, and the "Problem" of Minimal Music/Jonathan W. Bernard—The Question of Climax in Ruth Crawford's String Quartet, Mvt. 3/ Ellie M. Hisama—Does the Song Remain the Same? Questions of Authorship and Identification in the Music of Led Zeppelin/Dave Headlam (**A131**)—Theories of Chordal Shape, Aspects of Linguistics, and Their Roles in Structuring Berio's Sequenza IV for Piano/Richard Hermann—Stylistic Competencies, Musical Satire, and "This is Spinal Tap"/John Covach (**A70**)—Music Theory and the Postmodern Muse: An Afterword/Nicholas Cook.

C21 **McQuinn, Julie, ed.** *Popular Music and Multimedia.* Burlington, VT: Ashgate Publishing, 2011; 506p. ISBN 9780754629610; ML3470.P673 2011.

A volume in The Library of Essays on Popular Music (Allan Moore, series editor) containing 22 previously published essays. *Contents*: Introduction/Julie McQuinn—*I. Cross-Genre Analysis.* In the Air Tonight: Text, Intertextuality, and the Construction of Meaning/Robynn J. Stilwell—*II. Film.* Pop, Speed, and the "MTV Aesthetic"/Kay Dickinson—Torture Tunes: Tarantino, Popular Music and New Hollywood Ultraviolence/Lisa Coulthard—Remembering Pop: David Lynch and the Sound of the '60's/Mark Mazullo—Polyphony and Cultural Expression: Interpreting Musical Traditions in *Do the Right Thing*/ Victoria E. Johnson—From the Warehouse to the Multiplex: Techno and Rave Culture's Reconfiguration of Late 1990s Sci-Fi Spectacle as Musical Performance/Diana Sandars—The Music that Lola Ran To/Caryl Flinn— Celluloid Love Songs: Musical *modus operandi* and the Dramatic Aesthetics of Romantic Hindi Film/Natalie Sarrazin—The Edge of Seventeen: Class, Age and Popular Music in Richard Linklater's *School of Rock*/Jeff Smith—*III. Television.* "Reality goes pop!" Reality TV, Popular Music and Narratives of Stardom in *Pop Idol*/Su Holmes—Chewing Gum for the Ears: Children's Television and Popular Music/Karen Lury—In Perfect Harmony: Popular Music and Cola Advertising/Bethany Klein—It May Look Like a Living Room . . . : The Musical Number and the Sitcom/Robynn J. Stilwell—*Ally McBeal*'s Postmodern Soundtrack/Julie Brown—Nostalgia, Music and the Television Past Revisited in *American Dreams*/Faye Woods—*IV. Music Video.* Subjective Perspectives through Word, Image and Sound: Temporality, Narrative Agency and Embodiment in the Dixie Chicks' Video "Top of the World"/Lori Burns and Jada Watson—The Kindest Cut: Functions and Meanings of Music Video Editing/ Carol Vernallis—The Erotic Life of Machines/Steven Shaviro—Too Much, Tatu Young: Queering Politics in the World of Tatu/Sarah Kerton (**A153**)—*V. Video Games.* Grand Theft Auto? Popular Music and Intellectual Property in Video Games/Karen Collins—Dancing Machines: *Dance Dance Revolution*, Cybernetic Dance, and Musical Taste/Joanna Demers—Jacking the Dial: Radio, Race and Place in *Grand Theft Auto*/Kiri Miller.

Collections

C22 **Meriwether, Nicholas G., ed.** *All Graceful Instruments: The Contexts of the Grateful Dead Phenomenon.* Newcastle upon Tyne, UK: Cambridge Scholars Publishing, 2007; 236p. ISBN 1847180973; ML421.G72 2007.

Twelve essays whose origins lie in the interaction of Grateful Dead scholars at the annual meetings of the Southwest/Texas Popular & American Culture Associations. *Contents*: Introduction: "All Graceful Instruments": The Contexts of the Grateful Dead/Nicholas Meriwether—"Now is the Time Past Believing": Concealment, Ritual, and Death in the Grateful Dead's Approach to Improvisation/David Malvinni (**A171**)—Deadly Beauty: The Aesthetics of the Grateful Dead/Horace Fairlamb—Bobby, Béla, and Borrowing in "Victim or the Crime"/Shaugn O'Donnell (**A200**)—Robert Hunter, William Faulkner, and "It Must Have Been the Roses"/Nicholas G. Meriwether—Grateful Dead Musicking/Matthew Christen Tift—An American Nekyia: Terrapin Station and the Descent to the Underworld/Lans Smith—The Grateful Dead, Native American Novels and the Restoration of Oral Community/Christopher Norden—Black Muddy River: The Grateful Dead in the Continuum of American Folk Music/James Revell Carr—Grateful Rites, Dead Initiation/Mary Goodenough—"Songs of Our Own": The Deadhead Cultural Communication Code/Natalie Dollar—"It All Rolls into One": Rapture, Dionysus, Nietzsche, and the Grateful Dead/Stanley Spector—Dead Ahead: Using Logistics to Describe the Grateful Dead/F. Barry Barnes and Kenneth D. Mackenzie.

C23 **Middleton, Richard, ed.** *Reading Pop: Approaches to Textual Analysis in Popular Music.* Oxford: Oxford University Press, 2000; 388p. ISBN 0198166125; ML3470. R418 1999.

A collection of 16 articles previously published in *Popular Music*. *Contents*: Preface/Richard Middleton—Introduction: Locating the Popular Music Text/Richard Middleton—*I. Analysing the Music*. Randy Newman's Americana/Peter Winkler (**A264**)—Prince: Harmonic Analysis of "Anna Stesia"/Stan Hawkins (**A126**)—Analysing Popular Music: Theory, Method, and Practice/Philip Tagg (**A242**)—Popular Music Analysis and Musicology: Bridging the Gap/Richard Middleton (**A183**)—James Brown's "Superbad" and the Double-Voiced Utterance/David Brackett (**A31**)—"Maybellene": Meaning and the Listening Subject/Sean Cubitt—*II. Words and Music*. His Name Was in Lights: Chuck Berry's "Johnny B. Goode"/Timothy D. Taylor (**A244**)—Listening to Peter Gabriel's "I Have the Touch"/Umberto Fiori—Three Tributaries of "The River"/Dai Griffiths (**A122**)—Pity Peggy Sue/Barbara Bradby and Brian Torode (**A37**)—*III. Modes of Representation*. Progressive Rock and Psychedelic Coding in the Work of Jimi Hendrix/Sheila Whiteley (**A257**)—"The Hieroglyphics of Love": The Torch Singers and Interpretation/John Moore—Genre, Performance, and Ideology in the Early Songs of Irving Berlin/Charles Hamm—"Everbody's Lonesome for Somebody": Age, the Body, and Experience in the Music of Hank Williams/Richard Leppert and George Lipsitz—Postcolonialism on the Make: The Music of John Mellencamp, David Bowie, and John Zorn/Ellie Hisama—Structural Relationships of Music and Images in Music Video/Alf Björnberg (**A21**).

C24 **Mitsui, Tôru, ed.** *Popular Music: Intercultural Interpretations: International Association for the Study of Popular Music, Ninth International Conference on Popular Music.* Kanazawa, Japan: Kanazawa University, 1998; 558p. ISBN 4998068415; ML3470.P662 1998.

Sixty-seven essays, all but two of which were presented as conference papers at the ninth biennial meeting of the International Association for the Study of Popular Music. The conference's theme was "Intercultural Interpretations of Popular Music." *Contents*: Preface/Tôru Mitsui—*I. "East" and "West"?* Oriental Culture in Greece: Music and International Relations/Kevin Dawe—The Cultural Work of Miss Saigon: A Postcolonial Critique/Ellie M. Hisama—What Happens to Western Popular Music Histories When the "East" Gets a Look In?/David Hesmondhalgh—Non-Domestic Music in Japanese TV Commercials/Hideko Haguchi—Living in Confusion, Remembering Clearly: Rock in China/Jeroen de Kloet—Cantonese Popular Song: Hybridization of the East and West in the 1970s' Hong Kong/Ivy Oi-Kuen Man—A Jazz Novel in Prewar Japan: The Soundscape in Kawabata's *Asakusa Kerendai-dan*/Naoyuki Ishizaka—"Echoes" of the West: Kobo Abe, Haruki Murakami, and the Rock and Roll Imagination/Russell Reising—Soundscape, Post-Structuralism, and Music Education/Tadahiko Imada—Popular Music as Acquired Capital: Some Problems in Japanese Music Education/Kyôko Koizumi—*II. Intercultural Reception.* The Globalization of Music/Paul Williams—Dancing to Latin American Music: Exoticism and Creolization/Ute Bechdolf—Marketing British Pop: The Promotion of British Pop Acts and British Records in Japan/Mike Jones—Where Did Dance Music Come From? A Social History of the Taxi-Dance Hall in Japan, 1920s–1930s/Yoshikazu Nagai—Signifying China: The Exotic in Pre-War Japanese Popular Music/Edgar Pope—The Reception of Popular Music in the Early Stages of Acculturation in China: With Particular Reference to Jazz/Mamiko Naka—Was it Torture or Tune? First Japanese Music in the Western Theatre/Aya Mihara—Crossing Over: Japanese Popular Music Artists in the UK/Mark Percival—The Global and the Local: The Paradoxical Career of a Brazilian Death Metal Band within a Global Music Scene/Keith D. Harris—Korean Popular Music and Modes of Identification in Korea and America/Sarah Morelli—The Emotional Uses of Popular Music by Japanese Adolescents/Alan Wells, Ernest A. Hakanen, and Hiroshi Tokinoya—Mr. Big in Japan: Perception of Rock Music by Japanese Rock Fans/Yasushi Ogasawara—Limits of Musical Freedom/Johan Fornäs—*III. International Currents.* "Been All through the Nation..."/Paul Oliver—"Just in it for the Craic?": Irish Theme Pubs and Local Music Production/Abigail Gilmore—Elvis Presley and the Impulse Towards Transculturation/Rob Bowman—Dutch Radio: Valuing Pop Music through Institutional Changes/Wilfred Dolfsma—Class Acts? Taste and Popular Music/Martin Cloonan—A Tale of Two Festivals: Music and Festivals in Manchester, England, and Turku, Finland/Henri Terho—Local Music Policies within a Global Music Industry: Cultural Quarters in Manchester and Sheffield/Adam

Brown, Justin O'Connor, and Sara Cohen—"Diving in the River or Being It": Nature, Gender, and Rock Lyrics/Hillevi Ganetz—"I've Been Shushed at Bluebird": The Role of a Nashville, Tennessee, Café in Shaping Music and Musical Behavior/Amy R. Corin—The Allure of Sexuality in the Music of *The Jazz Singer* (1927): The Jewish Icon in Blackface Minstrelsy/Yûko Satô Nakamura—Autochthonisation of Rock Music in Rural Slovenia/Rajko Muršič—What's International About the International Bluegrass Music Association?/Neil V. Rosenberg—"I, Prince Jazzbo, Come to Stay, and I Will Never Be Late As I Would Tell You!"/Hasse Huss—*IV. Intercultural Production*. Rock Aesthetics and Nationalism/Motti Regev—"Something Old, Something New": Expatriate Musicians and Musical Authenticity/Andy Bennett—"Celtic Connections": Transnationalism or Localism in Popular Music?/Peter Symon—Changes in Conceptions of the "Authenticity" of Japanese Folksongs: A Case Study of Tôru Kasagi/Mamoru Tôya—Knockin' on China's Door/Dave Laing—Looking East: The Socialist Rock Alternative in the 1970s/Michael Rauhut—Early Czech Rock'n'Roll: Social Conditions and Four Sounds in Preserved Recordings—A Musicological Analysis of Melodies and Singing in Japanese Neo-Rockabilly/Terumasa Shimizu—Reception and Perception of Rock Music in India/Takako Inoue—"Brothers": The Indigenization of American Male Close-Harmony-Group Song Style in South Africa during the 1940s and 1950s/Christopher Ballantine—Rapping Around: Fad or Sign of Identity/Claire Levy—Salsa Musicians and the Performance of a Latin Style and Identity/Patria Román-Velázquez—Latin American Popular Music in Japan and the Issue of International Aesthetics/Steven Loza—Classification of Rhythm Patterns/Masato Yakô (**A267**)—Hamburg '60–'64: Cradle of British Rock?/Tony Sheridan—*V. The Pacific Rim*. Popular Music Beyond the Pacific: The Multi-Cultural Radio Station in Ôsaka/Hiroshi Ogawa—Local Space in the PNG Music Scene: String Band Sub-Styles/Denis Crowdy—"Popular Music in Yap?": A Study of the Conceptualization of Popular Music in a Non-Industrialized Island/Junko Konishi—The Papua New Guinean Music Industry and the World Music Market/Philip Hayward—The Invention of Heritage: Popular Music in Singapore/Lily L.L. Kong—East-West Synthesis or Cultural Hegemony? Questions on the Use of Indigenous Elements in Philippine Popular Music/Jonas and Amapola Baes—Localism, Nationalism, and Transnationalism in Pre-Postcolonial Hong Kong Popular Song/J. Lawrence Witzleben—Folk in China/Xin Tao—Shibuya-Kei (Shibuya Sound) and Globalization/Kôji Ônishi—Women in Japanese Popular Music: Setting the Subcultural Scene/Jennifer Milioto—The Rock Still Rolling: Local Subcultures/Masahiko Ôyama—Across a Crowded Room: Television and Rock in Australia in the Fifties/Bruce Johnson—"Brits and Pieces": The 1960s' "British Invasion" within Australia/Jon Fitzgerald—From the Australian Bush-Land to the Chill-Out Zones of Technoparties: The Didjeridu in the Labyrinth of Cultural Borderlands/Susanne Binas—New Zealand Music on the Internet: A Study of the NZPOP Mailing List/Tony Mitchell—Citing the Sound: New Zealand Indie Rock in North America/Geoff Stahl.

C25 **Moore, Allan, ed.** *The Cambridge Companion to Blues and Gospel Music.* Cambridge: Cambridge University Press, 2002; 216p. ISBN 0521001072; MT146.C36 2002.

Eleven essays on the development, performance, and recording of blues and gospel music. Includes chronology, illustrations, discography, and videography. *Contents*: Surveying the Field: Our Knowledge of Blues and Gospel Music/Allan Moore—Labels: Identifying Categories of Blues and Gospel/Jeff Todd Titon—The Development of the Blues/David Evans—The Development of Gospel Music/Don Cusic—Twelve Key Recordings/Graeme M. Boone (**A26**)—"Black Twice": Performance Conditions for Blues and Gospel Artists/Steve Tracy—Vocal Expression in the Blues and Gospel/Barb Jungr—The Guitar/Matt Backer—Keyboard Techniques/Adrian York—Imagery in the Lyrics: An Initial Approach/Guido van Rijn—Appropriations of Blues and Gospel in Popular Music/Dave Headlam.

C26 **Moore, Allan, ed.** *Analyzing Popular Music.* Cambridge: Cambridge University Press, 2003; 270p. ISBN 9780521100359; MT146.A54 2003.

Ten analytical essays covering various genres of music. The analyses are not ends unto themselves but are undertaken to answer larger related questions. *Contents*: Introduction/Allan Moore—Popular Music Analysis: Ten Apothegms and Four Instances/Rob Walser—From Lyric to Anti-Lyric: Analyzing the Words in Pop Song/Dai Griffiths (**A124**)—The Sound is "Out There": Score, Sound Design, and Exoticism in *The X-Files*/Robynn J. Stilwell—Feel the Beat Come Down: House Music as Rhetoric/Stan Hawkins (**A129**)—The Determining Role of Performance in the Articulation of Meaning: The Case of "Try a Little Tenderness"/Rob Bowman (**A30**)—Marxist Music Analysis Without Adorno: Popular Music and Urban Geography/Adam Krims (**A158**)—Jethro Tull and the Case for Modernism in Mass Culture/Allan F. Moore (**A188**)—Pangs of History in Late 1970s Rock/John Covach (**A74**)—Is Anybody Listening?/Chris Kennett—Talk and Text: Popular Music and Ethnomusicology/Martin Stokes.

C27 **Moore, Allan, ed.** *Critical Essays in Popular Musicology.* Burlington, VT: Ashgate Publishing, 2007; 608p. ISBN 9780754626473; ML3470.C75 2007.

A collection of 27 previously published essays. *Contents*: Introduction/Allan Moore—*I. Contexts for Addressing Texts. Theory.* "Black Music," "Afro-American Music," and "European Music"/Philip Tagg—A Theory of Musical Competence/Gino Stefani—Can We Get Rid of the "Popular" in Popular Music? A Virtual Symposium with Contributions from the International Advisory Editors of Popular Music/International Advisory Editors—Browsing Music Spaces: Categories and the Musical Mind/Franco Fabbri—The High Analysis of Low Music/Dai Griffiths—Second Thoughts on a Rock Aesthetic: The Band/Andrew Chester—Why I'll Never Teach Rock'n'Roll Again/Sean McCann—Authenticity as Authentication/Allan Moore—Intertextuality and Hypertextuality in Recorded Popular Music/Serge Lacasse (**A159**)—From Refrain to Rave: The Decline of Figure

Collections

and the Rise of Ground/Philip Tagg—What Does it Mean to Analyse Popular Music?/Adam Krims—*Music Theory*. The Formation of a Musical Style: Early Rock/Ronald Byrnside (**A53**)—Toward a Theory of Popular Harmony/Peter K. Winkler (**A263**)—On Aeolian Harmony in Contemporary Popular Music/Alf Björnberg (**A19**)—The So-Called "Flattened Seventh" in Rock/Allan Moore (**A186**)—Making Sense of Rock's Tonal Systems/Walter Everett (**A97**)—Incongruity and Predictability in British Dance-Band Music of the 1920s and 1930s/Derek B. Scott (**A227**)—Rhythm, Rhyme, and Rhetoric in the Music of Public Enemy/Robert Walser (**A255**)—*II. Addressing Texts*. Fantastic Remembrance in John Lennon's "Strawberry Fields Forever" and "Julia"/Walter Everett (**A90**)—The Rutles and the Use of Specific Models in Musical Satire/John R. Covach (**A69**)—The Aesthetics of Music Video: An Analysis of Madonna's "Cherish"/Carol Vernallis (**A252**)—"Gently Tender": The Incredible String Band's Early Albums/Charlie Ford (**A112**)—Cathy's Homecoming and the Other World: Kate Bush's "Wuthering Heights"/Nicky Losseff (**A165**)—Pulp, Pornography and Spectatorship: Subject Matter and Subject Position in Pulp's *This is Hardcore*/Nicola Dibben (**A82**)—Glamour and Evasion: The Fabulous Ambivalence of the Pet Shop Boys/Fred E. Maus (**A174**)—Vicars of "Wannabe": Authenticity and the Spice Girls/Elizabeth Eva Leach—Oh Boy! (Oh Boy!): Mutual Desirability and Musical Structure in the Buddy Group/Barbara Bradby (**A38**).

C28 **Perchard, Tom, ed.** *From Soul to Hip Hop*. Burlington, VT: Ashgate Publishing, 2011; 532p. ISBN 9780754629504; ML3479.F76 2014.

A volume in The Library of Essays on Popular Music (Allan Moore, series editor) containing 18 previously published essays. *Contents*: Introduction/Tom Perchard—*I. Style and Genre*. The Stax Sound: A Musicological Analysis/Rob Bowman (**A29**)—Questions of Genre in Black Popular Music/David Brackett (**A34**)—Turntablature: Notation, Legitimization, and the Art of the Hip-Hop DJ—A Vision of Love: An Etiquette of Vocal Ornamentation in African-American Popular Ballads of the 1990s/Richard Rischar—"Funky Drummer": New Orleans, James Brown, and the Rhythmic Transformation of American Popular Music/Alexander Stewart (**A238**)—The Construction of Jazz Rap as High Art in Hip-Hop Music/Justin A. Williams—*II. Theory, Analysis, and Historiography*. "That Ill, Tight Sound": Telepresence and Biopolitics in Post-Timbaland Rap Production/Dale Chapman—Goal-Directed Soul? Analyzing Rhythmic Teleology in African American Popular Music/Robert Fink (**A105**)—Accidents, Hooks, and Theory/Charles Kronengold—Soul Music: Its Sociological and Political Significance in American Popular Culture/Portia K. Maultsby—Doin' Damage in My Native Language: The Use of "Resistance Vernaculars" in Hip Hop in France, Italy, and Aotearoa/New Zealand/Tony Mitchell—Rap, Soul, and the Vortex at 33.3 rpm: Hip-Hop's Implements and African American Modernisms/Ed Pavlic—Who Hears Here? Black Music, Critical Bias, and the Musicological Skin Trade/Guthrie P. Ramsey, Jr.—*III. Identity*. "She's the Next One": Aretha Franklin's *Unforgettable: A Tribute to Dinah Washington* and the Black Women's Vocal Legacy/Michael Awkward—Sounds Authentic: Black Music, Ethnicity, and the

Challenge of a *Changing* Same/Paul Gilroy—Eminem's "My Name Is": Signifying Whiteness, Rearticulating Race/Loren Kajikawa—Men, Women, and Turntables: Gender and the DJ Battle/Mark Katz—Like Old Folk Songs Handed Down from Generation to Generation: History, Canon, and Community in B-Boy Culture/Joseph G. Schloss.

C29 **Plasketes, George, ed.** *Play it Again: Cover Songs in Popular Music.* Burlington, VT: Ashgate, 2010; 267p. ISBN 9780754668091; ML3470.P58 2010.

Fifteen essays on cover songs and their engagement of genre, gender, identity, and ideology. *Contents*: Introduction: Like a Version/George Plasketes—*I. Front Cover: Treatise.* Further Re-flections on "The Cover Age": A Collage and Chronicle/George Plasketes—*II. Under the Covers: History, Ideology, and Identity.* Charting Cultural Change, 1953-57: Song Assimilation through Cover Recording/B. Lee Cooper—The Cover Song as Historiography, Marker of Ideological Transformation/Sheldon Schiffer—Cover Up: Emergent Authenticity in a Japanese Popular Music Genre/Christine R. Yano—*III. The Song Remains the Same? Song and Album.* From Junk to Jesus: Recontextualizing "The Pusher"/Andrew G. Davis—David Bowie's *Pin-Ups*: Past as Prelude/Stuart Lenig—*IV. Look What They've Done to My Song: Gender, Identity, Media Makeovers.* Queering Cohen: Cover Versions as Subversions of Identity/Erik Steinskog—Covering and Un(covering) the Truth with "All Along the Watchtower": From Dylan to Hendrix and Beyond/Russell Reising—The Same Yet Different/Different Yet the Same: Bob Dylan Under the Cover of Covers/Greg Metcalf—*V. Don't Forget to Dance: Technique and Techno Transformations.* "Hide and Seek": A Case of Collegiate A Cappella "Microcovering"/Joshua S. Duchan (**A87**)—The Mashup Mindset: Will Pop Eat Itself?/David Tough—Camp Transitions: Genre Adaptation and the HI-NRG/Dance Cover Version/Lee Barron—*VI. Contemplating Covers.* In Defense of Cover Songs: Commerce and Credibility/Don Cusic—Artist Intentions: A Case for Quality Covers/Remy Miller—*VII. Back Cover: Epilogue.* Appreciating Cover Songs: Stereophony/Deena Weinstein.

C30 **Reising, Russell, ed.** *"Every Sound There Is": The Beatles'* Revolver *and the Transformation of Rock and Roll.* Burlington, VT: Ashgate, 2002; 278p. ISBN 0754605574; ML421.134.E94 2002.

Fourteen essays on the Beatles' album *Revolver*. The origins of the collection lie in a paper session at the BEATLES 2000 conference (see **C12** and particularly **A157**). Includes contributors' recollections and remembrances of the album. *Contents*: Introduction: "Of the Beginning"/Russell Reising—"When I'm in the Middle of a Dream": The Contributors Remember Revolver—*I. "Where Do They All Come From"? Revolver's Influences.* Detroit and Memphis: The Soul of *Revolver*/Walter Everett (**A95**)—*I'm* Eleanor Rigby: Female Identity and *Revolver*/Jacqueline Warwick—Sailing to the Sun: *Revolver's* Influence on Pink Floyd/Shaugn O'Donnell (**A198**)—*II. "It Is Shining": Revolver's Musicality. Revolver* as a Pivotal Art Work: Structure, Harmony, and Vocal Harmonization/Stephen Valdez—Tonal Family Resemblance in *Revolver*/Naphtali Wagner—A Flood of

Collections   113

Flat-Sevenths/Ger Tillekens—*III. "And Our Friends Were All Aboard": Revolver's Players.* "Tomorrow Never Knows": The Contribution of George Martin and His Production Team to the Beatles' New Sound/Kari McDonald and Sarah Hudson Kaufman—The Beatles for Everyone: Rearranging Base and Superstructure in the Rock Ballad/Cy Schleifer—Ringo Round *Revolver*: Rhythm, Timbre, and Tempo in Rock Drumming/Steven Baur—The Beatle Who Became a Man: *Revolver* and George Harrison's Metamorphosis/Matthew Bannister—Premature Turns: Thematic Disruption in the American Version of *Revolver*/Jim LeBlanc—*IV. "Here, There, and Everywhere": Revolver's Themes.* "Love is All and Love is Everyone": A Discussion of Four Musical Portraits/Sheila Whiteley—The Beatles, Postmodernism, and Ill-Tempered Musical Form: Cleaning My Gun; or, The Use of Accidentals in *Revolver*/Ronald Schleifer—"It Is Not Dying": *Revolver* and the Birth of Psychedelic Sound/Russell Reising.

C31   **Reising, Russell, ed.** *"Speak to Me": The Legacy of Pink Floyd's* The Dark Side of the Moon. Burlington, VT: Ashgate, 2005; 251p. ISBN 0754640191; ML421. P6S74 2005.

Fifteen essays on Pink Floyd's album *The Dark Side of the Moon*, addressing its "musical, philosophical, psychological, historical, thematic, and performative dimensions." Includes contributors' recollections of the album and an annotated bibliography. *Contents*: "Assorted Lunatics": Contributors' Biographical Notes—Foreword: The Floydian Slip/Craig Bailey—Introduction: Life on the Dark Side of the Moon/Russell Reising—*I. "Any Colour You Like": General Discussion.* On the Waxing and Waning: A Brief History of *The Dark Side of the Moon*/Russell Reising—"Matter of Fact It's All Dark": Audiovisual Stadium Rock Aesthetics in Pink Floyd's *The Dark Side of the Moon* Tour, 1973/Kimi Kärki—Dark Side of the Men: Pink Floyd, Classic Rock and White Masculinities/Matthew Bannister—"We're Not in Kansas Any More": Music, Myth and Narrative Structure in *The Dark Side of the Moon*/Lee Barron and Ian Inglis—*II. "Everything Under the Sun Is in Tune": Musical and Structural Discussions.* "Worked Out Within the Grooves": The Sound and Structure of *The Dark Side of the Moon*/Kevin J. Holm-Hudson—"On the Path": Tracing Tonal Coherence in *The Dark Side of the Moon*/Shaugn O'Donnell (**A199**)—The Keys to Quiet Desperation: Modulating Between Misery and Madness/Ger Tillekens—*III. "There's No Dark Side of the Moon": Theoretical Discussions.* Reversing Us and Them: Anti-Psychiatry and *The Dark Side of the Moon*/Nicola Spelman—Prismatic Passion: The Enigma of "The Great Gig in the Sky"/Sheila Whiteley—The Whole of the Moon: "Brain Damage," "Eclipse," and the Mythic Narrative of Pink Floyd/Peter Mills—Pink Floyd's Levinasian Ethics: Reading *The Dark Side of the Moon*'s Philosophical Architecture/Kenneth Womack—*IV. "Speak to Me": The Influence of* The Dark Side of the Moon. The Moons are Eclipsed by the Moon: Covering the Dark Side/Russell Reising—Eclipsing: The Influence of *The Dark Side of the Moon* on the Next Generation's Music through Radiohead's *OK Computer*/Benjamin Schleifer—"And if the Band You're in Starts Playing Different Tunes": An Interview with Mike Gordon of Phish/Russell Reising—The Jamaican Side of the Moon:

An Interview with Michael Goldwasser of Easy Star Records/Russell Reising—"Thought I'd Something More to Say": An Annotated Bibliography of Selected Reviews and Commentary on *The Dark Side of the Moon*/Mathew Bartkowiak.

C32   **Roe, Keith and Ulla Carlsson, eds.** *Popular Music Research: An Anthology from NORDICOM Sweden.* Gothenburg, Sweden: University of Gothenburg, 1990; 167p. ISSN 03491242; ML3499.5.S91P6 1990.

A collection of 11 articles from Swedish musicologists and sociologists. Includes a statistical profile of Swedish music consumption and a bibliography of Nordic literature. *Contents*: Foreword/Ulla Carlsson—Introduction/Keith Roe—The Implications of Structural Changes in the Music Industry for Media Policy and Music Activity: A Research Framework/Roger Wallis and Krister Malm—From a Whisper to a Scream: Music Video and Cultural Form/Robert Burnett—Popular Music and Youth Culture in Late Modernity/Johan Fornäs—Adolescents' Music Use: A Structural-Cultural Approach/Keith Roe—Children and Music: An Exploratory Study/Cecilia von Feilitzen and Keith Roe—Rock Tastes—On Rock as Symbolic Capital: A Study of Young People's Music Taste and Music Making/Mats Trondman—Trends in Popular Music Preferences in Sweden 1960–1988/Göran Nylöf—Music in Mass Media Studies: Reading Sounds for Example/Philip Tagg—The Meaning of Rock: Some Problems Concerning the Aesthetics of Popular Music/Per-Erik Brolinson and Holger Larsen—Sounding the Mainstream: An Analysis of the Songs Performed in the Swedish Eurovision Song Contest Semi-Finals 1959–1983/Alf Björnberg (**A20**)—Musical Acculturation: "Hound Dog" from Blues to Swedish Rock and Roll—Statistical Profile of Music Consumption in Sweden/Robert Burnett—Popular Music Research: A Selective Bibliography of Nordic [Denmark, Finland, Norway, and Sweden] Literature 1975–[1989].

C33   **Scott, Derek B., ed.** *The Ashgate Research Companion to Popular Musicology.* Burlington, VT: Ashgate, 2009; 557p. ISBN 9780754664765; ML3470.A84 2009.

Twenty-six essays written to familiarize scholars with current research and specific methodologies. *Contents*: Introduction/Derek B. Scott—*I. Film, Video, and Multimedia.* Trevor Jones's Score for *In the Name of the Father*/David Cooper—Music, Sound and the Moving Image: The Present and a Future?/Anahid Kassabian—Reinventing *Question Time*/Miguel Mera—Televised Live Performance, Looping Technology and the "Nu Folk": KT Tunstall on *Later . . . with Jools Holland*/John Richardson—*II. Technology and Studio Production.* Learning to Listen to Perfect Sound: Hi-Fi Culture and Changes in Modes of Listening, 1950–80/Alf Björnberg—Approaches to Analysing Recordings of Popular Music/Timothy Warner—The Art of Phonography: Sound, Technology and Music/Peter Wicke—*III. Gender and Sexuality.* Genre, Subjectivity, and Back-up Singing in Rock Music/Susan Fast—Notes on Musical Camp/Freya Jarman-Ivens—Who Are You? Research Strategies of the Unruly Feminine/Sheila Whiteley—"I'm a Man": Masculinities in Popular Music/Jason Lee Oakes—*IV. Identity and Ethnicity.* The Woven World: Unravelling the Mainstream and the Alternative in Greek

Popular Music/Kevin Dawe—Dayton Street Funk: The Layering of Multiple Identities/Portia K. Maultsby—Black, White and Brown on the Dance Floor: The New Meanings of Panjabiyat in the Twenty-First Century/Anjali Gera Roy—*V. Performance and Gesture*. Musical Persona: The Physical Performance of Popular Music/Philip Auslander—Vocal Performance and the Projection of Emotional Authenticity/Nicola Dibben—"Chelsea Rodgers" was a Model: Vocality in Prince of the Twenty-First Century/Stan Hawkins (**A130**)—Singing Style and White Masculinity/Jacqueline Warwick—Talking Music, Making Music: A Comparison between Rap and Techno/Antoine Hennion—*VI. Reception and Scenes*. Absolute Beginners: The Evolution of a British Popular Music Scene/Ian Inglis—Studying Reception and Scenes/Adam Krims—Interpretation: So What?/Allan F. Moore—Beyond the Master Narrative of Youth: Researching Ageing Popular Music Scenes/Nicola Smith—*VII. The Music Industry and Globalization*. Music and the Creative Knowledge Economy/Geraldine Bloustien—The Transnational Music Industry/Andreas Gebesmair—Pop Idol: Global Economy, Local Meanings/Tarja Rautiainen-Keskustalo.

C34 **Spicer, Mark and John Covach, eds.** *Sounding Out Pop: Analytical Essays in Popular Music*. Ann Arbor: The University of Michigan Press, 2010; 265p. ISBN 0472034000; ML3470.S635 2010.

Nine analytical essays covering a range of pop and rock music from the 1950s to the present. A wide range of approaches are offered, but all deal directly with the "music itself." *Contents*: Preface/Mark Spicer and John Covach—Leiber and Stoller, the Coasters, and the "Dramatic AABA" Form/John Covach (**A77**)—"Only the Lonely": Roy Orbison's Sweet West Texas Style/Albin Zak (**A270**)—Ego and Alter Ego: Artistic Interaction between Bob Dylan and Roger McGuinn/James Grier (**A121**)—Marvin Gaye as Vocal Composer/Andrew Flory (**A110**)—A Study of Maximally Smooth Voice Leading in the Mid-1970s Music of Genesis/Kevin Holm-Hudson (**A142**)—"Reggatta de Blanc": Analyzing Style in the Music of The Police/Mark Spicer (**A235**)—Vocal Authority and Listener Engagement: Musical and Narrative Expressive Strategies in the Songs of Female Pop-Rock Artists, 1993–95/Lori Burns (**A51**)—Recombinant Style Topics: the Past and Future of Sampling/Rebecca Leydon (**A163**)—"I'm Not Here, This Isn't Happening": The Vanishing Subject in Radiohead's *Kid A*/Marianne Tatom Letts (**A162**).

C35 **Spicer, Mark, ed.** *Rock Music*. Burlington, VT: Ashgate Publishing, 2011; 474p. ISBN 9780754629566; ML3534.R63346 2011.

A volume in The Library of Essays on Popular Music (Allan Moore, series editor) containing 20 previously published essays. *Contents*: Introduction/Mark Spicer—*I. Histories, Aesthetics, and Ideologies*. Prolegomena to Any Aesthetics of Rock Music/Bruce Baugh—Fans and Critics: Greil Marcus's *Mystery Train* as Rock 'n' Roll History/Mark Mazullo—Synergies and Reciprocities: The Dynamics of Musical and Professional Interaction between the Beatles and Bob Dylan/Ian Inglis—The Hippie Aesthetic: Cultural Positioning and Musical Ambition in Early Progressive Rock/John Covach—Consuming Nature: The Grateful Dead's

Performance of an Anticommercial Counterculture/Nadya Zimmerman—The Future is Now . . . and Then: Sonic Historiography in Post-1960s Rock/Kevin Holm-Hudson—Indie: The Institutional Politics and Aesthetics of a Popular Music Genre/David Hesmondhalgh—When Women Play the Bass: Instrument Specialization and Gender Interpretation in Alternative Rock Music/Mary Ann Clawson—All Singers are Dicks/Deena Weinstein—Intimacy and Distance: On Stipe's Queerness/Fred Maus—*II. Sounds, Structures and Styles*. The Melodic-Harmonic "Divorce" in Rock/David Temperley (**A246**)—Triadic Modal and Pentatonic Patterns in Rock Music/Nicole Biamonte (**A16**)—Transformation in Rock Harmony: An Explanatory Strategy/Christopher Doll (**A83**)—The Persona-Environment Relation in Recorded Song/Allan F. Moore—(Ac)cumulative Form in Pop-Rock Music/Mark Spicer (**A233**)—Every Inch of My Love: Led Zeppelin and the Problem of Cock Rock/Steve Waksman—Examining Rhythmic and Metric Practices in Led Zeppelin's Musical Style/John Brackett—Bob Dylan and Jimi Hendrix: Juxtaposition and Transformation "All Along the Watchtower"/Albin J. Zak III—The Learned vs. the Vernacular in the Songs of Billy Joel/Walter Everett—Sound, Text and Identity in Korn's "Hey Daddy"/Jonathan Pieslak.

C36 **Straw, Will, Stacey Johnson, Rebecca Sullivan, Paul Friedlander, with Gary Kennedy, eds.,** *Popular Music—Style and Identity: Seventh International Conference on Popular Music Studies.* Montreal: The Centre for Research on Canadian Cultural Industries and Institutions, 1993; 323p. ISBN 0771704593; ML3470. I58x 1993.

Fifty-five essays comprising the proceedings of the 1993 conference of the International Association for the Study of Popular Music in Stockton, California. Includes recollections of the conference. *Contents*: Introduction/Will Straw—The Stockton Conference: Recollections and Commentaries/Simon Frith, Paul Friedlander, and Anahid Kassabian—"Drumbeats, Pennywhistles, and All That Jazz": The Relationship Between Urban South African Musical Styles and Musical Meaning/Lara Allen—Sensation and Seduction: Sissel Kyrkjebø "Breathtakes" Norway—The Signifying Power of the Voice/Kate Augestad—The Identities of Race, Class, and Gender in the Repression of Early Black South African Jazz and Vaudeville (ca. 1920–1944)/Christopher Ballantine—Watching Pop Music Video Audiences/Ute Bechdolf—The Ins and Outs of Youth Broadcasting in (East) Germany/Susanne Binas—The Politics and Musical Practice of "Crossover"/David Brackett (**A32**)—Lesbians and Popular Music: Does it Matter Who is Singing?/Barbara Bradby—The End of the World as We Know It: Popular Music's Cultural Mobility/Marcus Breen—Not Taking the Rap: NWA Get Stranded on an Island of Realism/Martin Cloonan—Localizing Sound/Sara Cohen—We Can Work It Out/John Covach—Canadian Women in Country Music/Linda Daniel—American Karaoke Performers as Amateurs and Professionals/Robert S. Drew—For Love or Money? Austin Musicians' Discourse on the Idealist/Materialist Debate/Jeff Farley—Two Stories: Where Exactly is the Local?/Mark Fenster—"Old School—New School": An Examination of Changes in the Production and Consumption of Post-Disco Underground Dance Music in New York City/Kai Fikentscher—Black or White?

Stylistic Analysis of Early Motown "Crossover" Hits: 1963–1966/Jon Fitzgerald (**A106**)—Listen to Your Voice! Authenticity and Reflexivity in Karaoke, Rock, Rap, and Techno Music/Johan Fornäs—Body, Soul, and Modernity: A Comparative Study of Edith Södergram and Eva Dahlgren/Hillevi Ganetz—The Veneration of James Brown and George Clinton in Hip-Hop Music: Is It Live! Or Is It Re-Memory?/Kyra D. Gaunt (**A117**)—Rockin' the Imagined Local: New York Rock in a Reterritorialized World/Leslie C. Gay, Jr.—Quebec Sings "E Uassuian": The Coming of Age of a Local Music Industry/Line Grenier and Val Morrison—New Perspectives in Musicology: Musical Structures, Codes, and Meaning in 1990s Pop/Stan Hawkins (**A127**)—Australian Music Video: Industrial Spaces, Economics, and Style/Philip Hayward—Is This What You Call Change? Flexibility, Post-Fordism and the Music Industries/David Hesmondhalgh—Singing Not Together: Karaoke in São Paulo/Shuhei Hosokawa—Local Construction of Identity: Analysing Category-Work of an Amateur Music Group/Helmi Järviluoma—An American Accent: Gender and Cultural Reorientation in Australian Popular Music/Bruce Johnson—"Crossover" and the Politics of "Race"/Simon Jones—Recasting the Popular Music Studies' Conceptions of the Authentic and the Local in Light of Bell's Theorem/Steve Jones—Who Gets to Sound American in Hollywood Films?/Anahid Kassabian—The Adaptability of Karaoke in the United Kingdom/William H. Kelley—Technologies of Authorship in Disco/Carolyn Krasnow—Rock and Ritual: The Star-Cult as a Phenomenon of the Music Industry and as a Communications Stereotype of Modern Musical Culture/Kostanze Kriese—Institutional Practices in Alternative Music Scenes/Holly Kruse—An Examination of Industrial Practice: The Case of Wax Trax! Records/Stephen Lee—A Comparison of the Use and Appeal of Karaoke in Japan and Australia: How Has Karaoke Adapted to the Australian Culture?/Heather Macaw—Subculture, Rock Music, and Gender/Airi Mäki-Kulmala—He Waiata Na Aotearoa: Maori and Polynesian Music in New Zealand/Tony Mitchell—Karaoke Throughout the World (Introductory Remarks)/Toru Mitsui—Money for Nothing? The Future of Copyright Remuneration for the Use of Phonograms in Radio and the Blank Tape Levy/Fee/Jari Muikku—Newfoundland Vernacular Song/Peter Narváez—Sinéad O'Connor: Miniature Portrait of the Artist as an Angry Young Woman/Keith Negus—Karaoke in Japan: A Sociological Overview/Hiroshi Ogawa—The Influence of Czech Folklore on Czech Rock Music/Aleš Opekar—Music Knows No Borders: The Political Background of the GDR's International Rock Concerts in the Late Eighties/Michael Rauhut—A Hero to Most? Elvis, Myth, and the Politics of Race/Gilbert B. Rodman—The Garifuna & Creole Culture of Belize Explosion of Punta Rock/Jennifer Ryan—The Booth, the Floor, and the Wall: Dance Music and the Fear of Falling/Will Straw—(Dis)located? Rhetoric, Politics, Meaning and the Locality/John Street—What's That Sound? Listening to Popular Music, Revisited/Paul Théberge—Discothèques in Puerto Rico: Salsa vs. Rock/Patria Roman-Velásquez—Clamor and Community: Rhythm, Rhyme, and Rhetoric in the Music of Public Enemy/Robert Walser (**A255**)—Mick Jagger: An Analysis of Sexuality, Style, and Image/Sheila Whiteley—In Search of *Yaa Amponsah*/Peter Winkler.

C37 **Vulliamy, Graham and Ed Lee, eds.** *Pop, Rock and Ethnic Music in School.* Cambridge: Cambridge University Press, 1982; 244p. ISBN 0521233410; MT1.V84.

Fifteen essays on the practical application of popular music in the classroom and the attendant theoretical issues. *Contents*: Introduction/Graham Vulliamy and Ed Lee—*I. Classroom* Work. How Can I Use the Top Ten?/John Comer (**A64**)—Using Pop Music with Middle-School Classes/Michael Burnett (**A42**)—Rhythm and Percussion Work in Rock and Latin American Styles/John Comer—Examining Pop/Paul Farmer—*II. Aspects of Technique.* Rock and Blues Piano Accompaniments/John Comer (**A65**)—Bringing the Guitar into Your School/Ed Lee—The Foremost Medium: The Voice/Ed Lee—*III. Ethnic Musical Styles.* Background to West Indian Music/George Fisher and Piers Spencer—Teaching Steel Band Music/George Fisher—Reggae/Piers Spencer (**A231**)—African Drumming/Felix Cobbson—Glimpses of Indian Music/Leela Floyd—Balinese Music/Neil Sorrel—*IV. Alternatives.* The Central London Youth Project Music Workshop/Paul Crawford—Teaching Rock at the Basement Youth Club/Steward Knight.

C38 **Weiner, Robert G., ed.** *Perspectives on the Grateful Dead: Critical Writings.* Westport, CT: Greenwood, 1999; 272p. ISBN 0313305692; ML421.G72P47.

Twenty-two essays gathered to "examine the Deadhead phenomenon from many diverse perspectives." *Contents*: Foreword/Rebecca G. Adams—Introduction/Robert G. Weiner—Precisely How and Why I Didn't Kill Jerry: Ethnography, Surrealism, and *The Millennium Shows*/Philip E. Baruth—A Pilot Study in Dream Telepathy with the Grateful Dead/Stanley Krippner—Legally Dead: The Grateful Dead and American Legal Culture/David Fraser and Vaughan Black—The Grateful Dead Onstage in "World Music"/Thomas Vennum, Jr.—"No, but I've Been to Shows": Accepting the Dead and Rejecting the Deadheads/David L. Pelovitz—Why Are There So Many Jewish Deadheads?/Douglas M. Gertner—Bakhtinian Carnival, Corporate Capital, and the Last Decade of the Dead/Brad E. Lucas—Understanding "Show" as a Deadhead Speech Situation/Natalie Dollar—Is There a Day of the Month Effect in "Beat It on Down the Line?"/Robert K. Toutkoushian—The Grateful Dead Experience: A Factor Analytic Study of the Personalities of People Who Identify with the Grateful Dead/William McCown and Wendy Dulaney—"High Time" and Ambiguous Harmonic Function/Walter Everett (**A94**)—Space, Motion, and Other Musical Metaphors/Shaugn O'Donnell (**A197**)—The Grateful Dead Legendstock: Based on Alan Trist's *Water of Life: A Tale of the Grateful Dead*/Marjorie C. Luesebrink—The Grateful Dead vs. the American Dream?/Jason Palm—The Annotated "Ramble on Rose": An Installment in *The Annotated Grateful Dead Lyrics* (a Work in Progress)/David Dodd—"Laid My Proposition Down / Laid It on the Line": Gambling and the Storyteller in Robert Hunter's Lyrics/Anissa Craghead—Grateful Dead: Manifestations from the Collective Unconscious/Mary Goodenough—Clinging to the Edge of Magic: Shamanic Aspects of the Grateful Dead/Nancy Reist—The Grateful Dead as Community/Rachel Wilgoren—Deadhead Tales of the Supernatural: A Folkloristic Analysis/Revell Carr—The Piping of Heaven: Reckless Musings on Philosophical Taoism and the Grateful Dead Phenomenon/Joseph P. Noonan III—The Ripple Effect/Joseph Holt—Afterword: The Curriculum of Joy/Steve Silberman.

C39　**Whiteley, Sheila and Jennifer Rycenga, eds.** *Queering the Popular Pitch.* New York: Routledge, 2006; 308p. ISBN 041597805X; ML3470.Q44 2006.

Eighteen essays with roots in the 2003 Biennial Conference of the International Association for the Study of Popular Music, where debates raised by *Queering the Pitch: The New Lesbian and Gay Musicology* (Routledge, 1994) were brought into the discussion of popular music. *Contents*: Preface/Sheila Whiteley—Introduction/Sheila Whiteley—*I. Performing Lives, Hidden Histories.* What's That Smell? Queer Temporalities and Subcultural Lives/Judith Halberstam—Girl on Girl: Fat Femmes, Bio-Queens, and Redefining Drag/Rachel Devitt—Queering the Witch: Stevie Nicks and the Forging of Femininity at the Night of a Thousand Stevies/Jason Lee Oakes—Tickle Me Emo: Lesbian Balladeering, Straight-Boy Emo and the Politics of Affect/Karen Tongson—"Anders als die Anderen," or Queering the Song: Construction and Representation of Homosexuality in German Cabaret Song Recordings before 1933/Anno Mungen—*II. Queering Boundaries.* Tears and Screams: Performances of Pleasure and Pain in the Bolero/Vanessa Knights—Hey, Man, You're My Girlfriend! Poetic Genderfuck and Queer Hebrew in Eran Zur's Performance of Yona Wallach's Lyrics/Gilad Padva—Albita Rodríguez: Sexuality, Imaging, and Gender Construction in the Music of Exile/Mario Rey—Su Casa es Mi Casa: Latin House, Sexuality, Place/Stephen Amico (**A3**)—*III. Too Close for Comfort.* Too Much, Tatu Young: Queering Politics in the World of Tatu/Sarah Kerton (**A153**)—"I Am Not in a Box of Any Description": Sinéad O'Connor's Queer Outing/Emma Mayhew—Gender Crossings: A Neglected History in African American Music/Jeffrey Callen—Queer(ing) Masculinities in Heterosexist Rap Music/Freya Jarman-Ivens (**A146**)—Closeness and Distance: Songs about AIDS/Paul Attinello (**A6**)—*IV. Glamorous Excess.* Endless Caresses: Queer Exuberance in Large-Scale Form in Rock/Jennifer Rycenga (**A223**)—Popular Music and the Dynamics of Desire/Sheila Whiteley—Trans Glam: Gender Magic in the Film Musical/Lloyd Whitesell—On Male Queering in Mainstream Pop/Stan Hawkins.

C40　**Womack, Kenneth, ed.** *The Cambridge Companion to the Beatles.* Cambridge: Cambridge University Press, 2009; 316p. ISBN 9780521869652; ML421.B4C33.

Thirteen essays on the Beatles, their music, their influences, and particularly their recordings. Includes discography. *Contents*: Foreword: I Believe in Tomorrow: The Posthumous Life of the Beatles/Anthony DeCurtis—Introduction: Introducing the Beatles/Kenneth Womack—*I. Background.* Six Boys, Six Beatles: The Formative Years, 1950–1962/Dave Laing—The Beatles as Recording Artists/Jerry Zolten—*II. Works.* Rock and Roll Music/Howard Kramer—"Try Thinking More": *Rubber Soul* and the Beatles' Transformation of Pop/James M. Decker—Magical Mystery Tours and Other Trips: Yellow Submarines, Newspaper Taxis, and the

Beatles' Psychedelic Years/Russell Reising and Jim LeBlanc—Revolution/Ian Inglis—On Their Way Home: The Beatles in 1969 and 1970/Steve Hamelman—Apple Records/Bruce Spizer—The Solo Years/Michael Frontani—Any Time at All: The Beatles' Free Phrase Rhythms/Walter Everett (**A100**)—*III. History and Influence.* The Beatles as Zeitgeist/Sheila Whiteley—Beatles News: Product Line Extensions and the Rock Canon/Gary Burns—"An Abstraction, like Christmas": The Beatles for Sale and for Keeps/John Kimsey.

IV
Dissertations

D1 **Adam, Nathaniel.** "Coding OK Computer: Categorization and Characterization of Disruptive Harmonic and Rhythmic Events in Rock Music." Ph.D. diss., University of Michigan, 2011.

D2 **Attas, Robin.** "Meter as Process in Groove-Based Popular Music." Ph.D. diss., University of British Columbia, 2011.

D3 **Björnberg, Alf.** "En liten sång som alla andra: Melodifestivalen 1959–1983." Ph.D. diss., University of Gothenburg, 1987.

D4 **Boone, Christine.** "Mashups: History, Legality, and Aesthetics." Ph.D. diss., University of Texas at Austin, 2011.

D5 **Bowman, Durrell.** "Permanent Change: Rush, Musicians' Rock, and the Progressive Post-Counterculture." Ph.D. diss., University of California-Los Angeles, 2003.

D6 **Brackett, David.** "Three Studies in the Analysis of Popular Music." D.M.A. diss., Cornell University, 1991.

D7 **Brownell, John.** "The Changing Same: Asymmetry and Rhythmic Structure in Repetitive Idioms." Ph.D. diss., York University, 2003.

D8 **Carter, Paul.** "Retrogressive Harmonic Motion as Structural and Stylistic Characteristic of Pop-Rock Music." Ph.D. diss., University of Cincinnatti, 2005.

D9 **Clement, Brett.** "A Study of the Instrumental Music of Frank Zappa." Ph.D. diss., University of Cincinnatti, 2009.

D10   Cotner, John. "Archetypes of Progressiveness in Rock, ca. 1966–1973." Ph.D. diss., University of Wisconsin-Madison, 2001.

D11   Davis, Robert. "Who Got Da Funk? An Etymophony of Funk Music from the 1950s to 1979." Ph.D. diss., University of Montreal, 2005.

D12   de Clercq, Trevor. "Sections and Successions in Successful Songs: A Prototype Approach to Form in Rock Music." Ph.D. diss., University of Rochester, 2012.

D13   Doll, Christopher. "Listening to Rock Harmony." Ph.D. diss., Columbia University, 2007.

D14   Eggertson, Kristine. "'Where is the Meter?' An Investigation of Rhythmic Process in Björk's Music." Ph.D. diss., University of Saskatchewan, 2003.

D15   Endrinal, Christopher. "Form and Style in the Music of U2." Ph.D. diss., Florida State University, 2008.

D16   Fitzgerald, Jon. "Popular Songwriting 1963–1966: Stylistic Comparisons and Trends within the U.S. Top Forty." Ph.D. diss., Southern Cross University, 1996.

D17   Hawkins, Stan. "Stylistic Diversification in Prince of the Nineties: An Analysis of Diamonds and Pearls." Ph.D. diss., University of Oslo [Papers from the Department of Music and Theatre], 1992.

D18   Hoffman, Alan. "On the Nature of Rock and Roll: An Enquiry into the Aesthetic of a Musical Vernacular." Ph.D. diss., Yale University, 1983.

D19   Hughes, Bryn. "Harmonic Expectation in Twelve-Bar Blues Progressions." Ph.D. diss., Florida State University, 2011.

D20   Hughes, Tim. "Groove and Flow: Six Analytical Essays on the Music of Stevie Wonder." Ph.D. diss., University of Washington, 2003.

D21   Keesing, Hugo. "Youth in Transition: A Content Analysis of Two Decades of Popular Music." Ph.D. diss., Adelphi University, 1973.

D22   LaCasse, Serge. "'Listen to My Voice': The Evocative Power of Vocal Staging in Recorded Rock Music and Other Forms of Vocal Expression." Ph.D. diss., University of Liverpool, 2000.

D23   Lilja, Esa. "Theory and Analysis of Classic Heavy Metal Harmony." Ph.D. diss., University of Helsinki, 2009.

D24   Lupis, Giuseppe. "The Published Music of Keith Emerson: Expanding the Solo Piano Repertoire." Ph.D. diss., University of Georgia, 2006.

D25   Malawey, Victoria. "Temporal Process, Repetition, and Voice in Björk's Medúlla." Ph.D. diss., Indiana University, 2007.

D26   Mather, Olivia. "'Cosmic American Music': Place and the Country Rock Movement." Ph.D. diss., University of California-Los Angeles, 2006.

Dissertations

D27 **McCandless, Gregory.** "Rhythm and Meter in the Music of Dream Theater." Ph.D. diss., The Florida State University, 2010.

D28 **McDonald, Christopher.** "Grand Designs: A Musical, Social, and Ethnographic Study of Rush." Ph.D. diss., York University, 2002.

D29 **McGranahan, Liam.** "Mashnography: Creativity, Consumption, and Copyright in the Mashup Community." Ph.D. diss., Brown University, 2010.

D30 **Montgomery, David.** "The Rock Concept Album: Context and Analysis." Ph.D. diss., University of Toronto, 2002.

D31 **Morss, Benjamin.** "Pitch-Skipping in Rock Music." Ph.D. diss., University of California at Davis, 2000.

D32 **Neal, Jocelyn.** "Song Structure Determinants: Poetic Narrative, Phrase Structure, and Hypermeter in the Music of Jimmie Rodgers." Ph.D. diss., University of Rochester, 2002.

D33 **Nobile, Drew.** "A Structural Approach to the Analysis of Rock Music." Ph.D. diss., City University of New York, 2014.

D34 **Osborn, Brad.** "Beyond Verse and Chorus: Experimental Formal Structures in Post-Millennial Rock Music." Ph.D. diss., University of Washington, 2010.

D35 **Porter, Steven.** "Rhythm and Harmony in the Music of the Beatles." Ph.D. diss., City University of New York, 1979.

D36 **Ramaglia, Bellino.** "The Transcription, Analysis, and Study of Representative Recordings of Rock Music 1954–1969." Ed.D. diss., Columbia University, 1980.

D37 **Ripani, Richard.** "The New Blue Music: Changes in Melody, Harmony, Rhythm, and Form in Rhythm & Blues, 1950–1999." Ph.D. diss., University of Memphis, 2004.

D38 **Rischar, Richard.** "'One Sweet Day': Vocal Ornamentation and Style in the African-American Popular Ballad, 1991–1995." Ph.D. diss., University of North Carolina at Chapel Hill, 2000.

D39 **Rockwell, Joti.** "Drive, Lonesomeness, and the Genre of Bluegrass Music." Ph.D. diss., University of Chicago, 2011.

D40 **Rosenberg, Nancy.** "From Rock Music to Theory Pedagogy: Rethinking U.S. College Music Theory Education from a Popular Music Perspective." Ph.D. diss., Boston University, 2010.

D41 **Schneider, Thomas.** "Blues Cover Songs: The Intersection of Blues and Rock on the Popular Music Charts (1955–1995)." Ph.D. diss., University of Memphis, 2001.

D42 **Sonenberg, Daniel.** "'Who in the World Might She Be': A Contextual and Stylistic Approach to the Early Music of Joni Mitchell." D.M.A. diss., City University of New York, 2003.

D43 **Spicer, Mark.** "British Pop-Rock Music in the Post-Beatles Era: Three Analytical Studies." Ph.D. diss., Yale University, 2002.

D44 **Stephan-Robinson, Anna.** "Form in Paul Simon's Music." Ph.D. diss., Eastman School of Music, 2009.

D45 **Stoia, Nicholas.** "The Musical Frameworks of Five Blues Schemes." Ph.D. diss., City University of New York, 2008.

D46 **Summach, Jay.** "Form in Top-20 Rock Music, 1955–89." Ph.D. diss., Yale University, 2012.

D47 **Tagg, Philip.** "Kojak–50 Seconds of Television Music: Toward the Analysis of Affect in Popular Music" Ph.D. diss., University of Gothenburg, 1977.

D48 **Valdez, Stephen.** "The Development of the Electric Guitar Solo in Rock Music, 1954–1971." D.M.A. diss., University of Oregon, 1992.

D49 **Walsh, Brian.** "Structure, Function, and Process in the Early Song Cycles and Extended Songs of the Canadian Rock Group Rush." Ph.D. diss., The Ohio State University, 2002.

D50 **Williams, Justin.** "Musical Borrowing in Hip-Hop Music: Theoretical Frameworks and Case Studies." Ph.D. diss., University of Nottingham, 2010.

D51 **Zeiner-Henriksen, Hans.** "The 'PoumTchak' Pattern: Correspondences Between Rhythm, Sound, and Movement in Electronic Dance Music." Ph.D. diss., University of Oslo, 2010.

Song Index

Each title is followed by the entry numbers for all articles and books that make reference to the song. Boldface further indicates the appearance of a musical example or figure in the article or book. Different versions of a song are separated by artist (when artist is noted at all), and different songs with identical titles are indicated by bracketed numbers [1], [2], etc.

"1nce Again": A Tribe Called Quest **A158**
"2+2=5 (The Lukewarm)": Radiohead **A169**, **A204**, A206, A221
"2H.B.": Roxy Music A185
"3D": Big Jay McNeely B21
"3 O'Clock Shot": Strontium 90 A235
"4th Time Around": Bob Dylan **B8**
"4 W.D.": Jethro Tull A185
"5/4": Gorillaz B21
"5D Fifth Dimension": The Byrds A121
"6:00": Dream Theater A175
"7/4 Shoreline": Broken Social Scene A221
"7 & 7 Is": Love A43
"7 O'Clock News/Silent Night": Simon and Garfunkel B1
"9 to 5": Dolly Parton A43, A193
"10:45, Amsterdam Conversations": Funeral for a Friend A205
"12-Bar Original": The Beatles B7
"13th, The": The Cure A99
"15 Step": Radiohead **A169**, A206, A221
"19th Nervous Breakdown": The Rolling Stones A107, B8
"20th Century Boy": T. Rex A83, **A86**
"21st-Century Schizoid Man": King Crimson A99, **A152**, A185, B20, B21
"22": Leadbelly A240
"25 or 6 to 4": Chicago **B24**, A214
"26 Miles (Santa Catalina)": The Four Preps A97
"40": U2 A89
"43% Burnt": Dillinger Escape Plan **A203**
"44 Blues": Roosevelt Sykes **B26**
"46 and 2": Tool A205
"50 Ways to Leave Your Lover": Paul Simon A93, **A150**, B1
"59th Street Bridge Song (Feelin' Groovy), The": Simon and Garfunkel A93, B1

"96 Tears": ? And the Mysterians B8
"97 Bonnie and Clyde": Tori Amos A47; Eminem A47
"99 1/2 Won't Do": Wilson Pickett B8
"99 in the Shade": Bon Jovi A185
"99 Problems": Jay-Z B31
"100 Miles and Runnin'": N.W.A. **A2**
"1 2 3": Len Barry A95
"125th Street Congress": Weather Report A261
"300 M.P.H. Torrential Downpour Blues": White Stripes, The **A148**
"409": The Beach Boys A109, B15
"1000 Stars": Big Country A185, A187, B20
"1000 Umbrellas": XTC B20
"1983": Jimi Hendrix B3
"1952 Vincent Black Lightning": Richard Thompson B21
"1983 (A Merman I Should Turn to Be)" B3; Jimi Hendrix A17
"1984": David Bowie A19, B20
"1999": Prince A35, A80, A247
"2000 Light Years From Home": The Rolling Stones A99, B29
"2112": Rush **A28**

"Abacab": Genesis A55
"Abaddon's Bolero": Emerson, Lake, and Palmer A139
"A.B.C.'s of the U.S.A." A145
"ABC": The Jackson Five A232
"Abie Cohen" A168
"Abie Sings an Irish Song" **A168**
"About a Girl": Nirvana **A177**
"About to Rain *see* "(See the Sky) About to Rain"
"About You": Teenage Fanclub B20
"Abracadabra": Steve Miller Band A185

125

Song Index

"Absolute Beginners": The Jam A185, B20
"Absolutely Sweet Marie": Bob Dylan A121
"Ac-Cent-Tchu-Ate the Positive": B12, **B30**; Bing Crosby B4
"Accept Yourself": The Smiths A36
"Accidents Will Happen": Elvis Costello and the Attractions A185, B4
"Ace in the Hole" B10; Paul Simon A93, B1
"Achilles Last Stand": Led Zeppelin A185, A269
"Acorn Stomp" A145
"Acrobat": U2 A103
"Across the Night": Silverchair A205
"Across the Universe": The Beatles **A63**, A96, A98, B7, B8, **B18**, B20; Roger Waters A198
"Action": Sweet A43
"Act Naturally": The Beatles A98, B3, B7; Buck Owens B8
"Addictive": Truth Hurts A61
"Add Some Music to your Day": The Beach Boys B15; Brian Wilson B15
"Adelaide's Lament": **A41**
"Adhesive": Stone Temple Pilots A203
"Adieu to Old England": Askew Sisters B21
"Adios Hermanos": Paul Simon B1
"Adventures Close to Home": The Slits B20
"Adventures of Grandmaster Flash on the Wheels of Steel, The": Grandmaster Flash A184
"Adventures of Greggery Peccary": Frank Zappa A11
"Aenima": Tool A205
"Africa": Toto A219
"African Waltz": Johnny Dankworth B8
"Afterglow": Genesis A185
"After Laughter (Comes Tears)": Wendy Rene A99
"Afterlife": Dream Theater A175
"After Midnight": JJ Cale A16, A40; Eric Clapton A185, B20, B24
"Afternoon Delight": Starland Vocal Band A43
"After the Ball" A120, A219, B19, B24, **B27**
"After the Day": Barclay James Harvest A185
"After the Flood": Van der Graaf Generator A185
"After the Game": The Survivors B15
"After the Gold Rush": Neil Young B6, B21
"After You, Who?" A228, **B10**, B30
"After You've Gone" A145, **B30**; The Versatile Four A227
"Against All Odds": Phil Collins A21, B24
"Agua Caliente" *see* "Sloop John B" A160

"Ain't Dat a Shame Medley" A145
"Ain't Got a Dime to My Name (Ho Ho Hum)" A14
"Ain't Got No Heart": Slade B21; Frank Zappa & the Mothers of Invention B21
"Ain't Got No Home": Clarence Frogman Henry A44
"Ain't Got No Tears Left" B12
"Ain't It Funky Now": James Brown A99
"Aint' It Grand to Be Blooming Well Dead" B16
"Ain't Misbehavin'" A145, **B30**; Louis Armstrong A119
"Ain't Nobody Gonna Take That From Me": Collin Raye A191
"Ain't Nobody Here but Us Chickens": Louis Jordan & His Tympani Five B21
"Ain't Nobody": Rufus and Chaka Khan A232, A252
"Ain't Nobody's Business": Earl Johnson and His Dixie Entertainers A240
"Ain't No More Cain": Ernest Williams **A161**
"Ain't No Mountain High Enough" A105; Marvin Gaye B21; Diana Ross A167, A185, B21, **B24**
"Ain't No Particular Way": Shania Twain A193
"Ain't No Sunshine": Bill Withers B24
"Ain't No Telling": The Jimi Hendrix Experience A185, B21
"Ain't Nuttin' but Music": D12 A146
"Ain't She Sweet": The Beatles B7, **B8**
"Ain't Talkin' 'Bout Love": Van Halen A55
"Ain't That a Kindness": Johnny Winter A185
"Ain't That a Shame" A145; Fats Domino A44, A95, A185, B8, **B24**, **B25**
"Ain't That Cute": Doris Troy B7
"Ain't That Loving You (For More Reasons Than One)": Johnnie Taylor A29
"Ain't That Peculiar": Marvin Gaye A95, A108
"Ain't That So": Roxy Music A185
"Ain't Too Proud to Beg" A105; Temptations A185
"Ain't We Got Fun" A145, B12, **B19**
"Ain't You Coming Back to Old New Hampshire, Molly?" **B27**
"Airbag": Radiohead A162
"Airplane": The Beach Boys B15
"Air That I Breathe": The Hollies B24
"Air": The Incredible String Band A112
"Aja": Steely Dan **A96**, A99
"Alabama Blues": Robert Wilkins **A239**, A240

Song Index

"Alabama Bound": Leadbelly A240; Jelly Roll Morton A240
"Alabama": Neil Young B6
"Alabammy Bound": Lonnie Donegan B8; Leadbelly A95
"Albatross": Fleetwood Mac B7
"Albuquerque": Neil Young **A88**, B6
"Al Capone": Prince Buster B20; Madness B20
"Alcen Los Manos": Sanocho A3
"Alexander" A145
"Alexander's Bagpipe Band" B30
"Alexander's Ragtime Band": A114, A168, A219, **A227**, B10, B12, B16, B19, B30
"Alfie": Joey Baron A217; Cilla Black A249, B21
"Alice Blue Gown": The Original Dixieland Jazz Band A227
"Alien Orifice": Frank Zappa **A60**
"Alison": Elvis Costello A99, A185, B4, B20, B21
"Alive and Well and Living In": Jethro Tull **B20**
"All Aboard for Broadway" B12
"All About Soul": Billy Joel A101
"All About the Benjamins": Puff Daddy B14
"All Alone" B30
"All Along the Watchtower" A19, B17; The Beatles B7; Bob Dylan **A16**, A99, A121, **B3**, B7, B8, **B21**, B32; Richie Havens B21; Jimi Hendrix A17, A101, A185, A247, **B21**, B24; U2 A193, B21
"All Apologies": Nirvana A80, A247
"All Around My Hat": Ned Corvan B19; Steeleye Span A64
"All Around the World": Jam A185
"All Around the World or the Myth of Fingerprints": Paul Simon A9
"All a Woman Needs": Joan Armatrading A136
"All Because of You" [1]: Paul Simon B1
"All Because of You" [2]: U2 A89
"All Bound Down": Haywood County Ramblers A240
"All by Myself" [1]: Eric Carmen A43, B24
"All by Myself" [2]: Big Bill Broonzy **B21**
"All by Myself" [3] A145
"All by Myself" [4] B30
"All Caps": Madvillain **A2**
"All Coons Look Alike to Me" A145
"All Day and All of the Night": The Kinks **A55**, **A97**, A99, A107, A121, **A155**, B4, B8, B20, B21
"All Dressed Up for School": The Beach Boys A160, B15
"Allergies": Paul Simon A93, B1

"Alley Oop": The Beach Boys B15; The Hollywood Argyles B15; Rory Storm and the Hurricanes B8
"All for Love": The Beatles B7
"All for the Best" A182
"All Good Naysayers, Speak Up! Or Forever Hold Your Peace!": Sufjan Stevens A221
"All Hail the Weed King": Guided By Voices A243
"Alligator": Grateful Dead A171, B17
"All I Have to Do Is Dream" **A133**, B8; The Everly Brothers A75, A76, A94, A97, A247, A270, B15, B24
"All I Know": Art Garfunkel A185
"All in a Mouse's Night": Genesis A185
"All I Need Is a Miracle": Mike + The Mechanics A269
"All I Need": Radiohead A205, **A206**
"All in Fun" **B30**
"All in the Game": Tommy Edwards A44
"All I Really Want to Do": Byrd A121, A185, B21; Bob Dylan B7
"All Is Well": Chicago B24
"All I've Got to Do": The Beatles A91, A98, A99, **A100**, **A194**, B7, **B8**, **B18**
"All I Wanna Do" [1]: Sheryl Crow **A83**
"All I Wanna Do" [2]: The Beach Boys B15
"All I Want" [1]: Gary Moore A185
"All I Want" [2]: Joni Mitchell **A260**
"All Mine": Portishead **A97**
"All My Life" [1]: Uriah Heep A185
"All My Life" [2]: Foo Fighters B21
"All My Love Belongs to You": Bullmoose Jackson A53
"All My Loving": The Beatles **A69**, A98, B3, B7, **B8**, B24
"All My Tomorrows" A14
"All My Trials": Joan Baez B8
"All Night Long (All Night)": Lionel Richie B24
"All of a Sudden My Heart Sings": Kathy Kirby B21
"All of Me" B12; Louis Armstrong **A119**
"All of My Friends Were There": The Kinks B20
"All of My Life": Phil Collins A250
"All of You" **A113**; Bobby Darin B21
"All or Nothing": Small Faces B21
"All or Nothing at All" A147
"All Over Again": The Beatles B8
"All Over Me": Blake Shelton A191
"All Revved Up & No Place to Go": Meat Loaf A185

"All Right Now": Free A185
"All She'd Say was 'Umh Hum' " A145
"All She Gets From the Iceman Is Ice" A145
"All Shook Up": Elvis Presley A44, A97, A99, B8, **B19**, B21, **B25**
"All Summer Long": The Beach Boys A160, B15; Brian Wilson B15
"All the Love in the World": The Corrs A193
"All the Love of the Universe": Santana A185
"All the Things She Said": t.A.T.u. **A153**
"All the Things You Are" **A114**, **A133**, **A147**, A167, A168, **A263**, **B10**, **B16**, **B19**, **B30**; Ann Lenner, Carrol Gibbons, and the Savoy Orpheans B21
"All the Way" A14, B10; Frank Sinatra A97
"All the Way from America": Joan Armatrading A136
"All the Young Dudes": Mott the Hoople A185, **B21**
"All Things Must Pass": The Beatles B7; George Harrison A185, **B3**, B7
"All This and Heaven Too" **B30**
"All This and More": Wedding Present A185
"All Those Years Ago": George Harrison B7
"All Through The Night" **B30**
"All Together Now": The Beatles B7, B8
"All You Need Is Cash": The Rutles B7
"All You Need Is Love": The Beatles A17, A43, **A63**, A75, A92, A99, A100, A156, A185, A195, A198, A221, **A234**, A259, B7, B8, **B18**, B20, B21, B29
"All Your Love": Willie Dixon A19
"Alma Mater": Alice Cooper A99
"Almost Blue": Elvis Costello B4
"Almost Grown": The Beatles B8; Chuck Berry A95, **B19**
"Alone Again Or": Love A43
"Alone Together" **B10**, **B30**
"Along Came Jones": The Coasters A77
"Along Comes Mary": The Association A43, A99
"Alpha Beta Gaga": Air A221
"Alpine Blues" A266
"Already Gone": The Eagles A173, A185, B24
"Already One": Neil Young B6
"Alright, Okay, You Win": Peggy Lee B8
"Alright": Janet Jackson B24
"Also Sprach Zarathustra": Deodato **A101**, B24
"Althea": Grateful Dead B17
"Altruist and the Needy Case, The": Dory Previn B21

"Always" B30
"Always and Only": The Beatles B8
"Always Late With Your Kisses": Lefty Frizzell A189
"Always on My Mind": The Pet Shop Boys A174
"Always Something There to Remind Me": Naked Eyes **A248**, **A250**
"Always Treat Her Like a Baby" B30
"Always True to You in My Fashion" B10
"Amado Mio" B12
"Amazing": David Bowie B20
"Amazing Grace" **B19**, **B23**, B27; Blind Boys of Alabama B20; Aretha Franklin **A161**, B21; Daniel Lanois B32
"Amazing Journey": The Who A99
"Ambulance Blues": Neil Young **A88**, B6
"Amelia": Joni Mitchell A260
"Amen Brother": The Winstons A104, **B5**
"America, I Love You" A147
"America Drinks and Goes Home": Jean-Luc Ponty A11; The Mothers of Invention A12
"American, The": Simple Minds A185
"American Beauty Rose" B30
"American Boy Soldier": Edgar Broughton Band B21
"American Cake Walk" A145
"American Fantasie" A145
"American in Paris, An" B30
"American Metaphysical Circus, The": The united States of America **A138**
"American Pie": Don McLean **A86**, **A225**, B24
"American Psycho": D12 A146
"American Trilogy": Mickey Newbury B21; Elvis Presley B21
"American Tune" B12; Paul Simon A93, A219, B1
"American Way of Love": The United States of America A138
"American Woman": Guess Who, The **A101**
"America": Simon and Garfunkel A105, A185, B1; Yes A71
"Am I Blue?" B12, **B19**, **B30**
"Am I Here?": Johnny Winter A185
"Am I The Man?": Jackie Wilson B25
"Am I Wry": Mew A205
"Amnesia": Datblygy A123
"Amnesia Vivace": The Mothers of Invention A11, A12
"Among My Souvenirs" B12
"Amos 'n' Andy" A145

Song Index

"Amusement Parks U.S.A.": The Beach Boys B15
"Anarchy in the U.K.": The Sex Pistols A80, A99, A247, B20, B21, B32
"Anastasia" B12
"Ancient, The": Yes **A223**
"And Her Daddy's a Millionaire": The Iveys B7
"And I Am All Alone" B30
"And I Love Her [Him]": The Beatles **A63**, A93, A98, A99, **A107**, A107, A185, **A194**, **A253**, B4, B7, **B8**, B20, B24; Esther Phillips A95
"Andrew Bardeen" B27
"And Russia Is Her Name" B12
"And She Was": Talking Heads **A16**, A99
"And So It Goes": Billy Joel B21
"And the Angels Sing" B12
"And the Dance Goes On": Mission A185
"And the Sun Will Shine": Paul Jones B7
"And the Wind Cries Mary": Jimi Hendrix A257
"And Through the Wire": Peter Gabriel A185
"And When I Die": Blood, Sweat and Tears A101
"Andy": Frank Zappa **A60**
"And You and I": Yes A71, **A166**, B20
"And Your Bird Can Sing": The Beatles A95, A185, **A198**, A259, **B7**, B8, B18
"And Your Dream Comes True": The Beach Boys B15
"Andy Warhol": David Bowie A185
"Angel" [1]: Aretha Franklin A43
"Angel" [2]: Natasha Bedingfield A219
"Angel" [3]: Aerosmith B24
"Angela": Toto A185
"Angel Baby": The Beatles B8; Rosie and the Originals **B25**
"Angelene": PJ Harvey A223
"Angel Eyes" [1]: Roxy Music A185
"Angel Eyes" [2] B30
"Angel in the Snow": Elliot Smith A221
"Angelo": Brotherhood of Man A235
"Angel of Mine": Eternal B21
"Angel Say No": Tommy Tutone A250
"Angels": Robbie Williams B21
"(The Angels Wanna Wear My) Red Shoes": Elvis Costello A185, B4
"Angels With Dirty Faces": Los Lobos B32
"Angels Would Fall": Melissa Etheridge A219
"Anger": Marvin Gaye A110
"Angie": The Rolling Stones A185, B24
"Angle Park": Big Country A185
"Animal": Def Leppard A185, B21

"Animal Nitrate": Suede B21
"Anji": Simon and Garfunkel B1
"Anna (Go to Him)": Arthur Alexander A95; The Beatles A98, B8
"Anna Lee, the Healer": The Beach Boys B7, B15
"Anna Stasia": Prince A79, **A126**, B13
"Annie": Elastica B21
"Anniversary Blue Yodel": Jimmie Rodgers A266
"Anniversary Song" B12
"Another Beatles Christmas Record": The Beatles B8
"Another Brick in the Wall": Pink Floyd **A16**, A103, A167, A185
"Another Dawn Is Breaking": Negasphere A149
"Another Day": Paul McCartney B7
"Another Day in Paradise": Phil Collins A185
"Another Galaxy": Paul Simon B1
"Another Girl": The Beatles A92, A98, **A254**, **A259**, B7, B8
"Another Man Done Gone" B27
"Another Morning": The Moody Blues A101
"Another Night Alone" B30
"Another One Bites the Dust": Queen A185
"Another Op'nin', Another Show" **B30**
"Another Satellite": XTC A185
"Another Saturday Night": Sam Cooke A108
"Another Ticket": Eric Clapton A185
"Another Time, Another Place": U2 A89, B21
"Anthem": Rush A28
"Anthrax": Gang of Four B21
"Anticipation": Carly Simon A99, **B24**
"Ant Music": Adam & Ants A185
"Anvil Chorus, The" A145
"Any Colour You Like": Pink Floyd A185, A199, B29
"Anyday": Derek & Dominos A185
"Any Kind of Pain": Frank Zappa A59
"Any King's Shilling": Elvis Costello B20
"Any Major Dude Will Tell You": Steely Dan A96
"Any Man of Mine": Shania Twain A193
"Any Old Place With You" B30
"Any Old Time" A145; Jimmie Rodgers A266
"Anyone Can Play Guitar": Radiohead A162
"Anyone Who Had a Heart": Shirley Bassey B8
"Any Place I Hang My Hat Is Home" B30
"Any Rags" A145
"Anything Goes" **B30**
"Anything You Can Do" B30

"Any Time at All": The Beatles A98, **A100**, A185, B7, B8, **B18**
"Any Time of the Year" B12
"Anyway Anyhow Anywhere": Who A185, B8, **B19**, B21
"Anyway You Want It": Dave Clark Five A107
"AOS": Yoko Ono **B7**
"Apache Dropout": Edgar Broughton Band B21
"Apache": The Beatles **B8**; The Incredible Bongo Band B31
"Aperçu": Kansas A72
"Apocalypse in 9/8": Genesis A221, **A232**
"Apples and Oranges": Pink Floyd **A198**
"Apple Scruffs": George Harrison A185, B18
"April Come She Will": Paul Simon B1; Simon and Garfunkel B7
"April in Paris" **A114, B10, B30**
"April Love": Pat Boone A97
"April Showers" B12, **B19**, B30
"Aqua Boogie (A psychoalphadiscobetabioaquadoloop)": Parliament A269
"Aqualung": Jethro Tull **A4**, A188, **B20**, B21
"Aquarela do Brasil" A211
"Arabian Night": Siouxsie & Banshees A185
"Are 'Friends' Electric": Tubeway Army A24, A39, B20
"Aren't You Glad": The Beach Boys B15
"Aren't You Glad You're You" A14, B10
"Are You Coming": Madness A185
"Are You Experienced?": The Jimi Hendrix Experience A17, B29, **A257**, A261
"Are You Lonesome Tonight": The Beatles B8; Elvis Presley A99, A259
"Are You Sincere": Andy Williams A97, B15
"Armageddon It": Def Leppard A185
"Armful of You, An" **B30**
"Armistice Day": Paul Simon B1
"Arms of Love": T'Pau A185
"Army of Me": Björk A97, B21
"Arnold Layne": Pink Floyd **A198**, B29
"Around the Universe in 80 Days": Klaatu A149
"Around the World": Daft Punk A205
"Arrangement, The": Joni Mitchell **A260**
"Arroz con Pollo": Bad Boy Orchestra A3
"Ars Moriendi": Mr. Bungle A163
"Artificial Energy": The Byrds B7, B8
"Artistry in Rhythm": B12; Stan Kenton B4

"Artists Only": Talking Heads A185
"Art of Dying, The": George Harrison A185, B7, B18, B21
"As Does the Sun": Look Blue Go Purple **A149**
"Asforteri 25": Caravan **A166**
"As Hard as It Is": Fine Young Cannibals A185, B20
"Ash Can Blues": Cliff Carlisle A240, A266
"Ashes in Your Mouth": Megadeth A97
"Ashes to Ashes": David Bowie A185, **A186**, B20
"As I Am": Dream Theater A175
"As I Lay Me Down": Sophie B. Hawkins A167
"Ask Me Now": Thelonius Monk A96
"Ask Me Why": The Beatles A76, A98, A195, B7, B8, B24
"Ask the Lonely": The Four Tops A95, A108
"As Long as I Live" B10, B30
"As Long as There's an Apple Tree" B3
"As Old as You're Young": Gentle Giant **A166**
"Aspirations": Gentle Giant A185
"As Sure as Eggs Is Eggs (Aching Men's Feet)": Genesis A232
"As Tears Go By": Marianne Faithfull A107, B8; The Rolling Stones A70, A107, A142, B32
"Astral Traveller": Yes B20
"Astral Weeks": Van Morrison B7, B20
"Astrilly": Ned Corvan B19
"Astronomy Domine": Pink Floyd A67, A198, A257, B19, B20, **B29**
"Asylum": Supertramp A185
"As You Said": Cream B7, B20
"At a Georgia Camp Meeting": A145, **B30**
"At Home He's a Tourist": Gang of Four B20
"Atlanta Blues": Louis Armstrong A119
"Atlanta Bound": Gene Autry A240
"Atlantic City": Bruce Springsteen B32
"Atlantis": Donovan B7
"Atlas": Battles A221
"At Last" B12, **B30**
"At Last (I Found a Love)": Marvin Gaye A110
"At Long Last Love" **A113, B10**, B30
"At My Window": The Beach Boys B15
"Atom Heart Mother": Pink Floyd A198, B20
"Atomic": Blondie A185, B20
"Atomic Dog": George Clinton A261, **B31**
"At Seventeen": Janis Ian A185
"At Sundown" B10, **B30**
"At The Devil's Ball" B30

Song Index

"At the Hop": Danny and the Juniors A44, A97, A185, B24
"At the Scene": Dave Clark Five A107
"At the Yiddish Wedding Jubilee" B12
"At the Yiddisher Ball" B12
"At the Zoo": Simon and Garfunkel A93, B1
"Attics of My Life": Grateful Dead B17
"Audio Verité": echolyn A72
"Auld Lang Syne" B30; The Beach Boys B15; The Beatles B7, B8; Brian Wilson B15
"Aunt Hagar's Blues" B12
"Autumn Almanac": Kinks A185
"Autumn in New York" B10, **B11**, **B30**
"Autumn Leaves" ["Les Feuilles Mortes"] **A133**, B7, B12
"Avalon" B12
"Ave Maria": Gracie Fields A227
"Aw, Enoch Powell": The Beatles B7
"Awaiting on You All": The Beatles B3; George Harrison A185
"Awake": Audrye Sessions A169
"Awaken": Yes A71, A166, A188, **A207**
"Away from the Numbers": Jam A185
"Away Out on the Mountain": Jimmie Rodgers **A266**
"Awful, Beautiful Life": Darryl Worley A191
"Axel F": Crazy Frog B21
"Axel Öman" **B25**
"Axis: Bold as Love": Jimi Hendrix A17
"Aybe Sea": Frank Zappa **A60**

"Baba O'Riley": The Who A43, A141, A182, **A246**, B4, **B24**
"Babbitt and the Bromide, The" B12
"Babe I'm Gonna Leave You": Joan Baez **A131**; Led Zeppelin A204, B7, B20
"Babes in the Wood, The" B27
"Babe": Styx A250, B24
"Baby, Baby, All The Time" **B30**
"Baby, I'm for Real": The Originals **A110**
"Baby, I Need your Loving" A95; The Four Tops **A84**
"Baby, It's Cold Outside" **B30**
"Baby, Let Me Hold Your Hand": Professor Longhair A238
"Baby, Won't You Please Come Home" **B30**
"Baby, You're a Rich Man": The Beatles A195, A198
"Baby Blue": The Beatles B8

"Baby Can Dance": David Bowie **B20**
"B-A-B-Y": Carla Thomas A29, **A29**
"Baby Doll": Sons of the Pioneers B21
"Baby Don't You Do It": Marvin Gaye **A106**, **A108**
"Baby Driver": Simon and Garfunkel A93, A185, B1
"Baby Face": The Savoy Orpheans A227
"Babyface": U2 A89, **B19**
"Baby Get Lost": Billie Holiday B4
"(Baby) Hully Gully": The Beach Boys B15; The Olympics A95, B8, B15
"Baby I Don't Care": Transvision Vamp A185
"Baby I Got the Death Rattle": Los Campecinos! A205
"Baby I Love You": Aretha Franklin A99
"Baby I'm a-Want You": Bread A143
"Baby I'm Yours": Barbara Lewis **A95**
"Baby I Need Your Loving": The Four Tops A97, A99, **A106**, **A108**
"Baby It's You": The Beatles A98, A259, **B8**; The Shirelles A95, A259, B15
"Baby Let's Play House": Elvis Presley A99, B19, B32; The Quarrymen B8
"Baby Let's Wait": The Young Rascals A110
"Baby Let Your Hair Grow Long": Brian Wilson B15
"Babylon": Don McLean A43
"Babylon Sisters": Steely Dan A99, A250
"Baby Love": Supremes A95, **A108**, A185, B21
"Baby Make It Soon": Marmalade A185
"Baby Now That I've Found You": Foundations A185
". . . Baby One More Time": Britney Spears A153
"Baby Please Don't Go": Big Joe Williams A123, A210; MC5 A210; Them A210, B21
"Baby's in Black": The Beatles **A91**, A98, B7, B8, B18
"Baby's Request": Paul McCartney and Wings A99
"Baby Stop Crying": Bob Dylan **A101**, A180
"Baby Take a Bow": Adam Faith B8
"Baby Talk" B15
"Baby What You Want Me to Do": Bob and Bobby B15; Jimmy Reed B15
"Baby You're a Rich Man": The Beatles A92, A98, B7, B8, B18
"Bachelor Boy": Cliff Richard A259

"Back Door Ladies": Jethro Tull A188
"Backdoor Love Affair": Z.Z. Top A185
"Back Door Man": The Doors A210
"Backdrifts": Radiohead **A169**
"Back Home Again": John Denver **A7**
"Back Home": The Beach Boys B15; Brian Wilson B15
"Back in Black": AC/DC **A16**, A80, A246, A247, A247, A247, A250
"Back in My Arms Again": The Supremes A95, A99, **A106, A108**, B8
"Back in NYC": Genesis A142, A232
"Back in the High Life": Steve Winwood A250, B24
"Back in the U.S.A.": Chuck Berry A254, B7, B24
"Back in the U.S.S.R.": The Beatles A16, A17, A98, A247, **A254**, B7, B8, B18, B24, B32
"Back Off Boogaloo": Ringo Starr B7
"Back of Love": Echo & The Bunnymen A185
"Back Seat of My Car": The Beatles B7; Paul and Linda McCartney B18
"Backstairs": Clannad **A186**
"Back Street" A95
"Backstreet": Edwin Starr A95
"Back to Back" [1]: The Chariot **A203, A204**
"Back to Back" [2] B30
"Back to Paradise": .38 Special A250
"Back to the Old House": The Smiths A36
"Back Where You Belong": .38 Special A250
"Backyard Boogie": Mack 10 B14
"Bad" [1]: U2 A7, A89
"Bad" [2]: Michael Jackson A35
"Bad, Bad, Leroy Brown" A97; Jim Croce A16, A99, **B24**
"Bad Bad Boy": Nazareth A185
"Bad Boy": The Beatles A98, A254, B3, B7, **B8**; Eric Clapton A185; Larry Williams A95
"Badge": Cream B3, B7
"Bad in Every Man, The" B30
"Bad Medicine": Bon Jovi A185
"Bad Moon Rising": Creedence Clearwater Revival A185, **B3, B24**
"Bad Penny Blues": The Humphrey Lyttleton Band B7
"Bad Romance": Lady Gaga **A236**
"Bad Sneakers": Steely Dan A99
"Bad to Me": The Beatles B4, **B8**; Billy J. Kramer and the Dakotas A107

"Bad to the Bone": George Thorogood A55
"Badlands": Bruce Springsteen A99
"Bagdad" A145
"Bag Full of Money": Roger McGuinn A121
"Baggy Trousers": Madness A185
"Baile Conmigo": Tony Rohr **A115**
"Baker Man, The": The Beach Boys B15
"Baker St. Muse": Jethro Tull B20
"Baker Street": Gerry Rafferty A185
"Bake That Matza Pie" B12
"Balada Sarpelui": Gheorghe Zamfir B25
"Bali Hai" B16
"Ballad of a Thin Man": Bob Dylan A99, A216, **A264**, B7
"Ballad of El Dorado, The" B12
"Ballad of Henry Darger, The": Natalie Merchant B21
"Ballad of Hollis Brown, The": Bob Dylan A180, A216, **B3**, B27
"Ballad of John and Yoko, The": Beatles, The
"Ballad of John and Yoko, The": The Beatles A17, A43, A98, A101, A185, A195, A250, B7, B8, B18
"Ballad of Ole' Betsy": The Beach Boys B15
"Ballad of Sir Frankie Crisp (Let It Roll)": George Harrison A185, B7, B18
"Ballad of the Green Berets, The": SSgt Barry Sadler B7, B25
"Ballad of the Social Director, The" B12
"Ballad of You & Me & Pooneil, The": Jefferson Airplane B3
"Ball and Chain": Janis Joplin B20, B21
"Ballet for a Rainy Day": XTC A185
"Ballin' the Jack" **A147**, B30
"Ball of Confusion (That's What the World Is Today)": The Temptations A144
"Ballroom Blitz": The Sweet **A85**
"Baltimore, Md., That's The Only Doctor for Me" B30
"Baltimore" [1]: Randy Newman **A264**
"Baltimore" [2]: Tori Amos A46
"Baltimore Oriole" B10, B12, **B30**
"Baltimore to Washington": Woody Guthrie A240
"Bamalong Blues": Jim Baxter **A240**
"Bambalina" B30
"Banana Boat Song, The" A238, B27; The Tarriers A97

Song Index

"Bananas": Queen Latifah B14
"Banda, A": Chico Buarque A211
"Band Contest, A" A145
"Bandiera Rossa" A242
"Bandit Cole Younger": Edward L. Crain **A240**
"Bandit": Neil Young B6
"Band on the Run": Paul McCartney and Wings A182, B7, B24
"Band Played On, The" B12, **B27**
"Band Played Waltzing Matilda, The": The Pogues B20
"Banging the Door": Public Image Ltd B20
"Banks of Fordie, The" **B27**
"Banks of the Newfoundland" **B24**
"Banks of the Ohio, The": Neil Young B6
"Banquet": Joni Mitchell A260
"Banshee Beat": Animal Collective **A204**
"Banty Rooster Blues": Charley Patton **B26**
"Barangrill": Joni Mitchell A260
"Barbara Allen" **B27**
"Barbara Ann": The Beach Boys A43, A185, B15, B24; The Regents B15; Brian Wilson B15
"Barbara Ellen" A264
"Barbara Song" B12
"Barbeque Blues": Barbeque Bob **B26**
"Barely Breathing": Duncan Sheik B24
"Bargain": The Who **A247**
"Bar Mitzvah Song" B12
"Barnyard": The Beach Boys B15; Brian Wilson B15
"Barracuda": Heart **A16**, **A247**
"Barrytown": Steely Dan **A96**, A99
"Barstool Blues": Neil Young **A33**, B6
"Basin Street Blues" B12, **B16**
"Basketball": Kurtis Blow **A2**
"Basket Case": Green Day B21
"Bastard": Ben Folds **A221**
"Bastille Day": Rush A28
"Bat Out of Hell": Meat Loaf A185
"Batteries Not Included": Jethro Tull A185, A188
"Battle, The": Blood, Sweat and Tears B3
"Battle of Evermore, The": Led Zeppelin **A149**, B20
"Battle of Glass Tears, The": King Crimson A152
"Battle of New Orleans": Lonnie Donegan B21
"Battleship of Maine, The": Red Patterson's Piedmont Log Rollers **A240**

"Beach Baby": First Class A141
"Beach Boy Stomp" ["Karate"]: The Beach Boys B15
"Beach Girl": The Nodaens B15
"Be a Child" **A209**
"Beachwood 4–5789": The Marvelettes A110
"Bearing Down": echolyn A72
"Beat, The": Elvis Costello and the Attractions A185, B4
"Beat Goes On, The": Orbit A43
"Beat It": Michael Jackson **A35**, **A222**, B28, B32
"Beatrice from Baltimore": The Beach Boys B15
"Beat Surrender": Jam A185
"Beautiful Boy": John Lennon B7
"Beautiful Dreamer" B30; The Beatles B8; Roy Orbison A270
"Beautiful Love" **A224**
"Beautiful Morning, A": The Rascals A101, B3
"Beautiful Ohio" B30
"Beautiful": Paul Simon B1
"Beautiful Song, A": Nazz B7
"Beauty Queen": Roxy Music A185
"Be-Bop-A-Lula": The Quarrymen B7; Gene Vincent A43, A44, A185, A247, B8
"Be-Bop Baby": Ricky Nelson A97
"Be-Bop Tango, The": Frank Zappa A27
"Be Careful, It's My Heart" B30
"Because" [1]: Dave Clark Five A43, A107
"Because" [2]: The Beatles A74, **A92**, A98, **A100**, A101, **A116**, A149, A156, **A234**, B7, B8, **B18**
"Because I Love You" A13
"Because of You": 98 Degrees B24
"Because the Night": Patti Smith **A16**
"Because You Loved Me": Celine Dion A167
"Because You're Beautiful" **A120**
"Beck's Bolero": Jeff Beck A185
"Becky's Got a Job in a Musical Show" **A168**
"Be Cool": Joni Mitchell A260
"Bedelia" A145, B12
"Bed on the Floor": Woody Guthrie A240
"Bed Spring Blues": Blind Lemon Jefferson A240
"Bed's Too Big Without You, The": The Police **A235**
"Bedtime Stories": Madonna **B13**
"Been All Around This World": The Grateful Dead A99
"Been Around the World": Puff Daddy and the Family A99, A159

"Beep Beep": The Playmates A93, A97; Louis Prima **B25**
"Beer Drinkers & Hell Raisers": Z.Z. Top A185
"Beese However": However **A72**
"Beeswing": Richard Thompson B20, B21
"Before the Bells Did Ring": Ned Corvan B19
"Begat, The" B30
"Beggar Man, The" **B27**
"Beggin Back": Blind Lemon Jefferson A240
"Beginning, A": The Beatles B7, B8
"Beginning of the End": The Beach Boys B15
"Beginnings": Chicago A214, B3, B7
"Beginning to See the Light": The Velvet Underground B32
"Begin the Beguine" A168, A228, B10, B12, B30; The Beatles B8
"Be Here in the Morning": The Beach Boys A125, B15
"Behind My Camel": Andy Summers A235
"Behind the Lines": Phil Collins A185
"Behind the Locked Door": George Harrison B18
"Behind These Hazel Eyes": Kelly Clarkson A219
"Behind the Sun": Red Hot Chili Peppers A99
"Being for the Benefit of Mr. Kite!": The Beatles A17, A90, A98, A99, A100, A138, A163, A167, **A253**, B7, B8, B18, **B20**, B24, B29
"Being with the One You Love": Brian Wilson B15
"Be Kind to a Man When He's Down": North Carolina Ridge Runners A240
"Belfast Child": Simple Minds A185
"Believe": Cher A24
"Believe It or Not": Grateful Dead B17
"Believe Me, Baby, I Lied": Trisha Yearwood A189
"Believe What You Say": Ricky Nelson A97
"Bell-Bottom Blues": Derek & Dominos A185
"Belles of Paris": The Beach Boys B15
"Bells, The": Bobby Taylor & The Vancouvers **A110**
"Bells for Her": Tori Amos **A51**
"Bells of Rhymney, The": The Byrds A121, A185, **B8**
"Bells of St. Mary's": Bing Crosby B4
"Belt": Say Anything A205
"Belz" B12

"Be My Baby": The Ronettes A36, A74, **A75**, A77, A80, A160, A247, B7, B32; Brian Wilson B15
"Be My Baby Tonight": John Michael Montgomery A191
"Be My Girl–Sally": The Police A235
"Ben Dewberry's Final Run": Jimmie Rodgers A266
"Bend Me Shape Me": Amen Corner B20, B21
"Bends, The": Radiohead A162
"Beneath a Festering Moon": Guided By Voices **A243**
"Bennie and the Jets": Elton John A43, A247
"Benny Bloom" A168
"Be Not Too Hard": Manfred Mann's Earth band **A182**
"Ben's Song": Sarah McLachlan **A154**
"Be Our Guest" **A202**
"Bermuda Shorts": The Delroys B15
"Bernadette" [1]: Four Tops A185
"Bernadette" [2]: Paul Simon B1
"Bernie's Tune" B12
"Besame Mucho" B12; The Beatles B7; The Coasters A95; Upton Green **B8**
"Bess, You Is My Woman Now" B12
"Best, The": Tina Turner A185, B24
"Best Day, The": George Strait A191
"Best Deceptions, The": Dashboard Confessional A205
"Be Still": The Beach Boys B7, B15
"Best Little Whorehouse in Texas": Too Much Trouble A146
"Best of My Love": The Eagles A173
"Best of Times, The": Dream Theater A175
"Best Thing for You, The" B12, B30
"Be Tender with Me Baby": Tina Turner A185
"Be True to Your School": The Beach Boys A109, B15; Toby Keith B15
"Bette Davis Eyes": Kim Carnes A43
"Better Be Good To Me" **B30**
"Better Luck Next Time" B30; The Beatles B8
"Better Than It Was": Fastball A99
"Between the Devil and the Deep Blue Sea" B10, **B30**; Louis Armstrong A119
"Between the Lines": T'Pau A185
"Beware of Darkness": George Harrison A185, B18, **B21**
"Be What You See": Paul McCartney B7
"Bewildered": James Brown A238, B4

Song Index

"Bewitched" **B10**, B30
"Bewlay Brothers, The": David Bowie A185, B20
"Beyond Belief": Elvis Costello **A124**
"Beyond Love": Negasphere **A149**
"Beyond the Blue Horizon" B10
"Beyond the Sea" ["La Mer"]: Bobby Darin A99, A123
"Beyond This Life": Dream Theater A175
"Bib Bop": Wings B18
"Bicycle Race": Queen A185, B21
"Biddle Street Blues": Henry Spaulding **B26**
"Bidin' My Time" B30
"Big Bad John": Jimmy Dean A99
"Big Beat, The" [1]: Fats Domino **B25**
"Big Beat, The" [2]: Billy Squier B31
"Big Bird": Eddie Floyd A29
"Big Black Woman Blues": Cream A132
"Big Boss Man" B17
"Big Bottom": Spinal Tap A70
"Big Boy Pete" B17
"Big Boys": Elvis Costello A185
"Big Bright Green Pleasure Machine, The": Simon and Garfunkel B1, B3
"Big Butter and Egg Man": Louis Armstrong and His Hot Five, Featuring May Alix B21
"Big Chief Blues": Furry Lewis B9
"Big Chief DeSoto" A145
"Big Chief Dynamite" B12
"Big City Blues" A145
"Big Country, The": Talking Heads A185
"Big Day": XTC B20
"Big Fat Woman": Leadbelly A240
"Big Fight, The": Stars A205
"Big Girl Now": Bob Dylan B21
"Big Girls Don't Cry": The Four Seasons A99, B15, B21
"Big Hunk O' Love": Elvis Presley A44
"Big Leg Blues": Hurt, Mississippi John B9
"Big Leg Emma": The Mothers of Invention A27
"Big-Legged Woman": Jerry Lee Lewis B7
"Big Love": Fleetwood Mac A185
"Big Man": The Four Preps A97
"Big Man in Town": The Four Freshmen A160
"Big Noise From Winnetka" B30
"Big Poppa": Notorious B.I.G. B31
"Big Railroad Blues" B17
"Big Shot": Billy Joel A250

"Big Sky": Hüsker Dü A210
"Big Star": Reel Big Fish A205
"Big Swifty": The Mothers A27
"Big Time": Neil Young B6
"Big Yellow Taxi": Joni Mitchell A123, **A260**, B21; see also "Got 'Til It's Gone"
"Bike": Pink Floyd **A198, B20**
"Biko": Peter Gabriel A185, B25
"Bill" B10, B30
"Bill and Ben": The Beatles B8
"Bill Bailey" A145, **B27**, **B30**
"Billie Jean": Michael Jackson A39, A43, A80, A85, A99, A247, A250, **A250**, B24
"Billy Budd": Morrissey B13
"Billy Hunt": Jam A185
"Billy Lyons and Stack O'Lee": Furry Lewis A240
"Billy's Blues": The Beatles B7
"Billy's Bonesthe": The Pogues B20
"Billy the Mountain": Mothers of Invention, The A11
"Bim-Bom": João Gilberto A211
"Bimini Bay" A145
"Bingo Flamingo": Röda Kapellet B25
"Biology": Girls Aloud B21
"Bird Dog": The Everly Brothers A97, A185, B15
"Birdhouse in Your Soul": They Might Be Giants A185
"Bird in a Gilded Cage, A" A219
"Bird in Flight": Toyah A185
"Birdland": Patti Smith A269
"Bird Nest Bound": Charley Patton A240
"Birds, The": Peter Hammill A185
"Birds": Neil Young **B6**
"Birds of Fire": Mahavishnu Orchestra A221
"Bird Song": Grateful Dead B17
"Birmingham Blues": Electric Light Orchestra A185
"Birmingham Boys, The" **B27**
"Birth": John Oswald A24
"Birthday": The Beatles A24, A98, A167, B7, B8, B18
"Bite the Bullet": Neil Young B6
"Bits and Pieces": Dave Clark Five A107, A185, B8, B16
"Bitters End": Roxy Music A185, B20, B21
"Bittersweet Samba": Herb Alpert and the Tijuana Brass A39
"Bitter Sweet Symphony": Verve, The A80, A247

"Bizarre Love Triangle": New Order A80, A247
"Black and Blue" B12
"Black and White": Greyhound B21
"Black Beauty" A145
"Blackberry Way": Move, The A185, B21
"Blackberry Winter" **A209**
"Blackbird": The Beatles **A63**, **A63**, A98, A221, A254, B7, B8, **B18**
"Black Bottom, The" B30
"Black Bottom Stomp" A145, B9
"Black Cat": Gentle Giant A166
"Black Cow": Steely Dan **A96**, A99
"Black Crow": Joni Mitchell A260
"Black Dog": Led Zeppelin A101
"Blackened": Metallica A24, B21
"Blackest Eyes": Porcupine Tree B21
"Black Eyes, Blue Tears": Shania Twain A193
"Black Ghost": Harry Pussy A210
"Black Is Black": Los Bravos A43
"Black": John Oswald A24
"Blackleg Miner, The": Louis Killen A64; Steeleye Span A64
"Black Magic Woman": Fleetwod Mac **A186**, **B21**; Santana B3
"Black Mountain Side": Led Zeppelin B20
"Black Napkins": Frank Zappa A27, **A60**
"Black or White": Michael Jackson A33, **A35**, B24
"Black Page, The": Frank Zappa **A27**
"Black Rose" [1]: Eric Clapton A185
"Black Rose" [2]: Sad Café A185
"Black Satin Dancer": Jethro Tull A188
"Black Star": Yngwie Malmsteen A143, B28
"Black Sweat": Prince A130
"Black-Throated Wind": Grateful Dead A171
"Black Tie Knife Fight": Drowning Man **A204**
"Black Velvet": Alana Myles B24
"Black Water": The Doobie Brothers A205
"Black Wednesday": Brian Wilson B15
"Blah-Blah-Blah" B30
"Blame It on Cain": Elvis Costello A185, B4
"Blame It on My Youth" **B30**
"Blazing Apostles": Be-Bop Deluxe A185
"Blazing Arrow": Blackalicious **A2**
"Bleed": Meshuggah **A203**
"Bleeker Street": Simon and Garfunkel B1
"Blessed": Simon and Garfunkel B1
"Blind Arthur's Breakdown": A145

"Blinded by the Light": Manfred Mann's Earth band **A182**, **A225**, A233
"Blind Faith": Dream Theater A175
"Blind Lemon Blues" B27
"Blitzkrieg Bop": Ramones, The A80, A181, A247
"Blonde in the Bleachers": Joni Mitchell A260
"Blood Brother" [1]: Mission A185
"Blood Brother" [2]: Keith Hudson A231
"Blood on Blood": Bon Jovi A185
"Blood on the Rooftops": Genesis A185
"Bloody Well Right": Supertramp A185
"Bloom": Radiohead A206
"Blow, Gabriel, Blow" B30
"Blowin' Down the Road": Woody Guthrie A240
"Blowin' Free": Wishbone Ash A185
"Blowin' in the Wind" A122, B19; The Beach Boys B15; The Beatles B7; Bob Dylan **A58**, A80, A216, A247, B3, B8
"Blow Out": Radiohead **A169**
"Blow Up the Outside World": Soundgarden **A54**
"Blow Wind Blow": Eric Clapton A185
"Blue, Blue, Blue" **B30**
"Blue Again" **B30**
"Blue Angel": Roy Orbison A270, B8, B25
"Blue Avenue": Roy Orbison A270
"Blue Bayou": Roy Orbison A160, B21
"Blueberry Hill": The Beach Boys B15; Fats Domino A44, A76, A80, A97, A185, A247, B15, **B20**, B21, **B25**
"Bluebirds in My Belfry" A14
"Blue Boy": Joni Mitchell **A260**
"Blue Christmas": The Beach Boys B15
"Blue Collar Man": Styx A141, B24
"Blue Guitar Stomp" A145
"Blue Jay Way": The Beatles **A63**, A76, A98, A99, **B3**, B7, **B18**, B32
"Blue Jean Blues": Z.Z. Top A185
"Bluejean Bop": The Beatles B8
"Blue": Joni Mitchell **A260**
"Blue Matter": John Scofield A256
"Blue Monday" [1]: Fats Domino B8
"Blue Monday" [2]: New Order **A233**, B21
"Blue Moon" A222, B10, B30; Bob Dylan A216; Marcels A43, B21, B15; Elvis Presley A99, A216, A268, A270, B32
"Blue Moon of Kentucky" B8; Bob Dylan A216; Elvis Presley A99, A268, B32

Song Index

"Blue Motel Room": Joni Mitchell A260
"Blue on Black": Kenny Wayne Shepherd A247
"Blue Orchids" **B30**
"Blue Piccadilly": Feeling, The **B21**
"Blue Prelude" B30
"Blue Rain" A14, B30
"Blue Room" B10, B12, B16, **B30**
"Blues Ain't Nothin' Else But": Ida Cox A240
"Blues Bleach": Steely Dan **A96**
"Blues": Blood, Sweat and Tears A43
"Blues for Alice": Charlie Parker **A263**
"Blues for the Muse": The Incredible String Band A112
"Blues in Orbit" B12
"Blues in the Night" B10, B12, **B30**
"Blue Skies": A119, A147, **A168**, A216, **B10**, B12, B30; Frank Sinatra **B21**
"Blue-Skinned Beast, The": Madness A185, **B20**
"Blues of Bechet": Sidney Bechet B32
"Blues Power": Eric Clapton A185
"Blues Skies" A114
"Blue Suede Shoes": The Beatles B7; Carl Perkins A44, A80, A247, B7, B8, B32; Elvis Presley B7
"Blues Variation": Emerson, Lake, & Palmer B20
"Blue Velvet": Tony Bennett B4
"Blue Yodel #1": Bob Wills & His Texas Playboys A240
"Blue Yodel #2": Jimmie Rodgers A266
"Blue Yodel #3": Jimmie Rodgers A266
"Blue Yodel #4": Jimmie Rodgers A266
"Blue Yodel #5": Jimmie Rodgers A266
"Blue Yodel #6": Jimmie Rodgers A266
"Blue Yodel #8": Jimmie Rodgers A266
"Blue Yodel #9": Louis Armstrong A119; Jimmie Rodgers A266
"Blue Yodel #10": Jimmie Rodgers A266
"Blue Yodel #11": Jimmie Rodgers A266
"Blue Yodel #12": Jimmie Rodgers A266
"Blue Yodel": Jimmie Rodgers **A266**
"Bob (Medley), The": Roxy Music **A149**
"Bobby Jean": Bruce Springsteen A99
"Bob Dylan's Blues": Bob Dylan A58, **A239**
"Bob in Dacron": Frank Zappa A11
"Bob McKinney": Henry Thomas **A240**
"Bob White" A145, **B30**
"Bo Diddley" A97; Bo Diddley A44, A80, A95, A247; Buddy Holly A38
"Body and Soul" A145, **A147**, B10, **B16**, B19, **B30**

"Bogey Music": Paul McCartney B7
"Bogus Man, The": Roxy Music A185, B20
"Bogus Pomp": Frank Zappa A11, A12
"Bohemian Rhapsody" A104; Queen A43, A74, A167, **A178**, A185, A205, A233, A247, A269, B21
"Bold as Love": Jimi Hendrix A185
"Bolero": Colosseum B21
"Boll Weevil, The": Woody Guthrie A240; W.A. Lindsey and Alvin Condor **A240**; Finious "Flatfoot" Rockmore A240
"Bomba Remix": Bad Boy Orchestra A3
"Bombast": The Fall B20
"Bomb in Wardour Street, A": Jam A185
"Boney Moronie": Larry Williams **B25**
"Bongo Bongo": Steve Miller Band A185
"Bongo on the Congo" B10
"Bonita Appelbaum": A Tribe Called Quest B22
"Bony Moronie": The Beatles B8; Larry Williams A95
"Boogie Awhile": John Lee Hooker **A8**
"Boogie Blues": Anita O'Day **A239**
"Boogie Chillen'": John Lee Hooker A8, A154, B21
"Boogie Nights": Heatwave B24
"Boogie Woodie": The Beach Boys A160, B15
"Boogie Woogie Blues": Albert Ammons **A238**
"Boogie Woogie Bugle Boy": Bette Midler A43
"Bookends": Simon and Garfunkel B1, **B3**
"Book of Love": The Monotones A44
"Book of Saturday": King Crimson A152, A185
"Book of the Seven Seals": Dixie Hummingbirds A238
"Boom Boom": John Lee Hooker A154
"Booster Fox Trot" A145
"Boot Leg" [1]: Booker T. and the MGs A29, 95
"Boot Leg" [2]: Creedence Clearwater Revival B3
"Bootlegging Blues": Jim Jackson **B26**
"Boot Scoot Boogie": Brooks and Dunn A189
"Boots of Spanish Leather": Bob Dylan A216, B7
"Bootylicious": Destiny's Child A39
"Boppin' the Blues": The Beatles B8
"Borderline": Madonna A252, **B24**
"Border Song": Aretha Franklin A123; Elton John A123

"Boredom" [1]: Procol Harum A185
"Boredom" [2]: Buzzcocks **A210**
"Boris the Spider": The Who A182
"Born Again": No Motiv A205
"Born at the Right Time": Paul Simon B1
"Born Cross-Eyed": Grateful Dead B17
"Born in Puerto Rico": Paul Simon B1
"Born in the 50s": Police A185
"Born in the U.S.A." B19; Bruce Springsteen A99
"Born to Be Blue" A147
"Born to Be My Baby": Bon Jovi A185, B20
"Born to Be Sold": Transvision Vamp A185
"Born to Be Together": The Ronettes A95
"Born to Be Wild": Slade B21; Steppenwolf **A16**, A167, A246, A247, B28, B21
"Born to Live and Born to Die": Foundations A185
"Born to Lose": Roy Trakin A270; Hank Williams B4
"Born Too Late" **B30**; The Poni-Tails B24
"Born to Run": Bruce Springsteen A80, A99, A247, A269, **B24**, B32
"Born Under a Bad Sign": Cream A132, A185; Booker T. Jones B20; Albert King A29, A55
"Borrow From Me" A145
"Botallan Sharab Diyan": Bally Sagoo A61
"Both Sides Now": Joni Mitchell A247, **A260**
"Bottle of Red Wine": Eric Clapton A185
"Bottom to the Top": Joan Armatrading A136
"Boulevard of Broken Dreams, The" B12
"Bounce Back": Dave Angel **B5**
"Bound Steel Blues": Bill Shepherd with Hayes Shepherd & Ed Webb A240
"Bow Wow Wow": Ned Corvan B19
"Box Car Blues" B9
"Boxer, The": Simon and Garfunkel A7, A93, A185, A247, B1, B7
"Boy in a Dress": Namoli Brennet A169
"Boy in the Bubble, The": Paul Simon A9
"Boy Is Mine, The": Brandy and Monica A158
"Boy Next Door, The" [1] **B30**
"Boy Next Door, The" [2] **B30**
"Boys and Girls Like You and Me" **B30**
"Boys Are Back in Town, The": Thin Lizzy A185, A232
"Boy's Best Friend, A": White Stripes, The A148
"Boys in the Band, The": Gentle Giant B20
"Boys Keep Singing": David Bowie A185
"Boys' Night Out, The" A14

"Boys": The Beatles A259, B8, B7; The Shirelles A95, A259
"Boy! What Love Has Done To Me!" B30
"Boy With the Thorn in His Side": The Smiths B13
"Brahms's Disco Dance No. 5": Disko Band A179
"Brain Damage": Pink Floyd A185, A199, A205, **B24**, B29
"Brain Freeze": Weird Al Yankovic **A202**
"Brain Salad Surgery": Emerson, Lake, & Palmer B20
"Brakeman's Blues, The": Jimmie Rodgers **A266**
"Brandenburger": The Nice B29
"Brand New Cadillac": The Clash A118, A210, B20
"Brand New Style": LSD B31
"Brazilian, The": Genesis B20
"Brazil": The Coasters A77
"Break and Enter": Prodigy **A233**
"Breakaway": Kelly Clarkson A169
"Break Away": The Beach Boys A185, B15
"Breakdown, The": Rufus Thomas A29
"Breakdown": Tom Petty A250, B24
"Breaking All Illusions": Dream Theater A175
"Breaking Up Is Hard to Do": Neil and Dara Sedaka A43
"Breakin' Up Is Hard to Do": Neil Sedaka B24
"Break on Through": The Doors **A16**, A167, A185
"Breaks, The": Kurtis Blow B31
"Break the News to Mother" B12
"Breakup Song (They Don't Write 'Em)": The Greg Kihn Band B24
"Breathe": Pink Floyd A185, A199, B24
"Breathless" [1]: The Coors A193, B24
"Breathless" [2]: Robert Fripp A218
"Breizh Positive": Ar Re Yaouank B21
"Brenda's Got a Baby": Tupac Shakur [2Pac] B31
"Brian Epstein Blues": The Beatles B7
"Bridge, The": Neil Young **A88**, B6
"Bridge of Sighs" [1]: Opeth B21
"Bridge of Sighs" [2]: Robin Trower **B21**
"Bridge Over Troubled Water" A264; Aretha Franklin A123, A265; Simon and Garfunkel A43, A80, A93, A123, A247, B1
"Bridges Burning": Mission A185

Song Index

"Bridges in the Sky": Dream Theater A175
"Brigg Fair": Martin Carthy B21; Joseph Taylor B21
"Bright Lights, Big City": Jimmy Reed A144
"Bright Star Shining in Glory" B9
"Brilliant Corners" A224
"Bring a Friend": Happy Mondays A185
"Bring Back Those Wonderful Days" A145
"Bring It on Home": Led Zeppelin **A186**, B7; Sonny Boy Williamson II A83
"Bring It on Home to Me": The Animals A108; Sam Cooke A95, A108, B8; Eddie Floyd A185
"Bring It Up": James Brown B3
"Bring on the Night": The Police A103, A235
"Bring the Boys Back Home": Pink Floyd A198
"Bring the Noise": Public Enemy A80, A99
"Bring the Pain": Missy Elliott A55
"Bring Up Breakdown" A145
"Broadford Bazaar": Jethro Tull A188
"Broadway Hotel": Al Stewart A185
"Broadway Melody" A145
"Brokedown Palace": The Grateful Dead **A16**
"Broken Arrow": Neil Young B6
"Broken Down Angel": Nazareth A185, B20
"Broken Wings": Mister Mister B24
"Brontosaurus": The Move A185, B21
"Bron-y-aur Stomp": Led Zeppelin A185
"Brooklyn (Owes the Charmer Under Me)": Steely Dan **A96**
"Brother, Can You Spare a Dime?" B10, B12, B27
"Brother Low Down" A145
"Brother Sport": Animal Collective A205
"Brown-Eyed Girl": Van Morrison A247
"Brown-Eyed Handsome Man": Chuck Berry A95, B8, B15
"Brown Girl in the Ring": Boney M **A64**
"Brown Shoes Don't Make It": Mothers of Invention, The A11
"Brown Sugar": The Rolling Stones **A16**, A35, **A97**, A99, **A155**, **B24**, B29
"Brush Up Your Shakespeare" B30
"B.S.U.R. (S.U.C.S.I.M.I.M.)": James Taylor **B24**
"Bucket's Got a Hole in It": Lil Johnson **A240**; Washboard Sam **A240**
"Buddy": Murrey Harman A270
"Bug, The": Roy Orbison A270

"Bugged at My Old Man": The Beach Boys A125
"Bugle Blow" A168
"Building a Mystery": Sarah McLachlan **A5**, **A84**, **A154**, A219
"Build Me Up, Break Me Down": Dream Theater A175
"Built for Comfort": UFO B20
"Bull Dog" B30
"Bulldog": The Fireballs B15
"Bull Doze Blues": Henry Thomas A240
"Bullet in the Head": Rage Against the Machine A205
"Bullet Proof . . . I Wish I Was": Radiohead **A169**
"Bullet the Blue Sky": U2 A103, A185
"Bull Session With Big Daddy": The Beach Boys A125
"Bully, The" B30
"Bumble Bee": Memphs Minnie **B26**
"Bunch of Rags, A" A145
"Bungle in the Jungle": Jethro Tull B24
"Bunkers": Vapors A185
"Burning Brudges": Pink Floyd A185
"Burning Down the House": Talking Heads A185
"Burning Heart": Survivor A250
"Burning Love": Elvis Presley A99
"Burning My Soul": Dream Theater **A175**
"Bury Me Beneath the Willow": Woody Guthrie A240
"Bury Me Under the Weeping Willow": The Carter Family A240; The Delmore Brothers A240
"Buscando Ildo": That Cuban Guy A3
"Bushfire": The B-52's A99
"Business Is Business" **A168**
"Bus Stop" [1]: David Bowie B20
"Bus Stop" [2]: The Hollies B7, B8, B24
"Busted": Ray Charles B21
"Busy Bodies": Elvis Costello A185
"Busy Doin' Nothin' ": The Beach Boys B15
"But a Memory": Frantic Bleep B21
"But Beautiful" A14
"Butch the Beach Boy" A145
"But in the Morning, No!" B30
"But Not for Me" B12, B30
"Butterfly": Charlie Gracie A97; Andy Williams A97

"Butterfly Collector": Jam A185
"Butterfly Kisses": Jeff Carson A191
"Butterfly on a Wheel": Mission A185
"Buttons and Bows" B30
"Buzz Buzz A-Diddle-It": The Beatles B8
"Bye Bye Blues": Ambrose and his Orchestra A227
"Bye Bye Johnny": Chuck Berry A244
"Bye Bye Love": The Everly Brothers B15, A97; The Quarrymen B8; Simon and Garfunkel B1
"Bye-Ya": Thelonius Monk A96
"By Myself" **B30**
"By Strauss" B30
"By the Beautiful Sea" A145
"By the Light of the Silvery Moon" B12
"By the Sycamore Tree" A145
"By the Time I Get to Arizona": Public Enemy A39
"By the Time I Get to Phoenix" B3; Glen Campbell **A34**; Isaac Hayes **A34**, A39, A269
"By the Way": The Big Three B8
"By-Tor and the Snow Dog": Rush A28

"Cabbage Greens": Champion Jack Dupree A238
"Cabfare": Souls of Mischief B22
"Cabinessence": The Beach Boys A125, A205, B15; Brian Wilson B15
"Cabin in the Sky" B30
"Ça C'est l'Amour" B12
"Cactus Tree": Joni Mitchell **A260**
"Cada Vez": Negrocan A3
"Cadillac Ranch": Chris LeDoux A190
"Cakewalk" A145
"Cake Walking Babies From Home" A145
"California (Here I Come)" B30
"California": Joni Mitchell **A260**
"California Calling": The Beach Boys B15
"California Dreamin'": The Mamas and the Papas **A65**, A99, A247, B7, B8
"California Dreaming" B3
"California Girl": Eddie Floyd A29
"California Girls": The Beach Boys A75, A95, A109, **A125**, A185, A247, B15
"California Good-Time Music": The United States of America A138
"California Here I Come" A145
"California Love": 2Pac A80, A247

"California Man": Cheap Trick B21; Move, The B21
"Call Any Vegetable": The Mothers of Invention **A99**
"Callin' Baton Rouge": Garth Brooks A191
"Calling Card": Madness B20
"Calling Me Home": Roy Fox and His Band A227
"Call Me" [1]: Blondie **A241**, B24
"Call Me" [2]: Chris Montez A99
"Call Me Irresponsible" A14, B10, B12, **B30**
"Call on Me": Chicago **A237**, B24
"Call to Arms": Soulfly A205
"Calvary Cross": Richard Thompson B21
"Calypso Breakdown": Ralph MacDonald A3, A179
"Camay": Ghostface Killa B14
"Camptown Races" A219, B30
"Canada": Runrig **B21**
"Canary in a Coalmine": The Police A235
"C and a Blues": Peetie Wheatstraw B9
"Candidate": David Bowie B20
"Candle in the Wind": Elton John A99
"Candle": Peter Hammill A185
"Candles in the Rain": Melanie A185
"Candy Man, The" A202, B12
"Candy Store Rock": Led Zeppelin A185
"Candy": The Astors **A29**
"Canhanibalmo Rag" A145
"Can I Forgive Him": Paul Simon B1
"Can I Get a Witness": Marvin Gaye A32, A85, **A106**, A108, B8, B15, B19; The Rolling Stones A85
"Can I Kick It?": A Tribe Called Quest **A1**, A123; see also "Walk on the Wild Side, A"
"Can It Be All So Simple": Raekwon **A158**, B14; The Wu-Tang Clan A99
"Canned Heat Blues": Tommy Johnson A266
"Cannon Ball Blues" A240; The Carter Family A240; Frank Hutchison A240
"Cannoning in B Major": echolyn A72
"Canon": Ani DiFranco A101
"Cans and Brahms": Yes B21
"Can't Believe You Wanna Leave": The Beatles B8; Fats Domino B7; Little Richard A95
"Can't Buy Me Love": The Beatles A76, **A91**, A106, A107, A185, A195, A196, A248, A254, B7, **B8**, B19, B20, B21
"Can't Explain": Who A185

"Can't Get Enough" [1]: Bad Company A74, A75, B24
"Can't Get Enough" [2]: Liz Torres A3
"Can't Get Indiana off My Mind" B10, B30
"Can't Get Out of This Mood" B30
"Can't Help Falling in Love": Elvis Presley A99, A103, A167
"Can't Help Lovin' Dat Man" **B10**, B12, **B30**
"Can't Help Singing" B30
"Can This Be Love" **B10**
"Cantor, The" B12
"Canto Triste": Brasil 66 B3
"Can't Run But": Paul Simon B1
"Can't Stand Losing You": The Police A235
"Can't Stay Away From You": Gloria Estefan B24
"Can't Stop": Boomtown Rats A185
"Can't Take My Eyes Off You": Boystown Gang A52; Frankie Valli A52
"Can't Wait Too Long": The Beach Boys B15
"Can't We Be Friends?" B10, **B30**
"Can't You See That She's Mine": Dave Clark Five A107
"Can-Utility and the Coastliners": Genesis B21
"Canyons of Your Mind": Bonzo Dog Doo-Dah Band A185, B21
"Can You Forgive Her?": The Pet Shop Boys A124, A174
"Cap in Hand": Jethro Tull B20
"Caprice Rag": James P. Johnson A172
"Captain Bobby Stout": Manfred Mann's Earth band **A182**
"Captain Kennedy": Neil Young B6
"Captain Soul": The Byrds A121
"Captain Walker": The Who A101
"Caramia": Indigo Girls A221
"Caravan" A147
"Caravan of Love": The Housemartins **B19**
"Car Crazy Cutie": The Beach Boys B15
"Card Cheat, The": The Clash A118
"Career Day": The Format A205
"Carefree Highway": Gordon Lightfoot B24
"Careful in Career": Simple Minds A185
"Careful With That Axe, Eugene": Pink Floyd **A68**, A198
"Carey": Joni Mitchell **A260**
"Caribbean Queen": Billy Ocean B24
"Carioca" B12, **B25**, B30
"Carl's Big Chance": The Beach Boys B15
"Carmichael": Neil Young B6

"Carnival Fugue": Focus **A166**
"Carol": The Beatles B8; Chuck Berry A95
"Carolina in My Mind": James Taylor B7
"Carolina in the Morning": A114, B10, **B30**
"Carolina Moon" B16
"Carolina Shout": James P. Johnson B9, **A172**; Fats Waller **A172**
"Caroline [1]": Fleetwood Mac A185
"Caroline [2]": Status Quo B21
"Caroline No": The Beach Boys A17, A99, A125, A160, B15; Timothy B. Schmit B15; Brian Wilson B15
"Car on a Hill": Joni Mitchell A260
"Caro Nome" B12
"Carribean Queen": Billy Ocean A250
"Carrie" A145
"Carrie Ann": Hollies A185
"Carried Away": George Strait A189
"Carrier Railroad (The Carrier Line), The": Sid Hemphill A240
"Carry Me Back To Old Virginny" B30
"Carry on Wayward Son": Kansas **A16**, A17, **A17**, A43, A72, A101, **A250**, B24
"Carry That Load": The Beatles **A116**
"Carry That Weight": The Beatles **A92**, A98, A149, **B7**, B18
"Carry Your Lantern High": The Rolling Stones B29
"Cars Are Cars": Paul Simon B1
"Cars": Gary Numan B20, B21
"Carve Dat Possum" A145
"Car Wash": Rose Royce A105
"Case of the Blues, A": The Beatles B7
"Case of You, A": Joni Mitchell **A260**
"Casey Jones" A145; Grateful Dead B17
"Casey's Wedding Night" B12
"Cash Flow Shuffle": echolyn A72
"Cash Machine": Hard-Fi B21
"Cassidy": Grateful Dead B17
"Cassius' Love vs. 'Sonny' Wilson": The Beach Boys B15
"Castle House Rag": James Reese Europe B9
"Castle of the King of the Birds": The Beatles **B7**
"Castles in the Sand": Stevie Wonder A95
"Castles in the Sky": Ian Van Dahl A3
"Castles Made of Sand": The Jimi Hendrix Experience A17, A40, B3
"Casual Look, A": The Beach Boys B15; The Six Teens B15

"Catcall": Chris Barber's Band B7
"Cat Called Domino": Roy Orbison A270
"Catch a Falling Star": Perry Como A97, A99
"Catch a Wave": The Beach Boys B15
"Catch Me If You Can": Eric Clapton A185
"Catch Us If You Can": Dave Clark Five A107
"Catherine": PJ Harvey A223
"Cathy's Clown": The Everly Brothers **A241**, A247, A259
"Cat People": David Bowie B20
"Cat's in the Cradle": Harry Chapin B24
"Cat's Squirrel": Cream A132, B3
"Catswalk [Catcall]": The Beatles **B8**
"Caught in a Web": Dream Theater A175
"Caught Up in the Rapture": Anita Baker A39
"Caught Up in You": .38 Special A250
"Cause I Love You": Rufus and Carla Thomas A29
"Caution, Do Not Stop on Tracks": Grateful Dead B17
"Cautious Repose, A": echolyn **A72**
"Caves of Altamira, The": Steely Dan **A96**
"Cayenne": The Beatles B7; The Quarrymen **B8**
"C.C. Rider": Bill Broonzy A240
"Cecilia": Simon and Garfunkel B1
"Ce fut en mai" **B19**
"Celebration Day": Led Zeppelin A185, B7
"Celeste Aida" B12
"Celibate Life, The": The Shins **A22**
"Cell Therapy": Goodie MoB B14
"Certain Smile, A" B12
"C'est La Vie": Bob Seger & The Silver Bullet Band B21
"Chain, The": Fleetwood Mac A185, A205, **A248**
"Chained and Bound": Otis Redding A29, B3
"Chain Lightning": Steely Dan A250
"Chain Reaction of Love": Brian Wilson B15
"Chains": The Beatles A98, A259, B7, **B8**; The Cookies A95, A259
"Chair, The": George Strait A191
"Chameleon": Creedence Clearwater B3
"Champagne Charlie" **B19** B19
"Champagne Supernova": Oasis A99
"Champion": Kanye West A261, B31
"Chance": Big Country A185
"Chance Meeting": Roxy Music A185, B20
"Chances Are": Johnny Mathis A97
"Change Gonna Come": Otis Redding B19

"Change Is Gonna Come, A": Sam Cooke A30, A32, A80, A108, A247
"Change of Seasons": Dream Theater A175
"Change Partners" B30
"Changes" [1]: David Bowie **A17**, **A99**, A185, A247, B7, B20
"Changes" [2]: Yes A55
"Changes" [3]: 2Pac A99, B31
"Changes" [4] **B30**
"Change What You Can": Marvin Gaye A110
"Change Your Mind" **B30**; Neil Young **A88**, B6
"Changing of the Guards": Bob Dylan A180
"Channel Z": The B-52's **A99**
"Chapter 24": Pink Floyd A185, A198
"Charades": The Enid A166
"Charleston" B30; The Savoy Orpheans A227
"Charlestonette" A145
"Charley, My Boy" A145, B30
"Charlie Brown": The Coasters A44, A77
"Charmer, The": Seth Lakeman B21
"Chattahoochie": Alan Jackson A189, A190
"Chattanooga Choo-Choo" B10, B12, A53
"Ch-Check It Out": Beastie Boys B31
"Cheaper To Keep Her": Johnnie Taylor A29
"Cheapster": Spiritualized B21
"Cheap Thrills": Frank Zappa & the Mothers of Invention B21
"Cheating on the Blues": Brooks and Dunn A190
"Checkers" A145
"Checkin' Up on My Baby" B17
"Check the Rhime": Tribe Called Quest, A **B31**
"Check to Cheek" B10
"Check Up": Lawrence Bruce A53
"Cheek to Cheek" A13, B30
"Cheese and Onions": Neil Innes A69
"Chega de Saudade": João Gilberto A211
"Chelsea" see "(I Don't Want to Go to) Chelsea"
"Chelsea Morning": Joni Mitchell **A260**
"Chelsea Rodgers": Prince A130
"Cherish": The Association A43, **A252**
"Cherokee" A147, **A224**
"Cherokee Louise": Joni Mitchell A221, A260
"Cherry, Cherry Coupe": The Beach Boys B15
"Cherry Cherry": Neil Diamond **A85**
"Cherry Red": Groundhogs B21
"Cherub Rock": Smashing Pumpkins A99
"Chest Fever": Band A43, A185, B32

Song Index

"Chestnut Mare": The Byrds A121
"Chewing Gum": Elvis Costello B4
"Cheyenne Anthem": Kansas A72
"Chicago (That Toddlin' Town)" B8, B12, B30
"Chicago Stomp" A145
"Chi-Chi's Café " John Lennon B7
"Chicken Hearted": Roy Orbison A270
"Chicken Strut": Meters A185
"Chicken You Can Roost Behind the Moon": Frank Stokes A240
"Childhood's End": Pink Floyd A185
"Child in Time": Deep Purple **A16**, A167, A185, A208, B20, B21
"Child Is Born, A" **A209**
"Child Is Father of the Man": The Beach Boys B15; Brian Wilson B15
"Childlike Faith in Childhood's End": Van Der Graaf Generator **B21**
"Child of a Few Hours Is Burning to Death, A": West Coast Pop Art Experimental band A43
"Child of Clay" B3
"Child of Winter": The Beach Boys B15
"Child": Peter Hammill A185
"Chile Bean" A145
"Chim Chim Cher-ee" **A133**, B12
"Chimes at the Meeting" B12
"Chimes of Freedom": The Byrds A121, A185
"Chinaberry Tree": Mew **A204**
"China Cat Sunflower": Grateful Dead A171, B17
"China Girl": David Bowie A101, B20
"China Grove": The Doobie Brothers **A248**, **B24**
"China": Tori Amos A6
"Chinatown": Thin Lizzy A185
"China White": He Is Legend A205
"Chinese Café": Joni Mitchell **A260**
"Chipmunk Song, The": The Chipmunks A97
"Chiquitita": ABBA B25
"Chirpy Chirpy Cheep Cheep": Middle of the Road B21
"Choice of Colors": The Impressions A53, A144
"Choo Choo Ch'Boogie": Louis Jordan A185, B4, B21
"Christine": Siouxsie & Banshees A185, B20
"Christine's Tune (Devil in Disguise)": The Flying Burrito Brothers A173
"Christmas in Killarney" B16
"Christmas Is for Children" A14
"Christmas Song, A": Jethro Tull A188

"Christmas": The Who A99
"Christmas Time (Is Here Again)": The Beatles B7
"Chrome-Plated Megaphone of Destiny, The": Mothers of Invention, The A11, A43
"Chronic": Dr. Dre A261, B31
"Chug-a-Lug": The Beach Boys B15
"Church Is Burning, A": Paul Simon B1
"Church Key": The Revels B15
"Cinderella Man": Rush A28
"Cindy" **B24**
"Cindy, Oh Cindy" A238
"Cindy, Oh Cindy": The Beach Boys B15
"Cinnamon Girl": Neil Young A88, B6
"Circle Game, The": Joni Mitchell A99, **A260**
"Circle Is Unbroken, The": The Incredible String Band A112
"Circle of Hands": Uriah Heep A185
"Circle": Sarah McLachlan **A154**
"Circles": The Beatles B7
"Circus Day in Dixie" A145
"Circus Lights": Deacon Blue A185
"Cirkus": King Crimson A138, A152, A218
"Citadel, The": The Rolling Stones B29
"City Blues": Brian Wilson and Eric Clapton B15
"City of Angels": Nik Kershaw A185
"City of Blinding Lights": U2 **A89**
"Clampdown" *see* "(Working for the) Clampdown"
"Clap Hands": Tom Waits A135
"Clapping Song": Shirley Ellis A135
"Clap Yo' Hands" B10, **B30**
"Clarabella": The Beatles B8
"Clarabella": The Jodimars A95
"Clasp, The": Jethro Tull A188
"Claudette": The Beatles B8; Roy Orbison A270
"Clave, la": Isaac Santiago A3
"Clay": Echo & Bunnymen A185
"Cleanin' Out My Closet": Eminem A99, B31
"Cleanup Time": John Lennon and Yoko Ono B7
"Clementine": Grateful Dead B17
"Clevor Trever": Ian Dury A185
"Climbing Up the Walls": Radiohead A162
"Clocks": Coldplay B21
"Close (to the Edit)": The Art of Noise A104
"Close Action": Big Country A185
"Close Escape": Madness A185, B20

"Closer to Home / I'm Your Captain": Grand Funk Railroad B24
"Closer to the Heart": Rush A28
"Close to the Edge": Yes **A71**, A72, **A73**, A74, A101, A152, A207, **A224**, A229, A232, A269, B20
"Close to You" *see* "(They Long to Be) Close to You"
"Close Your Eyes" B10, B30
"Cloud Nine": The Temptations A95, **A105**, A144
"Clouds" **B30**
"Cloud Song": The United States of America A138
"Clouds Will Soon Roll By, The": Ambrose and his Orchestra A227
"Cloudy": Simon and Garfunkel B1
"Clubland": Elvis Costello and the Attractions B4
"C'mon Everybody": The Beatles B8; Eddie Cochran A185
"C'mon Marianne": The Four Seasons A99, B7
"C Moon": Wings B7
"Coal Miner's Daughter": Loretta Lynn A193
"Coal Train Robberies": Elvis Costello B4
"Coast, The": Paul Simon B1
"Cocaine Habit Blues": Memphis Jug Band A240
"Cocaine": J.J. Cale **A16**, A167; Eric Clapton B24
"Cocoanut Grove" A145
"Coco Jamboo": Mr. President B24
"Coconut": Nilsson B24
"Cocoon": Björk **A50**
"Coda: I Have a Dream": King Crimson B21
"Codex": Radiohead **A206**
"Cogs in Cogs": Gentle Giant A185
"Cohan's 'Rag Babe'" A145
"Cohen Family, The" B12
"Cohen Owes Me Ninety-Seven Dollars" **A168**
"Cohens, The" B12
"Cold, Cold, Heart": Tony Bennett B4; Hank Williams B4
"Cold as Ice": Foreigner **A74**
"Cold Blue Steel and Sweet Fire": Joni Mitchell **A260**
"Cold Cold Night": The White Stripes **A55**
"Cold Hard Bitch": Jet **A85**
"Cold Kisses": Richard Thompson B21
"Cold Morning Light": Todd Rundgren A99
"Cold Rain and Snow": Grateful Dead, The A25, B17

"Cold Sweat": James Brown A31, **A99**, A210, B4, B7, **B21**, B28
"Cold Turkey": The Plastic Ono Band A154, A185, B8, B7, B18, **B21**
"Cold War": Vapors A185
"Cold Wind to Valhalla": Jethro Tull A188, **B20**
"Collide": Leona Lewis & Avicii A212
"Colorado Bus Driver": Len Chandler A216
"Colour My World": Chicago B3, B24
"Colour of Love, The": Billy Ocean A250
"Colours": Donovan A185
"Colours in Her Hair": McFly B21
"Come a Little Closer": The Incredible String Band A112
"Come and Get It" [1]: Badfinger B7
"Come and Get It" [2]: The Tri-Five B15
"Come and Get These Memories": Martha and the Vandellas **A108**
"Come as You Are": Nirvana A80, A99, A246, A247
"Come Away Melinda": Uriah Heep A185
"Come Back to Me": Big Country B20
"Come Blow Your Horn" A14
"Come Dance with Me" A14
"Comedy Tonight" A41
"Come Fly with Me" A14
"Come Get to This": Marvin Gaye A110
"Come Go With Me": The Beach Boys B15; The Dell Vikings A44, A97, B15, B24; The Quarrymen B8
"Come Home": Dave Clark Five A107
"Come Home Father" **B19**, B19, A184
"Come In, Number 51, Your Time's Up": Pink Floyd A68
"Come in from the Cold": Joni Mitchell A260
"Come Josephine in My Flying Machine" A53, B12
"Come on and Pet Me" B30
"Come on Baby Let's Go Downtown": Neil Young B6
"Come on Down to My Boat": Every Mothers' Son **A99**
"Come on Eileen": Dexy's Midnight Runners A185
"Come on in My Kitchen": Robert Johnson A240
"Come on People" B8
"Come On": Rolling Stones B21
"Come on Up": The Rascals B3

Song Index

"Come Rain or Come Shine" **A15**, A147, **B10**, **B11**, B12, B30
"(Come Round Here) I'm the One You Need": The Miracles **A108**
"Come Sail Away": Styx **A141**, A250
"Comes a Time": Neil Young **A88**, B6
"Come See About Me": The Supremes A95, A99, **A106**, **A108**, B4
"Come See": Major Lance **A108**
"Comes Love" B12
"Come Softly To Me": The Fleetwoods B25
"Come Together": The Beatles A90, A92, A95, A98, A195, A246, B4, **B3**, B7, B8, **B18**
"Come to My Window": Melissa Etheridge B24
"Come With Me": Puff Daddy feat. Jimmy Page A159
"Comfortably Numb": Pink Floyd A185, A198
"Comin' Apart at Every Nail": Neil Young B6
"Coming Around Again": Carly Simon B24
"Coming Up (Live at Glasgow)": Paul McCartney B7
"Comin' in on a Wing and a Prayer" B10
"Common People": Pulp B21
"Commonwealth": The Beatles B7
"Commotion": Creedence Clearwater Revival A185
"Communication Breakdown": Led Zeppelin **A16**, A248
"Communication": Mario Più **B5**
"Computer Music": Suzie Q A128
"Concerto de Aranjuez": Miles Davis A217
"Concerto in Three Rhythms" B10
"Concrete and Clay": Unit 4+2 B21
"Conehead": Frank Zappa A27
"Confession" **B30**
"Confucius Say": Bing Crosby B4
"Conga": Miami Sound Machine A3
"Congratulations": Paul Simon B1
"Connected": James Ruskin **B5**
"Conquistador": Procol Harum A185, B20
"Consoler of the Lonely": Raconteurs B21
"Constantly" A14, A145
"Constant Motion": Dream Theater **A175**
"Contaminazione": Il Rovescio della Medaglia A166
"Continental, The" B30
"Continuing Story of Bungalow Bill, The": The Beatles A17, A43, **A63**, A98, A100, **A253**, B8, B7, B18

"Contract": Gang of Four B20
"Control": Janet Jackson B32
"Controversy": Prince B13
"Conversation": Joni Mitchell **A260**
"Convoy": C.W. McCall A43
"Cool, Cool, Cool of the Evening, The" B10
"Cool, Cool River, The": Paul Simon B1
"Cool, Cool Water": The Beach Boys B15
"Cool Drink of Blues": Tommy Johnson A266
"Cool Shake": The Del-Vikings B24
"Cool Water": John Lennon B8
"Coon Band Contest, A" A145
"Copper Head Mama": Bill Carlisle A240
"Coquette" B10; The Beatles B8; Fats Domino A95
"Corcovado" ["Quiet Nights of Quiet Stars"] A167, A211
"Corinna": Grateful Dead B17
"Corner Soul": The Clash B20
"Corn Whiskey Blues": J.T. "Funny Paper": Smith A240
"Corporal Clegg": Pink Floyd A198, B20
"Corrine, Corrina [Corrina, Corrina]": Too Bad Boys A240; The Beatles B8; Bob Dylan A58, A121, B7; Blind Lemon Jefferson A240, B7; Bob Wills & His Texas Playboys A240; James "Boodle It": Wiggins **A240**; The Quarrymen B7
"Cortez the Killer": Neil Young A7, **A155**, B6
"Cosmic Charlie": Grateful Dead B17
"Cosmic Thing": The B-52's A99
"Cosmik Debris": Frank Zappa A11
"Cossack Love Song" B12
"Cottage for Sale" B30
"Cotton-Eyed Joe, The" A189
"Cottonfield Blues": Garfield Akers A201, **B26**
"Cottonfields": The Beach Boys B15; Leadbelly A240
"Could You Use Me?" B12
"Council of Elrond, The": Enya **A54**
"Countdown" **A224**
"Countin' Teardrops": Emil Ford and the Checkmates B25
"Count Me in": Gary Lewis and the Playboys B4
"Count of Tuscany, The": Dream Theater **A175**
"Country Air": The Beach Boys B15
"Country Blues": Doc Boggs A210
"Country Cousin, The" B30
"Country Feelin's": Brian Wilson B15

"Country Girl": Crosby, Stills, Nash & Young B3
"Country Grammar (Hot . . .)": Nelly A99
"Country House": Blur B21
"Country Pie": Bob Dylan A99
"Country Style" A14
"County Fair": The Beach Boys B15
"Coup D-Etat": Level 42 A185
"Court and Spark": Joni Mitchell **A260**
"Court of the Common Plea": Marvin Gaye A110
"Court of the Crimson King": King Crimson A185, B20
"Cousin Kevin": The Who A99
"Cousin of Mine": Sam Cooke A108
"Covenant Woman": Bob Dylan A180
"Cover Me": Bruce Springsteen **A83**
"Cowboy Museum": George Harrison B7
"Cowboy's Last Ride, The": Jimmie Rodgers A266
"Cow Cow Blues": Cow Cow Davenport A238
"Cowgirl in the Sand": The Byrds A121; Neil Young **B6**
"Cowhand's Last Ride, The": Jimmie Rodgers A266
"Coyote": Joni Mitchell A260
"Coz I Luv You": Slade A185, B20, B21
"Crack at Your Love": The Beach Boys B15
"Crack City": David Bowie B20
"Crackin' Up": The Beatles B8; Bo Diddley A95
"Crack the Whip": Jasper Dailey B15
"Cradle's Empty, Baby's Gone" B30
"Crane Wife, The": The Decemberists **A205**
"Crash": David Byrne A99
"Crazy Blues" A145; Mamie Smith A8
"Crazy City": Barclay James Harvest A185
"Crazy Elbows" B30
"Crazy for You": Madonna A250
"Crazy in Love": Eminem A261, **B31**
"Crazy Little Thing Called Love": Queen **A16**, A185, A269
"Crazy Love, Vol. II": Paul Simon A9
"Crazy on You": Heart **A16**, A248
"Crazy": Patsy Cline A247
"Crazy Rhythm" **B30**
"Crazy Train": Ozzy Osbourne **A55**, **A250**
"Cream": Prince A79, **B13**
"Creep": Radiohead **A54**, A135, A162, **A169**
"Creeque Alley": The Mamas and the Papas A43, B20

"Creole Belles" A145
"Crickets Are Calling, The" B30
"Crime in the City": Neil Young B6
"Crime of the Century": Supertramp A46, A185, A186, B21
"Crimes of Paris, The": Elvis Costello B4
"Criminal": Eminem A146
"Criminal Minded": Boogie Down Productions A39
"Criminals": Atlas Sound A169
"Criminal World": David Bowie B20
"Crimson and Clover": Tommy James and the Shondells A43, **A101**, B7
"Crinoline Days" B30
"Crippled Inside": John Lennon B8, B18
"Crocodile Rock": Elton John B20, B21, **B24**
"Crooning" A145
"Croquet Habits": Freeny's Barn Dance Band **A239, A240**
"Cross-eyed Mary": Jethro Tull A188
"Crossfire": Jethro Tull A185
"Cross My Heart": Bruce Springsteen A99
"Cross Road [Crossroads] Blues": Blind Faith A132; Cream A43, **A132**, A176, B7; Derek and the Dominos A132; Robert Johnson A8, **A26**, A176, **A132**, B20, B21; Powerhouse A132
"Cross Street Swing" A145
"Crosstown Traffic": Jimi Hendrix A101
"Crowd, The": Roy Orbison A270
"Crowing, The": Coheed and Cambria **A205**
"Crown of Love": Arcade Fire A205, B21
"Crucify": Tori Amos **A46**
"Crunge, The": Led Zeppelin A99, B20
"Cry Baby Cry": The Beatles A98, A100, **A156, A157, A253, B7, B18**
"Cry": Brian Wilson B15
"Cry Cry Cry": Roxy Music A185
"Cry for a Shadow": The Beatles B7, **B8**
"Cry for Everyone": Gentle Giant B20
"Cryin' ": Aerosmith A167
"Cryin' for the Carolines": **A120**
"Crying, Waiting, Hoping": The Beatles **B8**; Buddy Holly **B8**
"Crying" [1]: George Harrison B7
"Crying" [2]: Roy Orbison A99, A247, A270, B21, B24
"Crying to the Sky": Be-Bop Deluxe A185

Song Index

"Cry Me a River": Julie London B8
"Cryptical Envelompent": The Grateful Dead A99, B17
"Crystal Clear": Goldie B21
"Crystalline": Bjork A205
"Crystal Ship, The": The Doors **B3**
"C-U-B-A" *see* "(I'll See You In) C-U-B-A"
"Cubanola Glide, The" A145
"Cubik (King's County Perspective)": 808 State **B5**
"Cuckoo Clock": The Beach Boys B15
"Cuckoo Is a Pretty Bird, The": Bob Dylan A216
"Cuckoo's Nest, The" **B27**
"Cuckoo Song" **A266**
"Cuddle Up a Little Closer" A145
"Cul-de-Sac": Genesis **A142**
"Cult of Personality": Living Colour A55, A99, **A97**
"Cumberland Blues": Grateful Dead B17
"Cumberland Gap": Lonnie Donegan B8
"Cum on Feel the Noize": Slade B21
"Cunning Cobbler, The" B27
"Cupid": Sam Cooke B21; The Spinners A250
"Cups and Cakes": Spinal Tap A69, **A70, A84**
"Cups": Underworld **B5**
"Curly": Move A185
"Custard Pie": Led Zeppelin A17, **A83, A86**
"Custom Machine": The Beach Boys B15
"Cut My Hair": Crosby, Stills, Nash & Young B3
"Cutter, The": Echo & Bunnymen A185
"C U When U Get There": Coolio B14
"Cycle of Sixty": GZR A221
"Cygnet Committee": David Bowie A185
"Cygnus . . . Vismund Cygnus": The Mars Volta **A203**
"Cygnus X-1": Rush **A28**, A175

"Daddy and Home": Jimmie Rodgers A266, B19
"Daddy Didn't Tell Me": The Astors A29
"Daddy Don't Live in That New York City No More": Steely Dan A96
"Daddy Pop": Prince A79, **B13**
"Daddy's Gonna Pay for Your Crashed Car": U2 A89, A103
"Daddy's Little Sunshine Boy": John Lennon B7
"Daddy Went Walkin'": Neil Young B6
"Daddy Wouldn't Buy Me a Bow Wow" A145

"Da Doo Ron Ron": The Crystals A160, A247, B15
"Daffodil Lament": The Cranberries A205
"Daikon Batake": U Totem A81
"Daily Growl, The": Lambchop B21
"Daisy" **B24**
"Dallas Rag" A145
"Damage Case": Motorhead A185, B21
"Damaged Goods": Fastball A99
"Dance, Dance, Dance": The Beach Boys A109, B15
"Dance, Mamma, Dance, Papa, Dance" A147
"Dance, The": Garth Brooks A193
"Dance Away": Roxy Music A185
"Danced": Toyah A185
"Dance for the One": Quintessence B21
"Dance in the Streets": The Beatles B8
"Dance of Eternity, The": Dream Theater A175
"Dance of Maya": The Mahavishnu Orchestra A73
"Dance on a Volcano": Genesis A221, B21
"Dancer, The": P.J. Harvey B21
"Dance the Night Away" [1]: Cream B7, B29
"Dance the Night Away" [2]: Van Halen A250
"Dance With Me Henry": Georgia Gibbs A44, A53
"Dancing Barefoot": The Patti Smith Group **A7**
"Dancing Days": Led Zeppelin A99, A185, A248
"Dancing in the Dark" [1] **A114, B10**, B30; Dave McKenna A114
"Dancing in the Dark" [2]: Bruce Springsteen A269
"Dancing in the Moonlight": Thin Lizzy A185
"Dancing in the Street" A105, B17; Martha and the Vandellas **A95**, A108, A110, A167, A247, B17; Van Halen A185
"Dancing on a Dime" B30
"Dancing on the Ceiling" B10, **B30**
"Dancing Queen": ABBA A185, A212, A247, B25
"Dancing With The Dead": Sting B25
"Dandelion": Rolling Stones A101
"Dandy": Herman's Hermit's A107
"Danger Bird": Neil Young B6
"Danger Heartbreak Dead Ahead": The Marvelettes A95
"Dangerous Kitchen, The": Frank Zappa A11
"Dangerous Veils": Jethro Tull A188

"Dangling Conversation, The": Simon and Garfunkel B1
"Daniel": Elton John A99, B24
"Danny Boy": The Beatles B7
"Danny's Song": Loggins and Messina B24
"Dardanella" A145
"Dark Ages": Jethro Tull A188, B20
"Dark Eternal Night, The": Dream Theater A175
"Dark Eyes" B12
"Darkey's Wail, A": Riley Puckett **A240**
"Dark Horse": George Harrison A101
"Darkies Awakening" A145
"Dark Matter": Porcupine Tree A221
"Dark Moon": Gale Storm A97
"Darkness": Van der Graaf Generator A185
"Dark Star": The Grateful Dead **A25**, A99, A171, B7, **B17**, B20
"Darktown Poker Club, the" A145
"Darktown Strutters Ball, The" B27, B30; The Beatles B8
"Darling Be Home Soon": Lovin' Spoonful B21; Slade B21
"Darling Lorraine": Paul Simon B1
"Darlin'": The Beach Boys A125, A185, B15
"Där Näckrosen Blommar" B25
"Darn That Dream" A14, B10, B30
"Daughter": Pearl Jam **A245**
"Daughters": John Mayer A169
"David Watts": The Jam A185, **B20**; The Kinks B20
"Dawn (Go Away)": The Four Seasons A99, B8
"Dawning Is the Day": The Moody Blues B7
"Dawntreader, The": Joni Mitchell **A260**
"Day After, The": Goodie MoB B14
"Day after Forever, The" A14
"Day after the Revolution, The": Pulp A82
"Day by Day": The Four Freshmen B15
"Daydream": The Lovin' Spoonful A95, B7, B8
"Day I Met Marie, The": Cliff Richard B21
"Day In-Day Out" **B30**
"Day in the Life, A" A97; The Beatles A22, A43, **A63**, A68, A71, **A76**, A80, A92, A95, A96, A98, A99, A100, A101, A134, **A157**, A224, A247, A253, B3, B8, **B18, B19, B20**, B21, B29, B32
"Day in the Life of a Fool, A" ["Black Orpheus"] B12

"Day in the Life of a Tree, A": The Beach Boys A125, B15
"Day Isn't Long Enough, The": The Four Freshmen A160, B15
"Day Is Past and Done, The" B27
"Day I Tried to Live, The": Soundgarden A221
"Day I Went Back to School, The": The Beatles B7
"Daylight": RAMP (Roy Ayers Music Project) B22
"Day-O (Banana Boat Song)" B17
"Days Between": The Grateful Dead B17
"Days": Kinks A185
"Days of Pearly Spencer": David McWilliams A185
"Daytona": Chris Rea A185
"Day Tripper" A97, B17; The Beatles A43, A55, **A83**, A91, A92, A95, A98, A99, A107, **A107**, A195, **A245**, B8, B7, B24
"Day Without Me, A": U2 A89, B20
"Dazed and Confused": Led Zeppelin A17, A269, B7
"D.C.B.A.-25": Jefferson Airplane A99
"Deacon Blues": Steely Dan **A101**, A269
"Dead and Lovely": Tom Waits **A222**
"Dead Drunk Blues": Margaret Johnson A240; Lillian Miller **B26**
"Dead End Street": The Kinks A185, B20, B21
"Dead Homiez": Ice Cube B14
"Dead in Magazines": Hopesfall **A204**
"Dead Leaves and the Dirty Ground": White Stripes, The A148
"Deadly Rhythm, The": Refused A205
"Dead Man's Curve": Jan and Dean A96, A109, B15
"Dead Man's Handle": Richard Thompson B21
"Dead!": My Chemical Romance B21
"Dead or Alive": Bon Jovi A250
"Dead": They Might Be Giants A185
"Deal": The Grateful Dead B17; Jerry Garcia A16
"Dear, Oh Dear!" **B30**
"Dear Delilah": Grapefruit B7
"Dear for Me" B12
"Dear Friend": Wings B18
"Dear Little Girl" B30
"Dearly Beloved" B10, **B30**
"Dear Mama": 2Pac B31, B14

Song Index

"Dear Old Sunny South By the Sea": Jimmie Rodgers **A266**
"Dear Prudence": The Beatles A92, A98, A259, B7, B8, **B18**, B20, B24
"Dear Sweet Impaler": Park A205
"Death Cab for Cutie": Bonzo Dog Doo Dah Band B7
"Death Don't Have No Mercy" B17; Grateful Dead A171
"Death Letter [Blues]": Son House **A148**; White Stripes, The **A148**
"Death of Emmet Till, The": Bob Dylan A216
"Death of Floyd Collins, The": Vernon Dalhart **A240**
"Death of Jimmie Rodgers, The": Gene Autry A266
"Death of Mother Nature Suite": Kansas A72
"Death or Glory": The Clash A118
"Death's Reply": The Rascals B7
"Deathwish": The Police A235
"December": All About Eve A185
"Deck the House": Akufen **A115**
"Dedicated Follower of Fashion": The Kinks A107, A185, B8, B20
"Dedicated to the One I Love": The Mamas and the Papas A99, B7
"De Do Do Do, De Da Da Da": The Police A235
"Deed I Do" A145, B30
"Deep Elm" A145
"Deep in a Dream" A14, B30
"Deep Night" B12
"Deep Purple": Brian Wilson B15
"Deep Song": Billie Holiday B4
"Dehra Dun": George Harrison B7
"Deirdre": The Beach Boys B15
"Deiro Rag" A145
"Déjà Vu": Crosby, Stills, Nash & Young B3, B7
"Delia": Blind Willie McTell A240
"Delirious": Prince A35
"Deliverance": Mission A185
"De-Lovely" B30
"De-Luxe": Lush A221
"Depression's Gone From Me Blues": Blind Blake **A240**
"Der Kommissar": Falco A19
"Desafinado" ["Off Key"]: João Gilberto A211
"Desecration Rag" A145
"Deseri": Mothers of Invention, The A11

"Desert Blues": Jimmie Rodgers A266
"Desert Drive": Brian Wilson B15
"Deserted Cities of the Heart": Cream **B20, B29**
"Desire": U2 A55, A89, A250
"Desolation Row": Bob Dylan **A7**, A141, A216, B7
"Desperado": The Eagles B24
"Desperate People": Living Colour A55
"Detroit, Lift up Your Weary Head!": Sufjan Stevens A221
"Detroit City": Bobby Bare B15
"Deutschland": Die Böhse Onkelz **B23**
"Devil Came from Kansas, The": Procol Harum A185
"Devil Doll": Roy Orbison A270
"Devil in His Heart" *see* "(There's a) Devil in His [Her] Heart"
"Devil in Me": 22-20S B21
"Devil Is Afraid of Music, The" B30
"Devil or Angel": Bobby Vee B24
"Devil's Child": Judas Priest A99
"Devil's Haircut": Beck A163
"Devil With a Blue Dress On": Mitch Ryder A108
"Devil Woman": Cliff Richard B8
"Devoted to You": The Beach Boys B15; The Everly Brothers B15
"Devotion": Weezer A221
"Dharma for One": Jethro Tull A188
"Dialogue": Chicago B24
"Diamond Dogs": David Bowie A185
"Diamond Head": The Beach Boys B15
"Diamond in the Rough": Shawn Colvin B32
"Diamonds and Gold": Tom Waits A221
"Diamonds and Pearls": Prince A79, **B13**
"Diamonds": Jet Harris and Tony Meehan B8
"Diamonds on the Soles of Her Shoes": Paul Simon A9
"Diana": Paul Anka A97, A185, B25
"Diary, The": The Beach Boys B15; Neil Sedaka B15
"Did It in a Minute": Hall and Oates A250
"Didn't Think So": The Great Society A99
"Didn't We" **A217**, B3; Gene Ammons **A217**; Michael Feinstein **A217**; Stan Getz **A217**; Richard Harris **A217**; Barbra Streisand **A217**
"Did She Jump or Was She Pushed": Richard and Linda Thompson B20

"Did You Ever Cross Over to Sneden's" **A209**
"Did You Ever See a Lassie?" A95
"Did Your Mother Come from Ireland?": Billy Cotton and His Band A227
"Different Finger": Elvis Costello and the Attractions B4
"Different Point of View, A": The Pet Shop Boys A174
"Difficult to Cure": Rainbow B28
"Diga-Diga-Doo" B12
"Dig a Pony": The Beatles A98, B7, B8, B18
"Digging in the Dirt": Peter Gabriel A159, B32
"Digging My Potatoes" B8
"Diggin' My Potatoes": Sonny Terry & Brownie McGhee A95
"Dig It": The Beatles A98, B7
"Dil Bharian": Panjabi MC A61
"Dilemma": Nelly featuring Kelly Rowland **A215**
"Dill Pickles Rag" A145
"Dim, Dim the Lights (I Want Some Atmosphere)": Bill Haley A97
"Diminuendo and Crescendo in Blue" A145; Duke Ellington A105
"Dimples": John Lee Hooker A144
"Dinah" A145, B30; Bing Crosby B8
"Dinah-Moe-Humm": Mothers of Invention, The A11
"Ding Dang": The Beach Boys B15
"Ding Dong the Witch Is Dead": Klaus Nomi A178
"Dinosaur": King Crimson **A54**, **A218**
"Dippermouth Blues" A219
"Directorate March, the" A145
"Dire Wolf": The Grateful Dead A171, B17
"Dirt Off Your Shoulder": Danger Mouse A24
"Dirty Day": U2 A89
"Dirty Diana": Michael Jackson A35
"Dirty Hangover Blues": W. Lee O'Daniel & His Hillbilly Boys A240
"Dirty Laundry": Don Henley A43
"Dirty Little Girl": Elton John B7
"Dirty Mack": Ice Cube A146
"Dirty Mind": Prince A250
"Dirty Overhalls": Woody Guthrie A240
"Dirty Pop": Skkatter A24
"Dirty South": Goodie MoB B14
"Dirty Water": The Standells A43
"Dirty White Boy": Foreigner A74, A250

"Dirty Work": Steely Dan A96
"Disappear" [1]: Madness A185
"Disappear" [2]: Dream Theater A175
"Discipline": King Crimson A221
"Disco Inferno": The Trammps A179
"Discothéque": U2 A89
"Dishes": Pulp A82
"Dissertation on the State of Bliss" B30
"Distant Lover": Marvin Gaye A110
"Distractions": Paul McCartney A185, B7, B20
"Dixie Boll Weevil": Fiddlin' John Carson A240
"Dixie Flyer Blues": DeFord Bailey B9
"Dixieland Band, The" B30
"Dizzy Miss Lizzy": The Beatles A98, A254, B8, B18; Larry Williams A95; Plastic Ono Band B7
"Dizzy's Business": Dizzy Gillespie **A96**
"Dock of the Bay" *see* "(Sittin' on the) Dock of the Bay"
"Doctor, Doctor": The Thompson Twins B32
"Doctor Pressure": Mylo A212
"Doctor Robert": The Beatles A63, **A92**, A95, A250, **A253**, B7, B8, B18
"Do-Do-Do" **B30**
"Does Anybody Really Know What Time It Is?": Chicago **A101**, A214, B3, **B24**
"Does Everyone Stare": The Police A235
"Dog, The": Rufus Thomas A29
"Dog Breath [Variations] [in the Year of the Plague]": Mothers of Invention, The A11, **A12**
"Doggie in the Window" B10
"Dogs" [1]: The Who B7
"Dogs" [2]: Pink Floyd A198, A207
"Dog Tribe": Fun-Da-Mental **A61**
"Do I Hear You Saying I Love You" B30
"Do I Love You" B10, B30
"Do I Love You Because You're Beautiful" B30
"Doina din Arges": Gheorghe Zamfir B25
"Doin' Dumb Shit": Ice Cube B14
"Doing It to Death" ["Gonna Have a Funky Good Time"]: Fred Wesley and the JBs A31, **A271**, B4
"Doing the Omralisk Schlagerfestival": Nationalteatern B25
"Doin' It": LL Cool J B14
"Doin' It the Old Fashioned Way": Roy Acuff B4
"Doin' That Rag": The Grateful Dead B17

Song Index

"Doin' What Comes Natur'lly" B10, B30
"Do It ('Til You're Satisfied)": B.T. Express A238
"Do It Again" [1]: The Beach Boys A185, B15
"Do It Again" [2]: Steely Dan **A7**
"Do It Again" [3] B10
"Do Lawd Do": Ida Cox A240
"Dollars and Cents": Radiohead A135, **A169**
"Doll Parts": Hole A124
"Dolly Dagger": The Jimi Hendrix Experience A101, **A257**, B29
"Dominique": The Singing Nun A99
"Domino Dancing": The Pet Shop Boys **A128, B13**
"Dominoes": Barrett, Syd A198
"Dona Dona" B12
"Donald, Where's your Troosers?": Andy Stewart B21
"Donna" [1]: Marty Wilde A185
"Donna" [2]: Ritchie Valens A44, B24, **B25**
"Donor, The": Judee Sill B21
"Do Not Expect Too Much From the End of the World": BradleyHeartVampire A205
"Do Nothing Till You Hear From Me" B30; Duke Ellington B4
"Don't Ask Me Why": Billy Joel A250
"Don't Back Down": The Beach Boys **A125**, B15
"Don't Be a Drop-Out": James Brown A31, A105, B4
"Don't Be Blue" A145
"Don't Be Cruel" B7, B8; American Spring B15; Elvis Presley A44, A99, B15, B19
"Don't Be Denied": Neil Young B6
"Don't Believe a Word": Thin Lizzy A185
"Don't Believe the Hype": Public Enemy **A24**
"Don't Believe What You Read": Boomtown Rats A185
"Don't Be Like That" A145
"Don't Be That Way" **B30**
"Don't Blame Me" B10, **B30**
"Don't Bother Me": The Beatles A76, A90, A98, A99, B7, **B8**
"Don't Bring Me Down" [1]: The Animals B8
"Don't Bring Me Down" [2]: E.L.O. **A16, A83**, A179, A248
"Don't Call Me Nigger, Whitey": Sly and the Family Stone **A55**
"Don't Call Us, We'll Call You": Sugarloaf/Jerry Corbetta A43, A248

"Don't Care": Kent Klark (Stewart Copeland) A235
"Don't Come Around Here No More": Tom Petty and the Heartbreakers B32
"Don't Come Home a Drinkin' (With Lovin' on Your Mind)": Loretta Lynn A193
"Don't Cry" [1]: Neil Young B6
"Don't Cry" [2]: Asia A71
"Don't Cry Joni": Conway Twitty A191
"Don't Cry No Tears": Neil Young B6
"Don't Dig No Pakistanis": The Beatles B7
"Don't Do Me Like That": Tom Petty A250
"Don't Doubt Yourself Babe": The Byrds A121
"Don't Ease Me In" B17; Grateful Dead A171; Henry Thomas A240
"Don't Eat the Yellow Snow": Frank Zappa A11, A221
"Don't": Elvis Presley A44, A99, A97
"Don't Ever Change": The Beatles A98; Buddy Holly and the Crickets A185, B8, B20
"Don't Ever Leave Me" B30
"Don't Explain": Billie Holiday B4
"(Don't Fear) The Reaper": Blue Öyster Cult A7, **A16**, A24, A43, A99, A167, A185, A247
"Don't Fence Me In" B30
"Don't Fight It": Wilson Pickett B8, B32
"Don't Forbid Me": The Beatles B8; Pat Boone A97
"Don't Get Around Much Anymore" B30; The Beatles B8; Duke Ellington A182
"Don't Get Me Wrong": The Pretenders B24
"Don't Go Away" A145
"Don't Go Away Mad": Motley Crue A250
"(Don't Go Back to) Rockville": REM A247
"Don't Go Home": The Jaguars B15
"Don't Go to Strangers": J.J. Cale B21
"Don't Have to Shop Around": The Mad Lads A29, A95
"Don't Hide Your Heart": Sheila Walsh A185
"Don't Hurt My Little Sister": The Beach Boys B15
"Don't Know Why": Eric Clapton A185, **B3**
"Don't Leave Me Here": Henry Thomas A240
"Don't Leave Me This Way": The Communards A123; Thelma Houston A123; Harold Melvin and the Blue Notes A123
"Don't Let Her Know She's an Angel": Brian Wilson B15
"Don't Let Him Go": REO Speedwagon **A250**

"Don't Let Him Steal Your Heart Away": Phil Collins A185, B20
"Don't Let It Bring You Down": Neil Young B6
"Don't Let It End": Styx A250
"Don't Let It Get You Down" [1]: Fine Young Cannibals A185
"Don't Let It Get You Down" [2] B30
"Don't Let It Rain on My Parade": Icicle Works A185, **A186**, **B20**, **B21**
"Don't Let Me Be Misunderstood": The Animals A185, A167, **B19**, B21, B24
"Don't Let Me Down": The Beatles A17, A43, A63, A98, A195, **B7**, **B8**
"Don't Let the Joneses Get you Down": The Temptations A105
"Don't Let the Sun Catch You Crying" B8; Ray Charles A95
"Don't Let the Sun Go Down on Me": Elton John A247, **B24**
"Don't Lie to Me": Jeanie and the Big Guys B8
"Don't Look at Me That Way" A113
"Don't Look Back" [1]: Fine Young Cannibals A185
"Don't Look Back" [2]: Boston A250
"Don't Look Back in Anger": Oasis B21, **B24**
"Don't Look Down": Lindsey Buckingham B24
"Don't Make Me Laugh, Bill" A145
"Don't Mess With Bill": The Marvelettes A108
"Don't Panic": Coldplay A167
"Don't Pass Me By": The Beatles A98, A234, B7, B8
"Don't Say Nothin' Bad (About My Baby)": The Cookies A38
"Don't Send Me Back to Petrograd" B12
"Don't Shoot Shotgun": Def Leppard A185
"Don't Sit on my Jimmy Shands": Richard Thompson B21
"Don't Sleep in the Subway": Petula Clark A185
"Don't Stand So Close to Me": The Police A7, A235, A248
"Don't Stop" [1]: Fleetwood Mac A185
"Don't Stop" [2]: Madonna **B13**
"Don't Stop Believin'": Journey A205, A250
"Don't Stop Me Now": Queen A185
"Don't Sweetheart Me": Lawrence Welk B4
"Don't Take Me Alive": Steely Dan A96
"Don't Take Me Home" A145

"Don't Take My Kindness for Weakness": The Soul Children A29
"Don't Take the Girl": Tim McGraw **A191**
"Don't Talk (Put Your Head on My Shoulder)": The Beach Boys **A160**, B15
"Don't Tell Me You Love Me": Night Ranger A250
"Don't Think Twice, It's All Right": Bob Dylan A121, A216
"Don't Throw Your Love Away": Searchers A185
"Don't Trust 'Em": Ice Cube B14
"Don't Wake Me Up Let Me Dream" A145
"Don't Worry, Baby": The Beach Boys B15, B24; Lorrie Morgan B15
"Don't Worry Baby": The Beach Boys **A84**, A99, A109, A160, A185, A247, B8
"Don't Worry Be Happy": Bobby McFerrin B24
"Don't Worry 'Bout Me" **B30**
"Don't Worry Kyoko (Mummy's Only Looking for Her Hand in the Snow)": Plastic Ono Band B7, B18
"Don't You Ever Learn?": Todd Rundgren **A59**
"Don't You Forget About Me": Simple Minds **A16**
"Don't You Know" B12
"Don't You Leave Me Here": Jelly Roll Morton A240
"Don't You Rock Me, Daddy-O": The Quarrymen B8
"Don't You Want Me": The Human League A248, A269
"Don't You Worry 'Bout a Thing": Stevie Wonder A43, A185
"Doo Dah Dey" B30
"Dooms Night": Azzido Da Bass **B5**
"Doors, The": Hello, I Love You A101
"Do Right to Me Baby (Do Unto Others)": Bob Dylan A180, A185
"Do Right Woman": Aretha Franklin B24
"Do the Funky Chicken": Rufus Thomas A29
"Do the Hucklebuck" B19; Roy Milton **B19**
"(Do the) Push and Pull": Rufus Thomas A29
"Do the Reggay": Toots and the Maytals A235
"Do the Strand": Roxy Music B20
"Do They Know It's Christmas?": Band Aid A205, B19, B25

Song Index

"Doubleback Alley": The Rutles A69
"Double Crossing Blues": The Robins A77
"Double Trouble": The Roots feat. Mos Def **B31**
"Double Vision": Foreigner A250
"Douglas Mountain" **A209**
"Douglas Traherne Harding": The Incredible String Band A112
"Do Wah Diddy Diddy": Manfred Mann B8
"Do What You Like": Blind Faith A43
"Down, Home": Spring B15
"Down Along the Cove": Bob Dylan B7
"Down Argentina Way": Marjorie Kingsley with Harry Roy's Dance Band B21
"(Down at) Papa Joe's": The Dixiebelles A95
"Down at the Twist and Shout": Mary Chapin Carpenter A191
"Down By the River" [1]: Neil Young A16, **A88**, B6
"Down By The River" [2] B30
"Down By The Sea" B30
"Down by the Seaside": Led Zeppelin A17
"Down Home Rag, The" A145, B30
"Down in Jungle Town": Bing Crosby B4
"Down in Mexico": The Coasters **A77**
"Down in Texas Blues": Jesse "Babyface" Thomas **A240**
"Down in the Bottom" B17
"Down in the Glen" **A227**
"Down in the Tube Station at Midnight": Jam A185
"Down Mexico Way" **B19**
"Down on Me": Big Brother and the Holding Co. A101, B7
"Down on the Brandywine Medley" A145
"Down on the Corner": Creedence Clearwater Revival A185, B20
"Down on the Highway": Bob Dylan A58
"Down on the Old Plantation" A145
"Down on You": Transvision Vamp A185
"Down Rodeo": Rage Against the Machine A205
"Down South Camp Meeting" A145
"Down the Dolce Vita": Peter Gabriel A185
"Down the Dustpipe": Status Quo B20
"Down the Highway": Bob Dylan **A18**
"Down the Line": The Beatles B8; Jerry Lee Lewis A270

"Down the Old Road to Home": Jimmie Rodgers A266
"Down to Earth" [1]: Curiosity Killed the Cat A185
"Down to Earth" [2]: The Bee Gees B3
"Downtown": Petula Clark B4, B21, **A241**
"Down to You": Joni Mitchell A260
"Down Under": Men at Work **A84**, B24
"Down With Love" B30
"Do Ya Think I'm Sexy": Rod Stewart A179
"Do You Believe in Magic": The Lovin' Spoonful **B24**
"Do You Believe?": Melanie B21
"Do You Feel Like We Do": Peter Frampton A43
"Do You Know the Way to San Jose" B3
"Do You Like Worms?": The Beach Boys B15
"Do You Love Me?" [1]: Brian Poole A185
"Do You Love Me?" [2] **B30**
"Do You Really Want to Hurt Me": Culture Club A43, A185
"Do You Remember": The Beach Boys B15
"Do You Wanna Dance": The Beach Boys B15; The Beatles B8; Bobby Freeman A44, A95, B15
"Do You Want Me": Slade **B21**
"Do You Want to Know a Secret?": The Beatles A95, A98, A107, **A107**, B4, B7, **B8**, **B18**; Billy J. Kramer and The Dakotas A185, B21
"Drag City": Jan and Dean **A109**, A125, B15
"Draggin'": Roger McGuinn A121
"Dragonfly": Goldie B21
"Drama": Erasure A185
"Drawn to the Rhythm": Sarah McLachlan **A5**
"Draw": Ringo Starr B18
"Dr. Dream": The Beatles A90
"Dreadlock Holiday": 10cc A235
"Dream, A": Jay-Z **B31**
"Dream (All I Have To Do)": The Everly Brothers A44
"Dream Angel": Brian Wilson B15
"Dream Baby" A147; The Beatles B8; The Quarrymen B7
"Dream Crazy": Level 42 A185
"Dreamer, The": All About Eve B21
"Dreamer": Supertramp A182, A185
"Dreaming, The": Kate Bush B20
"Dreaming of the Queen": The Pet Shop Boys A174, **B13**
"Dreaming": Orchestral Manoeuvres A185

"Dreaming with Tears in My Eyes": Jimmie Rodgers A266
"Dreamin'": Johnny Burnette A185
"Dream Lover": Bobby Darin **A241**, B21, B25
"Dreammare": Uriah Heep A185
"Dream Now": All About Eve A185
"Dream On": Aerosmith **A16**, **A101**, A247
"Dream/Pax/Nepenthe" B3
"Dream Police": Cheap Trick A250
"Dream Scene": George Harrison B7
"Dreams": Fleetwood Mac A59, A185, A248, B20, **B24**
"Dream Tango" B12
"Dream Weaver": Gary Wright B24
"Drei Six Cents" B12
"Dreyfus Court Marshal, The" B12
"Dr. Feelgood": Aretha Franklin A123
"Drifting Along With The Tide" B30
"Drilling a Home": George Harrison B7
"Drink Before the War": Sinéad O'Connor B32
"Drive (For Daddy Gene)": Alan Jackson A191
"Drive Back": Neil Young A33, B6
"Driven Insane": Gary Usher A160, B15
"Drive-In": The Beach Boys B15
"Drive My Car": The Beatles A76, A95, A98, A99, **A246**, A254, B7, B8, **B18**, **B20**
"Drop a Gem on 'Em": Mobb Deep B14
"Drop": Soft Machine B20
"Drop the Pilot": Joan Armatrading A136
"Drowning Man": U2 A103
"Drown Me": Soundgarden A55
"Dr. Robert": The Beatles A63, A185
"Drums in My Heart" B30
"Drums": The Grateful Dead B17
"Drumz": The Grateful Dead B17
"Drunkard's Child, A": Jimmie Rodgers **A266**
"Drunken Sailor, A" **A65**, A99, A126, **A231**, B12
"Drunken Spree": Skip James A240
"Dr. Wu": Steely Dan A96
"Dry Spell Blues" A145; Eddie "Son": House **B26**
"Dry Your Eyes": Streets, The B21
"Duane Joseph": The Juliana Theory A205
"Duck, The": Jackie Lee B21
"Ducks on a Pond": The Incredible String Band A112
"Duel of the Jester and the Tyrant": Return to Forever A73

"Du Gav Bara Löften": Vikingarna B25
"Duke of Earl": Gene Chandler A43
"Duke of Orchestral Prunes, The": Frank Zappa A12
"Duke of Prunes, The": The Mothers of Invention A11, A12
"Duke Regains His Chops, The": The Mothers of Invention A11, A12
"Duke's Travels/Duke's End": Genesis A142
"Duncan": Paul Simon B1
"Dunkin' Bagel" B12
"Dupree Blues": Willie Walker and Sam Brooks **B26**
"Dupree's Diamond Blues": The Grateful Dead B7, B17
"Dupree's Paradise": The Mothers A11, **A12**; Frank Zappa **A12**
"Duquesne Whistle": Bob Dylan A216
"Dust in the Wind": Kansas A72, B24
"Dust on the Moon" A145
"Dust Pneumonia Blues": Woody Guthrie B21
"D'yer Mak'er": Led Zeppelin A43, A167, A185, B21
"Dying Pickpocket Blues": Nolan "Barrelhouse": Welsh **B26**
"D'You Know What I Mean": Oasis **A246**

"Eagle and the Hawk, The": John Denver **B24**
"Eagle Laughs at You, The": Jackie Lomax B7
"Earl's Breakdown": Flatt and Scruggs **A220**
"Early 1970": Ringo Starr B7
"Early in the Morning": The Beatles B8; Louis Jordan **B25**
"Early Morning Blues": Blind Blake **B26**
"Earn Enough for Us": XTC B20
"Ears of Tin": Jethro Tull A188
"Earth Angel": The Crewcuts **B25**; Penguins A247, B21
"Earth Song": Michael Jackson A82
"Ease Back": Meters A185
"Easter Parade" B10
"East of Eden": Big Country A185
"East of the Sun" **B30**
"East St. Louis Blues (Fare You Well)": William Brown **A240**; Blind Willie McTell A240
"East St. Louis Toodle-oo": Steely Dan A96; Duke Ellington B9
"East Virginia Blues": Ashley & Foster A240
"Easy" [1]: Nik Kershaw A185

Song Index

"Easy" [2]: The Commodores A248
"Easy Come, Easy Go" **B30**
"Easy Living": Uriah Heep A185
"Easy Lover": Baily/Collins A250
"Easy Meat": Frank Zappa **A54**, **A60**
"Easy Money": King Crimson A152
"Easy Now": Eric Clapton A185
"Easy Rider": Leadbelly A240
"Easy Street" **B30**
"Easy to Love" *see* "(You'd Be So) Easy to Love"
"Easy Wind": The Grateful Dead B17
"Ebony and Ivory": Paul McCartney & Stevie Wonder A232, B7, B24
"Echo": Bob Dylan B32
"Echoes": Pink Floyd A198, A199, A207, A208, B29, B32
"Eclipse": Pink Floyd A185, A199, A205, B24, B29
"Eddie My Love": The Fontane Sisters A44
"Editions of You": Roxy Music A185
"Effigy": Creedence Clearwater B3
"Ego Tripping Out": Marvin Gaye A110
"Egyptian Ella" B12
"Eight Days a Week": The Beatles A16, A43, **A70**, **A76**, **A91**, A92, A98, A107, **A107**, A185, **A194**, B7, **B8**, B21, B21, **B24**
"Eight Miles High": The Byrds A17, A75, A121, A247, B7, B8
"Eiledon": Big Country A185, B20
"Einstein on the Beach (For an Eggman)": Counting Crows A246, A247
"Either Way": Wilco **A102**
"El Capitan March" A145
"El Condor Pasa" B12, **B25**; Los Calchakis B25; Simon and Garfunkel B1, B25
"Elder Greene Blues": Charley Patton A240
"Eldorado" [1]: Neil Young **A88**
"Eldorado" [2] B12
"Eleanor Rigby" B3; The Beatles A7, A43, A70, A71, A98, A99, A107, **A107**, A156, **A157**, A182, A185, A195, A198, **A230**, A233, A234, A247, A259, B3, **B7**, B8, **B18**, B21, B29, B32; Aretha Franklin A265; Vanilla Fudge A72, B21
"Elected": Alice Cooper **A16**
"Electioneering": Radiohead **A169**
"Electric Co. The": U2 A89
"Electric Eye": Judas Priest B28
"Electric Funeral": Black Sabbath A97, A99

"Electricity" [1]: Joni Mitchell A260
"Electricity" [2]: The Pet Shop Boys A174, B13
"Electricity" [3]: Orchestral Manoeuvres A185, B20
"Electricity" [4]: True Margrit A221
"Electric Light": PJ Harvey A223
"Elenore": Turtles B21
"Elephant's Wobble" A145
"Elephant Talk": King Crimson A224
"Elevation": U2 **A89**, A232
"Eleven, The": The Grateful Dead A25, A99, **A171**, B7, B17
"Eleven": Primus A221
"Eleventh Earl of Mar": Genesis A185
"Eli, Eli" B12
"Eli Green's Cake Walk" B12
"Eli's Coming": Three Dog Night A43
"El Loco": Bad Boy Orchestra A3
"El Loco Cha Cha": René Touzet **A85**
"Eloise (Hang on in There)" [2]: William Bell A29
"Eloise" [1]: Barry Ryan B21
"El Paso" B17
"El Pueblo Unido" **B25**
"Elsewhere": Sarah McLachlan **A154**
"El Sombrero de Gaspar" A145
"Elspeth of Nottingham": Focus B20
"Elvis Is Dead": Living Colour A99
"Elvis Presley and America": U2 A89, A185
"Emale": Prince **B13**
"Embarrassment": Madness A185
"Embraceable You": **A114**, A168, **A184**, **B10**, **B11**, B12, **B30**
"EMI": Jonathan Richman B4
"Emotionally Yours": Bob Dylan A99
"Emotions": Brenda Lee A96
"Empire State of Mind": Jay-Z featuring Alicia Keys **A84**
"Empty Cans": Streets, The B21
"Empty Cup, An": Roy Orbison **A270**
"End, The" [1]: The Beatles **A17**, **A92**, A99, **A100**, A101, **A116**, A250, B4, **B7**, B8, B18
"End, The" [2]: The Doors **A16**, A43, A82, A167, A269, **B3**
"End, The" [3]: My Chemical Romance B21
"Endless Enigma, The": Emerson, Lake, and Palmer A139, **A166**, **B24**
"Endless Harmony": The Beach Boys B15
"Endless Sacrifice": Dream Theater A175

"Endless Sleep": Larry Denton B15; Jody Reynolds B15
"End of the Innocence, The": Don Henley B24
"End of the Night": The Doors A99
"Engine 143": Carter Family, The A240
"England": The National A205
"English Breakfast": Fun-Da-Mental A61
"English Rose": Jam A185
"Enola Gay": Orchestral Manoeuvres A185, B20
"Enter Sandman": Metallica A80, A103, A151, A212, A247
"Entertainer, The": Billy Joel A99, A101
"Entre Mi Casa": Armand van Helden A3
"Entre Nous": Rush A245
"Entry": echolyn A72
"Envelopes": Frank Zappa A12
"Epic": Faith No More B21
"Epic Problem": Fugazi A205
"Epitaph": King Crimson A72, A185, A152, B7, B20, B21
"Erin-Go-Bragh": Dick Gaughan B21
"E.R.N.I.E.": Madness A185
"Erotomania": Dream Theater A175
"Eruption": Van Halen B28
"Esa Loca": Wepaman A3
"Escape Artists Never Die": Funeral for a Friend A205
"Esmeralda" B30
"Estimated Prophet": The Grateful Dead B17
"Et Cetera": Paul McCartney B7
"Eternity": The Grateful Dead B17
"Ether" [1]: Gang of Four B20
"Ether" [2]: Nas B31
"ethnik [sic]": Plastikman **A115**
"Eton Rifles": Jam A185, B20
"Europe Endless": Kraftwerk **A104**
"Evangeline": Icicle Works A185
"Eve Cost Adam Just One Bone" A145
"Evelina" **B30**
"Even Better Than the Real Thing": U2 A89, A103
"Even the Losers": Tom Petty A250
"Eve of Destruction": Barry McGuire A32, B8
"Everbody's Been Burned": The Byrds A121
"Everbody's Ever Got Somebody Caring": The Beatles B8
"Ever Fallen in Love": Fine Young Cannibals A185

"Everlasting Love": Love Affair A185
"Every [Ev'ry] Time We Say Goodbye" **B10**, **B30**, **A113**; Ella Fitzgerald B21; The Four Freshmen B15
"Everybody" A145
"Everybody Does It in Hawaii": Jimmie Rodgers A266
"Everybody Get Together": H.P. Lovecraft B21
"Everybody Hurts": R.E.M. A181
"Everybody Is a Star": Sly and the Family Stone **A84**
"Everybody Knows (I Still Love You)": Dave Clark Five A107
"Everybody Knows This Is Nowhere": Neil Young **B6**
"Everybody Loves a Clown": Gary Lewis and the Playboys B4
"Everybody Loves a Winner": William Bell A29
"Everybody Loves My Baby" A147, B30; Fletcher Henderson A119
"Everybody Loves to Play the Fool": Icicle Works A185
"Everybody Loves You Now": Billy Joel A99
"Everybody Needs Love": Marvin Gaye **A110**
"Everybody Needs Somebody to Love": Solomon Burke A95, A185
"Everybody Rag With Me" A145
"Everybody's Got Something to Hide Except Me and My Monkey": The Beatles B7, B18
"Everybody's Talking about Sadie Green": Memphis Jug Band A240
"Everybody's Trying to Be My Baby": The Beatles A92, A98, A254, B7, B8; Rex Griffin A266
"Everybody Two-Step" A145
"Everybody Wants a Key to My Cellar" A145
"Everybody Wants to Live": The Beach Boys B15
"Everybody Wants to Rule the World": Tears for Fears A185, A233, **A241**, A250
"Everybody Wants You": Billy Squier A247
"Every Breath You Take": The Police A75, A80, A99, A163, **A235**, A247, B21, B24
"Everyday" [1]: Buddy Holly A270, B8, B21, B32
"Everyday" [2]: Slade B20
"Every Day": Buddy Holly B24
"Everyday I Write the Book": Elvis Costello and the Attractions B4, B24

Song Index

"Everyday People": Sly and the Family Stone A99, A247, **B3**, B24
"Everyday Struggle": Notorious B.I.G. B14
"Everyday Will Be Like a Holiday": William Bell A29
"Every Heartbeat": Amy Grant B24
"Every Little Kiss": Bruce Hornsby A99
"Every Little Thing She Does Is Magic": The Police A235, A248
"Every Little Thing": The Beatles A76, A98, A100, B7, **B8**
"Every Man Oughta Have a Woman": William Bell A29
"Every Night":The Beatles B7; Paul McCartney B18, B20
"Everyone's Gone to the Moon": Jonathan King A185
"Everyone's in Love with You": The Beach Boys B15
"Everyone Thinks He Looks Daft": Wedding Present A185
"Every Step of the Way": Santana A185
"Every Tear from Every Eye": John McLaughlin A256
"Everything About It Is a Love Song": Paul Simon B1
"Everything Evil": Coheed and Cambria A205
"Everything Happens to Me" **A147**, B30
"(Everything I Do) I Do It for You": Bryan Adams **A183**, A202, B24
"Everything I Have Is Yours" B10, B16, **B30**
"Everything I Need": Brian Wilson B15; The Wilsons B15
"Everything in Its Right Place": Radiohead A7, **A97**, **A162**, **A169**, A221
"Everything I Own": Bread **B21**, B24
"Everything Is Good About You": The Supremes B3
"Everything Put Together Falls Apart": Paul Simon A93, B1
"Everything's Alright" [1]: The Newbeats B15
"Everything's Alright" [2]: Yvonne Elliman A43
"Everything's Gonna Be All Right" A145
"Everytime You Go Away": Paul Young B24, B32
"Everywhere": Fleetwood Mac A59
"Everywhere I Look" **A209**
"Everywhere I Roam": Metallica A252
"Everywhere It's Christmas": The Beatles B7

"Eveywhere": Fleetwood Mac A185
"Evil": Howlin' Wolf A75
"Evil Ways": Santana **A16**, **A75**, A101, A167
"Evil Woman": Electric Light Orchestra B24
"E Viva España" B25
"Ev'rybody Has the Right to Be Wrong" A14
"Ev'rybody's Doin' It Now" A168
"Ev'ry Day a Holiday" **B30**
"Ev'ry Little Bit Added to What You've Got" A145
"Ev'ry Sunday Afternoon" B30
"Ev'rything I Love" **B10**, **B30**
"Ev'rything I've Got" B30
"Ev'ry Time" **B30**
"Exactly like You" B10, B30
"Excitable": Def Leppard A185
"Excursions": Tribe Called Quest, A **B31**
"Exercise #4": Frank Zappa A12, A60
"Exiles": King Crimson A152, B20
"Exit": U2 A185, B20
"Exit Music (For a Film)": Radiohead **A143**, A169
"Exodus": Bob Marley and the Wailers A235
"Exodus Song, The" B12
"Experiment" B30
"Express": B.T. Express **A101**
"Expressway to Your Heart" A238
"Express Yourself": Madonna A66
"Expulsion, The": Frantic Bleep B21
"Eye in the Sky": Alan Parsons Project A43
"Eye of the Tiger": Survivor A247, B21
"Eyepennies": Sparklehorse B21
"Eyes of Fate, The": The Incredible String Band A112
"Eyes of the World": Grateful Dead A171, B17

"Fabulous": Charlie Gracie B8
"Facelift": Soft Machine B20
"Face the Fire": Dan Fogelberg **B24**
"Factory": Bruce Springsteen A99
"Factory Lass, The": Ned Corvan B19
"Faded Love": Patsy Cline **A189**
"Fa-Fa-Fa-Fa-Fa (Sad Song)": Otis Redding A29
"Fair Exchange": Be-Bop Deluxe A185
"Fair One" A145
"Fairy Tale": Brian Wilson B15
"Fairy Tale of New York": The Pogues A221
"Fairytalez": The Gravediggaz B14

Song Index

"Fais Pas Ça": Hackberry Ramblers **A240**
"Faithful Axe": Kenealley, Mike A72
"Faithfully": Journey A247, A250, **B24**
"Faith": Limp Bizkit **A83**; George Michael **A83**, A219
"Fake Plastic Trees": Radiohead A80, A162, **A169**, A247
"Fakin' It": Simon and Garfunkel B1, B3
"Fall Breaks and Back to Winter": The Beach Boys A125, B15
"Fallen Angel": Robbie Robertson B32
"Fallen": Sarah McLachlan **A5**
"Fallin'": Alicia Keys A221
"Falling Away with You": Muse B21
"Falling in Love Again (Can't Help It)": The Beatles **B8**; Klaus Nomi A178
"Fallin' in Love": American Spring B15
"Falling in Love With Love" B30
"Fall in Pieces": Velvet Revolver B21
"Fall on Me": R.E.M. A181
"Fall Out / Nothing Achieving": The Police A235
"Family Affair": Sly and the Family Stone A247
"Family Man": Fleetwood Mac A185
"Family of Man": Three Dog Night **B24**
"Family Snapshot": Peter Gabriel A185
"Fancy Meeting You" **B10**
"Fanfare for the Common Man": Emerson, Lake, & Palmer A235
"Fannie Mae": Buster Brown B15
"Fanny Blair" **B27**
"Fanny Mae": Buster Brown B24
"Fantastic Voyage": David Bowie B20
"Fantasy Fugue": Providence A166
"Fantasy Girl": .38 Special A250
"Fantasy Sequins": George Harrison B7
"Far Cry": Marvin Gaye **A110**
"Fare Missed the Train, The" B12
"Fare Thee Well, Cold Winter" B27
"Fare Three Blues": Johnnie Head A240
"Fare Three Honey Fare Thee Well": Georgia White A240
"Farewell Amanda" B12
"Farewell Farewell": Fairport Convention B20
"Farewell to Kings, A": Rush A28
"Far Far Away": Slade A185, B21
"Farmer John" B8
"Farmer's Daughter": The Beach Boys B15

"Farming" B30
"Farm on the Freeway": Jethro Tull A188
"Fascinating Rhythm" A227, **B11**, B12, B19, **B30**
"Fascination" [1]: David Bowie B20
"Fascination" [2] see "(Keep Feeling) Fascination"
"Fascination Street": The Cure A99
"Fascnating Rhythm" **A147**
"Fashion": David Bowie A178, A185, B20, B32
"Fast Car": Tracy Chapman A80, A247, A250, **A250**
"Fatal Tragedy": Dream Theater A175
"Fatal Wedding, The" B12
"Fat-Bottomed Girls": Queen B21
"Fate of Talmadge Osborne, The": Ernest Stoneman & Kahle Brewer **A240**
"Father, Father" B12
"Father Abraham" B12
"Father and Daughter": Paul Simon B1
"Fathfully": Journey **A250**
"Fat Old Sun": Pink Floyd A185
"Faust Arp": Radiohead **A169**, A205, **A205**, **A206**
"Favourite Shirts": Haircut 100 A185
"Fear, The": Pulp A82
"Feedback": The Grateful Dead B17
"Feed the Birds" A202
"Fee-Fi-Fo-Fum": Wayne Shorter **A203**
"Feelin' Blue": Creedence Clearwater **B3**
"Feeling I'm Falling" **B30**
"Feelings" B12
"Feeling Sentimental" **B30**
"Feelin' the Spirit" A145
"Feel It": Kate Bush A185
"Feel Like a Stranger": The Grateful Dead B17
"Feels Like the First Time": Foreigner **A74**
"Feel So Fine": Johnny Preston B15
"Felicidade, A" A211
"Fell on Black Days": Soundgarden A221
"Fembot in a Wet T-Shirt": Frank Zappa A11
"Feral": Radiohead **A169**
"Fergus Sings the Blues": Deacon Blue A185
"Fernando": ABBA A74, A159, A185, **A242**, B19, B20, B21, **B25**
"Ferry Cross the Mersey": The Beatmakers B8; Gerry & Pacemakers A185
"Festa": Sergio Mendes and Brasil 66 B3
"Festival": Sigur Ros A205

Song Index

"Feudin' and Fightin' " **B30**
"Fever" [1]: The Beatles B8; Little Willie John A44, A84; Peggy Lee A43; The McCoys A43
"Fever" [2]: Judas Priest A99
"Fiddle and the Drum, The": Joni Mitchell **A260**
"Fields of Fire": Big Country A185, A187
"Fifth of Beethoven, A": Walter Murphy and the Big Apple Band A43, A159, **A179**
"Fifty-First Anniversary": Jimi Hendrix B3
"Fifty Miles of Elbow Room": Rev. F.W. McGhee A240
"Fight for Your Right": The Beastie Boys A99
"Fightin' in the War with Spain": Wilmer Watts & the Lonely Eagles A240
"Fightin' Side of Me, The": Merle Haggard **B25**
"Fight Like a Brave": Red Hot Chili Peppers A99
"Fight the Power": Public Enemy A61, **A117**, **A255**, A261, B31
"Figure of Eight": Paul McCartney A185
"Fill Me In": Craig David B21
"Filthy Habits": Frank Zappa A11
"Final Countdown, The": Europe B21
"Finally Free": Dream Theater A175
"Final Silencing, The": Sin-Eater **A10**, B2
"Final Thrust, The": Procol Harum A185
"Find a Little Wood": Tyrannosaurus Rex B20
"Finders Keepers": The Beach Boys A160, B15
"Find My Fortune": R.E.O. Speedwagon A185
"F.I.N.E.": Aerosmith A246
"Fine and Dandy" [1] **B30**; The Beatles **B8**
"Fine Brown Flame": Nellie Lutcher A53
"Fine Romance, A" **B30**
"Fingerprints": Katy Perry A219
"Fingertips, Part II" A95; Little Stevie Wonder A43
"Fire" [1]: The Jimi Hendrix Experience A55, A257
"Fire" [2]: Crazy World of Arthur Brown A43, B21
"Fire" [3]: The Ohio Players A43, A99, A238
"Fire" [4]: Pointer Sisters A43
"Fire and Rain": James Taylor A99, A248, B3, B21, B24
"Fireball": Deep Purple A185
"Fire Brigade": The Move A185, B20
"Fire Escape": Fastball A99

"Firefly": Saves The Day A205
"Fire in the Hole": Steely Dan **A96**
"Fire in the Morning": Melissa Manchester A250
"Fire on the Mountain": The Grateful Dead **A16**, A167, **B17**
"Firewall": Bright Eyes A205
"Firework": Katy Perry **A248**
"Firm Biz": The Firm B14
"First Girl I Loved, The": The Incredible String Band A112
"First Heart, Might Dawn Dart": Tyrannosaurus Rex B20
"First Time, The" [1]: U2 A89
"First Time, The" [2]: Adam Faith B8
"First Time Ever I Saw Your Face, The": Roberta Flack A43
"First Time I Met the Blues, The": Cream A132
"First You Have Me High" B30
"Firth of Fifth": Genesis A229
"Fish, The": Yes A101
"fish (Schindleria Praematurus), the": Yes A99
"Fish Bowl Man": King's X A97
"Fishin' for Religion": Arrested Development **A127**
"Fish on the Sand": George Harrison B7
"Fit as a Fiddle" A147
"Five Bridges Suite": The Nice A71, A166, A207
"Five Five Five": Frank Zappa A221
"Five Foot Two, Eyes of Blue" B8
"Five Long Years": Cream A132
"Five Minutes With the Minstrels" A145
"Five O'Clock World": The Vogues **A84**
"Five to One": The Doors B3
"Five Years": David Bowie A185, B21
"Fixing a Hole": The Beatles A43, A90, A98, A234, B7, **B18**, **B20**, B29
"Fixin' to Die Blues": Bob Dylan A216; Bukka White A216
"Fix Up, Look Sharp": Dizzee Rascall B31
"F**k [Forget] You": Cee Lo Green A232
"Flame, The": Cheap Trick B24
"Flame of the West": Big Country A185, A187, **B20**
"Flaming Pie": Paul McCartney B7
"Flaming": Pink Floyd **A198**
"Flashback": Tha Alkaholiks B14

"Flashdance (What a Feeling)": Irene Cara A19
"Flashlight": Parliament A238
"Flash Tears the Roof Off": Grandmaster Flash A104
"Flight of the Rat": Deep Purple A185, B20
"Flirting on the Beach" A145
"Floating Bridge": Eric Clapton A185
"Floating Down the River on the Alabam'" A145
"Floating": The Moody Blues B8
"Flood, The": The Flying Lizards B20, B21
"Florida Rag" A145
"Flower Called Nowhere, The": Stereolab A221
"Flower in the Rain": Move A185
"Flower People" *see* "(Listen to the) Flower People"
"Flower Punk": The Mothers of Invention A27, B7
"Flowers in the Rain": Move A185
"Flowers Never Bend with the Rainfall": Paul Simon B1; Simon and Garfunkel B1
"Fly, The": U2 A103
"Fly Away": Lenny Kravitz A250
"Fly By Night": Rush A28
"Flyingdale Flyer": Jethro Tull **A188**
"Flying Down To Rio" **B30**
"Flying Dutchman": Jethro Tull A185, A188
"Flying High Again": Ozzy Osbourne **A54**
"Flying Saucer, The": Buchanan and Goodman A39
"Flying Saucer Rock and Roll": Billy Riley A270
"Flying": The Beatles A98, B7
"Flyin' Home": Lionel Hampton B19
"Fly Like an Eagle": Steve Miller Band A43, A185
"Fly Me to the Moon" A167, B30
"Fly on a Windshield": Genesis B20
"FM": Steely Dan A96
"Focus": Focus **B21**
"Fo' Day Blues": Peg Leg Howell **B26**
"Fo' de Lawd's Sake Play a Waltz" A145
"Foggy Day, A" **A114**, B10, **B19**, **B30**; Ella Fitzgerald B21; Frank Sinatra B21
"Foggy Notion": The Modern Lovers A210; The Velvet Underground A210
"Folks Who Lived on the Hill, The" B30
"Following the Sun Around" A145
"Follow the Boys": Connie Francis A99

"Follow the Fold" **A41**
"Follow You Down": The Gin Blossoms B24
"Follow You Follow Me": Genesis A142, A232
"Folsom Prison Blues": Johnny Cash A247
"Fool #1": The Beatles B8
"Fooled Around and Fell in Love": Elvin Bishop A43
"Fool for You, A": Ray Charles A95
"Fool for You, A": The Beatles B8
"Fooling Yourself (Angry Young Man)": Styx B24
"Fool in Love, A": Tina Turner **A161**
"Foolish Heart": The Grateful Dead B17
"Foolish Little Girl": The Shirelles A38
"Fool on the Hill": The Beatles A43, A90, A98, **A234**, **B7**, B8, **B18**
"Fools Fall in Love" [1]: The Drifters A53
"Fools Fall in Love" [2] B30
"Fools Like Me": The Beatles B8
"Fools Rush In" **B30**
"Fool Such as I" *see* "(Now and Then There's) A Fool Such as I"
"Fool to Cry": Rolling Stones A185
"For Crying Out Loud": Meat Loaf A185
"För Dina Bruna Ögons Skull" A19
"Fore Day Creep": Ida Cox A240
"Foreign Affair": Tina Turner A185
"Foreign Policy": The Buckinghams B7
"For Emily, Wherever I May Find Her": Simon and Garfunkel A7, B1
"Foresaken": Dream Theater A175
"Forever Man": Eric Clapton A271
"Forever": Spring B15
"Forever": The Beach Boys A160
"For Every Man There's a Woman" B12, B30
"Forever Young": Rod Stewart **B24**
"For Free": The Byrds A121; Joni Mitchell **A260**
"Forget Him": Bobby Rydell B8
"Forgotten Man, The" B3
"For John and Paul": Donovan B8
"For Me and My Gal" **B30**
"For No One" [1]: The Beatles **A63**, A70, A90, A98, A185, A198, A259, **B7**, B8, **B18**
"For No One" [2]: Barclay James Harvest A185
"For Once in My Life": Stevie Wonder A185, B21

"Forsaken": Dream Theater A175
"For Sentimental Reasons" *see* "(I Love You) for Sentimental Reasons"
"For The First Time" **B30**
"For the Roses": Joni Mitchell A260
"For the Sake of Days Gone By": Jimmie Rodgers A266
"For the Turnstiles": Neil Young B6
"For Those About to Rock (We Salute You)": AC/DC **A17, A250**
"Fortress Around Your Heart": Sting A250
"Fortunate Son": Creedence Clearwater Revival A43, A185, A247, B3, B24
"Fortune Teller": Benny Spellman A95, B8
"Forty-Nine Bye-Byes": Crosby, Stills, Nash & Young B3
"Forty-Second Street" B12
"Forty-Six & 2": Tool A175
"Forty-Six and Two": Tool A205
"Forty Thousand Headmen": Blood, Sweat and Tears B3
"For What It's Worth": Buffalo Springfield A247, B24
"For You, for Me, for Evermore" B10
"For You Blue" A147; The Beatles A98, A254, B7
"For Your Life": Led Zeppelin A185, B20
"For Your Love": The Yardbirds A185, B20, B21
"For Your Pleasure": Roxy Music A185
"For Your Precious Love": Curtis Mayfield A108
"Found a Job": Talking Heads A185
"Fountain of Lamneth, The": Rush A28
"Fountain of Salmacis, The": Genesis **A142**
"Fountain of Sorrow": Jackson Browne A124
"Four Horsemen": The Clash A118
"Four Sticks": Led Zeppelin A221
"Fourth Time Around": Bob Dylan A221
"Foxy [Foxey] Lady": The Jimi Hendrix Experience **A17**, A75, A101, A247, **A257**
"Fracture": King Crimson A28, B20, B21
"Frame by Frame": King Crimson A224
"Framed": The Robins A77
"Francine": Z.Z. Top A185
"Francis Massacre": Public Image Ltd B20
"Frankenstein": Edgar Winter Group A43
"Frankie and Albert": Charley Patton **A240**; Booker T. Sapps A240

"Frankie and Johnny": Gene Autry A240; Bill Broonzy A240; Sam Cooke **A239**; Jimmie Rodgers **A240, A266**
"Frankie Blues": Hazel Meyers A240; Bessie Smith A240; Mamie Smith A240
"Frankie Dean": Tom Darby & Jimmie Tarlton A240
"Frankie": Dykes Magic City Trio A240; Mississippi John Hurt A240, **B27**
"Franklin's Tower": The Grateful Dead B17
"Frank": Steve Vai B21
"Franky and Albert (Cooney and Delia)": John French and Gabriel Brown A240
"Frayed Ends of Sanity": Metallica **B20**
"Freak Like Me": Adina Howard A24, A39; Sugababes A24, A39
"Freak Out": Mothers of Invention, The B25
"Freddie's Dead": Curtis Mayfield A43
"Fred McDowell's Blues": Fred McDowell **A26**
"Free" B30
"Free as a Bird": The Beatles A95, B8, **B7**
"Free Bird": Lynyrd Skynyrd A43, A182, A269, B24
"Freedom" [1]: Rage Against the Machine A205
"Freedom" [2]: Grandmaster Flash A99
"Freedom" [3]: Jimi Hendrix A101
"Freedom" [4]: Charles Mingus A135
"Freedom at 21": Jack White **A148**
"Free Fallin'": Tom Petty and the Heartbreakers A80, A247, **A247**, A250, B21, **B24**
"Free Four": Pink Floyd A185
"Free Man in Paris": Joni Mitchell **A16**, A43, A260
"Freewill": Rush **A17**, A55
"Free Your Mind": En Vogue A39
"Freeze Out" A145
"Freight Train": The Quarrymen B8
"French Foreign Legion": Frank Sinatra A234
"French Kiss": L'il Louis & The World **A129**, B21
"Fresh Born": Deerhoof A205
"Fresh Garbage" B7; Spirit A99
"Freshman Year, The": The Four Freshmen B15
"Freshmen, The": The Verve Pipe B24
"Friday Night": The Beach Boys B15

"Friend Like You, A": Brian Wilson and Paul McCartney B15
"Friendly Birds": Touch, The A72
"Friend of the Devil": The Grateful Dead A173
"Friend of Yours, A" A14
"Friends" [1]: Arrival A185
"Friends" [2]: The Beach Boys B15
"Friendship" B10
"Frightened City, The": The Beatles B8
"Fritiof Andersson": Evert Taube B25
"From a Buick Six": Bob Dylan B4
"From a Deadbeat to an Old Greaser": Jethro Tull A188
"From a Jack to a King": Ned Miller A193
"From Another World" B30
"From a Window": The Beatles **A107**; Billy J. Kramer and the Dakotas A107, **B8**
"From Four Till Late": Robert Johnson A132, A240
"From Head to Toe": The Escorts B7
"From Jimmy with Tears": The Honeys B15
"From Me to You": The Beatles A74, A75, **A76**, A91, A98, A99, **A194**, A195, A213, A259, B7, **B8**
"From the Beginning": Emerson, Lake, & Palmer **A101**, B20
"From the Mouth of Gabriel": Sufjan Stevens A222
"From the Undertow": Tony Banks **A142**
"From This Moment On" [1]: Shania Twain **A193**
"From This Moment on" [2] B10, B30
"From Under the Covers": Beautiful South A185
"Front Porch Looking In": Lonestar A191
"Fuckin' Up": Neil Young B6
"Fuck Tha Police": N.W.A. A124, A146
"Fugue en Do Mineur": Séguin A166
"Fugue": Gentle Giant A166
"Fugue in D Minor": Egg A166
"Full Moon and Empty Arms" B15
"Fun, Fun, Fun": The Beach Boys A109, A160, B7, B8, B15, B24; Ricky van Shelton B15; Brian Wilson B15
"Funeral, The": Hank Williams B4
"Funeral for a Friend": Elton John A141
"Fun Fun Fun": Beach Boys A185
"Funkin' for Jamaica": Tom Browne A261, B31

"Funky Broadway": Dyke and the Blazers A238
"Funky Chicken": Rufus Thomas A185
"Funky Drummer": James Brown A104, A117, **A238**, A261, B5, B20, B22
"Funky Music": Johnny Winter A185
"Funky Pretty": The Beach Boys B15
"Funky Space Reincarnation": Marvin Gaye A110
"Funkytown": Lipps, Inc. A83, B24
"Funnies, The" B30
"Funny Boy": The Honeys B15
"Funny Face" B30
"Funny Little Something" **B30**
"Fun to Be Fooled" **A114**, B10, **B30**
"Furniture Man": Lil McClintock A240
"Furry Sings the Blues": Joni Mitchell A260
"Further to Fly": Paul Simon A93, B1
"Fur wen macht eine Frau sich schon?" A145
"Fury of the Storm": Dragonforce B21
"Future's So Bright, The": Timbuk 3 A250
"Fylingdale Flyer": Jethro Tull **B21**

"Galadriel": Barclay James Harvest A185
"Gal in Calico, A" B30
"Gallery, The": Joni Mitchell **A260**
"Gallow Pole": Led Zeppelin A185
"Gambling Man": Woody Guthrie A240
"Gambling Polka Dot Blues": Jimmie Rodgers A266
"Game, The": The Beatles B7
"Game of Love, The" [2]: Wayne Fontana and the Mindbenders B8
"Game of Love" [1]: Brian Poole A185
"Games Two Can Play": The Beach Boys B15
"Games Without Frontiers": Peter Gabriel A185
"Gamlbing Bar Room Blues": Jimmie Rodgers A266
"Gangsta, Gangsta": NWA B14
"Gangsta's Fairytale, A": Ice Cube B14
"Gangsta's Paradise": Coolio feat. L.V. A99, A123, A144, **A167**; see also "Pastime Paradise"
"Garden, The": PJ Harvey A223
"Garden of Delight": Mission A185
"Garden of Earthly Delights, The": The United States of America A138
"Garden of Weed": Lew Stone and His Band A227

Song Index

"Garden Party": Marillion B20
"Gasoline Kisses for Everyone": Park A205
"Gates of Delirium, The": Yes **A149**, A207
"Gates of Eden": Bob Dylan A216
"Gat Kirwani": George Harrison B7
"Gaucho": Steely Dan **A96**
"Gay Ranchero, A" B12
"G-Bop": Alison Brown **A220**
"Gee": Crows, The B15
"Geek USA": Smashing Pumpkins A205
"Gee Whiz": Carla Thomas A29
"General's Fast Asleep, The": Joe Loss and His Band A227
"Genesis, The": Nas A103
"Genevieve": Huey "Piano": Smith A238
"Genie in a Bottle": Christina Aguilera **A24**
"Gentleman Is a Dope, The" B30
"Gentle on My Mind": Glen Campbell A173
"Gentle Rain": Wild Turkey **B21**
"Gently Tender": The Incredible String Band **A112**, B20, B21
"George Jackson": Bob Dylan A101
"Georgia Bound": Blind Blake **A240**
"Georgia Brown Blues": Bill Cox A240
"Georgia Grind": Louis Armstrong A119
"Georgia on My Mind" B10, **B30**; Ray Charles A247, B7, B8
"Georgy Porgy": Toto A185
"Gerdundula": Status Quo A185
"Get a Chance with You": Jan and Dean B15
"Get a Job": The Silhouettes A44, A97, B24
"Get Away": Chicago A250
"Get Back on It": Neil Young B6
"Get Back": The Beatles A43, A90, A98, A185, A195, A247, B8, B7, B18
"Get Down and Get With It": Slade B20, B21
"Get Down Tonight": K.C. and the Sunshine Band B24
"Get Happy" B10, B12
"Get in the Sun": Joan Armatrading A136
"Get It On" [1]: Chase A43
"Get It On" [2]: T. Rex A185
"Get It": The Beatles B8
"Get My Hands on Some Lovin'": Marvin Gaye A110
"Get Off of My Cloud": The Rolling Stones A43, A99, A107, A185, B8, B21
"Get Off!": The Beatles B7

"Get Off Your Ass and Jam": Funkadelic A163
"Get on the Good Foot": James Brown A238
"Get on Your Boots": U2 A89
"Get Out of Town" **B10, B30**
"Get Ready" [1]: The Supremes B3; The Temptations A105, A108
"Get Ready" [2]: Eric Clapton A185
"Get Real Paid": Beck **A97**, A163
"Get Right Church": Reverend Gary Davis **A62**
"Get Thee Behind Me, Satan" B30; Almanac Singers, The A240
"Getting Better": The Beatles A90, A98, A167, B7, B8, B18, B29
"Getting Closer": Paul McCartney & Wings **A99**
"Getting' Hungry": Celebration B15; Brian Wilson B15
"Getting Nowhere Fast": Wedding Present A185
"Getting Some Fun Out of Life": Claude Thornhill **A263**
"Get Up (I Feel Like Being a) Sex Machine": James Brown A238, B21
"Get Up and Dance": Freedom B31
"Gettin' in Over My Head": Brian Wilson B15
"Gett Off": Prince A79, B13
"Ghetto Body Buddy": Broken Social Scene A221
"Ghetto Fantasy": Geto Boys B14
"Ghetto Gospel": Tupac Shakur [2Pac] **B31**
"Ghetto Musick": OutKast A99
"Ghose Love Score": Nightwish B21
"Ghostbusters": Ray Parker, Jr. A182
"Ghost": Neutral Milk Hotel A22
"Ghost of a Chance, A" **B30**
"Ghost of Smoky Joe, The" B12
"Ghost Riders in the Sky" A53
"Ghost Town": The Specials A185, A233, B19
"Giant for One Day": Gentle Giant A185
"Giant Steps" A224
"Gigolo" **B30**
"Gimme All Your Lovin'": ZZ Top A250
"Gimme Gimme Gimme": ABBA A185, B20
"Gimme Shelter": The Rolling Stones **A16**, A35, A43, A247
"Gimme Some Lovin'" B17; Spencer Davis Group **A16**

"Gimme Some Truth": John Lennon B18
"Gina Lola Breakdown": The Dixie Dregs A73
"Gin and Juice": the Gourds A24; Snoop Doggy Dogg A24, A99
"Ginseng Blues": Kentucky Ramblers A240
"Gipsy Eyes": The Jimi Hendrix Experience **B19**
"Girl, Inform Me": The Shins **A22**
"Girl Can't Help It" [1]: Journey B21
"Girl Can't Help It" [2]: Little Richard **A53**
"Girl Don't Tell Me": The Beach Boys A160, B15
"Girl Friend, The" B30
"Girlfriend": Beautiful South A185
"Girlfriend Is Better": Talking Heads A185
"Girl From Ipanema, The" ["Garota de Ipanema"] B12; Getz and Gilberto A99, **A211**, B7; Peri Ribiero A211
"Girl from New York City, The": The Beach Boys B15
"Girl From the North Country": Bob Dylan A58, A99, A216
"Girl Goodbye": Toto A185
"Girlie" B30; The Survivors B15
"Girl I Left Behind Me, The" B12
"Girl I Love, The" B30
"Girl in the Magnesium Dress, The": Frank Zappa A11, A27
"Girl Is Mine, The": Michael Jackson and Paul McCartney B7
"Girl of My Dreams" B8
"Girl on the Magazine Cover, The" B30
"Girl on the Wing": The Shins A22
"Girls, Girls, Girls": The Coasters A77
"Girl's Gotta Do What a Girl's Gotta Do, A": Mindy McCready A193
"Girls on Film": Duran Duran A36
"Girls on the Beach": The Beach Boys B15
"Girl's Song, The" **B3**
"Girl That I Marry, The" B10, B30
"Girl": The Beatles A92, A99, A98, B7, B8, **B18**, **B21**, **B24**
"Girl with Grey Eyes": Big Country A185
"Give a Little Bit": Supertramp B24
"Give Him Love": The Soul Children A29
"Give It up or Turnit a Loose": James Brown B31
"Give It Up": Victor Calderone A3
"Give Me Love (Give Me Peace on Earth)": George Harrison B7, B24

"Give Me Some Truth": The Beatles B7
"Give Me Strength": Eric Clapton A185
"Give Me The Simple Life" **B30**
"Give Me Your Hand" A145
"Give Me Your Tired, Your Poor" B12
"Give My Regards to Broadway" A145
"Give Peace a Chance": The Beatles B8; Plastic Ono Band A185, A233, B7
"Give the People What They Want": The O'Jays A238
"Give Up the Ghost": Radiohead **A169**
"Give Up the Goods": Mobb Deep B22
"Givin' the Dog a Bone": AC/DC A250
"Glada Bagarn i San Remo": Evert Taube B25
"Glad All Over": Dave Clark Five A107, A185, B8, **B20**; Rezillos **B20**, B21
"Glad to Be Unhappy" B10, **B30**
"Glad": Traffic B8
"Glass Box": George Harrison B7
"Glasses": Paul McCartney B7
"Glass Onion": The Beatles A43, A76, A98, A159, **A234**, B7, B8, B18
"Glass Prison, The": Dream Theater A175
"Glass Spider": David Bowie B20
"Glimpse of Heaven": The Strawbs B20
"Gloaming, The": Radiohead A206
"Gloomy Sunday" **A15**
"Gloria" **A155**; Tom Petty and the Heartbreakers A155; Patti Smith A55, **A78**, A269, B21; Them A43, **A78**, A85
"Glory Days" [1]: Bruce Springsteen A99
"Glory Days" [2]: Pulp A82
"Glory of Love": Peter Cetera B24
"Gloves for Snow Enthusiasts": Jesse Tree A205
"Glycerine": Bush **A202**
"Gnome, The": Pink Floyd SYD? A198
"Go Away Boy": The Honeys B15
"Go Back": Chalee Tennison A191
"Gob Is a Slob, A" B12
"Go Cry on Somebody Else's Shoulder": Frank Zappa & the Mothers of Invention A11, B21
"G.O.D. (Good Old Days)": Fastball A99
"God Bless America" A168, B30
"God Bless the Absentee": Paul Simon B1
"God Bless the USA": Lee Greenwood A189
"God Is a Good God": Fred Hammond **A161**
"God Is Love": Marvin Gaye A110
"God": John Lennon B7, B18

Song Index

"God Only Knows": The Beach Boys A80, A98, A99, A109, **A125**, **A160**, A185, A247, B7, B8, B15, B21, B32; Brian Wilson B15
"Go Down Gamblin": Blood, Sweat and Tears A43
"God Save America": Spirit of Memphis B21
"God Save the King" B10
"God Save the Queen" A242; The Sex Pistols A39, A118, A247
"Gods of War": Def Leppard A185, **A193**
"God Supreme" B12
"Gods Will Be Gods": Echo and the Bunnymen B20
"Go Go Go": Chuck Berry A244
"Go! Go! Go!": Roy Orbison A270
"Goin' Down": Monkees A185
"Goin' Down Slow": Howlin' Wolf **A186**
"Going Back": Neil Young B6
"Going Down in Louisiana, Way Down Behind the Sun": Muddy Waters A244
"Going Down the Road Feeling Bad" B17
"Going Down to Liverpool": Bangles A185
"Going My Way" A14; Bing Crosby B4
"Going to a Go-Go": The Miracles A95, A108
"Going to Germany": Cannon's Jug Stompers A240
"Going to Move to Alabama": Charley Patton A240
"Going Underground": The Jam B20, A185
"Going Up the Country": Canned Heat A43
"Goin' Hollywood" A145
"Goin' Home" **B27**
"Goin' On": The Beach Boys A160, B15
"Goin' Out of My Head": Little Anthony and the Imperials B8
"Gold Dust Woman": Fleetwood Mac A185, B20
"Golden Age, The" B10
"Golden Brown": The Stranglers A221
"Golden Earrings" B12
"Golden Gate Gospel Train": The Golden Gate Jubilee Quartet **A26**
"Golden Lady": Stevie Wonder A144, A185
"Golden Loom": The Byrds A121
"Golden Road (To Unlimited Devotion)": The Grateful Dead A105
"Golden Slumbers": The Beatles **A92, A116, B7, B8, B18**
"Golden Trumpets" A145

"Golden Vanity, The": Bob Dylan A216
"Golden Years": David Bowie A185, A247
"Goldfarb, That's I'm" B12
"Goldfinger": John Barry A43
"Goldheart Mountaintop Queen [Festering Moon] Directory, The": Guided By Voices **A243**
"Golem II, the Bionic Vapor Boy": Mr. Bungle **A163**
"Goliath": Mars Volta, The A205
"Go Little Boat" **B30**
"Golux's Song, The" **A209**
"Gomper": The Rolling Stones B29
"Gone, Gone, Gone (Done Moved On)": Robert Plant B21
"Gone" [1]: Ferlin Husky A97
"Gone" [2]: U2 A89
"Gone" [3]: Ben Folds A221
"Gone at Last": Paul Simon **A150**, B1
"Gone Gone Gone": The Beatles B8
"Gone With The Wind" B30
"Gonna Change My Way of Thinking": Bob Dylan A180, A185
"Gonna Die with My Hammer in My Hand": Williamson Brothers & Curry **A240**
"Gonna Hustle You": Jan and Dean B15; Brian Wilson B15
"Gonna Make You": Troggs, The B21
"Gonna Take It with Me When I Go": Tom Waits A221
"Go Now": Moody Blues A185, B7, B8
"Good Cigar Is a Smoke, A" B24
"Good Day Sunshine" B3; The Beatles A56, **A63**, **A63**, **A95**, A98, **A157**, A182, A185, A198, **A253**, A254, B3, **B7**, B8, **B18**, B21
"Good for Me" [1]: Otis Redding B3
"Good for Me" [2]: Amy Grant B24
"Good for Nothin' (But Love)" A14
"Good Golly, Miss Molly" B27; Little Richard A80, A95, A185, A238, A247, B7, **B25**; The Swinging Blue Jeans B8
"Good Lovin'": The Young Rascals, A101, A110, **A241**, A250
"Good Man Is Hard to Find, A" [1]: Sufjan Stevens A221
"Good Man Is Hard to Find, A" [2] A147
"Good Morning, Little Schoolgirl" B17; Ten Years After **A155**; Sonny Boy Williamson **A155**

"Good Morning Good Morning": The Beatles A92, A99, A221, **A245**, **B7**, B8, B18, B19, B20, B29
"Good Morning Heartache": Billie Holiday B4
"Good 'n Evil": Traci Lords A221
"Good News": Sam Cooke A108
"Good Night": The Beatles A98, B7, B21
"Good Rockin' Tonight": Wynonie Harris A53; Paul McCartney **B8**; Elvis Presley A99
"Good Thing, The" [2]: Talking Heads A185
"Good Thing" [1]: Fine Young Cannibals A185
"Good Times" [1]: Chic A24, A163, **A241**, B31
"Good Times" [2]: Sam Cooke A108
"Good Times Bad Times": Led Zeppelin A99, A141, B7, B8, B20
"Good Time": The Beach Boys B15; Spring B15
"Good Time Tonight": Bill Broonzy **A240**
"Good Timin'": The Beach Boys B15
"Good to Be Here": Lindisfarne B20, B21
"Good to My Baby": The Beach Boys A160, B15
"Good Vibrations": The Beach Boys A43, A71, A72, A80, A99, **A109**, **A125**, A160, A167, A185, A233, A247, A269, B7, B8, B15, B21, B32; Troggs, The B21; Brian Wilson B15, B21
"Good Year for the Roses" A33
"Good-Bye" **B30**
"Goodbye, John" **A209**
"Goodbye, Little Dream, Goodbye" A168
"Goodbye" [1]: Mary Hopkin **B7**
"Goodbye" [2]: Emmylou Harris B32
"Goodbye" [3]: Chicago **A237**
"Goodbye Blue Sky": Pink Floyd A205
"Good-Bye My Lady Love" A145
"Good-bye Summer! So Long Fall! Hello Winter Time!" A145
"Goodbye to Love": Carpenters A140, A185, **B21**
"Goodbye to Romance": Ozzy Osbourne B28
"Goodbye Yellow Brick Road": Elton John A99, **A225**, A248, B7, **B24**
"Goodnight, My Love": The Honeys B15; The McGuire Sisters B15
"Goodnight, Sweetheart" B30
"Goodnight My Love" A145
"Goodnight": The Beatles A234, **B18**
"Goodnight Tonight": Wings B7
"Goon Squad": Elvis Costello A185
"Goose-Step Mama": The Rutles A69
"Gospel According to Rasputin": Slade **B21**

"Gospel According to Tony Day, The": David Bowie B21
"Got a Date With an Angel": The Four Freshmen A160
"Got a Hold on Me": Christine McVie B24
"Go Tell Aunt Rhody" B30
"Go Tell It on the Mountain": Simon and Garfunkel B1
"Got My Mind Set on You": George Harrison B7, B8
"Got My Mojo Workin'": Alexis Korner B21
"Go to Sleep (Little Man Being Erased)": Radiohead **A203**, A221
"Go to the Mardi Gras" A238; Professor Longhair A238
"Gotta See Jane": R. Dean Taylor A185
"Gotta Serve Somebody": Bob Dylan A180, A185
"Got the Blues, Can't Be Satisfied": Mississippi John Hurt **A85**, A256, **B26**; Blind Lemon Jefferson **B26**
"Got 'Til It's Gone": Janet Jackson A123; *see also* "Big Yellow Taxi"
"Got to Be Certain": Kylie Minogue A185
"Got to Get You Into My Life" A97; The Beatles **A95**, A98, A99, A198, **A254**, **B7**, B8, **B18**
"Got to Get You Off My Mind": Solomon Burke A95
"Got to Know the Woman": The Beach Boys B15
"Government Walls": Jesus Jones B20
"Governor Al Smith for President": Carolina Night Hawks A240
"Go West": The Pet Shop Boys **A52**, A174, **B13**; The Village People **A52**, A174
"Go Your Own Way": Fleetwood Mac A185, **A245**, A247
"Grab This Thing": The Mar-Keys A29
"Grace": U2 A89
"Graceland": Paul Simon A9
"Graduation Day": The Beach Boys B15; The Four Freshmen B15
"Grand Conjuration, The": Opeth B21
"Grand Coolie Dam, The": The Beach Boys A125
"Grand Old Ivy" A41
"Grandpa (Tell Me 'Bout the Good Old Days)": The Judds A191

Song Index

"Grant It, Lord": Swan Silvertones B21
"Gråt Inga Tårar": Thorleifs B25
"Grave New World": The Strawbs B20
"Graveyard Dream Blues": Ida Cox **A240**
"Greasy Legs": George Harrison B7
"Great Balls of Fire": The Beatles B8; Jerry Lee Lewis A44, A75, A76, A80, A97, A185, A247, B7, B15, B21
"Great Curve, The": Talking Heads A99
"Great Day" B30
"Great Debate, The": Dream Theater A175
"Great Deceiver, The": King Crimson A218
"Great Divide, The": Big Country A185
"Greatest Actor Alive . . ., The": He Is Legend A205
"Great Frontier, Pt II: Come to Me Only With Playthings Now, The": Sufjan Stevens A221
"Great Gates of Kiev, The": Emerson, Lake, & Palmer B20
"Great Gig in the Sky, The": Pink Floyd A199, B29
"Great Pretender, The": The Platters A39, A44, A53, A99, B8, B25
"Green Fields of France, The": June Tabor B21; ["No Man's Land"] Men They Couldn't Hang B21; The Pogues B20
"Green Grass of Tunnel": Múm A204
"Green Grows the Lilacs": The Originals A110
"Green Manalishi": Fleetwood Mac A185
"Green Onions" B17; Booker T. and the MGs A29, A95, A185, A216, B24
"Green River Blues": Charlie Patton A238
"Green River": Creedence Clearwater B3
"Greensleeves" **A234**, B7, B8, B18
"Grenada" B25
"Grey Lagoons": Roxy Music A185
"Grimly Fiendish": The Damned B20, B21
"Groom's Still Waiting at the Altar": Bob Dylan A124
"Groove Machine": King's X **A55**
"Groovin'" B3; The Young Rascals A43, A110
"Groovy Kind of Love, A": Phil Collins A250; Wayne Fontana and the Mindbenders B8
"Ground Hog Blues": Rambling Thomas A240
"Grow Old With Me": John Lennon B7
"Grudge, The": Tool A221
"G-Spot Tornado": Frank Zappa A27, A60
"Guaranteed Eternal Sanctuary Man, The": Genesis **A142, A232**

"Guerilla Radio": Rage Against the Machine A205
"Guess I'll Go Away": Johnny Winter A185
"Guess I'm Dumb": Glen Campbell B15
"Guide Vocal": Genesis A142
"Guiltiness": Bob Marley and the Wailers A235
"Guilty of Being White": Minor Threat A210
"Guinnevere": Crosby, Stills, and Nash B7
"Guitar Blues": The Beatles B8; Carlisle & Ball A240
"Guitar Boogie": Arthur Smith B8
"Gully Low Blues": Louis Armstrong A119
"Gumboots": Paul Simon A9
"Guns of Brixton": The Clash A118, B20
"Guru Vandana": George Harrison B7
"Gustav Lindströms Visa" **B25**
"Gut Bucket Blues": Louis Armstrong A119
"Gut of the Quantifier": The Fall A185, B20
"Guys Do It All the Time": Mindy McCready A189, A193
"Gypsy Eyes": The Jimi Hendrix Experience A257, B29
"Gypsy in My Soul, The" B30
"Gypsy": Uriah Heep A185

"Hackensack" A224
"Had to Phone Ya": Spring B15
"Half a World Away": R.E.M. A181
"Half-Remarkable Question, The": The Incredible String Band A112
"Hallelujah!" B10, B24, **B30**
"Hallelujah, I Love Her So": The Beatles B7; Ray Charles A95; The Quarrymen B8
"Hallelujah": Jeff Buckley A7, A80, A167, A247, B21; Leaonard Cohen A7, A167, B21; k.d. lang A167
"Hallo Spaceboy": David Bowie B21
"Ha Llovido": Marina Rossell B21
"Ham Hound Crave" B9
"Handbags and Gladrags": Chris Farlowe B21
"Hand in Glove": Sandie Shaw A36; The Smiths A36
"Hand in Hand" [1]: Elvis Costello A185, B20
"Hand in Hand" [2]: Phil Collins A185
"Hand in My Pocket": Alanis Morissette **B24**
"Hand Me Down World": The Guess Who B24
"Hands Down": Dashboard Confessional **A205**
"Hands": Jewel A219

"Handsome Devil": The Smiths A36
"Handsome Territorial, The": Jack Hylton and His Orchestra A227
"Hand Song, The": Nickel Creek A191
"Hand That Feeds, the": nine Inch Nails A222
"Hand That Rocks the Cradle, The": The Smiths A36, A185
"Handy Man": Jimmy Jones A44, B24; James Taylor **B24**
"Hang 'Em High" [1]: Booker T. and the MGs A29
"Hang 'Em High" [2]: Van Halen A185
"Hangin' Around With You" **B30**
"Hanging Johnny" B27
"Hangin' on a Limb": Neil Young B6
"Hangin' Tree": Queens of the Stone Age A221
"Hang on Paul": The Nazz B7
"Hang on Sloopy": The McCoys A43, A85; Sandpipers A185
"Hang on to Your Ego": The Beach Boys A160, B15
"Hang on to Your Lids, Kids" **B30**
"Hang on to Your Life": Guess Who A43
"Hang on to Yourself": David Bowie **A84**, A185
"Hang Up My Rock and Roll Shoes": Chuck Willis A44, **B25**
"Hanky Panky": Tommy James and the Shondelles B7, B8
"Happening, The": The Supremes A185, B21
"Happiest Days of All": Carter Family, The A240
"Happiness Is an Option": The Pet Shop Boys A174
"Happiness Is a Thing Called Joe" **B30**
"Happiness Is a Warm Gun": The Beatles A76, A90, A92, A98, **A157**, A167, **A204**, A205, A221, **B7**, B8, B18; Bobby Bryant A157
"Happiness Runs": The Beatles B7
"Happiness Stan": The Small Faces A269
"Happy as The Day Is Long" B30
"Happy Birthday": Stevie Wonder B21
"Happy Days and Lonely Nights" B16
"Happy Days Are Here Again" A145; Jack Hylton and His Orchestra A227
"Happy Days": Brian Wilson A99, B15
"Happy Day": Talking Heads A99
"Happy-Go-Lucky Local": Duke Ellington B9
"Happy Hour": Housemartins A185

"Happy House": Siouxsie & Banshees A185
"Happy Hunting Horn" B30
"Happy Jack": The Who A99, A185
"Happy": Peter Hammill A185
"Happy Together": The Turtles A99, A185, A222, B7, B21, B24
"Happy Wanderer, The": The Beatles B7
"Happy Xmas (War Is Over)": Plastic Ono Band, The **A185**, B32
"Harbor Lights": Elvis Presley A99, A270
"Hard Day's Night, A": The Beatles A39, **A63**, A76, A91, A92, A95, A98, A99, A107, A185, **A194**, A195, **A246**, **A247**, A247, **A248**, A254, B7, **B8**, **B18**, **B19**, B20, B21, **B24**
"Harder, Better, Faster, Stronger": Daft Punk A205
"Hard Habit to Break": Chicago **A214**, A250
"Hard Headed Woman" B27; Elvis Presley A97, A99
"Hard Knock Life (Ghetto Anthem)": Jay-Z A99
"Hard Lovin' Man": Deep Purple A185
"Hard Oh Lawd": Ida Cox A240
"Hard Rain's A-Gonna Fall, A": Bob Dylan A58, A216, B7, B8
"Hard Time Killin' Floor Blues": R.L. Burnside B21; Skip James **A62**
"Hard to Explain": The Strokes A24
"Hard to Handle" B17
"Hard to Say": Dan Fogelberg B24
"Hard Working Woman": Mississippi Matilda A240
"Harlem on My Mind" B30
"Harmony" A14
"Harmony Bay" A145
"Harold Land": Yes B7
"Harper Valley P.T.A.": Jeannie C. Riley A193
"Harpies Bizarre": Elvis Costello B20
"Harry, You're a Beast": Mothers of Invention, The **A11**; Frank Zappa A11
"Harry Rag": The Kinks B20
"Harvester of Sorrow": Metallica A24
"Harvest Home": Big Country A185, A187
"Harvest Moon": Neil Young B6, B24
"Harz": Sensorama **B5**
"Hash Pipe": Weezer A83
"Hateful": The Clash A118
"Hats Off to (Roy) Harper": Led Zeppelin A185

"Hattie Blues": Big Bill Broonzy B21
"Haunted Heart" **B30**
"Haunted Road Blues": Tom Ashley A240
"Havana Moon": Chuck Berry A85
"Have a Cigar": Pink Floyd A198
"Have a Good Time": Paul Simon **A150**, B1
"Have I the Right": The Honeycombs B8, B21
"Have Mercy Judge": Chuck Berry A244
"Haven't Got a Clue": The Flaming Lips **A102**
"Haven't Got Time for the Pain": Carly Simon B24
"Have You Ever Been Away?": Beautiful South A185
"Have You Ever Been Lonely" B16
"Have You Ever Loved a Woman": Derek and the Dominos A185, B20
"Have You Ever Seen the Rain": Creedence Clearwater Revival A99, A185
"Have You Forgotten?" B10
"Have You Met Miss Jones?" **B30**
"Have You Noticed You're Alive": Buckinghams A43
"Have Yourself a Merry Little Christmas" B30
"Have You Seen the Rain": Creedence Clearwater Revival A185
"Have You Seen Your Mother Baby, Standing in the Shadow": The Rolling Stones A107
"Hawaii": The Beach Boys B15
"Hawg for You": Otis Redding B3
"Hawkmoon 269": U2 A89
"Hawks and Doves": Neil Young B6
"Hazy Shade of Winter, A": Simon and Garfunkel A43, B1, B3
"He, She, and Me" A145
"Head Down": Soundgarden **A177**
"Head Games": Foreigner A250
"Heading Out to the Highway": Judas Priest B28
"Head Over Heels": Tears for Fears **A59**
"Headphone Silence": Ane Brun **A222**
"Head Rag Hop": Romeo Nelson A238
"Heads Will Roll": Echo & Bunnymen A185
"Heads You Win, Tails, I Lose": The Beach Boys A160, B15
"Heard It on the X": Z.Z. Top A185
"Heard It Through the Grapevine": Marvin Gaye **A248**
"Hearing Aid": They Might Be Giants A185
"Hear Me Calling": Slade **B21**; Ten Years After B21

"Hear Me Lord": George Harrison A185, B7, B18
"Hearsay": The Soul Children A29
"Heartache Tonight": The Eagles B24
"Heart and Soul" [1] A147, A182, A222, B30; Al Bowlly & the Ray Nobel Orchestra B21; The Beach Boys B15; Cleftones B15
"Heart and Soul" [2]: Big Country B20, A185, A187
"Heartbeat": King Crimson A185; Buddy Holly A37, B8
"Heartbreaker": Led Zeppelin A55, B20, B7, B8
"Heartbreak Hotel": Elvis Presley **A7**, A44, **A75**, A76, A80, A99, A247, B8, **B19**, **B20**, B21, B24, B32; The Quarrymen B7
"Heartfeeder": String Driven Thing B21
"Heart Full of Soul": Yardbirds A43, B8
"Heart Is Quicker Than The Eye, The" **B30**
"Heartland": U2 A99
"Heart of Glass": Blondie A43, A179
"Heart of Gold": Neil Young B6
"Heart of Rock and Roll, The": Huey Lewis and the News A24
"Heart of Stone": The Rolling Stones A107, B3
"Heart of the Country": Paul McCartney B18
"Heart of the Matter": Don Henley B24
"Heart of the Sunrise": Yes B21
"Hearts and Bones": Paul Simon B1
"Heart-Shaped Box": Nirvana A205
"Hearts of Stone": The Fontane Sisters A44
"Heathen, The": Bob Marley and the Wailers A235
"Heat of the Moment": Asia A71, A269
"Heat on the Street": Phil Collins A250
"Heat Wave" [1] A13, B30
"Heat Wave" [2] *see* "(Love Is Like a) Heat Wave"
"Heave Away": Roger McGuinn A121
"Heaven" [1]: T'Pau A185
"Heaven" [2]: Bryan Adams A250
"Heaven" [3]: Joan Armatrading **A136**
"Heaven Can Wait" A14
"Heaven in My Arms" B30
"Heaven Knows I'm Miserable Now": The Smiths A36, B13
"Heavenly Homes": Be-Bop Deluxe A185
"Heavenly": The Beatles B8
"Heaven Sent": Dokken B28
"Heaven's in Here": David Bowie B20
"Heavy Duty": Spinal Tap A69, **A70**

"Heavy Horses": Jethro Tull A188, B20
"Heavy Love Affair": Marvin Gaye A110
"He Couldn't Get His Poor Old Body to Move": Brian Wilson B15
"He'd Have to Get Under – Get Out and Get Under" A145
"Heebie Jeebies": Louis Armstrong A119
"He Gives Speeches": The Beach Boys B15
"He Got Game": Public Enemy A123; see also "For What It's Worth"
"He Hit Me (And It Felt Like a Kiss) the crystals": The Crystals A45
"Heigh Ho!" **A202**
"Heilige Lieder": Die Böhse Onkelz **B23**
"He Is My Story": Arizona Dranes A205, A240
"Hejira": Joni Mitchell A260
"Helden": David Bowie A123
"Helen Wheels": Wings B7
"He'll Have to Go": Jim Reeves B8
"Hellhound Blues" A176
"Hellhound on my Trail": Robert Johnson A132, B7, B18
"Hell in a Bucket": The Grateful Dead B17
"Hello, Aloha, How Are You": Ronnie Munro and His Dance Orchestra A227
"Hello, Goodbye": The Beatles A195, B20
"Hello, I Love You": Doors A55, A185
"Hello, Ma Baby" A145, **B30**
"Hello, My Lover, Good-Bye" **B30**
"Hello, Young Lovers" B30
"Hello Goodbye": The Beatles A90, A92, A98, A185, **B7**, B8, B21, B32
"Hello": Lionel Richie A167
"Hello Little Girl": The Beatles B7, **B8**; The Fourmost A185, B8
"Hello Mabel": The Bonzo Dog Band B7
"Hello Mary Lou": Rick Nelson B8
"Hello Susie": Amen Corner A185, B21
"Hello There Angel": Marvin Gaye A110
"Hello Walls": Faron Young A191
"Hell's Kitchen": Dream Theater A175
"He Loves and She Loves" **B30**
"Help Is on Its Way": Little River Band B24
"H.E.L.P. Is on the Way": The Beach Boys B15
"Helpless": Crosby, Stills, Nash & Young **B3**; Neil Young B6
"Helplessly Hoping": Crosby, Stills, Nash & Young **B3**

"Helplessness Blues": The Fleet Foxes A205, B21
"Help Me, Rhonda": The Beach Boys A109, A160, B7, B15, **B24**; T. Graham Brown B15
"Help Me" [1]: Joni Mitchell A260, B24
"Help Me" [2]: Sonny Boy Williamson A216
"Help on the Way": The Grateful Dead B17
"Help the Aged": Pulp A82
"Help!": The Beatles A39, A43, **A69**, A76, A80, A90, A91, A95, A98, A99, A106, A107, A156, A195, A247, **A255**, A259, B7, **B8**, B18
"Helter Skelter": The Beatles B7, B8, B18, B21
"Here, My Dear": Marvin Gaye A110
"Here, There, and Everywhere" A95; The Beatles A16, A43, A94, A99, A167, B3, **B7**, B8, **B18**, B21, B24
"Here Am I" **B30**
"Here at the Western World": Steely Dan **A59**
"Here Comes My Girl": Tom Petty and the Heartbreakers A59, A248
"Here Comes Sunshine": The Grateful Dead A99, B17
"Here Comes the Flood": Peter Gabriel A185, **A186**, B21
"Here Comes the Moon": George Harrison B7
"Here Comes the Night" [1]: The Beach Boys B15
"Here Comes the Night" [2]: Them A185
"Here Comes the Sun": The Beatles **A16**, **A76**, A92, A98, A99, **A116**, A149, A185, **A245**, A248, A250, B3, B7, B8, B18, B21, B24
"Here Come the Bastards": Primus A221
"Here Come the Judge": Pigmeat Markham A99
"Here I Go Again": White Snake A250
"Here in My Arms" **B30**
"Here I Stand": Skunk Anansie B21
"Here Lies Love" B30
"Here's That Rainy Day" A14, B10, **B30**
"Here's To My Lady" **B30**
"Here's to You": Billy Ocean A250
"Here's What I'm Here For" B30
"Here There and Everywhere": The Beatles A90, A185
"Here Today" [1]: The Beach Boys **A160**, B15, B21; Brian Wilson B15
"Here Today" [2]: Paul McCartney B7, B8

Song Index

"Here We Are in the Years": Neil Young B6
"Here with Me": Michelle Branch B21
"Her Majesty": The Beatles A43, A92, **A116**, B8, B7, B21
"Hernando's Hideaway": John Lennon B7
"Heroes and Villains": Beach Boys A125, A167, A185, B7, B15, B21; Brian Wilson B15, B21
"Heroes": David Bowie A80, A247
"Heroine": Suede B20
"Heroin": The Velvet Underground **A67**, B32
"Hero Takes a Fall": Bangles A185
"He's a Devil in His Own Hometown" A145
"He's a Doll": The Honeys B15
"He's a Good Guy (Yes He Is)": the Marvelettes A95
"He's a Rebel": The Crystals A160, B7
"He's Gone": The Grateful Dead B17
"He's Good for Me" A147
"He's Got a Secret": Bangles A185
"He's Got the Whole World in His Hands": Laurie London A97
"Hesitation Blues": Leadbelly A240
"He's Misstra Know-It-all": Stevie Wonder A185
"He's So Fine": The Chiffons A43, A95
"He Was My Brother": Paul Simon B1; Simon and Garfunkel B1
"He Was Really Sayin' Something": The velvelettes A95
"He Was Too Good To Me" **B30**
"Hey, Bo Diddley": Bo Diddley **B19**
"Hey, Good Lookin'" B8
"Hey, Hey Georgie": The Beatles B7
"Hey, That's No Way to Say Goodbye": Leonard Cohen B21
"Hey Ba-Ba-Re-Bop": The Beatles B8; Lionel Hampton A95
"Hey Baby (They're Playing Our Song)": The Buckinghams B7
"Hey! Baby": The Beatles B8
"Hey Bo Diddley": Bo Diddley A38
"Hey Bulldog": The Beatles A43, A98, **A245**, **B7**, B8
"Hey Diddle Diddle": Marvin Gaye A110
"Hey Good Lookin'": Hank Williams **B4**
"Hey-Hey-Hey-Hey": Little Richard A95
"Hey-Hey-Hey-Hey": The Beatles A24, A254, B8

"Hey! Hey! Let 'Er Go" **A120**
"Hey Hey My My (Into the Black)": Neil Young A88, B6
"Hey! Jealous Lover": Frank Sinatra A97
"Hey Jealousy": The Gin Blossoms A205
"Hey Joe" A97; The Jimi Hendrix Experience **A16**, A99, A154, A167, A185, **A257**, B7, B19, B20, B21, **B24**, **B29**, B32; Robert Plant B21; Patti Smith A78
"Hey Jude" B17; The Beatles **A16**, A43, A75, A76, A80, **A83**, A92, A97, A98, A101, A154, A185, A195, A205, **A245**, A247, A259, A263, A269, B3, B7, B8, B21, B24
"Hey Jupiter": Tori Amos B21
"Hey Let's Twist": The Beatles B8
"Hey Little Girl" [1]: Professor Longhair A238
"Hey Little Girl" [2]: Major Lance A108
"Hey Little Tomboy": The Beach Boys B15
"Hey Little Twist": Joey Dee & the Starliters A95
"Hey Paula!": Paul and Paula **B25**
"Hey Tonight": Creedence Clearwater Revival A185
"Hey Ya": OutKast A34, A99
"Hey You": Pink Floyd A185
"Hide and Seek": Imogen Heap A87, A205
"Hide Away" B17
"Hideaway": Creedence Clearwater B3
"Hide Go Seek": The Honeys B15
"Hi-De-Ho": Blood, Sweat, and Tears A43, A185
"Hide in Your Shell": Supertramp A185
"Hide Your Love": The Rolling Stones **A86**
"High 5 (Rock the Catskills)": Beck A163
"High and Dry": Radiohead A162, **A169**, A169, A247
"High and Low" **B30**
"High Class Baby": Cliff Richard B8
"High Energy": Evelyn King A128
"Higher Ground": Stevie Wonder A144, A163, A185, A232
"Higher Hell": Echo and the Bunnymen A185, B20
"Higher Love": Steve Winwood A250, B32
"High Fidelity": Jurassic 5 A261, B31
"High Hopes" A14, B10
"High on the Mountain": Blood, Sweat and Tears B3
"High on You": Survivor A250

"High Powered Mama": Jimmie Rodgers A266
"High School Confidential": The Beatles B8
"High Time": The Grateful Dead **A94**, B17
"High Time We Went": Joe Cocker A43
"Highway 51": Bob Dylan A216
"Highway 61 Revisited": Bob Dylan A7
"Highway Patrolman": Bruce Springsteen A122
"Highways Are Happy Ways" A145
"Highway Star": Deep Purple B20, B28
"Hi-Heel Sneakers" B8, B17
"Hi Hi Hi": Wings B7
"Hi-Ho Silver Lining": Jeff Beck A185, B20
"Hill Where the Lord Hides": Eddie Russ A261
"Hip Hop Drunkies": Alkaholiks, Tha A146
"Hip-Hop Hooray": Naughty By Nature B14
"Hip Hop Is Dead": Nas B31
"Hip-Hop Lives": KRS-One B31
"Hip Hug-Her": Booker T. and the MGs A29
"Hippy Hippy Shake": Chan Romero B8; Swinging Blue Jeans A185, B8
"Hip to Be Square": Huey Lewis and the News B24
"Hiroshima": Gary Moore A185
"Hiroshima Sky Is Always Blue": Yoko Ono B7
"His Eye Is on the Sparrow" [1]: Mahalia Jackson **A161**
"His Eye Is on the Sparrow" [2]: Tanya Blount and Lauren Hill **A161**
"His Last Voyage": Gentle Giant **A166**
"His Latest Flame" *see* "(Marie's the Name) His Latest Flame"
"His Rocking Horse Ran Away" A14
"Hiszekeny": Venetian Snares A221
"Hit by Varèse, A": Chicago A237
"Hitch Hike": Marvin Gaye A95, A108, A110, B8
"Hit 'n Run Lover": Carole Jiani A128
"Hit the Road Jack": The Beatles B8; Ray Charles A43, A95, A99, A167, A185, B21
"Hobo Bill's Last Ride": Jimmie Rodgers A266
"Hobo Blues" A266
"Hobo's Blues": Paul Simon B1
"Hobo's Lullaby": Goebel Reeves A266
"Hobo's Meditation": Jimmie Rodgers A266
"Ho Hum": Ambrose and his Orchestra A227
"Hokum Blues": Paul Oliver A112
"Holding Back the Years": Simply Red A185

"Holding My Own": Darkness, The B21
"Hold Me" A145
"Hold Me, Thrill Me, Kiss Me": Mel Carter A43
"Hold Me Lord": Eric Clapton A185
"Hold Me Now": Thompson Twins A185
"Hold Me Tight": The Beatles A98, B7, **B8**, **B18**
"Hold My Hand" [1]: The Rutles **A69**
"Hold My Hand" [2]: Hootie and the Blowfish B24
"Hold On" [1]: Spiritualized B21
"Hold On" [2]: John Lennon **B18**
"Hold On! I'm Comin'": Sam and Dave A29, A95
"Hold on to Love": Gary Moore A185
"Hold on to Your Friends": Morrissey B13
"Hold the Heart": Big Country A185
"Hold the Line": Toto A185
"Hold What You've Got": Joe Tex B4
"Hold Your Head Up": Argent B21
"Hole in My Life": Police A185
"Hole in My Shoe": Traffic B21, B29
"Hole in the Heart Case, A": The Beatles B7
"Holiday" [1]: Weezer A221
"Holiday" [2]: Madonna A250
"Holiday in Berlin": Frank Zappa and the Mothers of Invention A11, **A60**
"Holidays": Brian Wilson B15
"Holidays in the Sun": Sex Pistols **B20**, B21
"Holland, 1945": Neutral Milk Hotel A22
"Hollywood Freaks": Beck A97
"Hollywood Nights": Bob Seger A250
"Holy Man": Scott McKenzie B7
"Homburg": Procol Harum A185, B20, B21
"Home, Sweet Home" B19 B19
"Home" [1]: Daughtry A247
"Home" [2]: Dream Theater A175
"Home" [3]: The Beatles B8
"Home Again": Carole King B24
"Home Again Blues" A145
"Home at Last": Steely Dan A96
"Home Call": Jimmie Rodgers A266
"Home Computer": Kraftwerk A163
"Home Front, The": Billy Bragg B21
"Homegrown": Neil Young B6
"Home in the Sky": The Incredible String Band A112
"Homeless": Paul Simon A9, A123
"Home of the Brave": jody Miller A32
"Home Sweet Home": Earl Scruggs **A220**

Song Index

"Home Tonight": Aerosmith A99
"Homeward Bound": Simon and Garfunkel A93, B1, B21, **B25**
"Honestly": Stryper A250
"Honey, I'm Home": Shania Twain **A193**
"Honey, Just [Won't You] Allow Me One More Chance": Bob Dylan A58; Henry Thomas A240
"Honey, Take a Whiff on Me": Blind Jesse Harris A240
"Honey": Bobby Goldsboro A93
"Honeycomb": Jimmie Rodgers A44, A97
"Honey Don't": The Beatles A98, A254, B8; Carl Perkins A254
"Honey Don't You Want a Man Like Me?": Frank Zappa A27
"Honey Hush": The Beatles B8
"Honey in the Honeycomb" B30
"(Honey) It's Tight Like That": Papa Too Sweet **A240**
"Honey Just Allow Me One More Chance": Bob Dylan B8
"Honeymoon Song (Bound By Love), The": The Beatles B8; Mary Hopkin B7
"Honey Pie": The Beatles A90, A98, B7, B8, **B18**
"Honeysuckle Rose" A145, **A147, A227**
"Hong Kong Blues" B8, B30
"Hong Kong Garden": Siouxsie and the Banshees A185, B20, B21
"Honkin' Down the Highway": The Beach Boys B15
"Honky Cat": Elton John A250
"Honky Tonk": The Beach Boys B15; Bill Doggett A44, **A53**, B15
"Honky Tonk Train Blues": Meade Lux Lewis **A238**, B19
"Honky Tonk Train": Lewis, Meade Lux B9
"Honky Tonk Women": The Rolling Stones A43, A121, A185, **A247**, B20, **B27**
"Honolulu Blues" A145
"Honorable Mr. So and So, The" B30
"Honor Thy Father": Dream Theater A175
"Hoochie Coochie Man" *see* "(I'm Your) Hoochie Coochie Man"
"Hook, The": Blues Traveler B24
"Hooked on Classics": Royal Philharmonic Orchestra A24
"Hooker with a Penis": Tool A205
"Hook": PJ Harvey A51

"Hope for the Hopeless": Sheila Walsh A185, B20
"Hope in Favour": Tractor **B21**
"Hope Springs Eternal": Icicle Works A185, B20, B21
"Hope You Niggas Sleep": Notorious B.I.G. A99
"Hopscotch March" A145
"Horny as a Dandy": Loo and Placido A212
"Horny Lil' Devil": Ice Cube A146
"Horse Latitudes": Doors, The A43
"Horse Told me, The" A14
"Horse With No Name, A": America B6, B24
"Hosanna" B3
"Hot as Sun": The Beatles B7, B8; Paul McCartney B18
"Hot Blooded": Foreigner A74
"Hotel California": The Eagles A80, **A99**, A167, A173, A247, A247, A248, A250, B24
"Hotel España": Røde Mor B25
"Hot Fun in the Summertime": Sly & The Family Stone B3
"Hot Harp": The Survivors B15
"Hot in Herre": Nelly A99
"Hot Love": T. Rex A185
"Hot Pants": James Brown A117
"Hots on for Nowhere": Led Zeppelin A185
"Hot Stuff": Donna Summer **A42**, A43, A80, A247
"Hotter": Brian Wilson B15
"Hotter Than That" B9
"Hot Time March" A145
"Hound Dog": Elvis Presley A75, A76, A77, A80, **A123, A241, A247**, A247, A250, B8, B21, B32; Big Mama Thornton **A123**, A170
"House Burning Down": Jimi Hendrix A17
"House of Cards": Radiohead **A169**
"House of the Blue Danube": Malcolm McLaren B21
"House of the Rising Sun": The Animals **A101**, A167, A185, A247, B8, B20, **B24**; Bob Dylan A216
"Housequake": Prince A130
"Houses of the Holy": Led Zeppelin A17
"House Where Nobody Lives, The": Tom Waits A221
"House With Love in It, A": The Beatles B8
"How About It" **B30**
"How About Me?" **A120**, B30
"How About That": Adam Faith B8

"How about You?" B10, **B30**
"How Are Things in Glocca Morra?" B10, B30
"How Beautiful You Are": Cyril Grantham B21
"How Can I Be Sure" B3; The Rascals A43, **B3**, B7
"How Can I Help You (To Say Goodbye)": Patty Loveless A191
"How Can You Expect to Be Taken Seriously?": The Pet Shop Boys A174
"How Can You Live in the Northeast?": Paul Simon B1
"How Could Little Red Riding Hood" A145
"How Could We Be Wrong" **B10**
"How Could We Still Be Dancin'": Brian Wilson and Elton John B15
"How Cruel": Joan Armatrading A136
"How Dare I Be So Beautiful": Genesis A232
"How Deep Is the Ocean" A147, A168, **B10**, B30; Dick Reynolds B15
"How Deep Is Your Love": The Bee Gees A167, A179, **A213**
"How Do You Do It?": The Beatles B7, B8; Gerry and the Pacemakers B20, B185, A259
"How Do You Quit (Someone You Love)": Carla Thomas A95
"How Do You Sleep": John Lennon **B18**
"How Do You Tell Someone": The Beatles B7
"How'd You Like to Be the Iceman" A145
"How'd You Like to Spoon with Me" B10, B30
"How High the Moon" A156, A147, A224, B16, **B30**; The Beatles B8; Les Paul and Mary Ford B32
"How Insensitive" ["Insensatez"] A211
"How": John Lennon **B18**
"How Little We Know" **B30**
"How Long, How Long [Blues]" B27; Leroy Carr A240, **B26**; Blind Lemon Jefferson A240
"How Long" [1] A145; Jed Davenport A240; Thomas "Jaybird": Jones A240
"How Long" [2]: Ace A182
"How Long?": Brownie McGhee **A239**, A240
"How Long 'Buck'": Skip James A240
"How Long Daddy, How Long": Ida Cox A240
"How Long Has This Been Going On?" A114, A147, A224, **B10**, **B11**, **B30**
"How Many Mics": The Fugees B22
"How Many More Times": Led Zeppelin A99
"How Many More Years": Howlin' Wolf **A210**

"How Much Is that Doggy in the Window": Lita Roza B21
"How's Chances" B30
"How's It Gonna Be": Third Eye Blind A247
"How Soon Is Now?": The Smiths A36, **A83**
"How Sweet It Is to Be Loved By You": Marvin Gaye A32, A106, **A108**, B4; Junior Walker and the All Stars A108, A185
"How the Heart Approaches What It Yearns": Paul Simon B1
"How to Disappear Completely (And Never Be Found)": Radiohead **A162**, **A169**
"How to Handle a Woman" A224
"How to Play Our Music": Reese and Santonio **B5**
"How to Succeed" **A41**
"How to Win Friends and Influence People" **B30**
"How Ya Gonna Keep 'Em Down on the Farm?" B30
"How You Ever Gonna Know": Garth Brooks **A190**
"How You Remind Me": Nickelback A248
"H": Tool **A203**
"Hucklebuck, The": Paul "Hucklebuck" Williams B9
"Hu-la Hu-la Cake Walk" A145
"Hully Gully" *see* "(Baby) Hully Gully"
"Human": Hank Snow B15
"Human Highway": Neil Young B6
"Human Nature" [1]: Madonna B13
"Human Nature" [2]: Michael Jackson A248
"Human Touch": Bruce Springsteen **A21**
"Humiliative": Meshuggah **A208**
"Humming Your Glum Times Away" A145
"Humpty Dumpty": Bob and Sheri B15
"Humpty Dumpty Heart" A14
"Hundred Years From Today, A" B30
"Hungarian Rag" A145
"Hungry Freaks, Daddy": The Mothers of Invention A67
"Hungry Heart": Bruce Springsteen A269
"Hungry Like the Wolf": Duran Duran A36, A43, A212, B24
"Hunter, The": Björk B32
"Hunting Bears": Radiohead A135, **A169**
"Hunting Girl": Jethro Tull A188, B20
"Hurdy Gurdy Man": Donovan A43, A185, B7
"Hurricane Eye": Paul Simon B1

Song Index   *175*

"Hurt, The": Aceyalone A221
"Hurt": Johnny Cash A24
"Hurts Like Teen Spirit": DJ Dangerous Orange **A24**
"Hurts So Bad": Little Anthony A32, B4
"Hushabye": The Beach Boys A160, B15; The Mystics A160, B15
"Hush": Deep Purple **A16**, A99, A167, B7
"Hush Your Mouth": Bo Diddley A38
"Hut of Baba Yaga, The": Emerson, Lake, & Palmer B20
"Hymn": Duncan Sheik A169
"Hymne à L'amour": Edith Piaf B25
"Hypnotize": Notorious B.I.G. B14
"Hysteria": Def Leppard A185

"I, Me, Mine": The Beatles B3
"I, Robot": Alan Parsons Project A17
"I Adore You" A145
"I Ain't Goin' Down": Shania Twain **A193**
"I Ain't Gonna Do It No More": Bertha "Chippie": Hill A240
"I Ain't Got Nobody" B16, B30
"I Ain't Got No Heart": Mothers of Invention, The A11
"I Ain't Mad at Cha": Tupac Shakur [2Pac] B31
"I Ain't Mad at Ya": 2Pac B14
"I Ain't No Quitter": Shania Twain A193
"I Ain't Superstitious" B17; Howlin' Wolf **A83**, **B21**; Jeff Beck Group A185, **B21**
"I Am a Child": Neil Young B6
"I Am a Pilgrim": Merle Travis B19
"I Am a Rock": Paul Simon B1; Simon and Garfunkel A93, B1, B8
"I Am Damo Suzuki": The Fall B20, B21
"I am Hated for Loving": Morrissey B13
"I Am Loved" B30
"I Am Stretched on Your Grave": Sinéad O'Connor A117
"I Am That Man": Brooks and Dunn A189
"I Am the Beat, The": The Look A185
"I Am the Man, Thomas": Bob Dylan A216
"I Am the Resurrection": Stone Roses A185
"I am the Tide": echolyn A72
"I Am the Walrus": The Beatles **A16**, **A17**, A43, A69, A90, A92, A98, A149, A185, A195, A218, **A225**, A232, A234, **B7**, B8, **B18**, B20, B24
"I Am Your Singer":: Wings B18

"Ian Underwood Whips It Out":: The Mothers of Invention A12
"I Been Gone a Long Time": Every Time I die A205
"I Believed All They Said" B30
"I Believe": Frankie Laine B21
"I Believe I Can Fly": R. Kelly A80, A247
"I Believe in You" [1] A147
"I Believe in You" [1]: Neil Young B6
"I Believe in You" [2] A147
"I Believe in You" [2]: Bob Dylan A180, A185
"I Call Your Name": The Beatles **A91**, A98, B8, B7, B21
"I Can Go to God in Prayer": Albertina walker **A161**
"I Can Hear Music": The Beach Boys A185, B15; Kathy Troccoli B15
"I Can Hear the Grass Grow": The Move B29
"I Can Help": Billy Swan A185
"I Can": Nas A261, B31
"I Cannot Believe It's True": Phil Collins A185
"I Cannot Sing the Old Songs": Claribel B25
"I Can See for Miles": The Who A101, A141, A185, **B3**, B7, B24
"I Can See Right Through You": The Honeys B15
"I Can't Afford to Dream" A145
"I Can't Be Satistied": Bill Broonzy A240
"I Can't Call It": De La Soul B14
"I Can't Drive 55": Sammy Hagar A55
"I Can Tell": Saosin A205
"I Can't Explain": The Who A97, A99, A248, B8
"I Can't Get Next to You": The Temptations A99, B24
"(I Can't Get No) Satisfaction" B17; The Beach Boys B15; Otis Redding A107; The Rolling Stones A7, A67, A74, A80, **A85**, A107, A184, A247, A250, **B3**, B8, B19, B20, B21, B29, B32
"I Can't Get Started" A145, B10, **B30**
"I Can't Give You Anything But Love" B10, B16; Louis Armstrong A119
"I Can't Go on Without You": Bullmose Jackson A53
"I Can't Help But Love You": Marvin Gaye A110
"I Can't Help Myself (Sugar Pie, Honey Bunch)": The Four Tops **A32**, A95, **A108**, B8, **B24**

"I Can't Hold Out": Eric Clapton A185
"I Can't Let Maggie Go": Honeybus B20, B21
"I Can't Make You Love Me": Bonnie Raitt A80, A247
"I Can't Quit You Baby": Led Zeppelin B20; Otis Rush B21
"I Can't": Radiohead **A169**
"I Can't See Nobody": The Bee Gees B3
"I Can't See Your Face": The Doors B3
"I Can't Stand It": Eric Clapton A185
"I Can't Stand Losing You": The Police A185, A219
"I Can't Stand Myself": James Brown A210, A238
"I Can't Stop Loving You": Ray Charles A185, A247
"I Cant Take My Eyes Off of You": The Pet Shop Boys A174
"I Can't Tell You Why": The Eagles A173
"I Can't Turn You Loose": Otis Redding A29
"Icarus": Paul Winter Consort A101
"Ice Cakes": The Dixie Dregs A73
"Ice Cream": Raekwon B14
"Ice Ice Baby": Vanilla Ice A99
"I Certainly Was Going Some" A145
"Ice": Sarah McLachlan **A49**
"Ice Water Blues" A145
"Icicle": Tori Amos A219
"Icky Thump": White Stripes, The A148
"I Concentrate on You": **A113**, **A114**, **B30**
"I Could Have Told You" A14
"I Could Never Be President": Johnnie Taylor A29
"I Could Never Take the Place of Your Man": Prince A144
"I Couldn't" A145
"I Could Write a Book" B30
"I Cover the Waterfront" **B10**, **B30**
"I Cried for You" **B30**
"Ida Cox's Lawdy, Lawdy Blues": Ida Cox A240
"Ida Red" A238
"Idea": The Bee Gees B3
"I'd Have You Anytime" B7, B8; The Beatles **B3**; George Harrison B18
"I Didn't Know About You" B30
"I Didn't Know What Time It Was" **A147**, **B10**, B30
"I Dig Love": George Harrison A185, B18
"I Dig Rock and Roll Music": Peter, Paul and Mary A43

"Idiot Bastard Son, The": Mothers of Invention, The A11, A12; Frank Zappa A11
"Idioteque": Radiohead A162
"Idiot Wind": Bob Dylan A122, B21
"I'd Know You Anywhere": Dorothy Carless B21
"I'd Like That": XTC **A97**
"I'd Like to Teach the World to Sing": The New Seekers B20
"I'd Love Just Once to See You": The Beach Boys B15
"I'd Love to Fall Asleep and Wake Up in My Mammy's Arms" A145
"I Do I Do I Do I Do I Do": ABBA **B25**
"I Do It for Your Love": Paul Simon **A93**, **A150**, B1
"I Do It for You" see "(Everything I Do) I Do It for You"
"I Don't Believe": Paul Simon B1
"I Don't Believe You": Bob Dylan **A33**
"I Don't Care Any More": Phil Collins A185
"I Don't Care if the Sun Don't Shine": The Beatles B8; Elvis Presley A99
"I Don't Have to Wonder": Garth Brooks **A190**
"I Don't Know" B8
"I Don't Know How to Love Him": Yvonne Elliman B24
"I Don't Know What Love Is Anymore": Troy Tate A36
"I Don't Know What You Want but I Can't Give It Anymore": The Pet Shop Boys A174
"I Don't Know Where I Stand": Joni Mitchell **A260**
"I Don't Know Why" B3
"I Don't Like It": Pauline Pantsdown A212
"I Don't Matter to Me": Phil Collins A185
"I Don't Mind": James Brown A238, B4
"I Don't Owe You Anything": The Smiths A36
"I Don't Remember": Peter Gabriel A185, **A186**
"I Don't Think I Will": James Bonamy A189
"I Don't Wanna Be a Soldier": John Lennon **B18**
"I Don't Wanna Be Called Yo Nigga": Public Enemy A99
"I Don't Wanna Cry": Mariah Carey A97
"I Don't Wanna Go on With You Like That": Elton John **A225**

Song Index 177

"I Don't Wanna Lose You" [1]: Tina Turner A185
"I Don't Wanna Lose You" [2]: REO Speedwagon A250
"(I Don't Want to Go to) Chelsea": Elvis Costello A124, A185, A247
"I Don't Want to Know": Fleetwood Mac A185
"I Don't Want to See You Again": Peter and Gordon A107, B8
"I Don't Want To Spoil The Party": The Beatles **A91**, A98, A107, **B8**, B18
"I Do": The Beach Boys B15; The Castells B15
"I'd Rather be a Minstrel Man than a Multimillionaire" A145
"I'd Rather Be With You": Bootsy Collins A39
"I'd Rather Be Your Lover": Madonna **B13**
"I'd Rather See a Minstrel Show": Bing Crosby B4
"I'd Really Love to See You Tonight": England Dan and John Ford Coley B24
"I Dreamed a Dream": Susan Boyle **A167**
"I Dream[ed] of a Hillbilly Heaven": Bill Anderson A191; Dolly Parton A191; Tex Ritter A191; Marty Stuart A191
"I Dream Too Much" B30
"Ieya": Toyah A185
"If 6 Was 9": The Jimi Hendrix Experience A40, A43, B7
"I Fancy Me Chances": The Beatles **B8**
"I Faw Down an' Go Boom" A145
"If": Bread B24
"If Dreams Come True" A145
"I Feel a Song Comin' On" B30
"I Feel Fine": The Beatles A98, A107, A195, A248, A254, B3, B4, B7, **B8**
"I Feel for You": Chaka Khan B19
"I Feel Free": Cream B29
"I Feel Love": Donna Summer A43, A235, B21
"I Feel So Bad": The Beatles B8
"I Feel the Earth Move": Carole King A99, B24
"If Everyone Was Listening": Supertramp A185
"If Heaven Aint a Lot Like Dixie": Hank Williams, Jr. A191
"If He Comes In, I'm Going Out" A145
"If I Can't": 50 Cent A99
"If I Can't Have You": Yvonne Elliman A179
"If I Could Be With You" A145, **B30**

"If I Could Be With You One Hour Tonight" A145; Louis Armstrong A119
"If I Could Build My Whole World Around You": Marvin Gaye A110
"If I Could Have Her Tonight": Neil Young B6
"If I Could See as Far Ahead as I Can See Behind" A145
"If I'd Been a Different Man" **B3**
"If I'd Been the One": .38 Special **A250**
"If I Ever Lose My Faith in You": Sting **B24**
"If I Fell": The Beatles **A90**, A91, A98, A99, B3, **B7**, **B8**, **B18**, B20, **B24**
"If I Forget You" **B30**
"If I Gave You" B30
"If I Had a Hammer": Pete Seeger B21
"If I Had a Talking Picture of You" A145
"If I Had the World to Give": The Grateful Dead B17
"If I Love Again" **B30**
"If I Loved You" B30
"If I'm Dreaming" **A120**
"If I Needed Someone": The Beatles A76, A92, A95, A98, A259, B7, B8, B18
"If I Ruled the World": Nas B31
"If I Should Die Tonight": Marvin Gaye A110
"If I Should Lose You" B30
"If It Can't Be You": Larry Denton B15
"If It's So Baby": The Robins A77
"If I Was Your Girlfriend": Prince B13
"If I Were a Bell": Miles Davis **A271**
"If I Were a Boy": Beyonce A219
"If I Were a Carpenter": Four Tops A185
"If I Were Not Upon the Stage": Paul McCartney B8
"If I Were You" B30
"If Leaving Me Is Easy": Phil Collins A185
"If Not for You": Bob Dylan A99; George Harrison A185, B7, B8
"I Forgot to Be Your Lover": William Bell A29
"I Forgot to Remember to Forget": The Beatles B8; Elvis Presley A99
"I Fought the Law": The Bobby Fuller Four A17, A99, A247
"I Found a Million Dollar Baby" A145, B10, **B30**
"I Found a New Baby": Lenny Tristano **A96**
"I Found Out": The Beatles **B18**; The Plastic Ono Band A90, A99
"If She Knew What She Wants": The Bangles B32

"If She Would Have Been Faithful": Chicago **A214**
"If Six Was Nine": Jimi Hendrix Experience, The A185, **B21**
"If There Is Someone Lovelier than You" **B10, B30**
"If There Is Something": Roxy Music A185
"If the River Was Whisky": Charlie Poole with the North Carolina Ramblers **A240**
"If They Move, Kill Them": Fairweather A205
"If This Isn't Love" B30
"If This World Were Mine": Marvin Gaye A110
"If Tomorrow Ever Comes": The Beatles **B8**
"If Women Ruled the World": Joan Armatrading A136
"If You Believe in Me" B30
"If You Can't Get Five, Take Two": Georgia White **A240**
"If You Could Read My Mind": Gordon Lightfoot B24
"If You Gotta Go, Go Now": Bob Dylan A216; ["Si Tu Dois Partir"] Fairport Convention A123
"If You Gotta Make a Fool of Somebody": The Beatles B8; James Ray A95
"If You Leave": Orchestral Manoeuvres in the Dark A36, A185
"If You Let Me Stay": Terence Trent d'Arby A185
"If You'll Be Mine" **B30**
"If You Please" A14
"If You're Gone": The Byrds A121
"(If You're Not in It for Love) I'm Outta Here!": Shania Twain A193
"If You're Ready (Come Go With Me)": The Staple Singers **A29**
"If You See My Saviour": Alex Bradford **A161**
"If You've Got Trouble": The Beatles B7, **B8**
"If You Wanna Touch Her, Ask!": Shania Twain **A192, A193**
"If You Wear That Velvet Dress": U2 A103
"I Get a Kick Out of You" A228, **B10, B30**; Frank Sinatra **A263**
"I Get Along Without You Very Well" **B30**
"I Get Around": The Beach Boys **A109**, A125, A185, A160, B8, B15, B24; Sawyer Brown B15
"I Get the Sun in the Morning" B10

"I Get Up I Get Down": Yes B21
"I Get Wild/Wild Gravity": Talking Heads A185
"Ignition": Trivium B21
"Ignoreland": R.E.M. A181
"I Got Ants in My Pants": James Brown A238
"I Got a Sure Thing": Ollie & The Nightingales A29
"I Got a Woman": The Beatles **B8**; Ray Charles A95, B8; Elvis Presley B8
"I Got It Bad and That Ain't Good" **B10, B30**
"I Got Lost in His Arms" B30
"I Got Love II": Marvin Gaye A110
"I Got Love": Marvin Gaye A110
"I Go to Extremes": Billy Joel A185, A250
"I Got Plenty of Nothin'" B16
"I Got Rhythm" A114, A147, A156, A168, A184, **A224**, B4, B8, **B10, B11**, B16, B19, B30; Ethel Merman B21
"I Got Stung": The Beatles B8
"I Gotta Dance to Keep From Cryin'": The Miracles **A106, A108**
"I Gotta Right to Sing the Blues" A48, B10, **B30**; Louis Armstrong **A48**; Billie Holiday A48
"I Got the Music in Me": The Kiki Dee Band A43
"I Got the News": Steely Dan A96, A99
"I Got the Sun in the Morning" A13, B30
"I Got to Find My Baby": The Beatles B8; Chuck Berry A95
"I Got To Love Somebody's Baby": Johnnie Taylor A29
"I Got You (I Feel Good)": James Brown A31, A95, A108, **A238**, A247, B4
"I Got You Babe": Sonny and Cher A32, A43, B21
"I Guess I'll Always Love You": Isley Brothers A185
"I Guess I'll Have to Change My Plan" B10, **B11**, B30
"I Guess I'll Have to Telegraph My Baby" A145
"I Guess I'm Lonely": Roy Orbison A270
"I Had a Dream": Johnnie Taylor A29
"I Had a Hard Day Last Night": Eartha Kitt B8
"I Had a King": Joni Mitchell **A260**
"I Had Myself a True Love" B30
"I Hadn't Anyone Till You" B30
"I Hate a Man Like You" A145

Song Index

"I Hate the White Man": Roy Harper B21
"I Have a Dream" ["Crejo en angelitos"]: ABBA B25
"I Have the Touch": Peter Gabriel A185, B21
"I Hear a Symphony" A105; The Supremes A43, A95, A99, A108
"I Heard It Through the Grapevine" A105; Marvin Gaye A99, A110, A144, **A245**, A247, B7, **B20**, **B24**, B32
"I Heard You Cried Last Night (and So Did I)": The Four Freshmen B15
"I Hear Music" B10, **B30**
"I Hear Ya Knockin'": Fats Domino **B25**
"I Helped You, Sick Man, When You were Sick and Down": Katherine Baker A240
"I Hope I Just Didn't Give Away the Ending": New Radicals B21
"I Hung My Head": Sting A221
"I Just Called to Say I Love You": Stevie Wonder B24
"I Just Couldn't Do Without You" **B30**
"I Just Don't Understand": The Beatles **B8**
"I Just Got My Pay": The Beach Boys B15
"I Just Want to Be with You": Chris Rea A185
"I Just Want to Make Love to You" B17
"I Just Wasn't Made for These Times": Brian Wilson B15
"I Just Wasn't Made for These Times": The Beach Boys **A160**
"I Keep Forgettin'": Artwoods B21
"Ikhnaton and Istacon and Their Band of Merry Men": Genesis A232
"I Knew I'd Want You": The Byrds A121
"I Knew Right Away": Alma Cogan B8
"I Knew the Moment I Lost You": Bob Wills & His Texas Playboys A240
"I Know": The Beatles B8; Fats Domino A95
"(I Know) I'm Losing You": John Lennon A99; The Supremes B3; The Temptations A97, A99, B7
"I Know It's a Sin" B17
"I Know That You Know" B10, **B30**
"I Know There's an Answer": The Beach Boys B7, B15, **A160**; Brian Wilson B15
"I Know There's Something Going On": Frida A19
"I Know What I Know": Paul Simon A9
"I Know What I Like": Huey Lewis and the News B24

"I Know What I Like (In Your Wardrobe)": Genesis A142
"I Know Why" A145
"I Know You Got Soul" [1]: James Brown A238
"I Know You Got Soul" [2]: Eric B. and Rakim A117
"I Know Your Heart" **B30**
"I Know You Rider" B17
"Iko Iko" A238, B17; The Dixie Cups A238; Dr. John A238
"I Learned From the Best": Whitney Houston A3
"I left My Heart at the Stage Door Canteen" A13
"I Let a Song Go out of My Heart" B10, B30
"I Like Bananas (Because They Have No Bones)": Henry Hall and the BBC Dance Orchestra A227
"I Like It": Gerry and the Pacemakers A185, B8
"I Like It Here" **A209**
"I Like It Like That": The Miracles **A108**
"I Like Love": Roy Orbison A270
"I Like the Likes of You" B10, **B30**
"I Like To Recognize The Tune" **B30**
"I Like What You're Doing": Carla Thomas A29
"I Like Your Style": The Originals A110
"I'll Always Be in Love with You" A145; Fats Domino A95, B8
"I'll Be a Bachelor 'Til I Die": Hank Williams B4
"I'll Be Around" **A209**
"I'll Be Back": The Beatles A43, A76, A98, A99, A185, **A253**, B7, **B8**, B18
"I'll Be Doggone": Marvin Gaye A32, A95, A108, B8
"I'll Be Gone, Long Gone": Mississippi Sheiks **A240**
"I'll Be Home for Christmas" A53
"I'll Be in Trouble": The Temptations **A108**
"I'll Be Leaving" B8
"I'll Be Loving You": New Kids A250
"I'll Be Missing You": Puff Daddy and Faith Evans feat. 112 A99, A163
"I'll Be on My Way": The Beatles **B8**
"I'll Be Seeing You" B10, **B30**; Bing Crosby **B4**; Hildegarde B4; Billie Holiday **B4**; Frank Sinatra with Tommy Dorsey and His Orchestra B4
"I'll Be The Other Woman": The Soul Children A29
"I'll Be There for You": Bon Jovi A185

"I'll Build a Stairway to Paradise" **A114**, B30; Paul Whiteman B8
"I'll Cry Instead": The Beatles A107, A185, **A194**, A250, A254, B7, B8, B18
"Illegal Business": KRS One B32
"I'll Feel a Whole Lot Better": The Byrds A33, A185, **B24**
"I'll Follow the Sun": The Beatles A98, B7, **B8**, **B18**
"I'll Get By (As Long as I Have You)" A145, **B30**; Billie Holiday B4; Harry James B4
"I'll Get You": The Beatles A195, B7, B8, B21
"I'll Give You a Ring": Paul McCartney B8
"I'll Go Crazy" B17; James Brown **B3**, B4, B17
"I'll Go Crazy If I Don't Go Crazy Tonight": U2 A89
"Illinois Enema Bandit, The": Frank Zappa A12, A27
"I'll Keep Holding On": The Marvelettes A95, A108
"I'll Know" A41
"I'll Lend You Anything" A145
"I'll Let You Hold My Hand": The Bootles A259
"I'll Never Let You Go (Little Darlin')": The Beatles B8
"I'll Never Smile Again" A53, **B10**
"I'll Only Miss Her When I Think of Her" A14
"I'll Remember April" B30
"I'll Run Your Hurt Away": Ruby Johnson A29
"I'll Sail This Ship Alone": Beautiful South A185
"(I'll See You In) C-U-B-A" B30
"I'll See You in My Dreams" B16, **B30**
"I'll Share It All With You" B30
"I'll Stick Around": Foo Fighters A205
"I'll Still Be Loving You": Kylie Minogue A185
"I'll String Along With You" B30
"I'll Take Care of You": Marvin Gaye A110
"I'll Take Romance" B30
"I'll Take You There": The Staple Singers A29
"I'll Tumble 4 Ya": Culture Club A36
"I'll Understand": The Soul Children A29
"I'll Wait for You": The Originals A110
"I'll Wait": Van Halen A250
"Ill Wind" **A114, B10, B30**
"I Looked at the Sun": Jonathan Kane A210
"I Looked Away": Derek and the Dominos **B20**

"I Look Out the Window": The Beatles **B7**
"I Lost It": Kenny Chesney A191
"I Lost My Little Girl": The Beatles **B8**
"I Lost My Sugar in Salt Lake City" B30
"I Love a Piano" A145, B30
"I Love How You Love Me": Jeff Mangum A22; The Paris Sisters B15
"I Love Louisa" B30
"I Love Paris" A168, B30
"I Love Rock and Roll": Joan Jett & The Blackhearts A43, B21
"I Loves You Porgy": Billie Holiday B4
"I Love the Night": Blue Öyster Cult **A59**
"I Love to Say Da Da": The Beach Boys B15
"I Love You" [1] **A113**, A228; Bing Crosby B4
"I Love You" [2]: Chris Clark A110
"I Love You Because": Elvis Presley A99; Jim Reeves A185
"I Love You (But You're Boring)": Beautiful South A185
"(I Love You) For Sentimental Reasons": Natalie Cole A30; Sam Cooke A30
"I Love You More Than Words Can Say": Otis Redding A29
"I Love You Sunday" A145
"I'm a Bad, Bad Man" B30
"I'm a Believer": The Monkees A182
"I'm a Boy": The Who A185, B8, B21
"I'm a Fool" B30
"I'm Afraid to Come Home in the Dark" A145
"Imagination" [1]: Tamia A35
"Imagination" [2] A14, **B10**, B30
"Imagine": John Lennon A80, A185, A247, B7, B8, **B18**, B19, B21
"I'm a Hog for You": The Beatles B8; The Coasters A95
"I'm a King Bee" B17
"I'm Alabama Bound": Papa Charlie Jackson **A240**
"I'm a Loser": The Beatles A76, A90, A91, A98, B7, **B8**
"I'm Already Taken": Steve Warner A191
"I'm a Man" [1]: Bo Diddley A216; The Yardbirds A43
"I'm a Man" [2]: Chicago B3
"I'm a Man" [3]: Pulp A82
"I'm a Man You Don't Meet Every Day": The Pogues B20
"I'm a Member of the Midnight Crew" A145

Song Index

"I'm an Old Cowhand" A145
"I'm a Ridin' Old Paint" B24
"(I'm a) Road Runner" B17; Jr. Walker and the All Stars A95, A105, **A108**
"I Married an Angel" A145, B10
"I'm Back": Eminem A146
"I'm Blessed": Paul Porter **A161**
"I'm Blue Again": Patsy Cline **B21**
"I'm Bugged at My Old Man": The Beach Boys B15
"I'm Coming Home": Deviants B21
"I'm Coming Virginia" A145, **B30**
"I'm Crazy About It" A145
"I'm Crying" [1]: Radiohead A143
"I'm Crying" [2]: The Animals **A16**
"I'm Down": The Beatles A76, A98, A195, B7, B8
"I'm Dying": Audio Sensory Theater A219
"I'm Eighteen": Alice Cooper **A16**
"I Me Mine": The Beatles A90, A98, B7, B8
"I": Meshuggah **A208**
"I'm Forever Blowing Bubbles": The Original Dixieland Jazz Band A227
"I'm Free (From The Chain Gang Now)": Jimmie Rodgers A266
"I'm Free": The Who A99, A185
"I'm Gettin' Sentimental Over You" **B30**
"I'm Glad There Is You" **A224, B30**
"I'm Going Back to Dixie" A145
"I'm Going Home": Ten Years After B21
"I'm Gone Before I Go" A145
"I'm Gonna Be a Wheel Someday": The Beatles B8; Fats Domino A95, A238
"I'm Gonna Build on That Shore": Sam Cooke A161
"I'm Gonna Charleston Back to Charleston" **B19** B19
"I'm Gonna Have You All": Manfred Mann's Earth band **A182**
"I'm Gonna Love You Too" A38
"I'm Gonna Love You To": The Beatles B8
"I'm Gonna Sit Right Down and Cry (Over You)": The Beatles B8
"I'm Gonna Sit Right Down and Write Myself a Letter" **B30**; Billy Williams A97
"I'm Gonna Tell God": The Soul Stirrers A205
"I'm Happy Just to Dance with You": The Beatles A185, A250, B3, B7, B8, B18, B20

"I'm Henry VIII, I Am": The Beatles B8; Herman's Hermits A32, A70, A71
"I'm Holdin' on to Love (To Save My Life)": Shania Twain **A193**
"I'm Hurtin'": Roy Orbison A270, B8
"I Might Be Wrong": Radiohead A135, **A169**
"I'm in Great Shape": Brian Wilson B15
"I'm in Love" **B3**; Billy J. Kramer B8; The Fourmost B8
"I'm in Love Again": Fats Domino A44, A95, **A264**, B8
"I'm in the Market for You" A145
"I'm in the Mood for Love" **B10**, B30
"I'm in the Mood": John Lee Hooker B21
"I'm Into Something Good": Herman's Hermits B8, B21
"I Missed Again": Phil Collins A185
"I Miss My Homies": Master P B14
"I Miss You": Kylie Minogue A185
"I'm Just a Child of Nature": The Beatles B7
"I'm Just Wild About Harry" **B30**
"I'm Leavin' Town (But I Sho' Don't Wanna Go)": William Harris A240
"I'm Left, You're Right, She's Gone": Elvis Presley A99
"I'm Lonely and Blue": Jimmie Rodgers A266
"I'm Lonesome Blues": Robert "Pete" Williams **A62**
"I'm Lonesome Too": Jimmie Rodgers A266
"I'm Looking Through You": The Beatles A76, A91, A98, B7, **B8**, B18
"I'm Losing You" *see* "(I Know) I'm Losing You"
"Immigrant Song": Led Zeppelin **A16**, A99, A101, A185, B20, B21
"I'm Needing You" A145
"I'm Nine Hundred Miles from Home": Fiddlin' John Carson A240
"I'm Nobody's Baby" **B30**
"I'm Not a Juvenile Delinquent": Frankie Lymon & The Teenagers A185, B21
"I'm Not Angry": Elvis Costello A185, B4
"I'm Not Down": The Clash A118
"I'm Not in Love": 10cc **A101**, A233
"I'm Not Moving": Phil Collins A185
"I'm Not Satisfied": Fine Young Cannibals A185
"I'm Not the Man I Used to Be": Fine Young Cannibals A185

"(I'm Not Your) Steppin' Stone" **A16**, B3; The Monkees **A97**, B7, B20
"I'm Old Fashioned" **B10**, **B30**
"I'm on a Plain": Nirvana A181
"I'm on a Trip to Your Heart": Sly & The Family Stone B3
"I'm Only Sleeping": The Beatles A70, A90, A98, A101, A138, A185, A198, **B7**, B8, **B18**, B21, B32
"I'm on the Crest of a Wave" **A120**
"I'm Outta Here!" see "(If You're Not in It for Love) I'm Outta Here!"
"Impatient Years, The" A14
"Impeach the President": The Honey Drippers A117, A261, B31
"Imperial Bedroom": Elvis Costello B4
"I'm Playing With Fire" B30
"I'm Putting All My Eggs in One Basket": Fred Astaire B21
"I'm Ready for Love": Martha and the Vandellas **A106**, **A108**, A185
"I'm Real": James Brown A117
"I'm Shakin": Little Willie John A148; White Stripes, The B7
"I'm Sick Y'All": Otis Redding **B3**
"I'm So Afraid": Fleetwood Mac B24
"I'm So Glad": Cream A132
"I'm So Glad I'm Twenty-One Years Old Today": Joe Dean A201, **B26**
"I'm So Glad We Had This Time Together (Carol's Theme)" **A202**
"I'm So Lonely": The Beach Boys B15
"I'm So Lonesome I Could Cry": Hank Williams **A83**, A247
"I'm So Proud": The Impressions **A108**
"I'm So Restless": Roger McGuinn A121
"I'm Sorry": Brenda Lee A99
"I'm Sorry I Ain't Got It" A145
"I'm Sorry We Met": Jimmie Rodgers A266
"I'm So Tired": The Beatles A99, B7, B8, **B18**, B21
"I'm So Young": The Beach Boys B15; The Students B15
"I'm Stepping Out": John Lennon B7
"I'm Sticking With You": The Rhythm Orchids A270
"I'm Still in Love With You Boy": Marcia Aitken A231

"I'm Talking About You": The Beatles **B8**; Chuck Berry A95; The Quarrymen B7
"I'm Telling You Now": Freddie and the Dreamers A185, B8, B20
"I'm the Greatest": Ringo Starr B7, B8
"I'm the One You Need" see "(Come Round Here) I'm the One You Need"
"I'm the Only One": Melissa Etheridge B24
"I'm the Slime": Frank Zappa and the Mothers A27, A55
"I'm the Urban Spaceman": The Bonzo Dog Band A185, B7
"I'm Thinking Tonight of My Blue Eyes": The Carter Family A240; Gene Autry A240
"I Must Be in Love": The Rutles A69
"I Must Have That Man": Lillie Delk Christian A119
"I Must Love You" B30
"I'm Waitin' for the Train to Come In" A53
"I'm Waiting for the Day": The Beach Boys **A160**, B15; Brian Wilson B15
"I'm Waiting for the Man": Velvet Underground A247
"I'm Walkin'": Fats Domino A97, **A238**, B24, **B25**; Ricky Nelson A44, A97
"I'm Wondering": Stevie Wonder A185
"I'm Your Angel" B10
"(I'm Your) Hoochie Coochie Man": Muddy Waters **A26**, A83, **A148**
"I'm Your Man": Wham **B19**
"I'm Yours" B30
"In a Big Country": Big Country A185
"In a Cage": Genesis B20
"In a Golden Coach" B16
"In a Little Second Hand Store": Henry Hall and the BBC Dance Orchestra A227
"In a Little While": U2 A89
"In a Lose, Lose Situation": Emery **A204**
"In Another Land": The Rolling Stones **B29**
"In Apple Blossom Time" A145
"In a Sentimental Mood" **A15**, B10, **B30**
"In a Station": Band A185
"In Bloom": Nirvana A80, A99, **A177**, A247
"In Blue Hawaii": Brian Wilson B15
"In Bluer Skies": Echo & Bunnymen A185
"In Coonland" A145
"In Crowd, The": Bryan Ferry A185, B21
"In Da Club": 50 Cent A99, **B31**

Song Index

"In Denial": The Pet Shop Boys A174
"In Dreams": Roy Orbison **A270**
"In Every Dreamhome a Heartache": Roxy Music A185
"In God's Country": U2 A185
"In Held 'Twas I'": Procol Harum A72
"In Limbo": Radiohead A162, **A169**
"In My Car": The Beach Boys B15
"In My Car (I'll Be the Driver)": Shania Twain **A193**
"In My Chair": Status Quo A185
"In My Childhood": The Beach Boys A160; Brian Wilson B15
"In My House": The Pet Shop Boys A174
"In My Life": Beatles, The **A7**, A80, A90, **A91**, A98, A247, B7, B8
"In My Merry Oldsmobile" A53
"In My Own Time": Family A185
"In My Room": The Beach Boys A99, A109, A125, B15; Brian Wilson B15
"In Other Words, Seventeen" **B30**
"In Our Bedroom After the War": Stars A205
"In Spite of All the Danger": The Beatles B7; The Quarrymen **B8**
"In the Aeroplane Over the Sea": Neutral Milk Hotel A22
"In the Air Tonight": Phil Collins A19, A43, A142, A185, A233, A235, B32
"In the Back of My Mind": The Beach Boys A160, B15
"In the Blood": Mudhoney A177
"In the Cage": Genesis A232
"In the City": The Jam A185, B20, B21; Razorlight B21
"In the Country" [1]: Chicago B3
"In the Country" [2]: Cliff Richard **B20**
"In the Court of the Crimson King": King Crimson B20
"In the End": Green Day B21
"In the Evening By The Moonlight" B30
"In the Flesh": Pink Floyd A185
"In the Garden": Bob Dylan A180
"In the Heart of the Dark" **B30**
"In the Heart of the Kentucky Hills" A145
"In the Hills of Tennessee": Jimmie Rodgers A266
"In the Jailhouse Now": Jimmie Rodgers A266

"In the Land of Harmony and Stop Stop Stop" A145
"In the Light": Led Zeppelin **A269**
"In the Midnight Hour" B3, B17; Wilson Pickett **A32**, **A95**, A99, **A97**, A185, A247, B4, B32; Billy Preston B7
"In the Mood" [1]: Glenn Miller **A234**, A270, **B21**
"In the Mood" [2]: Talib Kweli A261, B31
"In the Name of God": Dream Theater A175
"In the Park": George Harrison B7
"In the Parkin' Lot": The Beach Boys B15
"In the Pines" B17
"In the Presence of Enemies": Dream Theater A175
"In the Rain": Madness A185
"In the Right Church but in the Wrong Pew" A145
"In the Shade of the New Apple Tree" B30
"In the Still of the Night" **A113**, **B10**, B30; The Four Freshmen B15
"In the Still of the Nite": The Beach Boys B15; The Five Satins **A38**, A44, A80, A167, A247, **A263**, B15
"In the Summer of His Years": The Bee Gees B3
"In the Summertime": Mungo Jerry A55, A185
"In the Sweet By and By" A219
"In the Time of Our Lives": Iron Butterfly B3
"In the Wilderness": Genesis **A142**
"In the Year 2525": Zager and Evans A93, A185
"In This Life": Madonna A6
"In This Place": Robin Trower B21
"In Time": Sly and the Family Stone B32
"In Too Deep": Genesis A232
"In Walked Bud" A168; Thelonius Monk **A168**
"In Your Own Quiet Way" **A224**, **B30**
"In Zanzibar" A145
"In-a-Gadda-da-Vida": The Incredible Bongo Band B31; Iron Butterfly A28, A43, A72, **A101**, B3, B31; Rush A198
"Inbetweener": Sleeper A124
"Incarcerated Scarfaces": Raekwon B14
"Inca Roads": Frank Zappa A27, **A60**
"Incense and Peppermints": The Strawberry Alarm Clock A43, A99, B8
"Incident on 57th Street": Bruce Springsteen A269

"Incommunicado": Marillion A71
"Incurably Romantic" A14
"Independence Day": Martina McBride A167, A193
"Indiana" A145
"Indian Gin and Whiskey Dry": The Bee Gees B3
"Indian Summer" **B30**
"Indian Summer Sky": U2 A185
"Indian Sunset": Elton John **B31**
"Indian War Dance" A145
"Indiscreet" A14, **B30**
"Indoor Games": King Crimson A152
"Indoor Sports" A145
"I Need a Beat": LL Cool J A99
"I Need a Garden" B30
"I Need a Man": The Eurhythmics B13
"I Need a Miracle": the Grateful Dead A197
"I Need More Time": Meters A185
"I Need Your Love Tonight": Elvis Presley B8
"I Need You": The Beatles A76, A95, A98, A232, B7, B8
"I Never Found a Girl": Eddie Floyd A29
"I Never Has Seen Snow" **B30**
"I Never Loved a Man (The Way I Love You)": Aretha Franklin A99, A205, **A265**, B32
"I Never Loved Eva Braun": The Boomtown Rats A185, B20, B21
"I Never Realized" B30
"Infinite Space": Emerson, Lake, & Palmer A182
"Influência do Jazz, A": Carlos Lyra A211
"Information Overload": Living Colour A99
"Initials" B7
"Inner City Blues": Marvin Gaye A185
"Inner Light, The": The Beatles A90, A98, A195, B7, B8
"Innocence Faded": Dream Theater A175
"Innocent Ingenue Baby" A114, **A120**, B30
"Innocent Man": Billy Joel B24
"Insatiable": Prince A79, **B13**
"Inside of Me": Madonna B13
"Insomniac": Echobelly B21
"Instant Hot": The Slits B20
"Instant Karma (We All Shine On)": Plastic Ono Band A185, B7, B8, B18
"Intermezzo no. 1": ABBA B25
"International Rag, the" A145
"Interstellar Overdrive": Pink Floyd A185, A198, B7, B29

"Interview at the Ruins": Circle Takes the Square A205
"Intevrention": Arcade Fire A219
"Intolerance": Tool **A203**
"Into the Fire": Deep Purple A185
"Into the Great Wide Open": Tom Petty B24
"Into the Night": Benny Mardones A250
"Into the Sun": Grand Funk Railroad B21
"Introducing Palace Players": Mew A205
"Introduction": Chicago B24
"Intruder" [1]: Peter Gabriel A185, B21, **B23**, B32; Primus B23
"Intruder" [2]: Van Halen A185, B20
"Invalid Litter Department": At the Drive In A205
"Invisible Sun": The Police **A235**
"Invisible Touch": Genesis A72, A232, A250, **B24**
"Invocation and Ritual Dance of the Young Pumpkins": Mothers of Invention, The A11
"Inwards": Big Country A185
"I Only Have Eyes for You" B30; Flamingos A247
"I Put a Spell on You" **A133**; Nina Simone A95, **B8**
"I Really Love You": The Beatles B8
"I Remember April" B16
"I Remember": The Beatles B8; Eddie Cochran B21
"I Remember You": The Beatles B8
"Irish Washerwoman, The" B27
"I Robot": Alan Parsons Project **A233**
"Iron Man": Black Sabbath A17, A43, A55, **A55**, A99
"Iron Stone, The": The Incredible String Band A112
"Irresistable": The Corrs A193
"I Saw Her Standing There" B16; The Beatles A63, A91, A95, A98, A99, A107, **A194**, **A196**, A247, **A254**, A259, B7, **B8**, **B18**, **B19**, B24, B27
"I Saw the Light": Hank Williams B4
"I Say a Little Prayer": Dionne Warwick **A192**, B21
"I See It Now" **A209**
"I See Your Face Before Me" **B30**
"I Shall Be Free #10": Bob Dylan A99
"I Shall Be Released": The Band A185, B32; The Beatles B7; Bob Dylan B7, B8

Song Index

"I Shot the Sheriff": Eric Clapton A235, B20; Bob Marley A231, B20, B24; Warren G B14

"I Should be So Lucky": Kylie Minogue A185

"I Should Have Known Better" [1]: Jim Diamond A185

"I Should Have Known Better" [2]: The Beatles A91, A98, A99, **A100**, A185, B7, **B8**, B20, B21

"Is It Always Like This" **A209**

"Is It Like Today": World Party B32

"Island in a Stream": Mission A185

"Islands in the Stream": Kenny Rogers and Dolly Parton A193

"Island": T'Pau A185

"I Sleep on my Heart": Level 42 A185

"Isn't It a Pity" **B30**; The Beatles B7, B8; George Harrison **A83**, A185, B18, B21; John & Yoko with The Plastic Ono Band B32

"Isn't It Midnight": Fleetwood Mac A185

"Isn't It Romantic" B10, **B30**

"Isn't She Lovely": Stevie Wonder B21

"Isn't This a Lovely Day" **B10**, B30

"Isolation": John Lennon B7, **B18**

"Israelite": Desmond Dekker A185

"Is She Really Going Out With Him": Joe Jackson A71, A74

"Istanbul (not Constantinople)": They Might Be Giants A185

"I Started a Joke": The Bee Gees **B24**

"I Started Something I Couldn't Finish": The Smiths A36

"Is That All There Is?" A264; Peggy Lee A77

"Is There a Place Up There for Me?" A145

"Is This Desire?": PJ Harvey A223

"Is This Love": Survivor A250

"I Still Believe in You" B30

"I Still Haven't Found What I'm Looking For": U2 A22, A80, A99, A185, A247, B24

"I Still Look at You That Way" B30

"I Surrender, Dear" B10

"I Surrender All" A219

"Is You Is Or Is You Ain't My baby": Louis Jordan A185

"Is Your Love in Vain?": Bob Dylan A180

"It Ain't Always What You Do (It's Who You Let See You Do It)": The Soul Children A29

"It Ain't Easy": David Bowie A185

"It Ain't Gonna Rain No Mo?" A145

"It Ain't Hard to Tell": Nas A99

"It Ain't Me Babe": Bob Dylan **A225**; The Turtles B8

"It Ain't Necessarily So": Ian and the Zodiacs B8

"Italian X-Rays": Steve Miller Band A185

"It All Depends": Eric Clapton **A271**

"Itchycoo Park": The Small Faces A101, A185, B21

"It Could Happen to You" A14, B10, **B30**

"It Don't Come Easy": Ringo Starr B7

"It Don't Matter to Me" [1]: Bread B24

"It Don't Matter to Me" [2]: Phil Collins A185

"It Goes Like This" A145

"It Had to Be That way" A145

"It Had to Be You" **B30**

"I Thank You": Sam and Dave A29

"It Happened in Monterey" B16

"It Has Been Said": Eminem **B31**

"I Think I Can": Animal Collective A205

"I Think I'm Gonna Like It Here" A202

"I Think It's Going to Rain Today": Joe Cocker A264; Randy Newman **A264**

"I Think I Understand": Joni Mitchell **A260**

"I Think We're Alone Now": Tommy James and the Shondells **A241**

"I Thought About You" A14, A114

"I Thought I Was a Winner, or, I Don't Know, You Ain't So Warm" A145

"I Threw It All Away": The Beatles B7; Bob Dylan B7, B8

"It Hurt Me Too": Marvin Gaye A110

"It Hurts Me Too" B17

"It Is Well" A161

"It'll Be Me": The Beatles B8

"It Makes My Love Come Down" A145

"It Makes No Difference Now": Hank Williams B4

"It Might as Well Be Spring" **B30**

"It Might Be You": Stephen Bishop **B24**

"It Must Be Someone Like You" A185

"It Must Be True" **B30**

"It Never Dawned on Me" A145

"It Never Entered My mind" B30

"It Never Rains in Southern California": Albert Hammond A185

"It Only Happens When I Dance With You" **B30**

"It Only Hurts When I Breathe": Shania Twain A193

"It's a Blue World" A147; The Four Freshmen B15
"It's a Game": String Driven Thing A185
"It's a Grand Night for Singing" B30
"It's a Great Big Land" B30
"It's a Long, Long Way to Tipperary": The Beatles B8
"It's a Lovely Day Today" B30
"It's a Lovely Day Tomorrow" B10, B30
"It's a Man's World": Ice Cube and Yo-Yo B14; James Brown A247
"It's a Mistake": Men at Work B24
"It's a Most Unusual Day" **B30**
"It's a New Day": Skull Snaps A261
"It's a Sin": The Pet Shop Boys A174, B21
"It's a Sin to Tell a Lie": Henry Hall and the BBC Dance Orchestra A227
"It's a Small World (After All)" **A202**
"It Takes a Lot to Laugh": Bob Dylan B19
"It Takes Two": Marvin Gaye & Tammi Terrell A185
"It Tango": Laurie Anderson A99
"It Was a Good Day": Ice Cube B31
"It Wasn't My Fault" B30
"It Was So Beautiful" **B30**
"It Won't Be Long": The Beatles A76, A91, A100, B7, B8, **B18**, **B19**; Charley Patton A201, **B26**
"It Won't Be Wrong": The Byrds A121
"It's About Time": The Beach Boys B15
"It's All in the Game": Tommy Edwards A97
"It's All Over Now Baby Blue": The Byrds A121; Bob Dylan A121, A216
"It's All Over Now": The Rolling Stones **B20**
"It's All Right Now": Arizona Dranes A145, A240
"It's All Right": The Impressions A108
"It's All Too Much": The Beatles A98, B7
"It's Alright, Ma (I'm Only Bleeding)": Bob Dylan **A216**, B7
"It's Alright for You" [1]: The Byrds A121
"It's Alright for You" [2]: The Police A235
"It's Always You" A14, B27
"It's Bad for Me" **B30**
"It's Been So Long" **B30**
"It's De-Lovely" A113, **B10**
"It's Easy To Remember" **B30**
"It's for You": Cilla Black **B8**
"It's Getting Better": The Beatles B20

"It's Good to Be Here": Diagable Planets **B31**
"It's Got to Be Love" [1]: Marvin Gaye A110
"It's Got to Be Love" [2] **B30**
"It's Growing" A95; The Temptations **A108**
"It's Just a Matter of Time": Brook Benton A44
"It's Just a Thought": Creedence Clearwater B3
"It's Just for You": The Beatles **B7**
"It's Just the Blues": The Four Jumps of Five A110
"It's Lonely Out There": Pam Tillis A189
"It's Love-Love-Love": Guy Lombardo B4
"It's Midnight Cinderella": Garth Brooks A189
"It's Mine": Mobb Deep A158
"It's My Life" [1]: The Animals B8; Eric Burdon A185
"It's My Life" [2]: No Doubt A232; Talk Talk **A236**
"It's My Party": Bryan Ferry A123; Lesley Gore A123, B24
"It's Nice to Go Trav'ling" A14
"It's Nobody's Business But My Own" A145
"It's No Secret" [1]: Kylie Minogue A185
"It's No Secret" [2]: The Jefferson Airplane B7
"It's Not the Same for Us": Level 42 A185
"It's Not What You've Got" B30
"It's Now or Never": The Beatles B8; Johnny Powers A110; ["O Sole Mio"] Elvis Presley A99, A270, B7, **B25**
"It's Oh So Quiet": Bjork B21
"It's OK" [1]: Fine Young Cannibals A185
"It's OK" [2]: The Beach Boys B15
"It's Only a Paper Moon" B10, **B30**
"It's Only Goodbye": Gentle Giant A185
"It's Only Love" [1]: The Beatles A98, B7, B8
"It's Only Love" [2]: Bryan Adams A250
"It's Only Make Believe": Conway Twitty A97, **B25**
"It's Only Rock 'n Roll (But I Like It)": The Rolling Stones B24
"It's Over": Roy Orbison A270, B21, B25
"It's Over Now": The Beach Boys B15
"It's Rainin'": Kirk Franklin **A161**
"It's So Easy": Buddy Holly B8
"It's So Hard": John Lennon **B18**
"It's So Peaceful in the Country" **A209**
"It's the Dreamer in Me" B10
"It's the Hard Knock Life" A99
"It's the Same Old Song" A95; The Four Tops A32, A108, B8

Song Index   *187*

"It's the Talk of the Town" **B30**; Jack Hylton and His Orchestra A227
"It's Tight Like That" *see* "(Honey) It's Tight Like That"
"It's Time": Elvis Costello **A33**
"It's Time to Go Now": Gladys Knight and the Pips A110
"It's Too Late": Derek & Dominos A185
"It's Too Soon To Know": Pat Boone A97
"It's Trying to Say": The Beach Boys B15
"It's Wonderful": The Rascals A101, B7
"It's Wrong (Apartheid)": Stevie Wonder A99
"It's You": PJ Harvey A50
"I Understand": Freddie and the Dreamers B8
"I Used to Be Color Blind" B10, B30
"I Used to Love H.E.R.": Common B31
"I Used to Love You but It's All Over Now" A145
"Ivan Meets G.I. Joe": The Clash B20
"I've a Shooting Box in Scotland" B30
"I've Been Lonely for So Long": Frederick Knight **A185**
"I've Been Lonely Too Long": The Rascals B7
"I've Been Loving You Too Long": Otis Redding A29, A247
"(I've Been) Searchin' So Long": Chicago **B24**
"I've Been Thinking That You Love Me": The Beatles B8
"I've Done Everything for You": Rick Springfield A250
"I've Got a Boy Child" **B27**
"I've Got a Crush on You" **B30**, **B10**
"I've Got a Feeling I'm Falling" **A120**; Louis Armstrong **A119**
"I've Got a Feeling": The Beatles **A63**, **A63**, A98, A156, **B7**, B8, B18
"I've Got a Lovely Bunch of Coconuts" **B25**; The Beatles B7
"I've Got an Invitation to a Dance": Roy Fox and His Band A227
"I've Got a Story": Mary Wells A110
"I've Got Five Dollars" **B30**
"I've Got Money": James Brown **A238**
"I've Got My Captain Working for Me Now" A145
"I've Got My Fingers Crossed" A145
"I've Got My Love To Keep Me Warm" B30
"I've Got Sixpence": Billy Cotton and His Band A227

"I've Got Something in My Eye" A145
"I've Gotta Get a Message To You": Bee Gees B3, B7, B21
"I've Got the Music in Me": Kiki Dee Band, The A43
"I've Got the World on a String" B10, **B11**, **B30**; Louis Armstrong A119
"I've Got to Get a Message to You": The Bee Gees B24
"I've Got You on My Mind" A145, A228, B10, **B30**
"I've Got You Under My Skin" **A113**, A228, B10, **B11**, **B30**; Frank Sinatra B21
"I've Grown So Ugly": Robert Pete Williams A210
"I've Just Fallen for Someone": The Beatles B8
"I've Just Seen a Face": The Beatles A98, A99, B7, B8
"I've Loved Her So Long": Neil Young B6
"I've Never Been in Love Before": A41
"I've Never Seen a Straight Banana" A145
"I've Only Loved Three Women": Jimmie Rodgers A266
"I've Ranged, I've Roamed, I've Traveled": Jimmie Rodgers A266
"I've Seen All Good People": Yes A214, **A233**
"I've Seen That Movie Too": Elton John B21
"I've Told Ev'ry Little Star" **B30**
"I've Told You for the Last Time": Cream B3
"Ivory Tower": Otis Williams and his Charms B15
"Ivy" **B30**
"I Walk From the Hill": Big Country A187
"I Walk on Guided Splinters": Dr. john A222
"I Walk the Hill": Big Country A185, B20, B21
"I Walk the Line": Johnny Cash A44, A80, A247
"I Wanna Be Around": Brian Wilson B15
"I Wanna Be Loved" A114, B10
"I Wanna Be Sedated": Ramones A247
"I Wanna Be Your Dog": Sonic Youth A210; The Stooges A24
"I Wanna Be Your Man": The Beatles A95, A98, **B3**, B7, B8, B18, B19
"I Wanna Dance With Somebody": Whitney Houston A185
"I Wanna Go Back": Eddie Money A250
"I Wanna Pick You Up": The Beach Boys B15
"(I Wanna) Testify": Johnnie Taylor A29

"I Want a Dog": The Pet Shop Boys A174
"I Want a Good Woman": Carlisle & Ball A240
"I Want a Guy": The Marvelettes B8
"I Want a Lover": The Pet Shop Boys A174
"I Want a Man" **B30**
"I Want a New Drug": Huey Lewis & News A247
"I Want Candy": The Strangeloves A43
"I Want Someone": The Mad Lads A29
"I Want the One I Can't Have": The Smiths A36
"I Want to Be a Cowboy's Sweetheart": Patsy Montana A266
"I Want to Be Happy" B10
"I Want to Be with You" B10, **B30**
"I Want to Be with You Always": Lefty Frizzell A270
"I Want to Break Free": Queen A178
"I Want to Go Back There Again": Chris Clark A110
"I Want to Hold Your Hand" ["Komm, Gib Mir Deine Hand"]: The Beatles A7, **A17**, A63, A69, A74, **A75**, **A76**, A80, A85, A91, A92, A98, A99, A100, A107, A167, A182, A195, A233, **A241**, A247, B3, B4, B7, **B8**, B15, B21, B24
"I Want to Know What Love Is": Foreigner A7, B21, **B24**
"I Want to Know Where Tosti Went" A145
"I Want to Love You While the Music's Playing" A145
"I Want to Tell You": The Beatles A90, A92, A95, A185, A198, B7, B8, B18
"I Want to Thank You": Otis Redding B3
"I Want You, I Need You, I Love You": Elvis Presley A99
"I Want You" [1]: Bob Dylan A121, B4
"I Want You" [2]: Elvis Costello and the Attractions B4
"I Want You Back" [1] A238; The Jackson 5 A35, A232, A247
"I Want You Back" [2]: Bananarama A212
"I Want You By My Side" A145
"I Want You Now": Feeling, The B21
"I Want Your (Hands on Me)": Sinéad O'Connor B32
"I Want You (She's So Heavy)": The Beatles A43, **A63**, A91, A92, A95, A98, A167, A222, A223, A225, A259, B7, B8, **B18**, B21, **B23**

"I Want You to Want Me": Cheap Trick B21
"I Was Brought to My Senses": Sting A221
"I Was Doing All Right" **B30**
"I Was Kaiser Bill's Batman": The Mike Sammes Singers (Whistling Jack Smith) B7
"I Was Made to Love Her": The Beach Boys B15; Stevie Wonder A19, A96, A185, B8
"I Was Only Joking": Rod Stewart B24
"I Was So Young, You Were So Beautiful" B30
"I Went to Sleep": The Beach Boys B15
"I Will Always Love You": Whitney Houston B21; Dolly Parton A86
"I Will Do Anything for Love (But I Won't Do That)": Meatloaf **B21**
"I Will Put My Ship in Order": Ossian B21; June Tabor B21
"I Will Survive": Gloria Gaynor A5, A167, A185; The Pet Shop Boys A174
"I Will": The Beatles A98, **A100**, **A169**, B7, B8, B21
"I Wish I Could've Been There": John Anderson A191
"I Wish I Didn't Love You So" **A110**; Marvin Gaye **A110**
"I Wish It Would Rain Down": Phil Collins A185
"I Wish It Would Rain": Marvin Gaye A110; The Temptations A99
"I Wish I Were in Love Again" B10, B30
"I Wish": Skee-Lo B14
"I Wish": Stevie Wonder A234, **A236**
"I Woke Up in Love This Morning": The Partridge Family B24
"I Wonder If I Care as Much": The Beatles B8
"I Wonder What Became of Me" B10, B30
"I Wonder What's Become of Joe" A145
"I Wonder Why": Dion and the Belmonts A44
"I Won't Dance": A145, **B30**
"I Won't Hold You Back": Toto A250, B24
"I Won't Leave My Wooden Wife for You Sugar": The United States of America A138
"I Wouldn't Go That Far": Reba McEntire A191
"I Wouldn't Normally Do This Kind of Thing": The Pet Shop Boys A174
"I Wouldn't Want to Be Like You": The Alan Parsons Project B24
"Izzo (H.O.V.A.)": Jay-Z A35

Song Index

"Jabo": James Brown A238
"Jack and Diane": John Cougar **A250**
"Jack-a-Roe" B17; The Grateful Dead A99
"Jackhammer Blues": Woody Guthrie A240
"Jackin' for Beats": Ice Cube B22
"Jack in the Green": Jethro Tull A188, B20
"Jack of All Parades": Elvis Costello B4
"Jacksonville Blues": Nellie Florence **B26**
"Jacob's Ladder" [1]: Rush **A16**, A208
"Jacob's Ladder" [2]: Mark Wills A189
"Ja-Da" B30, B25
"Jailbreak": Thin Lizzy A185
"Jailhouse Blues, The": Sam Collins **B26**
"Jailhouse Rock" B27; Elvis Presley A64, **A75**, A77, A80, **A84**, A97, A247, B8, B19, **B24**
"J'ai Pres Parley": Hackberry Ramblers A240
"Jake! Jake! The Yiddisher Ball-Player" **A168**
"Jam" [1]: The Grateful Dead B17
"Jam" [2]: Michael Jackson A35
"Jamaica Farewell" A65
"Jambalaya (On the Bayou)" B8
"Jambi": Tool A221
"James": Billy Joel **A215**
"James & the Cold Gun": Kate Bush A185
"James Alley Blues": Richard "Rabbit" Brown **B26**
"Jamming": Bob Marley and the Wailers A235
"Jammin' Me": Tom Petty A225
"Jane Says": Jane's Addiction A248
"Japanese Sandman, The" B10, **B30**
"Jazz Concerto" B10
"Jazz Holiday, A" A145
"Jazz Thing": Gang Starr A261
"Jazz": Tribe Called Quest, A B31
"Jealous Guy": The Beatles A90; John Lennon B7, B8, **B18**
"Jealous Hearted Me": The Carter Family A240
"Jealous Lover" B30
"Jeane": Sandie Shaw A123; The Smiths A36, A123
"Jean Genie": David Bowie B21
"Jeanie With the Light Brown Hair" A219, **B11**, B30; Rory Storm and the Hurricanes B8
"Jeepers Creepers" B10, B16, B30
"Jelly Covered Cloud": The Scaffold B7
"Jelly Jungle (of Orange Marmalade)": The Lemon Pipers B7
"Jennifer Juniper" B7
"Jenny Jenny": Little Richard A95, B8

"Jerical": Jeff Mills **B5**
"Jericho": ADF A61
"Jerk, The": The Larks B32
"Jerry" B30
"Jerusalem" [1]: C.H.H. Parry A232
"Jerusalem" [2]: Herb Alpert A185
"Jerusalem Boogie": Peter Gabriel A232
"Jesamine": The Casuals B20, B21
"Jesse James": Ken Maynard A240
"Jessie's Dream": John Lennon **B7**
"Jessie's Girl": Rick Springfield A59
"Jesus Children of America": Stevie Wonder A185
"Jesus Christ Pose": Soundgarden A99
"Jesus Goin' Make Up My Dyin' Bed": Dock Reed, Vera Hall, and jesse Allison A26
"Jesus I'll Never Forget" A264
"Jesus Is Just Alright": The Byrds A121
"Jesus Is the Reason": Kirk Franklin **A161**
"Jesus Knows How Much We Can Bear": The Georgia Peach **A161**
"Jesus Left Chicago": Z.Z. Top A185
"Jesus Met the Woman at the Well": Swan Silvertones B21
"Jesus": Queen A221
"Jesus Thinks You're a Jerk": Frank Zappa A85
"Jet Airliner": The Steve Miller Band A101, A185
"Jet": Paul McCartney and Wings B7, B24
"Jig-Hop, The" B10
"Jim Dandy": LaVern Baker A44
"Jim Lee Blues – Part 1": Charley Patton A240
"Jimmie Rodgers Blues, The": Elton Britt A266
"Jimmie Rodgers's Last Blue Yodel": Jimmie Rodgers A266
"Jimmie Rodgers Visits the Carter Family": Jimmie Rodgers A266
"Jimmie's Mean Mama Blues": Jimmie Rodgers A266
"Jimmie's Texas Blues": Jimmie Rodgers A266
"Jimmie the Kid": Jimmie Rodgers A266
"Jimmy Jazz": The Clash A118, B20
"Jimmy Mack": Martha Reeves A185
"Jimmy Munro's Troubles": Ned Corvan **B19**
"Jive Talkin' ": The Bee Gees A179
"Joan of Arc": Orchestral Manoeuvres A185
"Job": Golden Gate Quartet B21
"Jock-a-Mo": Sugar Boy Crawford A238

"Joel": The Boo Radleys B20, B21
"John, John, Let's Hope for Peace": The Beatles B7; Plastic Ono Band B18
"John Allyn Smith Sails": Okkervil River A205
"John Barleycorn": Jethro Tull A188
"John Brown": Bob Dylan A216
"John Brown's Body" A196
"John Gaudie": Whippersnapper B21
"John Hardy": Ramblin' Jack Elliott A58
"John Henry": Arthur Bell A240; Reese Crenshaw A240; Lonnie Donegan B8; Woody Guthrie **A240**; Leadbelly **A240**; Sonny Terry & Brownie McGhee A95
"John Henry Was a Little Boy": J.E. Mainer's Mountaineers A240
"Johnny B. Goode" A76; The Beach Boys B15; Chuck Berry A7, A17, A75, A80, A84, A95, A185, **A244**, A247, B8, B15, **B21**
"Johnny Carson": The Beach Boys B15
"Johnny Don't Do It": 10cc B21
"Johnny Dunn's Cornet Blues" A145
"Johnny Get Angry": Joanie Sommers **A45**; k.d. lang **A45**
"Johnny One Note" B10, B30
"Johnny's So Long at the Fair" A209
"Johnny T": Slaughter and the Dogs A210
"John Walker's Blues": Steve Earle B21
"John Wesley Harding": Bob Dylan B7
"Jolly Coppers on Parade": Randy Newman **A264**
"Jonah in the Belly of the Whale": Norfolk Jubilee Singers A238
"Jonah": Paul Simon **A93**, B1
"Jones Crusher Love": Frank Zappa A27
"Jordu": Dizzy Gillespie A96
"Josie": Steely Dan A96
"Journey from Mariabronn": Kansas A72
"Journey Through the Past": Neil Young B6
"Journey to the Center of Your mind": Amboy Dukes, The **A101**
"Joy" [1]: PJ Harvey A223
"Joy" [2]: Apollo 100 A179
"Joy" [3]: Georgia State Mass Choir **A161**
"Joyride Cruise, A": The Survivors B15
"Joy to the World": Three Dog Night B24
"Jubilee (Junk)": The Beatles A90
"Judgement of the Moon and Stars": Joni Mitchell A260

"Judy" B30; The Beach Boys B15; Bobby Darin B25
"Judy in Disguise (With Glasses)": John Fred and his Playboy Band B7
"Judy Teen": Harley's Cockney Rebel A185, B20
"Jugband Blues": Pink Floyd A198, B7
"Jugni": Panjabi MC A61
"Juicy Fruit": Mtume B31
"Juicy": Notorious B.I.G. B14
"Juke Box Hero": Foreigner B24
"Julia" [1]: The Beatles **A24**, **A90**, **A97**, A99, A98, A100, A259, **B7**, B8, **B18**
"Julia" [2]: King's X A56
"Juliet": Four Pennies B21
"Jumbo Go Away": Frank Zappa A11
"Jump" [1]: Van Halen **A17**, A142, A232, **A236**, **A250**, B24
"Jump" [2]: Kriss Kross A35
"Jump Back": Rufus Thomas A95
"Jumpin' Jack Flash" A97; The Rolling Stones A43, **A55**, A99, A154, **A155**, A185, **A246**, A247, A248, B7, **B19**, **B24**
"Jumpin' Judy" A161
"Jump Steady Blues" A145
"June moon" A145
"Jungle": Electric Light Orchestra A185
"Jungle Fever" A145
"Jungleland": Bruce Springsteen A269
"Jungle Line, The": Joni Mitchell **A260**, B20, B21
"Jungle Love": Steve Miller Band A246
"Junior's Farm": Wings B7
"Junk": The Beatles B7, B8; Paul McCartney B18, B20
"Jupiter Forbid" B30
"Just a Dream": Jimmy Clanton A97
"Just a Few More Days": Carter Family, The A240
"Just a Friend": Biz Markie B14
"Just a Friend of the Family" A145
"Just a Girl": No Doubt A84
"Just Another Day in Paradise": Phil Vassar A191
"Just a Shadow": Big Country A185
"Just a Sinner": James Cleveland **A161**
"Just Because": Elvis Presley A99, B8
"Just Because I'm a Woman": Dolly Parton A193

Song Index

"Just Be Good to Me": The S.O.S. Band A252
"Just Call Me Joe": Sinéad O'Connor B32
"Just Friends" **B30**
"Just Fun": The Beatles **B8**
"Just Got Paid": Z.Z. Top A185
"Justify My Love": Madonna **A258**, B13
"Just in Time" B30
"Just in Time to See the Sun": Santana A185
"Just Let Me Breathe": Dream Theater A175
"Just Let Me Look at You" B30
"Just Like a Rainbow" A145
"Just Like a Woman": The Byrds A121; Judy Collins A123; Bob Dylan **A101**, A123, B21; Roberta Flack A123; Manfred Mann A185, B21
"Just Like Me": Paul Revere and the Raiders B8
"(Just Like) Starting Over": John Lennon A99, B7, B8, B24
"Just Like This Train": Joni Mitchell A260
"Just Once in My Life": The Beach Boys B15
"Just One Look": Doris Troy A95
"Just One of Those Funky Things": George Clinton B21
"Just One of Those Things" A113, B10, **B30**
"Just Plain Lonesome" A14
"Just": Radiohead A162, **A169**
"Just Take Me": Status Quo B20
"Just the Way You Are": Billy Joel **A247**, B24
"Just to Keep You Satisfied": Marvin Gaye A110
"Just Too Soon" A145
"Just Trying to Be": Jethro Tull A4
"Just What I Needed": The Cars **A17**, **A74**, A99, **B24**
"Just You 'n' Me": Chicago B24

"Kansas City Man Blues" A145
"Kansas City": The Beatles A24, A98, A254, B7, B8; Wilbert Harrison A44
"Karma Chameleon": Culture Club A250, B24
"Karma Police": Radiohead A56, A162, **A169**, A205
"Karn Evil 9": Emerson, Lake and Palmer A72, A138, A139, A182, B24
"Karucha Shokku": U Totem A81
"Kashmir": Led Zeppelin **A17**, A74, A159, A247, A269, **B20**
"Kathy's Song": Paul Simon B1
"Kaw-liga": Hank Williams A270, B4

"Kayleigh": Marillion A71
"K.C. Blues": Frank hutchison A240
"K.C. Moan": Memphis Jug Band A240, **B26**
"Keep a Knockin'": Little Richard A238
"Keep an Eye on Summer": The Beach Boys A160, B15; Brian Wilson B15
"Keep a Song in your Soul" A145
"(Keep Feeling) Fascination": The Human League A36
"Keep Getting' It On": Marvin Gaye A110
"Keeping It Moving": A Tribe Called Quest B14
"Keeping the Faith": Billy Joel A101
"Keepin' Myself for You" **B30**
"Keepin' Out of Mischief Now": Louis Armstrong A119
"Keep It Between the Lines": Ricky Van Shelton A191
"Keep It Greasey": Frank Zappa **A60**
"Keep Looking That Way": The Beatles B8
"Keep Moving": Madness A185
"Keep off the Grass" A145
"Keep on Growin'": Derek & The Dominos B21
"Keep on Loving You": REO Speedwagon A59, A248, **B24**
"Keep on Pushing": The Impressions A32, A108, A144
"Keep on Rolling": The Coasters A77
"Keep on Running": The Spencer Davis Group B8, B20
"Keep the Customer Satisfied": Simon and Garfunkel B1
"Keep Your Hands off My Baby": The Beatles B8; Little Eva A95
"Keep Your Head Up": 2Pac B31
"Kentucky Jubilee Singers" A145
"Kerry Dance, The" B12
"Kettle's On": Feeling, The B21
"Key to Highway 70": Brownie McGhee A240
"Key to My Door": Brownie McGhee A240
"Key to the Highway": Bill Broonzy **A240**; Derek and the Dominos A185, B21; Jazz Gillum **A240**
"Kick Inside, The": Kate Bush A185
"Kid A": Radiohead **A162**
"Kid Charlemagne": Steely Dan **A96**, A250
"Kidnapped": Gary Moore A185
"Kilburn Towers": The Bee Gees **B3**

"Kill 'Em at the Hot Club Tonite": Slade B21
"Killer on the Loose": Thin Lizzy A185, **A185**, B20
"Killer Queen": Queen A185
"Killer Wants to Go to College": Paul Simon B1
"Kill Eye": Crowded House B32
"Killing an Arab": The Cure **A137**
"Killing Game": Psycho **A149**
"Killing Hand, The": Dream Theater A175
"Killing Me Softly": Roberta Flack A24; Lori Lieberman A24
"Kill You": Eminem A99, A146
"Kimberly": Patti Smith A36
"Kim": Eminem A146
"Kind Hearted Woman Blues": Robert Johnson **A132**
"Kind of a Drag": The Buckinghams A101, B24
"Kind of Hush, A": Carpenters, The A140; Herman's Hermits A140
"Kind of Magic, A": Queen A16
"King Heroin": James Brown A117
"King Kong": The Mothers of Invention A11, A12
"King Midas in Reverse": The Hollies B7, B21
"King of Anything": Sara Bareilles A219
"King of Bohemia": Richard Thompson B20
"King of Carrot Flowers, The": Neutral Milk Hotel **A22**
"King of Fuh, The": George Harrison B7
"King of Pain": The Police A235
"King of Rags, The" A145
"King of Swing" B30
"King of the Road": Roger Miller **A190, A241**
"King of the World": Steely Dan **A96**
"King Porter Stomp" **B27**
"King Size Papa": Julia Lee and Her Boyfriends A53
"King Will Come, The": Wishbone Ash A185
"Kisses Sweeter Than Wine": Jimmie Rodgers A97
"Kiss From a Rose": Seal A221
"Kissin' and a-Huggin'": Joan Armatrading A136
"Kiss Me, Baby": The Beach Boys A160, B15; Brian Wilson B15
"Kiss Me, Honey, Do" A145
"Kiss Me Where It Smells Funny": The Bloodhound Gang A146

"Kiss of Life": Peter Gabriel A185
"Kiss on My List": Hall and Oates A250
"Kiss": Prince B13
"Kiss the Girl" A167
"Kiss Their Sons": Transvision Vamp A185
"Kite" [1]: U2 A89
"Kite" [2]: Kate Bush **A186**
"Kites": Simon Dupree and the Big Sound B20
"Kitten on the Keys" A145
"K-Jee": M.F.S.B A179
"K-K-K-Katy" A145
"Knife, The": Genesis B20
"Knights of the Jaguar": Aztec Mystic B5
"Knight": Tryannosaurus Rex B20
"Knives Out": Radiohead A135, A162, A205
"Knocking 'Round the Zoo": James Taylor B3, B4
"Knockin' on Heaven's Door": Roger McGuinn A121; see also "He Got Game"
"Knock Me Down": Red Hot Chili Peppers A99
"Knock on Wood": Eddie Floyd A29, **A29**, A95, A99, A185, B24
"Knocks Me Off My Feet": Stevie Wonder A97
"Knots": Gentle Giant A149, B20
"Know How": Nik Kershaw A185
"Knowing Me, Knowing You": ABBA A185, B25
"Know Who You Are": Slade B21
"Knuckleheadz": Raekwon A99
"Kodachrome": Paul Simon A93, B1, B24
"Kojak Theme": **A242**
"Koka Kola": The Clash A118
"Koko Joe": Don and Dewey **B25**
"Kokomo Blues": Kokomo Arnold A240; Scrapper Blackwell A240
"Kon Tiki": The Shadows A259, B8
"Kooks": David Bowie B21
"Kool Is Back": Funk Inc. A104; Kool and the Gang A261
"Kozmic Blues": Janis Joplin B3
"Kreen Akrore": Paul McCartney B32
"Kryptonite": Purple Ribbons All Stars **A1**

"La Bamba": A3, A184, B17, B19; Ritchie Valens A43, A44, A75, A85, B8
"Labelled With Love": Squeeze A124
"L.A. Blues": The Stooges A210
"Labour of Love": Hue & Cry A185
"Ladies' Man": Joni Mitchell A260

"Ladies of the Canyon": Joni Mitchell **A260**
"Ladies of the Road": King Crimson A152
"La-Do-Dada": Dale Hawkins B15
"Lads o' Tynside": Ned Corvan B19
"Lady, Be Good!" B10
"Lady, Play Your Mandolin" B30
"Lady" [1]: Styx A141
"Lady" [2]: Supertramp A182
"Lady Godiva": Peter and Gordon A71
"Lady in Red, The": DeBurgh, Chris A167
"Lady Is a Tramp" A147, B10, **B30**
"Lady Jane": The Rolling Stones A70, A71, A96, A107, **B3**, B29
"Lady Lady Lay": Bob Dylan A99
"Lady Madonna": The Beatles **A16**, A63, **A76**, A90, A96, A98, A99, A185, **A186**, A195, A234, A259, B7, B8, **B20**
"Lady Marmalade": Labelle A43, B24
"Lady of Spain" **B25**
"Lady of the Evening" A168, B30
"Lady of the Island": Crosby, Stills, Nash & Young **A99**, **A102**, B3
"Lady of the Lake": Starcastle **A72**
"Lady of the Valley": White Lion A250
"Lady's in Love with You, The" B10, **B30**
"Ladytron": Roxy Music A185, B20
"Lafayette Blues": The White Stripes A148
"La Fuente del Ritmo": Santana A185
"La Grange": ZZ Top A185, B21
"Laird o' Cockpen": Ned Corvan **B19**
"La Isla Bonita": Madonna **A24**, A258
"Lakeside Park": Rush A28
"Lambada": Kaoma B25
"La Mer": Trent Reznor A221
"Lana": The Beach Boys B15
"Land Ahoy": The Beach Boys B15
"Land of 1000 Dances": Wilson Pickett B4, B32; Patti Smith A78
"Land of Confusion": Genesis A232, B20
"Land of My Boyhood Dreams, The": Jimmie Rodgers A266
"Landslide of Love": Transvision Vamp A185, B20
"Lantern, The": The Rolling Stones **B3**
"La Penina": Carlos Mendes **B7**
"Lara's Theme" B27
"Lark's Tongues in Aspic": King Crimson A67, A141, **A152**, A224, **B20**, B21; Dream Theater B21

"Laser Love": After the Fire A185, B21
"Last Child": Aerosmith A99
"Last Dance, The" [3] A14
"Last Dance" [1]: Sarah McLachlan A154
"Last Dance" [2]: Donna Summer **A101**
"Last Gold Dollar": Ephraim Woodie and the Henpecked Husbands A240
"Last Kiss": J. Frank Wilson and the Cavaliers A43
"Last Night" [1]: The Mar-Keys A29
"Last Night" [2] A145
"Last Night I Had a Dream": Randy Newman **A264**
"Last Night I Had the Strangest Dream": Simon and Garfunkel B1
"Last Night on Earth": U2 A89
"Last Night on the Back Porch" B30
"Last Night When My Willie Came Home": Uncle Dave Macon A240
"Last Night When We Were Young" **B10**, B30
"Last of the Steam-powered Trains": The Kinks B20
"Last Resort": Papa-Roach **A22**
"Last Song, The": Elton John A6
"Last Song Ever Written, The": Stars A205
"Last Time, The" [1]: The Rolling Stones A16, A97, A107, A247, B8
"Last Time, The" [2]: Blind Boys of Alabama B21
"Last Time, The" see "(This Could Be) The Last Time"
"Last Time I Saw Paris, The" B30
"Last to Know, The": Asia **A59**
"Last Train to Clarksville": The Monkees **A241**, B8, **B24**
"Last Train to Liverpool": The Plummons A259
"Last Train to San Fernando": Johnny Duncan and the Bluegrass Boys, **B25**; The Quarrymen B8
"Last Trip to Tulsa": Neil Young B6
"Last Worthless Evening, The": Don Henley **A99**
"Las Vegas Tune" B7
"Late for Supper": Jerry Garcia A99
"Late Great Johnny Ace, The": Paul Simon B1
"Late in the Evening": Paul Simon **A7**, B1
"Lateralus": Tool B21
"L.A.": The Fall B20

"Låt Solen Värma Dig" A19
"Laugh Clown Laugh" **B16**
"Laughing Boy": Mary Wells A108
"Laughing Gnome, The": David Bowie B20
"Laundromat Blues": Albert King A29
"Laura" **A147**, **B16**, **B30**
"Lavender" [1]: Marillion A71
"Lavender" [2]: The Pendletones B15
"La Vie En Rose": Edith Piaf B21
"La Villa Strangiato": Rush A198, A208
"Lawd, You Make the Night Too Long" B12
"Lawdy, Lawdy Blues": Ida Cox **A240**
"Lawdy Miss Clawdy" B8; The Beatles B7; Elvis Presley B7; Lloyd Price A95, **B25**
"Law of the Jungle": Gary Moore A185
"L.A. Woman": Doors A185
"Lay Down Burden": Brian Wilson B15
"Lay Down Your Guns": Emerson Lake & Palmer A185
"Lay Down Your Weary Tune": The Byrds A121
"Lay It Down Slow": Spiritualized B21
"Layla" B19; Derek and the Dominos **A16**, **A17**, A19, A80, **A101**, A185, A247, A248, A250, B7, B19, B20, B24
"Lay Lady Lay": The Byrds A121; Bob Dylan **A54**, A185
"Lay Your Hands on Me" [1]: Bon Jovi A185, A250
"Lay Your Hands on Me" [2]: Peter Gabriel A185
"Lazy" B30
"Lazybones" **B30**
"Lazy Day": Spanky and Our Gang A43
"Lazy River" A147, B8, B25; Louis Armstrong A119
"Lazy River Road": The Grateful Dead B17
"Leader of the Pack": The Shangri-Las A45, **A77**, B19, B21
"Lead Me On": Amy Grant B24
"Lead Me To Love" B30
"Lead Me to the Rock": Heavenly Gospel Singers B21
"Leaf and Stream": Wishbone Ash A185
"League of Nations": Simple Minds A185
"Leah": Roy Orbison A270
"Learn How to Fall": Paul Simon B1
"Learnin' as You Go": Rick Trevino A189
"Learning How to Fly": Emerson Lake & Powell A185

"Learning How to Love You": George Harrison B7
"Learning to Fly": Emerson Lake & Powell A185
"Learning to Live": Dream Theater A175
"Learn to Fly": The Foo Fighters A167
"Leave It Out": Stray B21
"Leave My Kitten Alone": The Beatles B7, B8; Elvis Costello B4; Little Willie John A95, B4
"Leaves That Are Green": Paul Simon B1; Simon and Garfunkel B1
"Leaving Home": Charlie Poole with the North Carolina Ramblers A240
"Leaving It Up to You": John Clae A124
"Leaving Me Now": Level 42 A185
"Le Freak": Chic A99, A101, B24
"Left All Alone Again Blues" A145
"Left My Gal in the Mountains" A145
"Legalize My Name" B30
"Legend in Your Own Time": Carly Simon A99
"Legend of a Mind": The Moody Blues B7
"Legend of the Golden Arches, The": The Mothers of Invention **A12**
"Legs": ZZ Top A250
"Lemmings": Van der Graaf Generator B20, B21
"Lemon": U2 A103
"Lend Me Your Comb": The Beatles B7, **B8**; Carl Perkins A97
"Leningrad": Billy Joel A185, B21
"Leonora" B12
"Les deux hommes d'armes" B12
"Lesson in Survival": Joni Mitchell A260
"Lessons": Rush A28
"Less Than Zero": Elvis Costello A185
"Let Down": Radiohead A162, **A169**
"Let 'Em In": Wings B7
"Let George Do It" A145
"Let Him Run Wild": The Beach Boys B15; Brian Wilson B15
"Let It All Come Down": Simple Minds A185
"Let It Be Me": The Everly Brothers A160, B15
"Let It Be": The Beatles A80, A90, A98, A101, A123, A167, A195, **A245**, A247, A259, B7, B8, B18, B20, B24
"Let It Down": George Harrison A99, A185, B7, B18
"Let It End Ronald Selle": Ronald Selle **A213**

Song Index

"Let It Grow" [1]: The Grateful Dead B17
"Let It Grow" [2]: Eric Clapton **A16**, A185, B20, **B21**, B24
"Let It Rain": Eric Clapton A185, B3
"Let It Rock": Chuck Berry A244
"Let Me Be Your Sidetrack": Jimmie Rodgers A266
"(Let Me Be Your) Teddy Bear": Elvis Presley A97, A99, A270, B8
"Let Me Entertain You" B12
"Let Me Give All My Love to Thee" B30
"Let Me Go To Him" B3
"Let Me Look at You" B30
"Let Me Love You": Jeff Beck A185
"Let Me Ride": Dr. Dre A99, A261, B31
"Let Me Sleep on It": Meat Loaf A185
"Let My Love Open the Door": Pete Townshend A233
"Let's All Chant": Michael Zager Band A3
"Let's All Go Down the Strand" **B19** B19
"Let's Begin" B30
"Let's Break the Good News" A145
"Let's Call the Holy Rov" B12
"Let's Call the Whole Thing Off" B12, B30
"Let's Dance" [1]: David Bowie A19, A99, A101, A159, B20, B32
"Let's Dance" [2]: Chris Montez A185, B16
"Let's Do It" B10, **B30**
"Let's Do It, Let's Fall in Love" A113, A228
"Let's Face the Music and Dance" B30; Fred Astaire B21
"Let's Fall in Love" B30
"Let's Get It On": Marvin Gaye **A110**, A247, A250
"Let's Get Physical": Olivia Newton-John A185
"Let's Get Together": The Young Bloods B24
"Let's Go Away for a While": The Beach Boys **A160**; Brian Wilson B15
"Let's Go Crazy": Prince and the Revolution **A85**
"Let's Go Eat Worms in the Garden" B10
"Let's Go Get Stoned": Ray Charles **A264**
"Let's Go to Heaven in My Car": Brian Wilson B15
"Let's Go Trippin'": The Beach Boys B15; Dick Dale B15
"Let's Have Another Cup of Coffee" B10
"Let's Hear It for the Boy": Deniece Williams B24

"Let's Kiss and Make Up" **B30**
"Let Sleeping Dogs Lie": Mission A185
"Let's Live Before We Die" B15
"Let's Love": Johnny Mathis **A263**
"Let's Make the Water Turn Black": Mothers of Invention, The A11; Frank Zappa A11
"Let's Not Be Sensible" A14
"Let's Put Our Hearts Together": Brian Wilson B15
"Let's Put Out the Lights": Ambrose and his Orchestra A227
"Let's Roll": Neil Young B6
"Let's Say Goodnight Till the Morning" A145
"Let's See Action": Who A185
"Let's Shake Hands": The White Stripes A148
"Let's Spend the Night Together": The Rolling Stones A233, B7
"Let's Stay Together": Al Green A80, A247
"Let's Stick Together": Brian Wilson B15
"Let's Stomp": The Beatles B8
"Let's Submerge": X-Ray Spex **A210**
"Let's Take a Walk Around the Block" B30
"Letter, The": PJ Harvey **A50**
"Letterbox": They Might Be Giants A185
"Letter from Hiro": Vapors A185
"Letters, The": King Crimson A152
"Letter to the Liady Rabbi, A" B12
"Letter to the New York Post, A": Public Enemy A99
"Let That Liar Alone" A145
"Let The Good Times Roll": Louis Jordan **A85**; Shirley and Lee A44
"Let the Music Play": Johnny Winter A185
"Let There Be Love": The Bee Gees B3
"Let There Be More Light": Pink Floyd **A198**, B7
"Let the Wind Blow": The Beach Boys **A125**, B15
"Let the Wind Carry Me": Joni Mitchell **A260**
"Let Us Adore" B12
"Let Us Go Back to Church": James Moore A161
"Let Us Go on This Way": The Beach Boys B15
"Let Us Go to the Sheeny Wedding" B12
"Let Yourself Go" **B11**, B12, A168; James Brown A210
"Liar, Liar": Castaways A43
"Liberation": Chicago B3
"Liberty": The Grateful Dead B17

"License to Kill": Bob Dylan A99, A225
"Licking Stick": James Brown A238
"Lick My Love Pump": Spinal Tap A143
"Lie Dream of a Casino Soul": Fall, The A124
"Lie": Dream Theater A175
"Lies" [1] A147
"Lies" [2]: Gary Usher B15
"Life Goes On": 2Pac B14
"Life in a Glasshouse": Radiohead A135
"Life in Mono": Mono B21
"Life in the Factory": Drive-By Truckers B21
"Life in the Fast Lane": The Eagles A173, A248, **A225**
"Life Is a Rock (But the Radio Rolled Me)": Reunion A43
"Life Is for the Living": Brian Wilson B15
"Life of Jimmie Rodgers, The": Gene Autry A266
"Life on Mars?": David Bowie A99, A185, **B20, B21**
"Life": Sly & The Family Stone B3
"Life Stinks": Pere Ubu A210
"Lifting Shadows Off a Dream": Dream Theater **A175**
"Light My Fire": The Doors A17, A28, A43, A72, A101, **A101**, A185, A247, **A248**, A269, B20, B24; Jose Feliciano A43, A205
"Like a Hurricane": Neil Young **A88**, B6
"Like an Old Blues": Be-Bop Deluxe A185
"Like a Prayer": Madonna A66, A258
"Like a Rock": Bob Seger A340
"Like a Rolling Stone": Bob Dylan A16, A32, A43, A80, A96, A101, A121, A167, A216, A247, A269, B3, B4, B7, B8, B19, **B24**
"Like a Song . . .": U2 A89
"Like a Virgin": Madonna A234, A250, B13
"Like China": Phil Collins A185
"Like Clockwork": Boomtown Rats A185
"Like Dreamers Do": Applejacks B21; The Beatles B7, **B8**
"Like No Other Night": .38 Special A250
"Like Someone in Love": A14, **B30**
"Like Spinning Plates": Radiohead A135, **A169**
"Like to Get to Know You": Spanky and Our Gang B7
"Like Toy Soldiers": Eminem A234
"L'il Darlin'" B30
"Lilla Vackra Anna" **B25**
"Lilli Marlene" B25

"Lilywhite Lilith": Genesis B21
"Limb from Limb": Motorhead A185, B20
"Limehouse Blues" A147
"Limelight": Rush **A17**
"Lincoln County": Love Affair A185
"Linda" **B30**
"Lindbergh" A145
"Lines in the Sand": Dream Theater A175
"Linger Awhile" B30
"Link Track": The Beatles B7
"Lion Sleeps Tonight, The": Robert John A181; The Tokens A181, **B24**
"Lip Service": Elvis Costello A185
"Lips Like Oranges": Claire Bowditch A205
"Lips of Ashes": Porcupine Tree B21
"Lipstick Vogue": Elvis Costello A185, B20, B21
"Listen": Chicago B3
"Listening to You": The Who **A16**
"Listen to Her Heart": Tom Petty A250
"(Listen to) Flower People": Spinal Tap A69, **A70**
"Listen to the Music": The Doobie Brothers A173, A250, B24
"Listen to What the Man Said": Wings B7
"Listen to Your Heart" **A209**
"Lithium": Nirvana **A99**, A143, **A177**, **B20**, B21
"Lithium Sunset": Sting **A151**
"Little Beatle Boy": The Angels (I – little beatle boy) A259
"Little Bell": the Dixie Cups A95
"Little Bitty Pretty One": Thurston Harris A44
"Little Bluebird": Johnnie Taylor A29
"Little by Little" A145
"Little Child": The Beatles A98, B7, B8
"Little Cloud": The Incredible String Band B20
"Little Darlin'": The Diamonds A44, A97, B21, **B24**, A185
"Little Deuce Coupe": The Beach Boys A109, A185, B15; James House B15
"Little Egypt": The Coasters **A77**
"Little Egypt (Ying-Yang)": Coasters B15
"Little Girl Blue" **B30**
"Little Girl in Yellow": Tractor B21
"Little Girl I Once Knew, The": The Beach Boys **A109**, B8, B15; Brian Wilson B15
"Little Girl (You're My Miss America)": The Beach Boys B15

Song Index

"Little Green": Joni Mitchell **A260**
"Little Help From My Friends, A": The Beatles B18
"Little Honda": The Beach Boys B15; The Hondells A109
"Little House I Used to Live In": Frank Zappa and the Mothers of Invention A11, A27
"Little Igloo for Two" B10
"Little Jazz Bird" B30
"Little Jeannie": Elton John B24
"Little Kids": The Dixie Dregs A73
"Little Lies": Fleetwood Mac A59, A185, B20, B21
"Little Miss Lover": The Jimi Hendrix Experience **A86**, A185, B20
"Little Miss Strange": Otis Redding B3
"Little Moses": Bob Dylan A216
"Little Old Lady" B10, B30
"Little Old Lady (from Pasadena), The": The Beach Boys B15; Jan and Dean A93
"Little One" B30
"Little Pad": The Beach Boys B15
"Little Palaces": Elvis Costello B20, B21
"Little People": White Stripes, The A148
"Little Pink Houses": John Cougar Mellencamp A247
"Little Queenie": The Beatles B8; Chuck Berry A95
"Little Rain (For Clyde)": Tom Waits A221
"Little Red Book": Brian Wilson B15
"Little Red Corvette": Prince A35, A80, A247, B13
"Little Red Rooster": Willie Dixon A132; The Rolling Stones B16, B29, A257; Howlin' Wolf B20
"Little Rock": Reba McEntire **A190**
"Little Saint Nick": The Beach Boys B15; Brian Wilson B15
"Little Show, The" B10
"Little Star": The Elegants A97, B15
"Little Triggers": Elvis Costello and the Attractions A185, B4
"Little White Cloud That Cried, The": Johnnie Ray B8
"Little White Lies" A145, B8, B10
"Little Wing": The Jimi Hendrix Experience A17, **A40**, **B3**, B21
"Little Yellow Pills": Jackie Lomax B7
"Live 4 Love": Prince A79

"Live and Let Die": Wings A235, A250, B7
"Live": Bangles A185
"Live for Love": Prince **B13**
"Livery Stable Blues" A145
"Lives in the Balance": Jackson Browne A124
"Live Wire": Meters A185
"Living for the City": Stevie Wonder A43, A80, A85, **A101**, **A144**, **A236**, A247
"Living in a Moment": Ty Herndon A189
"Living in an Island": Boomtown Rats A185
"Living in Paradise": Elvis Costello A185, B20
"Living in Sin": Bon Jovi A185
"Living in the City": Stevie Wonder A185
"Living in the Past": Jethro Tull A43, A188, A221
"Living It Up": Rickie Lee Jones **A124**, A269
"Living Loving Maid (She's Just a Woman)": Led Zeppelin A101, B7, B21
"Livin' Lovin' Wreck": The Beatles B8
"Livin' on a Prayer": Bon Jovi **A16**, **A46**, A99, A250, A252, B28
"Livin' on Love": Alan Jackson A191
"Livin' Wreck": Deep Purple A185
"Liza" A145, B10, **B30**
"Lizard": King Crimson A152
"Llosgwch y Llosgach": Tystion A123
"Lobo Bobo" A211
"Locame": La Cubanita A3
"Loch Lomond" B27
"Loco-Motion, The": The Beatles B8; Little Eva A95, A185, B15, B24
"Locomotion": Orchestral Manoeuvres A185
"Locomotive Breath": Jethro Tull A43, A188
"Lodi": Creedence Clearwater Revival A185
"Logical Song, The": Supertramp **A149**, B24
"Lola" [1]: The Kinks **A16**, A185
"Lola" [2] B12
"Lollypop Mama": Wynonie Harris A53
"Lollipop": The Chordettes A44, A97, B15
"London Calling": The Clash A80, A118, A247
"London Rhythm" A145
"Lonely at the Top" A264
"Lonely Boy" [1]: Iron Butterfly B3
"Lonely Boy" [2]: Paul Anka B25
"Lonely Bull (El Solo Torro), The": Herb Alpert & The Tijuana Brass **A101**
"Lonely House" B12
"Lonely Ol' Night": John Cougar Mellencamp B24

"Lonely People": America B24
"Lonely Room": Mal Ryder and the Spirits B8
"Lonely Sea": The Beach Boys A160, B15
"Lonely Teardrops": Jackie Wilson A44
"Lonely this Christmas": Mud B21
"Lonely Too Long": The Young Rascals **B24**
"Loner, The": Neil Young B6
"Lone Ranger, The": Quantum Jump **A42**
"Lonesome Alimony Blues" A145
"Lonesome and a Long Way from Home": Eric Clapton A185
"Lonesome Blues": Ida Cox **A240**; Tommy Johnson **B26**, A201
"Lonesome Day Blues": Blind Willie McTell and Kate McTell A240
"Lonesome Death of Hattie Carroll, The": Bob Dylan B7
"Lonesome Home Blues": Tommy Johnson **B26**
"Lonesome Road, The" A145
"Lonesome Road Blues": Sam Collins A240
"Lonesome Swallow" A145
"Lonesome Tears": Beck **A54**, **A97**
"Lonesome Tears in My Eyes" B7; The Beatles **B8**
"Lonesome Town": The Beatles B8
"Long, Long Day": Paul Simon B1
"Long after Tonight Is Over" B3
"Long Ago (and Far Away)" A228, B10, B30
"Long and Winding Road, The": The Beatles A86, **A97**, A98, **B7**, B8, **B18**, B20
"Long Black Veil": Band A185
"Long Cool Woman (In a Black Dress)": The Hollies **A85**
"Long Distance Runaround": Yes A101
"Long Gone" [1]: Sonny Thompson A53
"Long Gone" [2]: Sonny Terry & Brownie McGhee A95
"Long Gone Lonesome Blues": Hank Williams A210, B4
"Long Haired Doney": R.L. burnside **A62**
"Long-Haired Lady": Paul McCartney **B18**
"Long Hot Summer Night": Jimi Hendrix A257
"Long Live Rock": The Who A141
"Long Lonely Night": Clyde McPhatter A53
"Long Lonesome Blues": Blind Lemon Jefferson A240, **B26**
"Long Long Day": Paul Simon **A93**

"Long Long Long": The Beatles A90, A98, **A100**, **B7**
"Long Tall Mama Blues": Jimmie Rodgers A266
"Long Tall Sally" **A133**, **B27**; The Beatles A254; Pat Boone B24; Little Richard A44, A80, A95, **A123**, A238, A247, B7, B8, B21, B24, B32
"Long Tall Texan": The Beach Boys B15; Doug Supernaw B15
"Long Time": Boston A246, B24
"Long Time Gone": The Dixie Chicks **A191**
"Long Train Runnin'": The Doobie Brothers **A247**, A167
"Longview": Green Day **A84**
"Look at Me": John Lennon B7, B8, **B18**
"Look at That": Paul Simon B1
"Look Away" [1]: Big Country A185, A187
"Look Away" [2]: Chicago **B24**
"Look Back in Anger": David Bowie A185, B20
"Look for the Silver Lining" B10, **B30**
"Lookin' for Love": Johnny Lee A154
"Looking at You" B30
"Looking for a Boy" **A120**, **B30**
"Looking for a New Mama": Jimmie Rodgers A266
"Looking for a Rainbow": Chris Rea A185
"Looking Glass": The Beatles B8
"Looking Out My Back Door": Creedence Clearwater Revival A185
"Look Into the Sun": Jethro Tull A4
"Look of Love, The" [1] A147, B3, B12
"Look of Love, The" [2]: ABC A19, A185
"Look Out for My Love": Neil Young B6
"Look Out for That Bolsheviki Man" B12
"Looks That Kill": Motley Crue A250
"Look to the Rainbow" B10, B30
"Look to Your Heart" A14
"Look Up": Johnny Winter A185
"Loop De Loop": The Beach Boys B15
"Loose": The Stooges A210
"L'Orchestra dei Fischietti": Stormy Six **A166**
"Lord, Do It": Kirvy Brown **A161**
"Lord Bateman" **B19**
"Lordly Nightshade": The Incredible String Band B7
"Lord Randal": Frank Harte B18
"Lord Send Me an Angel #1": Blind Willie McTell A240

"Lord's Prayer, The": The Beach Boys B15
"Lorelei" B30
"Lose My Breath": My Bloody Valentine A177
"Loser": Beck A80, **A222**, A247
"Lose Yourself": Eminem A247
"Losing End, The": Neil Young B6
"Losing My Religion": R.E.M. A80, A184, A247, B24
"Los Paranoias": The Beatles B7
"Lost at Birth": Public Enemy A99
"Lost Cause": beck **A83**
"Lost in France": Bonnie Tyler A185, B20
"Lost in the Supermarket": The Clash A118
"Lost John": Lonnie Donegan B8
"Lost Not Forgotten": Dream Theater A175
"Lost on France": Bonnie Tyler B20
"Lost Patrol": Big Country A185
"Lost Someone": James Brown B4
"Lost": Van Der Graf Generator A182
"Lost Wandering Blues": Gertrude "Ma" Rainey **B26**
"Lot of Livin' to Do": Pat Metheny Trio **A226**
"Lotta Love": Neil Young B6
"Lotta Lovin'": Gene Vincent B8
"Loudmouth": The Ramones A210
"Louie, Louie": The Beach Boys B15
"Louie Louie" A94, A184, B17; Richard Berry and the Pharoahs **A85**; The Feelies A85; The Kingsmen A27, A43, A75, A84, **A85**, A99, A141, A198, A247, A268, B21, B24, B32; Iggy Pop A85; Rockin' Robin Roberts and the Wailers A85; The Sonics **A85**; Travis Wommack A85
"Louise": Cream A132
"Louisiana Hayride" B10, B30
"Louisiana Purchase" B30
"Louisiana": Randy Newman A123, **A264**
"Louisiana Saturday Night": Mel McDaniel A191
"Louisville Burglar": The Hickory Nuts A240
"Lounding at the Waldorf" A145
"Love, Look Away" B30
"Love, Love, Love Me Honey": Patsy Cline B21
"Love, Love, Love": The Beatles B8
"Love, Me": Collin Raye A191
"Love, Need, and Want You": Patti LaBelle A215
"Love, Peace, and Happiness": The Lost Boyz B14

"Love, You Funny Thing!" **B30**
"Love" [1]: Joni Mitchell A260
"Love" [2]: Paul Simon B1
"Love" [3]: John and Yoko / Plastic Ono Band B7, B8, B18
"Love" [4] B10, B30
"Love and Affection" [1]: Def Leppard A185
"Love and Affection" [2]: Joan Armatrading **A136**
"Love and Affection" [3]: Marvin Gaye A110
"Love and Beauty": The Moody Blues B7
"Love and Happiness": Al Green A80, A247
"Love and Marriage" A14
"Love and Mercy": Brian Wilson A160, B15
"Love and Peace or Else": U2 A103
"Love and Regret": Deacon Blue A185
"Love and The Weather" B30
"Love Ain't for Keepin'": The Who **A16**
"Love at First Sight": Kylie Minogue A185
"Love Bites": Def Leppard A185, B20, B21
"Love Blind": Emerson Lake & Powell A185
"Love Bones": Johnnie Taylor A29
"Love Cats": Cure A185
"Love Child": Diana Ross A43, A99, A185
"Love Comes and Goes": Ed O.G. and Da Bulldogs B14
"Love Doesn't Last Long": Ringo Starr B18
"Love for Sale" [1] A41, A147, A168, A228, B10, B12, B30
"Love for Sale" [2]: Bon Jovi A185
"Love for Tender": Elvis Costello **B20**
"Love Grows": Edison Lighthouse B21
"Love Her Madly": Doors, The A43
"Love Hurts": Nazareth A185, **A247**, A248
"Love in a Void": Siouxsie and the Banshees A185, B20
"Love in Mind": Neil Young **B6**
"Love in My veins": Los Lonely Boys A222
"Love in the Open Air": Paul McCartney B7
"Love Is a Beautiful Thing": The Rascals B3
"Love Is a Bore" A14
"Love Is a Dancing Thing" **B30**
"Love Is All": The United States of America A138
"Love Is a Stranger": The Eurhythmics B13
"Love Is a Swingin' Thing": The Beatles B8; The Shirelles A95
"Love Is a Woman": The Beach Boys B15
"Love Is . . . ": Beautiful South A185

"Love Is Blindness": U2 A103
"Love Is Here and Now You're Gone": The Supremes A43, A99
"Love Is Here To Stay" B30
"(Love Is Like a) Heat Wave": Martha and the Vandellas **A106, A108**
"Love Is Like an Itching in My Heart": The Supremes **A106, A108**
"Love Is Love, Anywhere" B30
"Love Is Stronger than Justice (The Munificent Seven)": Sting A221
"Love Is Sweeping The Country" B30
"Love Is the Drug": Roxy Music B32
"Love Is the Sweetest Thing" B30; Al Bowlly & the Ray Nobel Orchestra B21
"Love Is Where You Find It" B12
"Love Letters in the Sand": Pat Boone A97
"Love Lies Bleeding": Elton John B24
"Love Lifted Me" A219
"Love Light" *see* "(Turn on Your) Love Light"
"Love Locked Out" **B30**
"Lovely Linda, The": Paul McCartney B8, B18
"Lovely Night, A" **B30**
"Lovely Rita": The Beatles A98, **A225**, A259, B7, B8, B18, B20, B29
"Lovely to Look At" **B10**, B30
"Love Me, and the World Is Mine" **B27**
"Love Me Do" B8; The Beatles A98, A107, **A107**, A195, A198, A247, **A259**, B7, **B16**, B18
"Love Me": Elvis Presley A97, **A99**
"Love Me or Leave Me" A147, **B10, B30**; Nina Simone B21
"Love Me Tender" B8; Elvis Presley A86, A99, A184, A216, A270, B19
"Love Me to a Yiddisha Melody" B12
"Love Me to Death": Mission A185
"Love Me to Pieces": Jill Corey A160
"Love Me Two Times": Doors, The **A16**, A43, A55, **A83**, A185
"Love Minus Zero / No Limit": Bob Dylan A216
"Love of a Boy and Girl, The": The Honeys B15
"Love of My Life": The Beatles B8
"Love of the Common Man": Todd Rundgren **A59**
"Love of the Loved": The Beatles B7, **B8**
"Love on a Two-Way Street": The Moments **A84**

"Love or Confusion": The Jimi Hendrix Experience **A257, B29**
"Love Potion No. 9": The Clovers A44, B24
"Lover" B30; Les Paul A140, B32
"Love Rescue Me": U2 B20
"Lover Man" A147, B30; Billie Holiday B4; Charlie Parker A96
"Lover's Concerto, A": The Toys A84, A93, A179, B7
"Lover's Leap": Genesis **A232**
"Lover's Question, A": Clyde McPhatter A44, A99
"Lover's Rock": The Clash A118
"Love Scene": George Harrison B7
"Love Shack": The B-52's A99
"Love She Can Count On, A": The Miracles A108
"Lovesick Blues": Hank Williams B4
"Loves Me Like a Rock": Paul Simon B1
"Loves Me Not": t.A.T.u. A153
"Love Song" [1]: The Damned B20
"Love Song" [2]: The Cure B24
"Love Story": Randy Newman **A264**
"Love Street": The Doors B3
"Love Takes Time": Mariah Carey B24
"Love That Burns": Fleetwood Mac B20
"Love the One You're With": Stephen Stills A232
"Love the Way You Lie": Eminem A219
"Love Thy Neighbor" B12
"Love to Be Loved": Peter Gabriel B32
"Love to Love You Baby": Donna Summer A43, A130, A182
"Love Turned The Light Out" **B30**
"Love und [sic] Romance": The Slits B20
"Love Walked In" B10, B30
"Love Walks In": Van Halen A250
"Love Will Find a Way" B30
"Love Will Keep Us Alive": The Eagles B24
"Love Will Keep Us Together": Captain and Tennille A99, B24
"Love Will Never Do": Janet Jackson A252
"Love Will Tear Us Apart": Joy Division A80, A247
"Love Will Turn You Around": Kenny Rogers **A248**
"Love Without End, Amen": George Strait A191
"Love You To": The Beatles A185, A198, A234, A259, B7, B18, B32

Song Index

"Lovin' Babe": Henry Thomas A240
"Lovin' You Lovin' Me": Eric Clapton A185, B3
"Lovin' You": Minnie Riperton A43
"Low Spark of High Heeled Boys, The": Traffic A43
"Luanne": Foreigner **B24**
"Luau": The Pendletones B15
"Lubbock or Leave It": The Dixie Chicks A55
"Lucifer Sam": Pink Floyd A185
"Lucille": Everly Brothers **B24**; Little Richard A44, **A53**, A73, A75, A95, A238, **B8**, B24
"Lucinda": Joe Cocker **A264**; Randy Newman **A264**
"Luck Be a Lady" **A41**, B12
"Luck of the Irish, The": John and Yoko/Plastic Ono Band B7, B8, B18
"Lucky Ball and Chain": They Might Be Giants A185
"Lucky Bird" B30
"Lucky Man": Emerson, Lake & Palmer A101, A141, A185
"Lucky Old Sun" A53
"Lucky": Radiohead A162, **A169**
"Lucky Rock Blues" A145
"Lucretia MacEvil": Blood, Sweat and Tears B3
"Lucy Blues": Uriah Heep A185
"Lucy in the Sky with Diamonds": The Beatles A17, A90, A92, A98, A99, A100, **A134**, A185, **A198**, A259, **B7**, B8, **B18**, B19, **B20**, B21, B29
"Lullaby of Broadway" B10, B30
"Lullaby of the Leaves" **B10**
"Lullaby Yodel": Jimmie Rodgers A266
"Lumpy Gravy (Main Theme)": Frank Zappa A11
"Lurgee": Radiohead **A169**
"Lust for Life": Iggy Pop A247
"Luv 'n' Haight": Sly & the Family Stone B21
"Luxury of Love": David Peaston B21
"Lyin' Eyes": The Eagles A185, **B24**
"Lying Still": Level 42 A185
"Lyre of Orpheus, The": Nick Cave and the Bad Seeds B21

"M62 Song": Doves B21
"Ma!" A145
"Ma Baker": Boney M A101
"MacArthur Park": Richard Harris A43, A269, B7, B21; Donna Summer **A101**
"Machinehead": Bush **A84**
"Mack the Knife" B10, B12, B16, B30; Bobby Darin A44, B7, B8, B15, B21
"Madalaine": Winger A250
"Madame Esther, Queen of Hester Street" B12
"Madame George": Van Morrison A269
"Made of Stone": Stone Roses A185
"Made You Look": Nas B31
"Mad Hatter's Song, The": The Incredible String Band A112, B20
"Madhouse" A145
"Madman Across the Water": Elton John A99
"Mad Man Moon": Genesis **A142**
"Madman": The Beatles B7
"Madness Is All in the Mind": Madness A185
"Madrigal": Rush A28
"Magdalene My Regal Zonophone": Procol Harum A185
"Maggie Campbell Blues": Tommy Johnson **B26**
"Maggie Mae": The Beatles A98, B7; The Quarrymen B8
"Maggie May": Rod Stewart A185, A247, B24
"Magical Mystery Tour": The Beatles **A63**, B7, B18, B24
"Magic Bus": The Who A141, A185
"Magic Carpet Ride": Steppenwolf B7
"Magic Garden" B3
"Magician, The": Return to Forever A73
"Magic Man": Heart A247, B24
"Magic Moments": Perry Como A97
"Magic": Olivia Newton-John A43
"Magnet and Steel": Walter Egan A248
"Magnetic Rag" B12
"Magneto and Titanium Man": Wings B7
"Magnificent Seven": The Clash B20
"Magnum Opus": Kansas A72
"Maharishi Song, The": John Lennon B7
"Mah Lindy Lou" **B30**
"Mahzel (Means Good Luck)" B12
"Maid of Judah" B12
"Maid of Orleans": Orchestral Maneuvers in the Dark B20
"Mailman, Bring Me No More Blues": The Beatles B7, B8
"Mailman Blues": The Beatles B8; Lloyd Price A95
"Maine Stein Song" B12
"Mainline Florida": Eric Clapton A185

"Mainstreet": Bob Seger A247, **A248**, **B24**
"Mairzy Doats": The Merry Macs B4
"Majestic Dance": Return to Forever A73
"Major Disaster": Gryphon B20
"Make a Wish": Brian Wilson B15
"Make Believe" B10, **B30**
"Make It Easy on Yourself" B3
"Make It Funky": James Brown **A117**, A238
"Make It With You": Bread A247, B24
"Make Me a Miracle": Jimmie Rodgers A160
"Make Me Feel Good, Kiddy-O" B12
"Make Me Smile": Chicago A17, **A101**, B24
"Make Music With Your Mouth": Biz Markie A39
"Make The Man Love Me" B30
"Make You Feel My Love": Bob Dylan A99
"Make Yourself": Incubus A221
"Making Flippy Floppy": Talking Heads A185
"Making Whoopee" B16
"Makin' Whoopee" B10, B12; Ray Charles **A263**
"Male Ego": The Beach Boys B15
"Mama Didn't Lie": Jan Bradley A108
"Mama": Genesis A233
"Mama Gets High": Blood, Sweat and Tears B3
"Mama Loochie": The Moonglows A110
"Mama Loves Papa" B30
"Mama Mia": ABBA A185, B25
"Mama Said": The Beatles B8; The Shirelles A95, B15; Spring B15
"Mama Says": The Beach Boys B15
"Mama 'T'ain't Long Fo' Day": Blind Willie McTell **B26**
"Mambo No. 5": Perez Prado A238
"Mambo No. 8": Perez Prado A238
"Mamma Mia": Abba B20
"Man, We Was Lonely": Paul McCartney B18
"Man and a Woman, A": U2 A89
"Manchild": Neneh Cherry A185, B20, B21
"Mandela Day": Simple Minds A185
"Mandelay Song": The Flying Lizards B20
"Mandjou": Salif Keita B20, B21
"M. and O. Blues": Willie Brown **B26**
"Mandolin Rain": Bruce Hornsby and the Range A250, B24
"Mandy" B30
"Mandy Is Two" **B30**
"Mandy Make Up Your Mind" B30
"Maneater": Hall and Oates A99

"Man Gave Names to All the Animals": Bob Dylan A180, A185
"Mangos" A238
"Manhã de Carnaval" A211
"Manhattan" B10, **B11**, B30, A219
"Manhattan Beach March" B12
"Manhattan Serenade" B30
"Man Holdin' On (To a Woman Lettin' Go), A": Ty Herndon **A191**
"Manic Depression": The Jimi Hendrix Experience **A55**, A221, B7
"Man! I Feel Like a Woman": Shania Twain **A190**, A193, B21
"Manifesto": Roxy Music A185
"Manimal": The Germs A210
"Man in a Suitcase": The Police A235
"Man in the Corner Shop": Jam A185
"Man in the Long Black Coat": Bob Dylan B32
"Man in the Mirror": Michael Jackson A35
"Man I Love, The" **A120**, **A263**, B10, B30
"Man Needs a Maid, A": Neil Young **A88**, A268, B6
"Mann für Mann": Störkraft **B23**
"Man[n]ish Boy": Muddy Waters A83, A216
"Man on the Flying Trapeze, The" **B19** B19
"Man on the Moon": R.E.M. A181, A248
"Man Out of Time": Elvis Costello B4
"Man Overboard": Status Quo B20
"Man River" B10
"Man Smart (Woman Smarter)" B17
"Man That Got Away, The" **A114**, **B10**, B30
"Man to Man": Joni Mitchell A260
"Manuela Run": Toto A185
"Man Who Sold the World": David Bowie A143
"Man with All the Toys, The": The Beach Boys A160, B15; Brian Wilson B15
"Man with the Child in His Eyes, The": Kate Bush A185, **B21**
"Man with the Golden Arm, The" A14
"Many Happy Returns": ABC B32
"Maple Leaf Rag" A145
"Ma Rainey": Memphis Minnie A240
"Marcella": The Beach Boys B15
"Marching Bands of Manhattan": Death Cab for Cutie A205
"Marching Home From the War March" A145
"Marching Through Georgia" B12
"March of the Black Queen, The": Queen A221

Song Index

"March of the Dwarfs" B12
"March of the Pigs": Nine Inch Nails A221
"Marcie": Joni Mitchell **A260**
"Mardi Gras Mambo": The Hawketts A238
"Maria" [1]: P.J. Proby B8
"Maria" [2] B16
"Marianne": Terry Gilkyson & The Easy Riders A97; The Hilltoppers A97
"Marie From Sunny Italy" B30
"Marie": Randy Newman A264
"(Marie's the Name) His Latest Flame": The Beatles B8
"Marine Hymn" B12
"Mariuch Dance da Hootch-a-Ma-Kootch" A145
"Mark Twain Suite" B30
"Marrakesh Express": Crosby, Stills & Nash B7, B21
"Marry a Yiddisher Boy" B12
"Marseillaise": **A234**, A242, B7, B19
"Mars": King Crimson A72
"Martelen": Kadril B21
"Martha": Jefferson Airplane A43, B3
"Martha My Dear": The Beatles A17, **A17**, A98, A100, A234, A259, B7, B8, B18, B21; Slade B21
"Mary Anne": Brian Wilson B15
"Mary Don't You Weep": The Swan Silvertones A123
"Mary Had a Little Lamb" **B24**, B24
"Mashed Potato Time": Dee Dee Sharp A44
"Master of Puppets": Metallica A221
"Masters of War": Bob Dylan A58, **B3**, B7, B8, **B19**
"Matchbox": The Beatles A98, A254; Carl Perkins B8
"Matchpoint of Our Love": The Beach Boys B15
"Material Girl": Madonna A66, B13, B21
"Matida Mother": Pink Floyd A185, **A198**
"Matilda": Harry Belafonte A238
"Matte Kudesai": King Crimson A218
"Matter of Trust, A": Billy Joel **B24**
"Matty Groves": Fairport Convention A185, B20
"Matzoh Balls" B12
"Maxwell's Silver Hammer": The Beatles A92, A98, B7, B8, B18
"Maya": The Incredible String Band A112, B7

"Maybe" **B30**
"Maybe Baby": The Beatles B8; Buddy Holly A185, B8, B21
"Maybe I'm Amazed": Paul McCartney **A16**, A38, B7, B8, **B18**, B24
"Maybe It's Because I Love You Too Much" B30
"Maybellene": The Beatles B8; Chuck Berry A44, A80, A95, A238, A247
"Maybe Tomorrow": The Iveys B7
"Mayor of Simpleton, The": XTC B4
"MCs Act Like They Don't Know": KRS-One A146, B14, B31
"Meadow Lark": Jack Hylton and His Orchestra A227
"Mean Black Cat Blues": Charley Patton **A240**
"Mean Conductor Blues": Ed Bell **B26**
"Me and Bobby McGee": Janis Joplin A241, A247, B24
"Me and Howard Hughes": Boomtown Rats A185
"Me and Julio Down by the Schoolyard": Paul Simon B1
"Me and My Gin": Bessie Smith **B26**
"Me and My Monkey": The Beatles **A16**
"Me and My Uncle" B17
"Me and the Devil Blues": Robert Johnson B21
"Mean Mistreater": Grand Funk Railroad B21
"Mean Mr. Mustard" A167; The Beatles **A63**, A92, A98, A149, **B7**, B8, B18
"Meant for You": The Beach Boys A125, B15
"Mean Time 'Till Failure": Sleepy Eyes of Death **A204**
"Mean To Me" **B30**
"Meanwhile. . .": Mary Hampton B21
"Mean Woman Blues": The Beatles B8
"Meat Is Murder": The Smiths A36
"Meccamputechture": The Mars Volta **A205**
"Mechanical World": Spirit B7
"Medicine Man": Barclay James Harvest A185
"Medieval Overture": Return to Forever A73
"Medley: The Lark in the Morning": Fairport Convention B21
"Medowlands (Calvary of the Steppes)" B12
"Meeting of the Spirits": Mahavishnu Orchestra A73
"Meeting Place, The": XTC A185
"Meet Me in My Dreams Tonight": Brian Wilson B15

"Meet Me in St. Louis, Louis" A219
"Melancholy" B30
"Melancholy Baby" **B11**
"Melinda" B12
"Melinda's Wedding Day" A145
"Mellow My Mind": Neil Young A88, B6
"Mellow Yellow": Donovan A43, B7, B8, B21, B29
"Melt Away": Brian Wilson B15
"Melt with You": Modern English A250
"Memories" B16
"Memories Are Made of This" **A167**; Kirlian Camera A167; Johnny Cash A167; Dean Martin A167
"Memories of You" **B16, B19**; Louis Armstrong A119
"Memory of a Free Festival": David Bowie A185
"Memphis Blues": W.C. Handy B9, B30, A145, A219, **A266**
"Memphis": The Beatles **B8**; Chuck Berry A33, A95, B15
"Memphis in June" B30
"Memphis Soul Stew": King Curtis B21
"Memphis Tennessee": Chuck Berry A185
"Memphis Train, The": Rufus Thomas A29
"Memphis Yodel" A266; Jimmie Rodgers A266
"Me Myself I": Joan Armatrading A136
"Mercury Blues": Steve Miller Band A185
"Mercy Blues": Ida Cox A240
"Mercy Mercy Me": Marvin Gaye A185
"Mercy Seat, The": Nick Cave and the Bad Seeds B21
"Mercy St.": Peter Gabriel A252
"Merlin the Magician": Rick Wakeman A149
"Merry Christmas, Baby": The Beach Boys B15
"Merry Xmas Everybody": Slade B21
"Mesmerizing": Liz Phair **A177**
"Message, The": Grandmaster Flash and the Furious Five **A1**, A80, A99, **A101, A221**, A247, A269
"Message From a Black Man": The Temptations A105
"Message in a Bottle": The Police A19, A185, A235, A250
"Messages": Orchestral Manoeuvres A185
"Message to You, Rudy, A": The Specials A118

"Messin' Around": Memphis Slim A53
"Metal Guru": T. Rex A36
"Metal on Metal": Kraftwerk A104
"Metamorphosis": The Pet Shop Boys A174
"Metaphor for an Older Man": The United States of America A138
"Me to the Future of You": Knifeworld **B21**
"Metropolis": Motorhead A185
"Metropolis Pt. I: The Miracle and the Sleeper": Dream Theater A175
"Mexicali Blues, The": Grateful Dead A171
"Mexican, The": Babe Ruth A104
"Mic Check": Aceyalone B14
"Michael Caine": Madness A185
"Michael from Mountains": Joni Mitchell **A260**
"Michelangelo": Björn Skif OR SKIFS? A20
"Michelle": The Beatles A43, A76, A95, A98, A99, A100, **A133**, A259, B7, **B8, B18**, B21, B24; David and Jonathan A107
"Mickey's Monkey": The Miracles **A106, A108**
"Mickey": Toni Basil A43
"Microbes": George Harrison B7
"Midas Touch": Saxon B21
"Middle Man": Living Colour A99
"Middle of the Road": The Pretenders **A16**
"Mideast Vacation": Neil Young **A88**, B6
"Midnight Rambler": The Rolling Stones A99, B29
"Midnight Rider": The Allman Brothers A222
"Midnight Rocks": Al Stewart A250
"Midnight Shift": The Beatles B8
"Midnight Special" B8; Creedence Clearwater Revival B24; Leadbelly **A240**
"Midnight": The Shadows B8
"Midnight Train to Georgia": Gladys Knight and the Pips **A124**, B21
"Mighty Quinn (Quinn the Eskimo), The" B17; Mannfred Mann **A225**
"Mighty Like a Rosenbloom" B12
"Mighty Man": The Beatles B8; Davy Jones A95
"Mike, Come Back to L.A.": The Beach Boys B15
"Milk Cow Blues": Bob Dylan A58
"Milkcow ['s Half] Blues [Boogie]": The Beatles B8; Robert Johnson A132; Elvis Presley A99, **B19**

Song Index

"Milk of Human Kindness, The": Procol Harum A185
"Million Miles, A": Wedding Present A185
"Mimi" B30
"Mind Game": John Lennon A185
"Mind Riot": Soundgarden A99
"Mind Your Own Business" [1]: Hank Williams B21
"Mind Your Own Business" [2]: Living Colour B21
"Mine" **B10**, B30
"Minglewood Blues": Cannon's Jug Stompers **B26**
"Ministry of Lost Souls, The": Dream Theater A175
"Minnie the Moocher" B12
"Minotaur's Song": The Incredible String Band A112
"Minstrel First Part – Just One Girl" A145
"Minstrel in the Gallery": Jethro Tull A188
"Minstrel Parade, The" B30
"Minstrel's Song": The Moody Blues B8
"Miracle, The": Emerson Lake & Powell A185
"Miracle Drug": U2 A86
"Miracle Man": Elvis Costello A185, B4
"Mirage": Siouxsie and the Banshees A185, B20
"Mirror": Dream Theater A175
"Miserable Lie": The Smiths A36
"Miserlou" B12
"Misery" [1] B16; The Beatles B7, B8, **B18**, **A90**, A98, **A194**
"Misery" [2]: Professor Longhair **A238**
"Misery Blues": Ida Cox A240
"Misirlou [Twist]": The Beach Boys A160, B15; Dick Dale A160, B15
"Miss America": Styx A141
"Miss Ann": The Beatles B7, B8; Little Richard A95, B7
"Miss Gradenko": The Police A235
"Missing": Everything But the Girl **A3**
"Missing You": John Waite A250, B24
"Mission Bell": Donnie Brooks A160
"Mission: Impossible": Lalo Schifrin A43
"Mission Impossible Theme / Norwegian Wood": Alan Copeland **A24**
"Mississippi Delta Blues": Jimmie Rodgers **A266**
"Mississippi Half-Step Uptown Toodleloo": The Grateful Dead B17

"Mississippi Moon": Jimmie Rodgers A266
"Mississippi Queen": Mountain **A16**, A43
"Mississippi Rag" **B27**
"Mississippi River Blues": Bill Broonzy **A240**; Jimmie Rodgers A266
"Miss Macbeth": Elvis Costello B20
"Miss Misery": Elliot Smith A221, **A222**
"Miss the Mississippi and You": Jimmie Rodgers A266
"Miss You": The Rolling Stones A179
"Mister Dooley" B12
"Mister Johnson, Turn Me Loose" **B30**
"Mister Mary Blues": Speedy Holmes A240
"Mister Meadowlark" **B30**
"Mister Music" A14
"Mister Snow" B30
"Mistletoe Bough, The": Ned Corvan B19
"Mistreatin' Mama": Walter "Furry": Lewis A201, **B26**
"Mistreatin' Woman Blues": Ida Cox A240
"Misty" A147
"Misty Islands of the Highlands": The Moonlight Revellers A227
"Misty Mountain Hop": Led Zeppelin A16
"Misunderstanding": Genesis A142
"Misunderstood": Dream Theater A175
"Mixed Salad" A145
"Mixed Up Confusion": Bob Dylan A121
"MLK": U2 A185
"Moanin' at Midnight": Howlin' Wolf B21
"Moanin' in the Mornin'" B10
"Moby Dick": Led Zeppelin B20
"Mocking Bird, The" A145
"Mockingbird" [1]: Barclay James Harvest A185, B21
"Mockingbird" [2]: Eminem **B31**
"Model Minstrels, The" A145
"Modern Day Bonnie and Clyde": Travis Tritt A191
"Modern Love" [1]: David Bowie A101
"Modern Love" [2]: Peter Gabriel A185
"Mofo": U2 A103
"Mojo Hand Blues": Ida Cox **A240**
"Moment of Surrender": U2 A89
"Moment of Truth": The Originals A110
"Momma, You're Just on My Mind": The Beatles B7; Bob Dylan B7, B8
"Momma Poppa Boogie" **A8**
"Mo Money, Mo Problems": Puff Daddy B14

"Mona (I Need You Baby)": The Rolling Stones **A83**
"Mona Lisa" B12
"Mona": The Beach Boys B15
"Monday, Monday": The Mamas and the Papas B8, B24
"Monday Date, A": Louis Armstrong A119
"Monday Morning": Pulp A82
"Mon Dieu": Charles Dumont B25
"Money (That's What I Want)": Barrett Strong A95, A105; The Beatles A98, B7, **B8**, B18; The Flying Lizards B20
"Money Can't Buy It": Annie Lennox A10, **A127**, **B13**
"Money Don't Matter 2 Night": Prince A79, **B13**
"Money for Nothing": Dire Straits **A101**, A248, B32
"Money Honey": Drifters B21
"Money Money Money": ABBA A185, B25
"Money Musk" B30
"Money": Pink Floyd A17, A19, A43, A64, A74, A99, **A101**, A185, **A198**, A199, A221, B21, B24, B29
"Mo 'n Herb's Vacation": Frank Zappa A12, A27
"Monkberry Moon Delight": Wings B7
"Monkees, The": Monkees B21
"Monkey in Your Soul": Steely Dan **A96**, B8
"Monkey Time, The": Major Lance **A108**
"Monk's Mood": Thelonius Monk A96
"Monster Mash": The Beach Boys B15
"Montana": Frank Zappa and the Mothers A27, **A60**
"Montego Bay": Sugar Cane B25
"Mood Indigo" **A15**, B10; Norman Petty Trio A121
"Moods for Moderns": Elvis Costello A185
"Moody's Mood" B10
"Moog Fugue": Gentle Giant **A166**
"Moog Raga": The Byrds A138
"Moon, Turn the Tides": Jimi Hendrix B3
"Moonage Daydream": David Bowie A185, B20
"Moon at the Window": Joni Mitchell A260
"Moonchild": King Crimson B20, B21
"Mooncoin Jig, The": Steeleye Span B21
"Moon Dawg": The Beach Boys A160; The Gamblers A160, B15

"Moonglow" B8, B30
"Moon Going Down": Charley Patton **A240**
"Moonlight and Pretzels" B10
"Moonlight and Roses" A227
"Moonlight and Skies": Jimmie Rodgers A266
"Moonlight Bay" B12; The Beatles B7, B8
"Moonlight Becomes You" A14, B10
"Moonlight Feels Right": Starbuck A43
"Moonlight Gambler": Frankie Laine A97
"Moonlight in Vermont": A156, B16, **B30**
"Moonlight on the Ganges" A147
"Moonlight Serenade": Glenn Miller B16
"Moon Rocks": Talking Heads A185
"Moonshine Lullaby" B30
"Moon Shines on the Moonshine, the" A145
"Moon Song" **B30**
"Moon Was Yellow, The" B12, **B30**
"Moovin' and Groovin'": Duane Eddy B8
"More and More" B30
"More I Cannot Wish You" **B30**
"More I See You, The" **B30**
"More Than a Feeling": Boston A16, A43, A75, **A101**, A205, **B24**
"More Than a Woman": The Bee Gees A179
"More Than I Can Say": The Beatles B8
"More Than Meets the Eye": Bangles A185
"More Than One": Phil Marks and the Originals **A53**
"More Than the Blues": All About Eve A185
"More Than Words Can Say": Otis Redding B3
"More Than You Know" **B10**, **B30**
"More Today Than Yesterday": The Spiral Staircase B7
"More Trouble Every Day": Mothers of Invention, The A11
"Morning Bell": Radiohead **A54**, A135, A162, **A169**, **A206**, A221
"Morning Dew" B17
"Morning Fog, The": Kate Bush A185
"Morning Glory": Oasis B7
"Morning Morgantown": Joni Mitchell **A260**
"Morning Mr. Magpie": Radiohead **A169**
"Morning Star, The" B12
"Morning Sun": Happy the Man **A72**, A73
"Moses" A168
"Moshe From Nova Scotia" B12
"Moss Garden": David Bowie B20
"Most Anything You Want": Iron Butterfly **B3**
"Most Beautiful Girl in the World, The" B30

Song Index

"Most Likely You Go Your Way (And I'll Go Mine)": Bob Dylan A121
"Most of All": The Moonglows A110
"Most of the Time": Status Quo A82
"Most Peculiar Man, A": Paul Simon B1; Simon and Garfunkel B1
"Moten Swing" A145
"Mother, the Queen of My Heart": Jimmie Rodgers A266
"Mother" [1]: The Police **A221**, A235
"Mother" [2]: John Lennon A90, B7, **B18**, B20
"Mother" [3]: Pink Floyd A198
"Mother and Child Reunion": Paul Simon A235, B1
"Mother Earth": Neil Young B6
"Mother India": Propa-Gandhi A61
"Motherless Children" A145; Eric Clapton A185; Bob Dylan A216
"Motherly Love": The Mothers of Invention A27
"Mother Nature's Son": The Beatles B7, B18
"Mother Popcorn (You Got to Have a Mother for Me)": James Brown A31, A53, A117, **A238**, B4
"Mothership Connection": Parliament A117
"Mother's Little Helper": The Rolling Stones A99, A107, B24
"Mothers of the Depressed": U2 A103
"Mother's Prayer, A" B12
"Mother Was a Lady": Jimmie Rodgers A266
"Motion Pictures": Neil Young **B6**
"Motion Picture Soundtrack": Radiohead A162
"Motorhead": Hawkwind B20
"Motor of Love": Paul McCartney A185
"Motorpsycho Nightmare": Bob Dylan B7
"Mountain Greenery" B16, **B30**
"Mountain of God, The": The Incredible String Band A112, B7
"Mountain of Love": The Beach Boys B15; Harold Dorman B15
"Mountain People": Super Furry Animals B21
"Mountains of the Moon": The Grateful Dead B17
"Mouse's Ear blues": Cliff Carlisle A266
"Mousetrap": Soft Machine B20
"Move, Members, Move": Courlander A238
"Move It": Cliff Richard B8, B20, **B21**
"Move It on Over": Hank Williams, Jr. A173, **B4**

"Move Out Little Mustang": Jan and Dean B15
"Move Over and Make Room for Me" B3
"Move Over": Janis Joplin B21; Slade B21
"Movie Magg": The Beatles B8
"Movin' In": Chicago **B3**
"Movin' ": REO Speedwagon A185
"Mozart Ballet – Piano Sonata in B Flat": Mothers of Invention, The A11
"Mr. Big Stuff": Jean Knight A185
"Mr. Blue Sky": Electric Light Orchestra A185, B20
"Mr. Brownstone": Guns n' Roses A99, A246
"Mr. Bubbleman": Fun-Da-Mental A61
"Mr. Chainsaw": Alkaline Trio A205
"Mr. Clean": The Jam B20
"Mr. Crowley": Ozzy Osbourne B28
"Mr. Gallagher and Mr. Sheen": Bing Crosby B4
"Mr. Green Genes": Mothers of Invention, The A11
"Mr. Jaws": Dickie Goodman A43
"Mr. Johnson's Blues No. 2": Lonnie Johnson **A240**
"Mr. Lee": The Bobbettes A44
"Mr. Loverman": Shabba Ranks **A61**
"Mr. Moonlight": The Beatles A43, A98, **A116**, B7, B8
"Mr. Moto": The Belairs B15
"Mr. Mustard": The Beatles **A116**
"Mr. Oxy Moron": Echolyn A72
"Mr. Pharmacist": Fall, The B21
"Mr. Pitiful": Otis Redding A29, A123
"Mr. Radio": Electric Light Orchestra A149
"Mr. Roboto": Styx A43
"Mrs. Brown, You've Got a Lovely Daughter": Herman's Hermits A70, B7, B8
"Mrs. O'Leary's Cow": Brian Wilson B15
"Mr. Soul": Neil Young B6
"Mr. Spaceman": The Byrds A121, A185
"Mr. Speaker Gets the Word": Madness A185
"Mrs. Robinson": Simon and Garfunkel A43, A93, A101, A167, A185, B1, B3, B7, B20, B21, B24
"Mrs. Vanderbilt": Paul McCartney and Wings **B24**
"Mr. Tambourine Man": The Byrds A33, A43, **A70**, **A121**, A185, A247, B8, B24, B32; Bob Dylan A180, A216, **A225**, A247, A268
"Mudmen": Pink Floyd A185

"Mueve la Cadera": Reel to Reel A3
"Mueve la Cintura": Septeto Nacional A205
"Mule Train" A53
"Mule Walk, The": James P. Johnson **A263**
"Mull of Kintyre": Wings **A64**, A235, B8
"Mumbo": Wings B18
"Mundian to Bach Ke": Panjabi MC A61
"Murder By Numbers": The Police A235
"Murder in the Skies": Gary Moore A185
"Murder on Music Row": George Strait & Alan Jackson A191
"Muscle Beach Party": Dick Dale B15
"Musetta's Waltz" B12
"Mushnik and Son" B12
"Musical Box, The": Genesis A232, B21
"Music Arcade": Neil Young B6
"Music Evolution": Buckshot Lefonque B14
"Music for Electric Violin and Low Budget Orchestra": Frank Zappa A11
"Music Makes Me" B30
"Music Makes Me Sentimental" A145
"Musicology": Prince A130
"Music to My Ears": 68 Beats A3
"Mustang Sally": Wilson Pickett B8, B32
"Must to Avoid, A": Herman's Hermits B8
"Muzzle": Smashing Pumpkins **A203**
"My, Oh, My": The Wreckers **A83**
"My Baby" [1]: The Temptations A108
"My Baby" [2]: Lil Romeo A35
"My Baby Knows How" A145
"My Baby Loves Me": Martha and the Vandellas A108
"My Baby Specializes": William Bell and Judy Clay A29
"My Back Pages": The Byrds **A121**; Bob Dylan **A121**, A216, B8
"My Backwards Walk": Frightened Rabbit A205
"My Beautiful Leah": PJ Harvey A223
"My Best Friend's Girl": The Cars **A74**
"My Black Mama": Son House A201, **B26**
"My Blue-Eyed Jane": Jimmie Rodgers A266
"My Blue Heaven" B10, B30; Jack Smith and Ambrose's Whispering Orchestra A227
"My Bonnie Lass She Smelleth": P.D.Q Bach A70
"My Bonnie (Lies Over the Ocean)": The Beatles B7, B18; Tony Sheridan B8
"My Boy and I" **B30**

"My Boyfriend's Back": The Angels A74
"My Boy Lollipop": Millie Small B21
"My Brave Face": Paul McCartney B7, B20
"My Bridal Gown" **B30**
"My Bucket's Got a Hole in It": Hank Williams B4
"My Buddy" B10, B30
"My Buddy Seat": Hondells B15
"My Carolina Sunshine Gal": Jimmie Rodgers A266
"My Castle in the Air" **B30**
"My Cherie Amour": Stevie Wonder **A99**
"My Cousin in Milwaukee" B30
"My Country 'Tis of Thee" B12
"My Dark Hour": The Steve Miller Band B7
"My Darling, My Darling" A41
"My Darling" [1] B12
"My Darling" [2]: Juliana Hatfield A218
"My Dear Wormwood": Echolyn A72
"My Defenses Are Down" B30
"My Diane": The Beach Boys B15
"My Ding-a-Ling": Chuck Berry A43
"My Faith Looks Up to Thee" A219
"My Fate Is in Your Hands" **A120**
"My Favorite Mistake": Sheryl Crow B24
"My Favorite Things" A147, B30; John Coltrane A261, B31; Outkast A261, B31
"My Favourite Dress": The Wedding Present A185, B20
"My First Love": Dick Dale B15
"My First Single": Eminem A146
"My First Song": Jay-Z A221
"My Forgotten Man" B12
"My Friend of Misery": Metallica A28
"My Funny Valentine": A147, A168, A216, B3, **B10**, B12, **B30**
"My Future Just Passed" **B30**
"My Gal Is a Highborn Lady" A145
"My Gal Sal" B30
"My Generation" A97; The Who A23, A43, A55, A80, A99, A185, A247, **B19**, B20, B21
"My Girl" A95; The Temptations A55, **A108**, A247, B4, B8, B24
"My Girl Has gone": the Miracles **A108**
"My God": Jethro Tull A4, B20
"My Good Gal's Gone Blues": Jimmie Rodgers A266
"My Guy": Mary Wells A95, A108, A185

Song Index

"My Harem" B10
"My Heart Belongs to Daddy" A168, B10, B12, B30
"My Heart Belongs to You": Arbee Stidham A53
"My Heart Goes Crazy" A14
"My Heart Is a Hobo" A14
"My Heart Is an Open Book": Carl Dobkins Jr. A44
"My Heart Is for You": Fred Hammond **A161**
"My Heart": Paramore A205
"My Heart Stood Still" **B10**, B30
"My Hillbilly Baby": Rex Griffin A266
"My Hometown": Bruce Springsteen A99
"My Honey's Lovin' Arms" **B30**
"My Ideal" B10, **B30**
"My Irish Rosie" A145
"My Iron Lung": Radiohead A162, **A169**
"My Kinda Love" **B30**
"My Kind of Town" A14, B30
"Mykonos": The Fleet Foxes A205
"My Little Bimbo" A145
"My Little Cousin" B12
"My Little Girl": Roxy Music A185
"My Little Irish Queen" A145
"My Little Lady": Jimmie Rodgers A266
"My Little Lovin' Sugar Babe" A145
"My Little Old Home Down in New Orleans": Jimmie Rodgers A266
"My Little Persian Rose" A145
"My Little Red Book" A147; Love A43; Manfred Mann B29
"My Little Town": Paul Simon A93, **A150**, B1
"My Little Yiddisha Queen" B12
"My Love An' My Mule" **B30**
"My Love Is Brighter Than the Brightest Sunshine": Petula Clark A185
"My Love My Life": ABBA B25
"My Love": Paul McCartney and Wings B7, **B24**
"My Lover's Prayer": Otis Redding A29
"My Mammy" B10
"My Man and I": Rosetta Tharpe A240
"My Man": Billie Holiday B4
"My Man Is on the Make" **A120**, B30
"My Man's Gone Now" B12
"My Melancholy Baby" B30
"My Michelle": Guns 'n' Roses A97

"My Money Never Runs Out" A145
"My Mother's Bible" A219
"My Mummy's Dead": John Lennon B18
"My My Hey Hey (Out of the Blue)": Neil Young A88, A99, B6
"My Name Is": Eminem A146, B31
"My Name Is Ticklish Reuben": Smyth County Ramblers A240
"My New House": Tha Fall A185
"My New Woman": Roger McGuinn A121
"My Old Dog": Lew Stone and His Band A227
"My Old Flame" **B30**
"My Old Kentucky Home" A219, A264
"My Old Man": Joni Mitchell **A260**, B4
"My Old Pal": Jimmie Rodgers A266
"My Ole Man's a Dustman": Lonnie Donegan A259
"My One and Only" **A120**, B12
"My Only Alibi": The Beach Boys B15
"My Own" A145
"My Pearl": Automatic Man A185
"My Prerogative": Bobby Brown B24
"My Pretty Girl" A145
"My Resistance Is Low" **B30**
"My Rival": Steely Dan A96
"My Rock": Swan Silvertones B21
"My Romance" B30
"My Rough and Rowdy Ways": Jimmie Rodgers A266
"My Sharona": The Knack **A16**, A27, **A97**, A99, **A101**, A250
"My Shiksa Goddess" B12
"My Shining Hour" **B30**
"My Silent Love" B10
"My Solution": The Beach Boys B15
"Mysterious Ways": U2 **A89**, A103, A232
"Mystery Dance": Elvis Costello A185, B4, B20
"Mystery of Number Five, The": Jimmie Rodgers A266
"Mystery Train" B8; Elvis Presley A80, A247, B19
"Mystic Eyes": Them A43
"Mystified": Fleetwood Mac A185
"My Stupid Mouth": John Mayer A247
"My Sunny Tennessee" A145
"My Surfin' Woodie" B15
"My Sweetheart's the Man in the Moon" B12
"My Sweetie Went Away" B30

"My Sweet Lord" B12; George Harrison A43, A95, A185, B7, B8, B18
"My Sweet Potato": Booker T. and the MGs A29
"My Time Ain't Long": Jimmie Rodgers A266
"My Time of Day" **A41**
"My True Love": Jack Scott A97, **B25**
"My Two Arms – You = Tears": Mary Wells A110
"My Very Good Friend the Milkman" B16
"My Way": Claude François B25; Frank Sinatra A123, B19, **B25**; Sid Vicious B19
"My White Bicycle" Nazareth A185; Tomorrow A70
"My Woman From Tokyo": Deep Purple A74
"My World Is Empty Without You": The Supremes A95, A99, **A106**, **A108**, B3

"Nagasaki" **A120**, B30
"Na Good Luck About the House": Ned Corvan B19
"Nah!": Shania Twain A193
"Name Game, The": Shirley Ellis B4
"Name": Goo Goo Dolls A247, **B24**
"Name of the Game, The": ABBA A185, B25
"Naminanu": Genesis A142
"Nananana": Steam A185
"Nancy" B10, B30
"Nancy (With the Laughing Face)" A14
"Nashville Nightingale" **A120**
"Nashville Skyline Rag": Bob Dylan A96, A99
"Nasty Mind": D12 A146
"Nat'an, Nat'an" B12
"Nathan Jones": Supremes A43
"Nathan LaFraneer": Joni Mitchell **A260**
"National Anthem, The": Radiohead **A162**, **A169**, **A206**
"National Front Disco, The": Morrissey B13
"Natural Beauty": Neil Young B6
"Natural Mystic": Bob Marley and the Wailers A235
"Natural Woman, A" *see* "(You Make Me Feel Like) A Natural Woman"
"Nature Boy" B12; Nat King Cole B7; Bobby Darin B7
"Nausea": Beck **A55**
"Naval Aviation in Art?": Frank Zappa A11
"Nearer My God to Thee" A219, A239, A240
"Nearer My Job to Thee": Joe Hill B25

"Nearness of You, The" B10, B30; The Four Freshmen B15
"Near the Woodland a Girl Is Ploughing" B12
"Near to the Heart of God" A219
"Neath the Weeping Willow Tree": The Hackberry Ramblers **A240**
"Neat Neat Neat": The Damned A210
"Necromancer, The": Rush A28
"Needle and the Damage Done, The": Neil Young A88, B6
"Needle to the Groove": Mantronix A104
"Need to Belong": Jerry Butler **A108**
"Need Your Love So Bad": Little Willie John B7; Fleetwood Mac B7
"Need Your Lovin' (Want You Back)": Marvin Gaye A110
"Negative Girl": Steely Dan **A96**, A222
"Nel Blu Dipinto Di Blu (Volare)": Domenico Modugno A97
"Nervous Boogie": Paul Gayton A238
"Nervous Breakdown": Black Flag A210
"Net": John Oswald A24
"Neuköln": David Bowie B20
"Nevada Johnny": Cliff Carlisle A266
"Ne Ver', Ne Boysia": t.A.T.u. A153
"Never Been to Spain": Three Dog Night B24
"Never Be Mine": Rocket's Tail B20
"Never Be the Same": Christopher Cross A250
"Never Can Say Goodbye": Gloria Gaynor **A101**; The Jackson 5 B3
"Never Comes the Day": The Moody Blues B7
"Never Die Young": James Taylor **A6**
"Never Enough": The Cure A103
"Never Going Back Again": Fleetwood Mac A185
"Never Gonna Give You Up": Rick Astley **A215**
"Never Grow Old": Aretha Franklin B21
"Never Knew Love Like This Before": Stephanie Mills B24
"Never Let Me Down": David Bowie A185
"Never Like This Before": William Bell A29
"Never My Love": The Association A101, **B3**
"Never No Mo' Blues": Jimmie Rodgers A266
"Never No More": Patsy Cline B21
"Never on Sunday" B12; The Beatles B7
"Never Said a Mumbalin' Word" B12
"New Day": Jackie Lomax B7
"New Delhi": Madness A185, B21

Song Index

"New Girl in School, The": Jan and Dean A109, B15
"New Kid in Town": The Eagles A99, **A111**
"New Millenium Cyanide Christ": Meshuggah **A208**
"New Millenium": Dream Theater A175
"New Orleans" B17; The Beatles B8; Leadbelly B21
"New Orleans Joys" A145
"New Pollution, The": Beck B32
"New Pony": Bob Dylan A180
"New Potato Caboose": The Grateful Dead B17
"New Rose": The Damned B20, B21
"New Slang": The Shins **A22**
"New Suit, The" B12
"New Sun in the Sky" **B30**
"New World": Strawbs B21
"New Year's Day": U2 A89, A103, B20
"New York, New York" [1] B12; Liza Minelli A178; Frank Sinatra A178, A202
"New York, New York" [2]: Nina Hagen **A178**
"New York City Boy": The Pet Shop Boys A174
"New York City Serenade": Bruce Springsteen A269
"New Yorkers, The" A145
"New York's Alright if You Like Saxophones": Derf Scratch A210
"New York State of Mind" B12
"News at Ten": Vapors A185, B21
"News of the World": Jam A185
"Newtown": The Slits B20
"Next Time, The": Cliff Richard A259
"Next to You": Police A185
"Nice Dream": Radiohead **A169**
"Nice Work if You Can Get It" A147, A167, **B10, B30**
"Nigga Ya Love to Hate": Ice Cube B14
"Nigga You Love to Hate, The": Ice Cube A99
"Night and Day": **A113, A114**, A168, **A228**, B10, B12, **B30**; Fred Astaire A228; Dr. Buzzard's Original Savannah Band A228; U2 A228
"Night Before, The": The Beatles A97, A98, **A194, A254**, B7, B8, B24
"Night Bloomin' Jasmine": Brian Wilson B15
"Night By Night": Steely Dan A96
"Night Fever": The Bee Gees A179
"Night Game": Paul Simon **A93, A150**, B1

"Night I Fell in Love, The": The Pet Shop Boys A146
"Night in the City": Joni Mitchell **A260**
"Night Is Young, The" **B10**
"Nightmare, The" A145
"Nightmare to Remember, A": Dream Theater A175
"Night Moves": Bob Seger **A16**
"Night of the Living Baseheads": Public Enemy A61, A99
"Night of the Swallow": Kate Bush B20
"Night on Bald Mountain": Bob James A217
"Night on Disco Mountain": David Shire A179
"Night Owl": James Taylor B3
"Night Rally": Elvis Costello and the Attractions A185, B4
"Night Ride Home": Joni Mitchell **A222**, A260
"Night School": Frank Zappa **A60**
"Night Shall Be Filled With Music" B12
"Nights in White Satin": The Moody Blues **A16**, A72, A101, A185, A248, B20, **B24**
"Nightswimming": R.E.M. **A124**, A181
"Night the Carousel Burnt Down, The": Todd Rundgren B7
"Night They Drove Old Dixie Down, The": Joan Baez A241, B24; The Band **B24**
"Night Time": Brian Wilson B15
"Night Train": James Brown **B19**
"Night Was Made for Love, The" **B30**
"Night Was So Young, The": The Beach Boys B15
"Night Watch, The": King Crimson A185, B20, B21
"Night We Called It a Day, The" B30
"Nine Hundred Miles from Home": Riley Puckett A240
"Nine Pound Hammer": Frank Blevins & His Tar Heel Rattlers A240; The Monroe Brothers A240
"Ninety-Nine Years Blues": Jimmie Rodgers A266
"Nitty Gritty": Gladys Knight and the Pips A53
"No, No, Nanette!" **B30**
"No. 9 Dream": John Lennon A185, B7
"No Action": Elvis Costello **A124**, B21
"Noah's Dove": 10,000 Maniacs **B24**
"No Analices": Milton Nascimento B25
"No Bed for Beatle John": John Lennon B7
"No Big Thing": The Honeys B15

"Noble Surfer": The Beach Boys B15
"Nobody" [1] A145; Perry Como B4; Bing Crosby B4
"Nobody" [2]: Paul Simon B1
"Nobody Breaks My Heart" B10
"Nobody But You": The Beatles B8; Dee Clark B25
"Nobody Cares if I'm Blue" A145
"Nobody Else But Me" **B30**
"Nobody Home": Pink Floyd A167, A185
"Nobody I Know": Peter and Gordon A107, **B8**
"Nobody Knows, Nobody Cares": Marion Williams **A161**
"Nobody Knows but Me": Jimmie Rodgers A266
"Nobody's Business": Willie Ford A240; Riley Puckett A240
"Nobody's Car": Jethro Tull **A188**
"Nobody's Child" B8
"Nobody's Dirty Business": Mississippi John Hurt A240
"Nobody's Fault": Aerosmith A97, A99
"Nobody's Fault but Mine": B17; Blind Willie Johnson **B21**
"Nobody's Heart Belongs to Me" **B30**
"Nobody Told Me": John Lennon B7
"No Cars Go": Arcade Fire A205
"No Excuses": Alice in Chains A246, **A247**, A248
"No Fear, No Hate, No Pain": The Eurythmics B20, B21
"No Feeling": Sex Pistols A43
"No Fun": Teen Idles A210; The Stooges A24, **A210**
"No Girl So Sweet": PJ Harvey A223
"No Good (Start the Dance)": Prodigy B21
"No Good Man": Billie Holiday B4
"No-Go Showboat": The Beach Boys B15
"No Hard Times": Jimmie Rodgers A266
"No Letter Today": Ted Daffan A270
"No Man's Land" *see* "Green Fields of France, The"
"No Matter What You Do": Frank Zappa A11
"No Mermaid": Sinead Lohan A169
"No Milk Today": Herman's Hermits A185
"No More Lonely Nights": Paul McCartney A198, B7
"No More Tears": Ozzy Osbourne A17

"No Mule's Fool": Family A185
"None But the Lonely Heart" A209
"No No Song": Ringo Starr B7
"No One Is Alone" B12
"No-One Left to Care": Michael Chapman B21
"No One Like You": Scorpions **A16**
"No One Needs to Know": Shania Twain A193
"No One's Fool" A145
"No Other Baby": The Vipers Skiffle group B8
"No Other One": Weezer A221
"No Particular Place to Go": Chuck Berry **A83**, A95, B24
"No Quarter": Led Zeppelin A99, A185
"No Reply": The Beatles A91, A98, B7, **B8**, B18, B24
"Normal People, The": Boomtown Rats A185
"North Country Girl" B16
"Northern Soul, A": The Verve B20, B21
"Norwegian Wood (This Bird Has Flown)": The Beatles **A24**, A39, A43, A70, A71, **A76**, A98, A221, A247, **A253**, **A254**, A259, B7, **B8**, **B18**, B20, B21, B24
"No Self Control": Peter Gabriel A185, B32
"Nosferatu Man": Slint A221
"No Stranger": Gentle Giant A185
"No Strings" B10
"No Surprises": Radiohead A143, A162, **A169**
"Not a Care in the World" B30
"Not Alone Anymore": The Traveling Wilburys B24
"Not as a Stranger" A14
"Not a Second Time": The Beatles A92, A95, A98, **A100**, B7, B8
"No Telephone in Heaven": The Carter Family **A240**
"No Tell Lover": Chicago B24
"Not Fade Away" A38, B17; Buddy Holly **A16**, A99, A247, B8, B20, B32; The Rolling Stones B20
"Not for All the Rice in China" B30
"Not Gonna Get Us": t.A.T.u. A153
"Not Guilty": The Beatles B7; George Harrison **B7**
"Nothin'" A145
"Nothin' But a Good Time": Poison B28
"Nothing But Heartaches" A95; The Supremes **A106**, **A108**
"Nothing But the Truth": Procol Harum A185

Song Index

"Nothing Can Be Done": Joni Mitchell A260
"Nothing Can Stop Me": Gene Chandler **A108**
"Nothing Compares 2 U": Sinead O'Connor A80, A247
"Nothing Could Be Sweeter" B30
"Nothing Is Easy": Jethro Tull A188
"Nothing Left": Johnny Winter A185
"Nothing's Too Good for My Baby": Stevie Wonder A95
"Nothing to Hold Me": Jesus Jones B20
"Nothing to Say": Jethro Tull B20
"Nothing Was Delivered": The Byrds A121
"Nothin' Shakin' (But the Leaves on the Trees)": The Beatles B8
"Nothin' to Lose": Josh Gracin A191
"Not Home Today": Madness A185
"No Time or Space": Bernie Krause B7
"No Time to Live": Johnny Winter A185
"No Time to Think": Bob Dylan A180
"Not Lately" A145
"Not One of Us": Peter Gabriel A185
"No Trouble But You" A145
"Not the Red Baron": Tori Amos A6
"Not to Touch the Earth": Doors A185
"No Two People": Danny Kaye and Jane Wyman B21
"Novacaine [sic]": Beck **A55**
"Now" B12, **B30**
"Nowadays Clancy Can't Even Sing": Neil Young B6
"Now and Then": The Beatles B7
"(Now and Then There's) A Fool Such as I": Elvis Presley A99, **B25**
"Nowhere Man": The Beatles **A33**, A70, A76, A90, A92, A98, A99, A107, A149, **A225**, B3, B7, B8, B18, B20, B29
"Nowhere to Run" A95; Martha and the Vandellas A94, A97, A99, **A106**, **A108**, B8
"Now I'm Here": Queen A185, B21, B32
"Now Is the Hour" B12; Bing Crosby B4
"Now It Can Be Told" **B10**, B30
"Now I've Got a Witness (Like Uncle Phil and Uncle Gene)": The Rolling Stones A85
"Now I Wanna Sniff Some Glue": The Ramones A210
"No Woman, No Cry": Bob Marley and the Wailers A80, **A83**, A185, A247, B21
"Now or Never": Yoko Ono B7
"Now's the Time to Fall in Love" B12

"Now That Everything's Been Said": Spring B15
"Now That You've Won Me": Marvin Gaye A110
"Now You Know": The Four Freshmen B15
"NSU": Cream A132
"Nuclear Attack": Gary Moore A185
"Nude": Radiohead **A169**
"Numb": U2 A89
"Number of the Beast, The": Iron Maiden **A16**, B28
"Number One" [1]: The Rutles A69
"Number One" [2]: Gentle Giant B20
"Number One" [3]: The Beach Boys B15
"Number Three Blues": Walter "Buddy Boy": Hawkins **B26**
"Nursery Rhyme": U.N.K.L.E A205
"Nuthin' But a 'G' Thang": Dr. Dre feat. Snoop Doggy Dogg A80, A99, A247, A261, **B31**
"Nutrocker": B. Bumble and the Stingers B24; Emerson, Lake & Palmer A101, B20
"Nymph Errant" B10

"Ob-La-Di, Ob-La-Da": The Beatles A77, A98, A234, A235, B7, B8, B18, B32
"Obscured by Clouds": Pink Floyd A185
"Obvious Child, The": Paul Simon B1
"Occasional Man, An" **B30**
"Ocean, The": Led Zeppelin A99, A185, A245, B20
"Oceans": Pearl Jam A99
"O Children": Nick Cave and the Bad Seeds B21
"Octavarium": Dream Theater A175
"October Song": The Incredible String Band **A112**
"Octopus's Garden": The Beatles **B7**, B8, B18, B21, A92, A167
"O Darling": The Beatles **B18**
"O Death, Where Is Thy Sting?" A145
"Odyssey": The Dixie Dregs A73
"Offering": Spooky Tooth B21
"O for a Thousand Tongues to Sing" A219
"Of Thee I Sing" B30
"Oh, Babe, What Would You Say?": Hurricane Smith A43
"Oh, Dem Golden Slippers" B30
"Oh, Happy Day": The Edwins Hawkins Singers **A26**

"Oh, How I Hate to Get Up in the Morning" B30
"Oh, Lady Be Good!" B30
"Oh, Marion": Paul Simon B1
"Oh, Mary, Don't You Weep" A99
"Oh, Mein Liebchen" B30
"Oh, Me! Oh, My!" B30
"Oh, Pretty Woman": Van Halen A185; Roy Orbison A43, A55, A270, B8, **B21**
"Oh, Promise Me" B30
"Oh, Susanna" **B24**, B30; The Byrds A121
"Oh, What a Beautiful Mornin'" B12
"Oh, You Beautiful Doll" A145
"Oh, You Nasty Man": Ray Noble and His Orchestra A227
"Oh Blackpool": Beautiful South A185
"Oh Boy!": Buddy Holly **A38**, A44, A185
"Oh! Carol": Neil Sedaka A44, B25
"Oh Comely": Neutral Milk Hotel A205
"Oh Daddy": Fleetwood Mac A185
"Oh! Darling": The Beatles **A63**, A92, A98, A167, B7, B8, B25
"Oh Darlin'": The Beach Boys B15
"Oh Gee! Oh, Joy!" **B30**
"Oh Gee! Oh Gosh! (My Feet Won't Behave)" A145
"Ohh Baby Baby": The Miracles A108
"O-H-I-O (O-MY O!)" A145
"Ohio": Crosby, Stills, Nash, and Young B32; Neil Young B6
"Oh Johnny! Oh Johnny! Oh!": Andrews Sisters B21
"Oh! Lawdy" A145
"Oh Lonesome Me": Neil Young B6, **A186**
"Oh! Look at Me Now" B30
"Oh Mein Papa" B25
"Oh My God": The Police A235
"Oh My Love": John Lennon B7, **B18**
"Oh No" **A11**; Mothers of Invention, The A11; Frank Zappa A11
"Oh to Be in Love": Kate Bush A185
"Oh Well": Fleetwood Mac A185, B21
"Oh Yoko!": John Lennon B7
"Oh You Blondy!" A145
"Oh! You Crazy Moon" A14
"Oh! You Pretty Things": David Bowie A185, B20
"Oi, Yoi, Yoi, Yoi (A Hebrew Love Song)" B12
"O Lawd, I'm on My Way" B12

"Old 97, The" B27
"Old Black Joe" B30
"Old Brown Shoe": The Beatles A98, A195, **B7**, B8
"Old Chisolm Trail, The" B24
"Old Country Waltz, The": Neil Young **A88**, B6
"Old Dan Tucker" A145, A219
"Old Deserted Barn" B30
"Old Devil Moon" B10, **B30**
"Old Eph's Vision" A145
"Old-Fashioned Garden, An" B30
"Old Fashioned Millionaire": Eartha Kitt B8
"Old Folks at Home" A219; The Beach Boys B15
"Old Folks Rag" A145
"Old Friends": Simon and Garfunkel A93, B1
"Old Ghosts": Jethro Tull A185
"Old Joe Clark" B27
"Old King Cole" B12
"Old Laughing Lady, The": Neil Young **A88**, B6
"Old Love Letters": Jimmie Rodgers A266
"Old MacDonald" B7
"Old Main Drag, The": The Pogues B20
"Old Man": Neil Young **A88**, B6
"Old Man River" A264
"Old Master Painter, The" A53; The Beach Boys B15; Brian Wilson B15
"Old Original Kokomo Blues" see "Kokomo Blues"
"Old Pal of My Heart": Jimmie Rodgers A266
"Old": Paul Simon B1
"Old Playmate" A145
"Old Ruben": Wade Mainer & Sons of the Mountaineers A240
"Old Rugged Cross, the" **A219**
"Old Shep": Elvis Presley B19
"Old Shoes and Leggins": Uncle Eck Dunford A240
"Old Time Rock and Roll": Bob Seger and the Silver Bullet Band **B24**
"Ole Faithful": Jack Jackson and His Orchestra A227
"Oliver's Army": Elvis Costello and the Attractions A185, B4
"Ol' Man River" A168, B10, B12, B30; Paul Robeson B21
"Ology": Living Colour A99
"Omaha Celebration": Pat Metheny A226
"Omnibus": Move A185

Song Index 215

"O.M.N.I.": Goodie MoB B14
"On a Beautiful Night With a Beautiful Girl" A145
"On a Carousel": The Hollies B7
"On a Clear Day You Can See Forever" **B30**
"On a Holiday": Brian Wilson B15, B21
"On Any Other Day": The Police A235
"On a Plain": Nirvana A99
"On a Slow Boat to China" B24 B24
"On Broadway" A97; The Beach Boys B15; George Benson B24; The Drifters A95, B8, B24
"Once and for Always" A14
"Once in a Blue Moon" B30
"Once Too Often" B12
"Once Upon a Time There Was an Ocean": Paul Simon B1
"One" [1]: U2 A80, **A89**, A103, A247, B21
"One" [2]: Metallica A24
"One After 909, The": The Beatles A91, A98, B7, **B8**, B18
"One Alone" B10
"One and One Is Two": The Fourmost B8
"One and Only": Chesney Hawkes **A186**
"One Better Day": Madness A185
"One Boy, One Girl": Collin Raye **A191**
"One Brown Mouse": Jethro Tull A188
"One By One All Day": The Shins **A22**
"One Day at a Time" ["Un Dydd Ar Y Tro"]: Trebor Edwards A123
"One Dimension": Simian B21
"One Fine Day": The Chiffons A96, B24
"One for My Baby" A85, B30
"One for Sorrow": Steps **B21**
"One for the Boys": Brian Wilson B15
"One for the Show": echolyn A72
"One for the Vine": Genesis A149
"One Girl, The" **B30**
"One Good Woman": Peter Cetera B24
"One Great Thing": Big Country B20
"One Headlight": The Wallflowers **A247**
"One Heartbeat": Smokey Robinson A250
"One Hundred Things": Deacon Blue A185
"One Hundred Years": Five for Fighting A247
"One I Love, The": R.E.M. **A16**, A167
"One I Love (Belongs to Somebody Else), The" B30
"One I Loved Back Then, The": George Jones A191

"One in a Million" [1]: The Platters B24
"One in a Million" [2]: The Pet Shop Boys **B13**
"One Kiss Led to Another": The Beach Boys B15; The Coasters A77, B15
"One Kiss": The Robins A77
"One Last Time": Dream Theater A175
"One Love" **B30**
"One Love / People Get Ready": Bob Marley and the Wailers A235
"One Man's Ceiling Is Another Man's Floor": Paul Simon **A93**, B1
"One Minute Woman": The Bee Gees B3
"One More Chance": The Pet Shop Boys A174
"One More Cup of Coffee": Bob Dylan A121, A216; Roger McGuinn A121
"One More Heartache": Marvin Gaye A108
"One More Night": Bob Dylan A99
"One More Red Nightmare": King Crimson A28
"One More Rounder Gone": Reese Du Pree A240
"One More Saturday Night": The Grateful Dead B17
"One More Time": The Clash B20
"One Morning in May" B10, **B30**
"One Nail Draws Another": U-Totem **A72**, **A81**
"One Night": Elvis Presley A97
"One Night With You": Elvis Presley **B25**
"One Note Samba": ["Samba De Uma Nota So"] **A133**, A211
"One of These Days" [1]: Neil Young B6
"One of These Days" [2]: Pink Floyd A99, A198
"One of These Days" [3]: Marvin Gaye A110
"One of These Days" [4]: Tim McGraw A191
"One of These Days" [5]: Paul McCartney B7
"One of These Nights": The Eagles A185, B24
"One of Us" [1]: ABBA A185, B25
"One of Us" [2]: Joan Osborne A219, B24
"One of Us Must Know (Sooner or Later)": Bob Dylan B4
"One Rainy Wish": The Jimi Hendrix Experience A185, B3, B7
"One Rose, The": Jimmie Rodgers A266
"One's on the Way": Loretta Lynn A193
"One Step Up": Bruce Springsteen A164
"One Sweet Day": Mariah Carey featuring Boyz II Men AND? A167

"Ones Who Help to Set the Sun, The": Dream Theater A175
"One Thing Leads to Another": The Fixx B24
"One Time Blues": Blind Blake **B26**
"One Time": King Crimson A218
"One Track Mind": The Beatles B8; Bobby Lewis A95
"One Tree Hill": U2 A185
"One Trick Pony": Paul Simon **A93**, B1
"One Way or Another": Blondie **A81**
"One Way Out": The Allman Brothers **A101**, B8
"One Way Road to Love": The Beach Boys B15
"One White Duck/O": Jethro Tull B20
"One You Can't Have, The": The Honeys B15
"On Linger Longer Island": Jack Harris and His Orchestra **A227**
"Only a Fool Would Say That": Steely Dan **A96**
"Only a Lonely Heart Sees": Felix Cavaliere A250
"Only a Matter of Time": Dream Theater A175
"Only a Northern Song": The Beatles A90, B7, B8
"Only a Pawn in Their Game": Bob Dylan B7, B8
"Only Joy in Town, The": Joni Mitchell A260
"Only Living Boy in New York, The": Simon and Garfunkel B1
"Only Living Boy in New York": Simon & Garfunkel A185
"Only Love Can Break Your Heart": Neil Young **A88**, A185, B6
"Only One, The": Transvision Vamp A185
"Only One Reason": All About Eve A185
"Only Shallow": My Bloody Valentine A22, **A177**
"Only Sixteen": Sam Cooke A44
"Only the Good Die Young": Billy Joel B8
"Only the Lonely (Know How I Feel)" A14; Roy Orbison A259, **A270**, B8, B21
"Only the Lonely": T'Pau A185
"Only the Wind": The Pet Shop Boys A174
"Only the Young": Journey A250
"Only Twelve": echolyn **A72**
"Only Wanna Be With You": Hootie and the Blowfish **B24**
"Only You": Child A64; The Platters A53, B21; Ringo Starr B7
"On My Death Bed": George Noble **A240**

"On My My": Ringo Starr B7
"On My Own" **A224**
"On My Radio": Selecter A185
"On Reflection": Gentle Giant A71, A166
"On The Alamo" **B30**
"On the Atcheson, Topeka, and the Santa Fe" B10; Bing Crosby B4
"On the Backs of Angels": Dream Theater A175
"On the Beach": Neil Young B6
"On the Beam" B30
"On the Beat Pete": Madness A185, B20
"On the Bed": George Harrison B7
"On the Bus": Frank Zappa **A60**
"On the Good Ship Lollipop" B10
"On the Limb": Johnny Winter A185
"On the Right Road" A145
"On the Road Again": Canned Heat A185
"On the Road to Mandalay" B10; Frank Sinatra A227
"On the Run": Pink Floyd A99, A199, B29
"On the Sea of Galilee": Carter Family, The A240
"On the Street Where You Live" **A224**
"On the Sunny Side of the Street": A145, B7, B10, B16, **B30**
"On the Western Skyline": Bruce Hornsby and the Range B24
"On With The Dance" **B30**
"On With the Show": The Rolling Stones B29
"Ooby Dooby": Roy Orbison A270
"Oodles of O's": De La Soul B14
"Ooh, Ooh, Ooooh": The Beatles B8
"Ooh Baby Baby": Smokey Robinson and the Miracles B4, B7
"Ooh! My Soul": The Beatles B8; Little Richard A95
"Ooooo": Steve Vai B21
"Oo You": Paul McCartney B8, B18
"Oozlin' Daddy Blues": Bill Cox & Cliff Hobbs A240
"Open Country Joy": Mahavishnu Orchestra A185, B20
"Opening Move": Gryphon **A166**
"Open Letter to the Lyrical Trainspotter, An": Mansun B21
"Open Sesame": Kool and the Gang A179
"Open Up": R.E.O. Speedwagon A185
"Open Up Your Lovin' Arms": The Beatles B8

Song Index

"Open Your Heart": Madonna A258, B13
"Opera Star": Neil Young B6
"Opportunities (Let's Make Lots of Money)": The Pet Shop Boys A174
"Opposites" A14
"Optimistic": Radiohead **A162, A169**
"Opus 17 (Don't You Worry 'Bout Me)": The Four Seasons A93
"Orange Air" B3
"Orange Blossom Special" A191
"Orange County Lumber Truck": The Mothers of Invention **A11**, A27
"Orange Crush": R.E.M. A181
"Orchids in the Moonlight" B30
"Ordinary Day": Vanessa Carlton **B21**
"Ordinary Pain": Stevie Wonder A269
"Oregon Trail": Woody Guthrie A240
"Original Blues": Bayless Rose **B26**
"Original Charleston Strut" A145
"Original Disco Man, The": James Brown A31, B4
"Original of the Species": U2 **A89**
"Original Stack O'Lee Blues": Long "Cleve" Reed and Little Harvey Hull A240
"Orinoco Flow": Enya B21
"Orion": Jethro Tull A185, A188
"Orphans": Deacon Blue A185
"O Sole Mio" B12
"O Superman": Laurie Anderson A182
"Other One, The": The Grateful Dead A99, B7, **B17**
"Ouch!": The Rutles **A69**
"Ou Est Le Soleil": Paul McCartney A185
"Our Boys Will Shine Tonight" B30
"Our Car Club": The Beach Boys B15
"Our Country": John Mellencamp A102
"Our Director" B12
"Our House" [1]: Madness A185, B21
"Our House" [2]: Crosby, Stills, and Nash B7
"Our Love Is Here to Stay" B10
"Our Prayer": The Beach Boys A125, B15; Brian Wilson B15
"Our Sweet Love": The Beach Boys B15
"Our Town" A14
"Our Way Across the Mountain, Ho!" B12
"Our Weekend Starts on Wednesday": Hey Mercedes **A203**
"Out-Bloody-Rageous": The Soft Machine A141

"Outcry": Dream Theater A175
"Out Demons Out": Edgar Broughton Band B20
"Out of Control" [1]: U2 A89
"Out of Control" [2]: L.H. and the Memphis Souls A95
"Out of My Dreams" **B30**
"Out of My Head": Fastball A99
"Out of Nowhere" **B10, B30**
"Out of Sight" A95; James Brown A31, A32, B4, **B19**
"Out of Step (With the World)": Minor Threat **A210**
"Out of the Night": Steve Miller Band A185
"Out of This World" B12, **B30**
"Out of Time": The Rolling Stones B8
"Out of Vogue": The Middle Class A210
"Out on the Tiles": Led Zeppelin A185, **A186**
"Out on the Weekend": Neil Young B6
"Outrage at Valdez": Frank Zappa A11, **A60**
"Outrageous": Paul Simon B1
"Outshined": Soundgarden A55, A221
"Outside Now, Again": Frank Zappa A11
"Outside Now": Frank Zappa A11, A27, **A60**
"Outside of That I Love You" B30
"Outside Woman Blues": Cream A132
"Outta Sight": James Brown A163
"Overkill": Motorhead A185
"Overlap": Ani DiFranco A51
"Over My Head": Fleetwood Mac A101, B24
"Overseas Stomp (Lindberg Hop)" B17
"Overs": Simon and Garfunkel A93, B1
"Over the Hills and Far Away": Led Zeppelin A17, A185
"Over the Rainbow": A168, A196, **B10, B11**, B12, **B19, B24**, B30; Judy Garland **A75**
"Over There" B30
"Overture (to Tommy)": The Who A99, A101
"Overture 1928": Dream Theater A175
"Over You": Aaron Neville A238
"Owner of a Lonely Heart": Yes A71, A72, A104, A261, A269
"Oxford Town": Bob Dylan A58, A184, B7, B8
"Oye Como Va": Santana **A101**, B3
"O Yoko": John Lennon B18

"Packard Goose": Frank Zappa **A60**
"Pack Jam": Jonzun Crew **A104**

"Packt Like Sardines in a Crushd Tin Box":
  Radiohead A17, A135, A162, A233, B21
"Pack Up Your Sins and Go to the Devil" B30
"Pagan Poetry": Bjork A205
"Paid in Full": Eric B. and Rakim A255, B31
"Pain in My Heart" B17; Otis Redding A29
"Pain in My Heart": Otis Redding **A29**
"Pain Is So Close to Pleasure": Queen A221
"Paint It Black": The Rolling Stones A70, A99, A107, A185, A247, B7, B21, B24
"Palaces of Gold": Martin Carthy B20
"Pale Shelter": Tears for Fears A59
"Palesteena" A145, B12
"Palisades Park": The Beach Boys B15; Freddy "Boom-Boom": Cannon B15
"Pal Like You, A" **B30**
"Paloma Blanca, Una": The George Baker Selection B25
"Pamela Jean": The Survivors B15
"Panama": Van Halen A250
"Pan American Blues": DeFord bailey B9
"Pandora's Box": Procol Harum A185
"Panic Attack": Dream Theater A175
"Panic in Detroit": David Bowie A185, B20
"Panic": The Smiths A36
"Panikattack": Plastikman **B5**
"Panique Celtique": Manau B21
"Panj Pind": Panjabi MC A61
"Papa Don't Take No Mess": James Brown A117, A238
"Papa Hobo": Paul Simon B1
"Papa Joe's" *see* "(Down at) Papa Joe's"
"Papa-Oom-Mow-Mow": The Beach Boys B15
"Paparazzi" [1]: Lady Gaga **A84**
"Paparazzi" [2]: Xzibit B14
"Papa's Got a Brand New Bag" A95; James Brown A31, **A32**, A83, A238, A247, B3, B4, **B19**
"Papa Was a Rolling Stone": The Temptations A108, A144, A247
"Pa-paya Mama": Perry Como A238
"Paperback Writer": The Beatles A99, A107, A195, A198, **B7**, B8, B29
"Paper Boy": Roy Orbison A270
"Paper Maché" A147
"Paper Moon" B12
"Paper Wings": Barclay James Harvest A185
"Pappa's Kleine Meid": The Spookrijders B14
"Paprika Plains": Joni Mitchell **A260**

"Paradise City": Guns n' Roses A99, B28
"Paradise": Uriah Heep A185
"Paranoia Blues": Paul Simon B1
"Paranoid" [1]: Black Sabbath **A16, A17, A55,** A99, A167, **B20**, B21, **B31**
"Paranoid" [2]: Grand Funk Railroad B21
"Paranoid Android": Radiohead **A17**, A80, A143, A162, **A169**, A221, A247, A269, B20, B21
"Pardners" A14
"Parker's Band": Steely Dan A96
"Parklife": Blur B21
"Part of Me": The Beach Boys B15
"Party Doll": Buddy Knox A44, A97, A270, B32
"Party Girl": Elvis Costello and the Attractions A185, B4
"Party Hard": Pulp A82
"Party Seacombe": George Harrison B7
"Party that Wrote 'Home, Sweet Home' Never Was a Married Man, The" A145
"Party": The Beatles B8
"Pasilda": Afro Medusa A3
"Passage to Bangkok, A": Rush A28
"Passing By": The Beach Boys A125, B15
"Passing the Time": Cream B7, **B20**
"Passin' Me By": The Pharcyde **A261**, B31
"Passion Play": Joni Mitchell A260
"Pass the Peas": James Brown A238
"Pastime Paradise": Stevie Wonder A144; *see also* "Gangsta's Paradise"
"Patent Leather Boots": Elton Britt A266
"Paths of Victory": The Byrds A121
"Patiently Waiting": 50 Cent A261, **B31**
"Patricia": Perez Prado Orch A97
"Patterns": Paul Simon B1, B3; Simon and Garfunkel B1
"Payback, The": James Brown **A55**
"Payback Is a Bitch": Liz Torres A3
"Pay It Back": Elvis Costello A185
"Pay Roll Blues": Lucille Bogan A240
"Pay Your Price": Motorhead A185
"Peace and Love for All" B12
"Peace Be Still": James Cleveland **A161**
"Peaceful Easy Feeling": The Eagles A38, A173
"Peaceful Valley" **B30**
"Peace in Our Time": Eddie Money A250
"Peace Like a River": Paul Simon B1

Song Index

"Peace of Mind": Boston A101, A219, A247, A250
"Peace Sells. . .But Who's Buying?": Megadeth B28
"Peaches III": Frank Zappa A11
"Peaches and Cream" [1]: Beck A163
"Peaches and Cream" [2]: The Beatles B8; Larry Williams A95
"Peaches En Regalia": Frank Zappa A11
"Peaches": P.U.S.A. A205
"Peach Pickin' Time in Georgia": Jimmie Rodgers A266
"Peach that Tastes the Sweetest Hangs the Highest on the Tree, the" A145
"Peak Hour": The Moody Blues B7
"Peanut Butter" B8
"Peanut Vendor, The": Louis Armstrong A119
"Pearl of the Quarter": Steely Dan **A96**
"Pearls, The": Jelly Roll Morton B7
"Pear Tree": We Were Promised Jetpacks A205
"Pease Porridge": De La Soul B14
"Peggy-O" B17; Simon and Garfunkel B1
"Peggy Sue": Buddy Holly **A37**, A38, A97, A185, A270, B8, **B19**, **B21**, B32
"Peggy Sue Got Married": Buddy Holly A270, B8, **B24**
"Peg o' My Heart" A145, B12, **B30**
"Peg": Steely Dan **A96**, **A225**
"Pelo Telefone" A211
"Penetration": The Stooges A210
"Pennies from Heaven" B10, B19; Bing Crosby **B4**; Billie Holiday **B4**
"Pennroyal Tea": Nirvana A205
"Penny Lane" A94, B8; The Beatles A69, A70, A74, **A75**, **A76**, A77, A84, A90, A98, A99, A101, A134, A185, A195, A198, A234, A248, A253, **B7**, **B18**, B19, B21, B32
"Penthouse Serenade" **B30**
"People Are Strange": Doors A185
"People Get Ready": The Impressions A32, A80, A108, A247
"People Got to Be Free": The Rascals A43, **B3**
"People Need Love": ABBA B25
"People Say": The Dixie Cups A95
"People's Parties": Joni Mitchell **A260**
"People Will Say We're in Love" B30
"Peppermint Twist": The Beatles B8; Joey Dee and the Starliters A95, B24
"Percy's Song": Bob Dylan A58

"Peregrine": Donovan B7
"Perfect Day, A" B30
"Perfect Day Elise, A": PJ Harvey A223
"Perfect Day": Lou Reed B21
"Perfect Kiss, The": New Order **A236**
"Perfect Nanny, The" A202
"Personality" A14
"Persona non Grata": Frank Zappa A12
"Peter Gun": Ray Anthony A44
"Peter Piper" B30
"Pet Sounds (Run James Run)": The Beach Boys **A160**
"Pet Sounds": Brian Wilson B15
"Phenagen": Public Image Ltd B20
"Philly Dog": The Mar-Keys A29
"Phoenix": Wishbone Ash A19
"Photograph" [1]: Ringo Starr B7
"Photograph" [2]: Def Leppard A250
"Physical Presence": Level 42 A185, B21
"Piano Concerto 1": Keith Emerson A166
"Piano Man": Doc Browne A185; Billy Joel A167, B21, B24
"Picasso Moon": The Grateful Dead B17
"Picasso": The Beatles B7
"Piccolino, The" B10, B12
"Pick a Bale of Cotton": Leadbelly B8
"Pickin' Petals Off O Daisies" **A120**
"Pickin' Up the Pieces": Poco **A173**
"Pick Poor Robin Clean" A145
"Pick Yourself Up" B12, B30
"Picnic" B30
"Picture of You, A": The Beatles B8
"Picture Perfect": echolyn A72
"Pictures of a City": King Crimson **A152**
"Pictures of Lily": The Who A185, B7
"Pictures of Matchstick Men": Status Quo B7
"Piece of My Heart": Big Brother & The Holding Company **A101**, B21; Nazareth B21
"Piece of the Pie": Randy Newman **A102**
"Pierce the Air": Sleepy Eyes of Death **A204**
"Piggies": The Beatles **A63**, A90, A98, B7, B8, B18, B20
"Piggy in the Middle": The Rutles A69
"Pig-Me & the Whore": Jethro Tull A185
"Pigs, Sheep and Wolves": Paul Simon B1
"Pigs Is Pigs": Every Time I Die **A203**
"Pigs on the Wing": Pink Floyd **A83**, B21
"Piku": Chemical Brothers **B5**

"Pilgrim's Progress": Procol Harum A185, B21
"Pilgrims": Van Der Graaf Generator **B21**
"Pill, The": Loretta Lynn A173
"Pillow for Your Head": The Beatles B7
"Pills and Soap": Elvis Costello and the Attractions **B4**
"P.I.M.P.": 50 Cent A99
"Pinball Wizard": The Who **A63**, A99, A141, A167, A185, B24
"Pinch Me": The Barenaked Ladies B24
"Pinetop's Boogie Woogie": Pinetop Smith A53
"Ping Pong Affair": The Slits B20
"Pinhead": The Ramones A210
"Pink Drink": Guided By Voices **A243**
"Pinwheel twist": The Beatles B8
"Pipi-pipippee" B12
"Pirate Jenny" B12
"Pirate of Penace, The": Joni Mitchell **A260**
"Pirates": Emerson, Lake and Palmer A71, A149
"Piss Factory": Patti Smith A124
"Pistol Packin' Papa": Jimmie Rodgers A266
"Pitter Patter": The Beach Boys B15
"PKNB": ADF A61
"Place in the Sun, A": Stevie Wonder A185
"Place to Be": Nick Drake A221
"Plague of Lighthouse Keepers, A": Van der Graaf Generator A207, B20
"Planet Rock": Afrika Bambaattaa **A104**, **B31**
"Planet Telex": Radiohead A85, **A169**
"Plastic People": The Mothers of Invention A11, A27, A99
"Playa Hater": Notorious B.I.G. B14
"Play a Simple Melody" B30; Bing Crosby B4
"Play at Your Own Risk": Planet Patrol A104
"Playboy Mansion, The": U2 A89
"Players Anthem": Junior M.A.F.I.A. B22
"Play Fiddle Play" B12
"Playground Twist": Siouxsie and the Banshees A185, B20
"Playing in the Band": Grateful Dead A221
"Play in Time": Jethro Tull A188
"Play That Barber Shop Chord" A145, **B30**
"Play That Funky Music": Wild Cherry **A55**, **A84**, A123, B24
"Play Your Part": Girl Talk A24
"Pleading" A145
"Pleasant Valley Sunday": The Monkees A99, A182

"Please, Please, Please": James Brown A238, A247
"Please" [1]: U2 A89
"Please" [2]: Bing Crosby B8
"Please Don't Bring Your Banjo Back": The Beatles B7
"Please Don't Drag That String Around": Elvis Presley B19
"Please Don't Tease": Cliff Richard B20
"Please Don't Tell My Wife" A145
"Please Go Home": The Rolling Stones **B3**, B8
"Please Let Me Wonder": The Beach Boys A160, B15
"Please Mr. Postman": The Beatles A24, A259, B8, B20; The Marvelettes A24, A43, A95, A110, A259, B20, B21
"Please Please Me" A97; The Beatles A69, **A91**, A98, A107, **A107**, **A124**, A195, A196, A198, A259, B4, B7, **B8**, **B16**, **B24**
"Please Send Me Someone to Love": The Moonglows A110
"Please Tell Me Why": Dave Clark Five A107
"Pledging My Love": Johnny Ace A270, B32
"Plenty of Jam Jars": The Ravellers B7
"P.L.K. Special" A145
"Plush": Stone Temple Pilots **A22**
"Pocahontas": Neil Young B6
"Pocketful of Miracles" A14
"Pocky-a-way": Meters A185
"Poem on the Underground Wall, A": Simon and Garfunkel B1
"Poems, Prayers, and Promises": John denver A182
"Poet's Justice": Uriah Heep A185
"Poinciana": Bing Crosby B4; Ahmad Jamal A238
"Point Me at the Sky": Pink Floyd A68, A198
"Poison": Alice Cooper A185
"Poison Ivy": The Coasters A77, **A84**, B8, **B25**
"Poker Chant" B12
"Poker Face": Lady Gaga A219, A232
"Police and Thieves": The Clash A118, A210; Junior Murvin A231
"Politician": Cream A132, B20
"Politicians in My Eyes": Death A210
"Politik": Coldplay A205
"Polka Dots and Moonbeams" A14, B30; The Four Freshmen B15
"Polly": Nirvana A124

Song Index

"Polly Perkins" B27
"Polythene Pam": The Beatles **A92, A116,** A149, **B7**, B8, B18
"Pomona for Empusa": Park A205
"Pompanola" **A120**
"Pom-Pom Play Girl": The Beach Boys B15
"Pony Blues": Charley Patton **B26, B27**
"Pool of Love": Les baxter A160
"Poontang Little, Poontang Small": Jimmie Strothers A240
"Poor Baby" B12
"Poorboy Shuffle": Creedence Clearwater **B3**
"Poor Butterfly" **B30**
"Poor Little Fool": Ricky Nelson A44, A97, B8
"Poor Man's Blues": Bessie Smith **B26**
"Poor Man's Roses, A": Patsy Cline A53
"Poor Me": Fats Domino **B25**; Adam Faith A259
"Poor You" **B30**
"Pop Goes the Weasel" **B27**
"Pop": N*Sync A24
"Pop Song 89": R.E.M. A181
"Porcupine": Echo & Bunnymen A185
"Porgy and Bess" B10
"Porrohman": Big Country A185
"Positively 4th Street": The Byrds A121; Bob Dylan B7
"Possession": Sarah McLachlan A154
"Postman": Living Colour B21
"Post-Modern Highrise Table Top Stomp": The Grateful Dead B17
"Pot, The": Tool A17
"Potter's Wheel": John Denver B21
"Pound for a Brown (On the Bus), A": The Mothers of Invention **A12**, A27, A60
"Pourquoi Es Tu Devenue Si Raisonnable?": The Wedding Present A123
"Pour Some Sugar on Me": Def Leppard A185, B20
"Powderfinger": Neil Young A88, A99, B6
"Power, The": Snap **B21**
"Power of Love " Huey Lewis A250
"Power to the People": John Lennon/Plastic Ono Band A185, B18
"Pow R. Toc H.": Pink Floyd A185, B7
"Prairie Lullaby": Jimmie Rodgers A266
"Praise You": Fatboy Slim B24
"Pravus": Meshuggah A175
"Prayer" B30

"Pray for Surf": The Honeys B15
"Preacher and the Slave, The" ["Pie in the Sky When You Die"]: Joe Hill B25
"Precious Angel": Bob Dylan A180, A185
"Precious Lord" *see* "Take My Hand, Precious Lord"
"Precious": The Jam A185, B20
"Predatory Wasp of the Palisades Is Out to Get Us!, The": Sufjan Stevens A205, A221
"Prelude": Chicago B3
"Prelude to a Kiss" A147, **A224, B10, B30**
"Prelude to the Afternoon of a Sexually Aroused Gas Mask": Mothers of Invention, The A11
"Pre-Road Downs": Crosby, Stills, and Nash B7
"Presente": El Aficiao A3
"Pressed in a Book": The Shins **A22**
"Pressed Rat and Warthog": Cream B20
"Prettiest Star, The": David Bowie **A83**, A185, B21
"Pretty Baby" A145, **B30**
"Pretty Ballerina": The Left Banke **A97**, A99, B7
"Pretty Boy": Randy Newman **A264**
"Pretty Flamingo": Manfred Mann B8, B21
"Pretty Girl Is Like a Melody, A" B30
"Pretty Little Baby": Marvin Gaye A32, A95, A110
"Pretty Mama Blues": Ivory Joe Hunter A53
"Pretty One": Roy Orbison A270
"Pretty Peggy-O": Bob Dylan A216
"Pretty Polly" **B27**
"Pretty Thing" [1]: Bo Diddley A38
"Pretty Vacant": The Sex Pistols A99, A124, A235, B4
"Pretty Woman" *see* "Oh, Pretty Woman"
"Pretzel Logic": Steely Dan **A96**
"Price of Love": Victor Calderone A3
"Pride (In the Name of Love)": U2 A103, A185
"Pride and Joy": Marvin Gaye A32, A108, A110, B8; Stevie Ray Vaughn A250
"Pride": Living Colour A99
"Priest, The": Joni Mitchell **A260**
"Primrose Hill": Madness A185
"Primrose Lane": Jerry Wallace A160
"Prison Bound Blues": Leroy Carr **B26**
"Prisoner of Love": David Bowie B20
"Prison Sex": Tool A205
"Prison Song": System of a Down B21
"Private Eyes": Hall and Oates A250

"Private Number": Judy Clay and William Bell A29, A185
"Private Sorrow": Pretty Things B21
"Problems": The Everly Brothers A97
"Proclamation": Gentle Giant A185
"Prodigal Son": Johnny Winter A185
"Progress?": Frank Zappa and the Mothers of Invention A11, A12
"Prohibition Blues" A145; Clayton McMichen A240
"Prologue" B3
"Promenade" [1]: U2 A185, B20
"Promenade" [2]: Emerson, Lake, & Palmer B20
"Promised Land": Cast **B20**
"Promises, Promises" B3
"Proof": Paul Simon B1, B32
"Prophets of War": Dream Theater A175
"Props Over Here": The Beatnuts B14
"Prose": echolyn **A72**
"Prospects": Madness A185, B20
"Prospeto's Speech": Loreena McKennitt B21
"Proud Mary" A97; Creedence Clearwater Revival A43, A99, A142, A185, A247, B20, B24; Ike and Tina Turner A43
"Prove Yourself": Radiohead **A169**
"Providence": King Crimson B20
"Prowling Night Hawk": Robert Lee McCoy A240
"PS I Love You": The Beatles A69, A96, **A97**, A98, A99, A107, A167, A195, B7, B8
"Psychedelic Shack": The Temptations A95
"Psycho Killer": Talking Heads **A83**, A99
"Psychotron": Megadeath A97
"Public Enemy No. 1": Public Enemy B21
"Puff": Kenny Lynch B8
"Pulk/Pull Revolving Doors": Radiohead A135
"Pull Harder on the Strings of Your Martyr": Trivium B21
"Pullman Porter's Parade" A145
"Pull Me Under": Dream Theater A175
"Pull Up the Roots": Talking Heads A185
"Pump It Up": Elvis Costello and the Attractions A185, B4
"Punchline": The Beach Boys B15
"Punch Up at a Wedding, A": Radiohead **A169**
"Punky's Dilemma": Simon and Garfunkel B1, B3
"Punky's Whips": Frank Zappa A27
"Puppies": The Incredible String Band **A112**

"Puppy Love": Donny Osmond B21
"Purple Bottle, The": Animal Collective A205
"Purple Haze": The Jimi Hendrix Experience A17, A43, A75, A80, **A83**, A101, A144, A159, A247, **A257**, B7, B24, B28, **B29**, B32
"Purple People Eater, The": B16; Sheb Wooley A97
"Purple Pills": D12 A146
"Purple Rain": Prince **A17**, A80, A247
"Purple Smoke": U Totem A81
"Purpostus" A145
"Push and Pull" *see* "(Do the) Push and Pull"
"Pusher, The": Steppenwolf **A85**
"Pushin' Too Hard": Seeds, The A43
"Push It" [1]: Garbage B20, B21
"Push It" [2]: Salt-n-Pepa A24
"Push It Along": A Tribe Called Quest **A1**
"Push It Like a Dog": Soulwax **A24**
"Pushit": Tool **A205**
"Push": Prince A79, **B13**
"Pussy Willow": Jethro Tull A185
"Put It There": Paul McCartney B8
"Put Me Off at Buffalo" A145
"Put on a Happy Face" B12
"Put on Your Tat-Ta Little Girlie" **B19** B19
"Put the Blame on Mame" B12
"Putting on the Style": The Quarrymen B8
"Puttin' on the Ritz": A168, A227, B10, B12, B30
"Put Your Dreams Away" B10
"Put Your Mind at Ease": Every Mother's Son A99
"Put Yourself in my Place": Isley Brothers A185
"Pyramid Song": Radiohead **A135**, A162, **A206**

"Quality": Paul Simon B1
"Quarter to Three": The Beatles B8
"Queen and Country": Jethro Tull **A186**
"Queen and the Soldier, The": Suzanne Vega B21
"Queen Bitch": David Bowie A185, B21
"Queen Is Dead, The": The Smiths A36
"Queen Jane Approximately": Bob Dylan B7
"Queen of the New Year": Deacon Blue A185
"Que Rico el Mambo": Perez Prado A238
"Que Sera Sera": Doris Day **B21**; Mary Hopkin B7

Song Index

"Questions 67 and 68": Chicago B24
"Question": The Moody Blues A101
"Que Te Gusta": 2nd Tribe A3
"Quick Joey Small": Slaughter and the Dogs A210
"Quick One, While He's Away, A": The Who B7
"Quicksand" [1]: Martha and the Vandellas **A106, A108**
"Quicksand" [2]: David Bowie **A83**
"Quien Será" B12
"Quiet" B12; Paul Simon B1
"Quiet Night" B10, **B30**
"Quiet Village": Les Baxter A160; Martin Denny A160
"Quizás" **B25**; Nat King Cole B25; Osvaldo Farrés B25

"Rabbi's Daughter, A" B12
"Race Through Space": Toyah A185
"Rachel": Pete Morton B21
"Raconteur Troubadour": Gentle Giant A166, B20
"Radar Love": Golden Earring **A16**
"Radio Play": John Lennon and Yoko Ono B7
"Radio Sweetheart": Elvis Costello B4
"Radio Times": Henry Hall and the BBC Dance Orchestra A227
"Ragdoll": Aerosmith A250
"Raggamuffin": Shabba Ranks **A61**
"Ragged William" A145
"Ragged Wood": The Fleet Foxes A205
"Ragging the Baby to Sleep" A145
"Rags to Riches": Tony Bennett B21
"Ragtime Annie" A145
"Ragtime Cowboy Joe" A145
"Ragtime Regiment Band" A145
"Ragtime Texas": Henry Thomas A58
"Ragtime Yodling [sic] Man, The" A266
"Railroad Bill" A240; Will Bennett A240; Frank Hutchison A240; Brownie McGhee A240; The Quarrymen B8
"Railroad Blues" A145
"Rain" [1]: The Beatles A70, **A90**, A98, A107, **A107**, A195, A198, B7, B8, B20, B21
"Rain" [2]: Poundhound **A55**
"Rainbow Eyes": Brian Wilson B15
"Rainbow": Russ Hamilton A97
"Rain Dance": Big Country A185
"Raindrops" [1]: Joel Melson A270

"Raindrops" [2]: The Honeys B15
"Raindrops Keep Fallin' on My Head" **B3**; B.J. Thomas A249
"Raining in My Heart": Buddy Holly A99, B8, B21
"Rain or Shine": Five Star A185
"Rain Song, The": Led Zeppelin A99, A185, A269
"Rain When I Die": Alice in Chains A221
"Rainy Day, Dream Away": The Jimi Hendrix Experience A17, B3
"Rainy Day Man": James Taylor B3
"Rainy Day Women #12 & 35": Bob Dylan A141, B7, B27
"Rainy Night House": Joni Mitchell **A260**
"Raised on Robbery": Joni Mitchell A260
"Raise Your Hand": Eddie Floyd A29
"Raising Hell": Run-DMC A99
"Raisins and Almonds" B12
"Ramble On": Procol Harum A185
"Rambling On": Procol Harum A185
"Ramblin' Man": The Allman Brothers band B24
"Ramblin' on My Mind": Robert Johnson A8; John Mayall (with Eric Clapton) A256
"Ramblin' Woman": The Beatles B7
"Ramona" B8
"Ram On": Paul McCartney B7, B18
"Ramrod": Duane Eddy B8
"Rape Me": Nirvana **A177, A202**
"Rapid Transit": Neil Young B6
"Rapper's Delight": The Sugarhill Gang A24, A261, B14, B31
"Rapture": Blondie A39, B14, **B24**
"Rapunzel": Pete Christlieb / Wayne Marsh Quintet A96
"Rational Gaze": Meshuggah **A208**
"Rattle Snake Daddy": Homer Callahan A240
"Rat Trap": The Boomtown Rats **A64**, A185, B20
"Raunchy": Ernie Freeman A97; Bill Justis Orch A44, A97, B8
"Rave On": Buddy Holly A247; Johnny and the Moondogs B8
"Ray of Light": Madonna A39
"Ray's Dad's Cadillac": Joni Mitchell A260
"Razamanaz": Nazareth A185
"Razor Love": Neil Young B6
"Razzamanazz": Nazareth B20

"RDNZL": Frank Zappa **A60**
"Reach Out I'll Be There": The Four Tops A99, **A106, A108**, A185, B7, B8, B21
"Reach Out of the Darkness": Friend and Lover A99
"React": Eric Sermon A61
"Ready Teddy": The Beatles B8; Little Richard A95
"Realest Killaz": 50 Cent B31
"Realest Niggaz": 50 Cent B31
"Real Gone Kid": Deacon Blue A185
"Real Life (I Never Was the Same Again)": Jeff Carson A191
"Real Love": The Beatles **B7**
"Really Free": John Otway & Wild Willy Barrett A185
"Really Gonna Rock": Gary Moore A185
"Real Slim Shady, The": Eminem A99, A146
"Real Turned On": Uriah Heep A185
"Reaper, The" see "(Don't Fear) the Reaper"
"Reason to Believe": Rod Stewart A185
"Re-Awakening": Peter Hammill A185
"Rebecca" B12
"Rebecca Lynn": Bryan White A191
"Rebel Girl": Bikini Kill A210
"Rebel Rouser": Duane Eddy A44
"Rebel-'Rouser": The Beatles B8
"Rebel Waltz": The Clash A221, B20
"Rebel Warrior": ADF A61
"Rebel Without a Pause": Public Enemy A39, A99
"Rebel Yell": Billy Idol A55
"Rebirth of Slick (Cool like Dat)": Diagable Planets **B31**
"Reborn": Walt J **B5**
"Recess in Heaven": Dan Grissom A53
"Reckless Blues": Bessie Smith featuring Louis Armstrong A48
"Reckoner": Radiohead **A206**
"Recreation": Bob and Sheri B15
"Red, Red, Rose, A" B27
"Red, White, and Blue Got the Golden Band" **A238**
"Red Bank Boogie": Count Basie A105
"Redemption": Blood, Sweat and Tears B3
"Redemption Day": Sheryl Crow A247
"Redemption Song": Bob Marley & The Wailers A80, A247
"Red Fox, The": Big Country A185

"Red Hill Mining Town": U2 A103, A185, A223, B20
"Red Hot": The Beatles B8
"Red House": The Jimi Hendrix Experience A256, A257
"Red Is the New Black": Funeral for a Friend A205
"Red": King Crimson A28, A208, A224, B21
"Red Lady Too": George Harrison **B7**
"Red Light Special": TLC B32
"Red Pepper: A Spicy Rag" A145
"Red Rain": Peter Gabriel A235
"Red Red Wine": UB40 A185
"Red River Rock": Johnny and the Hurricanes A44, A185
"Red Rubber Ball": The Cyrkle B8
"Red Sails": David Bowie A185
"Red Sails in the Sunset" B8, B12; Fats Domino A95
"Red Shoes" see "(The Angels Wanna Wear My) Red Shoes"
"Red Wing" A145
"Reel Around the Fountain": The Smiths A36, A185
"Reelin' and Rockin'" B7; The Beatles B8; Chuck Berry A95
"Reelin' in the Years": Steely Dan A43, **A96**
"Reese Crenshaw": John Henry **A239**
"Reet Petite": Jackie Wilson A185
"Reflections of My Life": Marmalade A185, B7
"Reflections": The Supremes A95
"Refugee": Tom Petty and the Heartbreakers A75, **A246**, B24
"Refuge of the Roads": Joni Mitchell A260
"Regatta de Blanc": The Police A235
"Regulate": Warren G. and Nate Dogg B31
"Rehab": Amy Winehouse B21
"Rejoyce": Jefferson Airplane A43, **B3**
"Relax" [1]: Frankie Goes to Hollywood A232, B24
"Relax" [2]: Leon Redbone A185
"Relic Mix, A": Derrick May A104
"Re-Make/Re-Model": Roxy Music A185
"Remember (Walkin' in the Sand)": The Shangri-Las A95, B7
"Remember a Day": Pink Floyd A99, A198
"Remember": John Lennon **B18**
"Remember Love": Plastic Ono Band B7
"Remember Me" [1]: British Sea Power B21

"Remember Me?" [2]: Eminem A146
"Remember the Time": Michael Jackson **A21**
"Remember Who You Are and What You Represent" B12
"Remembrance Day": Big Country A185
"Reminiscing" [1]: Buddy Holly **B8**
"Reminiscing" [2]: Little River Band **A250**
"Remniscin' in Tempo": Duke Ellington **A263**
"René and Georgette Magritte with Their Dog after the War": Paul Simon A21, A93, A124, B1
"Renegade": Styx **A16**, A141, A167
"Repentance": Dream Theater A175
"Repent Walpurgis": Procol Harum B7
"Requiem": King Crimson A185
"Rescue Me": Fontella Bass A95, A185
"Respectable": Mel & Kim A185
"Respect": Aretha Franklin A32, A80, **A170**, A185, A247, B21, B32; Otis Redding A29, A32, A95, **A170**, B8, B32, **B19**
"Respect Yourself": The Staple Singers A29, A144, A185
"Respiration": Black Star A158
"Rest in Peace": Gary Moore A185
"Restless" **B30**
"Restrospect for Life": Common B14
"Return of the B-Boy": The Pharcyde B31
"Return of the Gay Caballero, The" B12
"Return of the Giant Hogweed, The": Genesis A232
"Return of the Son of Monster Magnet, The": Mothers of Invention, The A11
"Return the Gift": Gang of Four A185, B20
"Return to Jericho": ADF A61
"Return to Me": Dean Martin A97
"Return to Sender": Elvis Presley A99, A185
"Reuben Oh Reuben": Emry Arthur A240
"Reuben Rag" A145
"Revelation (Mother Earth)": Ozzy Osbourne A97
"Revenue Man Blues": Charley Patton **A240**
"Reviewing the Situation" B12
"Revival": The Allman Brothers B7
"Revo-Lution, The": Rachel and the Revolvers B15
"Revolution": The Beatles A76, A92, A98, A100, A185, A195, B7, B8, B17, B18, B29
"Revolution 9": The Beatles A24, A92, A98, A99, A138, A157, A234, **B7**, B18, B20, B21

"Revolution Blues": Neil Young **B6**
"Revolution Rock": The Clash A118
"Revolution Will Not Be Televised, The": Gil-Scott Heron A82
"Reynardine": Fairport Convention A185
"Rhapsody in Blue" B10, B30
"Rhiannon": Fleetwood Mac A101, A185, B24
"Rhumbola" A145
"Rhymin' and Stealin'": The Beastie Boys A99
"Rhymin' Man": Frank Zappa A27
"Rhythm Is a Dancer": Snap **A21**
"Rhythm": Major Lance **A108**
"Rhythm of the Heat": Peter Gabriel A185, B20, B21
"Rhythm of the Night": DeBarge B24
"Rhythm of the Rain": The Cascades B25
"Rhythm of the Saints, The": Paul Simon B1
"Ribbon in the Sky": Stevie Wonder **A236**
"Richard Cory": Simon and Garfunkel B1
"Rich or Poor" B10
"Riddle, The": Nik Kershaw A185, B20, B21
"Ride a White Swan": T. Rex A185, B20
"Ride Cowboy Ride": Bon Jovi A185
"Ride My Llama": Neil Young A99, B6
"Ride My See Saw": The Moody Blues B7
"Ride on Time": Black Box A212, B21
"Riders on the Storm": The Doors **A16**, A39, A43, **A86**, A167, A185
"Ride the Wild Surf": Jan and Dean A109, B15
"Ride Wit Me": Nelly A99
"Ride Your Pony": Lee Dorsey A95, B8
"Riding on that Train Forty-Five": Wade Mainer A240
"Riding on the Wind": Judas Priest A99
"Riding the Scree": Genesis A142
"Ridin' the Storm Out": REO Speedwagon A43, A185, A246, B24
"Riffin' at the Ritz" A145
"Right as the Rain" **B30**
"Right Church but the Wrong Pew, the" A145
"Right": David Bowie B20
"Right Here, Right Now": Jesus Jones B20
"Right On": Marvin Gaye A185
"Right Profile, The": The Clash A118
"Right Round": Flo Rida featuring Ke$ha A232
"Right Thing to Do, The": Carly Simon A99, B24
"Rigor Mortis": Meters B21
"Rikki Don't Lose That Number": Steely Dan **A96**, A101, A247, **A248**, B21, B24

"Rimmin' at the Baths": Automatic Pilot A6
"Ring My Bell": Anita Ward **A42**, B21
"Ringo, I Love You": Bonnie Jo Mason (Cher) A259
"Ringo Boy": Dori Peyton A259
"Ring of Fire": Johnny Cash A7, A247
"Ringo's Theme (This Boy)": Beatles, The **A263**
"Ring Out Solstice Bells": Jethro Tull B20
"Ring Ring": ABBA A20, **B25**
"Ring Tail Tom": Cliff Carlisle A266
"Ring the Living Bell": Melanie A185
"Rio": Duran Duran **A248**
"Rio Grande": Brian Wilson B15
"Riot in Cell Block #9": The Robins A77
"Ripcord": Radiohead A17, **A169**
"Ripeness": Echo & Bunnymen A185
"Rip It Up" B8; The Beatles B7; Little Richard A83
"Ripple": The Grateful Dead B17
"Rise": Gabrielle A123; *see also* "Knockin' on Heaven's Door"
"Rise and Fall": Madness A185
"Rise in the Coals, The": Ned Corvan **B19**
"Rise 'N' Shine" **B30**
"Rishi Kesh Song, The": John Lennon B7
"Rita Mae": Eric Clapton A185
"Rite of Passage, A": Dream Theater A175
"River, The" [1]: PJ Harvey A223
"River, The" [2]: Bruce Springsteen **A122**
"River, The" [3]: Gentle Giant **B20**
"Riverboat Song": Ocean Colour Scene B20
"River Deep, Mountain High": Ike & Tina Turner A80, A247, B21
"River": Joni Mitchell **A260**
"River Man": Nick Drake A221
"River of Tears": Eric Clapton A221
"Rivers of Babylon": The Melodians **A222**
"Road, The": Chicago B3
"Roadhouse Blues": Doors A43, A185
"Road Movie to Berlin": They Might Be Giants A185
"Road Runner" [1] *see* "I'm a Road Runner"
"Road Runner" [2]: The Modern Lovers B4
"Road Runner" [3]: The Beatles B8; Bo Diddley A95, A198, B7
"Roadrunner": The Modern Lovers A210
"Road to Hell, The": Chris Rea A185, B20, B21
"Road to Morocco, The" A14
"Road to Our Dream": T'Pau A185

"Road to Your Soul": All About Eve A185
"Roam": The B-52's A99
"Robbery, Assault, and Battery": Genesis **A142**
"Robots, The": Kraftwerk B21
"Roc Boys": Jay-Z B31
"Rock-a-Bye Baby" **B27**
"Rock All Night Long": The Ravens A53
"Rock All Our Babies to Sleep": Jimmie Rodgers A266
"Rock-a My Soul in the Bosom of Abraham" B12
"Rock and Roll All Nite": Kiss A85
"Rock and Roll Bash": The Beach Boys B15
"Rock and Roll": Led Zeppelin A17, **A17**, A83, A101, A247, B21
"Rock and Roll Music": The Beatles A98, A247, B7, B8; Chuck Berry A76, A95, **A246**, B15, **B24**
"Rock Around the Clock" A76, B7; Bill Haley and His Comets A44, A75, A97, A99, A167, A185, A246, A247, B15, **B20**, B21, B24
"Rockaway Baby" B12
"Rock Climber": Gentle Giant A185
"Rocked in the Cradle of the Deep" B19 B19
"Rockestra Theme": Paul McCartney WINGS? A198
"Rocket 88": Delta Rhythm Kings B32
"Rocket": Def Leppard A185
"Rocket Man": Elton John A99, A167, A248, **B24**
"Rock House": Roy Orbison A270
"Rockin' and Tumblin'": Cream B19
"Rockin' Chair" **B30**; Louis Armstrong **A119**
"Rocking Surfer, The": The Beach Boys B15
"Rockin' in the Free World": Neil Young A80, A88, A247, B6
"Rockin' Pneumonia and the Boogie-Woogie Flu": Huey "Piano": Smith A44, A238
"Rockin' Robin": Bobby Day A44, A97
"R.O.C.K. in the U.S.A.": John Cougar Mellencamp **A16, A85**
"Rock Island": Jethro Tull A185, B21
"Rock Island Line": Chris Barber Band A132; Lonnie Denegan A132, B7, B8, B21
"Rockit": Herbie Hancock A55, **A101**
"Rock Lobster": The B-52's A17, A93, A202, A247
"Rockmaker": Toto A185
"Rock Me Amadeus": Falco **A202**

Song Index

"Rock'n Me": Steve Miller Band **A16**, A185, **A246**, B24
"Rock 'n' Roll Heaven": Righteous Brothers A43
"Rock 'n' Roll Nigger": Patti Smith A210
"Rock 'n' Roll Star": Oasis A99, B21
"Rock 'n' Roll Suicide": David Bowie A185
"Rock 'n' Roll With Me": David Bowie A185, B20
"Rock of Ages" A219
"Rock & Roll Hoochie Koo": Johnny Winter A185
"Rocks, Tonic, Juice, Magic": Save the Day **A205**
"Rock Show": Paul McCartney and Wings B24
"Rocks on the Road": Jethro Tull A188
"Rock the Joint": Jimmy Preston **A26**
"Rock This Country": Shania Twain A193
"Rockville" *see* "(Don't Go Back to) Rockville"
"Rocky Mountain Way": Joe Walsh A43, **A55**
"Rock You Like a Hurricane": Scorpions **A16**, **A85**
"Rock Your Baby": George McCrae B21
"Rocky Raccoon": The Beatles B7, B18
"Rocky Road Blues": Bill Monroe A210
"Roll Along Kentucky Moon": Jimmie Rodgers A266
"Roll and Tumble Blues": "Hambone": Willie Newbern **B26**
"Roll Another Number for the Road": Neil Young B6
"Roll Away the Stone": Mott the Hoople A185, B21
"Roll Dem bones": Bing Crosby B4
"Roll 'Em Pete": Joe Turner A240
"Roller Skating Child": The Beach Boys B15
"Rollin' and Tumblin' ": Muddy Waters **A132**, A210, **A246**
"Rolling and Rambling": Emmylou Harris **A190**; Robin and Linda Williams **A190**
"Roll Me Away": Bob Seger A250
"Roll Me Over in the Clover" B27
"Roll on Down the Highway": Bachman-Turner Overdrive B24
"Roll on Silver Moon": May McDonald A266; George P. Watson A266
"Roll Out the Barrel" B12
"Roll Over Beethoven" A104; The Beatles A254, B7, **B8**, B18; Chuck Berry A44, A80, A95, A167, A247, B8, B18, B21, **B24**; Electric Light Orchestra A43, B19
"Roll Plymouth Rock": Brian Wilson B15, B21
"Roll Right": Rage Against the Machine A205
"Roll Them Cotton Bales" A145
"Roll to Me": Del Amitri B24
"Roll With It": Oasis B24
"Roll with the Changes": REO Speedwagon A250
"Romance Is Dead": Parkway Drive A205
"Romantic Warrior": Return to Forever A73
"Romany Life" B12
"Romeo and Juliet": Dire Straits A185, B21
"Rome Wasn't Built in a Day": Al White and his HiLiters **A53**
"Ronde de Florette" B12
"Ronnie": The Four Seasons A99, A160
"Roof Is Leaking, The": Phil Collins A185
"Room in Heaven for Me": Carter Family, The A240
"Room Without Windows, A" B12
"Rooster, The": OutKast **A1**
"Root": Deftones **A205**
"Rosalie" B30
"Rosalinda's Eyes": Billy Joel B24
"Rosalita (Come Out Tonight)": Bruce Springsteen A269
"Rosanna": Toto A43, A250
"Rosa Parks": OutKast A99
"Rose, The": Bette Midler **A167**; Bianca Ryan A167
"Roseland Shuffle (Shoeshine Boy)": Count Basie **A263**
"Rosenbaum" B12
"Rose Room" A145, **B30**
"Roses" [1]: OutKast A99
"Roses" [2]: Nik Kershaw A185
"Roses Are Red (My Love)": The Beatles B8
"Roses Blue": Joni Mitchell **A260**
"Rosetta": The Fourmost B7, B8
"Rose von Chile, Die" B25
"Rosie": Joan Armatrading A136
"Roslagsvår" **B25**
"Rough Boy": ZZ Top A250
"Rough Music": Eliza Carthy B21
"Rough Ride": Paul McCartney A185
"Roundabout": Yes **A17**, A71, A99, **A101**, A224, **A229**, B20, B21
"Round and Round" [1]: Neil Young B6

"Round and Round" [2]: Perry Como A97, A99
"Round": Jethro Tull **A166**
"Round Midnight": Thelonius Monk A96
"Row Jimmy": The Grateful Dead A99
"Row! Row! Row!" A145
"Roxanne": The Police A185, A234, **A235**, B21
"Royal Garden Blues" A145, B16
"Royal Orleans": Led Zeppelin A185
"Royal Scam, The": Steely Dan A96
"Royla Orleans": Led Zeppelin B20
"Rubber Ball": Bobby Vee A185
"Rubber Bullets": 10cc B21
"Rubber Dolly": Woody Guthrie A240
"Rubber Ring": The Smiths A36, A143
"Rubber Shirt": Frank Zappa A11
"Ruby Baby": The Drifters A85
"Ruby Tuesday": Nazareth B21; The Rolling Stones A99, A233, B21
"Rudie Can't Fail": The Clash A118
"Rue the Day" **B27**
"Ruff Johnson's Harmony Band" A145
"Rumba": Armand van Helden A3
"Rumble": Link Wray B15
"Run, James, Run": Brian Wilson B15
"Run, Red, Run": The Coasters A77, B15
"Run-Around": Blues Traveler B24
"Run-Around Lover": Sharon Marie B15
"Runaway" [1]: The Beatles B8; Del Shannon A43, A99, A160, A167, A185, **A241**, B15, **B24**
"Runaway" [2]: Bon Jovi **A250**
"Runaway Child, Running Wild": The Temptations **A105**, A144
"Runaway Train": Soul Asylum **B24**
"Run for Your Life": The Beatles A92, A98, **A253**, B7, B8
"Run Home Slow": Frank Zappa A60
"Run Joe": Louis Jordan A53, **B25**
"Run": Leona Lewis B21
"Runnin' Down a Dream": Tom Petty A250
"Runnin'": Eminem **B31**
"Running Away": T'Pau A185
"Running Away With My Heart": Lone Star A189
"Running Dry": Neil Young B6
"Running Hard": Renaissance **A149**
"Running Scared": Roy Orbison A270, B25
"Running to Stand Still": U2 A89, A185

"Running Up That Hill": Kate Bush B20
"Running Wild": Charley Patton A240
"Runnin' Wild" [1] **B19**
"Runnin' Wild" [2]: Frankie Avalon B15
"Runnin' With the Devil": Van Halen B28
"Run of the Mill": The Beatles B3; George Harrison A185, B18
"Run Riot": Def Leppard A185
"Run That Body Down": Paul Simon B1
"Run through the Jungle": Creedence Clearwater Revival A185
"Run to Me": The Bee Gees **B24**
"Run to You": Bryan Adams A212, A250
"Run to Your Mama": Gary Moore A185
"Russian Doll" B12
"Russian Lullaby" A168, B12, B30
"Russian Rag" A145
"Russians": Sting A149
"Russia": The Flying Lizards B20
"Rusted Machines": Further Seems Forever A205
"Rusty and Dusty": Henry Hall and the BBC Dance Orchestra A227
"Ruthie Ruthie": Frank Zappa A27

"Sabotage": The Beastie Boys A80, A247
"Sabre Dance": B8
"Sacramento": Gary Usher B15
"Sacrificed Sons": Dream Theater **A175**
"Sacrificial Bonfire": XTC A185
"Sacrilege": Mission A185
"Saddle Up the Palomino": Neil Young B6
"Sadeness": Enigma A219
"Sad Eyed Lady of the Lowlands": Bob Dylan A269, **B7**
"Sadie Salome (Go Home)": A145, **A168**, B12
"Sad Jane": Frank Zappa A11
"Safe (Canon Song)": Chris Squire A166
"Safesurfer": Julian Cope A124
"Safeway Cart": Neil Young **A88**, B6
"Saga of Jenny, The" B12
"Sage, The": Emerson, Lake, & Palmer B20
"Said I Wasn't Gonna Tell Nobody": Sam and Dave **A29**
"Sail Away" [1]: Randy Newman A141, **A264**
"Sail Away" [2]: The Pet Shop Boys A174
"Sailing" [1]: Rod Stewart A185, B20
"Sailing" [2]: Christopher Cross A250
"Sailing Down the Chesapeake Bay" A145

Song Index

"Sail on, Sailor": The Beach Boys B15
"Sail On": The Commodores A205
"Sailor, The": Big Country A185, A187, B20
"Sailor's Plea, The": Jimmie Rodgers A266
"Sailor's Tale": King Crimson A152, B20
"Sail to the Moon": Radiohead **A169**, A206
"St. Alphonzo's Pancake Breakfast": Frank Zappa A60
"St. Ann" **B24** B24
"St. James Infirmary" B12; King Oliver B7
"St. Judy's Comet": Paul Simon B1
"Saint Louis Blues" B30
"St. Louis Blues" A145, A219, B7, B12; W.C. Handy B9; Bessie Smith **A26**, A48, **A176**; The Teen Kings A270
"St. Louis Tickle" A145
"Saint of Circumstance": The Grateful Dead B17
"Saint of Me": Rolling Stones A101
"St. Stephen": The Grateful Dead A25, **A99**, A171, A197
"Salamanders in the Sun": Steve Vai A60
"Sally Ann": Joe Brown **B8**
"Sally Go Round the Roses": the Jaynettes A95
"Sally": Gracie Fields A123; Paul McCartney B8; Gerry Monroe A123
"Sally Simpson": The Who **B24**
"Salsation": David Shire A179
"Salt Lake City": The Beach Boys B15
"Salty Dog, A": Procol Harum A43, A185, B21
"Salvacion por la Musica": Bloque A149
"Sam, You Made the Pants Too Long" B12
"Samantha": Madness A185
"Same Old Song and Dance, The" A14
"Same Situation, The": Joni Mitchell A260
"Same Way, The": Peter Green **A256**
"Sam Hall" B19
"Samuel" A145
"San" A145
"Sanctum Santorum": The Damned B20
"Sandy" B15
"San Francisco Bay Blues": The Beatles B8
"San Francisco": Scott McKenzie A70, B29
"San Jacinto": Peter Gabriel A185
"Sans Souci" A145
"Santa Ana Winds": The Beach Boys B15
"Sapphire Bullets of Pure Love": They Might Be Giants A185
"Sara": Fleetwood Mac A59, **A101**

"Sasha, the Passion of the Pascha" B12
"Sassi": Panjabi MC A61
"Satan Rejected My Soul": Morrissey B13
"Satellite" [1]: Elvis Costello B4
"Satellite" [2]: Dave Matthews Band A221
"Satellite of Love": Lou Reed A103
"Satellites": Doves B21
"Satin Doll" **A15**, **A147**, B30
"Satin Summer Nights": Paul Simon B1
"Satisfied Mind, A": Bob Dylan A180
"Saturday Morning in the City": Brian Wilson B15
"Saturday Night Forever": The Pet Shop Boys B13
"Saturday Night's Alright for Fighting": Elton John **A246**, **B24**
"Saucerful of Secrets": Pink Floyd A72, B20
"Saudade Fez um Samba" A211
"Save a Little Dram for Me" A145
"Save a Prayer": Duran Duran A185
"Saved": Bob Dylan A180
"Save Me" [1]: Queen B20
"Save Me" [2]: Fleetwood Mac B24
"Save the Best for Last": Vanessa Williams A167
"Save the Day": Brian Wilson B15
"Save the Last Dance for Me": The Drifters A95, A99, B7, B8
"Save the Life of My Child": Simon and Garfunkel B1
"Save the Whale": Nik Kershaw A185
"Save Your Heart for Me": Gary Lewis and the Playboys B4
"Saving All My Love for You": Whitney Houston A185
"Saviour Don't Pass Me By": Rosetta Tharpe A240
"Savoy Truffle": The Beatles A17, A90, A98, B7
"Sawdust Dance Floor" B8
"Say, Say, Say": Paul McCartney and Michael Jackson B7
"Say It (Over and Over Again)" **B30**
"Say It Isn't So" [1]: Hall and Oates A250
"Say It Isn't So" [2]: **B10**, B30
"Say It Loud–I'm Black and I'm Proud": James Brown A31, B4, B21
"Say It With Music" B30
"Say Mama": The Beatles B8
"Say One for Me" A14

"Say So!" B30
"Says Who? Says You, Says I!" **B30**
"Say The Word" B30
"Say Yes to Michigan!": Sufjan Stevens A221
"Say You Love Me": Fleetwood Mac A101, A247, B24
"Scandinavia" A145
"Scarborough Fair" B12; Martin Carthy A216; Simon and Garfunkel A182, B1, B3
"Scarecrow, The": Pink Floyd A198, B20
"Scarlet Begonias": The Grateful Dead **B17**
"Scarlet Ribbons" **B30**
"Scarred": Dream Theater A175
"Scary Monsters": David Bowie A185
"Scenario": A Tribe Called Quest **A1**
"Scenes From an Italian Restaurant": Billy Joel A269
"Scheherazade: Fugue for the Sultan": Renaissance A166
"Schism": Tool A205, A221
"School": Supertramp A185
"School Day": Chuck Berry A76, A97, A99, A167
"Schoolhouse Fire, The": The Dixon Brothers A240
"School's Out": Alice Cooper A99, B21
"Scientist, The": Coldplay A167
"Screamin' and Hollerin' Blues": Charley Patton A240
"Screaming Infidelities": Dashboard Confessional A205
"Screech Owl Blues": Ma Rainey A240
"Script for a Jester's Tear": Marillion A185
"Sea Breezes": Roxy Music A185, B20
"Sea Cruise": The Beach Boys B15; Frankie Ford A44, B15
"Seal Driver": Jethro Tull B20
"Sealed Tuna Bolero, The": Mothers of Invention, The A11
"Sealed With a Kiss": Brian Hyland B24; Gary Lewis and the Playboys B24; Bobby Vinton B24
"Sea of Love": Phil Phillips A44
"Searching' So Long" *see* "(I've Been) Searchin' So Long"
"Searchin'": The Beatles B7, **B8**; The Coasters A77, A95, A97, **B19**
"Search Is Over, The": Survivor A84
"Seaside Woman": Wings B7

"Season Cycle": XTC A185
"Sea Song": Robert Wyatt A59
"Season of the Witch": Vanilla Fudge A72
"Seasons in the Sun": Terry Jacks A43
"Secondary Modern": Elvis Costello **B20**
"Second Hand News": Fleetwood Mac A185, B24
"Second Line": Huey "Piano": Smith A238
"Seconds": The Human League A235, **B20**
"Second Time, The": Kim Wilde A19
"Second Time Around, The" A14, **B30**
"Secret Garden": T'Pau A185
"Secret Love": Kathy Kirby **B21**
"Secretly": Jimmie Rodgers A97
"Secret": Orchestral Manoeuvres A185
"Secrets": Van Halen A185
"Sedan Delivery": Neil Young B6
"Seductive Barry": Pulp A82
"Seeds of Love": Tears for Fears A185
"See Emily Play": Pink Floyd A198, B29
"Seeker, The": The Who **A16**
"Seeker, The": Who A185
"See Me, Feel Me": The Who A16, **A101**, A185, B7
"See My Friend": Kinks B21
"Seer, The": Big Country A185, A187
"See Saw" [1]: Pink Floyd A99
"See Saw" [2]: Don Covay A95, A185
"See See Rider": Wee Bea Booze A240; Leadbelly A240; Jelly Roll Morton A240; Ma Rainey A240
"See That My Grave Is Kept Clean": Bob Dylan A216; Blind Lemon Jefferson A216
"See the Child": Jane Siberry A124
"(See the Sky) About to Rain": The Byrds A121
"See You Later Alligator": Bill Haley A44
"See Yourself": George Harrison B7
"See You Sometime": Joni Mitchell A260
"Segnung": Popol Vuh **A149**
"Semi-detached Suburban Mr. James": Manfred Mann B20
"Send for Me" A145
"Send for Me if You Need Me": The Ravens A53
"Send in the Clowns" B12
"Send Me Some Lovin'": The Beatles B8; Little Richard A95
"Senior Service": Elvis Costello A185
"Señor (Tales of Yankee Power)": Bob Dylan A180

Song Index

"Señorita with a Necklace of Tears": Paul Simon B1
"Sensation": The Who A99
"Sense of Doubt": David Bowie B20
"Senses Working Overtime": XTC **A149**
"Sentimental Fool": Roxy Music A99
"Sentimental Journey" B7, **B30**
"Sentimental Me" B30
"Sentimental Mood" A167
"Separator": Radiohead A169
"September Gurls": Big Star A247
"September in the Rain" B10; The Beatles **B8**; The Platters A95
"September of My Years, The" A14
"September Song" B8, B10, B16, B30; The Platters A95
"Serenade in Blue" B10, B30
"Sesame Street" **A85**
"Set Fire to the Rain": Adele A222
"Set Me Free": Kinks A107, A185, B21
"Set the Controls for the Heart of the Sun": Pink Floyd A28, A68, A257, B29
"Set Up, The": Reel Big Fish A205
"Set You Free This Time": The Byrds A121
"Set Yourself on Fire": Stars A203, A205
"Seven Days": Sting A221
"Seven Nation Army": White Stripes, The **A148**
"Seven Stones": Genesis **A142**
"Seven Swans": Sufjan Stevens **A205**
"Seventh Son of a Seventh Son": Iron Maiden B28
"Seventy-Five": Touch, The A72
"Seven Wonders": Fleetwood Mac A185
"Seven Years": Saosin A205
"Several Species of Small Furry Animals Gathered Together in a Cave and Grooving with a Pict": Pink Floyd A198
"Severina": Mission A185
"Sex&Drugs&Rock&Roll": Ian Dury **A85**
"Sexual Healing": Marvin Gaye A110, A252
"Sexx Laws": Beck A163
"Sexy M.F.": Prince **B13**
"Sexy Sadie": The Beatles A76, A90, A92, A99, A100, A259, B7, B8, **B18**, B21
"Sgt. Pepper's Lonely Heart's Club Band": The Beatles A16, A19, **A76**, A98, **A198**, A247, **A254**, B7, B8, **B18**, B20, **B24**, B29
"Shadow": George Morton A77

"Shadow Knows, The": The Coasters A77
"Shadow of Fear": Madness A185, B20
"Shadow of the Hierophant": Steve Hackett **B21**
"Shadow of Your Smile, The" A147
"Shadows and Tall Trees": U2 A89, B20
"Shady Grove" B27
"Shahdoroba": Cyndi Walker A270
"Shake, Rattle, and Roll" A76; The Beach Boys B15; The Beatles B7, B8; Bill Haley and His Comets A75, B15, **B24**; Big Joe Turner A74, **A75**, A77, A84, A170, A247, B7, **B19**
"Shake a Hand": The Beatles B8; Little Richard A95
"Shakedown Street": The Grateful Dead B17
"Shake Down the Stars" A14
"Shake It and Brake It" A145
"Shake It Up": The Cars A182, B24
"Shake Me Wake Me (When It's Over)" A95; The Four Tops **A106**, **A108**
"Shake": Sam Cooke A108
"Shake the Disease": Depeche Mode **A54**
"Shakin' All Over": Johnny Kidd and the Pirates B8
"Shaking The Blues Away" B30
"Shall These Cheeks Go Dry": Marion Williams **A161**
"Shameless": Billy Joel A185
"Shanghaid 'n' Shanghai": Nazareth A185
"Shanghai Lil" B12
"Shangri-La": Steve Miller Band A185
"Shape of Things to Come": Slade A185, B21
"Shapes of Things": Jeff Beck B7; Gary Moore A185; The Yardbirds A70
"Share What You Got (But Keep What You Need)": William Bell A29
"Sharevari": Number of Names, A **B5**
"Share Your Love With Me": Aretha Franklin A53
"Sharing You": The Beatles B8
"Sharp Dressed Man": ZZ Top **A16**
"Shattered Fortress, The": Dream Theater A175
"Shazam": The Beatles B8
"Sh'boom": The Chords B21; Crew Cuts B21
"She Bangs the Drums": Stone Roses A185
"She Belongs to Me": Bob Dylan B7
"She Came in Through the Bathroom Window": The Beatles **A92**, **A116**, **B7**, B8, B18

"She Didn't Say 'Yes' " B10, **B30**
"She Don't Care About Time": The Byrds A121, B7, B8
"She Drives Me Crazy": Fine Young Cannibals A185
"She": Elvis Costello **A167**
"She Goes Down": Motley Crue A250
"She Has Funny Cars": The Jefferson Airplane B7
"Sheik of Araby, The" B30; The Beatles B7, B8; Sidney Bechet B32
"Sheila": The Beatles B8
"She Is More to be Pitied Than Censured" B12
"She Knows Me Too Well": The Beach Boys A125, A160, B15
"She Left Me By Myself": John Lee Hooker A8
"She Loves You": The Beatles A43, **A69**, **A76**, **A91**, A98, A99, A107, A131, A141, A185, A195, **A234**, A247, A259, B4, B7, B8, B18, B20, B21, B24; ["Sie Liebt Dich"] B19
"Shelter from the Storm": Bob Dylan A216
"Shelter of Your Arms": Paul Simon B1
"She Moves On": Paul Simon B1
"She Never Lets It Go to Her Heart": Tim McGraw A189
"She Really Meant to Keep It" A145
"She Rides with Me": Paul Petersen B15
"Sherri, She Needs Me": Brian Wilson B15
"Sherry": The Four Seasons B15, B21, B24
"She's a Beauty": The Tubes **A250**
"She's About a Mover": Sir Douglas Quintet, The B4
"She's a Hum Dum Dinger from Dingersville": Jimmy Davis B4
"She Said, 'Yeah' ": The Beatles B8
"She Said": Barclay James Harvest A185
"She Said She Said": The Beatles A90, A98, A99, A134, A184, A198, B3, **B7**, B8, B18
"She Said Yes": Rhett Akins A191
"She's Always a Woman": Billy Joel A5, **A97**, B24
"She's a Rainbow": The Rolling Stones **A101**, B29
"She's a Woman": The Beatles A98, A107, **A107**, A195, B7, B8, **B24**
"She Says That She Needs Me": Brian Wilson B15
"She's Crafty": The Beastie Boys A99
"She's Electric": Oasis A99, **B20**

"She's from Missouri" A14
"She's Funny That Way" B30
"She's Goin' Bald": The Beach Boys B15
"She's Gonna Make It": Garth Brooks **A190**
"She's Got It": Little Richard B8
"She's Got Rhythm": The Beach Boys B15
"She's Just My Style": Gary Lewis and the Playboys A99
"She Shook Me Cold": David Bowie **B21**
"She's Leaving Home": The Beatles **A91**, A98, A99, A100, A101, A105, A221, A259, B7, B8, **B18**, B29
"She's My Rock": Stoney Edwards A123
"She's My Summer Girl": Jan and Dean B15
"She's Not There": Santana A185; The Zombies A99, A248, B7, B8
"She's So Fine": Jimi Hendrix A185, B20
"She's So High": Tal Bachman A247
"She's So Modern": Boomtown Rats A185
"She's the One": Bruce Springsteen B32
"She Wandered Through the Garden Fence": Procol Harum A185
"She Was Happy Till She Met You": Jimmie Rodgers A266
"She Was": Mark Chesnutt A191
"She Wasn't Just a Tartar's Daughter" B12
"She Watch Channel Zero": Public Enemy A24
"She Wears Red Feathers": Guy Mitchell B21
"Shift, The": The Beach Boys B15
"Shimmy Like Kate": The Beatles B8; The Olympics A95
"Shine" A145, B30
"Shine on, Harvest Moon" A147, B12
"Shine on You Crazy Diamond": Pink Floyd A82, A198, A207, B25
"Shine on Your Shoes, A" B10, **B30**
"Shining Star" [1]: Earth, Wine and Fire A43, A55
"Shining Star" [2]: David Bowie B20
"Ship of Fools": Robert Plant B20
"Ships in the Night": Be-Bop Deluxe A185
"Ship without a Sail, A" **B10**, **B30**
"Shirley's Wild Accordion" B7
"Shiver": Coldplay A221
"Shiver Me Timbers": Tom Waits A221
"Shock the Monkey": Peter Gabriel A185
"Shoes" [1]: Patsy Cline A193
"Shoes" [2]: Shania Twain **A193**

Song Index

"Shoop Shoop Song (It's in His Kiss), The": Betty Everett A160
"Shooting Star": Bad Company A7
"Shoot the Curl": The Honeys B15
"Shoot the Moon": Mudhoney A177
"Shoot to Thrill": AC/DC A250
"Shoot You Down": Stone Roses A185
"Shop Around": Captain and Tennille B24; The Miracles A108, B24
"Shoplifters of the World Unite": The Smiths A36
"Shoplifting Clothes": Paul Simon B1
"Shoplifting": The Slits B20
"Shoppin' for Clothes": The Coasters A77
"Shortenin' Bread": The Beach Boys B15; Andrews Sisters B20; Spring B15
"Short Essay, A": echolyn A72
"Short Fat Fannie": The Beatles B8; Larry Williams A95
"Short People": Randy Newman **A264**
"Short Shorts": The Royal Teens A97
"Shotgun": Jr. Walker and the All Stars A32, A95
"Shot of Rhythm and Blues, A": Arthur Alexander A95; The Beatles B8
"Shots": Neil Young **A88**
"Shot Through the Heart" [Distinct from "You Give Love a Bad Name"]: Bon Jovi A250
"Shoulda Woulda Coulda": Beverly Knight B21
"Should Have Known": The Beatles A98
"Should I Stay or Should I Go": The Clash A80, A247
"Shout!": Isley Brothers A95, A105, A247, B7, B8
"Showdown": Electric Light Orchestra B21
"Show Me Heaven": Maria McKee A185
"Show Me Love": t.A.T.u. A153
"Show Me the Way": Peter Frampton **B24**
"Shut Down": The Beach Boys A109, B15
"Shut Up": The Bloodhound Gang A146
"Si a Vida E": The Pet Shop Boys **B13**
"Siberian Khatru": Yes A71, B20, B32
"Siberian Nights": Twilight 22 **A104**
"Sick Bed of Cuchulainn, The": The Pogues B20
"Sick of Myself": Matthew Sweet B32
"Side by Side" B12, B16, B25
"Side of a Hill, The": Paul Simon B1
"Sidewalks of New York, The" A219, **B27**

"Sidewalk Surfin'": Jan and Dean A109, B15
"Sidewinder Sleeps Tonite, The": R.E.M. **A181**
"Sighting": Dave Angel B5
"Signed Curtain": Matching Mole B21
"Signify": Count Basie B4
"Sign in Stranger": Steely Dan **A96**
"Sign O' the Times": Prince **A7**, **B13**
"Signs": Five Man Electrical Band A43
"Sign Your Name": Terrance T. D'Arby A250
"Silent Eyes": Paul Simon A93, **A150**, B1
"Silent Homecoming": Ringo Starr B18
"Silhouette" A145; Deacon Blue A185
"Silhouettes" B8; The Rays A97
"Silly Love Songs": Wings A182, B7
"Silver and Gold": U2 A89
"Silver Bell" A145
"Silver Bells" A182
"Silver Heels" A145
"Silver Machine": Hawkwind B20
"Silver Threads Among the Gold" B27
"Simon and Healy and Cohen (Skinners and Dealers in Hides)" B12
"Simple Desultory Philippic, A": Paul Simon B1; Simon and Garfunkel A182, B1, B4
"Simple Joys of Maidenhood, The" **A224**
"Simple Kind of Man": Lynyrd Skynyrd **A155**
"Simple Twist of Fate": Bob Dylan A99
"Simply Irresistible": Robert Palmer A250
"Since I Fell for You": Lenny Welch A95, B24
"Since I Lost My Baby": The Temptations A108
"Since I've Been Lovin' You": Led Zeppelin A185, B20, B21
"Sincerely": The Moonglows A110, B21
"Sing" A145
"Sing, Brothers" A145
"Sing, Sing, Sing" B12
"Singen und Tanzen": Die Böhse Onkelz **B23**
"Singer Not the Song, The": The Rolling Stones B8
"Sing for the Moment": Eminem B31
"Sing for Your Supper" B30
"Singing Om": George Harrison B7
"Singin' in the Rain" A145
"Sing It Again": Beck A221
"Single Girl" B27
"Sing Something Simple": The Incredible String Band A112
"Sing This All Together": The Rolling Stones B29
"Sinister Footwear": Frank Zappa A11, **A12**

Song Index

"Sinister Purpose": Creedence Clearwater B3
"Sins of Omission": Frantic Bleep B21
"Sir Duke": Stevie Wonder A55, A99
"Siren's Song, The" A114, B30
"Sirius": Alan Parsons Project A43
"Sisotowbell Lane": Joni Mitchell **A260**
"Sister Andrea": Mahavishnu Orchestra A185, B20
"Sister Golden Hair": America A167, **B24**
"Sister Ray": The Velvet Underground A210, A269
"Sisters, Oh Sisters": John and Yoko/Plastic Ono Band B18
"Sit Down, Stand Up": Radiohead **A169**, A205
"Sitting By the Riverside": The Kinks B20
"Sittin' in the Sun" B30
"(Sittin' On) The Dock of the Bay": Otis Redding A29, A80, A185, A247, B3, **B24**
"Sittin' on Top of the World": Bob Wills & His Texas Playboys A239, **A240**; The Carter Family **A240**; Cream **A132**, A185, B7; The Hackberry Ramblers, **A240**; Mississippi Sheiks, **A240**; Howlin' Wolf **A132**, B20
"Sit With the Guru": Strawberry Alarm Clock B7
"Six Degrees of Inner Turbulence": Dream Theater A175
"Sixteen Candles": The Crests A44
"Sixteen Saltines": White Stripes, The A148
"Sixteen Tons": Tennessee Ernie Ford B19
"Sixth of Tchaikovsky": Disko Band A179
"Sixty-Minute Man": Dominoes B21
"Skate King": Russell Gunn B31
"Ski-ing": George Harrison B7
"Skinny Leg Blues": Geeshie Wiley A240
"Skip a Rope": Henson Cargill **A189**
"Skip the Youth": Frightened Rabbit A205
"Skylark" **B10**, **B30**
"Sky Lit Up, The": PJ Harvey A223
"Sky Pilot": The Animals B7
"Slap That Bass" B30
"Slave" [1]: Prince B13
"Slave" [2]: The Temptations A105
"Sledgehammer": Peter Gabriel A142
"Sleep" B30
"Sleep, Baby, Sleep" **A209**; Charles Anderson A266; Ward Burton A266; Matt Keefe A266; Riley Puckett A266; Jimmie Rodgers **A266**; George P. Watson A266; Frank Wilson A266

"Sleepin' Bee, A" **A114**, B10, B30
"Sleeping in a Jar": The Mothers of Invention A12
"Sleeping In": Postal Service, The A204
"Sleep of the Just": Elvis Costello A186
"Sleep Talking Blues": Ma Rainey A240
"Sleep That Burns": Be-Bop Deluxe A185
"Sleepwalker": Megadeth A221
"Sleepy Time Gal" B10, **B30**
"Sleepy Time Time": Cream A132, B7
"Sleigh Ride in July" A14
"Slightly All the Time": Soft Machine B20
"Slim Jenkins' Place": Booker T. and the MGs A29
"Slip Away": Neil Young B6
"Slipknot": The Grateful Dead **B17**
"Slip of the Tongue": Whitesnake B20
"Slip on Through": Spring B15
"Slippery People": Talking Heads A185
"Slippin' and Slidin' ": The Beatles B8; Little Richard A95, A238
"Slip Slidin' Away": Paul Simon A185, B1
"Sloop John B": The Beach Boys A160, B15; The Cornells A160; Dick Dale A160; Lonnie Denegan A160; Collin Raye, B15; Jimmie Rodgers A160
"Slouching toward Bethlehem": Joni Mitchell A260
"Slowburn": Peter Gabriel A185
"Slowdown Sundown": Steve Winwood **A17**, A99
"Slow Down": The Beatles A98, A254, **B8**; Larry Williams A95
"Slow Drug, The": PJ Harvey A50
"Slowpoke": Neil Young B6
"Slow Train Coming": Bob Dylan A180, A185, B21
"Slow Walk": Sil Austin A44
"Smack Jack": Nina Hagen A178
"Small Fry" **B30**
"Smalltown Boy": Bronski Beat A21, A185
"Smash It Up": The Damned B20
"Smells Like Funky Music": DJ Lobsterdust **A84**
"Smells Like Nirvana": "Weird Al": Yankovic A159, A181
"Smells Like Teen Booty": 2 Many DJs A39
"Smells Like Teen Spirit": Nirvana **A16**, A24, A39, A80, **A84**, **A85**, **A97**, A99, A143, A181, A205, A234, A247, B21

Song Index

"Smile" [1]: Elastica B20
"Smile" [2]: The Fall A221
"Smile" [3]: Scarface B14
"Smiler, the" A145
"Smithers-Jones": Jam A185
"Smoke": Ben Folds Five A221
"Smoke Gets in Your Eyes": A145, A219, **B10**, **B11**, **B30**; The Platters B21, B24
"Smoke of a Distant Fire": The Sanford/Townsend Band B24
"Smoke on the Water": Deep Purple A16, A23, **A55**, A74, **A75**, A97, A99, **A101**, A233, **A246**, A248, B21, B24, B28, **B31**
"Smokestack Lightning" B17
"Smokey Joe's Café": The Beach Boys B15; The Robins A77, B15
"Smokin' in the Boys Room": Motley Crüe B28
"Smoky Moke(s)" A145
"Smooth Operator": Sade **B19**
"Smuggler's Blues": Glenn Frey A250
"Snake": R. Kelly A61
"Snap Your Fingers" A145
"Sneaky Feelings": Elvis Costello B4
"Snookey Ookums" A145
"Sober": Tool A167
"So Called Friend": Porcupine Tree A221
"So. Central Rain": R.E.M. A182
"Society Blues" A145
"Sock It to Me – Baby!": Mitch Ryder and the Detroit Wheels A43
"So Do I" **B30**
"Sofa (of my Lethargy)": Supergrass B20
"Sofa": Frank Zappa A27
"So Far Away" [1]: Carole King B24
"So Far Away" [2]: Dire Straits A99
"Soft as Spring" **A209**
"Soft Lights and Sweet Music" A168, B30
"Soft Parachutes": Paul Simon B1
"Soft Parade, The": The Doors B7
"So Hard": The Pet Shop Boys A174
"So Help Me (If I Don't Love You)" A14
"So How Come (No One Loves Me)": The Beatles B8
"So in Love" [1]: A228, **B10**, B12, B30
"So in Love" [2]: Orchestral Manoeuvres A185
"Solar" A224
"Sold! (The Grundy County Auction Incident)": John Michael Montgomery A191
"Soldier and Police War": Junior Murvin A231

"Soldier Boy": The Shirelles B8
"Soldier of Love (Lay Down Your Arms)": Arthur Alexander A95; The Beatles B8
"Soldiers of the Queen" **B19**
"Soldier's Sweetheart, The": Jimmie Rodgers A266
"Soldier's Things": Tom Waits A222
"Söldner": Störkraft **B23**
"Sole Survivor": Asia A185, **B20**
"Solid Gone": Madness A185
"Solid Love": Joni Mitchell A260
"Solid Rock": Bob Dylan A180
"So like Candy": Elvis Costello B20
"Soliloquy" B30
"Solitary Man": Johnny Cash B21
"Solitude" [1]: Billie Holiday B4
"Solitude" [2]: Peter Hammill A185
"So Lonely": The Police A185, A235
"So Long, Frank Lloyd Wright": Simon and Garfunkel **A93**, B1, B7, B21
"So Long, Samoa" B12
"Solsbury Hill": Peter Gabriel A185, A221, A233, B20
"So Many Stars": Brasil 66 B3
"Soma": Smashing Pumpkins A99
"Some Baby" A145
"Somebody" A145
"Somebody Else's Guy": Jocelyn Brown A232
"Somebody Help Me": The Spencer Davis Group B8, B20
"Somebody Lied" A145
"Somebody Loves Me" **B10**, B30
"Somebody's Sleeping in My Bed": Johnnie Taylor A29
"Somebody to Love" [1]: Jefferson Airplane A246, A247, **B24**
"Somebody to Love" [2]: Queen A185, B20
"Somebody Walkin' in My House": Howlin' Wolf **A186**, B20
"Someday, One Day": Simon & Garfunkel B3
"Someday, Someway": The Marvelettes A110
"Someday My Prince Will Come" B8
"Someday Never Comes": Creedence Clearwater Revival A185
"Some Days": The Quarrymen **B8**
"Some Days Are Better Than Others": U2 A89
"Some Day the Sun Won't Shine for You": Jethro Tull A188
"Someday You'll Realize You're Wrong" A145

Song Index

"Some Enchanted Evening" B12, B30
"Some Folks' Lives Roll Easy": Paul Simon **A150**, B1
"Some Happy Day": Charley Patton A240
"Somehow": Vapors A185
"Somehwere" A174
"Some Like It Hot" B10
"Some of These Days" A145, A147, B30
"Some of Your Love": The Beach Boys B15
"Someone, Someone": Brian Poole and the Tremeloes B8
"Someone Else's Baby": Adam Faith B8
"Someone Like You": Living Colour A99
"Someone Saved My Life Tonight": Elton John B24
"Someone to Call My Lover": Janet Jackson **A234**
"Someone to Watch Over Me" **A120, B10**, B30
"Some Other Guy" B7; Richie Barrett A95; The Beatles B8
"Some Other Time" B12
"Some People Never Know": Wings B18
"Some Summer Day": Charley Patton **A239, A240**
"Some Sunny Day" **A120**
"Some Sweet Day": Brian Wilson B15
"Some These Days I'll Be Gone": Charley Patton A240
"Something to Remember You By" A145
"Somethin' Doin?" A145
"Somethin' Else": Eddie Cochran A185
"Somethin' Goin' On": Blood, Sweat and Tears A43
"Something About England": The Clash A185, B20
"Something About You" [1]: The Four Tops A95, **A106, A108**
"Something About You" [2]: Level 42 A185
"Something and Nothing": Wedding Present A185
"Something for Nothing": Rush A28
"Something Happened on the Way to Heaven": Phil Collins A250
"Something in the Way She Moves": James Taylor B3, **B7**
"Something's Coming": Yes A71
"Something's Got a Hold of Me": Five Blind Boys of Alabama **A161**
"Something's Gotten Hold of my Heart": Gene Pitney A185

"Something's on the Move": Jethro Tull A185
"Something So Right": Paul Simon A99, B1
"Something Sort of Grandish" **B30**
"Something Special": Eric Clapton A185
"Something Stupid": Frank Sinatra B21
"Something": The Beatles **A63**, A76, A91, A98, A100, **A116**, A195, **B3, B7**, B8, B18, B24
"Something to Remember You By" B10, B30
"Something Wicked": 2Pac A146
"Something You Don't Expect" A145
"Something You Never Had Before" **B30**
"Sometimes I Feel Like a Motherless Child" B12
"Sometimes I'm Happy" B10, B30
"Sometimes in Winter": Blood, Sweat and Tears B3
"Sometimes When We Touch": Dan Hill **A167**
"Sometime World": Wishbone Ash A185
"Sometimes You Can't Make It on Your Own": U2 **A89**
"Somewhere" [1] B12
"Somewhere" [2]: P.J. Proby B8
"Somewhere" [3]: The Pet Shop Boys A52
"Somewhere along the Way" A14
"Somewhere Down Below the Mason Dixon Line": Jimmie Rodgers A266
"Somewhere Over the Rainbow" A174; Judy Garland B21
"Some Wonderful Sort of Someone" **B30**
"So Much for Pretending": Bryan White A189
"So Much in Love": The Tymes A95
"So Much Things to Say": Bob Marley and the Wailers A235
"So Much to Say, So Much to Give": Chicago **B3**
"Song #2": Marvin Gaye A110
"Song About the Moon": Paul Simon A93, B1
"Song Against Sex": Neutral Milk Hotel A22
"Songbird": Fleetwood Mac A185
"Song for a Belly Dancer" B12
"Song for America": Kansas **A72**
"Song for Children": Brian Wilson B15
"Song for Sharon": Joni Mitchell A260
"Song for the Asking": Simon and Garfunkel B1
"Song for Whoever": Beautiful South A185, B20
"Song Is Ended, The" B12, B30
"Song Is You, The" **A224**, B10, **B30**
"Song of Our Despair": Circulus B21
"Song of Songs, The" B12
"Song of the Hebrew Captive" B12
"Song of the Sewing Machine, The" B12

Song Index

"Song of the Wind": Santana A185
"Song Remains the Same, The": Led Zeppelin A99
"Songs From the Wood": Jethro Tull A188, B21, **B20**
"Songs to Aging Children Come": Joni Mitchell **A260**
"Song to a Seagull": Joni Mitchell **A260**
"Songwriter's Guid: Meurglys III": Van der Graaf Generator **A166**
"Son": Jethro Tull A185, A188
"Son of a Gun": JX A212
"Son of a Poor Man": R.E.O. Speedwagon A185
"Son of Mr. Green Genes": Frank Zappa A11
"Son of Orange County": Mothers of Invention, The **A11**; Frank Zappa A11
"Soon" [1] **B30**
"Soon" [2] **B30**
"Sooner or Later": Fastball A99
"Sophia": Témpano **A149**
"Sophisticated Lady" **B10**, B30
"Sophisticated Sissy": Rufus Thomas A29
"Sora ni Hikaru": Kenso **A149**
"So Rare": Jimmy Dorsey Orch A97
"Sorceress": Return to Forever A73
"Sorrowing Jew, The" B12
"Sorrow": The Merseys A185, B7
"Sorry But I'm Going to Have to Pass": The Coasters A77
"Sorry Seems to Be the Hardest Word": Elton John A167, B24
"Sorted for E's and Wizz": Pulp B20
"Sort of Homecoming, A": U2 A185, B20
"SOS": ABBA A141, A185, B25
"So Sincere": Gentle Giant A185
"So Special": Pretenders A185
"Sossity": Jethro Tull A188, B20
"Soul Bongo": Stevie Wonder A110
"Soul Crying Out": Simple Minds A185
"Soul Dressing": Booker T. and the MGs A29, A95
"Soul Finger": The Bar-Kays A29, A185
"Soul Food": Goodie MoB B14
"Soul Limbo": Booker T. and the MGs A29, A185
"Soul Love": David Bowie A185, A221, B20
"Soul Man" A238; Sam and Dave **A29**, A185, A205, B21, B24
"Soul Power": James Brown A31, A238, B4, B25
"Soul Searchin'": The Beach Boys B15

"Soul Survivor": The Rolling Stones A33, **A35**
"Sound and Vision": David Bowie A185, B20
"Sound Bwoy Bureill": Smif 'N Wessun B14
"Sound Chaser": Yes A71, A73
"Sound in 70 Cities": Simple Minds A185
"Sound of Muzak, The": Porcupine Tree B21
"Sound of Silence, The": Paul Simon B1; Simon and Garfunkel B1
"Sounds of Africa" A145
"Sounds of Silence, The" [1]: Simon and Garfunkel A93, **A97**, A99, A247, B24
"Sounds of Silence, The" [2]: The Beastie Boys A99
"Sour Milk Sea": Jackie Lomax **B7**
"South America, Take It Away": Bing Crosby B4
"South American": Brian Wilson B15
"South Bay Surfer": The Beach Boys B15
"South Bronx": KRS-One B31
"South California Purples": Chicago B7
"Southern Cannonball": Jimmie Rodgers A266
"Southern Cross": Crosby, Stills, and Nash A222
"Southern Man": Neil Young A185, B6, B20
"Southern Pacific": Neil Young **A88**, B6
"Southern Smiles Two-step" A145
"South of the Border": Henry Hall and the BBC Dance Orchestra **A227**; Andy Martin B25
"South Side of the Sky": Yes A71, A99, A269
"Souvenir": Orchestral Manoeuvres A185, B20
"Sovay": Martin Carthy B21
"So What" [1]: Miles Davis A60
"So What" [2]: No Motiv A205
"Sowing the Seeds of Love": Tears for Fears B20, B21
"So Young": The Ronettes B15
"So You Want to Be a Rock 'n' Roll Star": The Byrds A121, A185, A248, B7
"Soy Todo (amparame)": Los Van Van A205
"Space Is Deep": Hawkwind B20
"Space Oddity": David Bowie A74, B7, B21, **B24**
"Space": The Grateful Dead B17
"Spanish Bombs": The Clash A118
"Spanish Castle Magic": The Jimi Hendrix Experience **A97**, A99, A185, **A257**, B29
"Spanish Doll" A145
"Spanish Eyes": Al Martino B21
"Spanish Fire Dance" ["España Cani"]: The Beatles B8
"Spanish Harlem": Ben E. King A99

"Spanish Harlem Incident": The Byrds A121; Bob Dylan B8
"Spanish Jam": The Grateful Dead B17
"Spanish Shawl" A145
"Spanish Two Step": Bob Wills & His Texas Playboys A240
"Sparks": The Who A141
"Sparky's Dream": Teenage Fanclub B21
"Sparrow": Simon and Garfunkel B1
"Speaking of Kentucky Days": Jack Hylton and His Orchestra A227
"Speak Low" **B10**, **B30**
"Speak to Me" [1]: Jackie Lomax B7
"Speak to Me" [2]: Pink Floyd A138, A198, B29
"Speed King": Deep Purple A185
"Speed of Life": David Bowie B32
"Speedoo": The Cadillacs B15
"Speedway": Morrissey B13
"Spell, The": Uriah Heep A185
"Spellbound": Siouxsie and the Banshees A185, B20
"Spidergawd": Jerry Garcia A99
"Spider Man Blues": Bessie Smith B21
"Spies Like Us": Paul McCartney B7
"Spill the Wine": Eric Burdon A185
"Spin Me Round": Roxy Music A185
"Spinning Wheel": Blood, Sweat, and Tears A167, B3, B7
"Spiral Highway": Paul Simon B1
"Spirit in the Sky": Norma Greenbaum A185
"Spirit of America": The Beach Boys B15
"Spirit of Radio, The": Rush **A248**
"Spirit of Rock and Roll, The": Brian Wilson B15
"Spirit of the Land": Hothouse Flowers B21
"Spirits in the Material World": The Police **A235**, **A236**
"Spiritual Death of Howard Greer, The": Touch, The A72
"Spirit Voices": Paul Simon B1
"Splish Splash": Bobby Darin A44, A97
"Spoilt Victorian Child": The Fall A185, B20
"Spoonful": Cream A43, A132, B7, B19, **B20**, B21
"Spoonful of Sugar, A" A202
"Spoon Man": Soundgarden A245
"Spoonman": Soundgarden A221
"S'posin'" **B30**
"Spread": OutKast A99
"Spring Collection": Vapors A185

"Spring": John Oswald A24
"Spring Is Here" A114, B30
"Spring Song" B12
"Spring Will Be a Little Late This Year" **B30**
"Spy, The": Doors, The A43
"Squabblin'" A145
"Square One": Coldplay A102
"Squeeze Box": the Who B24
"Stack O'Lee [Stacko[a]lee] [Blues]": Lucious Curtis & Willie Ford A240; Fruit Jar Guzzlers A240; Woody Guthrie A240; ["Stagger Lee":] Mississippi John Hurt **A240**; Frank Hutchison A240; Lloyd Price A44; Ma Rainey **A240**
"Stagnation": Genesis A142
"Staircase (Mystery), The": Siouxsie and the Banshees A185, B20
"Stairway to Heaven": Led Zeppelin **A7**, **A16**, A43, A74, A80, A99, A185, A233, A247, **A247**, A269, B8, B20, B24, B28
"Stairway to the Stairs" A145
"Stakker Humanoid": Humanoid B21
"Stamped Ideas": Iron Butterfly B3
"Stand By Me" B20; The Beatles B8; Ben E. King A95, A167, A185, A247, B21, B24; Spyder Turner A101
"Stand By Your Man": Lyle Lovett A191; Tammy Wynette A165, A191, B19, B21
"Standing in the Shadows of Love": The Four Tops **A106**, **A108**, A185
"Standing on the Moon": The Grateful Dead B17
"Standin' in the Rain": Electric Light Orchestra A185
"Stand": Sly and the Family Stone A205, **B3**
"Star": David Bowie A185
"Star Dust" A168, **B30**; Ella Fitzgerald A168
"Stardust" A145, **B10**, B16; Louis Armstrong A119
"Stare of Death, The": True Dream A205
"Star Eyes" B16
"Starfish and Coffee": Prince B32
"Staring at the Sun": U2 A89
"Staring at the Sun": U2 A89
"Starless": King Crimson A28, A208, A224
"Starlight": Electric Light Orchestra A185
"Starlighter, The" **A209**
"Star Light Star Bright": Spring B15
"Starman": David Bowie A185, B20

Song Index

"Starrider": Foreigner A74
"Stars Fell on Alabama" **B30**
"Starship": MC5 A210
"Stars on 45": Stars on 45 A24
"Star Spangled Banner, The" A140, B12; The Jimi Hendrix Experience A67, A258, B8, B21, B28
"Stars": t.A.T.u. A153
"Start a New Life": R.E.O. Speedwagon A185
"Starting at the Bottom" B10
"Starting Over" *see* "(Just Like) Starting Over"
"Starting to Come to Me": Elvis Costello A33
"Start Me Up": Rolling Stones A17
"Start Talking Love": Magnum B20
"State of Grace": Billy Joel A185, A250
"Station to Station": David Bowie **A269**
"Status Back Baby": Mothers of Invention, The A11
"Status Seeker": Dream Theater A175
"Stay" [1]: The Beatles B8; Maurice Williams and the Zodiacs A94
"Stay" [2]: Pink Floyd A185
"Stay" [3]: Eternal B21
"Stay (Far Away, So Close!)": U2 A89, A103
"Stay as Sweet as You Are" B12
"Stay Clean": Motorhead A185
"Stayin' Alive": The Bee Gees A39, A179, A185, B25
"Stay or Leave": Dave Matthews A169
"Stay the Night": Chicago **A214**
"Stay with Me Baby": Shirley Brown A185, B21; Lorraine Ellison **B21**; Bette Midler **B21**
"Stay with Me": Mission A185
"Steady Rollin' Man": Eric Clapton A185
"Stealin'" B17
"Steaming Pipes": Happy the Man A73
"Steam": Peter Gabriel A142
"Steamy Window": Tina Turner A185
"Steel Guitar Blues": Roy Acuff & His Crazy Tennesseans A240
"Steeltown": Big Country A185, A187, **B20**
"Stefani, Gino" A67
"Stella Blue": The Grateful Dead A99
"Stella By Starlight": **A224**, B12; Dick Reynolds B15
"Stengah": Meshuggah **A208**
"Step Aside": Emerson Lake & Powell A185
"Step Inside Love": Cilla Black B7, B8, B21

"Stepping Closer to Your Heart": Marvin Gaye A110
"Steppin' Out" [1]: Paul Revere and the Raiders A27
"Steppin' Out" [2]: Electric Light Orchestra A185
"Steppin' Out" [3]: Joan Armatrading A136
"Steppin' Out With My Baby" A168, B12
"Steppin' Stone" *see* "(I'm Not Your) Steppin' Stone"
"Step Up": Bannock B14
"Sticks and Stones": The Beatles B8; Ray Charles A95
"Stick Shift": The Duals B15
"Stick to Me": Graham Parker A185
"Stick to Your Guns": Bon Jovi A185
"Still Crazy After All These Years": Paul Simon A93, **A97**, **A150**, A167, B1
"Still Falls the Rain": Roxy Music A185
"Still Haven't Found": U2 A250
"Still I Dream of It": Brian Wilson B15
"Still Ill": The Smiths A36, A185
"Still Life": Van der Graaf Generator A166
"Still Raining, Still Dreaming": Jimi Hendrix **B3**
"Still the Same": Bob Seger A250
"Still... You Turn Me On": Emerson, Lake, Palmer B24
"Stimulating and Exciting": Shine **A3**
"Stockholm Syndrome": Muse B21
"Stockyard Strut" A145
"Stoked": The Beach Boys B15
"Stolz": Die Böhse Onkelz **B23**
"Stone Free": Jimi Hendrix A257
"Stones in My Passway": Robert Johnson A132, B21
"Stonewall Blues": Memphis Jug Band A240
"Stood Up": Ricky Nelson A97
"Stop, Stop, Stop" A145
"Stop": Cissy Houston **A161**
"Stop Her on Sight": Edwin Starr A185
"Stop I Don't Wanna Hear It": Melanie A185
"Stop in the Name of Love": The Supremes A95, A99, **A106**, **A108**, A185, B21
"Stoppa Matchen": Hoola Bandoola Band B25
"Stop Whispering": Radiohead A162, **A169**
"Storm, The": Big Country A185
"Storm Angel": Sunday All Over the World A218
"Storm Front": Billy Joel A185, B21

"Stormy Monday": The Allman Brothers Band A99; Bobby Bland B21; Cream A132
"Stormy Weather": A156, A168, B7, B10, B12, B16, B30
"Story in Your Eyes, The": The Moody Blues A99, B24
"Story of Bo Diddley, The": Animals B21
"Story of My Life": Sharon Marie B15
"Straight Down the Middle" A14
"Straighten Up and Fly Right": The King Cole Trio B4
"Straight to the Heart": Sting A221
"Stranded in a Limousine": Paul Simon B1
"Strange Attraction": The Cure A99
"Strange Avenues": Jethro Tull A188
"Strange Boy, A": Joni Mitchell A260
"Strange Brew": Cream A132, B24, B29
"Strange Days": The Doors A43, **B3**
"Strange Déjà Vu " Dream Theater A175
"Strange Fruit": B12, B19; Billie Holiday **A47**, B4
"Strange Kind of Woman": Deep Purple B21
"Strange Magic": Electric Light Orchestra A179
"Strange Phenomena": Kate Bush A185
"Stranger, The": The Shadows B8
"Stranger Blues": Rosie Mae Moore **B26**
"Stranger in Paradise" A53
"Stranger in the House": George Jones and Elvis Costello B4
"Stranger on the Shore of Love": Stevie Wonder A99
"Strangers in the Night" B8, B12; Frank Sinatra B21
"Strange Things Happening Every Day": Sister Rosetta Tharpe A238
"Strawberry Fields Forever": The Beatles A43, A67, **A90**, A92, A98, A100, A101, A102, A124, A138, A195, A198, A207, **A234**, A247, **B7**, **B8**, **B18**, B19, B20, B21, B29, B32
"Stray Cat Strut": The Stray Cats A43, A99, A167
"Stream of Consciousness": Dream Theater A175
"Streetcar": Funeral for a Friend A205
"Street Fighting Man": The Rolling Stones A35, B7, B29
"Street Fighting Years": Simple Minds A185
"Street of Dreams" [1]: The Ink Spots **A263**
"Street of Dreams" [2]: The Damned B20

"Street Piano Medley" A145
"Streets of London": Ralph McTell A64, B21
"Street Spirit": Radiohead A162, **A169**, **B21**
"Stretch Out and Wait": The Smiths A36
"Strictly Confidential": Roxy Music A185
"Strictly Genteel": Frank Zappa and the Mothers A11, **A12**, **A59**
"Strict Time": Elvis Costello and the Attractions B4
"Strike Up The Band" B30
"String Bean Mama": Bill Carlisle A240
"Stringman": Neil Young B6
"String Quartet, The": Frank Zappa A12
"Strings of Life": Derrick May A104, B5
"Stroke of Genius, A": DJ Freelance Hellraiser **A24**
"Stroke of Luck, A": Garbage B21
"Stroll, The": The Diamonds A44, A97, B24
"Strolling Yodler [sic], The": Matt Keefe **A266**
"Strollin' ": Prince A79, **B13**
"Strong": Robbie Williams B21
"Stubborn Kind of Fellow": Marvin Gaye A110
"Stuck in a Moment You Can't Get Out Of": U2 A89
"Stuck Inside of Mobile With the Memphis Blues Again" B17
"Stuck in the Middle With You": Stealers Wheel A77
"Stuck on You": The Beatles B8; Elvis Presley B24
"Stuck With You": Huey Lewis and the News B24
"Stumble and Fall": Darlene Love A84
"Stumbling" **B30**
"Stupid Girl" [1]: Neil Young B6
"Stupid Girl" [2]: Garbage B32
"Stupid Puma": Don Caballero **A57**
"Style" A14
"Subdivisions": Rush A17
"Submarine": Genesis A142
"Submission": The Sex Pistols A210
"Substitute": The Who A185, **B20**
"Subterranean Homesick Alien": Radiohead A17, A143, **A169**
"Subterranean Homesick Blues" B19; Bob Dylan A27, A143, A184, A269, B4, B7, B8, B19
"Subtraction": Coheed and Cambria A205
"Suburbia": The Pet Shop Boys A174

Song Index *241*

"Such a Woman": Neil Young B6
"Suddenly" B10
"Suddenly It's Spring" A14
"Suddenly Last Summer": The Motels A250
"Suedehead": Morrissey **B13**
"Sue Me" A41
"Sueno": The Young Rascals A110
"Suffer Little Children": The Smiths A36
"Suffocating Sight": Trivium B21
"Suffocating the Bloom": echolyn A72
"Suffragette City": David Bowie **A16**, A185, B20
"Sugar Coated Sour": Dillinger Escape Plan **A204**
"Sugar Dumpling": Sam Cooke A108
"Sugaree": The Grateful Dead B17
"Sugarfoot": Hank Garland A270
"Sugar Hill": AZ B14
"Sugar Magnolia": The Grateful Dead **A101**, B17
"Sugar Mountain": Neil Young B6
"Sugar Shack": Jimmy Gilmer and the Fireballs **A241**
"Sugar Sugar": The Archies B21
"Sugar": System of a Down A205
"Sugartime": The McGuire Sisters A97
"Suicide Solution": Ozzy Osbourne B28
"Suicide": The Beatles B7
"Suitcase Blues" A145
"Suite: Judy Blue Eyes": Crosby, Stills, and Nash **A101**, A205, A269
"Sukiyaki": Kyu Sakamoto A43
"Sulk": Radiohead **A169**
"Sultans of Swing": Dire Straits A19, A99, A185
"Summer, Highland Falls": Billy Joel B24
"Summer '68": Pink Floyd A198
"Summer and Lightning": Electric Light Orchestra A185
"Summer Babe": Pavement A80, A247
"Summer Breeze": Seals and Crofts **B3**, B24
"Summer Days": Bob Dylan A216
"Summer in the City": Quincy Jones A261; The Lovin' Spoonful A99, B8, B15
"Summer Knows, The" B3
"Summer Means New Love": The Beach Boys B15
"Summer Moon, The": Vicki Kocher B15
"Summer Night" **B30**

"Summer Night City": ABBA A185
"Summer Nights": Van Halen A99
"Summer of '68": Pink Floyd B20
"Summer of '69": Bryan Adams A250
"Summer Rain": Johnny Rivers A43, B7
"Summer's Almost Gone": The Doors B3
"Summer's Cauldron": XTC B21
"Summer's Daughter" B3
"Summer Soldier": Barclay James Harvest A185
"Summer Song, A": Chad and Jeremy B8
"Summertime, Summertime": The Jaimees A44
"Summertime" [1] **A133**, A231, B9, B10, B12; The Beatles B7, B8; Sharon Marie B15
"Summertime" [2]: DJ Jazzy Jeff and the Fresh Prince B14
"Summertime Blues": The Beach Boys B15; Blue Cheer B28; Eddie Cochran A44, A80, A185, A247, B15; The Flying Lizards B20
"Sumpin' New": Coolio A99
"Sun Ain't Gonna Shine Any More, The": Walker Brothers B21
"Sun City": Artists United Against Apartheid B25
"Sunday" A145
"Sunday, Monday or Always" A14, B30
"Sunday Afternoon": Paul Simon B1
"Sunday All Over the World": Sunday All Over the World A218
"Sunday Bloody Sunday" [1]: John & Yoko / Plastic Ono Band A103, B18
"Sunday Bloody Sunday" [2]: U2 A89, A103, **A246**
"Sunday for Tea": Peter and Gordon A70
"Sunday Girl": Blondie **A42**
"Sunday Morning Fuddle, The": Ned Corvan **B19**
"Sunday Morning": Madness A185, **B20**
"Sunday's Best": Elvis Costello A185, A221
"Sunday Will Never Be the Same": Spanky and Our Gang A43
"Sundials": Alkaline Trio A205
"Sundown": Gordon Lightfoot B24
"Sun Is Burning, The": Simon and Garfunkel B1
"Sun King": The Beatles **A92**, A98, **A116**, A149, **B7**, B8, B18
"Sunny" B30; Bobby Hebb A93
"Sunny Afternoon": Kinks A107, A185, B8, B20

"Sunny Banks of Scotland": Ned Corvan B19
"Sunny Side Up" A145
"Sunrise, Sunset" B12
"Sun Set, The": The Moody Blues B7
"Sunset Medley" A145
"Sunset Trail, The": Ambrose and his Orchestra A227
"Sunshine, Sunshine": James Taylor B3, B4
"Sunshine" [1]: The Beach Boys B15
"Sunshine" [2]: Peter Hammill A185
"Sunshine" [3]: World Party B21, B32
"Sunshine Cake" A14
"Sunshine Every Day": Rattles A185
"Sunshine of My Life": Stevie Wonder A250
"Sunshine of Your Love": Cream **A16**, A43, **A55**, **A101**, A132, A185, A247, A248, B3, B8, B20, B21
"Sun Shines Brighter, The" B30
"Sunshine Special": Blind Lemon Jefferson **B26**; Memphis Minnie A201
"Sunshine Superman": Donovan A43, **A101**, B7, B8, B29
"Superbad": James Brown **A31**, A117, A184, A262, **B4**, B21
"Super Freak": Rick James A24, A202, A261
"Superman": Eminem A39
"Supernaturally": Nick Cave and the Bad Seeds B21
"Superstar" [1] **A85**; Murray Head A121, B24
"Superstar" [2] B3; Carpenters **A140**, B21; Sonic Youth A140
"Superstition": Stevie Wonder **A55**, A80, A144, A163, A232, A247
"Superstitious": Europe A250
"Super Trouper": ABBA A185, B25
"Supervixen": Garbage B21, B32
"Supper's Ready": Genesis A67, A141, A142, **A149**, A207, **A232**, B20, B21
"Supper Time" B30
"Suppertime" B12
"Sure Don't Feel Like Love": Paul Simon B1
"Surely God Is Able": Clara Ward A161
"Sure 'Nuff 'n' Yes I Do": Captain Beefheart A210
"Sure Thing" B30
"Sure to Fall": The Beatles **B8**; Carl Perkins A259
"Surf City": Jan and Dean A109, B15
"Surfer Girl": The Beach Boys A75, A109, A125, A160, B8, B15

"Surfer Joe and Moe the Sleaze": Neil Young B6
"Surfer Moon, The": The Beach Boys A160; Bob and Sheri B15
"Surfer's Holiday": Frankie, Annette, and Dick Dale B15
"Surfers Rule": The Beach Boys B15
"Surfin' Bird": Trashmen, The A43
"Surfin' Down the Swanee River": The Honeys B15
"Surfing Drums": Dick Dale B15
"Surfin' Safari": The Beach Boys A109, B15
"Surfin' ": The Beach Boys A109, A160, B15
"Surfin' U.S.A.": The Beach Boys A43, A109, A185, B7, B8, B15, B19, B21, B24
"Surfin' Wild": Jan and Dean B15
"Surfin' With the Alien": Joe Satriani B28
"Surf Jam": The Beach Boys B15
"Surf Route 101": Jan and Dean B15
"Surf's Up": The Beach Boys B15; Brian Wilson B15
"Surrender" [1] B12; Elvis Presley A99, B8
"Surrender" [2]: Cheap Trick A250
"Surrounded": Dream Theater A175
"Survival": Madonna **B13**
"Susan": The Buckinghams **A101**, B7
"Susie [Suzie] Q" **B27**; Creedence Clearwater Revival A43, A185,; Dale Hawkins A44
"Suspicious Minds": Elvis Presley A247
"Suzanne": Randy Newman A264
"Suzie Wong (The Cloud Song)" A14
"Suzy Parker": The Beatles B7
"Swamp": Talking Heads A185
"Swanee" A114, A145, B10, **B30**
"Swanee River" A145, B30, B15; The Beatles B8
"Sway" B12
"Sweet Adeline" B27
"Sweet and Easy to Love": Roy Orbison A270
"Sweet and Hot" **B30**
"Sweet and Lovely" A147, **B30**; Al Bowlly & the Ray Nobel Orchestra B21; Thelonius Monk A96
"Sweet and Low" B27
"Sweet and Low Down" **A120**, A145, **B10**, **B30**
"Sweet Baby James": James Taylor A99, B3, B24
"Sweet Box": Slade B21
"Sweet Child O' Mine": Guns n Roses **A16**, A17, A80, A247, **A247**, B28
"Sweet Dream": Jethro Tull A188, **B21**

Song Index   *243*

"Sweet Dreams Are Made of This": The Eurhythmics A269, B13
"Sweet Escape": Gwen Stefani **A215**
"Sweet Georgia Brown" A97, A145, A147, B10, **B19**, B25, **B27**, B30; The Beatles **B8**; The Coasters A95
"Sweet Home Alabama": Lynyrd Skynyrd A16, A43, A222, **B24**
"Sweet Home Chicago": Robert Johnson **A240**
"Sweet Is the Night": Electric Light Orchestra A185
"Sweet Little Sixteen" B8, **B27**; Chuck Berry A38, A43, A44, A95, A97, A185, B7, B15, B21
"Sweet Lorraine" **B10**, **B30**
"Sweet Mama Hurry Home": Jimmie Rodgers A266
"Sweet Man O' Mine" A145
"Sweet Maria" B12
"Sweet Mountain of Love": Spring B15
"Sweet Sacrifice": Evanescence B21
"Sweet Sarah Blues": Tom Darby & Jimmie Tarlton A240
"Sweet Soul Music": Arthur Conley A185
"Sweet Sue": Earl Burtnett B8
"Sweet Sue – Just You" B30
"Sweet Sweet": Smashing Pumpkins A99
"Sweet Talkin' Guy": The Chiffons A38
"Sweeter He Is, The": The Soul Children A29
"Sweetheart We Need Each Other" A145
"Sweetness": Yes A71
"Sweets for My Sweet": The Drifters A185, B15; Brian Wilson B15
"Sweet Thursday": Icicle Works A185
"Swingin' Down the Lane" **B30**
"Swinging on a Star" A14, B10; Bing Crosby B4
"Swing Low, Sweet Chariot" B9
"Swing Town": Steve Miller Band A185
"Swingtown": Steve Miller Band A250
"SWLABR (She Walks Like a Bearded Rainbow)": Cream B29
"S'Wonderful": **A120**, B10, B12, B30
"Sympathy for the Devil": The Rolling Stones **A16**, A80, A99, A247, A263, B7, B19, B21, B29
"Symphonic Waltzes" B10
"Symphony in X Major": Xzibit **A261**
"Symphony of Destruction": Megadeth **B31**
"Symptom of the Universe": Black Sabbath A167

"Synchronicity II": The Police A99, **A248**, A250
"Syncopated Walk, The" B30
"Synthetic Substitution": Melvin Bliss B22
"Szamar Madar": Venetian Snares A221

"Tabla and Pakavaj": George Harrison B7
"Table for Glasses": Jimmy Eat World **A205**
"Tag Team Partners": Living Colour A99
"Tahiti Trot" B10
"Taint Long for Day" A145
"[T]ain't Nobody's Business if I Do" A48; Billie Holiday A48, B4; Bessie Smith **A48**; Frank Stokes A240
"Taint So, My Honey, 'Taint So" B30
"Take a Chance on Me": ABBA A185, B20, B21
"Take a Letter, Maria": R.B. Greaves B24
"Take a Load Off Your Feet": The Beach Boys B15
"Take a Step Back": Simple Minds A185
"Take a Whiff on Me": Woody Guthrie A240; Leadbelly **A239**, **A240**
"Take Care of Your Homework": Johnnie Taylor A29
"Take Good Care of My Baby" A122; The Beatles **B8**, **B20**; Bobby Vee A185, **B20**
"Take It Away": Paul McCartney B7
"Take It Back": Cream A132, B7
"Take It Easy" A145; The Eagles A17, **A173**, B21
"Take It in Blood": Nas B14
"Take It off the Top": The Dixie Dregs A73
"Take It on the Run": REO Speedwagon B24
"Take It or Leave It": Madness A185
"Take It to the Limit": The Eagles A185, **B24**
"Take Me as I Am": Sugarland A219
"Take Me Back Again": Jimmie Rodgers A266
"Take Me Back to Manhattan" A113, A228
"Take Me for a Little While": Coverdale Page B21
"Take Me": Gentle Giant A185
"Take Me Home, Country Roads": John Denver **A241**, B21, B24; Olivia Newton-John A185
"Take Me I'm Yours": Squeeze A233
"Take Me in Your Arms": Gladys Knight A185
"Take Me to the Mardi Gras": Paul Simon A123, B1

"Take Me to the Pilot": Elton John B21
"Take Me to the River": Al Green A247, A80; Talking Heads A71, A185
"Take My Breath Away": Berlin A185
"Take My Hand, Precious Lord" **A26**; Alphabetical Four A240; Thomas A. Dorsey B9; Five Soul Stirrers of Houston A26; Mahalia Jackson A26; Clara Ward A26
"Take My Love" B12
"Take on Me": A-Ha A185, **B24**
"Take Out Some Insurance on Me, Baby" B8
"Take the 'A' Train" **B2**, B30
"Take the Long Way Home": Supertramp A248, B24
"Take the Money and Run": Steve Miller Band A43, A185, B24
"Take the Time": Dream Theater A175
"Take This Hammer" B8; Jesse Fuller A95
"Take Up the Stethoscope and Walk": Pink Floyd B29
"Take Your Burdens to the Lord": Blind Roosevelt Graves A240
"Taking a Chance on Love" B10, B30
"Taking a Trip to Carolina": The Beatles B7
"Taking Care of Businees": Bachman-Turner Overdrive **A246**
"Taking My Baby Uptown": Joan Armatrading A136
"Taking Steps to Russia" B30
"Taking Time Out": T'Pau A185
"Takin' It Back": Toto A185
"Takin' It In": James Taylor B3
"Tales of Brave Ulysses": Cream A99, B3, B7, B20
"Talking About My Baby": The Impressions **A108**
"Talking Drum, The": Robert fripp A67
"Talking in Your Sleep": The Romantics **A241**, B24
"Talkin' to Myself": Blind Willie McTell A240
"Talkin' World War III Blues": Bob Dylan A58, B7, B8
"Talk of the Town" A145
"Talk to Me": The Beach Boys B15; Little Willie John B15
"Tallahassee Lassie": Freddy "Boom-Boom": The Beach Boys B15; Cannon B15
"Tallest Man, the Broadest Shoulders, Pt. 1, The": Sufjan Stevens A221

"Tall Oak Tree": Dorsey Burnette B15
"Tall Ships Go": Big Country A185
"Tammy": Debbie Reynolds A97
"Tammy Tell Me True": The Beatles B8
"Tandoori Chicken": Ronnie Spector B7
"Tangerine" [1] **B16**
"Tangerine" [2]: Led Zeppelin A89, A99, A185
"Tangled Up in Blue": Bob Dylan A80, A216, A247
"Tango in the Night": Fleetwood Mac A185
"Tapestry": Carole King **B24**
"Ta Ra Ra Boom Deay" B19
"Tara's Theme" B12
"Tarkus": Emerson, Lake, and Palmer A207, A229
"Taste of Honey, A" **A133**, B8; The Beatles A95, B7; Lenny Welch A95
"Taut": P.J. Harvey B21
"Taxi": Harry Chapin A99
"Taxman": The Beatles **A16**, **A63**, A76, A77, A90, A95, A185, A198, A246, **B7**, B8, **B18**, B21, B32
"T.B. Blues" A266; Jimmie Rodgers A266
"Teacher, Teacher": .38 Special A250
"Teacher, The" [1]: Paul Simon B1
"Teacher, The" [2]: Big Country A185, A187
"Teach Your Children": Crosby, Stills, Nash & Young B3
"Tea for One": Led Zeppelin A185
"Tea for Two" A116, B9, B10, B16, **B30**
"Tea in the Sahara": The Police A235
"Teamwork" A14
"Tears" [1]: Ken Dodd B8, B19
"Tears" [2]: Rush A28
"Tears Dry on Their Own": Amy Winehouse B21
"Tears in Heaven": Eric Clapton A80, A99, A167, A247, B24
"Tears in the Morning": The Beach Boys B15
"Tears of a Clown": Smokey Robinson and the Miracles A163, B8
"Tears of Rage": The Band B20
"Tears on My Pillow": Little Anthony & The Imperials A44, A97
"Tear the Roof Off the Sucker (Give Up the Funk)": Parliament A261, **B31**
"Tear ya Down": Motorhead A185
"Tearz": Wu-Tang Clan A99
"Teddy Bear" *see* "(Let Me Be Your) Teddy Bear"

Song Index

"Teddy Bears' Picnic, The": Henry Hall and the BBC Dance Orchestra A227
"Teddy Boy": The Beatles B7; Paul McCartney **B18**
"Teen-Age Crush": Tommy Sands A97
"Teenage Dirtbag": Wheatus **B21**
"Teenage FBI": Guided By Voices A243
"Teenage Heaven": The Beatles B8
"Teenage Idol": Gary Moore A185
"Teenage Lobotomy": The Ramones B32
"Teenage Prostitute": Frank Zappa A11
"Teenager in Love" A222; Dion and the Belmonts A44
"Teenager's Romance, A": Ricky Nelson A97
"Teenage Wildlife": David Bowie B20
"Teenage Wind": Frank Zappa A60
"Teen Angel": Mark Dinning A44, A77, **A241**, B15, B24
"Teeter Totter Love": Jasper Dailey B15
"Telegram Sam": T. Rex A185
"Telegraph Road": Dire Straits A269
"Televised Green Smoke": Craig Carl **B5**
"Tell It Like It Is": Aaron Neville A43, A99
"Tell Laura I Love Her": Ray Peterson A77, B15, B25
"Tell Me, Little Gypsy" B30
"Tell Me" [1]: Bangles A185
"Tell Me" [2]: White Lion A250
"Tell Me (You're Coming Back)": Rolling Stones A107
"Tell Me Daddy": Julia Lee and Her Boyfriends A53
"Tell Me If You Can": The Beatles B8
"Tell Me Little Gypsy" A145
"Tell Me Something Good": Rufus and Chaka Khan **A17**
"Tell Me That It Isn't True": Bob Dylan A99
"Tell Me There's a Heaven": Chris Rea A185
"Tell Me What": Fine Young Cannibals A185
"Tell Me What You're Gonna Do": James Brown **B3**
"Tell Me What you See": The Beatles A98, B7, B8, B18
"Tell Me Why" [1]: The Beach Boys B15; The Belmonts B15
"Tell Me Why" [2]: The Beatles A185, B7, B8, B21
"Tell Me Why" [3]: Neil Young A185, B6
"Tell Me You Love Me" B12

"Tell Tale": Joan Armatrading A136
"Tell the Truth" [1]: Ray Charles **A238**
"Tell the Truth" [2]: Derek & Dominos A185
"Temple, The": Pink Floyd A43
"Temporary Like Achilles": Bob Dylan A121
"Temptation" [1] B12
"Temptation" [2]: Heaven 17 A36
"Temptation Eyes": The Grass Roots B24
"Ten Cents a Dance" B30
"Ten Commandments of Love": The Moonglows A110
"Ten Crack Commandments": Notorious B.I.G. B14
"Tenderloin": Blue Öyster Cult A99
"Tenderly" B30
"Tenderness": Paul Simon A93, B1
"Tender Trap, The" A14
"Ten Little Indians": The Beach Boys B15
"Tennessee": Carl Perkins **B8**
"Tennessee Jed": The Grateful Dead B17
"Tennessee Moon" A145
"Tennessee Waltz, The": Patti Page B15; Spring B15
"Tenth-Avenue Freeze-Out": Bruce Springsteen A101
"Tenting on the Old Camp Ground" A145
"Tenting To-Night" B24, **B24**
"Tequila": The Beatles B8; The Champs A44, A97
"Tequila Sunrise": Eagles A185
"Terminator X to the Edge of Panic": Public Enemy A99
"Terrapin Station": The Grateful Dead **B17**
"Terraplane Blues": Robert Johnson A132
"Tesla Girls": Orchestral Manoeuvres A185
"Testify" see "(I Wanna) Testify"
"Texas": Chris Rea A185
"Texas Flood": Stevie Ray Vaughan **A256**
"Tha' Lunatic": 2Pac A146
"Thanks for the Memory": Slade **B21**
"Thank You (Falettinme Be Mice Elf Agin)": Sly and the Family Stone A43, **A55**, A238, **A241**, B4, B19
"Thank You for Sending Me an Angel": Talking Heads A185
"Thank You for Talkin' to Me Africa": Sly and the Family Stone B4
"Thank You for the Music": ABBA B25

"Thank You Girl": The Beatles A98, A107, **A107**, A195, A259, B7, **B8**
"Thank You Guru Dev" **B3**
"Thank You": Led Zeppelin B21
"That Ain't Love": REO Speedwagon A250
"That Beautiful Rag" A145
"That Certain Feeling" **B30**
"That Christmas Feeling" A14
"That Day Is Done": Paul McCartney A185, B20
"That Feeling Is Gone" A145
"That Girl's Been Spying on Me": Billy Dean A189
"That Kazzatsky Dance" **A168**
"That'll be the Day": Buddy Holly A44, A75, A76, A80, A97, A185, A247, B7, **B8**, B24; The Quarrymen B8; Linda Ronstadt B24
"That Means a Lot": The Beatles B7, **B8**
"That Moment of Moments" **B30**
"That Old Black Magic" B10, B16, **B30**
"That Old Feeling" **B30**
"That Old Girl of Mine" A145
"That Ole Devil Called Love": Billie Holiday B4
"That's All" [1] B30
"That's All" [2]: Genesis **A55**
"That's All Right (Mama)" A216; The Beatles B8; Arthur Crudup A159; Elvis Presley A99, A159, A247
"That Same Song": The Beach Boys B15
"That's Another Scottish Story": Henry Hall and the BBC Dance Orchestra A227
"That's Entertainment": Jam, The A185, B21
"That's for Me" **B30**
"That's Gratitude" A145
"That's How I Love The Blues" **B30**
"That's How Strong My Love Is": Otis Redding A29, B20; The Rolling Stones B20
"That's It, I Quit, I'm Movin' On": Sam Cooke A160, B15
"That's It for the Other One": Grateful Dead, The A72
"That's Just the Way I Feel": Gary Usher B15
"That's Love" B30
"That Sly Old Gentleman" **B30**
"That's Me": Paul Simon B1
"That's My Job": Conway Twitty A191
"That's My Life (My Love and My Home)": Freddy (Alf) Lennon B8
"That's My Woman": The Beatles B8

"That's Not Her Style": Billy Joel A185
"That's Not Me": The Beach Boys A160, B15; Brian Wilson B15
"That Song About the Midway": Joni Mitchell **A260**
"That's Really Super, Supergirl": XTC A185
"That's the Doctor, Bill" A145
"That's the Kind of Baby for Me" A145
"That's the Way (I Like It)": K.C. and the Sunshine Band B24
"That's the Way God Planned It": Billy Preston B7
"That's the Way I've Always Heard It Should Be": Carly Simon A99
"That's the Way Love Goes": Janet Jackson A117
"That's the Way of the World": Earth, Wind, and Fire **A263**
"That Swaying Harmony" B12
"That's What Friends Are For" A249; Dionne and Friends A6
"That's What I Want for Christmas" B12
"That's What Love Is Made Of": The Miracles **A108**
"That's What Puts the Sweet in Home Sweet Home" A145
"That's When Your Heartaches Begin": The Beatles B7; Elvis Presley B8, B19
"That's Where I Belong": Paul Simon B1
"That's Where the Happy People Go": Trammps, The **A101**
"That's Why God Made the Movies": Paul Simon B1
"That's Why I'm Blue": Jimmie Rodgers A266
"That Was Your Mother": Paul Simon A9
"That Will Be Alright": Kansas Joe McCoy A201, **B26**
"That Wonderful Girl of Mine" B12
"That Wonderful Home Town of Mine" B12
"That Would Be Something": The Beatles B8; Paul McCartney **B18**
"That Yiddisha Professor" B12
"Theatre, The": The Pet Shop Boys A174
"Their Hearts Were Full of Spring": The Beach Boys **A125**, A160, B15; The Four Freshmen B15
"Their Satanic Majesties Request": The Rolling Stones B29
"Thela Hun Ginjeet": King Crimson A221

Song Index

"Thelma": Paul Simon B1
"Them Bones": Alice in Chains **A17**, **A97**, A221
"Theme for a Dream": The Beatles B8
"Theme for Great Cities": Simple Minds A185
"Theme from Dr. Kildaire (Three Stars Will Shine Tonight)": Richard Chamberlain A99
"Theme from Harry's Game": Clannad B21
"Theme from Shaft": Isaac Hayes A185
"Theme from The Apartment" B12
"Theme from The Family Way": Paul McCartney **B7**
"Theme from Z Cars": Johnny Keating B8
"Them There Eyes" B30; Billie Holiday B4
"Then Came You": Dionne Warwick and the Spinners **A248**
"Then He Kissed Me" A259; The Crystals A45, B15
"Then I Kissed Her": The Beach Boys B15
"Then We'll All Go Home" A145
"Then You'll Remember Me" A145
"There, There": Radiohead **A203**
"There Ain't No Sanity Clause": Damned, The B21
"There Goes a Tenner": Kate Bush B21
"There Goes My Baby": The Drifters A44, A77, A270
"There He Is (At My Door)": Martha and the Vandellas A110
"There Is a Balm": Mahalia Jackson **A161**
"There Is a Fountain Filled with Blood": Gidden Sisters A240
"There Is a Light That Never Goes Out": The Smiths A36
"There Is No Greater Love": Billie Holiday B4
"There Is No Language in our Lungs": XTC B21
"There Is No Time": Lou Reed A124
"There Is Power in the Blood" A219
"There'll Be a Hot Time in the Old Town Tonight" **A147**
"There'll Be Bluebirds Over the White Cliffs of Dover" A209
"There'll Be Sad Songs": Billy Ocean A250
"There'll Be Some Changes Made" **A147**, B30
"There Must Be an Angel": Eurythmics A185
"There Must Be a Place": Talking Heads A185
"There Once Was a Man" B12

"There's a Boat Dat's Leavin' Soon for New York" B12
"(There's a) Devil in His [Her] Heart": The Beatles A98, A259, B8; The Donays A95, A98, A259
"There's a Great Day Coming" B30
"There's a Kind of Hush": Herman's Hermits A70, A99
"There's a Little Bit of Irish in Sadie Cohen" B12
"There's a Lull in My Life" **B30**
"There's a Man": Marion Williams **A161**
"There's a Place" **B16**; The Beatles **A90**, A91, A98, **A100**, B7, **B8**, B18
"There's a Small Hotel" **B10**, **B30**
"There's a World": Neil Young A268
"There's No Action": Elvis Costello A185, **B20**
"There's No Business Like Show Business" B10, B12, B30
"There's No Other (Like My Baby)": The Beach Boys B15; The Crystals A160, B15
"There's No Sorrow": Spirit of Memphis B21
"There's No Tomorrow" B12
"There's No You" B30
"There's So Many": Brian Wilson B15
"There There": Radiohead **A169**
"There was a Time": James Brown and the Famous Flames A31, A43, A210, B4
"There Will Never Be Another You" **B10**, **B11**, **B30**, **A224**
"There You Are, Eddie": The Beatles B7
"These Are My Twisted Words": Radiohead **A169**
"These Arms of Mine": Otis Redding A29
"These Eyes": The Guess Who B24
"These Foolish Things" A33, **A96**, A145, **B19**
"These Things Take Time": The Smiths A36
"These Walls": Dream Theater A175
"They All Laughed" A145, B30
"They Always Follow Me Around" B30
"They Can't Take That Away From Me" A168, **B30**
"They Didn't Believe Me" A168, B10, **B30**
"They Don't Dance No Mo'": Goodie MoB B14
"(They Long to Be) Close to You" A147; The Carpenters **A249**; Richard Chamberlain **A249**; Dionne Warwick **A249**
"They Reminisce Over You": Pete Rock and C.L. Smooth B22

"They're on Their Way to Mexico" A145
"They're Red Hot": Robert Johnson A58
"They Say It's Wonderful" A13, **B10**, B30
"Thick as a Brick": Jethro Tull **A4**, **A188**, **A149**
"Thick as Thieves": Jam A185
"Thief in the Night": Sheila Walsh A185
"Thing or Two, A": The Beach Boys B15
"Things Are Looking Up" B10, **B30**
"Things": Bobby Darin B21
"Things 'Bout Coming My Way": Tampa Red **A239, A240**
"Things Can Only Get Better": Howard Jones A252
"Things That Dreams Are Made Of": The Human League B20
"Things That I Used to Do, The" B17
"Things We Do for Love, The": 10cc A99
"Things We Said Today": The Beatles A98, A99, A185, A195, A250, B3, B7, B8, **B18**, B19, B21
"Thingumybob": John Foster and Sons Ltd. Black Dyke Mills Band B7
"Thin Ice, The": Pink Floyd A185
"Think" [1]: James Brown A238, B4
"Think" [2]: Aretha Franklin **A230**, B7, B24
"Think for Yourself": The Beatles A43, A90, A247, **A254**, B7, B8
"Thinkin' 'Bout You Baby": Sharon Marie B15; Spring B15
"Thinking About You": Radiohead **A169**
"Thinking Blues": Bessie Smith A176
"Thinking of Linking": The Beatles B7, B8
"Thinking Round Corners": Jethro Tull A188
"Think It Over": Buddy Holly B8
"Think of Me With Kindness": Gentle Giant B20
"Think Too Much": Paul Simon A93, B1
"Third Man Theme, The" B30
"Third Stone from the Sun": The Jimi Hendrix Experience A40, A55
"Third World Man": Steely Dan A96
"Thirsty and Miserable": Black Flag A210
"Thirteen Collar" **B30**
"Thirteen": Frank Zappa A11
"Thirty Days" B8; Chuck Berry A95
"This Boy": The Beatles A91, A92, A98, A195, A221, B7, B8, B21
"This Can't Be Love" **B10**, **B30**
"This Car of Mine": The Beach Boys B15

"This Changing Light": Deacon Blue A185
"This Charming Man": The Smiths A36
"(This Could Be) The Last Time": The Rolling Stones **B19**
"This Diamond Ring": Gary Lewis and the Playboys **A32**, B4
"This Dying Soul": Dream Theater A175
"This Fire": Franz Ferdinand B21
"This Flight Tonight": Joni Mitchell **A260**; Nazareth A185, B20
"This Funny World" A168, B10, **B30**
"This Guitar (Can't Keep from Crying)": George Harrison B7
"This Guy's in Love with You" B3
"This Is Hardcore": Pulp A82
"This Is How It Feels": Inspiral Carpets B21
"This Is Love": George Harrison B7
"This Is My Country": The Impressions A144
"This Is Not Love": Jethro Tull **A186**
"This Isn't Love": Brian Wilson B15
"This Is Only The Beginning" B30
"This Is Rock and Roll": The Coasters A77
"This Is the Army, Mr. Jones" B12
"This Is the Life" [1]: Living Colour A99
"This Is The Life" [2]: Dream Theater A175
"This Joy": Vanessa Mitchell A3
"This Land Is Your Land": Dafyff Iwan A123; ["Mae'n Wlad I Mi"] Woody Guthrie B21
"This Little Girl of Mine": The Everly Brothers B15
"This Magic Moment": The Drifters **A33**
"This Must Be Love": Phil Collins A185
"This Must Be the Place": Talking Heads A185, B21
"This Night Has Opened My Eyes": The Smiths A36
"This Note's for You": Neil Young B6
"This Old Heart of Mine" A95; The Isley Brothers A108, A185
"This One": Paul McCartney A185, B20
"This Song" [1] B12
"This Song" [2]: George Harrison A43, A95, B7
"This Time the Dream's on Me" **B10**
"This Town Ain't Big Enough": Sparks A185
"This Town Is a Sealed Tuna Sandwich": Mothers of Invention, The A11
"This Wheel's on Fire": The Band A185; The Byrds A121

Song Index

"This Whole World": The Beach Boys A160, B15; Spring B15; Brian Wilson B15
"This Woman's Work": Kate Bush B21
"This Year's Girl": Elvis Costello A185, B21
"Thoroughly Modern Millie" A14
"Those Gambler Blues": Jimmie Rodgers A266
"Those Wedding Bells Shall Not Ring Out" B12
"Those Were the Days" [1] B12; Mary Hopkin B7
"Those Were the Days" [2]: Cream B7, B29
"Those Who Want to Buy": echolyn A72
"Thought I'd Died and Gone to Heaven": Bryan Adams **A21**
"Thoughts Without Words": Shadows Fall A205
"Thought @ Work": The Roots B31
"Thousand Island Park": Mahavishnu Orchestra B20
"Thou Swell": **B10**, **B30**; Count Basie B21
"THRAK": King Crimson A224
"Thrasher": Neil Young B6
"Three Blind Mice" B15
"Three Chords and the Truth": Sara Evans A193
"Three Coins in the Fountain" B8
"Three Cool Cats": The Beatles B7; The Coasters A77, A95, A160, B15; The Quarrymen B8
"Three Evils": Coheed and Cambria A205
"Three-fold Benediction" B12
"Three Girl Rhumba": Wire **A210**
"Three Legs": Paul McCartney B18
"Three Libras": A Perfect Circle A205
"Three Little Birds": Bob Marley and the Wailers A235
"Three O'Clock in the Morning" B30
"Three of a Perfect Pair": King Crimson A224
"Three Point One Four": The Bloodhound Gang A146
"Three Steps to Heaven": The Beatles B8; Eddie Cochran **B21**
"Three-Thirty Blues": The Beatles B8
"Thriller": Michael Jackson A202, B28
"Thrill Is Gone, the": B.B. King **A26**, A97
"Through a London Window": The Beatles B7
"Through My Sails": Neil Young A33
"Through the Fire": Chaka Khan B31
"Through These Walls": Phil Collins A185

"Through the Wire": Kanye West A261, B31
"Through the Years" B30
"Through With Buzz": Steely Dan **A96**, A99
"Through Your Hands": John Hiatt **A268**, **B32**
"Throw Back the Little Ones": Steely Dan **A96**
"Throw Down the Sword": Wishbone Ash A185, B20, B21
"Throwing It All Away": Genesis A232
"Throwing Stones": The Grateful Dead B17
"Thug for Life": Tupac Shakur [2Pac] **B31**
"Thuggish Ruggish Bone": Bone Thugs-n-Harmony B31
"Thugz Mansion": Nas **B31**; Tupac Shakur **B31**
"Thumbin' a Ride": The Beatles B8; The Coasters A95; Jackie Lomax B7
"Thunder": Prince A79, **B13**
"Thunder Road": Bruce Springsteen A7, A80, A122, A247
"Ticket to Ride": The Beatles A91, A92, A98, A107, A160, A195, A247, **A254**, **A259**, B3, B7, B8, B15, B21, B24; Vanilla Fudge A72
"Tico-Tico" B12
"Tide Is High, The": Blondie B32; The Paragons B32
"Tie Me Kangaroo Down, Sport": Rolf Harris B8
"Tiger Rag" A145
"Tighten Up My Thang": The Soul Children **A29**
"Tight Like This" A145
"Till I Die": The Beach Boys A125, B15
"Tillie's Downtown Now" A145
"('Till) I Kissed You": The Everly Brothers A44, B24
"Till Kingdom Come": Coldplay A167
"Till The Clouds Roll By" B30
"Till the End of the Day": The Kinks A121, A185, B20, B21
"Till the Morning Comes": Neil Young A185
"Till There Was You": The Beatles A98, B7; Peggy Lee B7, **B8**
"Till Times Get Better" A145
"Timbuctoo" A145
"Time" [1]: The Beatles B8
"Time" [2]: Pink Floyd A99, A185, A199, A205, **A225**, B24, B29
"Time" [3]: Anthrax **A208**
"Time After Time" [1] B30
"Time After Time" [2]: Cyndi Lauper B24

"Time Beat": Ray Cathode B8
"Time Fades Away": Neil Young B6
"Time for Action": Secret Affair A185, **A186**, B21
"Time for Tea": Madness A185
"Time Has Come Today": The Chambers Brothers A43, **A101**
"Time Is an Ocean": Paul Simon B1
"Time Is on My Side": The Rolling Stones A101
"Time Is Tight": Booker T. and the MGs A29
"Time Marches On": Tracy Lawrence A191
"Time of the Season": The Zombies A248
"Time on My Hands" B10, **B30**
"Time Out of Mind": Steely Dan A96
"Time's Beach": Frank Zappa A11
"Times They Are A-Changin', The": The Beach Boys B15; Bob Dylan A121, A216, A247, B16, B20, B21; Simon and Garfunkel B1
"Time to Get Alone": The Beach Boys A160, B15; Redwood B15
"Time Waits for No One": Helen Forrest B4
"Time Warp" A167
"Time Was" [1]: The Four Freshmen B15
"Time Was" [2]: Wishbone Ash A185
"Time Will Bring You Everything": The Beatles B8
"Time Will Crawl": David Bowie B20
"Time Will Tell": T'Pau A185
"Tin Angel": Joni Mitchell **A260**
"Ting, Ting, That's How the Bell Goes" **B19** B19
"Tin Man": America B24
"Tinnie Run": Wolfstone B21
"Tin Soldier Man": The Kinks B20
"Tiny Room" **B30**
"Tipitina": Professor Longhair **A238**
"Tip of My Tongue" B8
"Tipperary Christening, The" B12
"Tiptoes": Madness A185
"Tired Eyes": Neil Young B6
"Tired of Waiting for You": Kinks A107, A185, B21
"Tis So Sweet to Trust in Jesus" A219
"Titanic, The": Leadbelly **A240**
"Titanic Blues": Virginia Liston A240
"Titanic Man Blues": Ma Rainey A240
"Title of the Song": Darrell Scott **A191**
"Titties and Beer": Frank Zappa A11, A27

"TM Song": The Beach Boys B15
"Toad": Cream B20
"Toads of the Short Forest": Mothers of Invention, The A11
"To All the Girls I've Loved Before": Willie Nelson and Julio Iglesias A193
"To Be Alone With you": Bob Dylan B32
"To Be Free": Chicago B3
"Tobacco Road": Nashville Teens A185
"To Bring You My Love": PJ Harvey A55
"Toccata": Emerson Lake & Palmer B21
"To Cry You a Song": Jethro Tull B20
"Today, I Love Ev'rybody" B30
"Today, Tomorrow and Forever": Patsy Cline B21
"Today": Smashing Pumpkins A99
"Toddle, Introducing, 'Maori' " A145
"Todo Puerto Rico": Bad Boy Orchestra A3
"Together Again": Janet Jackson A6
"Together We Stand": Canned Heat A185
"To God Be the Glory" A219
"To Here Knows When": My Bloody Valentine **A22**
"To Keep My Love Alive" **B30**
"To Kingdom Come": Band A185
"To Know Him Is to Love Him": The Beatles **B8**; The Teddy Bears A97, A99, A160, B7, B15
"Tokolosche Man": John Kongos A185
"Tokyo": The Books A204
"To Life" B12
"To Love and Be Loved" A14
"To Love Somebody": The Bee Gees **B24**
"Tom, Dick Or Harry" B30
"Tomb of the Boom": Big Boi **A1**
"Tombstone Blues": Bob Dylan B7
"Tom Cat and Pussy Blues": Jimmy Davis B4
"Tom Dooley": The Kingston Trio A97
"Tomorrow" [1]: Wings B18
"Tomorrow" [2]: U2 A89
"Tomorrow Never Knows": The Beatles A75, **A76**, A90, A92, A95, **A97**, A98, A99, A134, A138, A185, A198, A250, **B7**, B8, **B18**, B21, B29, B32
"Tomorrow Night": Lonnie Johnson A53; Elvis Presley A99
"Tom Rushen Blues": Charley Patton **B27**
"Tones ('TuneX')": The Beach Boys B15
"Tongue": R.E.M. B32

Song Index

"Tonight" B12
"Tonight, Tonight, Tonight": Genesis A232, B20
"Tonight and the Rest of My Life": Nina Gordon A219
"Tonight I'll Be Staying Here With You": Bob Dylan A99
"Tonight Is Forever": The Pet Shop Boys A174
"Tonight Is So Right for Love": The Beatles B8
"Tonight Show, The": Dilly B7
"Tonight's the Night (Gonna Be Alright)": Janet Jackson A123; Rod Stewart A99, A123
"Tonight's the Night": Neil Young B6
"Tonight You Belong to Me": The Honeys B15; Patience and Prudence B15
"Too Bad About Sorrows": The Beatles **B8**
"Too Bad Boys": Bob Wills & His Texas Playboys A240
"Too Busy" A119
"Too Darn Hot" B30
"Too High": Stevie Wonder A185
"Too Kool to Kalypso": Kent Klark (Stewart Copeland) A235
"Too Late Now" **B10**, **B30**
"Too Many Parties and Too Many Pals": Hank Williams B4
"Too Many People": Paul McCartney B8, B18
"Too Marvelous for Words" **B10**, **B30**
"Too Much" [1]: Elvis Presley A97
"Too Much" [2]: The Velvet Underground A210
"Too Much monkey Business": The Beatles B8; Chuck Berry A95, B4,; Cream A132
"Too Much Mustard" A145
"Too Much Sugar": Brian Wilson B15
"Too Much Time on My Hands": Styx A141
"Toon Improvement Bill, The" **B19**
"Too Old to Rock 'n' Roll": Jethro Tull A188
"Too-Ra-Loo-Ra-Loo-Ra": Bing Crosby B4
"Toot Toot Tootsie (Goo'bye)": The Beatles B7
"Topango Windows": Spirit B7
"Topaz": The B-52's A99
"Top Hat" A145
"Top Hat, White Tie, and Tails" A168, B10, B30
"Top Man": Blur B20
"Top of the World": the Dixie Chicks A191
"Top o' the Morning" A14
"Topsy" A145

"Topsy II": Cozy Cole A97
"To Ramona": Bob Dylan **A225**
"Torchy": The Beatles B8
"To Speak Is a Sin": The Pet Shop Boys A174
"Tossin' and Turnin'": Ivy League **B20**; Bobby Lewis **A101**
"Total Eclipse": Klaus Nomi **A178**
"Total Eclipse of the Heart": Bonnie Tyler A167
"Totally Useless": 10000 Volts A185
"To the Steins" B12
"To the Water": Maire Brennan B21
"Touch a Hand, Make a Friend": The Staple Singers A29
"Touch and Go": Emerson, Lake, and Palmer A185
"Touch Me in the Morning": Diana Ross A248
"Touch Me": The Doors A101, A185, B7
"Touch of Grey": The Grateful Dead A155, B17
"Touch of Your Hand, The" B30
"To-Wa-Bac-A-Way" **A238**
"Town Called Malice, A": The Jam B20
"To What You Said" B12
"Toys in the Attic": Aerosmith A55, B24
"Toy Soldiers": Martika A234 (also see "Like Toy Soldiers")
"To Zion": Lauren Hill A99
"Traces of the Western Slope": Rickie Lee Jones A269
"Traces": The Classics IV A93, B8
"Track 8": Public Image Ltd B20
"Track": Kenny Larkin **B5**
"Tracks of My Tears, The" A95; Smokey Robinson and the Miracles A32, **A108**, A247, B4, B21
"Tracy": The Cuff Links A99, A185, **B20**
"Tradition" B12
"Tragedy": The Bee Gees **A241**
"Trail of the Lonesome Pine, The" A145
"Trailways Bus": Paul Simon B1
"Train 45": Grayson & Whitter A240
"Train Fare Blues": Muddy Waters **A75**
"Train in the Distance": Paul Simon B1
"Train in Vain": The Clash A118
"Train Kept a-Rollin', The": The Johnny Burnette Trio B8
"Trains" [1]: Vapors A185
"Trains" [2]: Porcupine Tree B21
"Train Time": Cream A132

"Train Whistle Blues": Jimmie Rodgers A266
"Trambone": Chet Atkins B8
"Trampled Underfoot": Led Zeppelin A16
"Tramp's Mother, The": Goebel Reeves A266
"Tramp the Dirt Down": Elvis Costello B4
"Transcendental Meditation": The Beach Boys B7, B15
"Trans Europe Express": Kraftwerk **A104**
"Transient Joy": Sunday All Over the World A218
"Trash": Roxy Music A185
"Travelin' Band": Creedence Clearwater Revival A185, B8
"Travelin' Blues": Jimmie Rodgers A266
"Travelin' Man": Ricky Nelson B15
"Traveller in Time": Uriah Heep A185
"Travelling Chess": Icicle Works A185
"Treasures Untold": Jimmie Rodgers A266
"Treat Me Right": Pat Benatar B24
"Treefingers": Radiohead **A162**
"Trees" B30
"Tres Palabras" B12
"Trial, The": Pink Floyd A185, A198, B21
"Trial of Tears": Dream Theater A175
"Tribal Anthem": 68 Beats A3
"Tribal Look": Toyah A185
"Tribute to a King" B3; William Bell A29; Otis Redding B3
"Trilogy": Emerson, Lake, and Palmer **A139**
"Triple Trouble": Beastie Boys B31
"Trip Through Your Wires": U2 A185
"Trip to the Fair, A": Renaissance A138
"Triste partida, A": Luís Gonzaga B25
"Trolley Song, The" A53, B30; Judy Garland B4
"Trombone Dixie": The Beach Boys B15
"Trouble" [1]: Dorothy Love Coates **A161**
"Trouble" [2]: The Flying Lizards B20
"Trouble Child": Joni Mitchell A260
"Trouble Every Day": Frank Zappa and the Mothers of Invention A11, A27, B7
"Trouble in Mind": Bertha (Chippie) Hill **A240**; Richard M. Jones A240; Rosetta Tharpe A240; Georgia White A240
"Trouble in Paradise": Huey Lewis A250
"Trouble Is a Man" **A209**
"Trouble Loves Me": Morrissey B13
"Trouble Minded Blues": Cliff Carlisle A240
"Trouble So Hard": Dora Reed, Henry Reed, and Vera Hall **A161**

"Truck Driver and His Mate, The": The Pet Shop Boys A174
"Truckin'": The Grateful Dead **A101**, B17
"True Colors": Cyndi Lauper A250
"True Fine Love": Steve Miller Band A250
"True Love Goodbye, A": Roy Orbison A270
"True Love Tends to Forget" A122; Bob Dylan A180
"True Love": The Beatles B8
"True Love Ways": Buddy Holly A270
"True": Spandau Ballet A36, A185, A250
"Trust Me (This Is Love)": Amanda Marshall **A167**
"Truth Hits Everybody": The Police A185, B21
"Try a Little Tenderness": The Commitments A30; Sam Cooke, **A30**; Bing Crosby **A30**; Ruth Etting A30; Aretha Franklin **A30**; Ted Lewis A30; Otis Redding A29, **A30**, A96; Frank Sinatra A30; Three Dog Night A30
"Trying to Get to You": Roy Orbison A270
"Tryin' to Get to You": Elvis Presley **A99**, B8
"Tryin' to Throw Your Arms Around the World": U2 A89, A103
"Try": Janis Joplin B3
"Try Me": James Brown A185
"Try Not to Breathe": R.E.M. **A181**, **B24**
"Try Not to Save Me": Two Tongues A205
"Try Some, Buy Some": Ronnie Spector B7
"Try to Forget" B30
"Try Too Hard": Dave Clark Five A107
"T Smidje": Laïs **B21**
"Tubthumping": Chumbawumba **A233**
"Tubular Bells": Mike Oldfield **A182**, A233
"Tuck Away My Lonesome Blues": W. Lee O'Daniel & His Hillbilly Boys A240; Jimmie Rodgers A266
"Tuck Me to Sleep in My Old 'Tucky Home" A145
"Tuesday [Forever] Afternoon [Tuedsay?]": The Moody Blues A72, A101, **A101**, B7
"Tuesday's Child": All About Eve A185
"Tulane": Chuck Berry A244
"Tulips From Amsterdam" B25
"Tulip Time in Sing Sing" B10
"Tumba la Caña" A3
"Tumba la Casa": Sancocho A3
"Tumbling Dice": The Rolling Stones A43, A246, B32

Song Index

"Tuna Fish Promenade": Mothers of Invention, The A11
"Tune Up" A224
"Tupelo Honey": Van Morrison A124, B21
"Turbulent Indigo": Joni Mitchell **A260**
"Turkey in the Straw" B27, B30
"Turn Around, Look at Me": Jerry Capehart B8
"Turn for the Worse": Dia Pason B2
"Turning Blue": Madness A185
"Turning Home": David Nail A205
"Turning Japanese": Vapors A185
"Turning Point": Brian Wilson B15
"Turn It into Love": Kylie Minogue A185
"Turn It on Again": Genesis A142
"Turn on the Heat" A145
"(Turn on Your) Love Light" B17; The Grateful Dead A25, A171
"Turn the Beat Around": Vicki Sue Robinson A3, B24
"Turn the Page": Bob Seger **A225**
"Turn to Stone": Electric Light Orchestra A185, B21, B24
"Turn! Turn! Turn!": The Byrds A33, A121, A185, B24; Mary Hopkin B7
"Turn Your Lights Down Low": Bob Marley and the Wailers A235
"Turtle Blues": Janis Joplin B3
"Turtle Dovin' ": The Coasters A77
"Tush": ZZ Top A55, A185
"Tutti Frutti" B27; Little Richard A43, A44, A73, A80, **A86**, A95, A181, A185, A238, A247, B8, B19, **B20**, B32
"TVC-15": David Bowie A101
"T.V. Eye": The Stooges **A210**
"Tweedle Dee" [1]: LaVern Baker A44
"Tweedle Dee" [2]: Chick Corea A114
"Twelfth of Never, The": Donny Osmond A259
"Twelfth Street Rag" B12
"Twelve-Bar Original": The Beatles B8
"Twelve Gate to the City": Rev. Gary Davis B21
"Twelve's Enough": echolyn A72
"Twenty-First Century Schizoid Man": King Crimson A72
"Twenty Flight Rock": Eddie Cochran B8
"Twenty-one Today" B16
"Twenty Small Cigars": Frank Zappa A12
"Twenty Years" A145

"Twiggy Voo" B19, **B19**
"Twilight": U2 B20
"Twilight Alehouse": Genesis A142
"Twilight Time": The Platters A97
"Twilight Zone, The": Rush A28, B21
"Twist, The": Hank Ballard B24; Chubby Checker A250, B24
"Twist and Shout" A97, A184, B16; The Beatles **A63**, A69, A92, A98, A99, A259, B7, **B8**, B18, B19, B20, **B24**; Isley Brothers A43, A95, A222, B7, B20, B24; The Top Notes A222
"Twisting": They Might Be Giants A185
"Two Big Eyes" B30
"Two Butchers": Steeleye Span B21
"Two Divided By Zero": The Pet Shop Boys A174
"Two Fingers": Jethro Tull A188
"Two Grey Rooms": Joni Mitchell A260
"Two Hands": King Crimson A185, A218
"Two-Headed Boy": Neutral Milk Hotel A22
"Two Hearts Are Better Than One" **B30**
"Two Hearts": Phil Collins A250
"Two Ladies in de Shade of de Banana Tree" **B30**
"Two Little Girls in Blue" **B19** B19
"Two Little Hitlers": Elvis Costello A185
"Two Minutes Silence": John Lennon B7
"Two of a Kind, Workin' on a Full House": Garth Brooks A191
"Two of Us": The Beatles A90, A99, A98, **A100**, **A245**, B7, B8, B18
"Two Princes": Spin Doctors **A245**
"Two Sisters of Mystery": Mandrill A39
"Two Sleepy People" B30
"Two Sparrows in a Hurricane": Tanya Tucker A191
"Two Ways to Fall": Barry and Holly Tashian A189; Ty Herndon A189
"Two Wrongs Don't Make a Right": Mary Wells A95
"Type": Living Colour A99

"U Can't Touch This": MC Hammer A24, **A202**, A261
"Uh-Uh Ooh-Ooh Look Out (Here It Comes)": Roberta Flack A24
"Ultraviolet (Light My Way)": U2 **A89**
"Um, Um, Um, Um, Um, Um": Major Lance A108

"Unbelievable" [1]: EMF A247
"Unbelievable" [2]: Diamond Rio A191
"Unchained Melody" A260; Roy Hamilton A44; Righteous Brothers A185, B21
"Unchained Melody": Joni Mitchell A260
"Uncle Albert / Admiral Halsey": Wings B7, B18
"Uncle Jack": Spirit B7
"Uncle John's Band": The Grateful Dead A101, A197, **B17**
"Uncle Meat [Variations]": Frank Zappa and the Mothers of Invention A11, **A12**, A27, **A60**
"Under a Blanket of Blue" B30
"Under African Skies": Paul Simon A9
"Under a Glass Moon": Dream Theater A175
"Undercover Agent for the Blues": Tina Turner A185
"Under Cover of the Night": The Rolling Stones A21
"Under My Thumb": The Rolling Stones B24
"Underneath the Arches": Henry Hall and the BBC Dance Orchestra A227
"Underneath the Streetlight": Joni Mitchell A260
"Under Pressure": Queen/David Bowie A185
"Under The Bamboo Tree" **B30**
"Under the Boardwalk": Drifters A185, B20; The Rolling Stones B20
"Under the Bridge": The Red Hot Chili Peppers A205, B32
"Under the Gun": Sheila Walsh A185
"Under the Hebrew Moon" B12
"Under the House": Public Image Ltd **B20**
"Under the Mersey Wall": George Harrison B7
"Under the Sea" **A202**
"Under the Ukelele [sic] Tree": Jack Hylton and His Orchestra A227
"Undertow" [1]: Genesis A142
"Undertow" [2]: Tool A205
"Underwater": The Frogmen B15
"Undressed to Kill": Jethro Tull A188
"Unexpected": Anonymous Bosch A212
"Unforgettable Fire, The": U2 A103, A185, B20
"Unforgettable": Natalie and Nat "King": Cole A101; Nat "King": Cole A101, B21
"Unforgiven, The": Metallica A28, A252
"Unknown Legend": Neil Young B6
"Unknown Soldier, The": The Doors B3

"Unlucky Blues" A145
"Until Jesus Calls Me Home": Sam Cooke A161
"Until the End of the World": U2 **A89**, A103
"Until The Real Thing Comes Along" **B30**
"Until Today" A145
"Untitled 1": Sigur Rós A205
"Up, Up, and Away" B3; The 5th Dimension A99, A105, B7
"Up Against It": The Pet Shop Boys **B13**
"Up Around the Bend": Creedence Clearwater Revival A16, A185, B24
"Up From the Skies": The Jimi Hendrix Experience A40, A101, **A257**, B3, B29
"Up Here in the North of England": Icicle Works A185
"Up in the Air": The Dixie Dregs A73
"Up Jumps the Boogie": Timbaland and Magoo B14
"Up on the Roof": Drifters A247, B24; Kenny Lynch B8; James Taylor B24
"Upper Room, The": Mahalia Jackson **A161**
"Up!": Shania Twain A191, **A193**
"Upside Down": Diana Ross B24
"Up the Pool": Jethro Tull A188
"Up Tight" A97
"Uptight (Everything's Alright)": Stevie Wonder **A95**, A99, A154, A185, B7
"Up to Me" [1]: Roger McGuinn A121
"Up to Me" [2]: Jethro Tull A188
"Uptown Girl": Billy Joel A167, A182
"Up Town": Roy Orbison A270
"Uptown": The Crystals A96
"Up Where We Belong": Joe Cocker & Jennifer Warnes A185
"Urge for Going": Joni Mitchell A260
"Urgent": Foreigner A74, A250
"Us and Them": Pink Floyd A185, A199, B24, B29
"Used to Be a Sweet Boy": Morrissey **B13**
"Use Your Imagination" B30

"Vacation": The Go-Go's **A250**
"Vacation Time": The Beatles B8; Chuck Berry A95
"Valencia": The Savoy-Orpheans A227
"Valentine's Day": Paul McCartney B18
"Valerie": Steve Winwood A250
"Valeska (My Russian Rose)" B12

Song Index 255

"Valley of the Dolls (Theme)": Dionne Warwick A99
"Vals i Gökottan": Evert Taube B25
"Vamos a Gozar": Lesson One A3
"Vampire Blues": Neil Young B6
"Vampires" [2]: The Pet Shop Boys A174
"Vampires, The" [1]: Paul Simon B1
"Vanity Fair": Mr. Bungle A163
"Variations on a Theme by Erik Satie": Blood, Sweat, and Tears A234, B3
"Varsity Drag" **A120**, B30
"Vegetable": Radiohead **A169**
"Vegetables": The Beach Boys A125, B7, B15; Brian Wilson B15
"Velveteen Doll": Roy Orbison A270
"Velvet Green": Jethro Tull A188, B20
"Ventura Highway": America A234
"Venus" [1]: Frankie Avalon A44
"Venus" [2]: Bananarama B24; Shocking Blue A185, B24
"Vera": Pink Floyd A185
"Veronica": Elvis Costello and Paul McCartney A99, B20
"Vertigo": U2 A89
"Very Cellular Song, A": The Incredible String Band A112, B20
"Very Early" A147
"Vicarious": Tool A205, A221
"Victim or the Crime": The Grateful Dead A99, **A200**, B17
"Victims of the Future": Gary Moore A185, B20, B21
"Victims of the Riddle": Toyah A185
"Victoria Gardens": Madness A185
"Victor Jara": Hoola Bandoola Band **B25**
"Victory": Puff Daddy A99
"Video Killed the Radio Star": The Buggles B32
"Vienna": Ultravox B20, B21
"View From the Afternoon, The": Arctic Monkey **B21**
"Viking": Peter Hammill A185
"Village Ghetto Land": Stevie Wonder B7
"Village Green Preservation Society": Kinks A185
"Village Green": The Kinks B20
"Village of the Sun": Frank Zappa **A59**
"Viola Lee Blues" B17
"Violent Side": Neil Young B6

"Violets for Your Furs" **B30**
"Virgil": Paul Simon B1
"Visions" [1]: Stevie Wonder A144, A185, B21
"Visions" [2]: Toyah A185
"Vision of Love": Mariah Carey B24
"Vision": Peter Hammill A185
"Viva Bobby Joe": Equals A185
"Vivaldi": Curved Air B21
"Vivienne" A228
"Vogue": Madonna A3, A258, B13
"Voices": Dream Theater A175
"Voices Inside My Head": The Police **A233**, A235
"Voices of Old People": Simon and Garfunkel B1
"Voices That Are Gone, The" **A264**
"Volunteers": Jefferson Airplane A99, B7
"Voodoo Child (Slight Return)": The Jimi Hendrix Experience **A16**, A17, A67, A247
"Voodoo Chile": The Jimi Hendrix Experience A19, A185, A269, **B3**, B20
"Voulez-Vous": ABBA A185, B20
"Voyeur": Kim Carnes A19
"VROOOM": King Crimson A224
"VROOOM VROOOM": King Crimson A224

"Wabash Blues" A145
"Wabash Cannonball" A191; The Quarrymen B8
"Wages Day": Deacon Blue A185
"Wah Wah": George Harrison A185, B18
"Wait, The": The Pretenders A221
"Waiter! Bring Me Water": Shania Twain A193
"Wait for an Answer": Heart B21
"Wait for Me": The Playmates B25
"Wait for Sleep": Dream Theater A175
"Waitin' for the Bus": Z.Z. Top A185
"Waiting, The": Tom Petty A250
"Waiting at the Church" B19 B19
"Waiting for a Certain Girl" A145
"Waiting for a Girl Like You": Foreigner A74
"Waiting for an Alibi": Thin Lizzy A185
"Waiting for a Train": Jimmie Rodgers A266, B8
"Waiting for the Big One": Peter Gabriel A185, **A186**
"Waiting for the End of the World": Elvis Costello A185, B20
"Waiting for the Robert E. Lee": A145, B19, B30
"Waiting for the Sun to Come Out" B30

"Waiting for the Weekend": Vapors A185
"Waiting for You": Edgar Broughton Band **B21**
"Wait": The Beatles A91, A92, A100, B7, B8, **B18**
"Wait Till The Cows Come Home" B30
"Wait 'Til the Sun Shines, Nellie" B12
"Wait Till You See Her" B30
"Wait Til the Clouds Roll By" B27
"Wait Until Tomorrow": Jimi Hendrix A185
"Wake Me I Am Dreaming": Love Affair A185, **B21**
"Wake Me up Before You Go-Go": Wham A185, A232
"Wake Me Up When September Ends": Green Day A5
"Wake the World": The Beach Boys B15
"Wake Up Alone": Amy Winehouse **A102**
"Wake Up Boo": The Boo Radleys B20
"Wake Up in the Morning": The Beatles **B8**
"Wake Up Little Susie": The Everly Brothers A44, A97, A216
"Wake Up": Rage Against the Machine A205
"Wake Up Sunshine": Chicago B7
"Walk, Don't Run": The Beatles B8; The Ventures A160
"Walk, The" [1]: The Beatles B7; Jimmy McCracklin B7
"Walk, The" [2]: Sawyer Brown **A191**
"Walk Away from Love": David Ruffin A43
"Walk Away Renee": Four Tops A185
"Walk Don't Run": Ventures A185
"Walk Don't Walk": Prince A79, **B13**
"Walkin' ": Beaver and Krause B21
"Walkin' Back to Happiness": Helen Shapiro B8
"Walking Blues": Robert Johnson A97
"Walking Down the Street": Nig-Heist A210
"Walking Happy" A14
"Walking in the Park With Eloise" [Jim McCartney]: Paul McCartney B7, **B8**
"Walking in Your Shadow": Uriah Heep A185
"Walking My Baby Home": John Lennon B8
"Walking on Air": King Crimson A218
"Walking on Broken Glass": Annie Lennox **B21**
"Walking on the Moon": The Police A235, A246
"Walking the Dog": B17; Rufus Thomas **A29**
"Walking With a Mountain": Icicle Works A185

"Walkin' My Baby Back Home" B30
"Walkin' the Back Streets": Little Milton A29
"Walkin' the Dog" B30
"Walkin' the Floor Over You": Ernest Tubb A53; Hank Williams B4
"Walkin' the Line": Brian Wilson B15
"Walk Like a Man": The Four Seasons A99, B15
"Walk Like and Egyptian": The Bangles B24
"Walk of Life": Dire Straits A99
"Walk On" [1]: Neil Young B6
"Walk On" [2]: U2 A89
"Walk on By" A147; Isaac Hayes A99; Dionne Warwick A247
"Walk on the Wild Side, A": Lou Reed A123, A124, A185; *see also* "Can I Kick It?"
"Walk Right Back": The Everly Brothers A259
"Walk Right In": The Rooftop Singers B8
"Walk This Way": Aerosmith A99, A225, **A248**; Run-DMC A99, B28
"Walk Upon the Water": Move A185
"Wall, The": Kansas A72, **A149**
"Wallflower": Peter Gabriel A185
"Wall of Love": Simple Minds A185
"Walls Come Tumbling Down": The Style Council B20, B21
"Walls": Emery A205
"Wall Street Shuffle": 10cc A19
"Waltz, The": Brian Wilson B15
"Waltz #2": Elliot Smith A221
"Waltz Darling": Malcolm McLaren B20
"Waltz Down The Aisle" B30
"Waltz for Debby" **A147**
"Waltz in Orbit": Ray Cathode B8
"Waltz in Springtime" B30
"Waltz in Swing Time" B30
"Waltz into Mischief": Madness A185
"Waltz of a New Moon": The Incredible String Band A112
"Wanderer, The": The Beach Boys B15; Dion B15
"Wandering in Dreamland" A145
"Wanderlust": Paul McCartney B7
"Wang Dang Doodel" B17
"Wang-Wang Blues" A145
"Wannabe": Spice Girls B24
"Wanted": Alan Jackson A191
"Wanted Dead or Alive": Bon Jovi **A16**, A55
"Wanted Man": Johnny Cash A216

Song Index

"WAOK Roll Call": The Roots B31
"War" [1]: The Temptations A105
"War" [2]: OutKast A99
"Warm and Beautiful": Wings B8
"Warmer Than a Whisper" A14
"Warm Fuzzy Feeling": Fastball A99
"Warm Sporran": Jethro Tull A188
"Warm": The Four Freshmen B15
"Warmth of the Sun": The Beach Boys A96, **A125**, A160, B15; Willie Nelson B15; Brian Wilson B15
"Warning": Black Sabbath **A83**
"Warning Sign": Talking Heads A185
"War of Man": Neil Young B6
"War Pigs / Luke's Wall": Black Sabbath A99
"Warrior": Wishbone Ash A185
"Wartime Prayers": Paul Simon B1
"Was a Sunny Day": Paul Simon A93, B1
"Washboard Blues" A145, **B30**
"Washington Bullets": The Clash B20
"Wasted on the Way": Crosby, Stills, and Nash **A247**
"Wasteland": Mission A185
"Watcher, The": Dr. Dre **B31**
"Watcher of the Skies": Genesis A142, A232, B20, **B21**
"Watching Rainbows": The Beatles **B7**
"Watching the Detectives": Elvis Costello A235
"Watching the Wheels": John Lennon A92, B7, B8, B24, B32
"Watch That Man": David Bowie B20
"Watch Your Step" [1]: The Beatles B8; Bobby Parker A95, **B8**
"Watch Your Step" [2]: Elvis Costello and the Attractions B4
"Water Boy" B12
"Waterfalls": TLC B32
"Waterfall": The Stone Roses B20
"Waterloo": ABBA A20, A185, B25
"Waterloo Sunset": The Kinks A185, A247, **B20, B21**, B29
"Watermelon in Easter Hay": Frank Zappa A11
"Watermelon Man": Mongo Santamaria B15
"Watermelon Party" A145
"Wave" A211
"Wave of Meditation": Pixies B21
"Waves of the Danube, The" B12
"Way, The": Fastball A99

"Way Back in the 1960s": The Incredible String Band A112
"Way Down in Alabama": Smyth County Ramblers A240
"Way Down Now": World Party **B32**
"Way Down South" A145
"Way Down Yonder in New Orleans" **B30**
"Wayfaring Stranger" B12
"Way I Am, The": Eminem A99
"Way It Is, The": Bruce Hornsby and the Range A99
"Way Over There": The Miracles A105
"Way That It Shows, The": Richard Thompson B21
"Wayward Girl Blues": Lottie Kimbrough **A239**, A240
"Wayward Son, The": Goebel Reeves A266
"Wayward Wind": The Beatles B8; Frank Ifield A259
"Way We Were, The": Gladys Knight and the Pips A158
"Way You Do the Things You Do, the": The Temptations **A108**
"Way You Look Tonight, The" A116, A168, **B10, B11, B30**; The Beatles B7; The Jaguars B15
"Way You Love Me, The": Faith Hill **A193**
"Way You Move, The": OutKast A99
"We Ain't": The Game A261, **B31**
"Weakest, The": Emery **A203**, A205
"Weakness": Inspiral Carpets B21
"We All Love Mother": Crowder Brothers A240
"We Are in Love": Adam Faith B8
"We Are Normal": The Bonzo Dog Band B7
"We Are the World": USA for Africa B25
"Wear My Ring Around Your Neck": Elvis Presley A97, B8
"Weasels Ripped My Flesh": Frank Zappa A208
"Weather Bird" B9
"Weather Report Suite": The Grateful Dead A171, B17
"Web, The": Marillion B20
"We Better Talk This Over": Bob Dylan A180
"We Bid You Goodnight" B17
"We Built This City": Starship A250, B24
"We Can Make It Baby": The Originals A110
"We Can Talk": The Band A185

"We Can't Use Each Other Anymore" A145
"We Can Work It Out": The Beatles A43, A90, A91, A98, A100, A107, **A107**, A195, A259, B7, B8, **B21**
"Wedding Bell Blues" B3
"Wedding Bells Are Breaking Up That Old Gang of Mine" B8
"Wedding Bells": The Beatles B8
"Wedding March" B12, B30
"Wedding Samba, The" B12
"We Didn't Start the Fire": Billy Joel A185, B21
"Wednesday Morning, 3 A.M.": Simon and Garfunkel B1
"We Don't Give a Damn About Our Friends": Girls on Top A24, A39
"We Don't Need Who You Think You Are": Skunk Anansie B20
"Weeping Wall": David Bowie B20
"Weep No More, My Baby" B10; The Beatles B8
"We Got Married": Paul McCarney A185, A198, B20
"We Gotta Get Out of This Place": The Animals B8
"We Got the Beat" [1]: The Go-Go's **A55**, B24
"We Got the Beat" [2]: Kweli, Talib **B31**
"We Go Together": The Moonglows A110
"We Have Heaven": Yes A99
"Weight, The": The Band A17, A185, A247, B24
"Weird Divide": The Shins A22
"Weird Fishes": Radiohead **A169**, A206
"Welcome to the Jungle": Guns N' Roses B28
"Welcome to the Machine": Pink Floyd A103, **A198**
"Welcome to the Room . . . Sara": Fleetwood Mac A185
"Welfare Mothers": Neil Young A99, B6
"We Like Birdland": Huey "Piano": Smith A238
"Well, Darling" B8
"Well, Well, Well": John Lennon **B18**
"Well . . . (Baby Please Don't Go)": The Beatles B8; The Olympics A95
"We'll Be the Same" **B30**
"We'll Be Together Again" **B30**
"We'll Build a New Church in the Morning" B30
"We'll Meet Again": The Byrds B7
"Well Respected Man, A": The Kinks A70, A107, A185

"We'll Run Away": The Beach Boys B15
"We'll See" B30
"Well Well Well": John Lennon B8
"We Love You": The Rolling Stones B7, B29
"Wendy": The Beach Boys B15
"We Open in Venice" B30
"We're a Happy Family": The Ramones A221
"We're All Alone": Rita Coolidge A235
"We're All One": Sheila Walsh A185
"We're All Water": John and Yoko/Plastic Ono Band B18
"We're an American Band": Grand Funk Railroad **A16**, A246, B24
"We're Going to Be Friends": White Stripes, The A148
"We're Gonna Make It": Little Milton A32
"We're Gonna Move" B8; Elvis Presley B7
"We're Gonna Rock": Gunther Lee Carr A53
"We're Having All the Fun": Fun Boy Three A19
"We're Oh So Starving": Panic! At the Disco A203
"Were Thine That Special Face" B12
"Werewolves of London": Warren Zevon A16, **B24**
"Were You There When They Crucified My Lord?" A264
"We Shall Overcome" B7
"We Shall Overcome": Pete Seeger B21
"We Sing Hallelujah": Richard and Linda Thompson B20
"West End Blues" A219, B9; Louis Armstrong A119
"West End Girls": The Pet Shop Boys **A174**, A185, B13
"West L.A. Fadeaway": The Grateful Dead B17
"West Virginia Fantasies": Chicago B3
"West Wind" B30
"We Used to Know": Jethro Tull A188, B21
"We've Got a Groovey Thing Goin'": Simon and Garfunkel B1
"We've Only Just Begun" B3; The Carpenters A101, **B3**
"We Want a Rock": They Might Be Giants A185
"We Will Rock You": Queen **A17**, A193
"We Wish You a Merry Christmas": The Rolling Stones B7
"Whadaya Want": The Robins A77

Song Index

"Whale, The": Electric Light Orchestra A185
"Whaler's Dues, The": Jethro Tull A188, B20
"Wharf Rat": The Grateful Dead B17
"What About Us?": The Coasters A77
"What a Crazy World We're Living In": Joe Brown and his Bruvvers B8
"What a Diff'rence a Day Made" **B30**
"What a Fool Believes": The Doobie Brothers **B24**
"What a Friend We Have in Jesus" A161, A219
"What Are We Here For?" **B30**
"What Are You Doing the Rest of Your Life" B3
"What a Way to Wanna Be": Shania Twain A193
"What Becomes of the Brokenhearted?": Jimmy Ruffin A185
"What Can I Do for You?": Bob Dylan A180
"What Can I Say After I'm Sorry" A145
"What Could I Do?": Swan Silvertones B21
"What Did I Have That I Don't Have?" B30
"What Did Your Last Servant Die Of?": Wedding Present A185
"What Difference Does It Make?": The Smiths A185
"What'd I Say": Ray Charles A44, **A55**, A80, A95, **A238**, A247, B21, B8
"What Does It Matter?" **A120**
"What Does Your Soul Look Like": DJ Shadow A269
"What Do We Do on a Dew Dew Dewy Day" A145
"What Do You Say": Reba McEntire A191
"What Do You Think I Am?" **B30**
"What Do You Want": Adam Faith B8
"What Do You Want to Make Those Eyes at Me For?": The Beatles B8
"Whatever" [1]: Iggy Pop B21
"Whatever" [2]: Oasis B21
"Whatever Gets You Through the Night": John Lennon A185, B7
"Whatever Would Robert Have Said?": Van der Graaf Generator A185
"What Goes On" B8; The Beatles A98, B7
"What Good Am I Without You": Marvin Gaye and Kim Weston A95
"What Have I Done to Deserve This?": The Pet Shop Boys A174
"What If": The Dixie Dregs A73
"What I Like About You": The Romantics **A16**, **A85**

"What Is and What Should Never Be": Led Zeppelin B7
"What Is Life?": The Beatles B3; George Harrison B7, B18, B24
"What Is Love" B30
"What Is There to Say" B10, **B30**
"What Is the Secret of Your Success": The Coasters A77
"What Is This Thing Called Love" **A96**, **A113**, A114, A228, B10, **B11**, B12, **B30**
"What It's All About": Girl Talk A24
"What It Takes": Aerosmith **A84**
"What I Was Warned About" **B30**
"What'll I Do" [1] B12, **A120**, A168, B30
"What'll I Do" [2]: Janet Jackson **A85**
"What'll I Wear to School Today": Sharon Marie B15
"What Makes You Happy": Liz Phair **A84**
"What Now My Love" ["Et Maintenant"]: Gilbert Bécaud B25
"What People Want Is a Family Life": Paul McCartney B8
"What Sarah Said": Death Cab for Cutie A221
"What's Become of the Baby": The Grateful Dead B7
"What's Easy for Two Is Hard for One": Mary Wells A108
"What's Going On": Marvin Gaye A80, A110, A185, A247, B32
"What's Good About Goodbye?" **B30**
"What's Happening?!?!": The Byrds A121
"What's It": Jimmie Rodgers **A266**
"What's Love Got to Do With It": Tina Turner B24
"What's New" B10, **B30**
"What's on My Mind": Kansas A72
"What's That You're Doing": Paul McCartney B7
"What's the Buzz": Jesus Christ Superstar Cast B24
"What's the New Mary Jane": The Beatles **B7**
"What's The Reason" A145
"What's the Reason I'm Not Pleasing You?": Fats Domino B8
"What's the Ugliest Part of Your Body": The Mothers B7
"What's the Use of Talking" **B30**
"What's Your Name": The Beatles B8
"What the World Needs Now" **A147**, B3

"What They Do": The Roots B14
"What Up Gangsta": 50 Cent A24
"What Used to Was, Used to Was, Now It Ain't!" B12
"What Would I Want, Sky": Animal Collective A205
"What Wouldn't I Do for That Man?" B12
"What You Need": The Fall B20
"What You're Doing": The Beatles A98, B7, **B8**, B18
"Wheel in the Sky": Journey B24
"Wheels Ain't Coming Down": Slade B21
"Wheels of Steel": Grandmaster Flash A104
"Whe I Grow Up " The Beach Boys A125
"When a Gypsy Makes His Violin Cry" B12
"When a Kid Who Came from the East Side Found a Sweet Society Rose" B12
"When Alice Comes Back to the Farm": Move A185
"When a Man Loves a Woman": The Beach Boys B15; Bette Midler A3; Percy Sledge A7, A99, A185, **A246**, A247, **B19**
"When an Old Cricketer Leaves the Crease": Roy Harper B21
"When a Prince of a Fella Meets a Cinderella" A14
"When a Woman Loves a Man" B30
"When Darkness Falls": Killswitch Engage **A203**
"When Doves Cry": Prince and the Revolution A80, A247, A250, A252
"When Do We Dance?" **B30**
"When Everybody Comes to Town" B7, B8
"When Girls Get Together": The Beach Boys B15
"When He Returns": Bob Dylan A180, A185
"When I Come Around": Green Day A247
"When I Come to the End of My Journey": Five Blind Boys of Alabama A161
"When I Fall in Love": Nat 'King' Cole B21
"When I Get Home": The Beatles B7, B8, B18, B20
"When I Get Mad I Just Play My Drums": Jasper Dailey B15
"When I Get Where I'm Going": Brad Paisley and Dolly Parton A167
"When I Grow Up (To Be a Man)": The Beach Boys **A109**, A160, B15
"When I Look at the World": U2 A89

"When I Lost You" A168, B30
"When I'm Dead and Gone": McGuinness Flint A185, B21
"When I'm Gone": Eminem B31
"When I'm Sixty-Four": The Beatles A64, A90, A98, A99, A167, B7, B8, **B18**, B29
"When I Need You": Leo Sayer A185
"When Irish Eyes Are Smiling": The Beatles B7
"When It Rains, It Really Pours": Elvis Presley A99
"When It's Apple Blossom Time in Normandy" A145
"When It's Sleepy Time Down South" B30
"When I Wake Up Early in the Morning": The Beatles A253
"When I Was Young": Eric Burdon A185
"When Jimmie Rodgers Said Goodbye": Dwight Butcher A266
"When Johnny Comes Marching Home": Bob Dylan A58; ["Johnny I Hardly Knew You"] B12, B27
"When Love Comes to Town": U2 A52, A89
"When Love Comes Your Way" B30
"When My Baby Smiles at Me" A145
"When My Blue Moon Turns to Gold Again": Hank Williams B4
"When My Dreamboat Comes home" A53
"When My Little Girl Is Smiling": The Beatles B8; The Drifters A95
"When No One Cares" A14
"When Numbers Get Serious": Paul Simon A93, B1
"When Something Is Wrong With My Baby": Sam and Dave A29, A170
"When Spirits Rise": Simple Minds A185
"When the Cactus Is in Bloom": Jimmie Rodgers A266
"When the Going Gets Tough": Billy Ocean B19
"When The Idle Poor Become The Idle Rich" B30
"When the Levee Breaks": Led Zeppelin A144, **A131**, B20, **B21**; Memphis Minnie **A131**
"When the Lovelight Starts Shining Through His Eyes": The Supremes **A106, A108**
"When the Midnight Choo Choo Leaves for Alabam'" A145
"When the Music's Over": The Doors A43, A82, B3

Song Index

"When the Red, Red Robin Comes Bob-Bob-Bobbin' Along": The Beatles B7
"When the Saints Go Marching In" A196, B8; The Beatles B7; Fats Domino A95
"When the Ship Comes In": Bob Dylan A180
"When the Sun Comes Out" **B10**, B12, **B30**
"When the War Is Over": Lindisfarne A185
"When the World Is Running Down, You Make the Best of What's Still Around": The Police **A235**
"When They Yodel Ragtime Songs in Tennessee" A266
"When We Was Fab": George Harrison B7
"When Will We Be Paid": The Staple Singers A29
"When You Are Available": The Originals A110
"When You Dance I Can Really Love": Neil Young B6
"When You Gonna Wake Up": Bob Dylan A180; George Harrison A185
"When You Got a Good Friend": Robert Johnson A97
"When You Kiss Me": Shania Twain A193
"When You're Smiling" B8
"When You're Young": Jam A185
"When Your Lonely Heart Breaks": Neil Young B6
"When Your Lover Has Gone" **B30**
"When You Walk in the Room": Jackie DeShannon A257; The Searchers B20
"When You Want 'Em, You Can't Get 'Em; When You've Got 'Em, You Don't Want 'Em" **B30**
"When You Were Mine": Icicle Works A185
"When You Wish Upon a Star" A109, **A202**
"Where, Oh Where?" B30
"Whereabouts": Stevie Wonder A99
"Where Are the Friends?": Koobas B21
"Where Are They Now?": Nas B31
"Where Are You?" B30
"Where Are You Now": Jimmy Harnen A250
"Where Are You Tonight (Journey Through Dark Heat)": Bob Dylan A180
"Where Can I Go?" B12
"Where Did Our Love Go?" A105, A106; Soft Cell B32; The Supremes A95, A108, A185, B21, B32
"Where Do You Go?" **A209**

"Where Has Love Been": Brian Wilson B15
"Where Have All the Flowers Gone": Pete Seeger B21
"Where Have All the Good Times Gone?": Van Halen A185
"Where Have You Been (All My Life)": Arthur Alexander A95; The Beatles B8
"Where Is the One?" **A209**
"Where It's At": Beck **A85**
"Where Love Has Gone" A14
"Where or When" **A224, B10**, B30; Dion & The Belmonts B21
"Where's That Little Girl (With The Little Green Hat)" **B30**
"Where's That Rainbow?" **B30**
"Where's the Party?": Madonna **A183**
"Where the Blue of the Night": Bing Crosby B4
"Where the Rose Is Sown": Big Country A185, A187, **B20**, B21
"Where the Shy Little Violets Grow" A145
"Where the Streets Have No Name": U2 **A52**, A89, A103, A185, B20, B21; The Pet Shop Boys **A52**, A174
"Where've You Been": Kathy Mattea A191
"Where You Are" **B30**
"Where You'll Find Me Now": Neutral Milk Hotel A22
"Which One Is It?": Frank Zappa A27
"While My Guitar Gently Weeps": The Beatles A76, A98, A234, A247, B7, B8, B18, **B24**
"While the Earth Sleeps": Peter Gabriel and Deep Forest A159
"While We're Young" **A209**
"While You See a Chance": Steve Winwood A99, A250, B24
"Whip It": Devo B24
"Whipped Cream" A145; Herb Alpert and the Tijuana Brass A39
"Whipped Cream Mixes, The": The Evolution Control Committee A24, A39
"Whipping Post": The Allman Brothers Band **A85**, A221
"Whippin' That Old T.B.": Jimmie Rodgers A266
"Whip-poor-will" B30
"Whiskey Man": The Who B3
"Whiskey Moan Blues": Clifford Gibson **B26**
"Whiskey Night": R.E.O. Speedwagon A185
"Whisky in the Jar": Thin Lizzy A185

"Whispering" B12, B16, B30; Paul Whiteman B8
"Whisper Your Mother's Name": Jimmie Rodgers A266
"Whistle In": The Beach Boys A125, B15
"Whistling About You": Harvey Fuqua A110
"Whistling in the Dark" [1] B10
"Whistling in the Dark" [2]: They Might Be Giants A185
"Whistling Rufus" A145
"White America": Eminem A146
"White Christmas" A13, A168, B10, B12, B16, B24, B30; Bing Crosby B4
"White Hammer": Van der Graaf Generator A185
"Whitehouse Blues": Charlie Poole with the North Carolina Ramblers **A239**, A240
"White Lines (Don't Don't Do It)": Grandmaster Flash A99
"White Minority": Black Flag A210
"White Mustang II": Daniel Lanois B32
"White Punks on Dope": Nina Hagen A178
"White Rabbit": Jefferson Airplane A43, A72, A101, A134, A185; Great Society A101, B7
"White Riot": The Clash B19
"White Room": Cream A43, **A101**, A185, A205, B7, B20
"Whiter Shade of Pale, A" A104; Procol Harum A67, A99, A141, A167, A185, A207, A247, B7, B19, **B21**, B29; Shorty Long A110
"White Ship, The": H.P. Lovecraft B21
"White Sport Coat (And a Pink Carnation), A": Marty Robbins A97
"Whitewater": Bela Fleck **A220**
"Who?" B30
"Who Am I (What's My Name)?": Snoop Doggy Dogg A99, A146, **A261**, **B31**
"Who Are the Brain Police": The Mothers of Invention A11, A101, A134, B7
"Who Are You": The Who A233, A250
"Who Can It Be Now?": Men at Work A250, **B24**
"Who Can I Turn To" **A209**
"Who Cares?" B10, **B30**
"Who Do You Love" [1]: Bo Diddley A247; Juicy Lucy A185; Quicksilver Messenger Service B7
"Who Do You Love" [2]: Steve Miller Band A185

"Who Do You Suppose Went and Married My Sister?" B12
"Who Do You Want for Your Love": Icicle Works A185
"Who Has Seen the Wind": Plastic Ono Band B7
"Who Knows": Jimi Hendrix **A155**
"Whole Lotta Love": Led Zeppelin A43, A55, A74, A75, A99, **A101**, **A131**, A132, A247 A247, **B19**, B20, B21, B32
"Whole Lotta Lovin' for You, A": Fats Domino A44
"Whole Lotta Shakin' Goin On" B15; The Beatles B8; Jerry Lee Lewis A44, A80, A97, A185, A247
"Whole World, The": OutKast A221
"Who'll Be the Fool tonight": Larson-Feiten Band A250
"Who'll Be the Next in Line": Kinks A107
"Who'll Stop the Rain?": Creedence Clearwater B3, B24
"Wholy Holy": Aretha Franklin **A161**; Marvin Gaye A185, B21
"Whoo Hah!! Got You All in Check": Busta Rhymes A24
"Who Put the Bomp": Viscounts B21
"Who Ran the Iron Horse": The Beach Boys A125
"Who's Crying Now": Journey **A250**, B24
"Whose Baby Are You?" B30
"Who's Gonna Ride Your Wild Horses": U2 A89, A103
"Who Shot Sam" B8
"Who's Lovin' You": The Jackson 5 A35
"Who's Making Love": Johnnie Taylor A29
"Who's Sorry Now" B16; Connie Francis A97
"Who's Yehoodi" B12
"Who Was That Masked Man": Van Morrison A185
"Who You Gonna Call": Missy Elliott A261
"Why, Oh Why?" B30
"Why (Can't You Love Me Again)" B8
"Why Can't a Man Stand Alone": Elvis Costello A33
"Why Can't This Be Love": Van Halen A99
"Why Can't You Behave?" B30
"Why Did You Give Me Your Love": Jimmie Rodgers A266

Song Index

"Why Does It Hurt When I Pee?": Frank Zappa A12
"Why Does Love Got to Be So Sad": Derek & Dominos A185
"Why Do Fools Fall in Love": The Beach Boys A160, B15; Frankie Lymon A44, A185, B15, B21
"Why Do I Love You" B10, B30
"Why Don't We Do It in the Road" B17; The Beatles A143, B7, B17, B18
"Why Don't We Love Together?": The Pet Shop Boys A174
"Why Don't You Do Right": Joe McCoy A167
"Why Don't You Write Me?": Simon and Garfunkel B1
"Why Go Anywhere at All?" **B30**
"Why Not Come Over Tonight" A145
"Why Should I Be Lonely?": Jimmie Rodgers A266
"Why Should I Care" B12, B30
"Why Shouldn't I?" **B10**, **B30**
"Why": The Byrds A121
"Why There's a Tear in My Eye": Jimmie Rodgers A266
"Why Was I Born?" B10, **B30**
"Wiblet, The": echolyn A72
"Wichita Lineman" **B3**; Glen Campbell A101
"Wich Stand": The Survivors B15
"Wicked Game": Chris Isaak A39
"Wide Boy": Nik Kershaw A185
"Wild Cat": Gene Vincent B8
"Wild Cats of Kilkenny": The Pogues B20
"Wild Cherry Rag" A145
"Wild-Eyed Boy From Freecloud": David Bowie B20
"Wildflower" B30
"Wild Honey" [1]: The Beach Boys A160, B15
"Wild Honey" [2]: U2 A89
"Wild Honey Pie": The Beatles A98, B7
"Wild Horses" [1]: The Rolling Stones B32
"Wild Horses" [2]: Nik Kershaw A185
"Wild in the Country": The Beatles B8
"Wild Is the Wind" [1]: David Bowie A185, B21; Nina Simone B21
"Wild Is the Wind" [2]: Bon Jovi A185
"Wild Night": Van Morrison B24
"Wild One" [1]: Bobby Rydell **A241**
"Wild One" [2]: Martha and the Vandellas A108

"Wild One" [3]: Thin Lizzy A185
"Wild Rose" B30
"Wild Thing" [1] **A155**; The Troggs A83, A85, A99, A185, B8, B20, B21
"Wild Thing" [2]: Tōn Loc B28
"Wild Things Run Fast": Joni Mitchell A260
"Wild Tiger Woman": Move A185
"Wild West Hero": Electric Light Orchestra A185, B20
"Wild Wild West": Will Smith A234
"Wild World": Cat Stevens A99, A167, B24
"Wilkins Street Stomp": Speckled Red A238
"William, It Was Really Nothing": The Smiths A36
"Willie and the Hand Jive": Johnny Otis Show A44, A185
"Willie the Weeper" B12
"Willing and Able": Prince A79, **B13**
"Willing": Lowell George A173
"Willow Farm": Genesis **A232**
"Willow": Joan Armatrading A136
"Willow Weep for Me" **A114**, **B10**, B30
"Will to Love": Neil Young A88, **B6**
"Willy": Joni Mitchell **A260**
"Will You [Still] Love Me Tomorrow" A259; The Beatles B8; Carole King B24; The Shirelles A45, A75, A95, A247, B24
"Will You Still Be Mine?" **B30**
"Wimoweh": Karl Denver B21; Weavers B21
"Winchester Cathedral": The New Vaudeville Band B7
"Wind, The": PJ Harvey A223
"Wind Chimes": The Beach Boys A125, B15; Brian Wilson B15
"Wind Cries Mary, The": The Jimi Hendrix Experience **A257**, B29
"Windfall, The": Joni Mitchell A260
"Windows of the World": Dionne Warwick A249
"Wind Quartets": Tyrannosaurus Rex B20
"Wind Up": Jethro Tull A188
"Wine": U2 A185
"Wine, Women, and Loud happy Songs": Ringo Starr B18
"Winner Takes It All": ABBA A185, **B21**, B25
"Winston's Walk": The Beatles B8
"Wintergreen for President" B12
"Winter Symphony": The Beach Boys B15
"Wintertime Love": The Doors B3

"Wipe Out": Surfaris A43, B15
"Wire": U2 A89, A185, B21
"Witch Doctor": David Seville [& The Chipmunks] A97
"Witch Doktor, the": Armand van Helden A3
"Witches Hat": The Incredible String Band A112
"Witchi Tai To": Topo D. Bil A185; Harper's Bizarre B21
"Witch's Promise, The": Jethro Tull A188
"Witchwood": Strawbs B21
"Witchy Woman": The Eagles A173, A185
"With a Girl Like You": The Troggs B8
"With a Gun": Steely Dan **A96**, A99
"With a Little Help from My Friends": The Beatles A43, **A65**, **A76**, A96, A98, **A157**, A185, A248, **B7**, B8, B20, B21, B29; Joe Cocker A43, B21
"With a Little Luck": Wings A97, A233, B7
"With a Shout": U2 A89
"With a Song in My Heart": B10, B12, **B30**
"With God on Our Side": Bob Dylan B7, B8, A184
"Within You Without You": The Beatles A67, A76, A90, A98, A100, A221, B7, B8, **B18**, B29
"With Me Tonight": The Beach Boys A125, B15
"With or Without You": U2 **A7**, A80, A99, A103, A247, A252, B20, B21
"Without a Song" B10, B30
"Without Expression": R.E.O. Speedwagon A185
"Without Her": Herb Alpert & the Tijuana Brass B21; Blood, Sweat and Tears B21
"Without Him": Lulu **B21**
"Without Me": Eminem A7
"Without You" [1] B12
"Without You" [2]: Mariah Carey B21; Nilsson A185, B21, B24
"With You With Me" B30
"Witness": ADF **A61**
"Wives and Lovers" A147; Jack Jones A249
"Wizard, The" [1]: Black Sabbath A55
"Wizard, The" [2]: Uriah Heep A185, B20
"Woke Up With the Blues in My Fingers" A145
"Wolf at the Door, A": Radiohead **A169**
"Woman" [1]: Peter and Gordon B8
"Woman" [2]: John Lennon B7, B8, **B24**
"Woman Don't Want to Love Me, The": Chicago **A237**
"Woman in Love, A" A41
"Woman in the Wall": Beautiful South A185
"Woman Is the Nigger of the World": John and Yoko/Plastic Ono Band A185, B18
"Woman of Heart and Mind": Joni Mitchell **A260**
"Woman's Got Soul": The Impressions **A108**
"Woman's Got the Power, A": Jennifer Holliday A3; Victoria Lace A3
"Woman to Woman": Shirley Brown A29
"Woman Woman Blues": Ishman Bracey A240
"Women": Def Leppard A185
"Wonderful City, The": Jimmie Rodgers A266
"Wonderful Dad" **B30**
"Wonderful in Young Life": Simple Minds A185
"Wonderful Land": The Shadows B8
"Wonderful": The Beach Boys A99, **A125**, B15; Brian Wilson B15
"Wonderful Time Up There, A": Pat Boone A97
"Wonderful Tonight": Eric Clapton **A101**, A167, B24
"Wonderful Woman": The Smiths A36
"Wonderful World": Sam Cooke B21
"Wonderin'": Neil Young B6
"Wonder of You, The" B12
"Wonder of You, The": Elvis Presley B21
"Wonderous Stories": Yes A232, A233
"Wonderwall": The Mike Flowers Pops A159; Oasis A159
"Wonderwall to be Here": George Harrison B7
"Wond'ring Aloud": Jethro Tull A4
"Wontcha Come Out Tonight": The Beach Boys B15
"Won't Get Fooled Again": The Who A43, **A101**, A141, **A182**, A247, B24
"Won't You Be My Baby": Johnny Devlin and the Devils B8
"Won't You Come Home, Bill Bailey": Bobby Darin B21
"Won't You Please Say Goodbye": The Beatles **B8**
"Wooden Heart" ["Muss I Denn zum Staedele Hinaus"]: The Beatles B8
"Wooden Soldier and the China Doll, The" B30

Song Index

"Woodman, Spare That Tree" A145, B12, B19
"Woods of Darney, The": Richard Thompson B20
"Woodstock": Crosby, Stills, and Nash **A246, A248**; Joni Mitchell **A260**
"Wooly Bully": Sam the Sham and the Pharaohs B8
"Word, The": The Beatles A76, A92, A98, A246, A250, **A254**, B7, B8, **B18**, B19
"Words Get in the Way": Gloria Estefan B24
"Words": Neil Young A88, B6
"Words of Love" [1]: The Beatles A98, B32,; Buddy Holly B24, B32
"Words of Love" [2]: The Mamas and the Papas B7
"Words that Maketh Murder, The": PJ Harvey A205
"Words Without Music" **B30**
"Word Up": Cameo A250
"Wordy Rappinghood": The Tom Tom Club B14
"Workers of World, Awaken": Joe Hill B25
"Working Class Hero": John Lennon / Plastic Ono Band A43, B18, B21
"(Working for the) Clampdown": The Clash A118
"Working in a Coalmine": Lee Dorsey B21
"Working John Working Joe": Jethro Tull A185
"Working Man Blues" A145
"Working Man": Rush A28
"Working on the Highway": Bruce Springsteen B32
"Work That Thang Out": Lanelle Collins **A161**
"Work With Me, Annie": Hank Ballard and the Midnighters A53, A170
"World I Know, The": Collective Soul B24
"World Is in My Arms, The" B30
"World Is Lit by Lightning, The": Deacon Blue A185, B21
"World Is Mine, The" B30
"World Is Waiting for the Sunrise": Les Paul and Mary Ford B8
"World Is Yours, The": Nas A99
"World Machine": Level 42 A185
"World to Win, A" B12
"World Without Love, A": Peter and Gordon A107, **B8**
"Worried Any How Blues": Ida Cox A240
"Worried Blues": Frank Hutchison A240

"Worried Life Blues, The": Minnie Lee Whitehead A240
"Worried Life Blues": David Edwards A240; Big Maceo A240
"Worried Man Blues": The Quarrymen B8
"Worrying You Off My Mind": Big Bill Broonzy **A240**
"Worthless Thing": Elvis Costello B4
"Wots . . . Uh the Deal": Pink Floyd A185
"Would?": Alice in Chains A167, A205
"Wouldn't It Be Loverly": Peter Sellers B7
"Wouldn't It Be Nice": The Beach Boys A99, A101, A109, **A160**, A167, A185, A214, B8, B15; Elton John B15; Brian Wilson B15
"Would You Believe?": Roxy Music A185, B20
"Would You Like to Take a Walk?" B12, **B30**
"Wowie Zowie": Mothers of Invention, The A11
"Wow": Kate Bush A59
"Wrack My Brain": Ringo Starr B7
"Wrap It Up": The Robins A77
"Wrapped Around Your Finger": The Police A235, A250, **B24**
"Wrappin' It Up" A145
"Wreck": Gentle Giant A166
"Wreck of the [Southern] Old [Southern] 97": Vernon Dalhart **A240**; Woody Guthrie A240; Kelly Harrell A240; Ernest Stoneman, A240
"Wreck of the Edmund Fitzgerald, The": Gordon Lightfoot A7
"Wreck of the John B., The": The Kingston Trio B15
"Writen' Paper Blues": Blind Willie McTell **B26**
"Wrong 'em Boyo": The Clash A118
"Wrong Road, The": The Hall Brothers A240
"Wu-Gambinos": Raekwon B14; Wu-Tang Clan **A2**
"Wunderbar" B30
"Wuthering Heights": Kate Bush A59, **A165**, A185, B21

"Xanadu": Rush **A28**
"X-Tasy": Missy Elliott **A102**

"Ya Got Me" B12
"Yah Mo B There": Michael McDonald and James Ingram A252

"Ya Hozna": Frank Zappa A27
"Yah-ta-ta, Yah-ta-ta (Talk, Talk, Talk)" A14
"Yakety Yak": The Beatles B8; The Coasters A44, A77, A95, A97
"Yama, Yama Man, the" A145
"Yan-kee" **B30**
"Yankee Doodle Blues" **A120**
"Yankiana Rag" A145
"Ya Playin' Yaself": Jeru Tha Damaja B22
"Yassassin": David Bowie A185
"Ya Ya": The Beatles B8; Lee Dorsey A95, B7; John Lennon B7
"Yeah, 'Cause You're a Surefire Bet to Win My Lips": The Beatles B8
"Year 1": X A210
"Year From Today, A" A145
"Years Ago": Jimmie Rodgers A266
"Years Roll Along": The Beatles B8
"Yellow Bird" A238
"Yellow Dog Blues" B30
"Yellow Girl Blues": Alger "Texas": Alexander **B26**
"Yellow Rainbow": Move A185
"Yellow Submarine": The Beatles A92, A98, A107, **A107**, A185, A195, A198, B3, B7, B8, B18, B29
"Yer Blues": The Beatles A254, B7, B8, **B18**
"Yes, My Darling Daughter" B12
"Yes, Sir, That's My Baby" B10; Jack Hylton and His Orchestra A227
"Yes, the River Knows": The Doors B3
"Yes, We Have No Bananas" B16
"Yes I'm Ready": Barbara Mason A95
"Yes It Is": The Beatles A90, A91, A92, A98, A100, A195, A232, A234, B7, B8
"Yessir, That's My Baby" B19, **B19**
"Yesterday" **A96**, A145; The Beatles A70, A80, A90, **A91**, A98, A99, A100, A107, A142, A156, A157, A247, A259, B3, B7, B8, **B18**, B21, B24, B32
"Yesterday, When I Was Mad": The Pet Shop Boys **A128**, **B13**
"Yesterdays" **B10**, B12, **B30**; The Four Freshmen B15; Dizzy Gillespie **A96**
"Yesterday's Papers": The Rolling Stones A70
"Yester-me, Yester-you, Yerster-day": Stevie Wonder B21
"Yiddisha Professor" **A168**
"Yiddisha Rag, The" B12

"Yiddle, on Your Fiddle, Play Some Ragtime" **A168**, B12
"Y.M.C.A.": Village People B21
"Yodeling Cowboy, The": Jimmie Rodgers A266
"Yodeling My Way Back Home": Jimmie Rodgers A266
"Yodeling Ranger, The": Jimmie Rodgers A266
"Yo Mama": Frank Zappa A60
"Yonkle, the Cowboy Jew" B12
"You, My Love" A14
"You" [1]: Marvin Gaye A110
"You" [2]: Radiohead **A169**
"You [You'll] Know What to Do": George Harrison B8
"You Ain't Goin' Nowhere": The Byrds A121
"You Ain't Heard Nothing Yet" A145
"You Ain't Talking to Me" A145
"You Always Hurt the One You Love": The Mills Brothers B4
"You and I, Part II": Fleetwood Mac A185
"You and Me": Neil Young B6
"You and My Old Guitar": Jimmie Rodgers A266
"You and the Night and the Music" **B10**, B12
"You and Whose Army?": Radiohead A135, **A169**, A205
"You and Your Love" **B30**
"You Are for Loving" **B30**
"You Are": Lionel Richie A43
"You Are Love" B10, B30
"You Are My Sunshine" B8, B10; The Beatles B7; Jimmy Davis B4
"You Are the Sunshine of My Life": Stevie Wonder A99, B24
"You Are Too Beautiful" **B10**, **B30**
"You Belong to Me": Elvis Costello A185
"You Belong to the City": Glenn Frey A250
"You Better Move On": Arthur Alexander A95; The Beatles B8
"You Better You Bet": The Who A233
"You Bowed Down": Elvis Costello A33
"You Came a Long Way From St. Louis" B30
"You Can All Join In": Traffic B7
"You Can Call Me Al": Paul Simon A7, A9, B21
"You Can Do Magic": America A43
"You Can't Always Get What You Want": The Rolling Stones A99, **A101**, A121, A247, B24

Song Index

"You Can't Catch Me": The Beatles B8; Chuck Berry A95, B7
"You Can't Dance": LL Cool J A99
"You Can Tell the World": Simon and Garfunkel B1
"You Can't Do That": The Beatles A95, A98, A185, A195, A254, B7, B8, B16, **B18**
"You Can't Fool Your Dreams" **B30**
"You Can't Get a Man With a Gun" B30
"You Can't Get Away From It" A145
"You Can't Hurry Love": Phil Collins A185, **B20**; The Supremes **A99**, A101, **A106**, **A108**, B8, **B20**
"You Can't Lose Me": Faith Hill A189
"You Can't Trust Nobody" A145
"You Could Be Happy": Snow Patrol B21
"You Could Be Mine": Guns N' Roses A89
"You Couldn't Be Cuter" **B30**
"(You'd Be So) Easy to Love" **A113**, A228, **B10**, B30
"You'd Be So Nice to Come Home To" **A113**, A147, **B10**, B12
"You'd Better Love Me" **B30**
"You Didn't Have to Be So Nice": The Lovin' Spoonful B7, B15
"You Didn't Try to Call Me": The Mothers of Invention A27
"You Don't Have to Be a Star (To Be in My Show)": Marilyn McCoo and Billy Davis, Jr. B24
"You Don't Have to Cry": Crosby, Stills, Nash, and Young B3
"You Don't Have to Know the Language" A14
"You Don't Have to Say You Love Me": Dusty Springfield A123, B21
"You Don't Know How It Feels": Tom Petty B24
"You Don't Know Like I Know": Sam and Dave A29, A95
"You Don't Know Me": Helen Shapiro A259
"You Don't Know What Love Is" **B30**
"You Don't Love Me" B17
"You Don't Mess Around With Jim": Jim Croce B24
"You Don't Miss Your Water": William Bell **A29**
"You Don't Own Me": Lesley Gore A45
"You Don't Understand" A145
"You Don't Understand Me": The Beatles B8; Bobby Freeman A95

"You Do Something to Me" **B30**
"You Dream Flat Tires": Joni Mitchell A260
"You Fool You": Roy Orbison A270
"You Forgot Your Gloves" **B30**
"You Gave Me the Answer": Paul McCartney Wings? B8
"You Give Love a Bad Name": Bon Jovi A99
"You Gonna Quit Me Baby": Blind Blake A240
"You Good Thing (Is About to End)": Mable John A29
"You Got Me Floatin'": The Jimi Hendrix Experience A40, **A155**
"You Got Me Hummin'": Sam and Dave **A29**
"You Got Me": The Roots **A222**
"You Go to My Head" **B10**, **B30**
"You Gotta Go to Work": Rex Griffin A266
"You Got to Wet It" A145
"You Have Cast Your Shadow on the Sea" **B30**
"You Just Gotta Know My Mind": Donovan B29
"You Keep It All In": Beautiful South A185
"You Keep Me Hangin' On": The Supremes A99, **A106**, **A108**, A185, B3, **B24**; Vanilla Fudge A72
"You Know My Name (Look Up the Number)": The Beatles A195, B7, B8
"You Know What to Do": The Beatles B7
"You Know What You Could Be": The Incredible String Band A112
"You Learn": Alanis Morissette B24
"You Leave Me Breathless" **B30**
"You Like Me Too Much": The Beatles A98, B7, B8
"You Little Trust Maker": Tymes **B21**
"You'll Accomp'ny Me": Bob Seger A250
"You'll Always Be My Baby": Sara Evans A191
"You'll Be Mine": The Beatles **B7**; The Quarrymen **B8**
"You'll Get Yours" A14
"You'll Never Know" B10
"You'll Never Need a Doctor No More" A145
"You'll Never Walk Alone" **B16**; The Beatmakers B8; Gerry and the Pacemakers B16, B21
"You Lost the Sweetest Boy": Mary Wells **A106, A108**
"You Made Me Love You" A145
"You Made Me Realize": My Bloody Valentine A22

"You Make Loving Fun": Fleetwood Mac A85, A185, **B24**
"(You Make Me Feel Like) A Natural Woman" A217; Aretha Franklin A24, A217, B24; Carole King A24, A182, A217, B24
"You Make Me Feel So Young" **B30**
"You May Be Right": Billy Joel B24
"You May Leave But This Will Bring You Back": Memphis Jug Band A240
"You Might Already Have Me, Rossi": BradleyHeartVampire A205
"You Might": Nik Kershaw A185
"You Might Think": The Cars A99, B24
"You Must Be Evil": Chris Rea A185
"You Must Believe Me": The Impressions **A108**
"You Need a Mess of Help to Stand Alone": The Beach Boys B15
"You Needed Me": Boyzone A167; Anne Murray A167
"You Need Love": Muddy Waters **A131**
"You Never Can Tell": Chuck Berry A95, B21
"You Never Even Call Me by My Name": David Allan Coe A191
"You Never Give Me Your Money": The Beatles **A92**, A98, A100, **A116**, A149, A167, **B7**, B8, **B18**
"Young Americans": David Bowie A101, **A101**, A185, B20
"Young Blood": The Beatles **B8**; The Coasters A44, A53, A77, A95
"Young Boy": Paul McCartney B7
"Young Love": Tab Hunter A44, A97; Sonny James A97
"Young Lust": Pink Floyd A103, A185
"Young Man Is Gone, A": The Beach Boys A160, B15
"Young Man's Fancy, A" **B30**
"Young Ones, The": Cliff Richard A259
"You Oughta Be in Pictures" B10
"You Oughta Know": Alanis Morrisette A51, A246, A247, A248
"Your Cheatin' Heart": Ray Charles A123; Joni James A123, B4; Frankie Laine A123; Hank Williams with his Drifting Cowboys A123
"Your Constant Heart": Deacon Blue A185
"Your Dream" B30
"You're a Bad Influence on Me" B30
"You're a Builder Upper" B30
"You're a Grand Old Rag" A145

"You're a Great Big Blue-Eyed Baby" A145
"You're a Heartbreaker": Elvis Presley A99
"You're a Heavenly Thing" B10, **B30**
"You're All I Need to Get By": Marvin Gaye & Tammi Terrell A185; Method Man featuring Mary J. Bluge A123, B14
"You Really Got a Hold on Me": The Beatles A98, B7, B8, B20; The Miracles A95, A108, B7, B20
"You Really Got Me": The Kinks **A16**, A43, **A55**, A107, A155, A184, A185, **A210**, A247, B8, B20, B21, B28
"You're a Sweetheart" **B30**
"You're a Wonderful One": Marvin Gaye **A106**, A108
"You're Blasé" **B30**
"You're Breaking My Heart" B12
"You're Dangerous" A14
"You're Driving Me Crazy" B10, B30; The Temperance Seven A259, B8
"You're Getting to Be a Habit with Me" B10, **B30**
"You're Going to Lose That Girl": The Beatles A91, A98, A99, A100, A259, A167, **B3**, B7, **B8, B18**, B21, **B24**
"You're Gonna Make Me Lonesome When You Go": Bob Dylan B8
"You're Gonna Miss Me": Muddy Waters B21
"You're Here and I'm Here" **B30**
"You're Just in Love" B30
"You're Kind": Paul Simon A93, **A150**, B1
"You're Laughing at Me" B30
"You're Lonely and I'm Lonely" B30
"You're Lost, Little Girl": The Doors B3
"You're Mama Don't Dance": Loggins and Messina B24
"You're My Baby": Johnny Cash A270
"You're My Everything": The Temptations A99
"You're My World": Cilla Black B8
"You're No Good": Linda Ronstadt A99, B24; Swinging Blue Jeans A185
"You're Okay" A145
"You're Pretty When I'm Drunk": The Bloodhound Gang A146
"You're Sixteen": Johnny Burnette A185, B21; Ringo Starr B7; Rory Storm and the Hurricanes B8
"You're Smiling Face": James Taylor B24
"You're So Good to Me": The Beach Boys B8, B15, A185

Song Index

"(You're So Square) Baby I Don't Care": The Beatles B8
"You're So Vain": Carly Simon A99, B21
"You're Still a Mystery": Brian Wilson B15
"You're Still My Man": Whitney Houston A185
"You're Still the One": Shania Twain **A111**, A193
"(You're the) Devil in Disguise": Elvis Presley A99
"You're the Inspiration": Chicago **A214**, B24
"You're the Mother Type" **B30**
"You're the One" [1] A95; The Originals A110
"You're the One" [2]: Paul Simon B1
"You're the Top" A168, A219, A228, B10, **B30**
"You're the Voice": John Farnham A185, **A186**
"You're Too Far Away" **B10**
"You're What's Happening (In the World Today)": Marvin Gaye A110
"Your Feet's Too Big" B8; Fats Waller A95
"Your Gold Teeth": Steely Dan **A96**
"Your Good Thing": Lou Rawls A53
"Your Imagination": Brian Wilson A160, B15
"Your Love Is Forever": George Harrison B7
"Your Love": The Outfield A250
"Your Mother Should Know": The Beatles A90, A92, **A100**, B7, B8, **B18**
"Your Old Standby": Mary Wells A108
"Your Own Choice": Procol Harum A185
"Your Own Special Way": Genesis A185, **B21**
"Your Racist Friend": They Might Be Giants A185
"Yours Is No Disgrace": Yes **A72**
"Your Smiling Face": James Taylor A167
"Your Song": Elton John A17, A234, A247, B20, B21, B24
"Your Southern Can Is Mine": Blind Willie McTell B7; The White Stripes B7
"Yours Sincerely" **B30**
"Your Summer Dream": The Beach Boys A160, B15
"Your True Love": Carl Perkins B8
"Your Unchanging Love": Marvin Gaye A110
"Your Warm & Tender Love": Chris Rea A185
"You Said": Madness A185
"You Said Something" B30
"You Send Me": Sam Cooke A30, A44, A97, A108, A247
"You Shook Me All Night Long": AC/DC A212

"You Shook Me": Jeff Beck A185, **B21**; Willie Dixon B21; Led Zeppelin **A186**, A269, **B21**; Muddy Waters, B21
"You Should Be Dancing": The Bee Gees A43, A179
"You Spin Me Round (Like a Record)": Dead or Alive A185, A232
"You Still Believe in Me": The Beach Boys **A160**, B15
"You Sure Love to Ball": Marvin Gaye A110
"You Think of Ev'rything" A14
"You Took Advantage of Me" B10, **B30**
"You Took the Words Right Out of My Mouth": Meat Loaf A185
"You Tore Me Down": The Flamin' Groovies A99
"You Turned The Tables on Me" **B30**
"You Turn Me On (I'm a Radio)": Joni Mitchell A260
"You've Been a Good Old Wagon" A145, **B19**, **B27**, **B30**
"You've Been Cheating": The Impressions **A108**
"You've Been in Love Too Long": Martha and the Vandellas A108
"You've Got a Friend": Carole King A99, B4; James Taylor A241, B4
"You've Got Another Thing Comin'": Judas Priest A99
"You've Got Everything Now": The Smiths A36, A185
"You've Got Me Thinking": Jackie Lomax B7
"You've Got the Power": James Brown B4
"You've Got the Style": Athlete B21
"You've Got to Be Modernistic" A145; James P. Johnson A172
"You've Got to Hi-De-Hi": Hackberry Ramblers A240
"You've Got to Hide Your Love Away": The Beatles A76, A90, A98, **A100**, A221, B7, B8, **B18**, B24; Silkie A107
"You've Got to See Mama Ev'ry Night" A145
"You've Lost That Lovin' Feelin'": The Righteous Brothers A32, A75, A77, **A85**, **A242**, A247, B4, B7, B24, **B25**, B32; Brian Wilson B15
"You've Made Me So Very Happy": Blood, Sweat, and Tears B24
"You've Touched Me": Brian Wilson B15

"You Want Her Too": Paul McCartney A185
"You Were Made for Me": Freddie and the Dreamers A70
"You Were Meant for Me" B30; The Beatles B8
"You Were Never Lovelier" B10
"You Were on My Mind": We Five A99
"You Win Again": The Beatles B8
"You Win My Love": Shania Twain A193
"You Won't See Me": The Beatles **A91**, A98, **A194**, B7, B8, B20
"You Wreck me": Tom Petty **A155**
"Y Teimlad": Datblygy A123; Super Furry Animals A123
"Ytse Jam, The": Dream Theater **A175**
"YYZ": Rush **A17**, A167

"Zéphyre et Flore" B10
"Ziggy Stardust": David Bowie A185, B20
"Zing! Went the Strings of My Heart": Lew Stone and His Band A227
"Zip-A-Dee-Doo-Dah": Bob B. Soxx and the Blue Jeans B32
"Zip Coon" B19 B19
"Zizzy Ze Zum Zum" A145
"Zomby Woof": Mothers of Invention, The A11
"Zonky" A145
"Zoo Station": U2 A103, **B32**
"Zoot Allures": Frank Zappa A27, A60
"Zo Simpel": Osdorp Posse B14
"Zulu": Armand van Helden A3

Subject Index

.38 Special A250
2nd Tribe A3
2Pac A247
3 Notes and Runnin' A163
5th Dimension, The A105, B3
10cc A19, A99, A101, B21
22–20S B21
24K B14
50 Cent A24, A99, B31
68 Beats A3
98 Degrees B24
808 State B5
10,000 Maniacs B24
10000 Volts A185

ABBA A20, A74, A141, A159, A185, A212, A242, A247, B19, B20, B21, B25
Abbott, H. Porter A7, A51
Abbott, Kingsley B15
ABC A19, A185, B32
Abrahams, Roger D. B4
Abrams, Maurie B12
accelerando A8
accent A53, A210, A240, A250; linguistic A58; rhythmic B16
Accept B28
accident A43
accompaniment B26
accordion A227, B25
AC/DC A16, A17, A80, A212, A246, A247, A250, B28
Ace A182
Ace, Johnny A270, B32
Aceyalone A221
Achron, Joseph B12
Acuff, Roy A240, B4
Acuff-Rose A270
Adam and the Ants A185
Adams, Bryan A21, A183, A212, A250, B24
Adams, John A72
Adams, Kyle A261

Adele A222
ADF A61
Adler, Jacob B12
Adler, Richard B12
Adorno, Theodor A79, A115, A131, A158, A182, A184, A188, A196, B4, B19, B20, B21, B22, B28
Aerosmith A16, A55, A84, A97, A99, A101, A167, A225, A246, A247, A248, A250, B24, B28
aesthetics B2, B20
affect B2, A134
Aficiao, El A3
African American Music A32, A35, A62, A105, A108, A119, A161, A176, A262, B4, B5, B9, B14, B19
African Music A251, A262, B5, B9, B18, B19, B27
Afro Medusa A3
After the Fire A185, B21
Agawu, Kofi A102, A105, A163, A183, A205, A235, B4, B5
Ager, Milton B30
Agmon, Eyton A16, A68
Aguilera, Christina A24
Aha B24
A-Ha A185
Ahlert, Fred B30
AIDS A6, A128
Air A221
Aitken, Marcia A231
Aitken, Matt A185
Akers, Garfield A201, B26
Akins, Rhett A191
Akron, OH A10
Akst, Harry B30
Akufen A115
Alberti Bass A141
Albini, Steve B32
Aldwell, Edward A86
aleatoric music B7

Alexander, Alger "Texas" B26
Alexander, Arthur A95
Alice in Chains A97, A167, A205, A221, A246, A247, A248
Alkaholics, Tha B14
Alkaline Trio A205
All About Eve A185, B21
Allanbrook, Wye A163
Allen, Ernest, Jr. B22
Allen, Harry B22
Allen, Woody B12
Allison, Jesse A26
alliteration A124, A225
Allman Brothers, The A85, A99, A101, A221, A222, B8, B7, B24
Almanac Singers, The A240
Alpert, Herb A39, A101, A185, B21
Alphabetical Four A240
Altamont B29
Altena, Edward Van B12
Alter, Louis B30
amateur A192
Amazin' Blue A87
ambience B32
ambiguity A135, B5, B22
Amboy Dukes, The A101
Ambrose, Bert A227, B21
Amburn, Ellis A270
Amen Corner A185, B20, B21
America B24
America (band) A43, A167, A234
American Record Company A132
American Songbook A114, A168, B11, B30
American Spring B15
Ammons, Albert A238
Ammons, Gene A217
Amos, Tori A6, A46, A47, A51, B21
Amsterdam B14
anacrusis A17, A68, B5; extended A100
analysis B19; auditory stream A8, B6; paradigmatic A159, B4, B19; poetic A216; Schenkerian A13, A40, A41, A45, A46, A49, A56, A86, A90, A91, A93, A97, A99, A143, A150, A184, A186, A194, A199, A214, A253, B8, B10, B19; spectral B4; waveform A193, A204, A265
Anderson, Benedict B22, B31
Anderson, Charles A266
Anderson, Ian A4, A188, B20

Anderson, John A191
Anderson, Jon A71, A72, A198, A207, A223
Anderson, Laurie A99, A182
Anderson, T.J. B9
Andersson, Benny B25
Andersson, Stig B25
Andrews Sisters, The B4, B12, B21
androgyneity B13, B28
Angel, Dave B5
Angel, The B22
Angels, The [1] A259
Angels, The [2] A74
Animal Collective A204, A205
Animals, The A16, A101, A108, A132, A167, A185, A247, B8, B19, B21, B24
Anka, Paul A97, A185, B25
Anthony, Ray A44
Anthrax A208
Apollo 100 A179
Appadurai, Arjun B22
Appalachian music B27
Applejacks B21
Arab music A137, B27
Arcade Fire A205, B21
Archies, The B21
Argent B21
aria A178
Arlen, Harold A114, B10, B11, B12, B30
Armatrading, Joan A136
Armstrong, Louis A48, A119, A176, B4, B12, B16, B19, B21
Arnheim, Gus B30
Arnheim, Rudolph A102
Arnold, Kokomo A240
Arom, Simha B22
arpeggio B27, B28
arranging A12, A87, A109, A130, A156, A160, A249, B6, B32
Arrested Development A127
Ar Re Yaouank B21
Arrival A185
Ars Nova A53
Art Ensemble of Chicago B9
Arthur, Emry A240
articulation A225, B19
Artists United Against Apartheid B25
art mark A163
Art of Noise, The A104
Artusi, G.M. A53

Subject Index

Artwoods B21
Asaf'ev, Boris A183
Ashby, Arved A12
Asher, Jane B8, B7
Asher, Peter B7, B8
Asher, Tony A160, B15
Ashley, Tom Clarence A240
Ashton, Gardner and Dyke B7
Asia A59, A71, A185, B20
Askew Sisters B21
Aspden, Suzanne A178
Aspinall, Neil B7, B8
Association, The A43, B3
assonance A225
Astaire, Fred A228, B7, B10, B12, B21
Astley, Rick A215
Astors, The A29
A Team, The A270
Athlete B21
Atkins, Chet A270, B8
Atkins, Juan B5
Atkinson, Brooks A228
Atlanta B14
Atlantic Records A77, A95
Atlas, Raphael A142
Atlas Sound A169
atonality A53, A72, A73, A99
Attali, Jacques A162, A163, B22
Atwood, Margaret A181
Auden, W.H. B13
audience B14
Auster, Paul A181
Austin, Billy B12
authenticity A47, A52, A68, A148, A170, A218, A229, B4, B5, B13, B14, B19, B21, B22, B28, B31, B32
authorship A131, A170, A217
Automatic Man A185
Automatic Pilot A6
Autry, Gene A240, A266
Avalon, Frankie A44, B8
Avicii A212
Awadu, Keidi Obi B22
Axis of Awesome A219
Ayers, Roy B22
AZ B14
Azerrad, Michael A137
Aztec Mystic B5
Azzido Da Bass B5

B-52's, The A17, A93, A99, A247
Babbitt, Milton A81, B12, B28
Babe Ruth (group) A104
Babo, Lamartino A211
Babyface *see* Edmonds, Kenneth
Bach, Johann Sebastian A46, A71, A99, A141, A222, A261, B7, B8, B16, B19, B25, B27, B28, B32
Bacharach, Burt A6, A147, B3, B8, B15, B21, B30
Bachman, Tal A247
Bachman-Turner Overdrive A246, B24
backbeat A17, A95, A203, A233, A244, A271, B5, B8, B19, B21; in stride piano A172
Bad Boy Orchestra A3
Bad Company A74, A75, B24
Badfinger B7
Badman, Keith B15
Baer, Abel B30
Baez, Joan A99, A131, A241, B8, B24
Bagemihl, Bruce A223
bagpipes A186, A187, B27
Bailey, Derek B17
Bailey, Philip A250
Bailey, Robert A116, A214, B8
BaileyShea, Matthew A241
Baker, Arthur A104
Baker, Belle A168, B12
Baker, Ginger A132, B20, B29
Baker, Houston A. B4
Baker, Jack B12
Baker, Katherine A240
Bakhtin, Mikhail A34, A51, A261, B4, B6, B13, B28
balance (panning) A36
Ball, Marcia A123
ballad A37, A125, A270, B10, B19
Ballard, Florence A99
Ballard, Hank A11, A53, B24
Bambaataa, Afrika B31
Bananarama A212, B24
Band, The A17, A43, A185, A247, B7, B20, B24, B32
Band Aid A205, B19, B25
Bangles A185, B24, B32
Bang on a Can A72
Bangs, Lester B6
banjo A173, A220, A227, B27
Banks, Tony A141, A142, A232

Bannock B14
Baraka, Amiri (LeRoi Jones) A30, A255
Barbeque Bob B26
Barber, Adrian B8
Barber, Chris A132, B7
barbershop harmony A263, A264, B27
Barclay James Harvest A185, B21
Barenaked Ladies, The B24
Bar-Kays, The A29, A185
Barlow, Barriemore B20
Barnard, Stephen B20
Baron, Joey A217
Baroque music B27
Barrett, Richie A95
Barrett, Syd A199, B29
Barrett, Wild Willy A185
Barri, Steve B15
Barris, Harry B30
Barroso, Ary A211
Barrow, Steve A235
Barry, Jeff A106
Barry, John A43
Barry, Len A95
Barsalou, Lawrence A271
Barthes, Roland A38, A122, A183, A225, A227, A258, B4, B13, B19
Bartky, Sandra Lee A49
Bartók, Béla A71, A114, A157, A200, B3, B19, B27
Bashe, Philip B28
Basie, Count A105, A263, B4, B16, B21
Basil, Toni A43
bass A29, A98; bass guitar A130, A238, B2
Bassey, Shirley B8
Bassman, George B30
Bataille, George A223
Batári, M. A183
Bates, Ian A59
Bates, Simon A185
Batten, Jennifer B28
Battles A221
Baudrillard, Jean A82, B4
Baur, Steven B8
Baxter, Andrew A240
Baxter, Jim A240
Baxter, Les B15
Bayes, Nora B12
Bazilian, Eric A219
B. Bumble and the Stingers B24

Beach, David A86
Beach Boys, The A17, A22, A43, A71, A75, A80, A84, A95, A99, A109, A125, A160, A167, A185, A205, A214, A224, A247, A269, B7, B8, B15, B16, B19, B21, B24, B32
Beadle, Jeremy J. B22
Bearden, Romare B22
Beastie Boys, The A80, A99, A247, B14, B31
beatboxing A221
Beat Brothers B8
Beatles, The A16, A17, A19, A24, A33, A39, A43, A46, A55, A56, A63, A64, A67, A68, A69, A70, A71, A72, A73, A74, A75, A76, A77, A80, A83, A84, A85, A86, A90, A91, A92, A93, A94, A95, A96, A98, A99, A100, A101, A102, A107, A116, A121, A123, A124, A132, A133, A134, A138, A141, A143, A149, A154, A156, A159, A160, A167, A182, A184, A185, A186, A194, A195, A198, A204, A205, A207, A213, A221, A222, A225, A230, A232, A233, A234, A235, A241, A245, A246, A247, A248, A250, A253, A254, A259, A263, A263, A269, B3, B4, B7, B8, B16, B19, B20, B21, B23, B24, B25, B27, B28, B29, B31, B32
Beatmakers, The B8
Beatnuts, The B14
beats B31; breakbeat B5, B22, B31; breakdown B5; chopping B22; flipping B22
Beautiful South A185
Beaver and Krause B21
Bebee, Roger A163
Be-Bop Deluxe A185
Bécaud, Gilbert B25
Bechet, Sidney B32
Beck A54, A55, A80, A83, A85, A97, A163, A221, A222, A247, B32
Beck, Jeff A132, A185, B7, B29
Becker, Howard B22
Becker, Judith B21
Becker, Walter A96
Becky songs B12
Beebe, Roger A163
Bee Gees, The A43, A167, A179, A185, A213, A241, B3, B7, B21, B24, B25
Beethoven, Ludwig van A92, A97, A99, A116, A147, A166, A179, A183, A227, A234, A245, B5, B8, B16, B17, B18, B19, B21, B25, B28, B31, B32

Subject Index

Beiderbecke, Bix B16, B19
Belafonte, Harry A238, B17
Belairs, The B15
Belknap, Ray B28
Bell, Al A29
Bell, Arthur A240
Bell, Ed B26
Bell, William A29, A99, A185
Belleville Three, The B5
Belmonts, The B15
Belz, Carl B32
Benatar, Pat B24
Beni B. B22
Benjamin, Benny A106, A108
Benjamin, Walter B4, B19, B32
Benjamin, William A237
Bennett, Tony B10, B21
Bennett, Will A240
Bennett and the Rebel Rousers, Cliff B7
Benson, George B24
Bent, Ian A109, A156
Berberian, Cathy B17
Berg, Alban A114, A178
Berger, Harris B22
Berio, Luciano A24, B7, B17, B32
Berland, Jody B14
Berle, Milton B12
Berlin (group) A185
Berlin, Edward B12
Berlin, Irving A13, A120, A168, A228, B10, B11, B12, B19, B27, B30
Berlioz, Hector A116, A232
Berman, Marshall B28
Bernard, Jonathan A27, A73, A99
Bernie, Ben B30
Bernstein, Leonard B12, B16
Berry, Chuck A17, A33, A53, A75, A76, A80, A83, A85, A95, A97, A99, A125, A160, A167, A185, A238, A244, A246, A254, B4, B7, B8, B9, B15, B18, B19, B21, B24, B25, B27, B28, B32
Berry, Jan B15
Berry, Richard A85, B15
Berry, Venise A255
Berry, Wallace A208
Best, Mona B8
Best, Peter B8
Betterton, Rosemary A45
Bhagwat, Anil B7

bhangra A61
Biamonte, Nicole A205
Big Bill Broonzy B21
Big Boi A1
Big Brother and the Holding Company A101, B7
Big Country A185, A187, B20, B21
Big Maceo A240
Big Pun(isher) B14
Big Star A247
Big Three, The B8
Bikini Kill A210
Billboard magazine A32, A107, A241
biology A152
Bishop, Elvin A43
Bishop, Joe B30
Bishop, Stephen B24
Bixler-Zavala, Cedric A205
Bizet, Georges B12
Biz Markie B14
Bjork A50, A51, A97, A205, B21, B32
Björnberg, Alf A46, B19
Black, Cilla A249, B7, B8, B21
Black Ace A62
Blackalicious A2
Black Box A212, B21
Black Combo, The Bill B8
Black Dyke Mills Band, The B7
Black Flag A210
Blacking, John A183, A220, A255, B19, B28
Blackjacks B8
Black Keys, The A148
Blackmore, Richie B28
Black Orpheus B14
Black Sabbath A16, A17, A43, A55, A83, A97, A99, A167, B20, B21, B28, B31
Black Sheep A1
Black Star A158
Black Thought B14
Blackwell, Scrapper A240
Blaine, Hal B15
Blake, Eubie B19, B30
Blake, Ginger B15
Blake, Tchad B32
Bland, Bobby B21
Bland, James A. B30
Blevins, Frank A240
Blige, Mary J. A123, B14
Blind Blake A240, B26

Blind Boys of Alabama B21
Blind Faith A43, B17
Bliss, Melvin B22
Blitzstein, Marc B12
Blondie A42, A43, A179, A185, A241, B24, B32
Blood, Sweat, and Tears A43, A167, A185, A234, B3, B7, B19, B21, B24
Bloodhound Gang, The A146
Bloom, Harold A234
Bloom, Rube B30
Bloom, Sol B12
Bloomfield, Terry A82
Bloque A149
Blount, Tanya A161
Blow, Kurtis A2, B31
Blue Cheer B28
bluegrass music A173, A220, B19, B27
blue note A14, A23, A26, A170, A180, A239, A251, A254, A256, A264, B19, B26, B27
Blue Öyster Cult A7, A16, A24, A43, A59, A99, A167, A185, A247, B28
blues A8, A26, A40, A62, A131, A132, A144, A148, A170, A172, A176, A180, A201, A210, A235, A239, A240, A254, A264, B6, B9, B19, B26, B27, B28, B29, B32; country A238, B26; vaudeville blues B26
Bluesbreakers, The B29
Blues Traveler B24
Blur B20, B21
BMI B19
Bobbettes, The A44
Bob B. Soxx and the Blue Jeans B15
Bob & Sheri B15
Boccherini, Luigi A70
Bock, Jerry B12
Bogan, Lucille A240
Boggs, Doc A210
Bohlman, Philip B21
Boland, Clay B30
bolero A270
Bomb Squad A261
Bonamy, James A189
Bonds, Mark Evan B9
Bones, Frankie B5
Bone Thugs 'N' Harmony B14, B31
Boney M A64
Bonham, John A131, B20, B32
Bon Iver A102

Bon Jovi A16, A46, A55, A99, A185, A250, A252, B28
Bonner, Juke Boy A62
Bono A7, A52, A103, B32
Bono, Sonny A32
Bonzo Dog [Doo Dah] Band, The A185, B7, B21
boogaloo A238
boogie A238
boogie woogie A8, A238, B19
Booker T. and the MGs A29, A95, A185, A216, B24
Books, The A204
Boomtown Rats, The A64, A185, B20, B21
Boone, Graeme A171
Boone, Pat A97, A123, B19, B24, B32
Boo Radleys, The B20, B21
Booth, David A270
Booth, Wayne A51
Booze, Wee Bea A240
Bordieu, Pierre B6
Boretz, Benjamin, B32
Borlagdan, Joseph A212
Borneman, Ernest A176
Borodin, Alexander B25
borrowing A71
Bosch, Anonymous A212
bossa nova A211
Boston A16, A43, A75, A101, A205, A246, A247, A250, B24
Bottrill, David B32
Bouhafa, Faris A137
Boulez, Pierre A11, A12, B17
Bourdieu, Pierre B4, B19
Bowditch, Claire A205
Bowie, David A16, A19, A80, A83, A84, A99, A101, A103, A123, A143, A159, A185, A186, A221, A247, A269, B7, B13, B20, B21, B24, B32
Bowles, Jimmy and Judy B15
Bowlly, Al A227, B21
Bowman, Brooks B30
Bowman, Euday B12
Boyarin, Daniel B22
Boyer, Horace Clarence A161
Boyle, Susan A167
Boyz II Men A167
Bozzio, Terry A11, A27
Bracewell, Michael B13

Subject Index

Bracey, Ishmon A240, B26
Brackett, David A7, A22, A99, B13, B21
Bradby, Barbara A7, B19
Bradford, Alex A161
Bradford, Perry B26
Bradley, Dick B20, B21
Bradley, Harold Ray A270
Bradley, Jan A108
BradleyHeartVampire A205
Bragg, Billy B21
Braham, David B12
Braham, John Joseph B12
Brahms, Johannes A99, A166, A222, B8, B12, B21, B28, B30
Bramlett, Bonnie A140
Branch, Michelle B21
Brandwein, Naftule B12
Brandy A158
Braxton, Anthony B9
Brazilian music A211
Bread A247, B24
Brecht, Bertold B4, B12, B19
Brecker, Michael B1
Bregman, Albert A8
Brennan, Maire B21
Brennan, Tim B14
Brennet, Namoli A169
Brewer, Kahle A240
Brice, Fanny B12
Bright Eyes A205
Brill Building A77, A106, A108
British Sea Power B21
Britt, Elton A266
Britz, Chuck B15
Broadway A41, A113, A168, A228, B19
Brockman, Polk B26
Brogan, Daniel A181
Broken Social Scene A221
Bronski Beat A21, A185
Brontë, Emily A165
Brooklyn B14
Brooks, Garth A189, A190, A191, A193
Brooks, Harry B30
Brooks, John Benson B30
Brooks, Sam B26
Brooks, Shelton B30
Brooks and Dunn A189, A190
Broonzy, Big Bill A240, B21, B26, B27
Brotherhood of Man A235

Broughton, Edgar B21
Broughton, Frank B5
Brown, Alison A220
Brown, Arthur A43
Brown, Bobby B24
Brown, Buster B24
Brown, Charles B9
Brown, James A32, A35, A43, A53, A55, A83, A95, A99, A104, A105, A117, A163, A184, A185, A210, A238, A255, A262, A271, B3, B4, B5, B7, B19, B20, B21, B22, B31
Brown, Jason Robert B12
Brown, Jema A31
Brown, Joe B8
Brown, Kirvy A161
Brown, Les B30
Brown, Lew A120, B12, B30
Brown, Matthew A99
Brown, Nacio Herb B12, B30
Brown, Peter (artist) B7
Brown, Peter (writer) B8
Brown, Richard "Rabbit" B26
Brown, Scott A172
Brown, Shirley A29, A185, B21
Brown, William A240
Brown, Willie B26
Browne, Doc A185
Browne, Jackson A124
Browne, Tom B31
Brubeck, Dave A93, A224
Bruce, Jack A132, B7, B20, B29
Bruce, Lawrence A53
Bruford, Bill A71, A207
Brun, Ane A222
Bryan, Alfred B12
B.T. Express A101, A238
Buarque, Chico A211
bubblegum pop A163
Buck, Peter A181
Buckingham, Lindsey B24
Buckinghams, The A43, A101, B7, B24
Buckley, Jeff A80, B21
Buffalo Springfield A247, B24
Buggles, The B32
Bühler, Karl A115
Burdon, Eric A185
Burke, Johnny B11
Burke, Solomon A95, A185
Burkhart, Charles A116

Burleigh, Harry T. B9
Burnett, Carol A202
Burnett, Ernest M. B30
Burnett, Robert A158
Burnette, Johnny A122, A185, B8, B21
Burns, Gary A250, B20
Burns, Lori A205
Burnside, R.L. A62, B21
Burroughs, William B7
Burstein, Poundie A116
Burtnett, Earl B8
Burton, Val B30
Burton, Ward A266
Burwell, Cliff B10, B30
Bush A84
Bush, Frank B12
Bush, Kate A59, A165, A185, A186, B20, B21
Bushkin, Joe B30
Busta Rhymes A1, A24
Butcher, Dwight A266
Butler, Jerry A108
Butler, Judith B13
Butler, Mark A115, A135, A144, A208, A217
Buzby, Christopher A72
Buzzcocks A210
Byrd, William A185, B27
Byrds, The A33, A43, A70, A75, A121, A138, A247, A248, B7, B8, B21, B24, B32
Byrne, David A99, A178
Byrnside, Ronald B20, B21
Byron, Don B12

C.L. Smooth B22
Caccini, Giulio A53
cadence A5, A14, A40, A44, A45, A86, A88, A99, A174, A186, A190, A226, A232, A247, B27; authentic A172; auxilary A214, A254; half A172; Landini A247; plagal A33, A45, A183, A186, A194; plagal (double) A5, A16, A43, A92, A96, A97, A100, A180, A263, B7, B8
Cadwallader, Allen A86
Caesar, Irvin B30
Cage, John A11, A99, B17, B18
Cahn, Sammy B12, B30
Cain, Edward L. A240
cakewalk B9, B27
Calderone, Victor A3
Cale, J.J. A16, A40, A167, B21

Cale, John A124
call and response A170, B4, B9, B19, B21, B27
Callahan, Fred B. B30
Callahan, Homer A240
Callaway, Helen B22
Calloway, Cab B12
Cameo A250
Camilleri, Lelio B21
camp B13
Campbell, Glen A34, A173, B15
Campbell, James A30
Camus, Albert A137
Canadian music B14
Canned Heat A43, A185, B17
Cannon, Freddy Boom-Boom B15
Cannon, Gus B26
Cannon, Hughie B30
Cannon's Jug Stompers A240, B26
Canterbury scene A73, A166, A207
cantor B12
Cantor, Eddie B12220
Capehart, Jerry
Cantwell, Robert A B8
capitalism B28
Capitol Records A39, A160, A162, B15, B32
Caplin, William A205, A240
capo A4, B1
a cappella A26, A87, A178, A221, B15
Captain and Tennille B24
Captain Beefheart A210
Capuzzo, Guy A84, A142, A205, A250
Cara, Irene A19
Caravan A166
cardinality B5
Carey, Danny A205
Carey, Mariah A97, A167, B21, B24
Cargill, Henson A189
Caribbean music B27
caricature A69
Carl, Craig B5
Carless, Dorothy B21
Carleton, Bob B30
Carlin, Peter Ames B15
Carlisle & Ball A240
Carlisle, Bill A240
Carlisle, Cliff A240, A266
Carlos, Walter/Wendy A141, A261
Carmen, Eric A43, B24
Carmichael, Hoagy B8, B10, B11, B12, B30

Carnes, Kim A19, A43
Carolina Night Hawks A240
Carpenter, Karen B31
Carpenter, Mary Chapin A191
Carpenters A140, A185, A249, B3, B21
Carr, Gunther Lee A53
Carr, Leon B12
Carr, Leroy A240, B26
Carraba, Chris A205
Carradine, Keith A66
Cars, The A17, A74, A99, A182, B24
Carson, Fiddlin' John A240
Carson, Jeff A191
Carter Family, The A240
Carter, Bo B26
Carter, Mel A43
Carthy, Eliza B21
Carthy, Martin B20, B21
Caryll, Ivan B30
Cascades, The B25
Casey, Edward A22
Casey, Kenneth B30
Cash, Johnny A7, A24, A44, A80, A247, A270, B21
Casman, Nellie B12
Cass and the Casanovas B8
Cast B20
Castaways A43
Castells, The B15
Casuals, The B20, B21
Cateforis, Theo A203
Cavaliere, Felix A250
Cave, Nick A162, B21
Cecil, Malcolm A144
Celebrated Working Men's Band B18
celesta A98, A200
cello A98
Celtic music B27
Cento A159
centricity A55, A56, A200; sectional A56
Certeau, Michel de B4
Cetera, Peter B24
chaccone/passacaglia A74, A149
Chad and Jeremy B8
Chafe, Eric A134
Challengers, The B15
Chamberlain, Richard A249
Chambers Brothers A43, A101
Chambers, Iain B19, B20

Champs, The A44, A97
Chancellor, Justin A205
Chandler, Chas A40
Chandler, Gene A43, A108
chant A134
Chapin, Harry A99, B24
Chaplin, Saul B12, B30
Chapman, Michael B21
Chapman, Norman B8
Chapman, Tracy A80, A247, A250
charango B25
Chariot, The A203, A204
Charles, Ray A43, A44, A55, A80, A95, A123, A167, A185, A238, A247, A263, A264, B7, B8, B9, B15, B16, B21
Charleston, The B11
Chase, Newell B30
Chatman, Seymour A51
Cheap Trick A250, B7, B21, B24
Checker, Chubby A250, B15
Chemical Brothers B5
Cher A32, A259
Cherlin, Michael A142
Chernoff, John A115, B4, B22, B27
Cherry, Neneh A185, B20, B21
Chesney, Kenny A191
Chesnutt, Mark A191
Chess Records A110, A132, B32
Chess, Leonard B32
Chester, Andrew A67, A184
Chic A24, A163, A241, B24, B31
Chicago (band) A17, A101, A214, A237, A250, B3, B7, B24
Chicago (city) B5, B14, B32
Chiccarell, Joe B32
Chiffons, The A43, A95, A96, B24
Child A64
Chipmunks, The A97
Choclair B14
Chopin, Frédéric A97, A99, A116, A142, A211, A214, A215, A264, B27
chord: "sus" A86, A226; added-sixth A45, A86, A91, A93, A99, A114, B10; augmented A63; augmented-sixth A14, A15, A160, A167, A169, B3, B23; cadential six-four A160; chromatic mediant A54, A72, A111, A116, A138, A142, A177,; common-tone diminished seventh A167, B7, B8; diminished seventh A14, A63, A93, A100,

A114, A234, A251; dominant seventh A86, A261, B20; eleventh B3; extensions A60, A96; half-diminished seventh A81, A113, B10; major seventh A113, A114, A228, B10; minor seventh A14; mystic chord A114; Neapolitan A93, A139, A150, A169, A234, B3, B7, B8, B18; ninth A14, A209, A263, B3; Petrouchka A139; pivot A93; pop or soul dominant A226; power chord A16, A80, A86, A88, A99, A155, A177, A210, B7, B28; secondary dominant A63, A147, A167, B3, B7, B8; seventh chord A254, A256, A263, B3; six-four B10; slash chord A86, A96, A142, A226; thirteenth A14, B3; Tristan chord A113, A116, A232, B10
Chordettes, The A44, A97, B15
Chords, The B21
Christian, Lillie Delk A119
Christian, Roger A160, B15
Christianity A180
chromaticism A93, A260, B3
Chubby Checker B24
Chuck D A39, A255
Chumbawumba A233
church B9, B26
Churchill, Winston A232
circle of fifths A14, A96, A147, A150, A207, A214, A263, A264, B10, B19, B28
Circle Takes the Square A205
Circulus B21
Clannad A186, B21
Clanton, Jimmy A97
Clapton, Eric A16, A19, A80, A99, A101, A132, A160, A167, A185, A221, A235, A247, A250, A256, A257, A271, B7, B17, B19, B20, B24, B28, B29
Claribel B25
Clarida, Bob B21
Clark Five, The Dave A43, A107, B8, B16, B20
Clark, Chris A110
Clark, Dee B25
Clark, Petula A185, A241, B4, B21
Clarke, Eric A50, B21
Clarke, Martin A162
Clarkson, Kelly A169
Clash, The A80, A118, A185, A210, A221, A247, B19, B20
class B26

classical ("art") music A12, A52, A71, A74, A105, A114, A141, A149, A178, A179, B5, B13, B20, B27, B28, B32
Classics IV, The A93, B8
Clausen, Alf A202
clave A3, A17
Clavinet A233
Clay, Judy A29, A99, A185
Claypool, Les B23
Clayton Skiffle Group, the Eddie B8
Clayton, Adam A103
Clearmountain, Bob B32
Cleftones, The B15
Clement, Jack A270
Clendinning, Jane A55, A86
Cleveland, James A161
Clifford, James B14, B22
climax A204, A205
Cline, Patsy A53, A189, A193, A247, B21
Clinton, George A117, A238, B13, B21, B31
Clovers, The A44, B24
Clovis, New Mexico B32
clubbing B5
Coasters, The (Billy J. Kramer) B8
Coasters, The (Carl Gardner) A44, A53, A77, A84, A95, A97, B8, B15, B19, B25
Coates, Dorothy Love A161
Cobain, Kurt A99, A181, B17, B31, B32
Cobb, Will B12
Coburn, Richard B30
Cochran, Eddie A44, A80, A185, A247, B8, B15, B21
Cocker, Jarvis A82
Cocker, Joe A43, A185, A264, B21
Cockney Rebel A185
Cocteau Twins B32
Coe, David Allan A191
Cogan, Alma B8
Cogan, Robert A22, A78, A88, B4
Cogbill, Tommy A265
cognition A40
Coheed and Cambria A205
Cohen, A.M. A8
Cohen, Leonard A7, B21
Cohn, Dorri A51
Cohn, Richard A54, A142, A220, B5
Cohon, Baruch J. B12
Coker, Wilson B19
Coldplay A102, A167, A205, A221, B21

Cole, Bob B30
Cole, Cozy A97
Cole, Nat "King" B4, B7, B21, B25, B31
Coleman, Jaybird B26
Coleman, Ornette B9, B18, B7
Coleman, Ray B8
Coliauta, Vinnie A27
collage A24, A131
Collective Soul B24
Collingwood, R.G. B18
Collins, Albert B8
Collins, Bootsy A117, A238
Collins, Judy A123
Collins, Lanelle A161
Collins, Phil A19, A43, A142, A185, A232, A235, A250, A264, B20, B24, B32
Collins, Ray A11
Collins, Sam A240, B26
Collyer, David Sorin A93, A150
Colosseum B21
Coltrane, John A224, B9, B17, B31
Columbia Records A121
Colvin, Shawn B32
Combs, Sean "Puffy" (Puff Daddy) A159, A163, B14, B31
Comden, Betty B12
Commodores, The A205, A248
Common B14, B31
Communards, the A123
Como, Perry A97, A99, A238, B4
complexity A27
Compton B14
concept album A160, A162, A199, A269, B15
conceptual blending B6
conceptual model A271
concrete music A198, A199
Condor, Alvin A240
Cone, Edward T. A162, B4, B5, B7
Confrey, Zez B30
Conley, Arthur A185
Connelly, Reg A30
Connolly, Ray A259
Conrad, Con B30
Considine, J.D. B22
Constanten, Tom A25, A99, A171
contour A5, A14, A107, A108, A252, B26, B30, A201
contrafact A168
Cook, Nicholas A50, A183, A217, B21

Cook, Will Marion B9, B12
Cooke, Deryck A134, A140, B20, B21
Cooke, Sam A32, A80, A95, A97, A108, A161, A239, B7, B8, B21
Cookies, The A95
Coolidge, Rita A140, A235
Coolio A99, A123, A224, B14
Cooper, Alice A16, A99, A185, B21, B28, B29
Coopersmith, Harry B12
Coots, J. Fred B30
Copa, The A30
Cope, Julian A124
Copeland, Alan A24
Copeland, Stewart A178, A235
Copland, Aaron B12, B16
copyphrase A202
copyright A30, A202, A212, A213
Coral Records A270
Corbetta, Jerry A43
Corday, Leo B12
Corea, Chick A73, A114
Corelli, Arcangelo A92
Cornells, The B15
coro/sono A205
corporate rock A74
Corrs, The A193, B24
Corvan, Ned B19
Coslow, Sam B12, B30
Costello, Elvis A7, A33, A74, A95, A99, A124, A167, A185, A186, A221, A235, A247, B4, B20, B21, B24
Cotton, Billy A227
Cotton, Elizabeth A62
counterculture A166, B17, B19, B29
counterpoint A25, A72, A99, A166, A200, A237; double counterpoint A215
Counting Crows A246, A247
country music A151, A173, A189, A190, A191, A193, A240, A266, B4, B6, B18, B19, B26, B28, B32
Coupland, Douglas A181, A234
Courlander A238
Covach, John A22, A51, A67, A81, A99, A141, A142, A143, A191, A205, A232, A235, A207
Covay, Don A185
cover song A24, A27, A30, A34, A47, A52, A53, A75, A123, A131, A159, A170, A217, B8, B21
Coward, Noël B13, B30

Cox, Bill A240
Cox, Ida A240
Coyle, Michael A170
Crain, Edward L. A240
Cramer, Floyd A270, B8
Cranberries, The A205
Crawford, Joan B12
Crawford, Sugar Boy A238
Crazy Frog B21
Crazy Horse A88, B6
Crazy World of Arthur Brown B21
Cream A16, A43, A55, A99, A101, A132, A141, A176, A185, A205, A247, A248, B3, B7, B17, B19, B20, B21, B24, B29
Creamer, Henry B12, B30
Creation Records A22
Cree B14
Creedence Clearwater Revival A16, A43, A99, A185, A247, B3, B8, B20, B24
Crenshaw, Reese A240
Crests, The A44
Crew Cuts, The B21, B25
Crickets, The A97, A185, B20
Croce, Jim B24
crooning A227, B19
Cropper, Steve A29, A30, A95, A256, B8, B32
Crosby, Bing A14, A168, B4, B8, B12, B16, B19, B32
Crosby, David A121, A173, A260, B7, B8
Crosby, Stills, and Nash (and Young) A101, A102, A205, A222, A246, A247, A248, A269, B3, B4, B6, B7, B21, B32
cross relations A151, A177, A222, B18
cross-domain mapping B21
Cross, Christopher A250
crossover A12, A32, A35, A73, A193, B13
Crow, Sheryl A83, A247, B24, B32, A247
Crowder Brothers A240
Crowley, Daniel J. B22
Crows, The B15
Crystals, The A45, A160, A247, B7, B15, B32
Cubanita, La A3
Cubitt, Sean A258, B19
cuerpo A205
Cuff Links, The A99, A185, B20
culture B2, B6
Culture Club A36, A43, A185, A250, B24
Cumming, Naomi A88, B21
Cure, The A99, A103, A137, A185, B24

Curiosity Killed the Cat A185
Curtis Mayfield A108
Curtis, King B8
Curtis, Lucious & Willie Ford A240
Curved Air A235, B21
Cusic, Don A217
Cusick, Suzanne A143, B14
Cutler, Chris B19
Cutting Records A3
cutting rhythm A66
Cypress Hill B14
Cyrkle, The B8

D12 A146
Daffan, Ted A270, B4
Daft Punk A205
Dahlhaus, Carl B4
Dale, Dick B15
Dalhart, Vernon A240
Dalton, Peter A235
Damasio, Antonio B21
Damned, The A210, B20, B21
dance A189, B9, B18, B19, B27
Dance, Daryl Cumber B22
dance band A227
dance music A115, B5, B13, B19; ambient B5; breakdance B31; Hi-NRG A128; house A3, A129, B5; line dancing A189
Danger Mouse A24, A39, A163
Dankworth, Johnny B8
Danny and the Juniors A44, A97, A185, B24
Danzig, Evelyn B30
D'Arby, Terence Trent A185, A250
Darby, Tom A240
Darcy, Warren A163
Darin, Bobby A44, A97, A123, A241, B7, B8, B15, B21, B25
Darkness, The B21
Dashboard Confessional A205
Datblygy A123
Daugherty, Michael A72
Daughtry A247
Dave Clark Five A107, A185, B8
Davenant, Sir William B16
Davenport, Cow Cow A238
Davenport, Jed A240
David, Benny B30
David, Craig B21
David, Hal A249, B12

Subject Index

David, Jimmy B30
David, Mack B8
David and Jonathan A107
Davies, Dave B8
Davies, Ray A107
Davis, Billy, Jr. B24
Davis, Jimmy B4
Davis, Miles A73, A217, A271, B9, B17
Davis, Rev. Gary A62, B21
Davis, Rod B8
Davis, Sammy, Jr. B12
Davis, Spencer A132
Davis Group, The Spencer B8
Day, Aidan A7
Day, Bobby A44, A97
D, Chuck A39
Deacon Blue A185, B21
Dead or Alive A185, A232
Dead Weather, The B7
Dean, Billy A189
Dean, James B15
Dean, Joe A201, B26
Dean, Winton A122
Death A210
Death Cab for Cutie A205, A221
Death Row Records B31
DeBarge B24
DeBurgh, Chris A167
Debussy, Claude A53, A114, A227, B3, B10, B16, B19, B27, B30
Decemberists, The A162, A205
deceptive harmonic motion A219, B1
Decker, Jeffrey Louis B22
deClercq, Trevor A222
DeCurtis, Anthony A103, A137, A181
Dee, Joey, and the Starli[gh]ters A95, B24
Dee, Kiki A43
Deep Forest A159
Deep Purple A16, A23, A55, A74, A75, A97, A99, A101, A167, A185, A208, A233, A246, A248, B7, B20, B21, B24, B28, B31
Deerhoof A205
Deevoy, Adrian A51
Def Leppard A185, A193, A250, B20, B21, B28, B32
Deftones A205
Dekker, Desmond A185
Del Amitri B24
Delaney, William W. B12
Delaney and Bonnie and Friends B7
DeLange, Eddie B30
De La Soul A1, B14
Del Barco, Mandalit B22
Deleuze, Gilles B17
Délibes, Léo A178
Dell-Vikings B24
Delmore Brothers A240, B4
Delroys, The B15
Delta Rhythm Kings B32
Del-Tones, The B15
Del Vikings, The A44, A97, B24
Dempsey, Michael A137
Dennett, Daniel A152
Denniker, Paul B30
Dennis, Matt A147, B30
Denny, Martin B15
DeNora, Tia A50
Denton, Larry B15
Denver, John A7, A182, A241, B21, B24
Denver, Karl B21
Deodato A101, B24
dePaul, Gene B30
Depeche Mode A54
Dere, Karen B22
Derek and the Dominos A16, A80, A101, A185, A247, A248, B7, B19, B20, B21, B24
Derf Scratch A210
Derrida, Jacques A34, B17
Derry and the Seniors B8
DeShannon, Jackie A257
Desper, Stephen B15
DeSylva, Buddy A120
detuning A158
Deviants B21
Devlin, Johnny B8
Devo B24
Dexter, Dave, Jr. B8
Dexy's Midnight Runners A185
Diagable Planets B31
Diamond, Jim A185
Diamond, Neil A85
Diamond Rio A191
Diamonds, The A44, A97, A185, B15, B21, B24
Dia Pason B2
Dibben, Nicola B21
Dibdin, Charles B16
Dickinson, Jim B32
Dickinson, Reverend Emmett B26

Diddley, Bo A38, A44, A80, A95, A198, A216, A238, A247, B7, B17, B19
Dietrich, Marlene B8
Dietz, Howard B10, B11
DiFranco, Ani A51
Dillinger Escape Plan A203, A204, A208
Dillon, Will A120
Dilly B7
DiMeola, Al A93, A255
Dinning, Mark A44, A241, B24
Dion B15
Dion, Celine A167
Dion and the Belmonts A44, B21
Dire Straits A19, A99, A101, A185, A248, A269, B21, B32
disco music A52, A179, A182, B5, B13, B19, B25
discourse A143, B13, B28
Disko Band A179
Disney A141, A202
dissonance A103, A239, A256
distortion A43, A177, B6, B32
Dixiebelles, The A95
Dixie Chicks, The A55, A191
Dixie Cups, The A95, A238
Dixie Dregs, The A73
Dixie Hummingbirds A238, B1
Dixon, Willie A19, A131, A132, B17, B21
Dixon Brothers, The A240
DJ A129, B5, B14, B22; scratching B19; turntabling A221, B5
DJ B-Mello B22
DJ Dangerous Orange A24
DJ Freelance Hellraiser A24
DJ Impact B5
DJ Jazzy Jay B22
DJ Kool Akiem B22
DJ Kool Herc B31
DJ Lobsterdust A84
DJ Mixx Messiah B22
DJ O-Dub B22
DJ Pierre B5
DJ Premier B22
DJ Quik B22
DJ Roach B14
DJ Shadow B22
DJ Shiva B5
DJ Topspin B22
Doane, Randal A163
Dockwray, Ruth B21

Dodd, Ken B8, B19
Doe, Andrew B15
Doggett, Bill A44, A53, B15
Dokken B28
Doll, Christopher A56
Domino B22
Domino, Fats A44, A76, A80, A95, A97, A185, A238, A247, A264, B7, B8, B15, B20, B21, B24, B25
Dominoes, The B21
Donaldson, Walter B10, B19, B30
Don and Dewey B25
Donat, Robert B10
Donays, The A95
Don Caballero A57, A208
Donegan, Lonnie A132, A259, B7, B8, B21
Donovan A43, A101, A185, B7, B8, B21, B29
Doobie Brothers, The A74, A167, A173, A205, A247, A248, A250, B24
Doors, The A16, A17, A43, A55, A72, A82, A83, A86, A99, A101, A148, A167, A185, A210, A247, A248, A269, B3, B7, B8, B20, B24, B29
doo-wop A33, B15, B19, B21
Doran, Terry B7
Dorsey, Jimmy B30
Dorsey, Lee A95, B7, B8, B21
Dorsey, Thomas A26, A161, B9
Dorsey, Tommy B4, B10
double emploi A86
Douglas, Craig B8
Douglas, Jack B32
Douglas, Steve B15
Doves B21
Dowd, Tom A101, A238, B32
Dowland, John A178
Down Beat magazine A53
Downhill Battle A163
Doyle, Peter B21
Doyle, Walter B12
Dozier, Lamont A95, A99, A106, A108, B32
Dragonforce B21
Drake, Nick A221
Dranes, Juanita "Arizona" A205, A240
Dr. Buzzard's Original Savannah Band A228
Dr. Dre A80, A99, A247, A261, B31
Dream Theater A175, B21
Drew, David B12

Drifters, The A33, A44, A53, A77, A85, A95, A99, A185, A247, A270, B7, B8, B20, B21, B24
Drifting Cowboys, The B4
Drive-By Truckers B21
At the Drive In A205
Dr. John A222, A238
Drowning Man A204
drugs B5, B18, B29; LSD A134
drums A17, A29, A98, A203, A208, A231, A238, A261, B2, B5, B9, B20, B28, B31; drum machine A255, B5, B22, B31, B32; kick drum A3, A146, A241, B5; patterns A221, A267
Duals, The B15
Dubin, Al B10
DuBois, W.E.B. B22
Dudley, Shannon B22
Duke, Vernon B10, B11, B30
Dukelsky, Vladimir B30
Dumont, Charles B25
Duncan, Johnny B25
Duncan, Robert B28
Dunford, Uncle Eck A240
Dunhill Records A121
Dunn, Donald "Duck" A29, A95, B8, B32
Dunn, Trevor A163
Dunne, Irene B10
Dunphy, Eamon A103
Dupree, Champion Jack A238
Du Pree, Reese A240
Duran Duran A36, A43, A185, A212, A248, B24
Durant, Alan B19
Dury, Ian A85, A185
Dust Brothers, The A261
Dvořák, Antonín A215, B12, B27
Dyer, Richard A261
Dyke and the Blazers A238
Dykes Magic City Trio A240
Dylan, Bob A7, A11, A16, A18, A27, A32, A33, A43, A54, A58, A80, A96, A99, A101, A121, A122, A123, A124, A143, A167, A173, A180, A184, A185, A216, A221, A225, A239, A247, A264, A268, A269, B3, B4, B6, B7, B8, B15, B16, B17, B18, B19, B21, B24, B27, B29, B32
dynamics A43
Dyson, Michael Eric A110, B14, B22

Eagles, The A17, A80, A111, A167, A173, A185, A225, A247, A248, A250, B21, B24
Eagleton, Terry B28
Earle, Steve B21
Earth, Wind, and Fire A43, A55, A263, B7
Eastman, John B7
Eastman, Linda A90
Echo and the Bunnymen A185, B20
Echobelly B21
echolyn A72
eclecticism A163
Eco, Umberto A140, B19
Eddy, Duane A44, B8, B15
Edens, Roger B12
Edge, The A103
Edison Lighthouse B21
edited versions A159
editing A43
Edmonds, Kenneth "Babyface" B32
Edmonton B14
Edmunds, Ben A110
Ed O.G. and Da Bulldogs B14
Edwards, David A240
Edwards, Gus B12
Edwards, Tommy A44, A97
Edwards, Trebor A123
Eerola, Tuomas B8
Egan, Walter A248
Egg A166
Egypt B27
Ehrenreich, Barbara B28
Eightball and MJG B14
Eindhoven B14
Eisler, Hans B19
Elastica B20, B21
Electric Light Orchestra A16, A43, A83, A149, A179, A185, A248, B7, B19, B21, B24
Elegants, The A97, B15
Elgar A227
Elgar, Edward B19, B27
Eliot, T.S. A18, B16
Eliscu, Edward B10
elision A190, A270
Elliman, Yvonne A43, A179, B24
Ellingson, Ter B22
Ellington, Duke A15, A105, A147, A182, A263, B8, B9, B11, B12, B16, B19, B30
Elliot, Joe B28
Elliott, Brad B15

Elliott, Missy A55, A102, A261
Elliott, Ramblin Jack B8
Ellis, Alfred "Pee Wee" A238
Ellis, Shirley A135, B4
Ellstein, Abe B12
Elman, Mischa B12
Elman, Ziggy B12
embodiment A50, A155
Emerick, Geoff B7, B8, B32
Emerson, Ida B30
Emerson, Keith A71, A72, A73, A141, A166, A139, A232
Emerson, Lake, and Palmer A71, A72, A73, A74, A101, A138, A139, A141, A149, A166, A182, A185, A207, A229, A232, A235, B20, B21, B24, B28
Emery A203, A204, A205
EMF A247
Eminem A7, A47, A146, A234, A247, B31
emotion A23
Empson, William A122
engineer B32
England Dan and John Ford Coley B24
English; Black English B4, B22; Standard English A31, B4
Enid, The A72, A166
enjambment A2
Ennis, Phillip A44
Eno, Brian A22, A103, B1, B20, B32
Ensemble Modern, The A11, A12
Enya B21
Enzensberger, Hans Magnus B19
Epstein, Brian A95, B7, B8, B16
Epstein, Dena B4, B22, B27
Equals A185
Erasure A185
Eric B. and Rakim A117, A255, B31
Erlewine, Stephen Thomas A51
Erskine, Peter A71
Ertegun, Ahmet A77
Ertegun, Neshui A77
Escorts, The B7
Escot, Pozzi A22
Eshun, Kodwo B22
Esparaza, Sharon Marie B15
Estefan, Gloria B24
Esu-Elegbara B9
Eternal B21
Etheridge, Melissa A136, A219, B24

ethnography B2
ethnomusicology A10, A105, A255, B2, B4, B14, B19, B22, B28
Europe (band) A250, B21
Eurovision Song Contest A153
Eurythmics, The A185, A269, B20, B21
Evand, David A266
Evanescence B21
Evans, Bill A114, A147, B1
Evans, Faith B31
Evans, Gil B9
Evans, Malcolm B7, B8
Evans, Sara A191, A193
Evans and McLain A240
Everett, Betty B15
Everett, Walter A5, A16, A22, A56, A59, A63, A67, A80, A83, A86, A121, A142, A143, A154, A162, A191, A194, A198, A200, A205, A208, A215, A222, A232, A241, A269, B20
Everly Brothers, The A44, A75, A76, A94, A97, A185, A216, A241, A247, A259, A270, B1, B7, B15, B24
Every Mothers' Son A99
Everything But the Girl A3
Every Time I Die A203, A205
Evolution Control Committee, The A24, A39
exotica A160

Fab 5 Freddy B31
Fabbri, Franco B19, B21
Fabian, Johannes A182, B22
Fagen, Donald A96
Fain, Sammy B12, B30
Fairlight A104
Fairport Convention A123, A185, B20, B21
Fairweather A205
Faith, Adam A259, B8, B16
Faithfull, Marianne A107, B7, B8
Faith No More B21
Falco A19
Fales, Cornelia A22, B5
Fall, The A124, A185, A221, B20, B21
Fältskog, Agnetha B25
Fame Studios B32
Family A185, B7
Family Guy A202
Family Stone, The A43
fans B14

Subject Index

Farlowe, Chris B21
Farnham, John A185, A186
Farrés, Osvaldo B25
Farrow, Prudence B7
Fast, Susan A269, B6
Fastball A99
Fatboy Slim B24
Fauconnier, Gilles B21
Feather, Leonard A119, A227
feedback B17, B29
Feelies, The A85
Feeling, The B21
Feinstein, Michael A217
Feld, Steven B22
Feldman, Jerome B21
Feldman, Morton A138
Feliciano, Jose A205
feminism A45, A49, A66, A170, B13
Fender Rhodes A72, A98, A182
Fenoulhet, Paul B8
Ferdinand, Franz B21
Fernando, S.H., Jr. B22
Ferry, Bryan A123, A185, B21
Field Hippies, Joe Byrd and A138
Fields, Dorothy B10, B12
Fields, Gracie A123, A227, B16
Fifth Dimension, The A99, B7
figured bass B10
Fikentscher, Kai B5, B22
Fillmore, Charles B21
Fillyau, Clayton A238
film music A264, B1, B19, B25
film theory B14
Fine Young Cannibals A185
Fink, Robert A163, A182
Finnegan, Ruth B22
Fiori, Umberto B19
Fireballs, The B15
First Class A141
Fischer, Carl B30
Fish, Stanley A261
Fisher, Doris B12
Fisher, Fred B12, B30
Fiske, John B28
Fisk Jubilee Singers, The B9, B16
Fitzgerald, Ella A168, B12, B19, B21
Five Blind Boys of Alabama A161
Five for Fighting A247
Five Keys, The B15

Five Man Electrical Band A43
Five Percent Nation B14
Five Satins, The A38, A44, A80, A167, A247, A263, B15
Five Soul Stirrers of Houston A26
Five Star A185
Fixx, The B24
Flack, Roberta A24, A43, A123
Flaming Lips, The A102
Flamingos A247
Flamin' Groovies, The A99
Flanagan, Bill A103
Flanigan, Bob A160, B15
Flatt, Lester A220
Flavor Flav A255
Fleck, Bela A220
Fleet Foxes, The A205, B21
Fleetwood Mac A59, A85, A101, A132, A185, A186, A205, A245, A247, A248, B7, B20, B21, B24, B29
Fleetwoods, The B15, B25
Flint, McGuinness B21
Flippo, Chet B4
Florence, Nellie B26
Flores, Juan B22
Flo Rida A232
flow A2, A61, A144, A252, A261, B14, B31
Flowerpot Men, The B29
Floyd, Eddie A29, A95, A185, B24
Floyd, Samuel A., Jr. A48, A110, A238, B4, B21, B31
flute B25
Fluxus B7
Flye, Tom B32
Flying Burrito Brothers, The A173
Flying Lizards, The B20, B21
FM radio A141, A269
Focus A166, B20
Fogelberg, Dan B24
Folds Ben A221
folk music A58, A180, A188, B4, B19, B26
Fonda, Peter B7
Fong-Torres, Ben A35
Fontana and the Mindbenders, Wayne B8
Fontane Sisters, The A44
Fontella Bass A185
Foo Fighters, The A167, A205, B21
Fool, The B7
Forbes, Rand A138

Ford, Charles B21
Ford, Emil B25
Ford, Frankie A44
Ford, Lita A255, B28
Ford, Mary B8, B32
Ford, Robben A256
Ford, Tennessee Ernie B19
Ford, Willie A240
Foreigner A74, A141, A193, A250, B21, B24
form A12, A13, A14, A17, A21, A52, A66, A68, A75, A77, A80, A99, A109, A113, A125, A132, A139, A143, A144, A152, A190, A191, A194, A195, A196, A199, A205, A229, A269, B1, B2, B5, B10, B11, B30; 12-bar blues A22, A53, A75, A77, A86, A109, A132, A144, A148, A176, A201, A210, A239, A240, A244, A247, A251, A254, A256, A266, B7, B20, B27; 32-bar song form A227; AAA strophic A107; AAB (bar form) A26, A76, A132, A156, A210, A240, B10, B26; AABA A5, A13, A14, A20, A26, A30, A41, A71, A74, A76, A77, A106, A107, A108, A109, A113, A119, A120, A139, A144, A147, A150, A156, A160, A168, A191, A193, A194, A195, A196, A205, A209, A224, A240, A241, A270, B3, B10, B15, B21; AABB A240; ABA (ternary) A11, A58, A72, A75, A76, A132, A156, A270, B10; ABAB' A147, A195, A209, A217, A224, A270, B3; ABAC A209; accumulative A233; album form A163, A223; arch form A81; binary A14, A126; bridge A75, A89, A191, B7, B8; chorus A75, A84, A89, A191, A230, A241, B7, B8; coda A75, A89, B3; compound binary A205; cumulative A205, A233; double period A113, B10; formal function A205, A224; interlude A75, A89; introduction A228, B5; outro B5; period A46, A100, B10; phrase A5, A39, A78, A93, A124, A175, A189, A225, A252; phrase expansion A5, A190; postchorus A232; prechorus A182, A191, A241; recapitulation A205; refrain (sectional) A13, A75, B10, B27; refrain (subsection) A241, B7, B8; retransition A194; rondo A72, A222, B27; sentence A194, A241; simple verse A75; sonata form A72, A81, A163, B27; srdc, B7, B8; strophic A196, A241; terminally climactic A205; ternary B27; theme and variations B15; through-composition A204; verse A13, A75, A89, A241, B2, B8
Forman, Murray B22
Format, The A205
Fort, Joel B29
Forte, Allen A13, A14, A184, A228, A232
Foster, David B32
Foster, Fred A270
Foster, Gwen A240
Foster, Leroy "Baby Face" A132
Foster, Stephen A121, A264, B15, B27, B30
Foucault, Michel A131, B4, B28
Foundations A185
Four Freshmen, The A125, A160, B15
Fourmost, The A185, B7, B8
Four Pennies B21
Four Preps, The A97
Four Seasons, The A43, A93, A99, B7, B8, B15, B21, B24
Four Tops, The A32, A84, A95, A97, A99, A106, A108, A185, B7, B8, B21, B24
Fox, Roy A227
Foxy Brown B14
Fragos, George B12
Frampton, Peter A43, B24
France B14
Francis, Connie A97
François, Claude B25
Frankie Goes to Hollywood B24
Franklin, Aretha A32, A43, A53, A80, A99, A123, A161, A170, A185, A205, A217, A230, A247, A265, B7, B9, B21, B24, B32
Franklin, Kirk A161
Franklin, Reverend Clarence LaVaughn A170
Frantic Bleep B21
Fraser, Robert B7
Fred and his Playboy Band, John B7
Freddie and the Dreamers A70, A185, B8
Free A132, A185
Freeberg, Stan B25
Freed, Alan A53
Freed, Arthur B30
Freedom B31
Freeman, Bobby A95
Freeman, Ernie A97
Freeman, L.E. B30
Freeny's Barn Dance Band A239, A240

Subject Index

French, Jay Jay B28
French, John and Gabriel Brown A240
French music B27
Fresstyle Fellowship B14
Freud, Sigmund A82, A115, A133, A134, B19
Frey, Glenn A173, A250
Fricke, David A163, B28
Frida A19
Friedwald, Will A48
Friend, Cliff B30
Friend and Lover A99
Frightened Rabbit A205
Friml, Rudolf B30
Fripp, Robert A28, A67, A71, A218, A224, B20
Frith, Fred A72
Frith, Simon A7, A21, A34, A40, A50, A51, A66, A70, A124, A128, A143, A163, A201, A225, B4, B6, B13, B14, B19, B21, B28
Frizzell, Lefty A189, A270
Froom, Mitchell B32
Frost, David B7
Frug, Simon B12
Fruit Jar Guzzlers A240
Fugazi A205
Fugees, The B22
fugue A166, A200; fugato A71, B15
Fuller, Bobby A99
Fuller, Jesse A95
Fun Boy Three A19
function (harmonic) A16, A111
Fun-Da-Mental A61
fundamental line (Urlinie) A41, A97, A99, A113, B19
fundamental structure (Ursatz) A86, A147, A183, B19
Funeral For a Friend A205
funk A238, B5, B13, B19
Funkadelic A163, A255
Funk Brothers, The A270
Funk Inc. A104
Fuqua, Harvey A110
Furay, Ritchie A173
Furia, Philip B12
Furnes, Odd Torleiv A205
Further Seems Forever A205
Fusilli, jim B15
fusion A72, A73, B2
Fux A215

Gabriel, Jill A232
Gabriel, Peter A51, A72, A73, A142, A159, A185, A186, A221, A232, B20, B21, B23, B25, B32
Gabrielle A123
Gadd, Steve B1
Gage, Pete A136
Gaillard, Bulee B12
Gaines, Donna B28
Gallo, Armando A142, A232
Gamblers, The B15
Game, The B31
Gammon, Vic B19
Gammond, Peter B10
Gang of Four A185, B20, B21
gapped cycles A205
Garbage B20, B21, B32
Garcia, Jerry A16, A25, A94, A99, A171, A200, B17
Gardner, Carl A77
Gardner, Elysa A103
Garfunkel, Art A185, B1
Garland, Hank "Sugarfoot" A270
Garland, Judy A75, B10, B12, B21
Garry, Len B8
Garson, Greer B10
Garth Brooks A191
Gates, Henry Louis, Jr. A31, A48, A115, A170, A255, A256, A261, B4, B9, B14, B22, B31
Gates, Reverend J.M. B26
Gaughan, Dick B21
Gaunt, Kyra D. B22
Gauss, Carl Friedrich A57
Gay, John B16
Gaye, Anna A110
Gaye, Marvin A32, A51, A80, A85, A95, A99, A106, A110, A142, A144, A185, A245, A248, A250, B4, B7, B8, B19, B20, B21, B24, B32
Gay Metal Society B28
Gaynor, Gloria A5, A101, A167, A185
Gayton, Paul A238
Gebirtig, Mordecai B12
Geertz, Clifford B19
gender A38, A45, A82, A130, A136, A141, A153, A170, A173, A174, A259, B5, B6, B13, B14, B19, B22, B28

Genesis A28, A55, A67, A71, A72, A141, A142, A149, A154, A185, A207, A221, A229, A232, A250, A269, B20, B21, B24
Genette, Gérard A7, A159
genre A32, A34, A97, A163, B5, B14, B19, B28
Gentle Giant A71, A72, A73, A141, A149, A166, A185, B20
geography A158, B14
George, Lowell A173
George, Nelson B22
George Baker Selection, The B25
Georgia Peach, The A161
Georgia State Mass Choir A161
Gerber, Alex B12
German music B27
Germs, The A210
Gerry and the Pacemakers A185, A259, B8, B16, B21
Gershwin, George A114, A120, A147, A224, B8, B9, B10, B11, B12, B15, B16, B19, B30
Gershwin, Ira A224, B8, B10, B11, B12
gestalt theory A10
gesture A50, A88, A155, A183, B32
Geto Boys B14
Getz, Stan A99, A217, B7
G-Funk B14
Ghostface Killa B14
Gibbons, Billy B28
Gibbons, Carrol B21
Gibbons, Orlando B16
Gibbs, A. Harrington B30
Gibbs, Georgia A44, A53
Gibbs, Raymond B21
Gibran, Kahlil B7
Gibson, Clifford B26
Gibson, James J. B21
Gidden Sisters A240
Giddons, Anthony B2
Gideon, Melville B30
Gil, Gilberto A211
Gilbert, Jeremy B20
Gilbert and Sullivan A178, B16
Gilberto, Astrud A99, A211
Gilberto, João A211
Gilkyson, Terry A97
Gillespie, Dizzy A96, B9, B16
Gillett, Charles B20
Gillum, Jazz A240
Gilmer, Jimmy A241

Gilmore, Voyle B8
Gilmour, David A68, A198, B29
Gilrod, Louis B12
Gilroy, Paul A61, B14, B22
Gil-Scott Heron A82
Gimble A87
Gin Blossoms, The B24
Ginsberg, Allen B7, B29
Gioia, Ted A48
Girard, Chuck B15
girl groups A38, A45
Girls Aloud B21
Girls on Top A24
Girl Talk A24
Gjerdingen, Robert A70
glam rock A178, B28
Glass, Philip A81, A175, A182, A222, B1
glockenspiel A40
Glover, Corey A99
Glover, Tony A99
Gluck, Christoph W. B25
Godchaux, Keith B17
Goehr, Lydia B32
Goetschus, Percy A223
Goetz, E. Ray B30
Goffin, Gerry A106, A108, B8
Go-Go's, The A55, A250, B24
Gold, Ernest B12
Goldberg, Isaac A228
Golden Earring A16
Golden Gate Quartet A26, B21
Goldfaden, Abraham B12
Goldie B21
Goldsboro, Bobby A93
Gombosi, Otto A240
Gonzaga, Luís B25
Gonzalez, Michael B22
Goodie MoB B14
Goodman, Benny A168
Goodman, Dickie A43
Goodman, Nelson A102, B32
Goodwin, Andrew A66, A252, B13, B22
Goo Goo Dolls, The A247, B24
Goons, The B7
Gordon, Mack A14, A224, B11, B12, B30
Gordon, Nina A219
Gordy, Berry A105, A106, A108, A110, B8
Gordy, George A110
Gordy Records A110

Subject Index

Gore, Lesley A32, A45, A123, B24
Gore, Tipper B28
Gorillaz B21
Gorney, Jay B12
gospel music A26, A105, A106, A161, A264, B4, B9, B18, B19, B28
Gould, Glenn B32
Gouldstone, David B20
Gourds, The A24
Grable, Betty B12
Gracie, Charlie A97, B8
Gracin, Josh A191
Gracyck, Theodore A27, B6, B21, B32
Graham, Bill A103
Graham, Larry A238
Grainger, Percy B19, B21
grammar A18
Grammy Awards A217
Gramsci, Antonio A30, B19
Granata, Charles L. B15
Grande Ole Opry B4
Grand Funk [Railroad] A16, A246, B21, B24
Grandmaster Flash A80, A101, A104, A184, A221, A247, A269, B14, B31
Grant, Amy B24
Grantham, Cyril B21
Grapefruit B7
Grappelli, Stephane A93
Grass Roots, The B24
Grateful Dead, The A16, A25, A94, A99, A101, A148, A155, A167, A171, A173, A197, A221, A232, B7, B17, B20, B29
Gray, Dobie B19
Grayson, Kathryn B12
Grayson and Whitter A240
Great Society, The B7
Greaves, R.B. B24
Green, Adolph B12
Green, Al A80
Green, Archie B19
Green, Bud B30
Green, Grant A247, B22
Green, John A147, B30
Green, Lucy B19, B20, B21
Green, Peter A256
Greenbaum, Norma A185
Green Day A5, A84, A247, B21
Greenway, John A266
Greenwich, Ellie A106, A107

Greenwood, Colin A143, A162
Greenwood, Jonny A143, A162
Greenwood, Lee A189
Gretty, Jim B8
Grever, Maria B30
Greyhound B21
Grey Tuesday A163
Grieg, Edvard A222, B12
Griffes, Charles B3
Griffin, Rex A266
Griffiths, Dai A50, A162, A217, B20, B21
Grigsby, James A72, A81
Grimaldi, Joseph B16
Grissom, Dan A53
groove A8, A105, A129, A144, A172, A183, A203, A204, A233, A235, A255, A265, A271, B2, B5, B22
Gross, Larry A153
Gross, Walter B30
Grossberg, Lawrence A3, A38, A163, B6, B19, B21
Grossman, Stefan B1
ground bass A240
Groundhogs B21
Group A240
Grusin, Dave B1
Gryphon A166, B20
Guck, Marion, A197
Guess Who, The A43, A101, B24
Guided By Voices A243
guitar A29, A40, A54, A82, A92, A98, A132, A155, A211, A235, A256, B2, B6, B29; 12-string A90; acoustic A4, A98; distortion A98, A257, B6; electric A22, B19, B28; fingering A4, A62, A164, A186, A257, B1, B20; harmonics A99; rhythm guitar A231; slide A23, A132; solo A88, A182, B28; steel guitar A151; tablature A155; timbre A23, A67, A98, A121, B8, B28; tuning A98, A132, B1; voicings A33, B20
Gunn, Russell B31
Guns N' Roses A16, A17, A80, A89, A97, A246, A247, B28
Guralnick, Peter A269
Guthrie, Robin B32
Guthrie, Woody A238, A240, B8, B21, B27
Guy, Billy A77
Guy, Buddy B28
Gypsy music B17
GZR A221

habañera A30
Habermas, Jurgen B19
Hackberry Ramblers, The A240
Hackett, Steve A73
Haddad, Albert and Eddy B15
Hagar, Sammy A55
Hagen, Nina A178, A232
Hager, Steven B22
Haggar, Merle B25
Haggart, Bob B30
Haircut 100 A185
Halbersberg, Elianne B28
Halee, Roy B1
Halevi, Yehudah B12
Halévy, Jacques Fromental B12
Haley, Bill A44, A75, A97, A167, A185, A246, B16, B18, B20, B21, B24
Hall, Adelaide B12
Hall, Arsenio B14
Hall, Henry A227
Hall, Jim A270
Hall, Vera A26, A161
Hall and Oates A250, B22, B32
Hall Brothers, The A240
Hamilton, Ord B30
Hamilton, Russ A97
Hamm, Charles A147, A168, B10, B19
Hammer, Jan A73
Hammerstein, Oscar, II A14, B10, B12
Hammill, Peter A185
Hammond, Albert A185
Hammond, Fred A161
Hammond, Ian B8
Hammond, John B32
Hammond organ A29
Hampton, Lionel A95, B12, B19
Hampton, Mary B21
Hancock, Herbie A55, A101
Handel, George F. A92, A245, B16, B19, B25, B27
Handman, Lou B30
Handy, W.C. A119, A266, B9, B12, B19, B26, B27, B30
Hanighen, Bernard B30
Hansen, Mark B.N. A162
Hanslick, Eduard A184
Hanton, Colin B8
Happy Mondays A185
Happy the Man A72, A73

Harbach, Otto B10
Harburg, E.Y. A99, B10, B12
Harde, Erin A162
Hard-Fi B21
Hardt, Michael A158
Harlambos, Michael B22
Harlem Square Club A30
Harman, Murrey "Buddy" A270
Harmonettes, The A87
harmonica A36, A58, A259, B6, B27
harmonium A98, A156
harmony A16, A43, A46, A80, A83, A86, A97, A99, A125, A126, A154, A185, A229, A246, A252, B2, B6, B9, B11, B13, B19; quartal A185, A260; syntax A234
Harms, T.B. B10
Harnen, Jimmy A250
Harney, Ben B30
Harnick, Sheldon B12
harp A140
Harper, Roy B21
Harper's Bizarre B21
harpsichord A90, A98
Harrell, Kelly A240
Harrigan, Edward B12
Harris, Blind Jesse A240
Harris, Charles K. A120, B12, B19
Harris, Emmylou B32
Harris, Jack A227
Harris, Jet B8
Harris, Jimmy "Jam" A117
Harris, Richard A43, A217, A269, B7, B21
Harris, Rolf B8
Harris, Thurston A44
Harris, William A240
Harris, Wynonie A53
Harrison, Daniel A15, A16, A72, A99
Harrison, George A43, A83, A90, A92, A95, A99, A100, A185, A234, B7, B8, B18, B21, B24, B29, B32
Harrison, Harold (father) B8
Harrison, Harry (brother) B8
Harrison, Louise B8
Harrison, Pete B8
Harrison, Wilbert A44, B7
Harry, Bill B8
Harry Pussy A210
Hart, Lorenz A14, A114, A120, A224, B10, B11, B12

Subject Index

Hart, Mickey A171, B17
Hart, Moss A228
Harte, Frank B18
Hartman, Tom A200, B8
Harum, Procol A185
Harvey, David A158
Harvey, PJ A51, A55, A188, A205, A223, B21
Hasty, Christopher A50, B5
Hatch, David B20
Hatch, Tony A107, B8
Hatfield, Juliana A218
Hatten, Robert A88, A141, A155, A234, B6
Havens, Richie B21
Hawkes, Chesney A186
Hawketts, The A238
Hawkins, Dale A44
Hawkins, Edwin A26
Hawkins, Roger A265
Hawkins, Ronnie B8
Hawkins, Sophie B. A224
Hawkins, Stan A10, A52
Hawkins, Walter "Buddy Boy" B26
Hawkwind B20
Haydn, Franz J. A251, B27, B31
Hayes, Isaac A29, A34, A110, A185, A269
Haymes, Bob B30
Haywood County Ramblers A240
Hayworth, Rita B12
Head, Johnnie A240
Head, Murray A121, B24
Headbanger's Ball B28
Headlam, Dave A208
Heap, Imogen A87, A205
Heart A16, A247, A248, B21, B24
Heatwave B24
Heaven 17 A36
Heavenly Gospel Singers B21
Hebb, Bobby A93
Hebdige, Dick A57, A178, A255, B19, B20, B21
Hefti, Neil B30
Heidegger, Martin B17
Heiftez, Jascha B12
Heinonen, Yrjö B8
He is Legend A205
Helfman, Max B12
Helmet A57
hemiola A17, A214, A244, B27
Hemphill, Sid A145, A240

Henderson, Fletcher A119, A168, B9, B12, B16
Henderson, Ray A120
Hendricks, Jon A168
Hendrix Jimi A16, A17, A40, A43, A55, A67, A71, A72, A75, A80, A83, A86, A97, A99, A101, A121, A132, A148, A155, A159, A167, A185, A221, A247, A256, A257, B3, B7, B8, B17, B19, B20, B24, B28, B29, B31, B32
Henley, Don A43, A99, A173, B24
Hennion, Antoine B19
Henry, John A239
Henry Cow A72
Hentof, Nat B16
Hepokoski, James A163
Herbert, Victor B12, B30
Herman, Andrew B22
Herman, Jerry B12
Herman's Hermits A32, A70, A71, A99, A107, A140, A185, B7, B8, B21
Herndon, Ty A189, A191
Heron, Gil-Scott A117, B22
Herron, Joel B12
Herskovits, Melville A262, B22
Hesmondhalgh, David A158
Hesse, Herman A71
heterophony A68, B27
Hewson, Richard B7
hexatonic pole A99
Heylin, Clinton A74, A121
Hey Mercedes A203
Heyward, DuBose B12
Heywood, Donald B30
Hiam, Jonathan A36
Hiatt, John A268, B32
Hickman, Art B30
Hickory Nuts, The A240
Hicks, Robert B26
Hidalgo, David B32
hierarchy A40
Hill, Bertha "Chippie" A240
Hill, Dan A167
Hill, Dave B13
Hill, Faith A189, A193
Hill, Joe B25
Hill, Lauren A99
hillbilly music A32, A161, A266, B27
Hillman, Chris A121
Hillman, James A143

Hilltoppers, The A97
Hi-Lo's, The B15
Hindemith, Paul A53, A116, A237
Hines, Earl A172
hip-hop A2, A24, A61, A99, A117, A158, A221, A261, B22, B31, B32
Hirsch, Walter B30
Hirsh, Marc A219
Hjort, Christopher A121
Hodeir, André A263
Hoffman, Al B12
Hole A124
Holiday, Billie A48, B4, B12, B19
Holiner, Mann A47, B30
Holland B14
Holland, Brian A95, A99, A106, A108, B32
Holland, Eddie A95, A99, A108, B32
Holland, Jools A106, A235
Hollander, Frederick B30
Holliday, Jennifer A3
Hollies, The A85, A148, A185, B7, B8, B21, B24
Holloway, Loleatta A212
Holly, Buddy A16, A37, A74, A75, A76, A80, A97, A99, A185, A270, B7, B8, B15, B19, B20, B21, B24, B32
Hollywood B19
Holst, Gustav A11, A227, B7
Homer, Ben B30
Hondells, The A109, B15
Honegger, Arthur B3
Honeybus B21
Honeycombs, The B8, B21
Honey Drippers, The A117, B31
Honeys, the B15
hook A43, A108, A192, A193, A250, A261, B15, B19
Hook, Julian A54
Hooker, John Lee A8, A144, A256, A257, B21, B27
hooks, bell A170
Hoola Bandoola Band B25
Hootie and the Blowfish B24
Hopesfall A204
Hopkin, Mary B7
Hopkins, Lightnin' A62
Hopkins, Nicky B7
Hopkins, Pandora A265
Hopper, Hal B30

Horkheimer, Max B19
Horne, Lena B12
Horner, Bruce A51
horns A95
Hornsby, Bruce A250, B24
Hosokawa, Shuhei B19
Hothouse Flowers B21
House, Son A148, A201, B26, B27
Housemartins, The A185, B19
Houston B14
Houston, Cissy A161
Houston, Thelma A123
Houston, Whitney A3, A185, B21
Howard, Adina A24
Howard, Eugene B12
Howard, Harlan A193
Howard, Joseph E. B30
Howard, Willie B12
Howe, Steve A71, A73, A229
Howell, Peg Leg A207, A223, B26
Howlett, Mike A235
Howlin' Wolf A75, A83, A132, A186, A210, B9, B17, B19, B20, B21, B26, B28, B32
Hubbell, Raymond B30
Hubbs, Nadine A162
Hudson, Garth B32
Hudson, Will B30
Hue & Cry A185
Hughes, Langston B12
Hughes, Timothy S. A162, A163
Hull, Little Harvey A240
Human League, The B20, A36, A235, A248, A269
Humanoid B21
humor A39, A69
Humphrey Lyttleton Band, The B7
Hunter, Ivory Joe A53, A70
Hunter, James A143
Hunter, Janis A110
Hunter, Robert A25, A94, A99, B17
Hunter, Tab A97, A171
Huron, David A80, A135
Hurt, Mississippi John A85, A240, A256, B26, B27
Hurwitz, Moshe Halevi B12
Hüsker Dü A210
Husky, Ferlin A97
Husserl, Edmund A10
Hutchison, Frank A240

Hutton, Danny B15
Hyer, Brian A54, A142
Hyland, Brian B24
Hyler, Tammy A193
Hylton, Jack A227
hymnody A219
hypertextuality A159

Ian, Janis A185
Ian and the Zodiacs B8
Ibrahim, Anwar A162, B21
Ice Cube A99, B14, B22, B31
Ice T A255, B14
Icicle Works A185, A186, B20, B21
iconicity B6
Idelsohn, Abraham Z. B12
identity A123, B13, B14
idiolect A188, A235, B19
Idle, Eric A69
Idol, Billy A55
Ifield, Frank A259
Iggy Pop A85, A103, A247, B21, B32
Il Rovescio della Medaglia A166
Imberty, M. B19
imformation processing A40
immanence A223
Impressions A32, A53, A80, A108, A144, A247
improvisation A43, A64, A65, A72, A73, A119, A138, A149, A152, A161, A171, A172, A210, A227, A229, B2, B5, B6, B9, B16, B17, B19, B26, B27
Incas, Los B1
Incredible Bongo Band, The B31
Incredible String Band, The A112, B7, B20, B21
Incubus A221
Indian Music A61, A254, B18
indie music A22
Indigo Girls A221
individualism A28
ineffability A88
influence A28, A95, A133, A234
information theory B19
Ingelf, Stan A156
Ink Spots, The A263, B8
Innes, Neil A69, B7
Inspiral Carpets B21
instrumental A159, B15
instrumentation A9, A43, A68, A70, A98, A107, A108, A156, A233, A249

internal rhyme A270
interruption B7, B8
intertextuality A31, A69, A78, A101, A141, A159, A170, A182, A234, A261, B21
interval A82, A167, A169
intonation B27
introduction A5
inversion A60, A63, A167, A207, A226; chord A94; operation A207
IQ A72
Ireland, John B7
Irish music B12
Iron Butterfly A43, A72, A101, B3, B31
Iron Maiden A16, B28
irony A150, A151, B1
Islam A61, A70, A96, B13, B27
Isley Brothers, The A43, A95, A105, A108, A185, A247, B7, B8, B20, B24
Israels, Chuck A93, A150
Italian music B27
Ives, Charles A11, A53, A102, A138, B17
Iveys, The B7
Ivy League B20
Iwan, Dafyff A123

Jablonski, Edward B10
Jackendoff, Ray A100, A208, A245, A250, B5
Jacks, Terry A43
Jackson, Al A29, A30, A95, B32
Jackson, Alan A189, A190, A191
Jackson, Bullmoose A53
Jackson, Jack A227
Jackson, Janet A6, A85, A110, A117, A123, A234, A252, B24, B32
Jackson, Jim B26
Jackson, Joe A71, A74
Jackson, Lil' Son A62
Jackson, Mahalia A21, A26, A161, B9
Jackson, Michael A33, A35, A80, A82, A85, A99, A222, A247, A248, A250, B7, B24, B28, B32
Jackson, Papa Charlie A240
Jackson, Tony B30
Jackson, Travis A110
Jackson Five, The [The Jacksons] A35, A232, A247, A255, B3
Jacobs, Jacob B12
Jagger, Mick A7, A78, A107, B7, B8, B29, B32
Jaguars, The B15

Jaimees, The A44
Jake One B22
Jakobson, Roman B4, B19
jam (jamming) A25, A185, A232, B17
Jam, The A269, B13, B20, B21
Jamaica B14
Jamal, Ahmad A238
Jamerson, James A99, A108, B8
James, Bob A217, B22
James, Dick B7, B8
James, Elmore A132
James, Henry A7
James, Joni A123, B4
James, Paul B11
James, Rick A24
James, Skip A240, A62
James, Sonny A97
James, Tommy A43, A101, A241
James, William B2
James and the Shondells, Tommy A106, B7, B8
James Brown A108, A247
Jameson, Fredric A79, A163, B4, B7, B14, B19, B28, B22
Jan and Dean A93, A109, A125, A160, B15
Jane's Addiction A248
Janis Joplin A247
Jansch, Bert B16
Jardine, Al A109, A160, B15
Jason, Will B30
Jassinowsky, Pinchos B12
Jay, Adam B5
Jaynettes, The A95
Jay-Z A39, A61, A84, A99, A163, A221, B14, B31
jazz A15, A71, A93, A119, A132, A168, A235, A238, B2, B9, B14, B16, B17, B19, B27, B28, B31, B32; bebop B9; big bands B9; theory A185
Jean, Wyclef B22
Jeanie and the Big Guys B8
Jeff Buckley A224, A247
Jefferson, Blind Lemon A216, A240, A62, B26
Jefferson Airplane A43, A99, A134, A138, A185, A246, A247, B3, B7, B17, B24, B29
J.E. Mainer's Mountaineers A240
Jenkins, Gordon B30
Jenkins, John B16
Jeru Tha Damaja B14, B22
Jesse Tree A205

Jesus Jones B20
Jet A85
Jethro Tull A4, A43, A71, A72, A101, A149, A166, A185, A186, A188, A221, B20, B21, B24
Jett, Joan A43, B21
Jewel A219
Je-Wel A270
Jewish music A168, A228, B12
Jew's harp B27
Jim Croce A16
Jimi Hendrix A19, A247, B21
Jimmy Dorsey Orchestra A97
Jimmy Eat World A205
Jimmy Rogers A44
Jobim, Antônio Carlos A211
Jodimars, The A95
Joel, Billy A5, A97, A99, A101, A167, A182, A185, A215, A232, A247, A250, A269, B7, B8, B21, B24
John, Elton A6, A17, A43, A123, A141, A167, A225, A234, A246, A247, A248, A250, B7, B15, B21, B24, B31
John, "Little" Willie A44, A84, A95, A148, B7, B15
John, Mable A29
Johnny and the Hurricanes A44, A185
Johnny and the Moondogs B8
Johnny and the Rainbows B8
Johns, Donald A14
Johns, Glyn A173, B7
Johnson, Blind Willie A62
Johnson, Earl A240
Johnson, Elvie A62
Johnson, James P. A172, A263, B9, B30
Johnson, James Weldon A120
Johnson, Jesse B26
Johnson, J. Rosamond B12
Johnson, Lil A240
Johnson, Lonnie A53, A240
Johnson, Margaret A240
Johnson, Mark A197, B6, B21
Johnson, Robert A26, A58, A97, A99, A132, A176, A240, B7, B18, B20, B21, B26, B28
Johnson, Rosamond A120
Johnson, Ruby A29
Johnson, Shelby A130
Johnson, Tommy A266, A201, B26
Johnson, Willie "Blind" B17
Johnston, Arthur B30

Johnston, Bruce B15
Jolson, Al A168, B12, B19
Jonas, Oswald A100
Jones, Alan Rankin B30
Jones, A.M. A262
Jones, Booker T. A29, A30, B20
Jones, Brian B7, B29
Jones, Davy A95
Jones, Del B22
Jones, George A191, B4
Jones, Isham B30
Jones, Jack A249
Jones, Jimmy A44, B24
Jones, John Paul A269, B7
Jones, Paul B7
Jones, Quincy A93, A131, B32
Jones, Richard M. A240
Jones, Ron A202
Jones, Thomas "Jaybird" A240
Jones, Tom B8
Jonzun Crew A104
Joplin, Janis A241, B3, B7, B19, B20, B21, B24
Joplin, Scott A251, B9, B19, B30
Jordan, Louis A53, A85, A185, B4, B12, B19, B21, B25
Jordanaires, The B8
Josephson, Nora S. A232
Journey A205, A247, A250, B21, B24
Journey, Jimmi B5
Journeymen, The B15
Joyce, Mike A36
Joy Division A80, A247
Judas Priest A73, B28
Judds, The A191
Juicy Lucy A185
juke joint B26
Juliana Theory, The A205
Jung, Carl A134, A143
Jungle Brothers, The A1, B14
Junior M.A.F.I.A. B22
Junior Murvin A231
Junior Walker and the All Stars A95, A105, A108, A185
Jurassic 5 B31
Justis, Bill A270, B8
JX A212

Kadril A97, B21
Kaempfert, Bert B8, B12

Kahn, Douglas B32
Kahn, Gus B12
Kahn, Roger Wolfe B30
Kaihan, Maewa B12
Kalich, Jacob B12
Kalinich, Steve B15
Kaminsky, Peter B1
Kane, Jonathan A210
Kansas A16, A17, A43, A72, A73, A141, A149, A250, B24
Kant, Immanuel A70, B21
Kanter, Kenneth B12
Kantner, Paul B17
Kaoma B25
Kaper, Bronislau B12
Kardinal Offishall B14
Karp, Sophie B12
Karpinski, Gary A224
Kass, Ron B7
Katz, M A261
Katz, Mark A110
Katzenelenbogen, Judah B12
Kaye, Danny B21
K.C. and the Sunshine Band A44, B24
Keating, Johnny B8
Keefe, Matt A266
Keenan, Maynard James A205
Keil, Charles A105, A184, A250, A256, A262, A265, B4, B19, B22
Keita, Salif B20, B21
Kelley, Robin D.G. B14, B22
Kellner, Douglas B13
Kelly, R. A80, A247
Kendrick, Nat A238
Kenso A149
Kentucky Ramblers A240
Kerman, David A81
Kerman, Joseph A40, A183
Kern, Jerome A79, A143, A147, A224, B10, B12, B16, B19, B30
Kerr, Anita A270
Kershaw, Nik A185, B20, B21
Kesey, Ken B7
Ke$ha A232
Kessel, Barney A77
Kestrels, The B8
key A14, A43, A44, A52, A63, A93, A154, A160, A165, A191, A214, A232, B1, B27
Keyes, Cheryl A1, A255, B14, B22

Keys, Alicia A84, A221
Khan, Chaka B19
Kidd, Johnny B8
Kihn, Greg B24
Killen, Louis A64
Killswitch Engage A203
Kimbrough, Lottie A239, A240
King, Adolf B12
King, Albert A29, A55, A132
King, B.B. A26, A97, A132, A257, B7, B19, B29
King, Ben E. A77, A95, A99, A167, A185, A247, B21, B24
King, Carole A106, A108, A182, A217, B8, B24
King, Earl A238
King, Jonathan A185
King Crimson A28, A54, A67, A72, A73, A99, A138, A141, A152, A175, A185, A208, A218, A221, B7, B20, B21
King Curtis A77, B21
King Otto B22
King Records A117
Kingsley, Marjorie B21
Kingsmen, The A27, A43, A75, A84, A85, A99, A141, A198, A247, A268, B21, B24, B32
Kingston Trio, The A97, B15
King's X A55, A56, A97
Kinks, The A16, A43, A55, A70, A97, A107, A121, A132, A155, A184, A185, A210, A247, B4, B8, B20, B21, B29
Kirby, Kathy B21
Kiss A85, B28
Kitt, Eartha B8
Kivy, Peter A102, B9
Klaatu A149
Klein, Allen B7
klezmer music B12
Klumpenhouwer, Henry A54
Knack, The A16, A27, A97, A99, A101, A250
Knechtel, Larry B1
Knight, Beverly B21
Knight, Frederick A185
Knight, Gladys A53, A110, A124, A158, A185, B21
Knight, Jean A185
Knight, Suge B31
Knopfler, Mark A99
Knox, Buddy A97, B32
Knuckles, Frankie B5
Koechlin, Charles B3

Koehler, Ted B10, B11, B12
Kong, Leslie A235
Kongos, John A185
Koobas B21
Kool and the Gang A179, A238
Kool DJ Herc B22
Kopfton A113, B10
Kopp, David A155
Korner, Alexis B21
Kornfeld, Artie B15
Korsyn, Kevin A143, A234
Koschmider, Bruno B8
Kostelanetz, Richard A138
Kostenbaum, Wayne A143, A153
Kostka, Stefan A111
Kövecses, Zoltán B21
Kraftwerk A104, A163, B21
Kramer, Billy J. A107, A185, B8, B21
Kramer, Eddie A40
Kramer, Jonathan A139, A182, A205, B20
Kramer, Lawrence A102, A174, B9, B23
Kramer, Richard A40
Krause, Bernie B7
Kravitz, Lenny A250
Krebs, Harald A208, A214, A220, A253, B5
Kresa, Helmy A13, B10
Kreutzmann, Bill B17
Krims, Adam A1, A261, B22, B31
Kristeva, Julia B13, A38
KRS One A78, A101, B14, B31, B32
Krumhansl, Carol A142
Kubik, Gerhard B27
Kubrick, Stanley A141
Kumalo, Bakithi B1
Kurth, Ernst A183
Kurtz, Manny B12
Kweli, Talib A15, A261, B31
Kylea B22

LaBelle, Patti A43, A215, B24
Lacan, Jacques A146, B13, B19
Lacasse, Serge A24, A101, A261, B21
Lace, Victoria A3
Lacey, Rubin B26
Ladefoged, Peter A78
Lady Gaga A84, A232
Ladysmith Black Mambazo B1
Laine, Frankie A97, A123, B21
Laing, Dave A37, A38, B19

Subject Index

Laitz, Steven A86, A210
Lakeman, Seth B21
Lakoff, George A197, B6
Lambchop B21
Lambert, Constant A168, B12, B16
lament bass A166, A199, A235
Lamm, Robert A237
Landy, Eugene B15
Lane, Burton B10, B12, B30
Lang, David A72
lang, k.d. A45, A136
Lange, Johnny B30
Lange, Robert John "Mutt" A192, A193, B32
Langer, Susanne B32
Langham, Richard B8
Langlois, Tony A129
Langston, Tony B26
language A18, B32
Lanois, Daniel B32
Larkin, Kenny B5
Larks, the B32
Larson-Feiten Band A250
Laske, Otto B19
Last Poets, The B31
Latvala, Dick B17
Lauper, Cyndi A250, B24
Laurents, Arthur B12
LaVern Baker A44
Lavitz, T A73
Lawrence, Jack B12
Lawrence, Tracy A191
layering A158, A160, A233, A261, B5, B14
Layton, Turner B30
Leach, Sam B8
Leadbelly [Huddie Ledbetter] A62, A95, A239, A240, B8, B21, B27
Leaders of the New School A1
leading tone A59, A60
Leadon, Bernie A173
lead sheet A13, A111, A157, A265, B16
Leaf, David B15
Leander, Mike B7
Leary, Timothy A134, B7, B18, B29
Lebedeff, Aaron B12
Lebieg, Earl B30
Leckie, John B32
LeDoux, Chris A190
Led Zeppelin A7, A16, A17, A43, A55, A74, A75, A80, A83, A86, A89, A101, A131,
    A132, A141, A149, A167, A185, A186, A221, A233, A245, A247, A248, A269, B7, B8, B19, B20, B21, B24, B28, B32
Lee, Brenda A99
Lee, Geddy A28
Lee, Jackie B21
Lee, Julia A53
Lee, Peggy A77, B7, B8
Lefebvre, Henri B19
Left Banke, The A97, A99, B7
Lehak, Ned B30
Lehrdahl A100
Leiber A108
Leiber, Jerry A77
Lemare, Jules B30
Lemon Pipers, The B7
Lennon, Alfred B8
Lennon, Freddie (Alf) B8
Lennon, John A43, A80, A90, A92, A93, A100, A107, A134, A157, A185, A234, A247, B7, B8, B15, B18, B19, B21, B23, B24, B29, B31, B32
Lennon, Julian B8
Lennon [Twist], Cynthia Powell B8
Lennox, Annie A10, A127, B13
Lerdahl, Fred A208, A245, A246, A250, B5
Lerner, Alan Jay A224, B10
Lesgold, Allan A40
Lesh, Phil A25, B17
Leslie (speaker) A40, B32
Leslie, Edgar B12
Lessig, Lawrence A24
Lesson One A3
Lester, Joel A208
Lester, Richard B8
Levant, Oscar B30
Level 42 A185, B21
Levine, Larry B32
Levine, Lawrence W. B22, B28
Levinson, Jerrold A224
Lévi-Strauss, Claude A183, A201, B19
Levitin, Daniel A140
Lewandowski, Louis B12
Lewin, David A54, A142, A203, A220, A232
Lewis, Barbara A95
Lewis, Bobby A95, A101
Lewis, Furry A240
Lewis, Gary, and the Playboys A32, A99, B4, B24

Lewis, Huey A182, A247, A248, A250, B24
Lewis, Jerry Lee A44, A75, A76, A80, A97, A185, A238, A247, A270, B7, B8, B15, B21
Lewis, Leona A212, B21
Lewis, Meade Lux A238, B19
Lewis, Morgan B30
Lewis, Sam B12
Lewis, Terry A117
Lewis, Walter "Furry" A201, B26
Lewisohn, Mark B7, B8
L.H. and the Memphis Souls A95
libertarianism A28
Lidov, David A88, A102, A182, B6
Lieber, Jerry B8, B12, B15
Lifeson, Alex A28
Lightfoot, Gordon B24
Li'l Kim B14
Lil' Louis A129
L'il Louis & The World B21
Lillywhite, Steve B32
Lindisfarne A185, B20, B21
Lindsay, W.A. A240
Lindsay-Hogg, Michael B7
linear intervallic pattern A92, A215
linguistics B19
Lippmann, Edward B20
Lipps, Inc. A83, B24
Lipscomb, Mance A62
Lipsitz, George B14, B22
listening B19; listening modes A163, A183
Liston, Virginia A240
Liszt, Franz A232, B27
Little, "Little" Jack B30
Little Anthony A44, A97, B8, B28
Little Eva [Boyd] A95, A185, B8, B24
Little Milton A29, A32
Little Richard A43, A44, A53, A73, A75, A80, A83, A86, A95, A123, A181, A185, A238, A247, A254, B7, B8, B9, B15, B19, B20, B21, B24, B25, B32
Little River Band A250, B24
Little Walter A132
Livgren, Kerry A72
Living Colour A55, A97, B21, B28
Livingston, Jerry B30
LL Cool J A99, B14
Lloyd, A.L. B16
Loesser, Frank A41, A110, B12, B30
Loewe, Frederick A224

Logan, Joshua B12
Loggins and Messina B24
Lohan, Sinéad A169
Lomax, Alan A30, B19, B27
Lomax, Jackie B7
London, Julie B8
London, Justin A206, A220
London, Laurie A97
London Symphony Orchestra A11
Lonestar A189, A191
Loo and Placido A212
Look, The A185
Look Blue Go Purple A149
loop A115, A203, A222, A261, B5, B22
Lord, Jon B28
Lord-Alge, Tom B32
Lords, Traci A221
Lorenzo, Ange B30
Los Angeles B14, B31, B32
Los Calchakis B25
Los Campecinos! A205
Los Lobos B32
Los Lonely Boys A222
Loss, Joe A227
Los Van Van A205
Loughnane, Lee A237
Louisiana B27
Love (group) A43, B29
Love, Andrew A29
Love, Darlene B15
Love, Mike A109, A125, A160, B7, B15
Love Affair A185
Lovecraft, H.P. B21
Loveless, Patty A191
Loven, Jeff B28
Lovett, Lyle A191
Lovin' Spoonful, The A95, A99, B7, B8, B15, B21, B24
Lowe, Chris A128
Lowe, Lisa A3
LSD B31
lullaby B12
Lulu B7
Lunceford, jimmie B10
Lush A221
Lutcher, Nellie A53
lute B27
Luttrell, Terry A72
Lyman, Abe B30

Subject Index

Lymon, Frankie A44, A185, B15, B21
Lynch, George B28
Lynch, Kenny B8
Lyngstad, Anni-Frid B25
Lynn, Loretta A193
Lynn, Vera B18
Lynyrd Skynyrd A16, A43, A155, A182, A222, A269, B24
Lyra, Carlos A211
lyre B27
lyrics A37, A43, A58, A109, A122, A124, A181, A191, B4, B6, B10, B11, B13, B19, B26, B28, B30

Maas, Timo B5
Macan, Edward A67, A71, A73, A141, A143, A229, B20
MacDonald, Ballard B12
MacDonald, Ralph A179
Mack, Cecil B30
Mackey, Steve A72
Macon, Uncle Dave A240
Madeira, Paul B30
Mad Lads, The A29, A95
Madness A185, B20, B21
Madonna A3, A6, A24, A39, A66, A183, A234, A250, A252, A258, B13, B21, B24
madrigal A149
Magritte, René B7
Maharishi, The B18
Mahavishnu Orchestra, The A73, A185, A221, B20
Mahler A150, B25
Mahler, Gustav A232
Mainer, J.E. A240
Mainer, Wade A240
Maines, Natalie A191
mainstream A22
Major Lance A108
Malm, Krister B20
Malmsteen, Yngwie A143, B28
Malone, Bill C. A266
Malotte, Albert Hay B15
Mamas and the Papas, The A43, A247, B7, B8, B24
Manau B21
Manchester, Melissa A250
Mancini, Henry B16
mandolin A227

Maness, Jay Dee A163
Manger, Itsik B12
Mann, Barry A108
Mann, Manfred A132, A182, A185, A225, B7, B8, B16, B21, B29
Mann, William B8
Manson, Charles B29
Mansun B21
Mantronix A104
Manuel, Richard B32
Manvell, Roger A66
Marcels A43, B15, B21
March, Frederic B10
Marchand, Pierre A154
Marcus, Greil A269, B4, B32
Mardas, "Magic" Alexis B7
Mardin, Arif B32
Mardones, Benny A250
Margouleff, Robert A144
Marillion A71, A72, A185, B20
Mar-Keys, The A29
Marks, David B15
Marks, Edward B12
Marks, Gerald B12
Marks, Phil A53
Marley, Bob A80, A83, A185, A235, B20, B21
Marley Marl A117
Marmalade A185, B7
Maróthy, János A183
Marr, Johnny A36, A83, B13
Marriott, Robert B14
Marron, Gordon A138
Marsalis, Branford A255
Marsalis, Wynton A255, B31
Marsh, Dave A144
Marsh, Mike A205
Marshall, Amanda A106, A167
Marshall, Wolf B28
Mars Volta, The A203, A205
Martha and the Vandellas A94, A95, A97, A99, A106, A108, A110, A167, A247, B8
Martika A234
Martin, Andy B25
Martin, Carl B26
Martin, Dean A97, A167, B8
Martin, George A90, A92, A101, A134, A156, A196, A234, B7, B8, B18, B23, B32
Martin, Henry A99
Martin, Hugh B30

Martino, Al B21
Marvelettes A43, A95, A108, A110, A259, B8, B20, B21
Marvin, Elizabeth West A55, A86
Marvin, Hank B8
Marvin Gaye A108, A185, A247
Marx, A.B. A205
Marx, Groucho B12
Marx, Karl B19; Marxism B14; Marxist analysis A158
mashup A24, A159, A212
Masilda, Lulu B1
Mason, Barbara A39, A95
Mason, Nick A198
Massenburg, George A268, B32
Matassa, Cosimo B32
Matching Mole B21
mathematics A206
Mathis, Johnny A97, A263, B12
Mattea, Kathy A191
Matthews, Dave A169
Max Panic B2
May, Brian A178
May, Derrick A104, B5
Mayall, John A256, B8, B29
Mayer, John A169, A247
Mayfield, Curtis A43, A108, A144
Maynard, Ken A240
MC5 A210, B29
McBride, Martina A193
McCall, C.W. A43
McCarthy, Joe B12
McCartney, Gin B8
McCartney, James B8
McCartney, Linda Eastman B7
McCartney, Mary Mohin B8
McCartney, Michael B7, B8
McCartney, Paul A16, A72, A90, A92, A95, A99, A107, A134, A156, A160, A167, A178, A182, A185, A198, A234, A235, A250, B4, B7, B8, B15, B18, B19, B20, B24, B29, B32
McClary, Susan A45, A66, A141, A142, A146, A223, B13, B14, B28
McClintock, Lil A240
McColl, Ewan B16
McCoo, Marilyn B24
McCoy, Charley B26
McCoy, Joe A167
McCoy, Kansas Joe A131, A201, B26

McCoy, Robert Lee A240
McCoys, The A43, A85
McCracklin, Jimmy B7
McCrae, George B21
McCready, Mindy A189, A193
McDaniel, Mel A191
McDonald, Chris A22
McDonald, May A266
McDowell, Fred A26, B26
McEntire, Reba A190, A191, A193
McFarland, Thomas B32
McFerrin, Bobby B24
McFly B21
McGhee, Brownie A95, A239, A240, B8, B21
McGhee, Rev. F.W. A240
McGough and McGear B7
McGrath, Fulton B30
McGraw, Tim A189, A191
McGuinn, Roger A121, A33, B8
McGuinness Flint A185
McGuire, Barry A32, B8
McGuire Sisters, The A97
MC Hammer A24, A202
McHugh, Jimmy B10, B30
McKee, Maria A185
McKeen, William A121
McKenna, Tyrone A163
McKennitt, Loreena B21
McKenzie, Scott A70, B7, B29
McKernan, Ronald C. "Pigpen" B17
McLachlan, Sarah A5, A49, A84, A154, A219
McLaren, Malcolm A118, A178, B20, B21
McLaughlin, John A73
McLean, Don A86, A225, A256, B24
McLeod, Kembrew A39
McLuhan, Marshall B19
McMichen, Clayton A240
McNally, Dennis B17
McNeely, Big Jay B21
McParland, Stephen J. B15
McPhatter, Clyde A53, A99
McRobbie, Angela B19
McTell, "Blind" Willie A148, A240, B26
McTell, Kate A240
McTell, Ralph A64, B21
McVie, Christine B24
McWilliams, David A185
meaning A30, B32
Meat Loaf A101, A103, A183, A185, B2

medley A24, A92
Meehan, Tony B8
Megadeth A97, A221, B28, B31
Mehldau, Brad A143
Mehrdeutigkeit A15
Meisner, Randy A173
melancholy B25
Melanie A185, B21
Melcher, Terry B15
melisma A34, A87, B18
Mel & Kim A185
Mellencamp, John [Cougar] A16, A85, A102, A247, A250, B24
Mellers, Wilfrid A71, A76, A134, B7, B8, B16, B19, B20
Mellotron A71, A98, A142, A152, A224, B8
Melly, George A218, B18, B20
Melnick, Jeffrey B12
Melodians, The A222
melodica A231
melody A30, A42, A43, A46, A109, A113, A225, A246, B6, B8, B9, B10, B11, B19, B30
Melody Maker B29
Melson, Joe A270
Melson, Joel A270
Melvin, Harold A123
memory A90, A122
Memphis B32
Memphis Horns (Mar-Keys) A29, A30
Memphis Jug Band A240, B26
Memphis Minnie A131, A201, A240, B26
Memphis Slim A53
Men at Work A84, A250, B24
Mendelssohn, Felix A227
Mendes, Carlos B7
Mendes, Sergio B3
Menescal, Roberto A211
Menken, Alan A202
Men They Couldn't Hang B21
Mercer, Johnny A14, B10, B11, B12, B15
Merchant, Natalie B21
Mercury, Freddie A269
Merge Records A22
Merleau-Ponty, Maurice A22
Merman, Ethel A178, B21
Merriam, Alan A262, B20, B22
Merrill, Blanche B12
Merseybeats A185
Merseys, The B7

Meshuggah A175, A203, A208
Messina, Jim A173
Metallica A24, A28, A80, A103, A151, A212, A221, A247, A252, B20, B21, B28
metaphor A6, A45, A197, B6, B28
meter A17, A28, A38, A43, A44, A53, A71, A99, A112, A121, A132, A135, A144, A145, A152, A171, A175, A189, A204, A206, A221, A229, A232, A238, B5, B16, B20; hypermeter A5, A17, A92, A99, A100, A110, A125, A129, A151, A175, A189, A190, A193, A203, A207, A228, A233, A247, A270, B5, B7, B8, B21; metric dissonance A208, B5; metric modulation A203; mixed A203, A208, A218; time signature A208, B5
Meters, The A185, A238, B21
Metheny, Pat A226
Method Man A123
Metz, Theodore A147
Metzer, David A261
Mew A205, A204
Meyer, George B30
Meyer, Joseph B30
Meyer, Leonard B. A69, A70, A105, A234, A240, B20, B21
Meyerowitz, David B12
Meyers, Hazel A240
MF DOOM A2
M.F.S.B A179
MGM B10
Miami A3, B14
Miami Sound Machine A3
Michael, George A83
microphone A29, B32
Middle Class, The A210
Middle of the Road B21
Middleton, Jason A163
Middleton, Richard A21, A30, A46, A47, A67, A78, A88, A115, A143, A185, A196, A205, A207, A216, A220, A227, A235, A237, A246, A261, B4, B5, B6, B13, B20, B21, B29, B31, B32
MIDI B5
Midler, Bette A3, A43, A140
Mike Flowers Pops, The A159
Milano, Dominic A142, A224
Milchberg, Jorge B1
Miles, Barry A156, B7

Milhaud, Darius A53, B3, B16
Miller, Bernie B12
Miller, Glenn A234, B16
Miller, Jody A32
Miller, Lillian B26
Miller, Ned A193
Miller, Roger A190, A241
Miller, Steve A16, A43, A185, A246, A250, B7, B24
Mills, Irving B12, B30
Mills, Jeff B5
Mills, Kerry B30
Mills, Stephanie B24
Millward, Stephen B20
Milton, Roy B19
Milward, John B15
Mingus, Charles A135, A162
minimalism A57, A182, B5
Minnear, Kerry A72
Minogue, Kylie A185
Minor Threat A210
minstrelsy A227, B19
Miracles, The A32, A95, A105, A106, A108, B4, B7, B20, B24
Miranda, Carmen A211
misogyny A146, B28
Mission A185
Mississippi B27
Mississippi Matilda A240
Mississippi Sheiks A240
Mitchell, Guy B21
Mitchell, Joni A16, A51, A99, A121, A123, A124, A221, A222, A247, A260, B4, B20, B21, B24
Mitchell, Mitch A40, B7
Mitchell, Tony B13
Mitchell, Vanessa A3
Mitchell, William A116
Mitchell-Kernan, Claudia B22
mixing A36, A43, A156, B32; sound-box A36
Mobb Deep A158, B14, B22
mode A16, A23, A28, A46, A59, A60, A68, A71, A72, A88, A97, A99, A134, A177, A186, A232, A248, A260, B1, B3, B12, B13, B16, B17, B19, B20, B21, B27, B28; Aeolian A16, A19, A42, A55, A56, A59, A60, A88, A96, A97, A99, A108, A126, A140, A154, A180, A185, A186, A207, A235, A246, A248, A260, B3, B12, B18, B19, B20, B21, B28; Dorian A5, A16, A25, A55, A56, A59, A60, A71, A80, A93, A99, A127, A130, A149, A154, A167, A169, A185, A186, A200, A207, A248, A253, A254, A256, A260, B3, B7, B20, B21, B28; Ionian A56, A59, A60, A80, A88, A107, A108, A185, A186, A207, A248, B20, B21; Jewish B12; Locrian A16, A59, A167, A185, B2, B20, B21, B28; Lydian A59, A60, A93, A96, A175, A185, A248, A260, B3, B8, B18, B20, B21; Mixolydian A16, A25, A39, A59, A60, A63, A66, A72, A76, A78, A80, A94, A97, A99, A107, A108, A149, A154, A166, A167, A169, A180, A185, A186, A222, A232, A235, A248, A253, A254, A256, A260, A269, B3, B7, B8, B18, B20, B21; mixture A13, A63, A90, A91, A93, A96, A99, A125, A139, A151, A160, A165, A168, A174, A232, A243, B10, B18; Phrygian A16, A55, A57, A59, A72, A88, A97, A134, A139, A149, A167, A185, A186, A200, A232, A248, B3, B7, B20, B21, B27, B28
Modern English A250
Modern Jazz Quartet, The B7
Modern Lovers, The A210
Modugno, Domenico A97
modulation A14, A41, A52, A63, A84, A93, A97, A102, A108, A125, A150, A165, A186, A191, A192, A193, A214, B7, B8, B16, B27; common-tone A125; direct A41; transient B16
Molenda, Michael A235
Molino, Jean A140
Moman, Chips A29, A265, B32
Moments, The A84
Monaco, Bob A43
Monaco, James B30
Money, Eddie A250
Monica A158
Monk, Thelonius A96, A168
Monkees A97, A99, A182, A185, A241, B7, B8, B20, B21, B24
Mono (band) B21
monody A180
Monotones, The A44
Monro, Matt B8
Monroe, Bill A210, A220
Monroe, Gerry A123
Monroe, Marilyn A66

Monroe Brothers, The A240
Monson, Ingrid A143, A261, A271, B6, B22, B31
Montana, Patsy A266
Monterey Pops Festival B17, B29
Monteverdi, Claudio A53, B28
Montez, Chris A185, B16
Montgomery, John Michael A191
Montreal B14
Monument Records A77, A270
mood music B19
Moody Blues A16, A72, A99, A101, A185, A198, A248, B7, B8, B24
Moog A92; MiniMoog A72, A73, A182
Moonglows B21
Moonlight Revellers, The A227
Moore, Allan F. A5, A16, A36, A46, A47, A54, A80, A99, A162, A183, A196, A207, A218, A222, A235, B20, B21
Moore, Bob A270
Moore, Gary A185, B20, B21
Moore, James A161
Moore, Rosie Mae B26
Moore, Scotty B8
Moore, Tommy B8
Moraes, Vinícius de A211
Moraz, Patrick A71
Moreira, Airto B1
Moret, Neil B30
Morgenstern, Rod A73
Morissette, Alanis A51, A247, B24
Morley, Thomas B16
Morreall, John A70
Morris, Charles A140, A246, A248
Morris, Richard A110
Morris, Robert A15
Morrison, Dorothy A26
Morrison, Jim A72, A99
Morrison, Toni A117
Morrison, Van A14, A78, A103, A124, A185, A247, A269, B7, B20, B21, B24
Morrissey (Steven) A124
Morse, Steve A73
Morss, Benjamin A36, B13
Morthland, John A32
Mortimer B7
Morton, Jelly Roll A238, A240, B7, B9, B27
Morton, Pete B21
Mos Def B31

Moskowitz, Dorothy A138
Mosser, Kurt A217
Motels, The A250
Mothers [of Invention], The A11, A12, A27, A43, A67, A134, A138, B7, B25, B29
motive A14, A52, A113, A116, A207, A252
Mötley Crüe A250, B28
Motloheloa, Forere B1
Motörhead A185, B20, B21, B28
Motown B19
Motown Records A32, A95, A105, A106, A108, A110, A230, B4, B9, B32
Mott the Hoople A185, B21
Mountain A16, A43
Move, The A185, B21, B29
Moylan, William B. B21
Mozart, Wolfgang Amadeus A70, A111, A141, A163, A246, A261, B16, B18, B20, B27, B31
Mr. Bungle A163
Mr. Mister B24
Mr. President B24
Mr. Supreme B22
Mtume B31
MTV B13, B28
Mud B21
Muddy Waters A26, A75, A83, A131, A132, A148, A210, A216, A244, A246, B21, B26, B28
Mudhoney A177
Muir, Lewis F. B30
multiplication (pc-set) A15
Mulvey, Laura B28
Mungo Jerry A55, A185
Munro, Ronnie A227
Murphy, Scott A250
Murphy, Walter A43
Murray, Albert A176
Murray, Anne A167
Murray, Mitch A179, A202, B8
Muscle Shoals A93, A265, B1
Muse B21
Muse, Clarence B30
museme A19, A227, A242, A256, A261, B25
music hall A235, B19
musicology B14, B19; queer musicology A223
music publishing A213, B12
music therapy A23
music video A21, A66, A252, A258, B13, B14, B28

Mussorgsky, Modest A179, A222, B27
My Bloody Valentine A22, A177
My Chemical Romance B21
Mydland, Brent B17
Myles, Alana B24
Mylo A212
Myrow, Josef A200, B30
? And the Mysterians B8
Mystics, The B15
Mystikal B14

Nail, David A205
Naked Eyes A248, A250
narrative A6, A7, A21, A51, A139, A150, A160, A191, A252, B13, B32
Nas A152, B14, B31
Nascimento, Milton A211, B1, B25
Nash, Graham B7
Nash, Ogden B10
Nashville Teens A185
Nate Dogg B31
National, The A205
Nationalteatern B25
Nation of Islam B14
Native American music A238, B18
Native Tongues B14, B31
Nattiez, Jean-Jacques B19, B20
Naughty by Nature B14
Nazareth A185, A247, A248, B20, B21
Nazz B7
Neal, Jocelyn A5
Nederhop B14
Negasphere A149
Negrocan A3
Negus, Keith A158
Negus I B22
Nelly A99
Nelson, Havelock B22
Nelson, Rick[y] A44, A97, A215, A225, B8, B15
Nelson, Romeo A238
Nelson, Willie A168
neo-Riemannian theory A142
neo-romanticism A152
Nerk Twins B8
Nesmith, Michael A54, A155, A173
Nettl, Bruno A20, A109, A265, B20
Neutral Milk Hotel A22, A205
Neville, Aaron A43, A99, A123

Neville, Richard A238, B29
Neville Brothers B17
Nevin, Ethelbert B30
Newbern, "Hambone" B26
Newbury, Mickey B21
Newby, Chas B8, B32
New Kids [on the Block] A250
New Lost City Ramblers B17
Newman, Alfred B12
Newman, Floyd A29
Newman, Randy A123, A141, A264
New Order A80, A232, A233, A247, B21
New Orleans A238, B14, B27, B32
Newport Folk Festival A102, A121
New Radicals B21
New Riders of the Purple Sage A173
New Seekers, The B20
Newton-John, Olivia A43, A185
New Vaudeville Band, The B7
New York City A3, B14, B27
Nguini, Vincent B1
Nice, The A68, A71, A72, A166, A207, B29
Nichols, Alberta B30
Nicholson, Stuart A73
Nickelback A248
Nickel Creek A191
Nielsen, Lorri A146
Nietzsche, Friedrich A18
Nig-Heist A210
Night Ranger A250
Nightwish B21, B28
Niles, Abbe A119
Nilsson, Harry B7, B21, B24, A185
Nine Inch Nails A222
Nirvana A16, A24, A80, A84, A85, A97, A99, A124, A143, A159, A167, A177, A181, A205, A221, A234, A246, A247, B7, B20, B21, B32
Nitzsche, Jack B32
Noble, George A240
Noble, Ray A224, A227, B30
No Doubt A84
noise A183
Nomi, Klaus A178
No Motiv A205
non-harmonic tone A63, A86, A93, A167, A239; anticipation A38; appoggiatura A185, B6, B25; neighbor A14, A25, A45, A55, A90, A174, A246, B10; passing tone B27; pedal

Subject Index

A60, A63, A72, A74, A86, A95, A125, A142, A222, A260; suspension A33, A40, A63, A226, A260
Noone, Peter A70, A107
Norberg, Bob B15
Norfleet, Dawn B22
Norfolk Jubilee Singers A238
North Carolina Ridge Runners A240
Norworth, Jack B12
nostalgia A38, A52, A227, A266, B17
notation A268, B5, B32; Nashville number system A189
Notorious B.I.G. A99, B14, B31
Nozick, Robert A40
N*Sync A24
Nugent, Ted B28
Numan, Gary B20, B21
Number of Names, A B51
Nurmesjärvi, Terhi B8
NWA A124, B14
N.W.A. A2, B31

Oakland, Ben B30
Oasis A159, B7, B24
objectivity A99, A246, B20, B21, B28
Ocean, Billy A250, B19, B24
O'Connor, Sinéad A80, A117, A247, B32
O'Daniel, W. Lee A240
O'Day, Anita A239
O'Dell, Denis B7
O'Donnell, Shaugn B17
Offenbach, Jacques B12
Offord, Eddie B32
O'Grady, Terence B8
Ohio Players, The A99
Oi Musik B19, B23
O'Jays, The A238
Okediji, Moyo A43, A238, B22
Okely, Judith B22
Okkervil River A205
Oldfield, Mike A101
Oliver, King B7
Oliver, Paul A112, A182, B19, B22, B27
Ollie and The Nightingales A29
Olshanetsky, Alexander B12
Olwage, Grant A22
Olympics, The A95, B8
OMD A36
ondes Martenot A162

Ong, Walter A206, A252, A255, A265
Ono, Yoko B7, B18, B32
Onward Brass Band, The B1
opera A53, A71, A178, B19
Opeth B21
Orbison, Roy A55, A259, A269, A270, B8, B15, B21, B24, B25
Orchestral Maneuvers in the Dark A185, B20
Orff, Carl A231
organ A52, A71, A98, B28; Farfisa B25
Original Dixieland Jazz Band, The A227, B16
Originals, The A110
ornamentation A29, A149
Osborne, Joan A219, B24
Osbourne, Ozzy A17, A54, A55, A97, A250, A255, B28
Osby, Greg B31
oscillation A253
Osdorp Posse B14
Osmond, Donny A259, B21
Ossian B21
ostinato A53, B19, B27
Oswald, John A159, A164
Otis, Johnny A44, A185, A270
Otway, John A185
Outfield, The A250
OutKast A1, A24, A34, A39, A99, A221, B14, B31
Overstreet, W. Benton A147
Owens, Buck B8
Ozimek, Chris B2, B30

Pachelbel, Johann B28
Padgham, Hugh B32
Padovani, Henri A235
Paganini, Nicolo B28, B16
Page, Coverdale B21
Page, Jimmy A131, A269, B7, B28, B32
Page, Patti A97
Paisley, Brad A167
Paley, Andy B15
Palmer, Jack B30
Palmer, Robert (artist) A250
Palmer, Robert (author) B4
Panic! At the Disco A203
Panjabi MC A61
panning A130
Pantsdown, Pauline A212
Papa Too Sweet A240

Paragons, the B32
parallel fifths A40, A46, A49, A96, A97, A228, A232
Paramore A205
paraphrase A202
Pareles, Jon B22
Parish, Mitchell B12
Park A205
Parker, Bobby A95, B8
Parker, Charlie A263, B16, B31
Parker, Graham A185
Parker, Maceo A117
Parker, Ray, Jr. A182
Parks, Van Dyke A109, A125, B15
Parkway Drive A205
Parliament/Funkadelic A238, B31
parlour music B27
Parnes, Larry B8
parody A11, A69, A159
Parry, C. Hubert H. A70, A232, B13
Parsons, Alan A17, A43, A198, A233, B7
Parsons, Arrand A213
Parsons, Gram A173
Pärt, Arvo A222
Partch, Harry B18
Parton, Dolly A45, A86, A167, A193
Partridge Family, The B24
passamezzo moderno A240, B27
Passaro, Joanne B22
passing tone A246, B10
Passmore, Mark Thomas B15
Pasternak, Velvel B12
pastiche A159, A261, B12
Pater, Walter A79, A237
Patinkin, Mandy B12
Patterson, Red A240
Patterson's Piedmont Log Rollers, Red A240
Patton, Charley A201, A238, A239, A240, B26, B27
Paul, Les B8, B32
Paul, Steven B32
Paul and Paula B25
Pavarotti, Luciano A178
Pavement A80, A247
Payne, Dorothy A111
Payne, Rufus (Tee-Tot) B4
Pearl Jam A245
Pearson, Ewan B20
Peart, Neil A28

Peaston, David B21
pedagogy A42, A55, A64, A86, A111, A164, A167, A169, A185, A221, A222, A224, A231; ear training A169, A224; form and analysis A224; rhythm A111, A221
Pederson, Herb A163
Peer, Ralph A266, B26
Peirce, Charles S. A102, A140, B21
Pendletones, The B15
Pendragon A72
Penguins A247, B21
Pepys, Samuel B16
Peraino, Judith A143
perception A10, A245, B2
percussion A125, A267
Pere Ubu A210
Perfect Circle, A A205
performance A25, A30, A43, A216, A227, B2, B13, B19
Perfume A221
Perkins, Carl A80, A97, A99, A254, A259, B7, B8, B32
Perkins, Frank B30
Perkins, William Eric B22
Perlmutter, Arnold B12
Perry, Katy A248
persona A7, A58, B21
Peter, Paul, and Mary A121
Peter and Gordon A70, B8
Petersen, Paul A71, A107, B15
Peterson, Ray B25
Petkere, Bernice A43, B30
Pet Shop Boys, The A124, A185, B21, A174, A128
Petty, Norman A270, B32
Petty, Tom A75, A80, A155, A225, A246, A247, A248, A250, B21, B24, B32
Peyton, Dori A259
Phair, Liz A84, A177
Pharcyde, The A261, B31
Phat Pockets B14
phenomenology A203, B6
Phillips, Esther A95
Phillips, Phil A44
Phillips, Sam A270
Phiri, Chikapa Ray B1
Phish B17
phonetics A18, A87, B32
phonology A18

Piaf, Edith B21, B25
Piaget, Jean B19
piano A53, A65, A90, A98, A172, B2; classical A65; keyboard A54, A231, A232; stride piano A172
Piano, Harry M. B12
Picardy third A103
Pickering, Michael B21
Pickett, Wilson A32, A63, A93, A95, A97, A143, A149, A185, A247, B4, B8, B17, B32
Picon, Molly B12
Pierson, Kate A99
Pieslak, Jonathan A175
Pinkard, Maceo B30
Pink Floyd A16, A19, A28, A43, A64, A67, A68, A74, A82, A83, A101, A103, A132, A138, A162, A167, A185, A198, A199, A205, A207, A208, A221, A225, B7, B17, B19, B20, B21, B24, B25, B29, B32
Piston, Walter A86
pitch A43; pitch class A142; pitch-class set A232
Pitney, Gene A56, A114, A185, A237, B8
Più, Mario A14, A114, B5
Pixies B21
plagal harmonic motion A16, A56, A86, A106, A186, A247; *see also* cadence; plagal
Planet Patrol A104
Plant, Robert A269, B21, B28
Plastic Ono Band, The A43, A131, A154, A185, A233, B7, B8, B18, B32
Plastikman A115
Platters, The A44, A53, A95, A97, A99, B5, B8, B15, B21, B24, B25
Playford, John B16
playlet A77
Playmates, The A93, A97, B25
pleasure A115, A223
Plummons, The A259
Plunderphonics A159
Poco A173
poetics B14
poetry A18
Pogues, The B20
Pointer Sisters, The A43
Poirer, Lucien A159
Poison A221, B28
Police, The A19, A75, A80, A103, A185, A221, A232, A233, A234, A235, A246, A247, A248, A250, B21, B24

polka B19, B27
Pollack, Alan B8
Pollard, Robert A243
polyphony A90, A130, A200
Poni-Tails, The B24
Ponty, Jean-Luc A11
Poole, Brian A185, B8
Poole, Charlie A239, A240
Popol Vuh A149
Popper, Karl A40
Porcupine Tree A221, B21
Porter, Bill A270
Porter, Cole A41, A113, A114, A147, B8, B10, B11, B12, B30
Porter, David A29
Porter, John A36
Porter, Linda A228
Porter, Paul A161
Porterfield, Nolan A266
post-Fordism B14
Portishead A97
postmodernism A21, A79, B14, B19, B22, B28
posture A88
Potter, Russell B14, B22
Poundhound A55
Powell, Bud A168
Powell, Cozy A72
Powell, Eleanor B10
Powers, Johnny A110
Power Station Studios B32
practice B2
Prado, Perez A238
Preiss, Byron B15
Presley, Elvis A7, A35, A44, A53, A64, A75, A76, A77, A80, A84, A86, A97, A99, A123, A159, A167, A184, A185, A241, A247, A250, A259, A268, A270, B7, B8, B15, B16, B18, B19, B20, B21, B24, B25, B31, B32
Preston, Billy B7
Preston, Jimmy A26
Preston, Johnny B15
Pretenders, The A16, A185, A221, B24
Pretty Things A132, B21
Previn, Dory B21
Price, Charles B8
Price, Lloyd A44, A95
Prima, Louis B25
Primus B23

Prince A7, A17, A79, A80, A85, A126, A130, A144, A221, A247, A250, B13, B25, B32
Prince, Peter Mark A72
Prince Buster B20
Prince Paul B22
Priore, Domenic B15
Proby, P.J. B8
process A115
Procol Harum A43, A67, A71, A141, A207, A224, A247, B7, B19, B21, B29
Prodigy A233, B21,
producer B32
Professor Longhair A238
Progler, J.A. B22
progression; Aeolian A16, A97, A214, A235, B28; harmonic A43, A44, A80, A83, A94, A162, B8, B10; linear A14, A93, A96, A99, A113
prolongation A25, A63, A91, A93, A111, A263, B7, B8
Propa-Gandhi A61
Providence A166
psalms B12
psalm tone A134
psychedelia A25, A40, A72, A74, A134, A138, A257, B29
Psycho A149
psychology A40, A68, A143, A198; Gestalt A102
Public Enemy A24, A39, A61, A80, A117, A123, A255, B14, B21, B22, B31
Public Image Ltd B20
Puccini A178
Puckett, Riley A240
Pulp A82
pulse A157, A203, A266; pivot pulse A203, B20, B21
Purcell, Henry A178, B27
P.U.S.A. A205

Q-Tip A1, B14
Quantum Jump A42
Quarrymen, The B7, B8
Queen A16, A17, A43, A74, A99, A149, A167, A178, A185, A205, A221, A233, A247, A269, B21, B32
Queen Latifah A1, B14
Queens of the Stone Age A221, A255
Queensrÿche B28

Quicksilver Messenger Service B7
Quiet Riot B28
Quintessence B21
quodlibet A166, A233
quotation A11, A159, A261, B31

race A34, A35, A136, A230, A244; racism A137
race records A32, B26
Rachel and the Revolvers B15
Raconteurs, The B21
Radano, Ronald A105
radio B28
Radiohead A17, A54, A56, A80, A85, A97, A135, A143, A162, A169, A203, A204, A205, A206, A221, A233, A247, A269, B7, B20, B21
Raekwon A158, B14
Rafferty, Gerry A185
raga A134
Rage Against the Machine A205
ragtime A254, B9, B19, B27
Rahn, Jay A172
Rainbow B28
Rainey, Gertrude "Ma" A176, A240, B26
Rainger, Ralph B30
Raitt, Bonnie A80, A247
Rakim B14
Raksin, David A147, B30
Ram, Samuel "Buck" B12
Rambling Thomas A240
Rameau A15, B16
Ramirez, Roger B30
Ramones, The A80, A181, A221, A247, B32
Ramsey, Guthrie A110
Rand, Ayn A28
Randolph, "Boots" A270
range A25, A44, A107, A165
rap A1, A2, A24, A61, A117, A146, A158, A255, B19, B22, B28, B31, B32; bohemian rap B14; gangsta rap B14; party rap B14; reality B14
Rascall, Dizzee B31
Rascals, The [Young] A110, B3, B24, B30
Ratner, Leonard A163
Ratoff, Gregory B12
Ratt A43, A101, A241, A250, B3, B7, B8, B28
Rattles A70, A185, A235
Ravel A72

Subject Index 311

Ravellers, The B7
Ravens, The A53
Rawls, Lou A53, A222, B3, B16
Ray, James A95, B8
Ray, Johnnie B8
Ray Cathode (George Martin and Maddalena Fagandini) B8
Raye, Collin A191
Rays, The A97
Razorlight B21
RCA Records A270
Rea, Chris B21
recitative A232
recorder A178, A196, A234
record stores A34, A185
Redbone, Leon A185
Redding, Noel B29
Redding, Otis A99, B17, B19, B24, B32
Redhead, Steve A40, B21
Red Hot Chili Peppers, The A205
Reed, Dock A26, A29, A32, A80, A95, A107, A123, A170, A185, A247, B3, B8, B18, B20, B32
Reed, Dora A161
Reed, Edward S. B21
Reed, Henry A161
Reed, James Mathis "Jimmy" B17
Reed, Jimmy A8, B15
Reed, Les B8
Reed, Long "Cleve" A144, A240
Reed, Lou A124
Reel Big Fish A205
Reel to Reel A3
Rees, David A123, A185, A188, B21, B32
Reese and Santonio B5
Reeves, Goebel A266
Reeves, Jim A185
Reeves, Martha A185
Refused A205
Regents, The B8, B15
reggae A118, A235; dub A231
Reich, Charles A166, A231, B17, B21
Reich, Steve A81, A233
Reimann, Hugo A142, A175, A182, A222
Reingold, Isaac B12
R.E.M. A16, A80, A124, A167, A181, A182, A184, A247, A248, B24, B32
remix A159
Renaissance music B27

Rene, Leone B30
Rene, Otis A3, A24, B30
REO Speedwagon A185, A246, A248, B24
repetition A205, A250, B19
Resnicoff, Matt B28
Respighi, Ottorino A115, A129, A144, A146, A182, B3, B22
Return to Forever A73
Reum, Peter B15
Reunion A43
Revels, The B15
Revere, Paul, and the Raiders A27, B8
Reynolds, Debbie A97
Reynolds, Dick B15
Reynolds, Simon A51, A129, B5, B20
Rezillos, The B20, B21
Reznor, Trent A221
rhetoric A255, B4, B32
Rhoads, Randy B28
rhyme A38, A122, A124, A144, A225, A243, A255, B11, B14
rhythm A8, A38, A43, A53, A105, A132, A190, A206, A221, A238, A245, A252, A262, A267, B5, B9, B11, B20, B27, B19; Balkan A157; beat B5; beat class A220, A233, B14; Charleston B10; diatonic rhythm B5; foxtrot B10; harmonic rhythm A121, A122, A207, A230, A252, A270, B25; phrase rhythm A5, A100, A208, A224; polyrhythm A11, A71, A117, A208, A218, A221, A255, A262, B4, B26, B27; shuffle A238; time signature A157; *see also* subdivision
rhythm and blues A11, A32, A77, A95, A238, A270, B14, B19, B32; soul music A29, A105
Ribiero, Peri A211
Ricci, Alfredo B2
Richard, Cliff A259, B8, B16, B20, B21
Richard[s], Keith A107, A132, B7, B8, B29
Richards, Ron B8
Richie, Lionel A43, A167, B12, B24
Richman, Jonathan B4
Rick Rock A261
Ricoeur, Paul B21
Riegger, Wallingford B3
Rietveld, Hillegonda B5
riff A8, A22, A42, A55, A85, A108, A131, A132, A155, A167, A210, A233, A256, B23

Righteous Brothers, The A43, A75, A85, A185, A126, A242, A247, B4, B7, B15, B21, B24, B25, B32
Riley, Jack B15
Riley, Jeannie C. A193
Riley, Terry A141, A233
Riley, Tim A182, B7, B8
Riordan, James A43
Riperton, Minnie A43
Ripley, John W. B12
Rite of Spring, The A232
Ritter, Tex A191
Ritts, Herb A252
ritual A171
Ritz, David A77, A110
Rivers, Johnny A43, B7
Robbins, Elizabeth "Bett" B8
Robbins, Jerome B12
Robbins, Marty A97
Roberts, Lenny B22
Roberts, Robin A85
Robertson, Robbie A33, B32
Robertson, Stuart A227
Robeson, Paul B21
Robin, Leo B12, B30
Robins, The A11, A77
Robinson, Bill "Bojangles" B12
Robinson, J. Bradford A55
Robinson, Smokey B4, B8, B21, A106, A108, A247, A250
Robinson, Vicki Sue B24
Robison, Willard B30
Robles, Daniel B1
rock A105, A188, B6, B19, B32; classic rock A17; country rock A173; death metal A10; experimental A205; folk rock A15, A32, A33; hard rock A28, B2; heavy metal A28, A97, A132, A175, A208, B2, B19, B28, B32; lo-fi A243; math rock A57, A167, A203, A204; new wave A71, A74; progressive metal A175; progressive rock A67, A71, A72, A73, A141, A149, A166, A175, A207, A218, A232, A235, A257, A269, B29; punk A71, A167, A210, A235, A118, B19, B32; Rock, Pete B22; rock and roll A37, A44, A80, A178, B19; Rock Steady Crew B31; shoegaze A22; soft rock A173
Rocket's Tail A238, B20

Rockmore, Finious "Flatfoot" A240
Rockwell, John A269
Röda Kapellet B25
Røde Mor B25
Rodgers, Jimmie A97, A160, A240, A266, B8, B15, B19
Rodgers, Richard A14, A114, A120, A147, A168, A224, A228, B10, B11, B12, B30
Roe, Tommy B8
Roeder, John A142, A208
Rogan, Johnny A121
Rogers, Ginger B12
Rogers, Kenny A193, A248
Roger Waters A198, A199
Rogin, Michael B22
Rohr, Tony A115
Rolling Stone (magazine) A80
Rolling Stones, The A16, A17, A21, A33, A35, A43, A55, A67, A70, A71, A74, A80, A83, A85, A86, A96, A97, A101, A107, A121, A132, A155, A179, A184, A185, A218, A229, A233, A246, A247, A248, A250, A257, A263, B3, B7, B8, B15, B16, B17, B19, B20, B21, B24, B27, B29, B32
Rollins, Henry A33
Roman numeral, A83, A86, B10
Romantics, The A16, A85, A241, B24
Romberg, Sigmund B10, B30
Rome, Harold B12
Romero, Chan B8
Ronell, Ann A114, B10, B30
Ronettes, The A36, A74, A75, A80, A95, A160, A247, B7, B15, B32
Ronson, Mark B21
Ronstadt, Linda B1, B24
Rooftop Singers, The B8
Roots, The A222, B14, B22, B31
Ros, Sigur A205
Rose, Arnold A48
Rose, Axl B28
Rose, Bayless B26
Rose, Billy B12
Rose, Fred B30
Rose, Tricia A158, A163, A238, A255, A261, B13, B14, B22
Rose, Vincent B30
Rose, Wesley A270
Rose, William "Billy" B10

Rosen, Charles A163, A253, B23
Rosenblatt, Yossele B12
Rose Royce A105
Rosie and the Originals B25
Ross, Diana A43, A136, A167, A185, A248, B21, B24
Ross, Jerry B12
Rossell, Marina B21
Rossini, Gioachino A251
Roth, Bill B2
Roth, David Lee B28
Rothstein, Edward A57
Rothstein, William A5
Rotten, Johnny A178, B20
Rourke, Andy A36, A100, A208, A240, B5
Rovell, Diane B15
Rovell, Marilyn B15
Rowland, Kelly A215
Roxy Music A149, A185, B20, B21, B32
Royal Philharmonic Orchestra A24
Royal Teens, The A97
Roy Hamilton A44
Roy Orbison A247
Roza, Lita B21
rubato A52, B27
Rubens, Paul B30
Rubenstein, Anton B12
Rubin, Rick B32
Ruffin, David A43
Ruffin, Jimmy A185
Rufus A17
rumba B27
Rumshinsky, Joseph M. B12
Rundgren, Todd A59, B7, B31
Run-D.M.C. A99
Rush A16, A17, A28, A55, A125, A167, A175, A208, A245, A248, B21, B28
Rush, Otis B21
Ruskin, James B5
Russell, Bernie B12
Russell, George A59, A60
Russell, Leon A140, A256, B7, B15
Russell, Tony A240, A266
Russian music B12
Rutherford, Michael A142
Rutles, The A69, B7
Ruwet, Nicolas B19
Ryan, Barry B21

Rydell, Bobby A241, B8
Ryder, Mal B8
Ryder, Mitch A43, A108
RZA B14, B22

Sad Café A185
Sade B19
Sadler, Ssgt Barry B7, B25
Sager, Carole Bayer A6
Sagoo, Baljit "Bally" A61
Said, Edward A137, A249, A265, B22
Saint-Saens, Camille A178
Sakamoto, Kyu A43
Saladin, Dann A10, B2
Salt-n-Pepa A24
Salzer, Felix A237
Sam and Dave A29, A95, A185, A205, B21, B24
Samarotto, Frank A205
samba A211
Sam Cooke A44, A108, A247
Saminsky, Lazare B12
Sammes Singers, The Mike B7
sampling A24, A61, A104, A117, A163, A212, A234, A261, B5, B19, B22, B32
Sampson, Edgar B30
Samson S. B22
Sam the Sham and the Pharaohs B8
Sandler, David B15
Sandler, Jocob Koppel B12
Sandpipers, The A185
Sands, Tommy A97
Sanford/Townsend Band, The B24
Sanocho A3
Santana A16, A75, A101, A167, A185, B3
Santiago, Isaac A3
Santly, Lester B30
Saosin A205
Sapps, Booker T. A240
Sargeant, Winthrop A263
Sartre, Jean-Paul A137
Saslaw, Janna A197
Satanism B28
Satie, Erik A234
satire A11
Satriani, Joe B28
Satterfield, Tom B3, B30
Saturday Night Fever A179

Saturday Night Live A74
Saunders, Ben A163
Saussure, Ferdinand de B21
Saves the Day A69, A205
Savoy Orpheans A227, B21
Sawyer, Keith B5
Sawyer Brown A191
Saxon B20, B21
saxophone A149
Say Anything A205
Sayer, Leo A185
Sayrs, Elizabeth A32
Scaduto, Anthony A121
Scaffold, The B7
scale A63, A248, B3, B28; altered A15; altered blues scale A55; blues A55, A65, A106, A256, B3; diatonic A81, A167, A246; harmonic minor A143; hexatonic A93, A107, A108, A114; Lydian dominant A15, A71, A185, B28; major A106; octatonic A97, A139, A169, A226, A256, B4; pentatonic A16, A19, A40, A55, A80, A92, A97, A99, A106, A107, A108, A114, A144, A168, A170, A180, A246, A248, A256, A257, A264, B7, B9, B10, B18, B19, B25, B27; scale degree A55, A91, A209; whole tone A72, A149, B10
Scarlatti, Domenico A114, A251
Scepter Records A249
Schachter, Carl A86, A240
Schaeffer, Pierre A159
Schaffner, Nicholas A68
Schenker, Heinrich A46, B19
Schenker, Michael B28
Scherzinger, Martin A83, A99, A131, A206, A213, B5, B23
Schickele, Peter A70
Schifrin, Lalo A43
Schloss, Joseph A110, A261, B31
Schmalfeldt, Janet A194
Schmidt, Patricia B21
Schneider, Fred A99
Schoenberg, Arnold A53, A71, A72, A81, A86, A113, A114, A115, A147, A178, A185, A188, A228, B3, B16, B19
Scholem, Isaac B12
Schönberg, Claude-Michel A224
Schonberger, John B30
Schopenhauer, Arthur A70

Schreiber, Ryan A163
Schubert, Franz A54, A69, A104, A142, A150, A253, B12, B18, B19, B25, B27, B28
Schuller, Gunther A48, A119, A156, B10, B16
Schumann, Robert A150, A253, B8, B19, B27
Schwartz, Abe B12, B28
Schwartz, Arthur B10, B11, B12, B30
Schwartz, Jean B12
Schwartz, Stephen B12
science fiction A28
Scofield, John A256
Scorpions A16, A85, B28
Scott, Bobby A110
Scott, Darrell A191
Scott, Elizabeth A227
Scott, Jack A97, B25
Scott, Jimmy B7
Scott, Richard A222
Scottish music B27
Scriabin, Alexander A114
Scruggs, Earl A220
Scruton, Roger A70
Seal A221, B3
Seals and Crofts B3, B24
Searchers A185
second line A238
Secret Affair A185, A186
Secunda, Sholom B12
Sedaka, Neil A44, B21, B24, B25
Sedgwick, Eve Kosofsky A146
Seeds, The A43
Seeger, Charles B4, B19
Seeger, Pete A168, A265, B8, B21
Seekers, The B8
Seger, Bob A16, A225, A247, A248, A250, B21, B24
Séguin A166
Selecter A185
Selle, Ronald A213
Sellers, Peter B7, B8
Sells, Dan Gillespie B21
Selznick, David O. B12
semiotics A21, A54, A88, A102, A126, A140, A242, B6, B13, B19, B25, B28
Sensorama B5
Septeto Nacional A205
sequence A14, A54, A93, A125, A167, A209, A213, A214, A215, B19
Seress, Rezso A15

Subject Index

serialism A81; retrograde A207; retrograde inversion A207; serial operations A72, A207
Serman, Jimmy B30
Sermon, Eric A61
Sesame Street B22
Sessions, Audrye A169
Seville, David A97
Sex Pistols, The A43, A74, A80, A99, A118, A124, A178, A210, A235, A247, B4, B21, B28, B32
Sexton, Adam B22
sexuality A38, A82, A136, A258, A259, B13, B19; homosexuality A3, A52, A128, A136, A146, A153, A174, A223, B28
Shabalala, Joseph B1
Shabba Ranks A61
Shadows, The A259, B8
Shadows Fall A205
Shakespeare, William A7, B16
Shakur, Afeni B31
Shakur, Tupac (2Pac) A80, B14, B31
Shangri-Las A45, A95, B7, B8, B19, B21
Shankar, Ravi B7, B8
Shannon, Del A43, A99, A167, A185, A241, B8, B15, B24
Shapiro, Helen A259, B8
Sharp, Cecil B16, B19, B21, B27
Sharp, Dee Dee A44
Shavers, Charlie B12
Shaw, Arnold A131
Shaw, George Bernard B27
Shaw, Sandie A36, A123
sheet music A14, A65, A228
Sheik, Duncan A157, A169, B24
Shelton, Blake A191
Shelton, Ricky Van A191
Shenson, Walter B8
Shepard, Kenny Wayne A247
Shepherd, Bill A240
Shepherd, John A88, B19, B20
Sheridan, Tony A19, B7, B8
Shield, William B16
Shields, Kevin A22
Shiga, John A24
Shine A3
Shins, The A22
Shire, David A179
Shirelles, The A45, A75, A95, A247, A259, B8, B15, B24

Shirinda, General M.D. B1
Shirley and Lee A44
Shocking Blue A185, B24
Shocklee, Hank A117, A255
Shore, Dinah B21
Shorter, Wayne A203
Shotton, Pete B8
Shusterman, Richard B14
Sibelius, Jean A71
Siberry, Jane A51, A124
sibilance A30, A130
Sicko, Dan B5
signification A21, A31, A47, A48, A57, A103, A115, A170, A176, A183, A184, A187, A218, A256, A261, B4, B9, B19, B22
Sigur Rós A205
Sil Austin A44
Silhouettes, The A97, B24
Silkie A107
Sill, Judee B21
Silouettes, The A44
Silverchair A205
Silvers, Louis B30
Simian B21
Simon, Carly B21, B24
Simon, Paul A7, A9, A21, A93, A97, A99, A123, A124, A150, A167, A185, A264, B1, B12, B21, B24, B32
Simon and Garfunkel A7, A43, A80, A93, A97, A123, A167, A182, A185, A247, B3, B4, B7, B8, B17, B21, B24, B25
Simone, Nina A95, B8, B21
Simple Minds A16, A185
Simply Red A185
Simpsons, The A202
Sinatra, Frank A14, A97, A123, A160, A263, B4, B10, B12, B15, B16, B21, B25
Sin-Eater (band) B2
singer-songwriters A219, B19
singing A18; scat singing A119; sprechstimme (speech-singing) A99, A119
Siouxsie and the Banshees A185, B20, B21
Sir Douglas Quintet, The B4
Sirmay, Albert A228
Six Teens, The B15
ska A222, B19
Skkatter A24
Skunk Anansie B21
Slade A185, B20, B21

Slaughter and the Dogs A210
slavery B9
Slayer B28
Sledge, Percy A99, A185, A247, B19
Sleeper A124
Sleepy Eyes of Death A7, A204, A246
Sless, David B21
Slint A221
Slits, the B20
Sloan, Allen A73
Sloan, Phil B15
Sloane, A. Baldwin A120, B30
Slobin, Mark B22
Sly and the Family Stone A55, A84, A205, A238, A241, A247, A255, B3, B4, B19, B21, B24, B32
Small, Christopher A30, A255, B20, B28
Small, Mille B21
Small, Solomon B12
Smallboy, Rex B14
Small Faces, The A72, A185, A269, B7, B20, B21
Smashing Pumpkins A203, A205
Smith, Arthur B8
Smith, Barbara A153
Smith, Bessie A26, A48, A176, A240, B9, B21, B26
Smith, Bill B8
Smith, Elliot A221, A222
Smith, Huey "Piano" A44, A238
Smith, Jack A227
Smith, J.T. "Funny Paper" A240
Smith, Lucius B27
Smith, Mamie A240, B26
Smith, Mary Elizabeth Stanley ("Mimi") B8
Smith, Neil A158
Smith, Norman B8
Smith, Patti A7, A16, A36, A55, A78, A124, A269, B21
Smith, Pinetop A53
Smith, Robert A137
Smith, Will A234, B14
Smitherman, Geneva B22
Smiths, The A36, A83, A123, A124, A143, A185, B13
Smyth County Ramblers A240
Snap A21
Snead, James A255, B4, B22
Sniader Lanser, Susan A51

Snider, Dee B28
Snoop [Doggy] Dogg A24, A99, B14, B31, A261
Snow, Phoebe B1
Snow Patrol B21
Soft Cell B32
Soft Machine, The A72, A141, A207, A235, B20
Sokrates B14
Solie, Ruth A79
Solis, Gabriel A217
Solomon, Maynard A133
Solomon, Robert C. B21
somatics A183
Sommers, Joanie A45
Sondheim, Stephen A41
song cycle A199, A223
songwriting A14, A76, A42, A93, A108, A116, A133, A150, A191, A193, A205, B1, B8, B16, B30, B32
Sonics, The A85
Sonic Youth A140, A210
Sonny and Cher B21
sonority A18
Sons Of the Pioneers B21
Soul Asylum B24
Soul Children, The A29
Soulfly A205
Souls of Mischief B22
Soul Stirrers, The A205
Soulwax A24
Soundgarden A55, A99, A167, A177, A221, A245
Sounds Incorporated B7, B8
Sousa, John Philip A251, B27
South B14
space A183
Spaeth, Sigmund A213, B12
Spandau Ballet A36, A185, A250
Spanish music B27
Spanky and Our Gang A43, B7
Sparklehorse B21
Spark Records A77
Sparks A185
Spaulding, Henry B26
Specials, The A185, B19
Speckled Red A238
Specs B22
Spector, Phil A36, A71, A109, A125, B7, B8, B15, B18, B19, B32
Spector, Ronnie B7

Subject Index

spectrogram A216
spectrograph A22
Speedy Holmes A240
Spellman, Benny A95, B8
Spencer, Herbert A70
Spencer, J. B31
Spencer Davis Group, The A16, B20
Spice Girls B24
Spicer, Mark A22, A83, A99, A115, A142, A162, A163, A205
Spinal Tap A69, A84, A143
Spin Doctors A245
Spinetti, Victor A70, B7
Spinners, The A248, A250
Spiral Staircase, The B7
Spirit B7
Spirit of Memphis B21
spiritual B9, B12, B27
Spiritualized B21
Spitzer, John A131
Spooky Tooth B21
Sppokrijders B14
Spring *see* American Spring
Springfield, Dusty A123, A178, B21
Springfield, Rick A250
Springsteen, Bruce A7, A21, A25, A80, A83, A122, A164, A182, A269, B24, B32
Squeeze A124
Squier, Billy A247, B31
Squire, Chris A166, A207
Stampp, Kenneth B27
Standells, The A43
Stanley B5
Staple Singers, The A29, A99, A185
Starbuck A43
Starcastle A72
Starkey, Maureen Cox B7
Starland Vocal Band A43
Starr, Edwin A185
Starr, Ringo A92, B7, B8, B18, B29
Stars A203, A205
Starship A250, B24
Stars on 45 A24
Star Wars A202
Status Quo A82, A185, B7, B20, B21
Stax A29, B32
Stax Records A30, A32, A95
Steam A185
Stearns, Marshall B16

Steedman, Mark B19
Steeleye Span A64, B21
Steely Dan A43, A59, A74, A96, A101, A142, A222, A225, A232, A247, A248, A250, B8, B21, B24
Stefani, Gino A188, A225, B4, B19, B20, B21
Stefani, Gwen A215
Stein, Deborah A41
Steinberg, Lewis A29
Steiner, Max B12
Stephenson, Ken A5, A80, A89, A205, A222
Stephenson, William A110
Steppenwolf A16, A85, A167, A246, A247, B7, B21, B28
Stereolab A221
Stern, Daniel A134
Stevens, Cat A99, A167, B24
Stevens, Sufjan A205, A221
Stevenson, William A108
Stewart, Al A185, A250
Stewart, Andy B21
Stewart, Art A110
Stewart, James "Jimmy" B10
Stewart, Rod A29, A99, A123, A179, A185, A247, B24
Sticky Fingaz A146
Stidham, Arbee A53
Still, William Grant B9
Stills, Stephen A269, A232
Stimela B1
Sting A149, A151, A221, A235, A250, B24, B25, B32
Stipe, Michael A181
Stockhausen, Karlheinz A138, B7, B17, B19
Stokes, Frank A11, A92, A240
Stokes, Geoffrey B20
Stokes, Martin B14
Stokes, Niall A103
Stokowski, Leopold B32
Stoller, Mike A77, A108, B8, B12
Stolzoff, Norman C. B22
Stone, Lew A227
Stoneman, Ernest A240
Stone Roses, The A185, B20
Stone Temple Pilots A203
Stooges, The A24, A210
Storm, Gale A97
Storm, Rory B8
Stormy Six A166

Stover, Elgie A110
Strait, George A189, A191
Strange, Billy B15
Stranglers, The A99, A221
Straus, Joseph N. A55, A56
Strauss, Johann A215, A251, B27
Strauss, Neil A57, A163
Strauss, Richard B12
Stravinsky, Igor A11, A12, A53, A71, A104, A114, A139, A141, A187, A232, B3, B12, B16, B19, B20, B27
Straw, Will B22, B28
Strawberry Alarm Clock, The A43, A99, B7, B8
Strawbs, The B20, B21
Stray Cats, The A43, A99, A167
Strayhorn, Billy B11, B30
Streets, The B21
Streisand, Barbra A217
Strickland, Keith A99
Strickland, Lily B30
String Driven Thing A185, B21
Strokes, The A24
Stroman, Phill [sic] B22
Strong, Barrett A95, A105
Strothers, Jimmie A240
Stryper A250, B28
Stubblefield, Clyde A238, B22
Students, The B15
studio techniques A29, A36, A92, A126, B19, B32; chorus A90, B32; compression A140, B8; demo recording A110; double-tracking B7; echo B7, B32; effects A98; EQ B32; fadeout A126, A227, B23, B27; flanging B32; gate B32; limiter B7, B32; multitracking A29, A74, A90, A92, A98, A119, A125, A160, B19, B32; pan B32; sequencing B5
Stuessy, Joe B28
Sturgeon, Theodore B17
style A29, A53, A103, A235, A270, B19; polystylism A163
Style Council, The B20, B21
Styne, Jule B12, B30
Styx A16, A43, A141, A167, A250, B24
subculture A118, B19
subdivision A20, A107, A238, A157; straight A109; swing A108, A109, A132, A238, B8
Subotnick, Morton A141
Subotnick, Rose Rosengard A183
substitution A83, B3, B25; chord A147; melodic A113; tritone A15, A102, A172, A214, A263, B10, B23
Suede B20, B21
Suessdorf, Karl B30
Suesse, Dana B10
Sufjan Stevens A205, A222
Sugababes A24
Sugar Cane B25
Sugarhill Gang A24, A101, B31
Sugarloaf A43, A248
suicide B28
Sullivan, Ed B7
Sullivan, Sir Arthur B30
Sulzer, Salomon B12
Summer, Donna A42, A43, A80, A101, A130, A136, A182, A247, B21
Summers, Andy A235
Sunday All Over the World A218
Sun Studio A270
Super Furry Animals A123, B21
Supergrass B20
Super Stocks, The B15
Supertramp A46, A141, A149, A182, A185, A186, A248, B21, B24
Supremes, The A11, A43, A95, A106, A108, A185, B3, B4, B7, B8, B20, B24, B32
Surfaris, The A43, B15
surprise B1
Survivor A247, A250, B6, B21
Survivors, The B15
Suskin, Steven B10
Sutcliffe, Stuart Fergusson Victor B8
Swan, Billy A185
Swan, E. A. B30
Swan Silvertones A123, A246, A264, B21
Sweatman, Wilbur B30
Swedien, Bruce B32
Swedish music A20, B25
Sweet, Matthew B32
Sweet, The A43, A85
Swift, Kay B10, B11, B30
Swinging Blue Jeans, The A185, B8
swing music A238
Swiss, Thomas B22
Sykes, Roosevelt B26
Sylvester, Victor B8
synaesthesia A134
synchronicity B17

syncopation A37, A106, A132, A145, A170, A187, A191, A245, A250, A262, B5, B16, B19, B27
synthesizer A138, A141, A163, A235, B5, B6, B23; synth-pop A235
System of a Down A205, B21
Szwed, John A119, A139

Tab Hunter A44
Tabor, June B21
Tagg, Philip A19, A34, A88, A131, A140, A187, A217, A266, B6, B19, B20, B21, B28
Talking Heads A16, A71, A83, A185, B21
Talk Talk A232
Talmy, Leonard B21
tambourine A252
Tamla Records *see* Motown Records
Tamm, Eric A218
Tampa Red A239, A240
tango B27
Tanner, Tony A122
tape loops A92, A98
Tarasti, Eero A140, B9
Tarkovsky, Andrey A66
Tarlton, Jimmie A240
Tarras, David B12
Tarriers, The A97
Tashian, Barry and Holly A189
Tate, Greg B22
Tate, Troy A36
t.A.T.u. A153
Tatum, Art A172, B9, B10
Taube, Evert B25
Tauber, Chaim B12
Tauber, Doris B30
taxonomy A43, A163
Taylor, Alistair B7
Taylor, Derek B7
Taylor, James A6, A99, A167, A241, A248, B3, B4, B7, B21, B24
Taylor, Johnnie A29
Taylor, Joseph B21
Taylor, R. Dean A185
Taylor, Teddy "King Size" B8
Taylor, Timothy B21
Tchaikovsky, Peter Ilych A11, A71, A141, A222, B12, B27, B30
Tears For Fears A59, A185, A241, A250, B20, B21

technology B5
Teddy Bears, The A97, A99, B7
Tee, Richard B1
Teenage Fanclub B20, B21
teleology A105
Témpano A149
Temperance Seven, The A259, B8
Temperley, David A16, A59, A222, A225, A240, A250, B5, B21
tempo A8, A43, A99, A107, A108, A203, A221, B2, B22
Temptations, The A55, A95, A97, A105, A108, A185, A247, B4, B7, B8, B24
Tenaglia, Danny B5
tendency tone A60
Tennant, Neil A128, A174, B13
Tenney, James A52, A159
Tennison, Chalee A191
tension A13
Ten Years After A132, A155, B21
Terrell, Tammi A110
Terry, Sonny A95, B8, B21
Tesla B28
Tex, Joe B4
Texas A270
text-music relations A1, A2, A9, A13, A45, A71, A93, A112, A125, A132, A264, B1
texture A68, A252, B5, B6
Tha Fall A185
Tharpe, Sister Rosetta A238, A240
That Cuban Guy A3
Théberge, Paul A129, B22
Them A43, A85, A123, A185, B13, B21
therapy A133
They Might Be Giants A185
Thin Lizzy A185, B20, B28
Third Eye Blind A247
Third Man Records A148
Thomas, B.J. A249
Thomas, Carla A29, A95
Thomas, Chris B7
Thomas, Craig A188
Thomas, Henry A58, A240, B17
Thomas, Jesse "Babyface" A240
Thomas, Joe B15
Thomas, Rambling A240
Thomas, Rufus A29, A95, A185, B17
Thompson, Flora B16
Thompson, Linda B20

Thompson, Richard B20, B21
Thompson, Robert Farris B22
Thompson, Sonny A53
Thompson Twins, The A185, B32
Thoreau, Henry David B15
Thorleifs B25
Thornhill, Claude A263
Thornton, "Big Mama" A77, A83, A123
Thorogood, George A55
Threadgill, Henry A255
Three Dog Night A43, B24
Three Stripped Gears A239
Tillis, Pam A189
Tilzer, Harry Von B12
Timbaland B22
timbre A22, A23, A29, A30, A32, A61, A86, A88, A93, A98, A132, A140, A141, A161, A177, A192, A225, A252, A255, A268, B6, B13, B14, B32
Timbuk 3 A250
time A139
Tin Pan Alley A30, A75, A119, A168, A228, B12, B19, B21, B32
Tiomkin, Dimitri B12
Tipton, Glenn B28
Tirro, Frank B10
Titelman, Russ B15
Titon, Jeff Todd A244, B19
TLC B32
Tobias, Charles A256, B12
Tobias, Harry B30
Tobler, John B15
toccata A149
Tokens, The A181, B15, B24
Tolhurst, Laurence A137
Tomkins, Silvan A3
Tomlinson, Gary B14
Tommy Tutone A250
Tomorrow A70, B7
tonality A56; bitonality A102, B27; directed A41, A60, A97; dual A56, A92, A214, A253; monotonality A41, A56, A214; polytonality A116, A165, A260; sectional A56
tonicization A56, A59, A111, B7, B8
tonnetz A72, A93, A96, A116, A155
Tony Bennett B4
Too Bad Boys A240
Tool A17, A167, A175, A203, A205, A221, B21

Toop, David A255, B22, B31
Too $hort B14
Top 40 A108
topics A163
topic theory A235
Top Notes, The A222
Topo D. Bil A185
Torke, Michael A72
Tornados B8
Torode, Brian B19
Toronto B14
Torrence, Dean B15
Torres, Liz A3
Torry, Clare A199
Tosches, Nick A266
Toto A43, A185, A250, B24
Touzet, René A85
Tovey, Donald B27
Tower of Power A238
Townsend, Ed A110
Townshend, Ken B7
Townshend, Pete A52, A99, A141
Toyah A185
Toynbee, Jason B21
Toys, The A84, A93, A179, B7
T'Pau A185
Tracey, William B30
Tractor B21
Traffic A43, B7, B8, B21, B29
Trammps, The A101, A179
trance A8
transcription A132, A156, A157, A265, A268, B5, B22, B28
transformation A83, A155, A220, B19; cross-type A54
Transvision Vamp A185
Trash B7
Trashmen, The A43
Traveling Wilburys, The B7, B24
travesty A159
Travis, Merle B19
tresillo A3, A17
Trevino, Rick A189
T. Rex A36, A83, A86, A185
triad A16
Tribble, Kim A193
Tribe Called Quest, A A1, A123, A158, B14, B22, B31

Tri-Five, The B15
Trilling, Ilya B12
Tristano, Lennie A96
tritone A93, A149, B25
Tritt, Travis A191
Trivium A41, A96, A263, B21
Troggs, The A83, A85, A99, A185, B8, B20, B21
Troup, Bobby B30
Trower, Robin B21
Troy, Doris A95, B7
True Dream A205
True Margrit A221
trumpet A119
Truth Hurts A61
Tubb, Ernest A53
Tubes, The A250
Tubeway Army A24, B20
Tucker, Henry A264
Tucker, Ken B20
Tucker, Tanya A191
Tucker, Tom B32
Tulving, Endel A133
Türk, D.G. A163
turnaround A266
Turner, Big Joe A74, A75, A240, B7, B19
Turner, Ike A43, A80, A247, B21
Turner, J. Layton B12
Turner, Mark B21
Turner, Tina A43, A80, A136, A161, A185, A247, B24
Turtles, The A185, A222, B7, B8, B21, B24
Twain, Shania A111, A190, A191, A192, A193, B21
Twelfth Night A72
twelve-tone music A72
Twiggy B7
Twilight 22 A104
Twista B14
Twisted Sister B28
Twitty, Conway A97, A191, B25
Twomey, Kathleen B8
Two Tongues A205
Tyler, Bonnie A185
Tymes, The A95
Tyndall, Robert A156
Tyrannosaurus Rex B20
Tyrell, Steve A249
Tystion A123

U2 A7, A52, A55, A80, A81, A86, A89, A99, A103, A185, A228, A232, A246, A247, A250, A252, B20, B21, B24, B32
UB40 A185
UFO (band) B28
Ultravox B20
Ulvaeus, Björn B25
Underworld B5, B20, B21
Unit 4+2 B21
United States of America, The A138
U.N.K.L.E A205
Upton Green B8
Uriah Heep A185, B20
Urtext A13
USA for Africa B25
Usher, Gary A160, B15
U Totem A72

Vai, Steve A12
Valens, Ritchie A43, A44, A60, A75, A85, B8, B21, B24, B25, B28
Valentin, Val B32
Vallee, Rudy A227, B12
vamp A6, A95, A147, A216
Van Alstyne, Egbert A120, B12, B30
Vance, Jay B28
Van Dahl, Ian A3
Van Deburg, William L. B22
Van der Graaf Generator A72, A166, A182, A185, A207, B20, B21
van der Merwe, Peter A23, A256, B19
Van Dyke, Earl A106
Van Halen A17, A55, A99, A108, A141, A185, A232, A250, B24, B28
Van Halen, Eddie A35, B28, B32
Van Helden, Armand A3
Van Heusen, Jimmy B10, B11, B12, B30
Vanilla Fudge A72
Van Shelton, Ricky A191
Vapors A185, B21
Varèse, Edgard B7, B17, B21
variation A11, A53, A149, A156, A237, A270, B27
Vassar, Phil A191
Vaughan, Ivan B8
Vaughan, Stevie Ray A250, A256
Vaughan Williams, Ralph A227, B3, B16, B18, B21

Vee, Bobby A185, B20, B24
Vega, Suzanne B21
Veloso, Caetano A211
Velvelettes, The A95
Velvet Revolver B21
Velvet Underground, The A67, A210, A247, A269, B32
Venet, Nick B15
Venetian Snares A221
Ventures, The A185, B15
Verdi, Giuseppe B12, B27
Versatile Four, The A227
Verve A247
Verve, The A80, B20, B21
Verve Pipe, The B24
Vibrants, The B15
Vibrations, The B15
Vicious, Sid B19
Vickers, Mike B7
Vidacovich, johnny A238
Vig, Butch B32
Vikingarna B25
Village People, The A52, A179, B21
Villa Lobos, Heitor A211, A235
Vincent, Gene A43, A44, A174, A185, A247, B7, B8
Vinton, Bobby B8, B24
violence B28
violin B12
Vipers Skiffle Group, The B8
virtuosity A74
Visconti, Tony B32
Viscounts B21
Vitamin D A82, A178, A229, B22, B28
Vivaldi, Antonio B28
vocalese A168
vocoder B6
Vogler, Abbé A15
Vogues, the A84, A181
voice A37, A47, A48, A50, A51, A52, A53, A58, A79, A99, A119, A132, A161, A165, A170, A178, A210, A225, A227, A259, A264, A265, B6, B19, B20; background vocals A107, A231; diction B26; falsetto A98, B15; range A20, A87, A130; register A136; timbre A58, A127, B16
voice leading A46, A49, A97, A99, A142, A154, A160, A194, A263, B8, B10
Vološinov, V.N. B28

Von Tilzer, Harry A120
Voodoo B18
Voorman, Klaus B7
Vulliamy, Graham B20

Wagner, Naphtali A83, A215, B8
Wagner, Richard A116, B27
Waite, John A250, B24
Waits, Tom A135, A221, A222
Wakeman, Rick A71, A73, A74, A149, A162, A207, A229
Walcott, Derek B1
Walker, Albertina A161
Walker, Junior A108
Walker, Willie B26
Walker Brothers B21
Waller, Fats A95, A119, A120, A147, A172, B30
Waller, Gordon B8
Wallflowers, The A247
Wallinger, Karl B32
Wallis, Roger B20
Walser, Robert A46, A88, A103, A131, A143, A208, A256, B6, B14, B21, B22
Walsh, Joe A43, A55
Walsh, Sheila A185
Walt J B5
waltz B19, B27
Wang, Oliver B22
Ward, Anita A42, B21
Ward, Clara A26, A161
Ward, Ed B20
Ward, John A240
Warfield, Charles B30
Warhol, Andy B7
Warner, Timothy A22
Warner Brothers B15
Warnes, Jennifer A185
Warren, Harry A120, A224, B10, B11, B12, B30
Warren G. B31
Warshavsky, Harry B12
Warwick, Dionne A99, A192, A247, A248, A249, B21
Warwick, Jacqueline B8
Washboard Sam A240
Washington, Booker T. B22
Washington, Dinah B8
Washington, Ned B11
W.A.S.P. (band) B28
Waterman, Richard Alan A262, B4

Subject Index

Waters, Ethel B12
Waters, John A103
Waters, Roger B29
Waters, Simon A163
Watson, George P. A266
Watts, Wilmer, and the Lonely Eagles A240
Waxman, Franz B12
Wayne, Artie B12
Weathersby, Alan B26
Weaver, Derry B15
Weavers B21
Webb, Jimmy A34, A217, B3, B15
Weber, Gottfried A15
Webern A11, A81
Webster, Paul Francis B12
Wedding Present, The A53, A114, A123, A185, B20
Weezer A83, A221
We Five A99
Weil, Cynthia A108
Weill, Kurt B10, B12, B16, B27, B30, B32
Weinger, Harry A110
Weinstein, Deena B28
Weir, Bob B17
Weisethaunet, Hans B21
Weisman, Benjamin A208, B8
Welch, Bruce A25, A99, A200, B8
Welch, Lenny A95, B8, B24
Weller, Paul B20
Wells, Mary A108, A110, A185, B8
Wellstood, Dick A95, A106, A172
Welsh, Nolan "Barrelhouse" B26
Wepaman A3
Wermuth, Mir B14
Werner, Craig A144
Werner, Eric B12
Wesker, Arnold B16
Wesley, Fred A31, A271, B4
West, Cornel A255
West, Kanye A261, B31
Westberry, Kent B8
West Coast Pop Art Experimental band A43
Western Studios B15
Weston, Kim A95
Wetton, John A72
Wexler, Jerry A77
We Were Promised Jetpacks A205
Whalley, Nigel B8
Wham A185, B19

Wheeler, Elizabeth A. A95, A265, B22, B32
Whippersnapper B21
Whisler, Larry B2
Whitaker, Stanley A73spelling?
Whitburn, Joel A32
White, Alan A53, A207
White, Bryan A148, A189, A191
White, Bukka A216
White, Edward R. B12
White, Evelyn A170
White, Georgia A240
White, Jack A148
White, John Wallace A217
White, Lenny A73
White, Robert A108
White, Timothy B8, B15
Whitehead, Minnie Lee A240
Whitehouse, Fred B12
Whiteley, Sheila B20
White Lion A250
Whiteman, Paul B8, B10
White Snake A250, B16, B28
White Stripes, The A55, B4
Whitfield, Norman A110
Whiting, Richard B10
Who, The A16, A23, A43, A55, A63, A80, A97, A101, A105, A132, A141, A162, A167, A182, A185, A246, A247, A248, A250, B3, B4, B7, B8, B19, B20, B21, B24, B28, B29, B30
Wicke, Peter A88, B19, B20
Wiggins, James "Boodle It" A240
Wilco A102
Wild Cherry A55, A84, B24
Wilde, Kim A19
Wilde, Marty A185
Wilde, Oscar B13
Wilder, Alec A209, B19
Wiley, Geeshie A240
Wilkin, Marijohn B8
Wilkins, Robert A228, A240, B10
Willcocks, David B7
Williams, Andy A97, B15
Williams, Bert B12
Williams, Big Joe A123
Williams, Billy A97
Williams, Clarence B12, B30
Williams, Deniece B24
Williams, Ernest A161

Williams, Hank A83, A123, A210, A247, A270, B4, B21
Williams, Hank, Jr. A173, A191
Williams, Ian A57
Williams, John A202
Williams, Larry A95, A254, B7, B25
Williams, Marion A161
Williams, Maurice A94
Williams, Raymond B19, B21
Williams, Robbie B21
Williams, Robert "Pete" A62, A210
Williams, Robin and Linda A190
Williams, Spencer B12, B30
Williams, Vanessa A167
Williams-Jones, Pearl A161
Williamson, Sonny Boy A83, A132, A155, A216, B26
Williamson Brothers & Curry A240
Willis, Chick B25
Willis, Mark A189
Willis, Paul B19, B20
Willis, Victor A52
Wills, Bob A240
Wilson, Audree B15
Wilson, Brian A99, A109, A125, A239, A269, B7, B8, B15, B21, B32
Wilson, Carl A125, B7, B15
Wilson, Cindy A99, A160
Wilson, Dennis A160, B15
Wilson, Frank A266
Wilson, Harold B21
Wilson, Jackie A44, A108, A185
Wilson, J. Frank A43
Wilson, Murry B15
Wilson, Olly B9
Wilson, Teddy A172, B25
Wimsat, William Upski B22
Winehouse, Amy B4, B21, B22
Winger A250
Wings A64, A97, A102, A182, B7, B8, B18, B24
Winkler, Peter B19
Winstons, The B5
Winter, Edgar A43
Winter, Johnny A83, A185
Winter's Bane A104, B2
Winwood, Steve A250, B17, B24
Wire A17, A210, B32
Wise, Fred B8
Wishbone Ash A19, A185

Withers, Bill B24
Witmark, Isidore B12
Wittgenstein, Ludwig B20, B21
Wohl, Herman B12
Wolf, Hugo A41
Wolf, Jack B12
Wolf, Stacy A143
Wolfson, Mack B12
Wolfstone B21
Wommack, Travis A85
Wonder, Stevie A19, A43, A55, A80, A85, A95, A96, A97, A99, A101, A110, A154, A163, A185, A232, A234, A247, A250, A269, B7, B8, B15, B21, B24
Woodie, Ephraim A240
Woods, Alyssa A51
Woods, Harry A30
Woodson, Craig A138
Woodstock B29
Wooley, Sheb A97
world music A93, B19
World-Pacific Studios B15
World Party B21
Worley, Darryl A191
Wray, Link A44, B15, B32
Wreckers, The A83
Wrecking Crew, The A270, B15, B32
Wright, Charles A238
Wright, Gary A160, B24
Wright, Rick A198
Wrubel, Allie B30
Wu-Tang Clan A2, B14
Wyatt, Robert A207
Wyman, Jane B21
Wynette, Tammy A165, B19

X A210
X-Ray Spex A210
XTC A97, A185, B21
xylophone A227
Xzibit A261

Yablokoff, Herman A149, B4, B12, B20, B21
Yamami, Wynn A149
Yankovic, "Weird Al" A159
Yardbirds, The B8, B17, A181, A185
Yearwood, Trisha A189
Yellen, Jack A43, A70, B12, B20, B21, B29
Yes A73, A233, B7

Subject Index

Yeston, Maury A17, A55, A71, A72, A74, A99, A101, A104, A141, A149, A152, A166, A188, A207, A208, A214, A218, A223, A229, A269, B20, B21, B32
Yingish songs B12
yodeling A266, B5
Yorke, Thom A143
Youmans, Vincent B10, B12, A58
Young, Angus B28
Young, Faron A191
Young, Joe B12, B30
Young, Lester A263
Young, Neil A16, B24
Young, Paul A7, A33, A80, A88, A155, A185, A186, A247, A268, B6, B21, B24, B32
Young, Roy B8
Young, Victor B12, B30
Young Bloods, The B24
Your Hit Parade B10

Zadeh, Lofti A. A224
Zager and Evans A93
Zagorski-Thomas, Simon B21
Zak, Albin B6
Zamfir, Gheorge A185, B25
Zapp B31
Zappa, Frank A36, A110, A121, A163, A208, B19, B21
Zarlino, Gioseffo A134
Zbikowski, Lawrence B6
Zevon, Warren A11, A12, A16, A27, A54, A55, A59, A60, A85, A138, A221, A268, B7, B20, B21, B24, B29
Ziegfeld, Florenz A155, A168, A197, B21
Zollo, Paul B1
Zombies, The A99
Zorn, John A163
ZZ Top A16

Author/Editor Index

Aarden, Bret C2
Adam, Nathaniel D1
Adams, Kyle A1, A2
Adams, Rebecca C38
Albiez, Sean C3
Allen, Lara C19, C36
Amico, Stephen A3, C3, C39
Ancelet, Barry Jean C5
Anderson, Roger A4
Attas, Robin A5, D3
Attinello, Paul A6, C39
Auerbach, Brent C2
Augestad, Kate C36
Auner, Joseph C9
Auslander, Philip C33
Auster, Albert C9
Averill, Gage C19
Awkward, Michael C28

Backer, Matt C25
Baes, Amapola C24
Baes, Jonas C24
Bailey, Craig C31
BaileyShea, Matthew A7
Baily, John C19
Baker, Ejima C14
Baker, Geoffrey C19
Bakrania, Falu C3
Balfour, Ian C1
Ballantine, Christopher C13, C19, C24, C36
Balliger, Robin C17
Bannister, Matthew C12, C30, C31
Barber-Kersovan, Alenka C16
Barendregt, Bart C19
Barnes, F. Barry C22
Barron, Lee C29, C31
Bartkowiak, Mathew C31
Baruth, Philip E. C38
Baugh, Bruce C35
Baur, Steven C30
Beaud, Paul C16

Bechdolf, Ute C24, C36
Beebe, Roger C1
Benadon, Fernando A8
Bennett, Andy C18, C24
Bennighof, James A9, B1
Berger, Harris A10, B2
Berger, Rolf C12
Bernard, Jonathan A11, A12, C6, C20
Berry, David Carson A13, A14
Biamonte, Nicole A15, A16, A17, C2, C35
Bickford, Tyler A18
Biermann, Benjamin C2
Binas, Susanne C24, C36
Björnberg, Alf A19, A20, A21, C23, C27, C32, C33, D2
Black, Vaughan C38
Blake, David A22
Bloustien, Geraldine C33
Blum, Stephen C19
Bobbitt, Richard B3
Bolelli, Roberto A23
Boone, Christine A24, D4
Boone, Graeme A25, A26, C4, C25
Borders, James A27, C6
Bostock, Mathonwy C2
Bowman, Durrell A28, C15, D5
Bowman, Rob A29, A30, C24, C26, C28
Brackett, David A31, A32, A33, A34, A35, B4, C13, C17, C23, C28, C36, D6
Brackett, John A36, C35
Bradby, Barbara A37, A38, C3, C9, C23, C27, C36
Breen, Marcus C36
Brocken, Mike C18
Brolinson, Per-Erik C32
Brøvig-Hanssen, Ragnhild A39
Brown, Adam C24
Brown, Julie C21
Brown, Matthew A40, C4
Brownell, John D7
Buchanan, Donna C5, C19

Buchler, Michael A41
Buckland, Fiona C3
Burnett, Michael A42, C37
Burnett, Robert C32
Burns, Gary A43, C18, C40
Burns, Joe A44
Burns, Lori A45, A46, A47, A48, A49, A50, A51, C2, C4, C6, C21, C34
Butler, Mark A52, B5, C3
Byrnside, Ronald A53, C7, C27

Callen, Jeffrey C39
Capuzzo, Guy A54, A55, A56
Carlsson, Ulla C32
Carr, James Revell C22
Carr, Revell C38
Carter, Paul D8
Cascone, Kim C3
Catefortis, Theo A57, C15
Chapman, Dale C9, C28
Chen, Szu-Wei C19
Cherlin, Michael A58
Chester, Andrew C27
Clarke, Eric C9
Clawson, Mary Ann C35
Clement, Brett A59, A60, D9
Clements, Carl A61, C14
Clendinning, Jane Piper C20
Cloonan, Martin C9, C18, C24, C36
Cobbson, Felix C37
Cogan, Robert C20
Cohen, Andrew A62
Cohen, Sara C5, C17, C24, C36
Collaros, Pandel A63, C12
Collins, John C16
Collins, Karen C21
Comer, John A64, A65, C37
Cook, Guy C18
Cook, Nicholas A66
Cooper, B. Lee C29
Cooper, David C33
Corin, Amy C24
Cotner, John A67, A68, C15, D10
Coulthard, Lisa C21
Covach, John A69, A70, A71, A72, A73, A74, A75, A76, A77, C4, C6, C20, C26, C27, C34, C35, C36
Coyle, Michael C1
Craghead, Anissa C38

Crawford, Paul C37
Crowdy, Denis C24
Cubitt, Sean C23
Cusic, Don C25, C29
Daley, Mike A78

D'Andrea, Anthony C3
Daniel, Linda C36
Danielsen, Anne A79, C9
Davis, Andrew C29
Davis, Robert D11
Dawe, Kevin C24, C33
Decker, James C40
de Clercq, Trevor A80, D12
de Kloet, Jeroen C24
Demers, Joanna C21
Derfler, Brandon A81
Devitt, Rachel C39
DeWitt, Mark C5
Diamond, Beverley C5
Dibben, Nicola A82, C9, C27, C33
Dickinson, Kay C9, C21
Dodd, David C38
Dolfsma, Wilfrid C24
Doll, Christopher A83, A84, A85, A86, C35, D13
Dollar, Natalie C22, C38
Drew, Robert C36
Dubuc, Tamar C2
Duchan, Joshua A87, C29
Dugaw, Diane C5
Dulaney, Wendy C38
Dyer, Richard C3

Echard, William A88, B6
Eerola, Tuomas C10, C11
Eggertson, Kristine D14
Eigtved, Michael C8
Einbrodt, Ulrich C12
Endrinal, Christopher A89, D15
Evans, David C5, C25
Everett, Walter A90, A91, A92, A93, A94, A95, A96, A97, A98, A99, A100, A101, A102, B7, B8, C4, C6, C12, C20, C27, C30, C35, C38, C40

Fabbri, Franco C16, C27
Fairbairn, Hazel C5
Fairlamb, Horace C22
Farley, Jeff C36

Author/Editor Index

Farmelo, Allen C5
Farmer, Paul C37
Fast, Susan A103, C6, C9, C33
Fenster, Mark C17, C36
Ferreira, Pedro Peixoto C3
Fikentscher, Kai C3, C36
Fink, Robert A104, A105, C1, C28
Fiori, Umberto C23
Fisher, George C37
Fitzgerald, Jon A106, A107, A108, A109, C9, C18, C24, C36, D16
Flinn, Caryl C21
Flory, Andrew A110, C34
Floyd, Jr., Samuel B9
Floyd, Leela C37
Folio, Cynthia C20
Folse, Stuart A111
Ford, Charles A112, C27
Fornäs, Johan C24, C32, C36
Forte, Allen A113, A114, B10, B11
Fox, Aaron A. C5
Fraser, David C38
Friedlander, Paul C36
Frith, Simon C9, C16, C36
Frontani, Michael C40
Fuchs, Cynthia C17
Fulbrook, Denise C1

Gammon, Vic C16
Ganetz, Hillevi C24, C36
Garcia, Luis-Manuel A115
Gauldin, Robert A116
Gaunt, Kyra A117, C36
Gay, Jr., Leslie C36
Gebesmair, Andreas C33
Gelbart, Matthew A118
Gertner, Douglas C38
Gilbert, Jeremy C3
Gilmore, Abigail C24
Gilroy, Paul C28
Gioia, Ted A8
Givan, Benjamin A119
Gloag, Kenneth C12
Goodenough, Mary C22, C38
Goodwin, Andrew C9
Gopinath, Sumanth A58
Gottlieb, Jack B12
Grajeda, Tony C1
Graziano, John A120

Green, Lucy C17
Grenier, Line C36
Grier, James A121, C34
Griffiths, Dai A122, A123, A124, C13, C23, C26, C27
Grossberg, Lawrence C1
Grymes, James A. C2
Guilbault, Jocelyne C13, C19

Haguchi, Hideko C24
Hakanen, Ernest C24
Halberstam, Judith C39
Hamelman, Steve C40
Hamm, Charles C7, C16, C23
Hannan, Michael C12
Harkins, Paul A39
Harris, Keith C24
Harrison, Daniel A125, C4
Hassanpour, Amir C19
Hautamäki, Tarja C8
Hawkins, Stan A126, A127, A128, A129, A130, B13, C9, C23, C26, C33, C36, C39, D17
Hawley, Laura A50
Hayward, Philip C24, C36
Headlam, Dave A131, A132, C4, C20, C25
Heinonen, Yrjö. A133, A134, A156, C10, C11, C12
Hennion, Antoine C9, C16, C33
Herd, Judith Ann C19
Hermann, Richard C20
Hesmondhalgh, David C13, C24, C35, C36
Hesselink, Nathan D. A135
Heuger, Markus C12
Hill, Trent C1
Hisama, Ellie A136, A137, C6, C14, C20, C23, C24
Ho, Wai-Chung C19
Hoffman, Alan D18
Holmes, Su C21
Holm-Hudson, Kevin A138, A139, A140, A141, A142, C15, C31, C34, C35
Holt, Joseph C38
Horn, David C16
Horner, Bruce C17
Hosokawa, Shuhei C13, C36
Hubbs, Nadine A143, C6
Hudson-Kaufman, Sarah C12
Hughes, Bryn D19
Hughes, James R. C2
Hughes, Timothy A144, C6, D20

Hughes, Walter C3
Huq, Rupa C13
Huron, David A145
Huss, Hasse C24
Hustwitt, Mark C9

Imada, Tadahiko C24
Inglis, Ian C18, C31, C33, C35, C40
Inoue, Takako C24
Ishizaka, Naoyuki C24

Jacbson, Marion S. C5
Jackson, Richard C16
Jarman-Ivens, Freya A146, C33, C39
Järviluoma, Helmi C36
Jensen-Moulton, Stephanie C14
Johns, Donald A147
Johnson, Bruce C12, C24, C36
Johnson, Nicholas A148
Johnson, Stacey C36
Johnson, Victoria C21
Jones, Mike C24
Jones, Simon C36
Jones, Steve C36
Josephson, Nors A149
Jungr, Barb C25

Kajikawa, Loren C28
Kaminsky, Peter A150, A151
Kärki, Kimi C31
Karl, Gregory A152, C15
Kassabian, Anahid C13, C17, C33, C36
Katz, Mark C28
Kaufman, Sarah Hudson C30
Keesing, Hugo D21
Kelley, William C36
Kennedy, Gary C36
Kennett, Chris C26
Kerstetter, Kathleen C2
Kerton, Sarah A153, C21, C39
Kimsey, John C40
Kisliuk, Michelle C5
Klein, Bethany C21
Klotz, Sebastian C3
Knight, Stewart C37
Knights, Vanessa C39
Koizumi, Kyôko C24
Kong, Lily C19, C24
Konishi, Junko C24

Koozin, Timothy A154, A155, C6
Koskimäki, Jouni A156, A157, C10, C11, C12
Kramer, Howard C40
Kramer, Jonathan C20
Krasnow, Carolyn C36
Kriese, Kostanze C36
Krims, Adam A158, B14, C26, C27, C33
Krippner, Stanley C38
Kronengold, Charles C28
Kruse, Holly C17, C36
Kubik, Gerhard C5
Kun, Josh C1
Kurkela, Vesa C8

Lacasse, Serge A159, C27, D22
Lafrance, Marc A50, C2
Laing, Dave C24, C40
Lambert, Philip A160, B15
Langlois, Tony C19
Larkin, Brian C19
Larsen, Holger C32
Lawrence, Time C3
Leach, Elizabeth Eva C27
LeBlanc, Jim C30, C40
Lee, Edward B16, C37
Lee, Stephen C36
Legg, Andrew A161
Leisiö, Timo C8
Lemish, Dafna C9
Lenig, Stuart C29
Leppert, Richard C23
Letts, Marianne Tatom A162, A243, C34
Levy, Claire C24
Leydon, Rebecca A163, C34
Lilja, Esa D23
Lilliestam, Lars C8, C32
Lipsitz, George C23
London, Justin A164
Losseff, Nicky A165, C27
Lott, Eric C5
Loza, Susana C3, C24
Lucas, Brad C38
Luesebrink, Marjorie C38
Lundberg, Mattias A166
Lupis, Giuseppe D24
Lury, Karen C21

Maasø, Arnt C9
Macaw, Heather C36

Mackenzie, Kenneth C22
MacLachlan, Heather A167, C2
Madrid, Alejandro C3
Magee, Jeffrey A168
Mäkelä, Janne C12
Mäkelä, Tomi C12
Mäki-Kulmala, Airi C36
Malawey, Victoria A169, A170, C2, D25
Malbon, Ben C3
Malm, Krister C16, C32
Malvinni, David A171, B17, C22
Mamula, Stephen C19
Man, Ivy Oi-Kuen C24
Manuel, Peter C5, C19
Marcus, Scott C19
Marshall, P. David C18
Marshall, Wayne C2
Martin, Henry A172
Marvin, Elizabeth West C20
Mather, Olivia Carter A173, D26
Maultsby, Portia C28, C33
Maus, Fred A174, C27, C35
Maxwell, Ian C13
Mayhew, Emma C39
Mazullo, Mark C21, C35
McCandless, Gregory A175, D27
McCann, Sean C27
McCarthy, Len C12
McClary, Susan A176
McCown, William C38
McDonald, Chris A177, D28
McDonald, Kari C12, C30
McGranahan, Liam D29
McLeod, Kembrew C3
McLeod, Ken A178, A179, C9
McQuinn, Julie C21
Mead, Andrew C20
Meier, Leslie M. C9
Mellers, Wilfrid A180, B18
Mera, Miguel C33
Mercer, Neil C18
Mercer-Taylor, Peter A181, A182
Meriwether, Nicholas C22
Metcalf, Greg C29
Middleton, Jason C1
Middleton, Richard A183, A184, B19, C8, C17, C23
Mihara, Aya C24
Milioto, Jennifer C24

Miller, Kiri C21
Miller, Remy C29
Mills, Peter C31
Mitchell, Tony C24, C28, C36
Mitsui, Tôru C24, C36
Miyakawa, Felicia C28
Montgomery, David D30
Moore, Allan A185, A186, A187, A188, B20, B21, C25, C26, C27, C33, C35
Moore, John C23
Morelli, Sarah C24
Morris, Robert C20
Morrison, Val C36
Morss, Benjamin D31
Muikku, Jari C36
Mulder, Juul C12
Muncie, John C18
Mungen, Anno C39
Muršič, Rajko C24

Nagai, Yoshikazu C24
Naka, Mamiko C24
Nakamura, Yûko Satô C24
Narváez, Peter C36
Neal, Jocelyn A189, A190, A191, A192, A193, C6, D32
Neaverson, Bob C18
Neff, Ali Colleen C2
Negus, Keith C13, C36
Nestiev, Israel C16
Nettl, Bruno C7
Niemi, Seppo C11
Nobile, Drew A194, D33
Noonan III, Joseph C38
Norden, Christopher C22
Nurmesjärvi, Terhi A195, A196, C10, C11, C12
Nylöf, Göran C32
Nyong'o, Tavia C3

Oakes, Jason Lee C33, C39
O'Connor, Justin C24
O'Donnell, Shaugn A197, A198, A199, A200, C22, C30, C31, C38
Ogasawara, Yasushi C24
Ogawa, Hiroshi C24, C36
Oliver, Paul A201, C16, C24
Ommen, Ann A145
Ônishi, Kôji C24
Opekar, Aleš C24, C36

Orosz, Jeremy A202
Osborn, Brad A203, A204, A205, A206, D34
Ôyama, Masahiko C24

Padva, Gilad C39
Palm, Jason C38
Palmer, John A207
Parks, Lisa C1
Pavlic, Ed C28
Pegley, Karen C9
Pelovitz, David C38
Peña, Manuel C5
Pennanen, Risto Pekka C8
Perchard, Tom C28
Percival, Mark C24
Pettan, Svanibor C5
Pickering, Michael C13
Pier, David C14
Pieslak, Jonathan A208, C35
Pini, Maria C3
Plasketes, George C29
Pope, Edgar C24
Porter, Steven D35
Potter, Russell C17
Prather, Ronald A209
Price, Charles Gower C12

Race, Kane C3
Ramaglia, Bellino D36
Ramsey, Jr., Guthrie C28
Rapport, Evan A210, C14
Rauhut, Michael C24, C36
Rautiainen-Keskustalo, Tarja C8, C33
Regev, Motti C13, C24
Reily, Suzel Ana A211, C19
Reising, Russell C24, C29, C30, C31, C40
Reist, Nancy C38
Renzo, Adrian A212
Rey, Mario C39
Reynolds, M. Fletcher A213
Ricci, Adam A214, A215
Richards, Paul C16
Richardson, John C9, C10, C33
Riley, Tim C12
Rings, Steven A216
Ripani, Richard D37
Rischar, Richard C28, D38
Robinson, Thomas A217

Robison, Brian A218, A219, C15
Rockwell, Joti A220, D39
Rodgers, Tara C3
Rodman, Gilbert C17, C36
Roe, Keith C32
Román-Velázquez, Patria C13, C24, C36
Rosenberg, Nancy A221, A222, C2, D40
Rosenberg, Neil C24
Rosing, Helmut C16
Roy, Anjali Gera C33
Ryan, Jennifer C36
Rycenga, Jennifer A223, C15, C39

Saada-Ophir, Galit C19
Saldanha, Arun C3
Salley, Keith A224, A225, C2
Samuels, David C5
Sandars, Diana C21
Sanjek, David C9, C17
Sarrazin, Natalie C21
Saunders, Ben C1
Savage, Jon C9
Schenkius, Patrick A226
Schiffer, Sheldon C29
Schleifer, Ben C31
Schleifer, Cy C30
Schleifer, Ronald C30
Schloss, Joseph B22, C28
Schneider, Thomas D41
Schulz, Dorothea C19
Schwarz, David B23
Scott, Derek A227, C12, C27, C33
Shaftel, Matthew A228
Shank, Barry C5
Shaviro, Steven C21
Sheinbaum, John A229, A230, C1, C15
Shepherd, John C17
Sheridan, Tony C24
Shimizu, Terumasa C24
Shumway, David C17
Silberman, Steve C38
Smith, Hope Munro C2
Smith, Jeff C21
Smith, Lans C22
Smith, Nicola C33
Snell, Karen C2
Sonenberg, Daniel D42
Sorrell, Neil C37

Author/Editor Index

Spector, Stanley C22
Spelman, Nicola C31
Spencer, Piers A231, C37
Spicer, Mark A232, A233, A234, A235, A236, C6, C34, C35, D43
Spizer, Bruce C40
St. John, Graham C3
Stahl, Geoff C24
Stefani, Gino C27
Steingo, Gavin C3
Steinholt, Yngvar C19
Steinskog, Erik C29
Stephan-Robinson, Anna D44
Stephenson, Ken A237, B24
Stewart, Alexander A238, C5, C28
Stilwell, Robynn C21, C26
Stoia, Nicholas A239, A240, D45
Stokes, Martin C19, C26
Straw, Will C13, C17, C36
Street, John C36
Sullivan, Rebecca C36
Summach, Jay A241, D46
Suutari, Pekka C8
Swedenburg, Ted C19
Swiss, Thomas C17
Symon, Peter C24

Tagg, Philip A242, B25, C3, C16, C23, C27, C32, D47
Tao, Xin C24
Tatit, Luiz C13
Taylor, Timothy A244, C23
Temperley, David A80, A245, A246, A247, A248, C35
Terho, Henri C24
Théberge, Paul C17, C36
Thompson, Gordon C12
Thornton, Sarah C3
Tift, Matthew Christian C22
Tillekens, Ger C12, C30, C31
Titon, Jeff Todd B26, C25
Toft, Robert A249, C9
Tokinoya, Hiroshi C24
Tolvanen, Hannu C12
Tongson, Karen C39
Torode, Brian A37, C23
Toubin, Jonathan C14
Tough, David C29

Toutkoushian, Robert C38
Tôya, Mamoru C24
Toynbee, Jason C13
Tracy, Steve C25
Traut, Don A250
Trondman, Mats C32
Turino, Thomas C19

Valdez, Stephen C12, C30, D48
van der Merwe, Peter A251, B27, C8
van Rijn, Guido C25
van Zanten, Wim C19
Vennum, Jr., Thomas C38
Vernallis, Carol A252, C21, C27
von der Horst, Dirk C15
von Feilitzen, Cecilia C32
Vulliamy, Graham C37

Wagner, Naphtali A253, A254, C12, C30
Waksman, Steve C35
Wald, Gayle C1
Wallis, Roger C16, C32
Walser, Robert A255, B28, C9, C26, C27, C36
Walsh, Brian D49
Warner, Timothy C33
Warwick, Jacqueline C12, C30, C33
Watson, Jada C21
Weiner, Robert C38
Weinstein, Deena C15, C17, C29, C35
Weisethaunet, Hans A256
Wells, Alan C24
Whiteley, Sheila A257, A258, A259, B29, C12, C23, C30, C31, C33, C36, C39, C40
Whitesell, Lloyd A260, C39
Whitley, Ed C18
Wicke, Peter C33
Wilder, Alec B30
Wilgoren, Rachell C38
Williams, Justin A261, B31, C28, D50
Williams, Paul C24
Williams-Jones, Pearl C5
Wilson, Olly A262, C5
Winkler, Peter A263, A264, A265, C23, C27, C36
Wise, Timothy A266
Witzleben, Lawrence C24
Womack, Kenneth C31, C40

Wood, Robert C14
Woods, Alyssa A47, C2
Woods, Faye C21

Yakô, Masato A267, C24
Yano, Christine C19, C29
York, Adrian C25

Zak, Albin A268, A269, A270, B32, C6, C34, C35
Zanes, Warren C1
Zbikowski, Lawrence A271, C9
Zeiner-Henriksen, Hans D51
Zimmerman, Nadya C35
Zolten, Jerry C40
Zuberi, Nabeel C13

Year Index

1970: B16
1972: B30
1973: B18, D21
1974: A262
1975: A53, C7
1976: B3
1977: B26
1978: A263
1979: D35
1980: D36
1981: A180
1982: A42, A64, A65, A201, A231, A242, C16, C37
1983: D18
1984: A37
1986: A90
1987: A43, D2
1988: A4, A122, A264
1989: A19, B27
1990: A20, A69, A116, A164, A209, A257, B19, C32
1991: B25, D6
1992: A31, A91, A126, A149, A150, A185, A213, A244, B29, D17, D48
1993: A9, A113, A147, A183, B20, B28, C36
1994: A21, A32, A227
1995: A29, A70, A92, A106, A112, A117, A127, A131, A186, A251, A255, B4, B10, C8, C20
1996: A62, A211, B9, D16
1997: A25, A40, A45, A71, A78, A79, A93, A125, A128, A132, A258, A265, B23, C4, D47
1998: A66, A133, A156, A187, A189, A195, A252, A267, C10, C24
1999: A10, A11, A13, A72, A94, A107, A136, A165, A184, A197, A228, A245, B2, B7, C17, C38
2000: A12, A14, A27, A46, A63, A67, A73, A81, A88, A103, A114, A134, A137, A143, A151, A154, A157, A168, A176, A177, A190, A196, A214, A232, A238, A243, B14, C11, C18, C23, D22, D31, D38
2001: A82, A174, A178, A207, A253, A256, B8, B11, B32, C12, D10, D41
2002: A26, A28, A38, A57, A68, A95, A123, A138, A139, A140, A152, A198, A218, A229, A230, A260, B13, B24, C1, C13, C15, C25, C30, D28, D30, D32, D43, D49
2003: A30, A44, A52, A74, A124, A129, A158, A188, A254, C26, D5, D7, D14, D20, D42
2004: A47, A54, A96, A97, A111, A119, A233, A237, A271, B12, B22, D37
2005: A33, A34, A48, A49, A61, A75, A104, A115, A141, A172, A181, A199, A250, A268, B6, C14, C31, D8, D11
2006: A3, A6, A23, A76, A98, A145, A146, A153, A179, A223, A259, B5, C39, D24, D26
2007: A18, A108, A159, A171, A191, A192, A200, A208, A246, B1, B15, C22, C27, D13, D25
2008: A1, A15, A41, A50, A99, A144, A160, A193, A269, C6, D15, D45
2009: A2, A8, A55, A56, A58, A83, A100, A109, A130, A220, A234, C33, C40, D9, D23, D44
2010: A16, A51, A77, A87, A101, A110, A121, A142, A161, A162, A163, A203, A235, A239, A249, A266, A270, C29, C34, D27, D29, D34, D40, D50, D51
2011: A5, A80, A84, A85, A89, A105, A118, A155, A167, A194, A204, A215, A221, A224, A225, A226, A236, A241, A247, A248, C2, C3, C5, C9, C19, C21, C28, C35, D1, D3, D4, D19, D39
2012: A22, A35, A39, A102, A169, B21, D12, D46
2013: A24, A36, A59, A86, A120, A135, A173, A175, A182, A205, A212, A216, A219, A240, B17, B31
2014: A7, A17, A60, A148, A166, A170, A202, A206, A210, A217, A222, A261, D33

Taylor & Francis eBooks

Helping you to choose the right eBooks for your Library

Add Routledge titles to your library's digital collection today. Taylor and Francis ebooks contains over 50,000 titles in the Humanities, Social Sciences, Behavioural Sciences, Built Environment and Law.

Choose from a range of subject packages or create your own!

Benefits for you
- Free MARC records
- COUNTER-compliant usage statistics
- Flexible purchase and pricing options
- All titles DRM-free.

Benefits for your user
- Off-site, anytime access via Athens or referring URL
- Print or copy pages or chapters
- Full content search
- Bookmark, highlight and annotate text
- Access to thousands of pages of quality research at the click of a button.

REQUEST YOUR FREE INSTITUTIONAL TRIAL TODAY

Free Trials Available
We offer free trials to qualifying academic, corporate and government customers.

eCollections – Choose from over 30 subject eCollections, including:

Archaeology	Language Learning
Architecture	Law
Asian Studies	Literature
Business & Management	Media & Communication
Classical Studies	Middle East Studies
Construction	Music
Creative & Media Arts	Philosophy
Criminology & Criminal Justice	Planning
Economics	Politics
Education	Psychology & Mental Health
Energy	Religion
Engineering	Security
English Language & Linguistics	Social Work
Environment & Sustainability	Sociology
Geography	Sport
Health Studies	Theatre & Performance
History	Tourism, Hospitality & Events

For more information, pricing enquiries or to order a free trial, please contact your local sales team:
www.tandfebooks.com/page/sales

Routledge
Taylor & Francis Group

The home of Routledge books

www.tandfebooks.com